JOHN CONSTANTINE, HELLBLAZER: TAINTED LOVE

GARTH ENNIS Writer

STEVE DILLON Artist

Tom Ziuko Stuart Chaifetz Colorists

Gaspar Saladino Letterer

Francesco Francavilla Cover Art

Glenn Fabry Original Series Covers

STUART MOORE Editor – Original Series
JULIE ROTTENBERG Assistant Editor – Original Series
SCOTT NYBAKKEN Editor
ROBBIN BROSTERMAN Design Director – Books
ROBBIE BIEDERMAN Publication Design

SHELLY BOND Executive Editor – Vertigo
HANK KANALZ Senior VP – Vertigo and Integrated Publishing

DIANE NELSON President
DAN DIDIO and JIM LEE Co-Publishers
GEOFF JOHNS Chief Creative Officer
JOHN ROOD Executive VP – Sales,
Marketing and Business Development
AMY GENKINS Senior VP – Business and Legal Affairs
NAIRI GARDINER Senior VP – Finance
JEFF BOISON VP – Publishing Planning
MARK CHIARELLO VP – Art Direction and Design
JOHN CUNNINGHAM VP – Marketing
TERRI CUNNINGHAM VP – Editorial Administration
ALISON GILL Senior VP – Manufacturing and Operations
JAY KOGAN VP – Business and Legal Affairs, Publishing

JACK MAHAN VP – Business Affairs, Talent
NICK NAPOLITANO VP – Manufacturing Administration
SUE POHJA VP – Book Sales
COURTNEY SIMMONS Senior VP – Publicity
BOB WAYNE Senior VP – Sales

JOHN CONSTANTINE, HELLBLAZER: TAINTED LOVE

DC Comics, 1700 Broadway, New York, NY 10019
A Warner Bros. Entertainment Company
Printed in the USA. First Printing.
ISBN: 978-1-4012-4303-6

LIBRARY OF CONGRESS CATALOGING-IN-PUBLICATION DATA

ENNIS, GARTH, AUTHOR.
JOHN CONSTANTINE, HELLBLAZER. VOLUME 7, TAINTED LOVE / GARTH ENNIS; [ILLUSTRATED BY] STEVE DILLON.
  PAGES CM
  ISBN 978-1-4012-4303-6 (PBK.)
1. GRAPHIC NOVELS. I. DILLON, STEVE, ILLUSTRATOR. II. TITLE. III. TITLE: TAINTED LOVE.
PN6728.H383E46 2014
741.5'973—DC23
                    2013036108

SUSTAINABLE
FORESTRY
INITIATIVE
Certified Chain of Custody
Promoting Sustainable Forestry
www.sfiprogram.org
SFI-01042
APPLIES TO TEXT STOCK ONLY

"WE NEVER LIKED YOU ANYWAY."

This is a book about lives being ground into shit.

It's funny stuff.

I imagine a lot of you holding this book in your hands, or between your stumps or whatever, are familiar with the names Ennis and Dillon from PREACHER, which, in addition to being the best regular comic published today, is also bloody funny. This book has its funny bits, too; the piss jokes and liberal sprinklings of rabbit shit are the bad seeds of PREACHER's screaming laugh track.

The rest of you, I guess, might have flicked through this volume and are having problems with the fact that I am characterizing such things as The Death of Hope, Horrible Beatings, Disgusting Murder, Sexual Treachery, The Killing of Love and Stark Religious Horror as funny. Tough. Garth and Steve are comfortable with these themes. It may be gallows humor, but they're at least stopping to draw a cock on the wood before they swing.

Garth Ennis is the Irishman who started writing comics in order to escape from university, characterizing the students he was locked up with as "a pack of wankers." As I write this, the bastard's just starting a month-long trip across the States with his mate Jeff, while I sit here locked in my Essex castle writing the intro for his book. It's a rough old life, being in comics. Steve Dillon has been drawing comics professionally since he was about four years old. He has about eighty-five kids and lives in Luton, because somebody has to.

This book comprises the opening shots of their collaboration. Garth had already been writing HELLBLAZER for a couple of years, taking great joy in making previous regular artist Will Simpsons draw disgusting things. Will, an excellent artist, responded gamely and professionally, as he always does, but his heart was never in the horror. Will is a very nice man, and so his

waking hours are not consumed with daydreams of gratuitous claret and eviscerated royalty. It was fine work, but what Steve brought to the book, in addition to his phenomenal storytelling skills (and I don't think there's a better storyteller than Steve Dillon in the monthly comic-book business right now), was an utter relish for the punished meat and torn skin. I guess that when you've worked for British publishers for as long as Steve had, you develop a higher and finer touch for these things. Garth responded in the only way he could, being Garth: he turned up the volume.

But before I get too far into that, it's worth spending a few moments with the other important character in the book: John Constantine. Frequently painted as a mystic investigator in some kind of bastardized Chandlerian tradition — Society's Knight riding against the Bad Craziness in the dark — John is one of horror fiction's more complex characters. Rather than Philip Marlowe with a magic kit, John is instead Society's Bastard,

locked inside the world he hates, angry and twisted, holding a small, poisoned set of ethics to his chest. And that last point is possibly the only thing that really makes him different from the rest of them. That's what makes him wake with anger and lie down with it. That little voice that says Fucking People Over Is Wrong, and No One Else Should Have To Live Like This.

In the (Christ! It's damn near a) decade since his creation, John Constantine has gone from the young English occult wideboy of Alan Moore's initial vision to the troubled and aging adrenaline addict of Jamie Delano's bleakly poetic writing, who grew crushed by the appalling weight of his own terrible life during Jamie's often brilliant forty episodes. The strength of the character, that has him remain so clearly the same man even when viewed through two or three different writers' eyes, is that he is a terrific mouthpiece for anger.

Jamie's final episode of his run on the book saw John finding some kind of personal closure, having finally turned

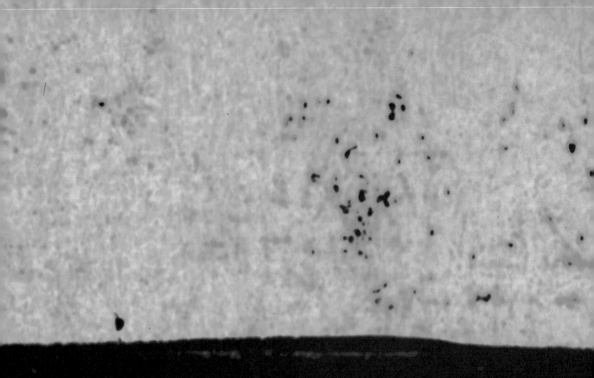

his anger inward. Once Garth got moving — and "Fear and Loathing" really does signal Garth hitting top speed on HELLBLAZER — John Constantine, forty and fucked off, got angry with *everything*. It works because John is very clearly given things worth protecting from the world. In this piece, his anchor and his grail is his girlfriend Kit. A complex piece of work in herself, and John's superior in pretty much everything, she's another facet of the strong, intelligent woman that Garth's been writing (probably unconsciously) from his earliest work, *Troubled Souls*, to PREACHER. The world in which he wants to live with her is symbolized by the clasp of friendship, another major theme of Garth's run on HELLBLAZER and best displayed in the "party issue" contained in this book.

What's John protecting these things from? Authority. With a capital A. These are stories about what authority does to people, about the poison in its foundations. You can substitute Authority for Government, for The Establishment, even for God, and it all means the same

thing: someone exerting control they did not earn and do not deserve, grinding lives into shit largely because they feel like it. This is where Garth and Steve found the anger, in people using our fear on us, locking us in the black iron prison of mediocrity and ignorance.

What follows is among the very best horror work of the 1990s. It retains the occult connections, but what sets it apart from the sad, played-out "dark fantasies" that you'll find on the shelf next to it is its clear knowledge that real horror is perpetrated not by eye-rolling pantomime monsters, or pale things in black with stupid names. Real horror comes only from people. Just people. They're the scariest things in the world.

Hold on, let me light up here... okay, where's the checklist? I've pretty much covered the "I know Garth, which is why I'm writing this" bit, done the quick bio bit, done the history bit and the sad litcrit bit, praised Garth and Steve to the skies so's I can get drinks out of 'em... right, I'm finished. Now go and read the sodding book.

—WARREN ELLIS
SOUTHEND
AUGUST 1996

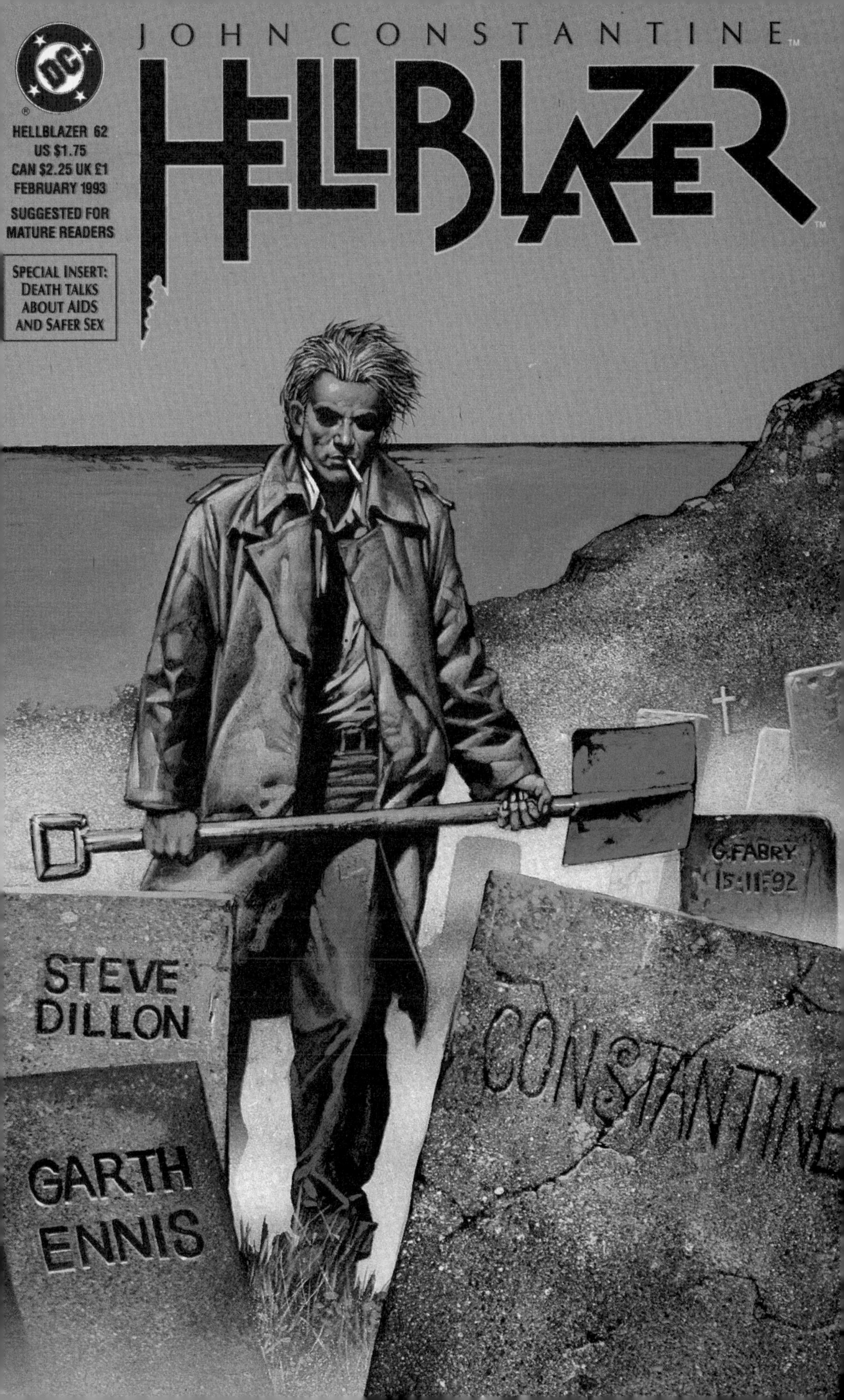

JOHN CONSTANTINE
HELLBLAZER
HELLBLAZER 62
US $1.75
CAN $2.25 UK £1
FEBRUARY 1993
SUGGESTED FOR MATURE READERS
SPECIAL INSERT: DEATH TALKS ABOUT AIDS AND SAFER SEX
G.FABRY
15:11:92
STEVE DILLON
GARTH ENNIS
CONSTANTINE

JOHN CONSTANTINE, HELLBLAZER: TAINTED LOVE

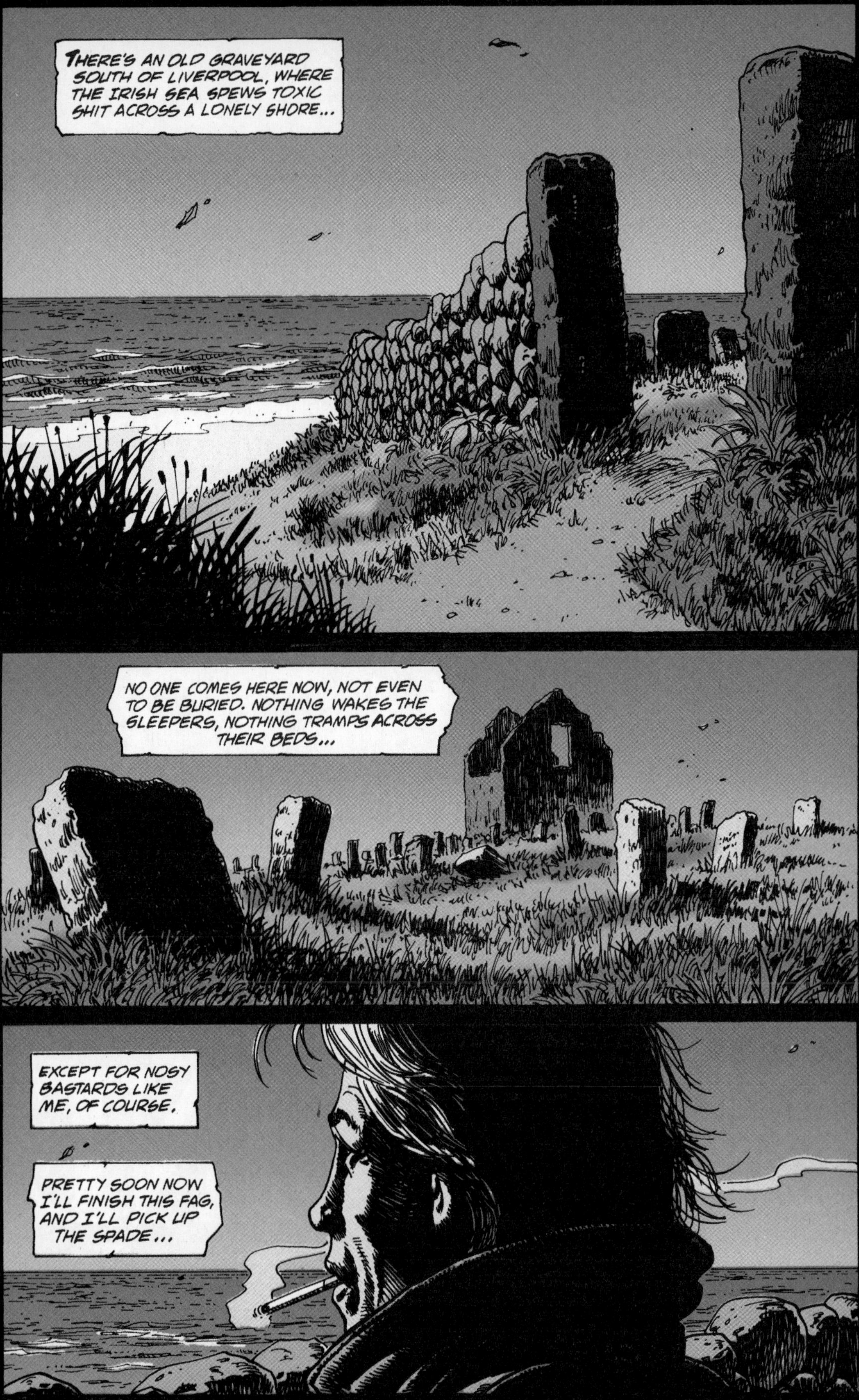
THERE'S AN OLD GRAVEYARD SOUTH OF LIVERPOOL, WHERE THE IRISH SEA SPEWS TOXIC SHIT ACROSS A LONELY SHORE...
NO ONE COMES HERE NOW, NOT EVEN TO BE BURIED. NOTHING WAKES THE SLEEPERS, NOTHING TRAMPS ACROSS THEIR BEDS...
EXCEPT FOR NOSY BASTARDS LIKE ME, OF COURSE.
PRETTY SOON NOW I'LL FINISH THIS FAG, AND I'LL PICK UP THE SPADE...

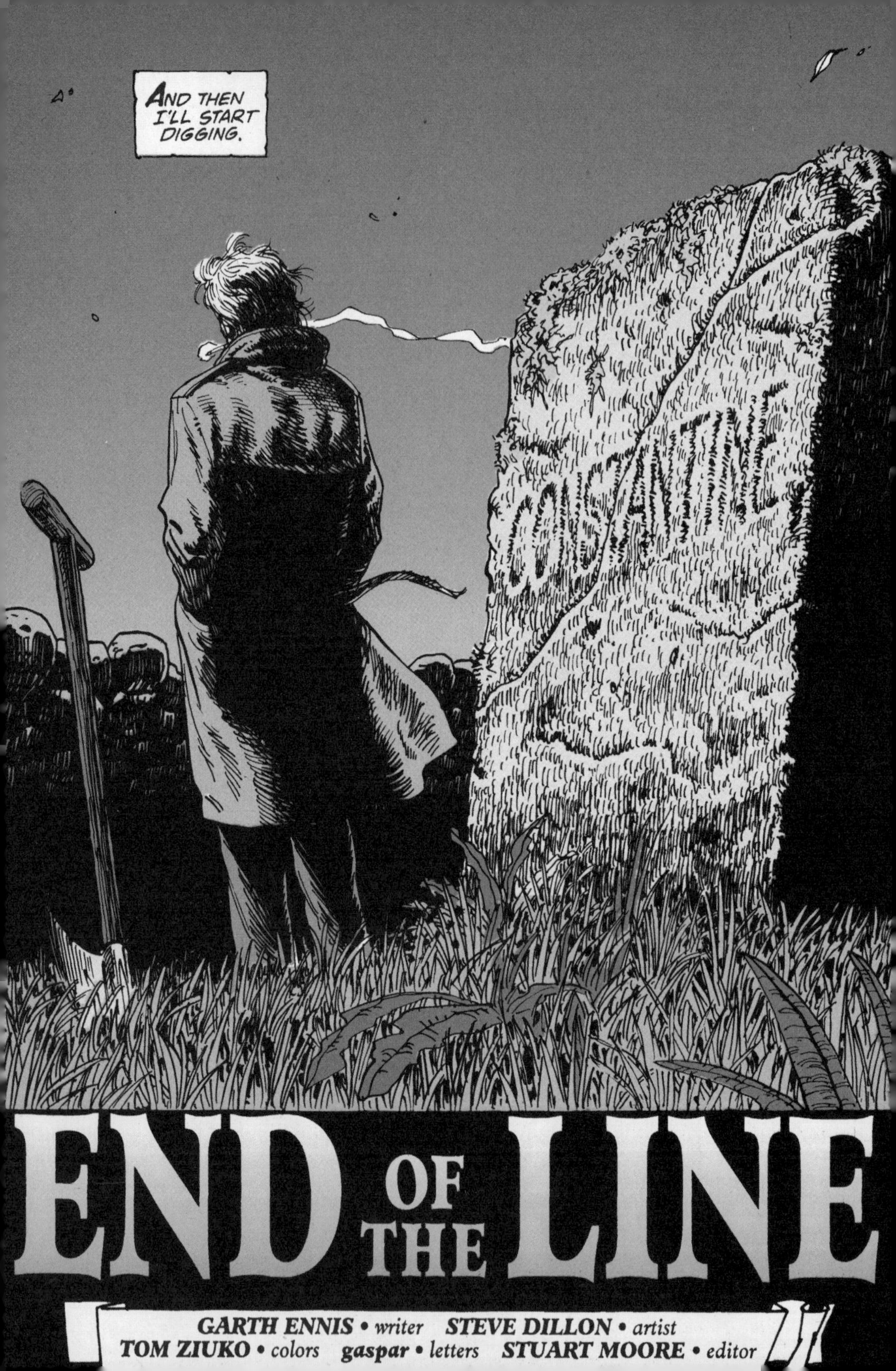
AND THEN I'LL START DIGGING.
CONSTANTINE
END OF THE LINE
GARTH ENNIS • writer STEVE DILLON • artist
TOM ZIUKO • colors gaspar • letters STUART MOORE • editor

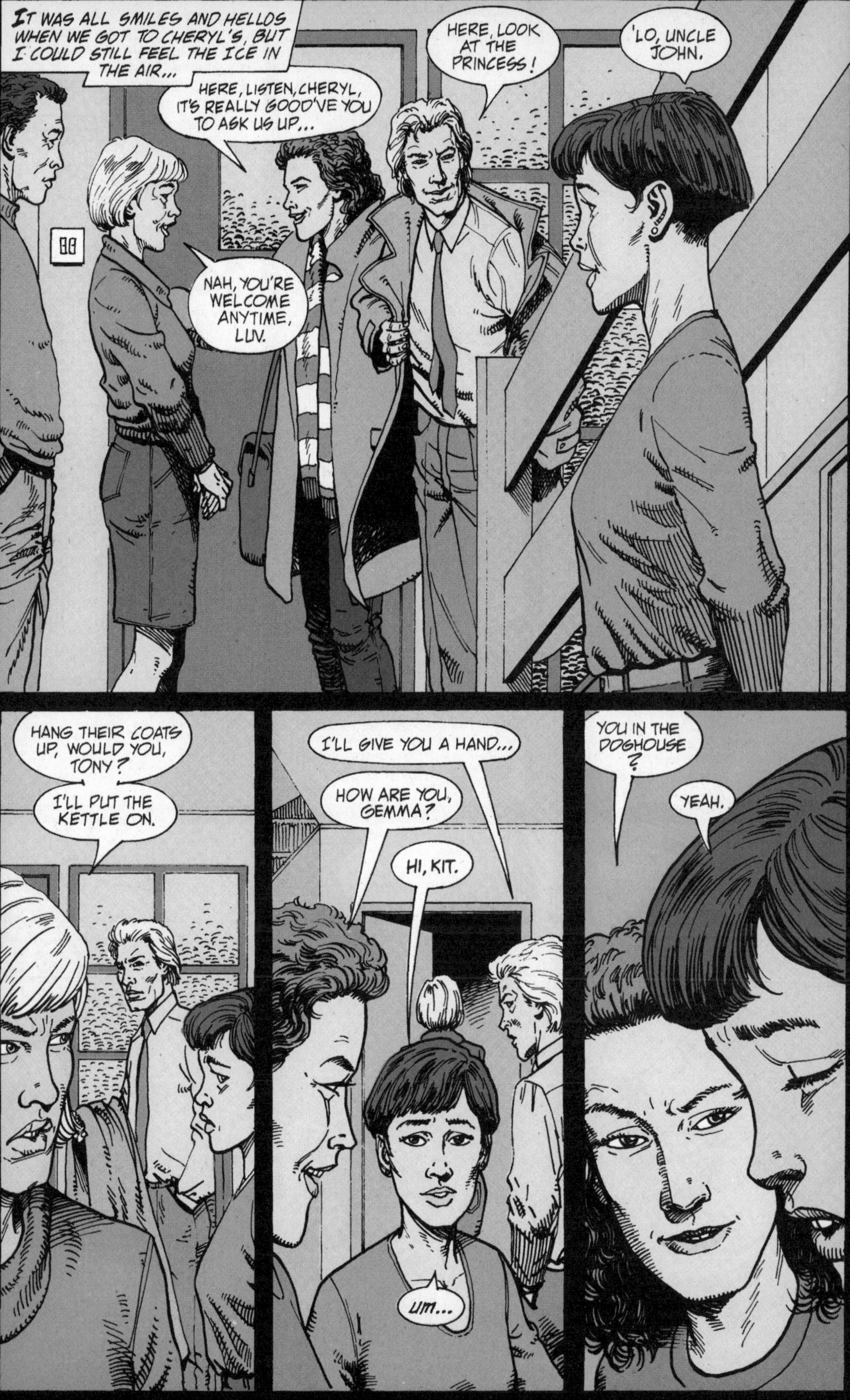

IT WAS ALL SMILES AND HELLOS WHEN WE GOT TO CHERYL'S, BUT I COULD STILL FEEL THE ICE IN THE AIR...
HERE, LISTEN, CHERYL, IT'S REALLY GOOD'VE YOU TO ASK US UP...
HERE, LOOK AT THE PRINCESS!
'LO, UNCLE JOHN.
NAH, YOU'RE WELCOME ANYTIME, LUV.
HANG THEIR COATS UP, WOULD YOU, TONY?
I'LL PUT THE KETTLE ON.
I'LL GIVE YOU A HAND...
HOW ARE YOU, GEMMA?
HI, KIT.
UM...
YOU IN THE DOGHOUSE?
YEAH.

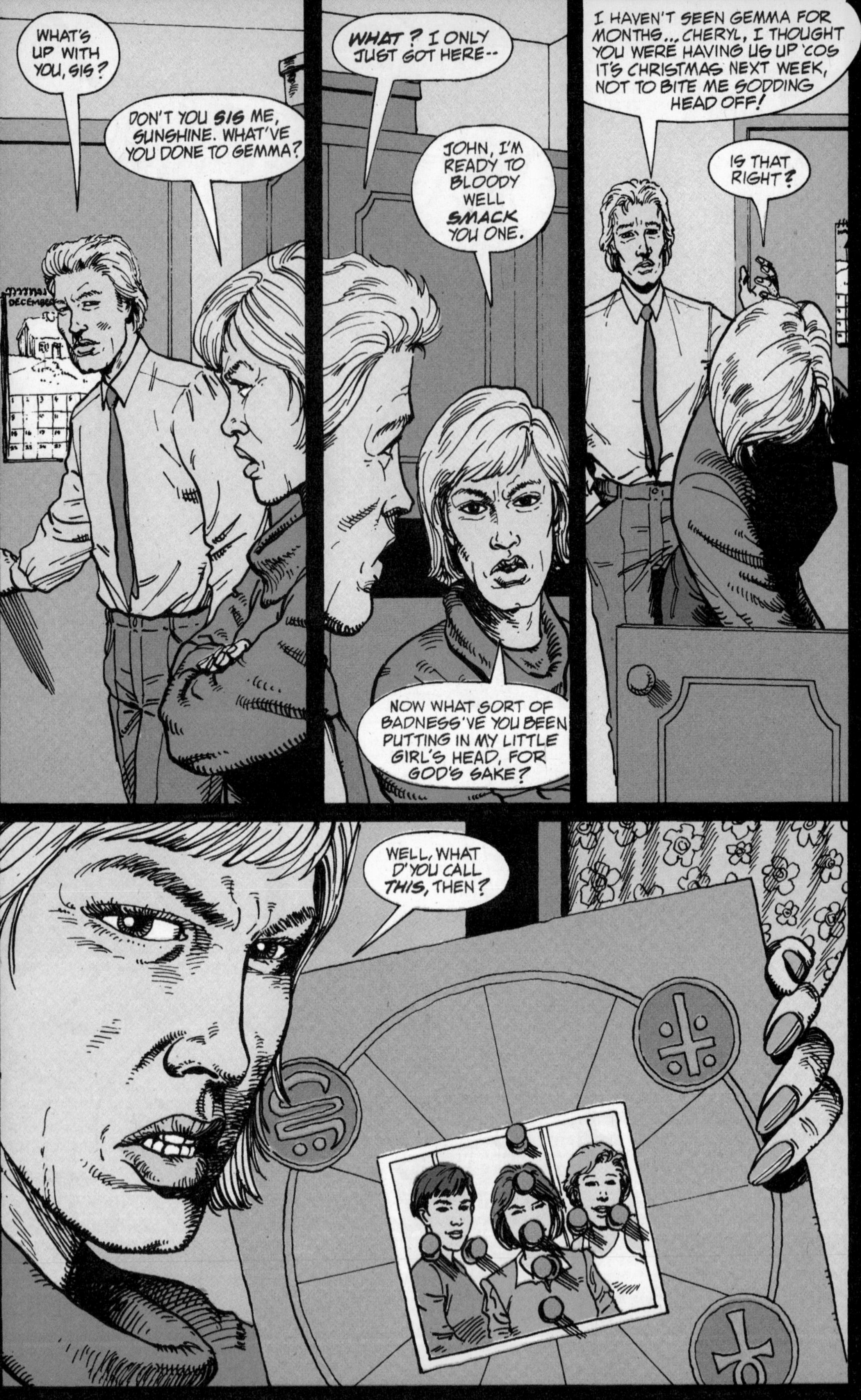
WHAT'S UP WITH YOU, SIS?
DON'T YOU SIS ME, SUNSHINE. WHAT'VE YOU DONE TO GEMMA?
WHAT? I ONLY JUST GOT HERE--
JOHN, I'M READY TO BLOODY WELL SMACK YOU ONE.
NOW WHAT SORT OF BADNESS'VE YOU BEEN PUTTING IN MY LITTLE GIRL'S HEAD, FOR GOD'S SAKE?
I HAVEN'T SEEN GEMMA FOR MONTHS... CHERYL, I THOUGHT YOU WERE HAVING US UP 'COS IT'S CHRISTMAS NEXT WEEK, NOT TO BITE ME SODDING HEAD OFF!
IS THAT RIGHT?
WELL, WHAT D'YOU CALL THIS, THEN?

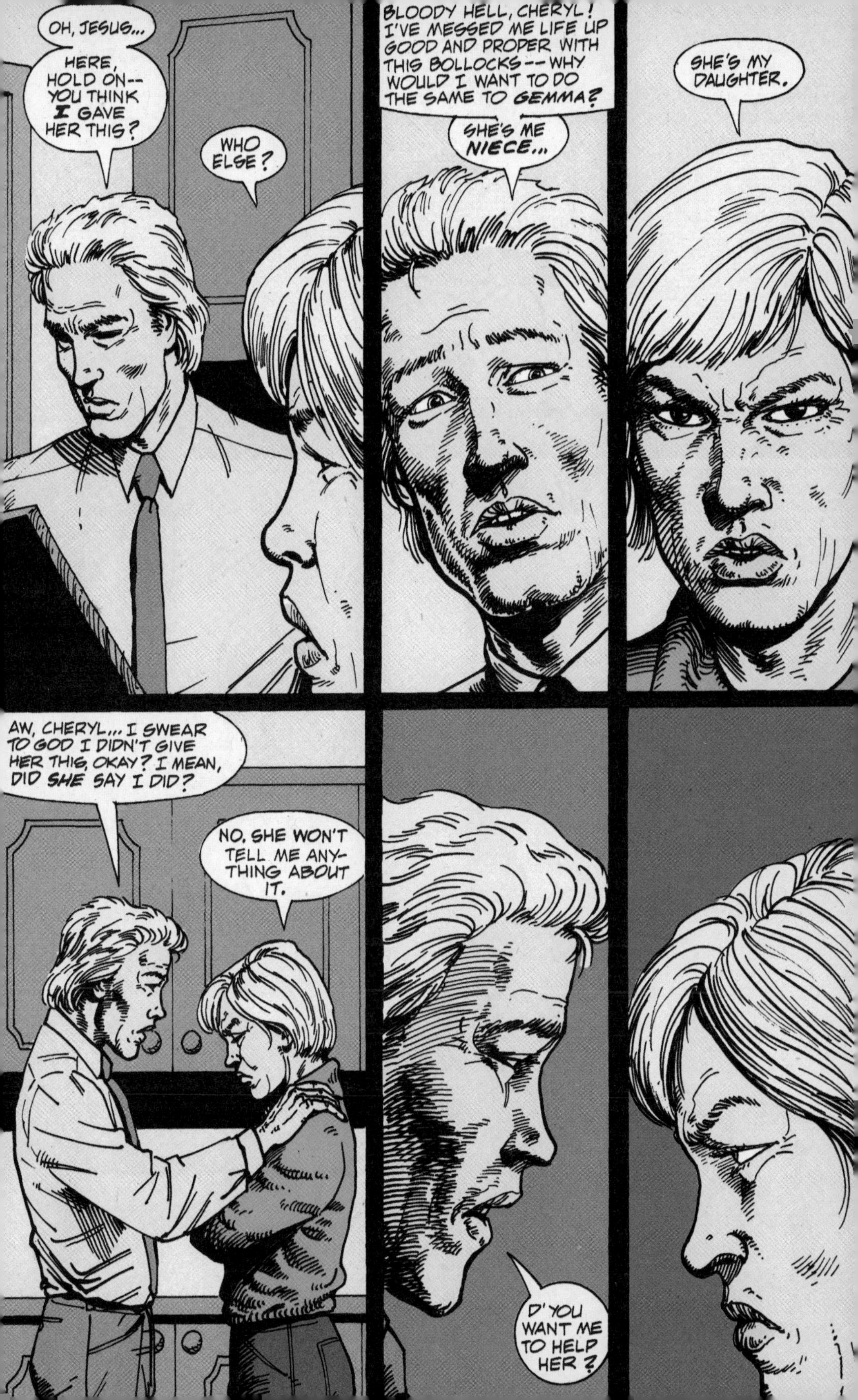
OH, JESUS...
HERE, HOLD ON-- YOU THINK I GAVE HER THIS?
WHO ELSE?
BLOODY HELL, CHERYL! I'VE MESSED ME LIFE UP GOOD AND PROPER WITH THIS BOLLOCKS-- WHY WOULD I WANT TO DO THE SAME TO GEMMA?
SHE'S ME NIECE...
SHE'S MY DAUGHTER.
AW, CHERYL... I SWEAR TO GOD I DIDN'T GIVE HER THIS, OKAY? I MEAN, DID SHE SAY I DID?
NO. SHE WON'T TELL ME ANYTHING ABOUT IT.
D'YOU WANT ME TO HELP HER?

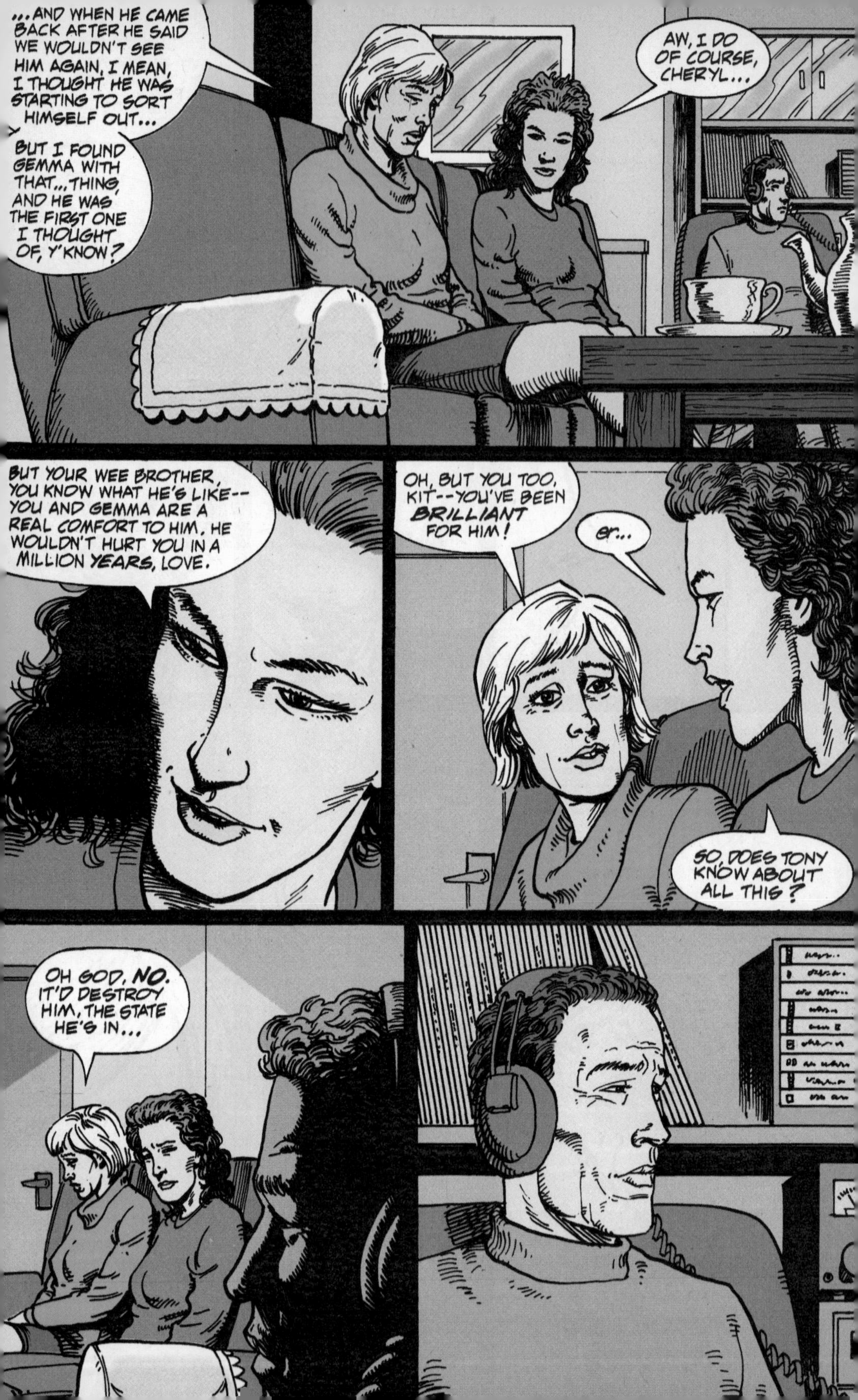
...AND WHEN HE CAME BACK AFTER HE SAID WE WOULDN'T SEE HIM AGAIN, I MEAN, I THOUGHT HE WAS STARTING TO SORT HIMSELF OUT...
BUT I FOUND GEMMA WITH THAT...THING, AND HE WAS THE FIRST ONE I THOUGHT OF, Y'KNOW?
AW, I DO OF COURSE, CHERYL...
BUT YOUR WEE BROTHER, YOU KNOW WHAT HE'S LIKE-- YOU AND GEMMA ARE A REAL COMFORT TO HIM. HE WOULDN'T HURT YOU IN A MILLION YEARS, LOVE.
OH, BUT YOU TOO, KIT--YOU'VE BEEN BRILLIANT FOR HIM!
er...
SO, DOES TONY KNOW ABOUT ALL THIS?
OH GOD, NO. IT'D DESTROY HIM, THE STATE HE'S IN...

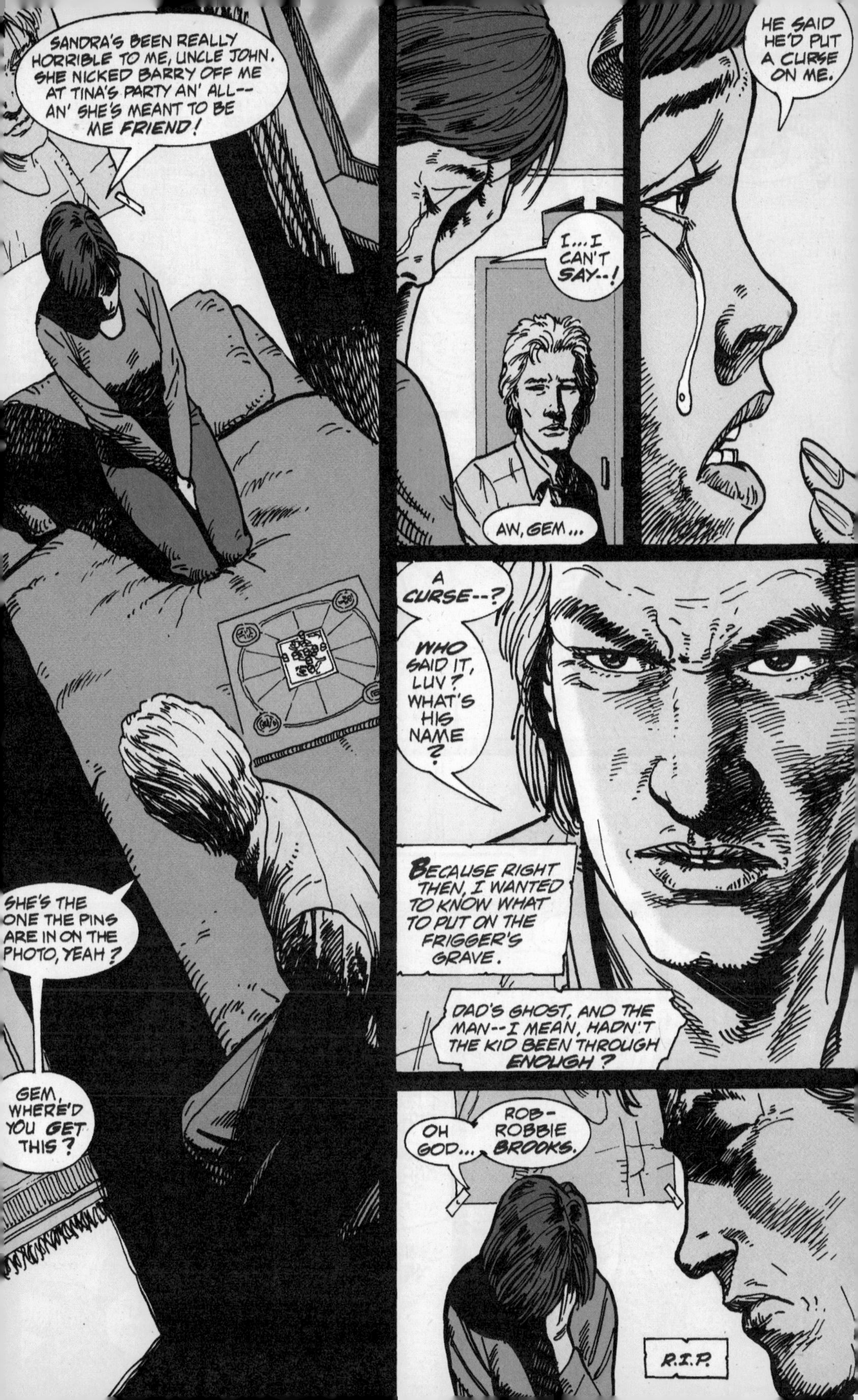

SANDRA'S BEEN REALLY HORRIBLE TO ME, UNCLE JOHN. SHE NICKED BARRY OFF ME AT TINA'S PARTY AN' ALL-- AN' SHE'S MEANT TO BE ME FRIEND!
SHE'S THE ONE THE PINS ARE IN ON THE PHOTO, YEAH?
GEM, WHERE'D YOU GET THIS?
I... I CAN'T SAY--!
AW, GEM...
HE SAID HE'D PUT A CURSE ON ME.
A CURSE--?
WHO SAID IT, LUV? WHAT'S HIS NAME?
BECAUSE RIGHT THEN, I WANTED TO KNOW WHAT TO PUT ON THE FRIGGER'S GRAVE.
DAD'S GHOST, AND THE MAN--I MEAN, HADN'T THE KID BEEN THROUGH ENOUGH?
OH GOD...
ROB- ROBBIE BROOKS.
R.I.P.

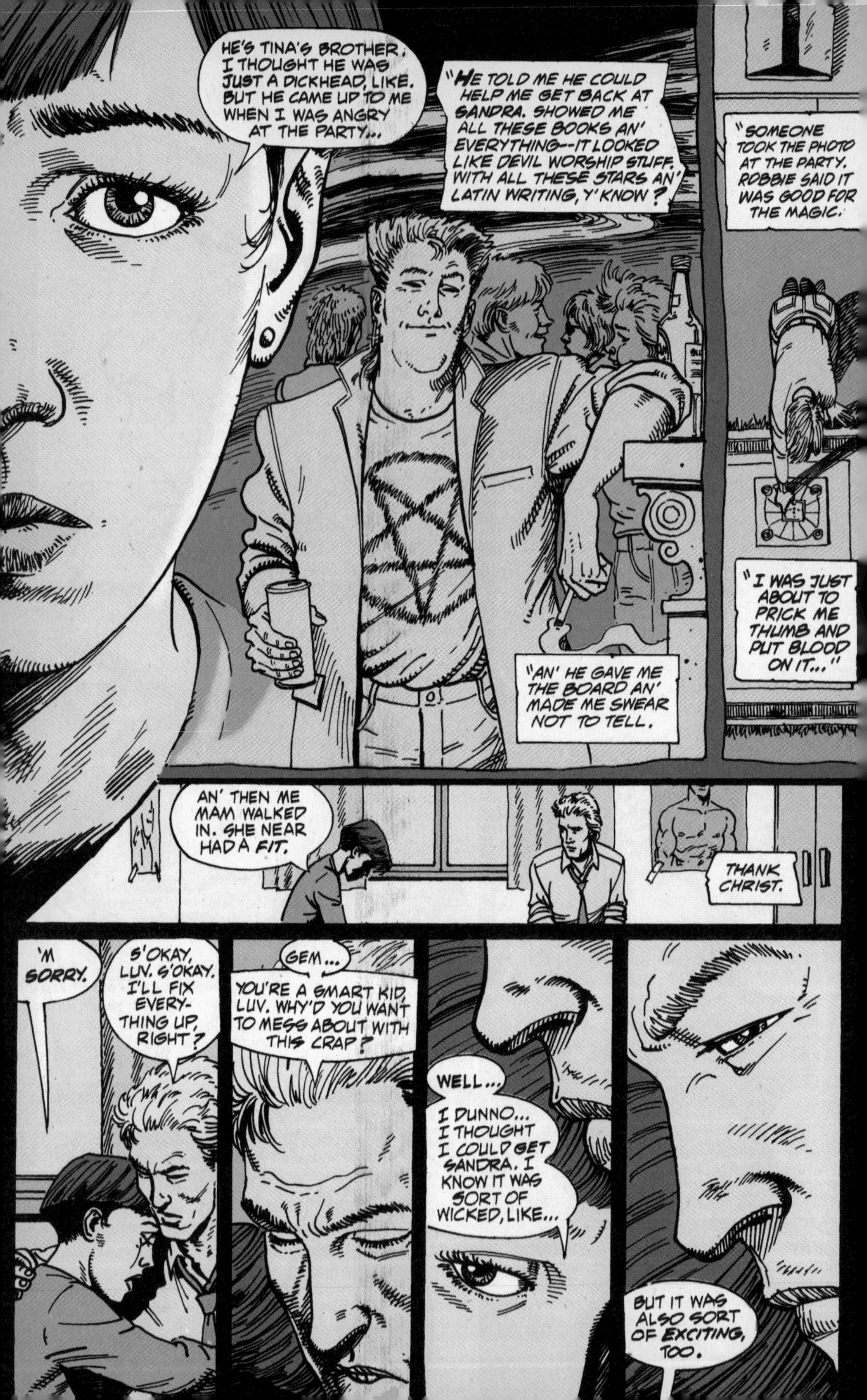
HE'S TINA'S BROTHER. I THOUGHT HE WAS JUST A DICKHEAD, LIKE. BUT HE CAME UP TO ME WHEN I WAS ANGRY AT THE PARTY...
"HE TOLD ME HE COULD HELP ME GET BACK AT SANDRA. SHOWED ME ALL THESE BOOKS AN' EVERYTHING--IT LOOKED LIKE DEVIL WORSHIP STUFF. WITH ALL THESE STARS AN' LATIN WRITING, Y'KNOW?
"SOMEONE TOOK THE PHOTO AT THE PARTY. ROBBIE SAID IT WAS GOOD FOR THE MAGIC.
"AN' HE GAVE ME THE BOARD AN' MADE ME SWEAR NOT TO TELL.
"I WAS JUST ABOUT TO PRICK ME THUMB AND PUT BLOOD ON IT..."
AN' THEN ME MAM WALKED IN. SHE NEAR HAD A FIT.
THANK CHRIST.
'M SORRY.
S'OKAY, LUV. S'OKAY. I'LL FIX EVERY-THING UP, RIGHT?
GEM...
YOU'RE A SMART KID, LUV. WHY'D YOU WANT TO MESS ABOUT WITH THIS CRAP?
WELL...
I DUNNO... I THOUGHT I COULD GET SANDRA. I KNOW IT WAS SORT OF WICKED, LIKE...
BUT IT WAS ALSO SORT OF EXCITING, TOO.

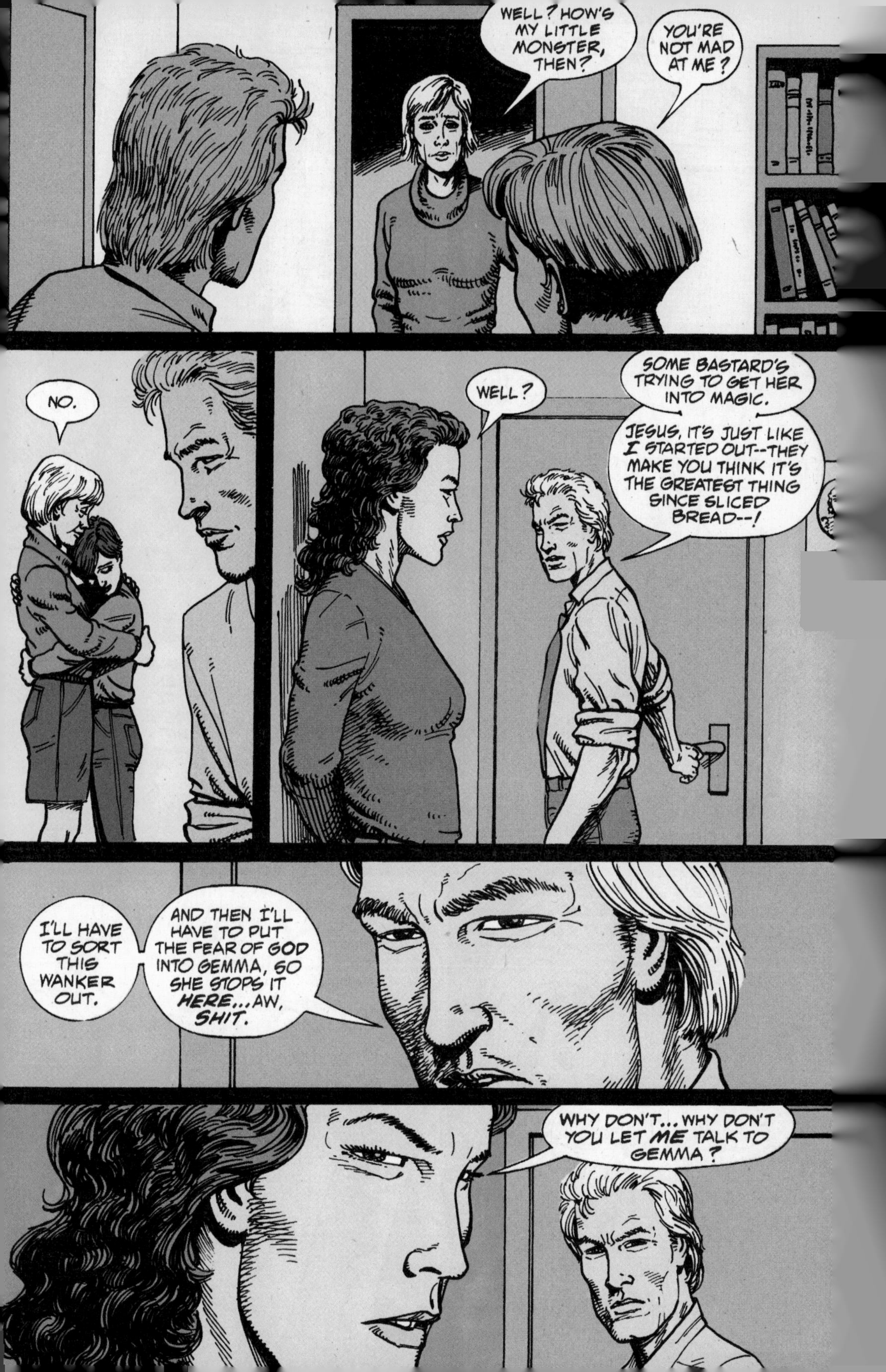
WELL? HOW'S MY LITTLE MONSTER, THEN?
YOU'RE NOT MAD AT ME?
NO.
WELL?
SOME BASTARD'S TRYING TO GET HER INTO MAGIC.
JESUS, IT'S JUST LIKE I STARTED OUT--THEY MAKE YOU THINK IT'S THE GREATEST THING SINCE SLICED BREAD--!
I'LL HAVE TO SORT THIS WANKER OUT.
AND THEN I'LL HAVE TO PUT THE FEAR OF GOD INTO GEMMA, SO SHE STOPS IT HERE... AW, SHIT.
WHY DON'T... WHY DON'T YOU LET ME TALK TO GEMMA?

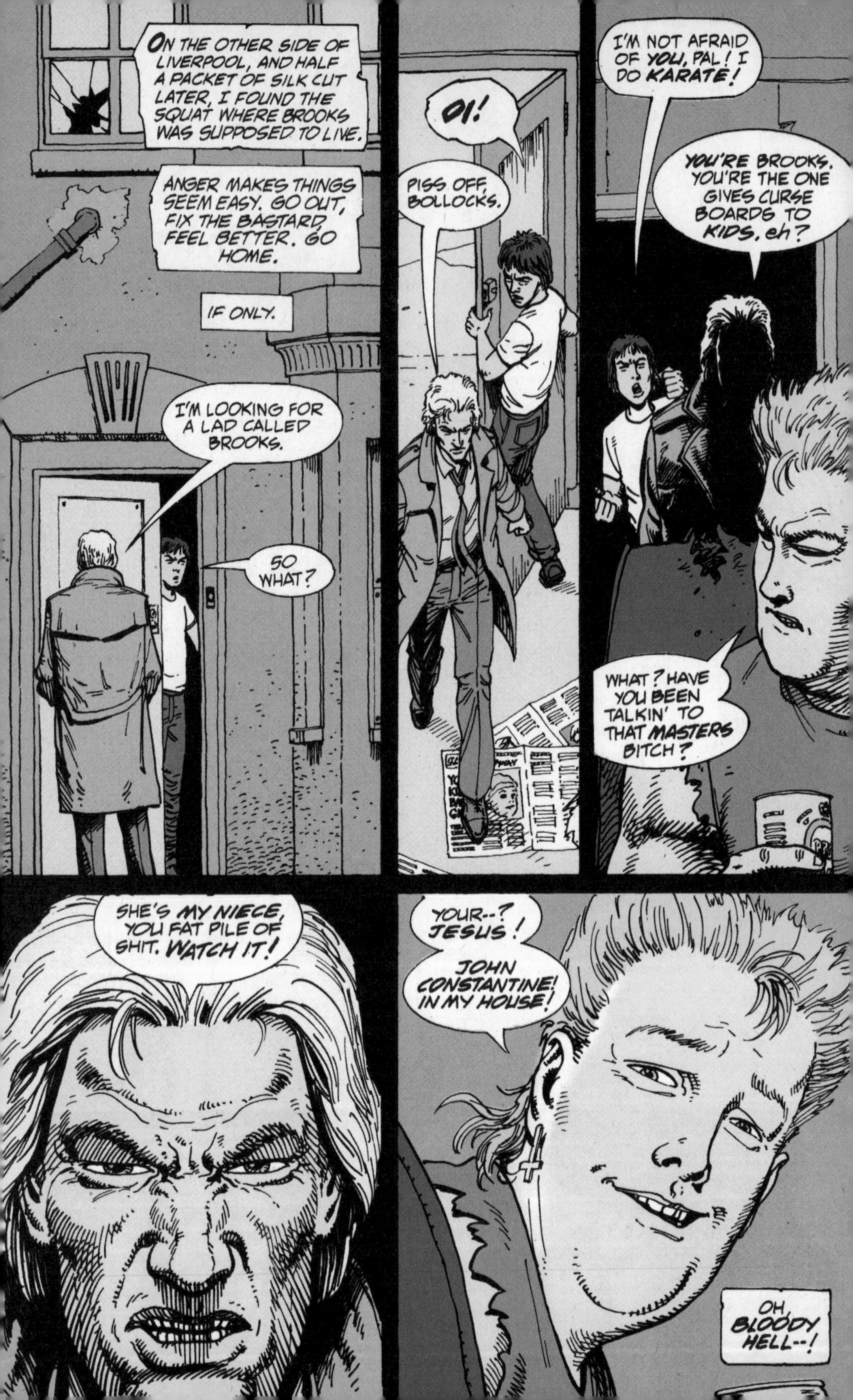
ON THE OTHER SIDE OF LIVERPOOL, AND HALF A PACKET OF SILK CUT LATER, I FOUND THE SQUAT WHERE BROOKS WAS SUPPOSED TO LIVE.
ANGER MAKES THINGS SEEM EASY. GO OUT, FIX THE BASTARD, FEEL BETTER. GO HOME.
IF ONLY.
I'M LOOKING FOR A LAD CALLED BROOKS.
SO WHAT?
OI!
PISS OFF, BOLLOCKS.
I'M NOT AFRAID OF YOU, PAL! I DO KARATE!
YOU'RE BROOKS. YOU'RE THE ONE GIVES CURSE BOARDS TO KIDS, eh?
WHAT? HAVE YOU BEEN TALKIN' TO THAT MASTERS BITCH?
SHE'S MY NIECE, YOU FAT PILE OF SHIT. WATCH IT!
YOUR--? JESUS!
JOHN CONSTANTINE! IN MY HOUSE!
OH, BLOODY HELL--!

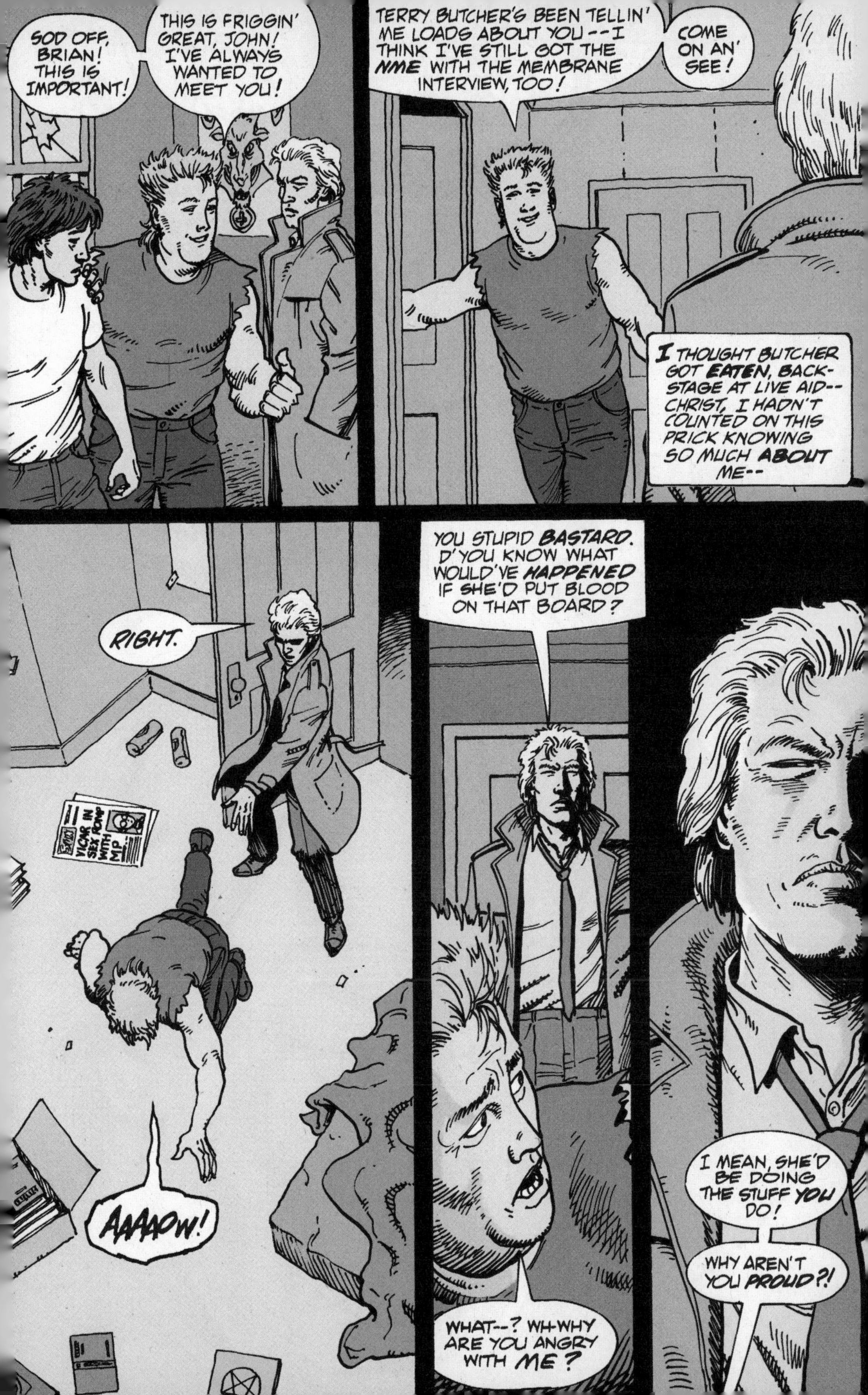
SOD OFF, BRIAN! THIS IS IMPORTANT!
THIS IS FRIGGIN' GREAT, JOHN! I'VE ALWAYS WANTED TO MEET YOU!
TERRY BUTCHER'S BEEN TELLIN' ME LOADS ABOUT YOU -- I THINK I'VE STILL GOT THE NME WITH THE MEMBRANE INTERVIEW, TOO!
COME ON AN' SEE!
I THOUGHT BUTCHER GOT EATEN, BACKSTAGE AT LIVE AID-- CHRIST, I HADN'T COUNTED ON THIS PRICK KNOWING SO MUCH ABOUT ME--
RIGHT.
VICAR IN SEX ROW WITH MP
AAAAOW!
YOU STUPID BASTARD. D'YOU KNOW WHAT WOULD'VE HAPPENED IF SHE'D PUT BLOOD ON THAT BOARD?
WHAT--? WH-WHY ARE YOU ANGRY WITH ME?
I MEAN, SHE'D BE DOING THE STUFF YOU DO!
WHY AREN'T YOU PROUD?!

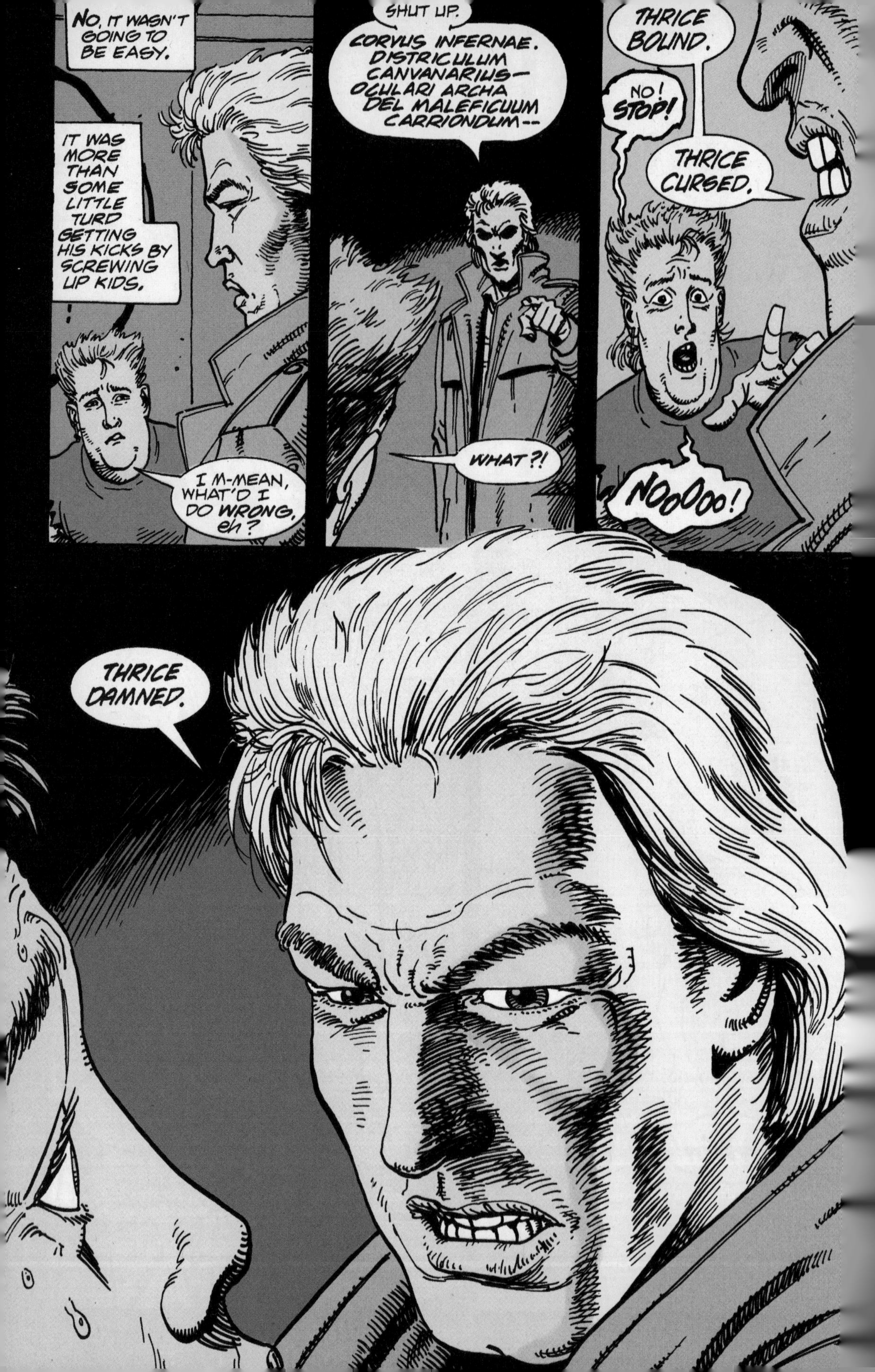

NO, IT WASN'T GOING TO BE EASY.
IT WAS MORE THAN SOME LITTLE TURD GETTING HIS KICKS BY SCREWING UP KIDS.
I M-MEAN, WHAT'D I DO WRONG, eh?
SHUT UP.
CORVUS INFERNAE. DISTRICULUM CANVANARIUS-OCULARI ARCHA DEL MALEFICUUM CARRIONDUM--
WHAT?!
THRICE BOUND.
NO! STOP!
THRICE CURSED.
NOOOOO!
THRICE DAMNED.

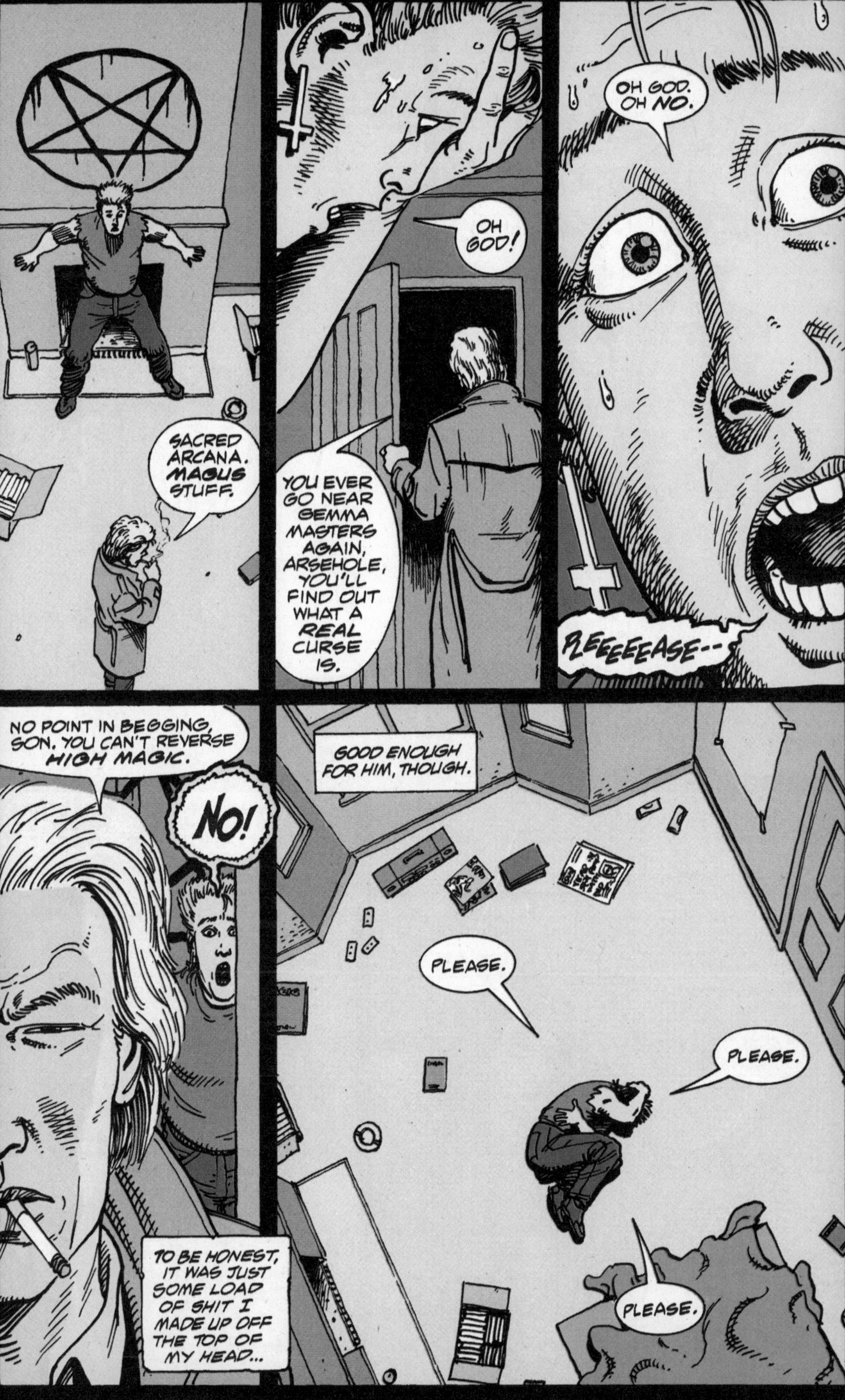
SACRED ARCANA. MAGUS STUFF.
OH GOD!
YOU EVER GO NEAR GEMMA MASTERS AGAIN, ARSEHOLE, YOU'LL FIND OUT WHAT A REAL CURSE IS.
OH GOD. OH NO.
PLEEEEEEASE--
NO POINT IN BEGGING, SON. YOU CAN'T REVERSE HIGH MAGIC.
NO!
TO BE HONEST, IT WAS JUST SOME LOAD OF SHIT I MADE UP OFF THE TOP OF MY HEAD...
GOOD ENOUGH FOR HIM, THOUGH.
PLEASE.
PLEASE.
PLEASE.

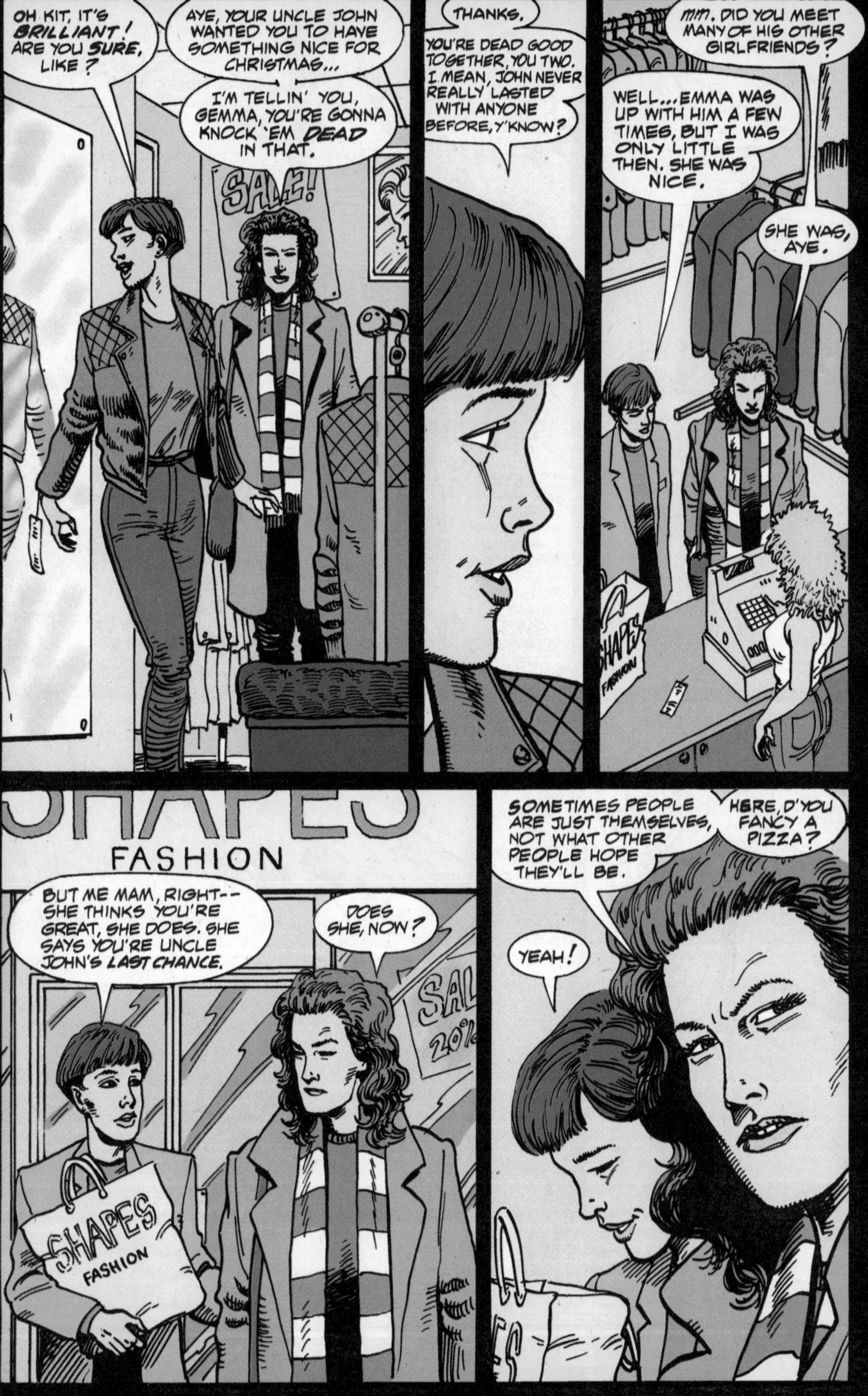

OH KIT, IT'S BRILLIANT! ARE YOU SURE, LIKE?
AYE, YOUR UNCLE JOHN WANTED YOU TO HAVE SOMETHING NICE FOR CHRISTMAS...
I'M TELLIN' YOU, GEMMA, YOU'RE GONNA KNOCK 'EM DEAD IN THAT.
SALE!
THANKS.
YOU'RE DEAD GOOD TOGETHER, YOU TWO. I MEAN, JOHN NEVER REALLY LASTED WITH ANYONE BEFORE, Y'KNOW?
MM. DID YOU MEET MANY OF HIS OTHER GIRLFRIENDS?
WELL...EMMA WAS UP WITH HIM A FEW TIMES, BUT I WAS ONLY LITTLE THEN. SHE WAS NICE.
SHE WAS, AYE.
SHAPES FASHION
SHAPES
FASHION
BUT ME MAM, RIGHT--SHE THINKS YOU'RE GREAT, SHE DOES. SHE SAYS YOU'RE UNCLE JOHN'S LAST CHANCE.
DOES SHE, NOW?
SHAPES FASHION
SOMETIMES PEOPLE ARE JUST THEMSELVES, NOT WHAT OTHER PEOPLE HOPE THEY'LL BE.
HERE, D'YOU FANCY A PIZZA?
YEAH!

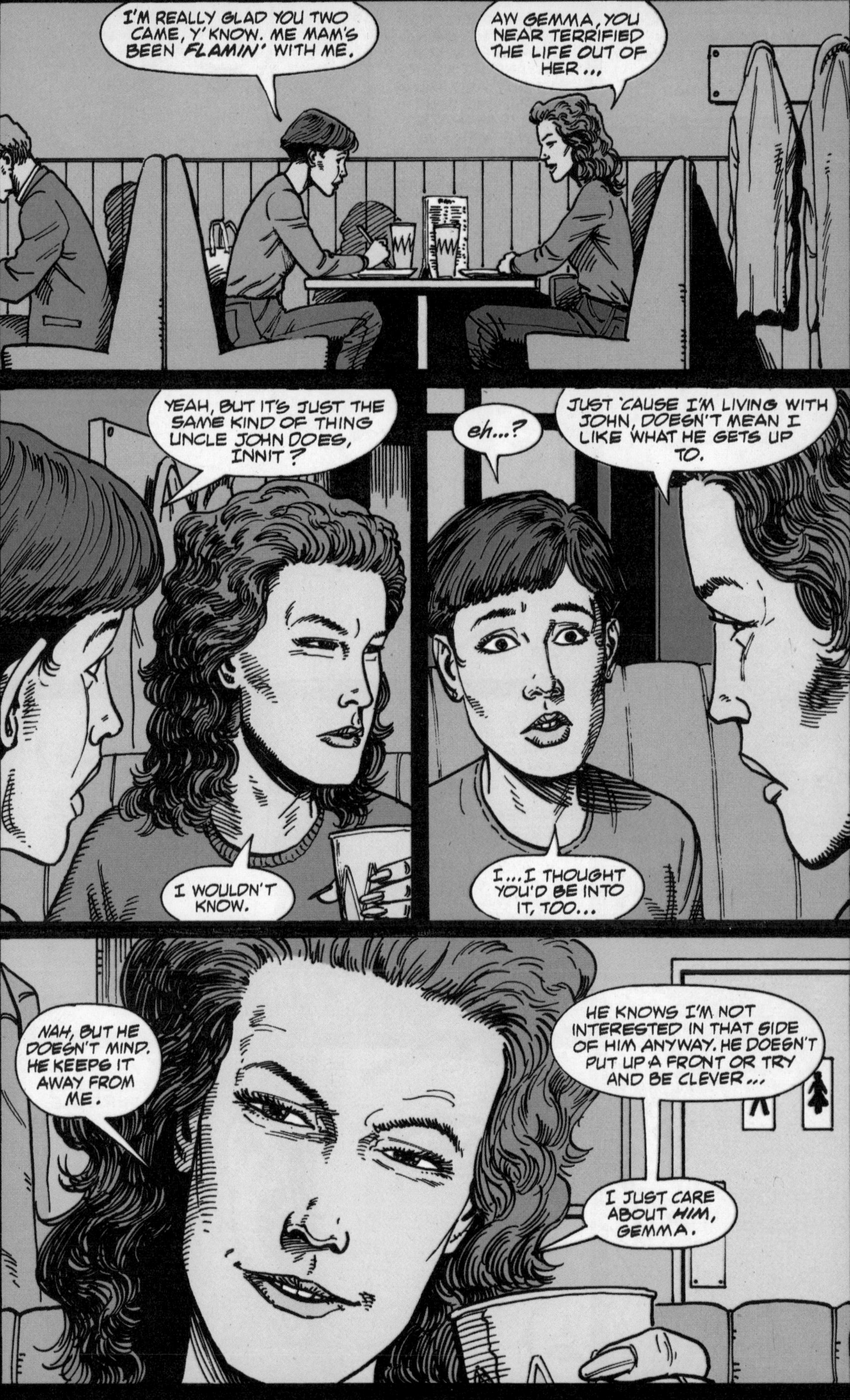

I'M REALLY GLAD YOU TWO CAME, Y'KNOW. ME MAM'S BEEN *FLAMIN'* WITH ME.
AW GEMMA, YOU NEAR TERRIFIED THE LIFE OUT OF HER...
YEAH, BUT IT'S JUST THE SAME KIND OF THING UNCLE JOHN DOES, INNIT?
I WOULDN'T KNOW.
eh...?
JUST 'CAUSE I'M LIVING WITH JOHN, DOESN'T MEAN I LIKE WHAT HE GETS UP TO.
I...I THOUGHT YOU'D BE INTO IT, TOO...
NAH, BUT HE DOESN'T MIND. HE KEEPS IT AWAY FROM ME.
HE KNOWS I'M NOT INTERESTED IN THAT SIDE OF HIM ANYWAY. HE DOESN'T PUT UP A FRONT OR TRY AND BE CLEVER...
I JUST CARE ABOUT *HIM*, GEMMA.

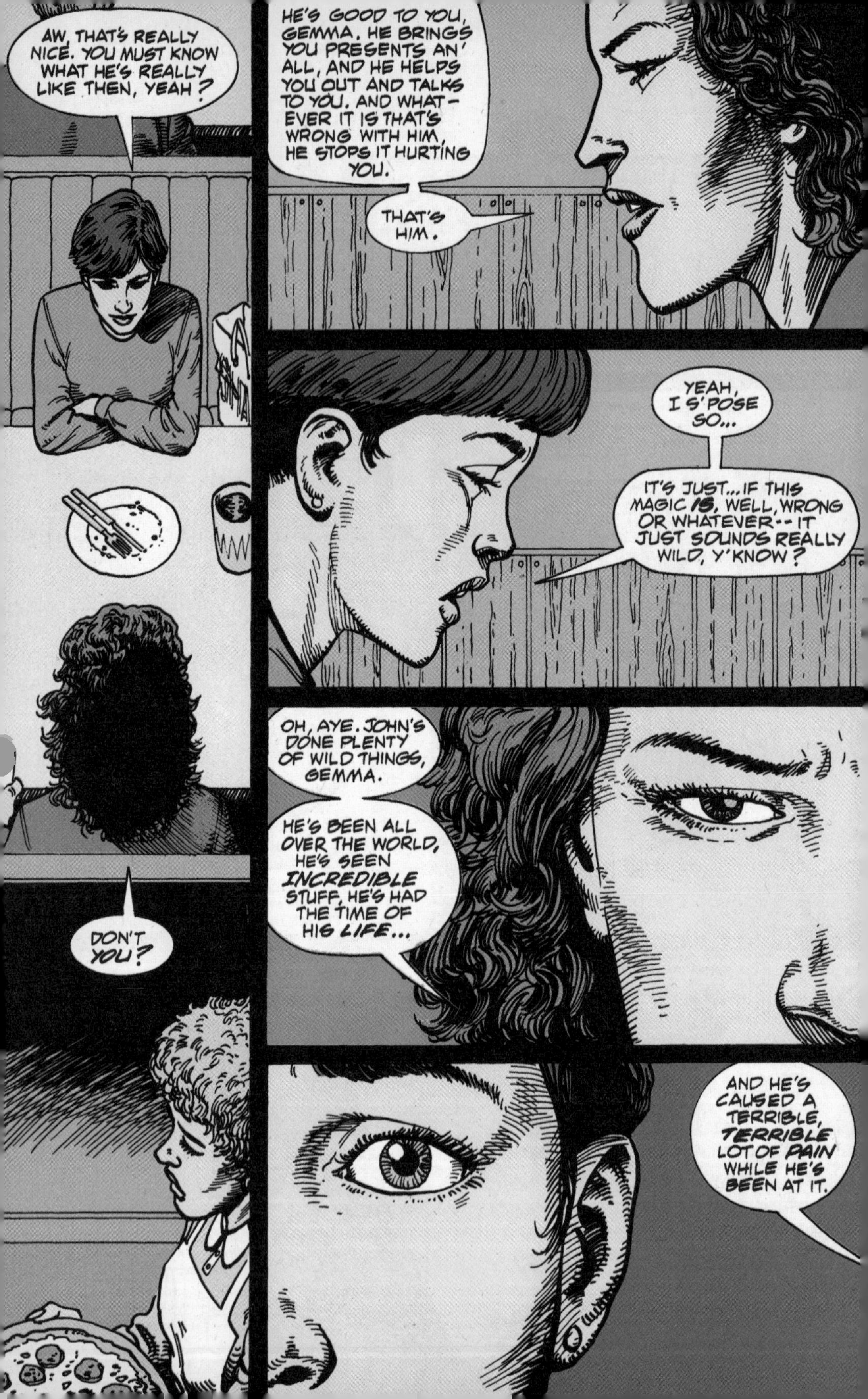
AW, THAT'S REALLY NICE. YOU MUST KNOW WHAT HE'S REALLY LIKE THEN, YEAH?
HE'S GOOD TO YOU, GEMMA. HE BRINGS YOU PRESENTS AN' ALL, AND HE HELPS YOU OUT AND TALKS TO YOU. AND WHAT-EVER IT IS THAT'S WRONG WITH HIM, HE STOPS IT HURTING YOU.
THAT'S HIM.
YEAH, I S'POSE SO...
IT'S JUST... IF THIS MAGIC *IS*, WELL, WRONG OR WHATEVER-- IT JUST SOUNDS REALLY WILD, Y'KNOW?
OH, AYE. JOHN'S DONE PLENTY OF WILD THINGS, GEMMA.
HE'S BEEN ALL OVER THE WORLD, HE'S SEEN *INCREDIBLE* STUFF, HE'S HAD THE TIME OF HIS *LIFE*...
DON'T *YOU*?
AND HE'S CAUSED A TERRIBLE, *TERRIBLE* LOT OF *PAIN* WHILE HE'S BEEN AT IT.

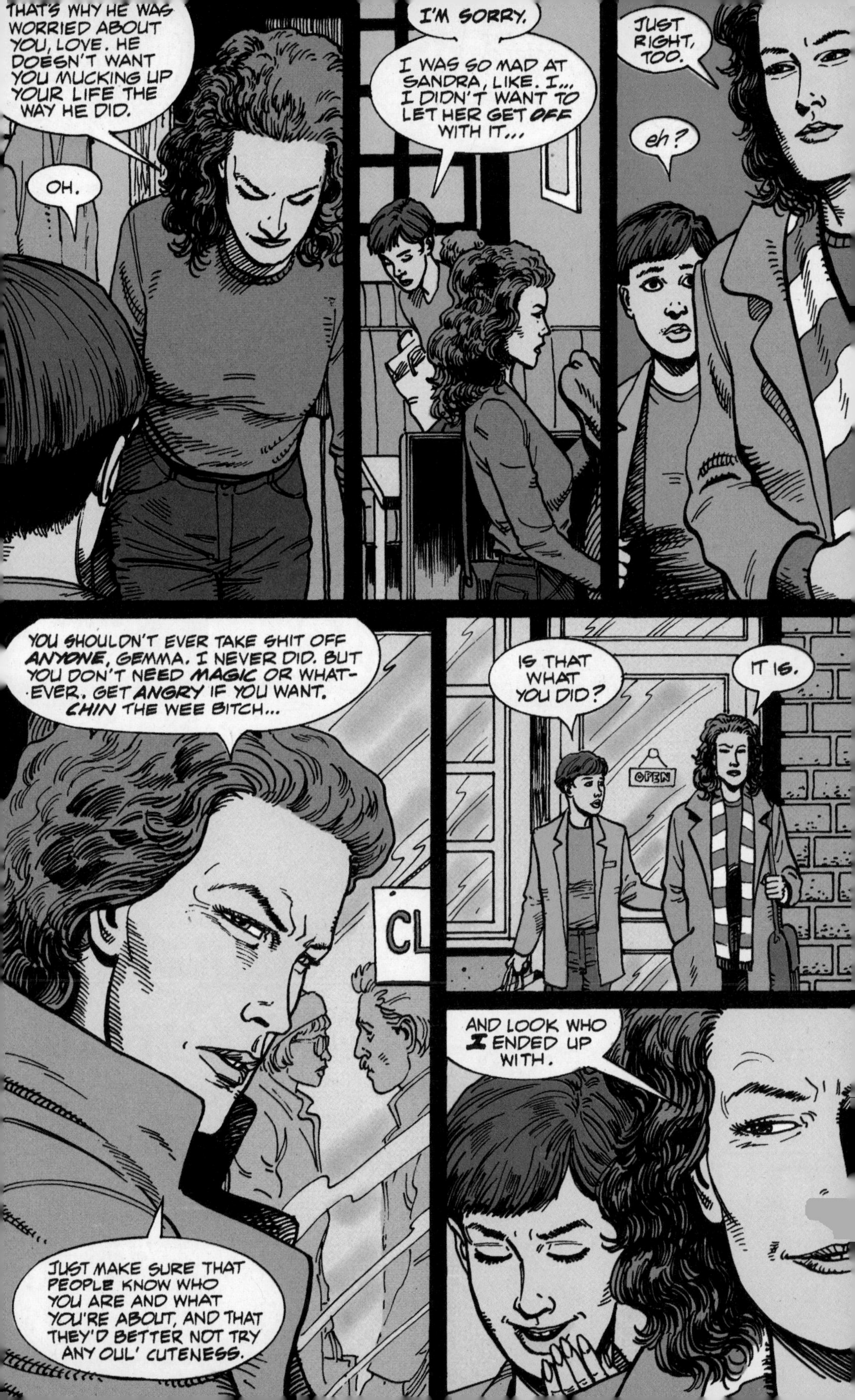

THAT'S WHY HE WAS WORRIED ABOUT YOU, LOVE. HE DOESN'T WANT YOU MUCKING UP YOUR LIFE THE WAY HE DID.
OH.
I'M SORRY.
I WAS SO MAD AT SANDRA, LIKE. I... I DIDN'T WANT TO LET HER GET OFF WITH IT...
JUST RIGHT, TOO.
eh?
YOU SHOULDN'T EVER TAKE SHIT OFF ANYONE, GEMMA. I NEVER DID. BUT YOU DON'T NEED MAGIC OR WHAT-EVER. GET ANGRY IF YOU WANT. CHIN THE WEE BITCH...
JUST MAKE SURE THAT PEOPLE KNOW WHO YOU ARE AND WHAT YOU'RE ABOUT, AND THAT THEY'D BETTER NOT TRY ANY OUL' CUTENESS.
IS THAT WHAT YOU DID?
IT IS.
OPEN
AND LOOK WHO I ENDED UP WITH.

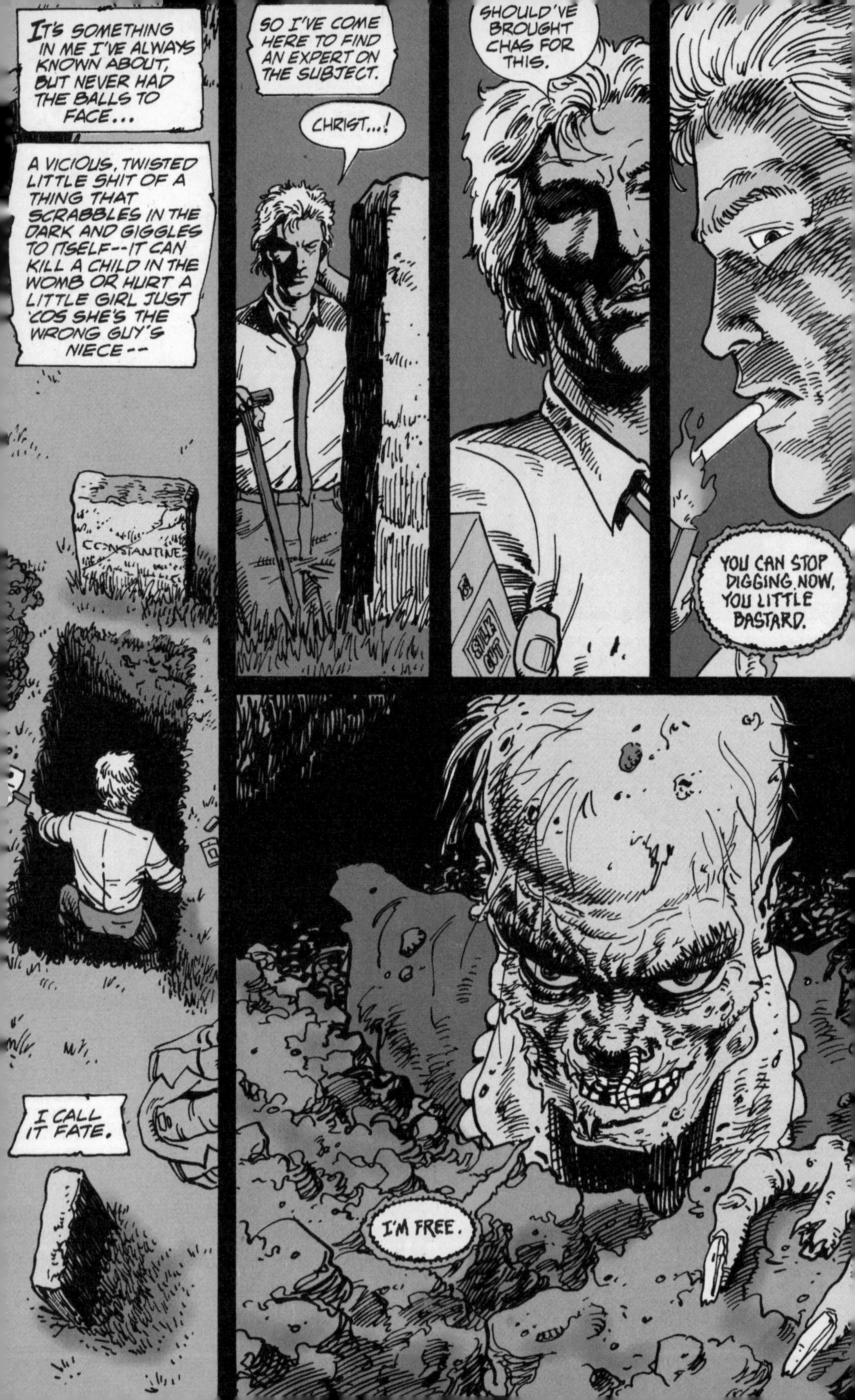
IT'S SOMETHING IN ME I'VE ALWAYS KNOWN ABOUT, BUT NEVER HAD THE BALLS TO FACE...
A VICIOUS, TWISTED LITTLE SHIT OF A THING THAT SCRABBLES IN THE DARK AND GIGGLES TO ITSELF--IT CAN KILL A CHILD IN THE WOMB OR HURT A LITTLE GIRL JUST 'COS SHE'S THE WRONG GUY'S NIECE--
SO I'VE COME HERE TO FIND AN EXPERT ON THE SUBJECT.
CHRIST...!
SHOULD'VE BROUGHT CHAS FOR THIS.
YOU CAN STOP DIGGING NOW, YOU LITTLE BASTARD.
I CALL IT FATE.
I'M FREE.

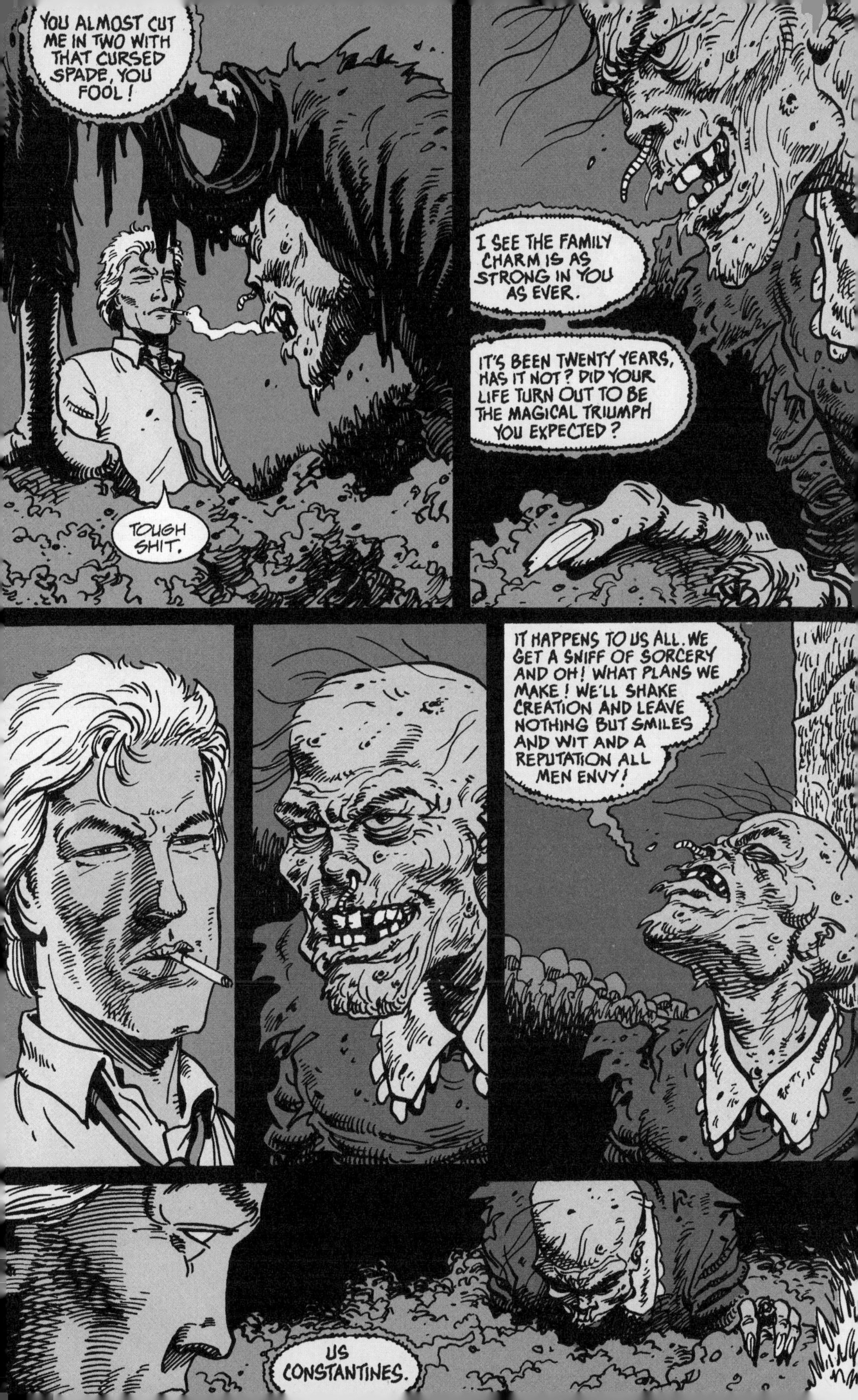
YOU ALMOST CUT ME IN TWO WITH THAT CURSED SPADE, YOU FOOL!
TOUGH SHIT.
I SEE THE FAMILY CHARM IS AS STRONG IN YOU AS EVER.
IT'S BEEN TWENTY YEARS, HAS IT NOT? DID YOUR LIFE TURN OUT TO BE THE MAGICAL TRIUMPH YOU EXPECTED?
IT HAPPENS TO US ALL. WE GET A SNIFF OF SORCERY AND OH! WHAT PLANS WE MAKE! WE'LL SHAKE CREATION AND LEAVE NOTHING BUT SMILES AND WIT AND A REPUTATION ALL MEN ENVY!
US CONSTANTINES.

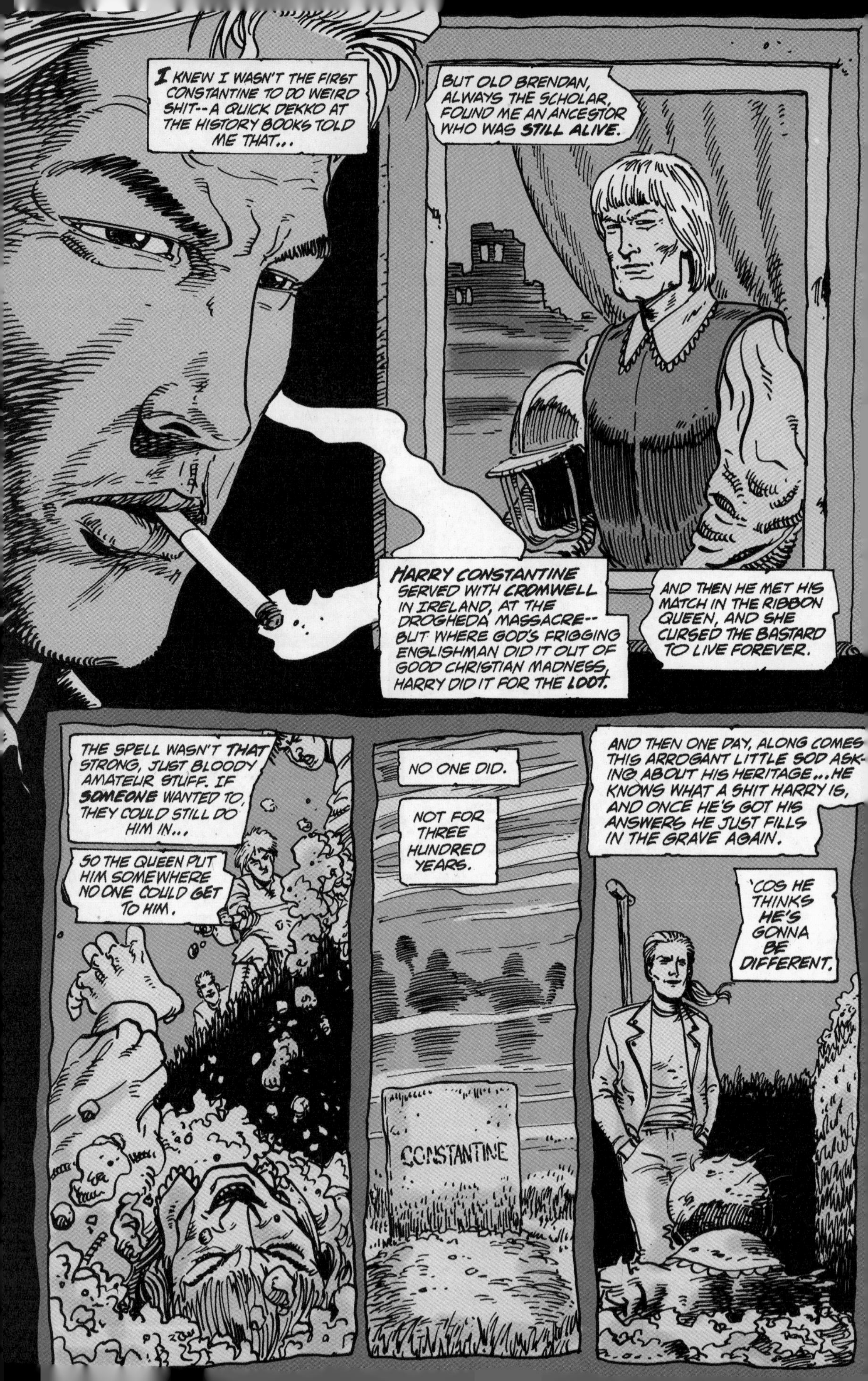
I KNEW I WASN'T THE FIRST CONSTANTINE TO DO WEIRD SHIT--A QUICK DEKKO AT THE HISTORY BOOKS TOLD ME THAT...
BUT OLD BRENDAN, ALWAYS THE SCHOLAR, FOUND ME AN ANCESTOR WHO WAS STILL ALIVE.
HARRY CONSTANTINE SERVED WITH CROMWELL IN IRELAND, AT THE DROGHEDA MASSACRE-- BUT WHERE GOD'S FRIGGING ENGLISHMAN DID IT OUT OF GOOD CHRISTIAN MADNESS, HARRY DID IT FOR THE LOOT.
AND THEN HE MET HIS MATCH IN THE RIBBON QUEEN, AND SHE CURSED THE BASTARD TO LIVE FOREVER.
THE SPELL WASN'T THAT STRONG, JUST BLOODY AMATEUR STUFF. IF SOMEONE WANTED TO, THEY COULD STILL DO HIM IN...
SO THE QUEEN PUT HIM SOMEWHERE NO ONE COULD GET TO HIM.
NO ONE DID.
NOT FOR THREE HUNDRED YEARS.
CONSTANTINE
AND THEN ONE DAY, ALONG COMES THIS ARROGANT LITTLE SOD ASKING ABOUT HIS HERITAGE... HE KNOWS WHAT A SHIT HARRY IS, AND ONCE HE'S GOT HIS ANSWERS HE JUST FILLS IN THE GRAVE AGAIN.
'COS HE THINKS HE'S GONNA BE DIFFERENT.

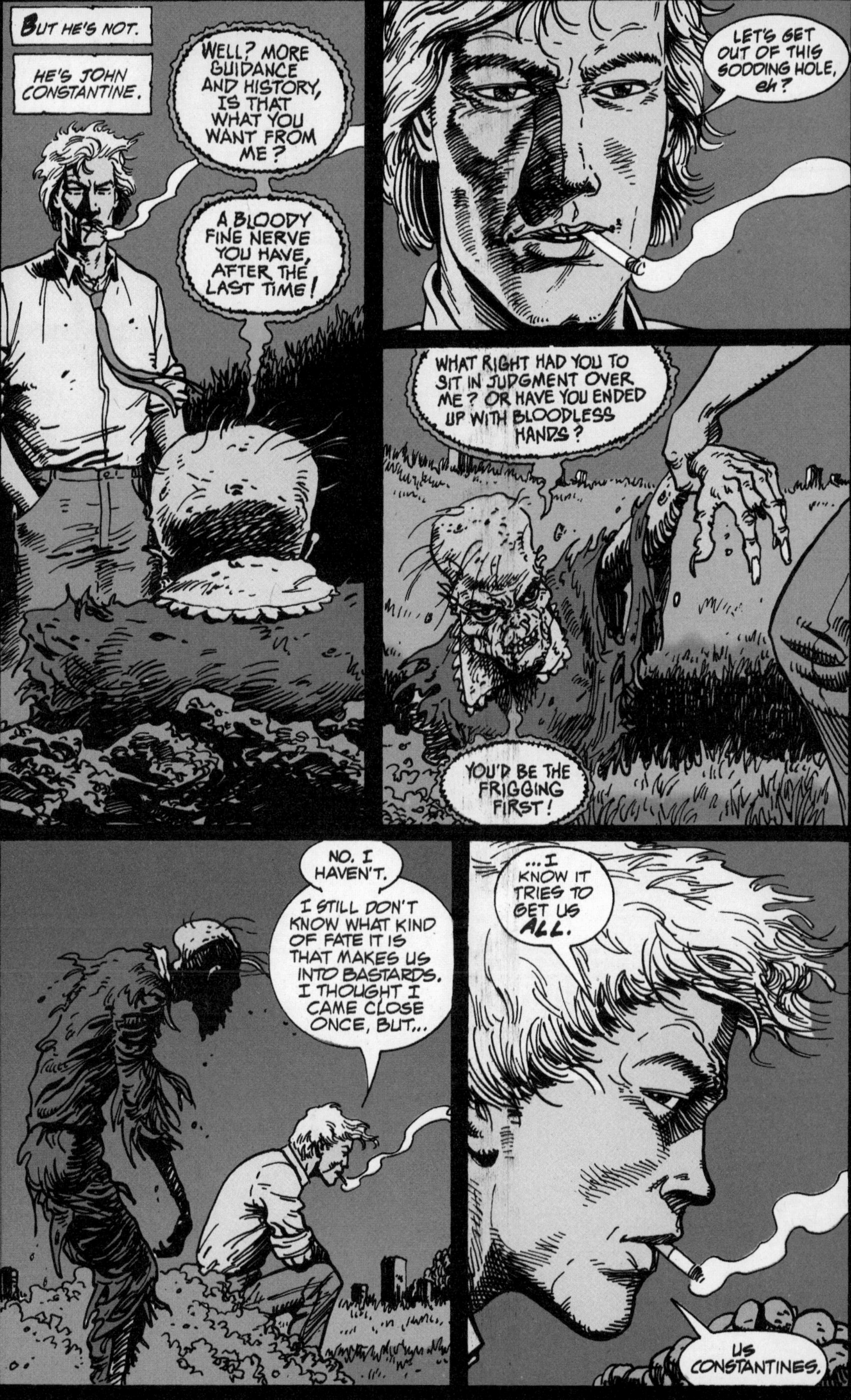
BUT HE'S NOT.
HE'S JOHN CONSTANTINE.
WELL? MORE GUIDANCE AND HISTORY, IS THAT WHAT YOU WANT FROM ME?
A BLOODY FINE NERVE YOU HAVE, AFTER THE LAST TIME!
LET'S GET OUT OF THIS SODDING HOLE, eh?
WHAT RIGHT HAD YOU TO SIT IN JUDGMENT OVER ME? OR HAVE YOU ENDED UP WITH BLOODLESS HANDS?
YOU'D BE THE FRIGGING FIRST!
NO. I HAVEN'T.
I STILL DON'T KNOW WHAT KIND OF FATE IT IS THAT MAKES US INTO BASTARDS. I THOUGHT I CAME CLOSE ONCE, BUT...
...I KNOW IT TRIES TO GET US ALL.
US CONSTANTINES.

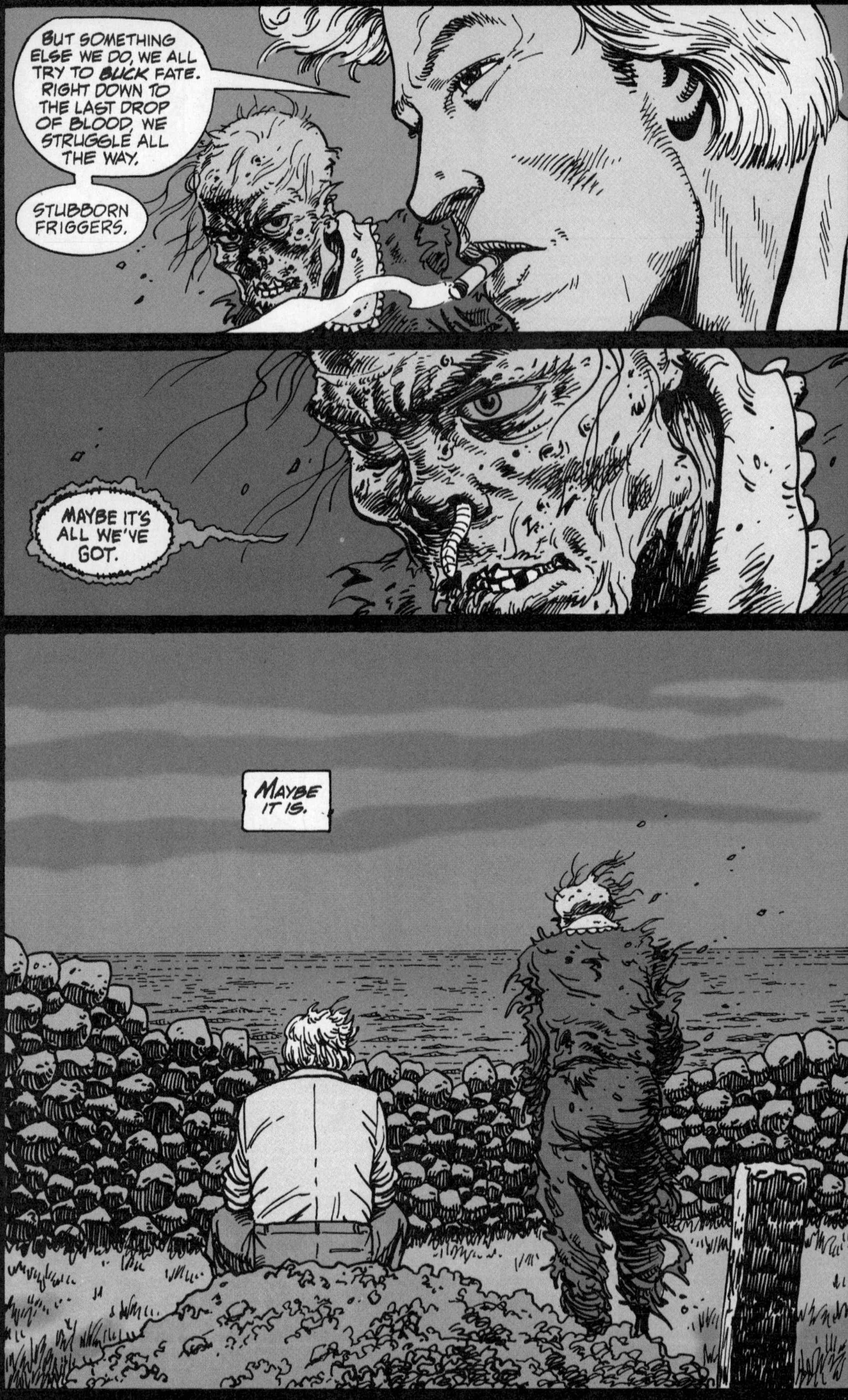
BUT SOMETHING ELSE WE DO, WE ALL TRY TO BUCK FATE. RIGHT DOWN TO THE LAST DROP OF BLOOD, WE STRUGGLE ALL THE WAY.
STUBBORN FRIGGERS.
MAYBE IT'S ALL WE'VE GOT.
MAYBE IT IS.

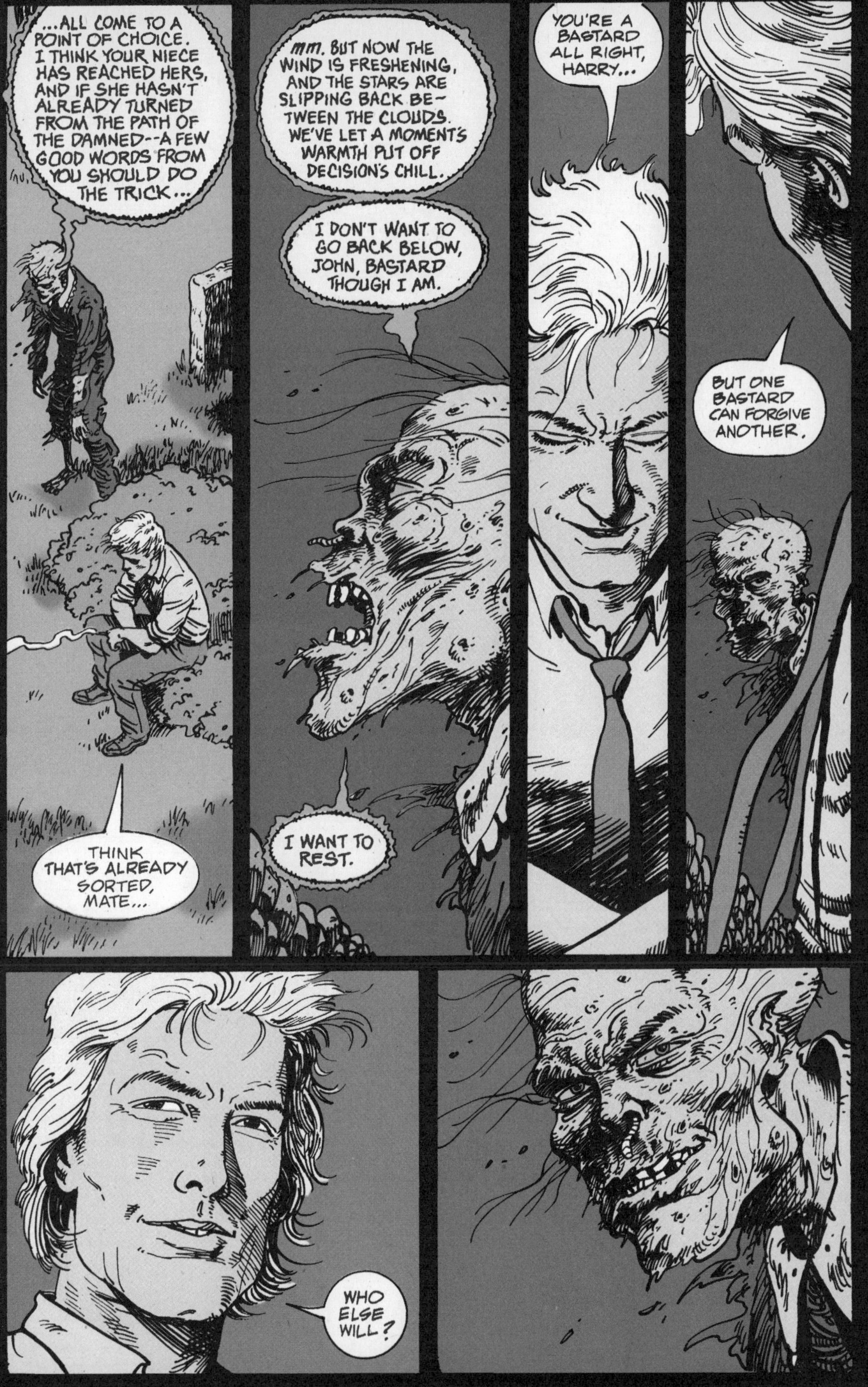
...ALL COME TO A POINT OF CHOICE. I THINK YOUR NIECE HAS REACHED HERS, AND IF SHE HASN'T ALREADY TURNED FROM THE PATH OF THE DAMNED--A FEW GOOD WORDS FROM YOU SHOULD DO THE TRICK...
THINK THAT'S ALREADY SORTED, MATE...
MM. BUT NOW THE WIND IS FRESHENING, AND THE STARS ARE SLIPPING BACK BE-TWEEN THE CLOUDS. WE'VE LET A MOMENT'S WARMTH PUT OFF DECISION'S CHILL.
I DON'T WANT TO GO BACK BELOW, JOHN, BASTARD THOUGH I AM.
I WANT TO REST.
YOU'RE A BASTARD ALL RIGHT, HARRY...
BUT ONE BASTARD CAN FORGIVE ANOTHER.
WHO ELSE WILL?

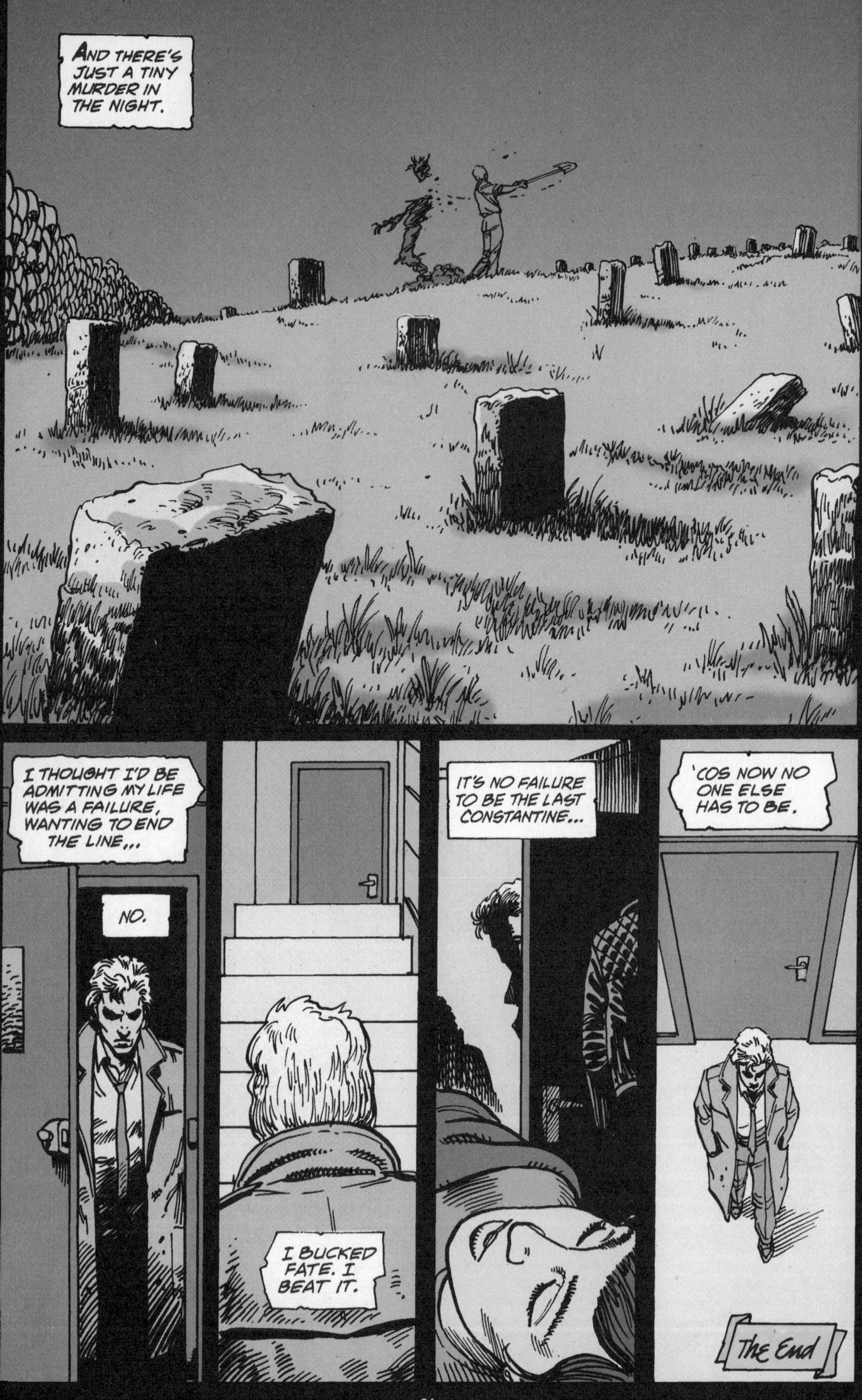
AND THERE'S JUST A TINY MURDER IN THE NIGHT.
I THOUGHT I'D BE ADMITTING MY LIFE WAS A FAILURE, WANTING TO END THE LINE...
NO.
I BUCKED FATE. I BEAT IT.
IT'S NO FAILURE TO BE THE LAST CONSTANTINE...
'COS NOW NO ONE ELSE HAS TO BE.
THE END

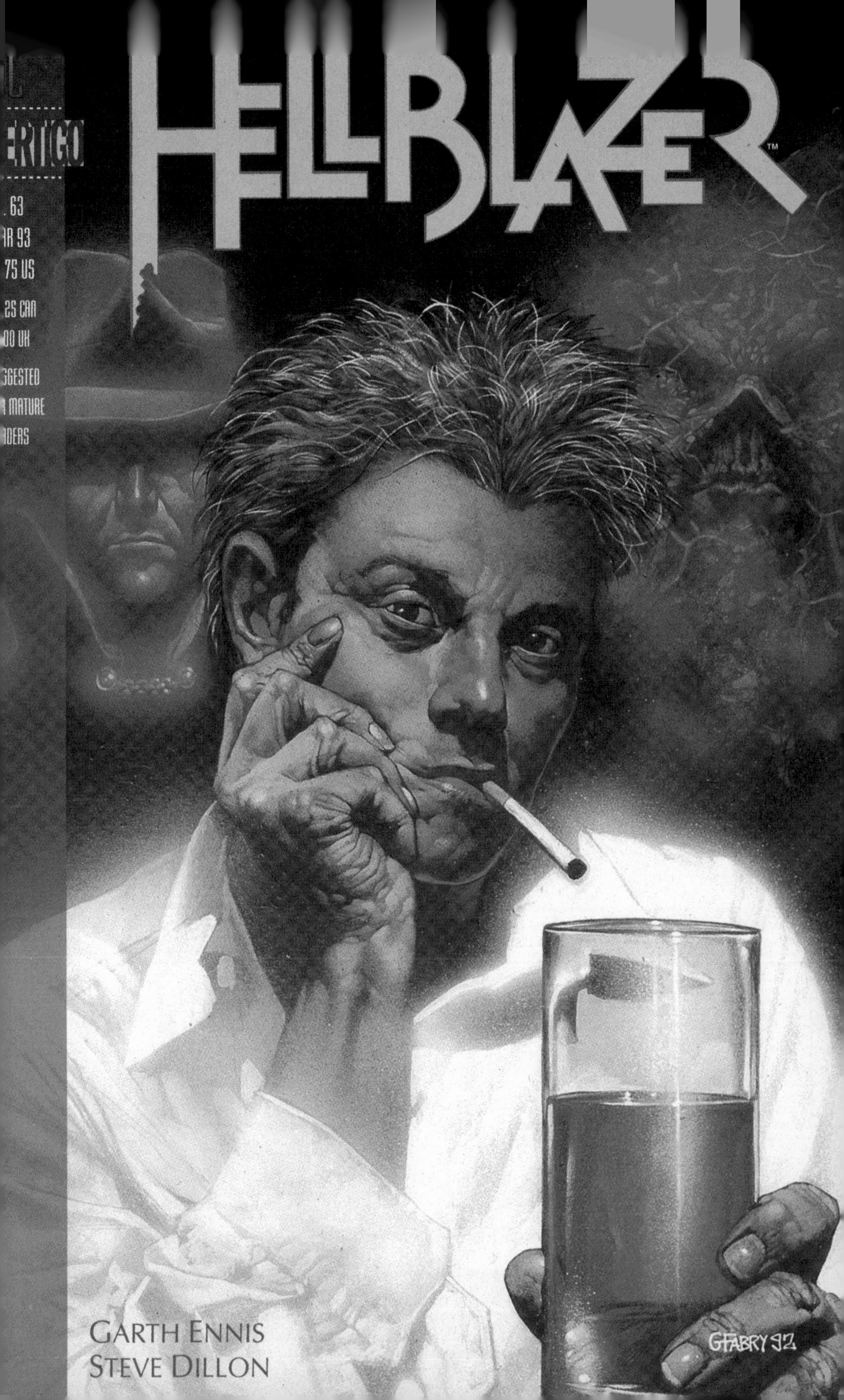
HELLBLAZER™
GARTH ENNIS
STEVE DILLON
GFABRY 92

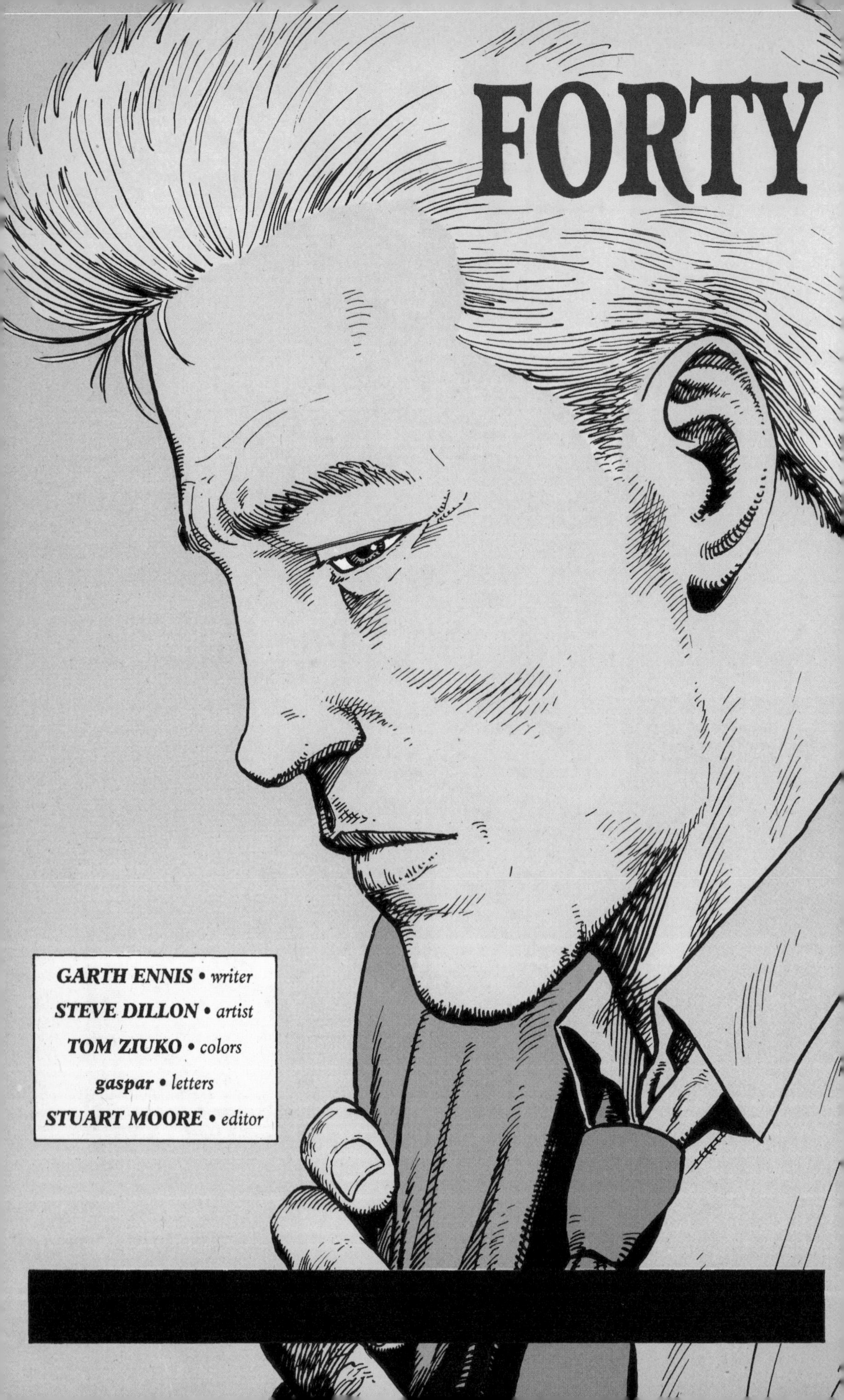
FORTY
GARTH ENNIS • writer
STEVE DILLON • artist
TOM ZIUKO • colors
gaspar • letters
STUART MOORE • editor

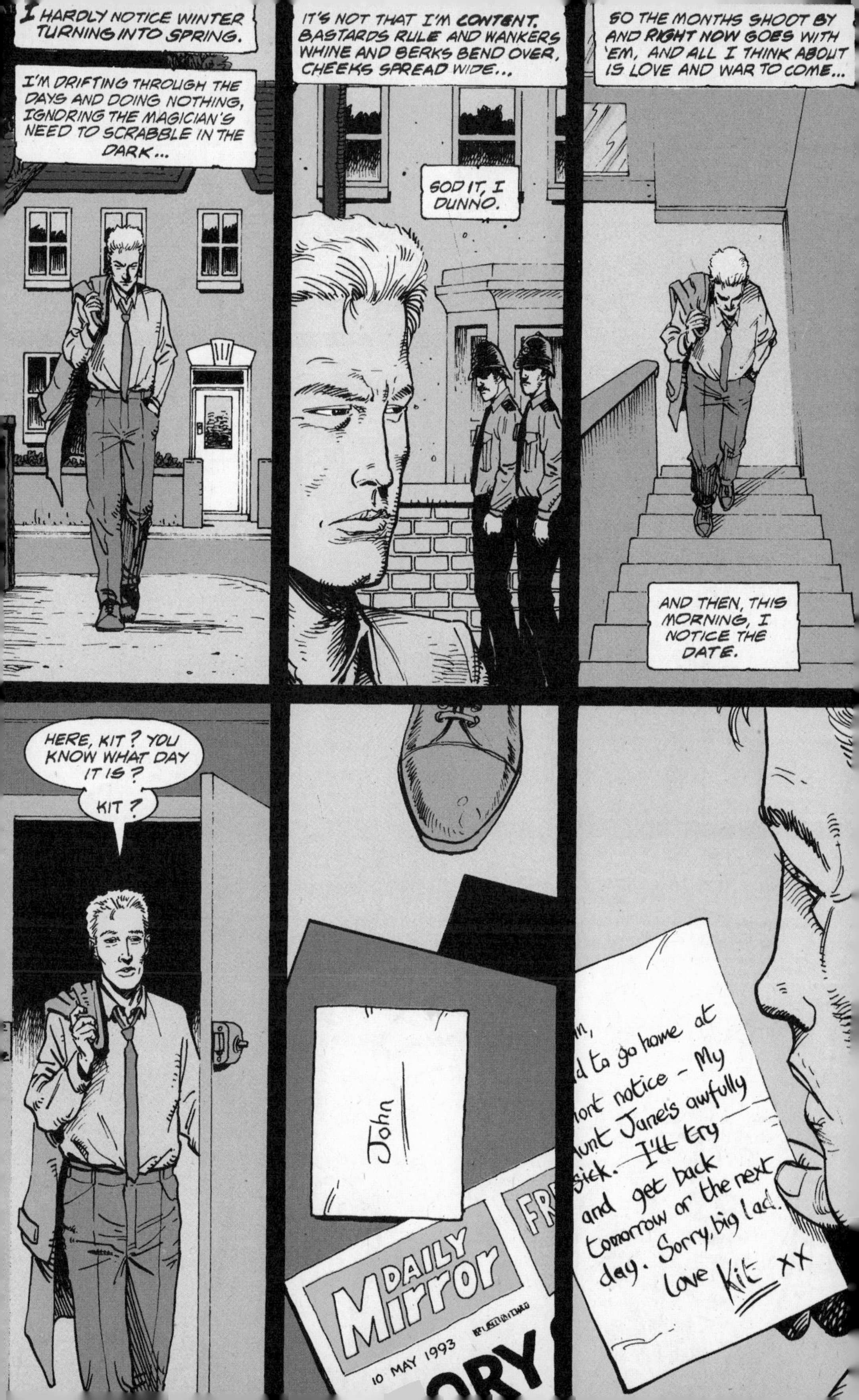
I HARDLY NOTICE WINTER TURNING INTO SPRING.
I'M DRIFTING THROUGH THE DAYS AND DOING NOTHING, IGNORING THE MAGICIAN'S NEED TO SCRABBLE IN THE DARK...
IT'S NOT THAT I'M CONTENT. BASTARDS RULE AND WANKERS WHINE AND BERKS BEND OVER, CHEEKS SPREAD WIDE...
SOD IT, I DUNNO.
SO THE MONTHS SHOOT BY AND RIGHT NOW GOES WITH 'EM, AND ALL I THINK ABOUT IS LOVE AND WAR TO COME...
AND THEN, THIS MORNING, I NOTICE THE DATE.
HERE, KIT? YOU KNOW WHAT DAY IT IS?
KIT?
John
DAILY Mirror
10 MAY 1993
d to go home at
hort notice - My
unt Jane's awfully
sick. I'll try
and get back
tomorrow or the next
day. Sorry, big lad.
love Kit xx

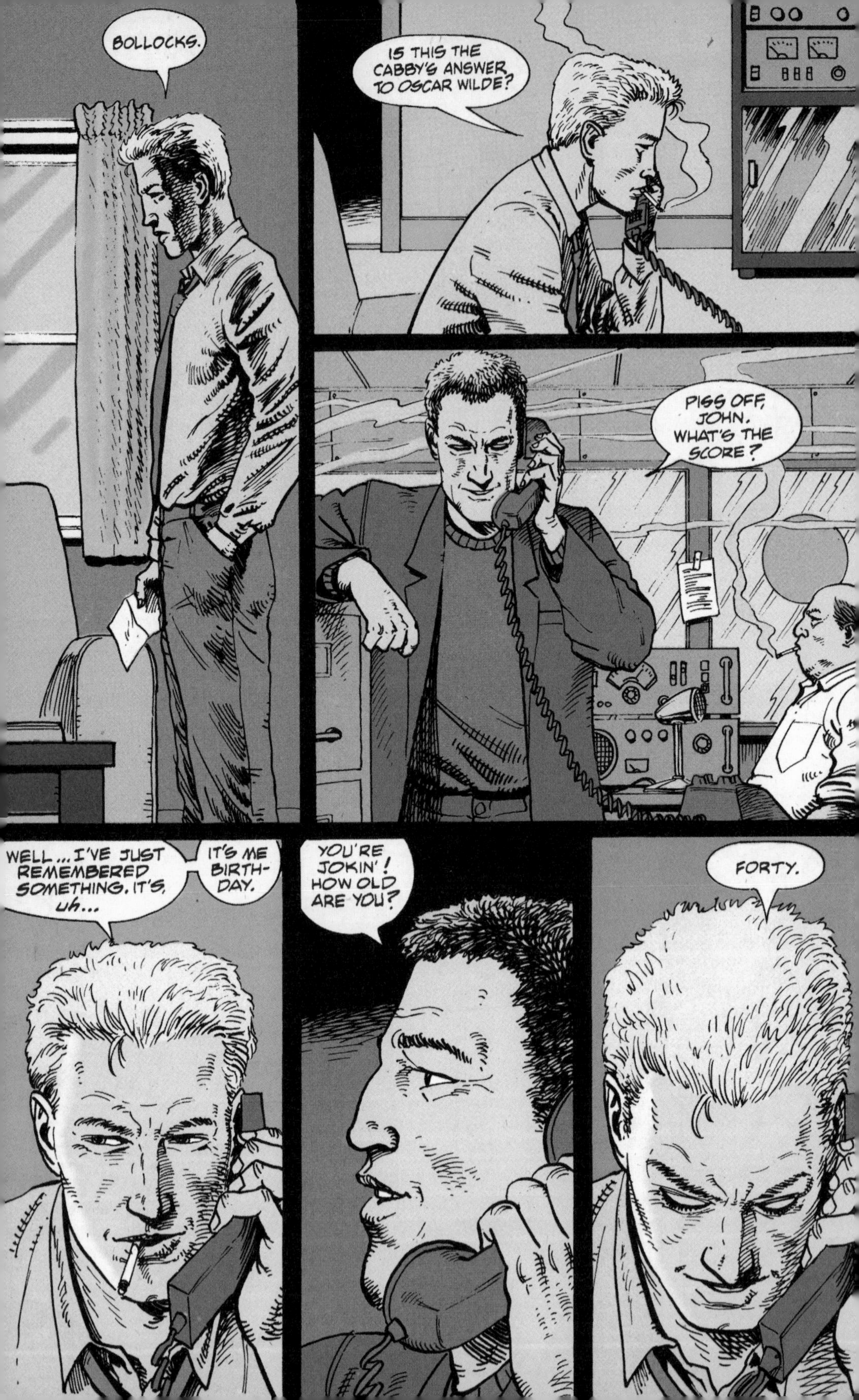
BOLLOCKS.
IS THIS THE CABBY'S ANSWER TO OSCAR WILDE?
PISS OFF, JOHN. WHAT'S THE SCORE?
WELL... I'VE JUST REMEMBERED SOMETHING. IT'S, uh...
IT'S ME BIRTH-DAY.
YOU'RE JOKIN'! HOW OLD ARE YOU?
FORTY.

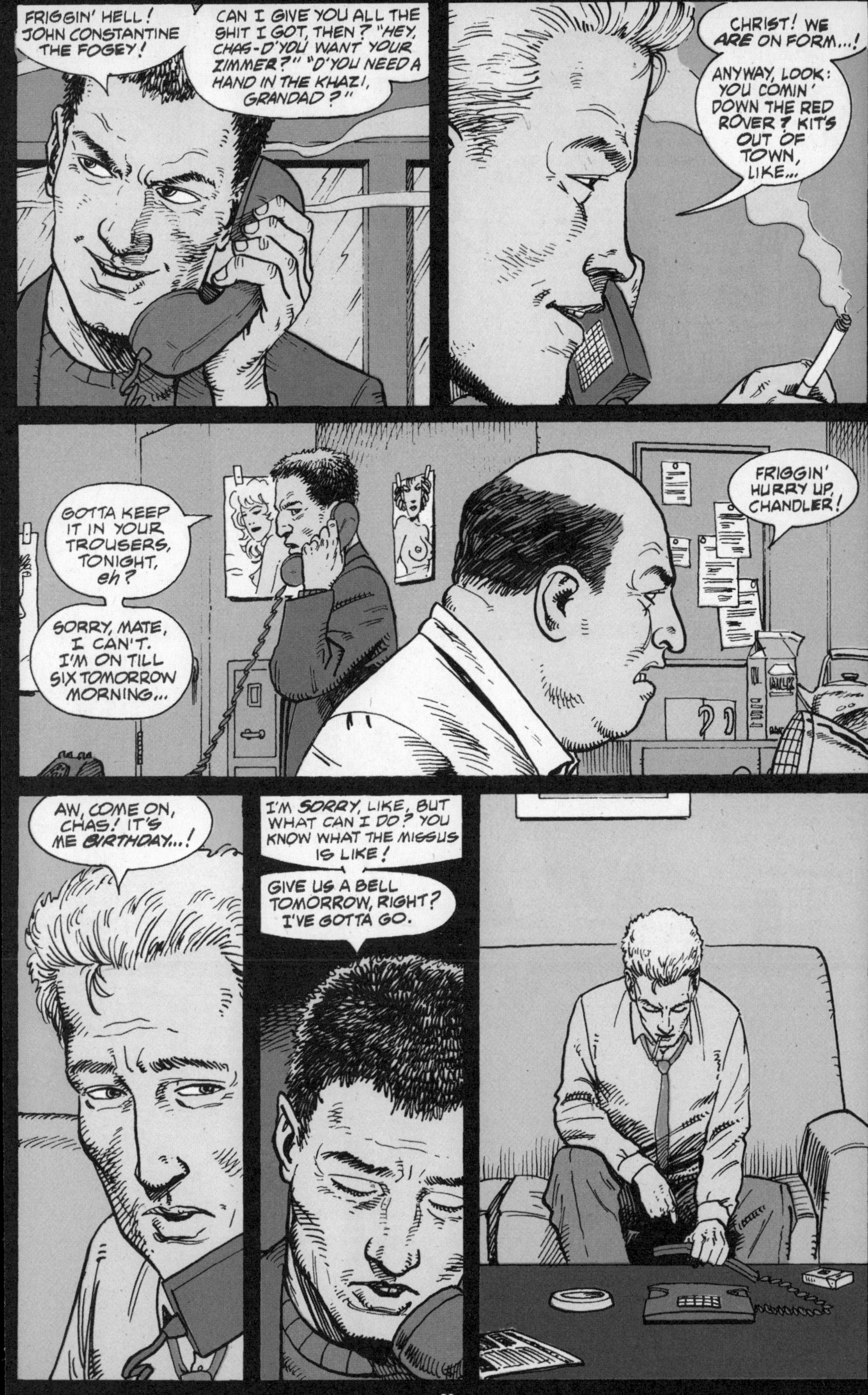
FRIGGIN' HELL! JOHN CONSTANTINE THE FOGEY!
CAN I GIVE YOU ALL THE SHIT I GOT, THEN? "HEY, CHAS-D'YOU WANT YOUR ZIMMER?" "D'YOU NEED A HAND IN THE KHAZI, GRANDAD?"
CHRIST! WE ARE ON FORM...!
ANYWAY, LOOK: YOU COMIN' DOWN THE RED ROVER? KIT'S OUT OF TOWN, LIKE...
GOTTA KEEP IT IN YOUR TROUSERS, TONIGHT, eh?
SORRY, MATE, I CAN'T. I'M ON TILL SIX TOMORROW MORNING...
FRIGGIN' HURRY UP, CHANDLER!
AW, COME ON, CHAS! IT'S ME BIRTHDAY...!
I'M SORRY, LIKE, BUT WHAT CAN I DO? YOU KNOW WHAT THE MISSUS IS LIKE!
GIVE US A BELL TOMORROW, RIGHT? I'VE GOTTA GO.

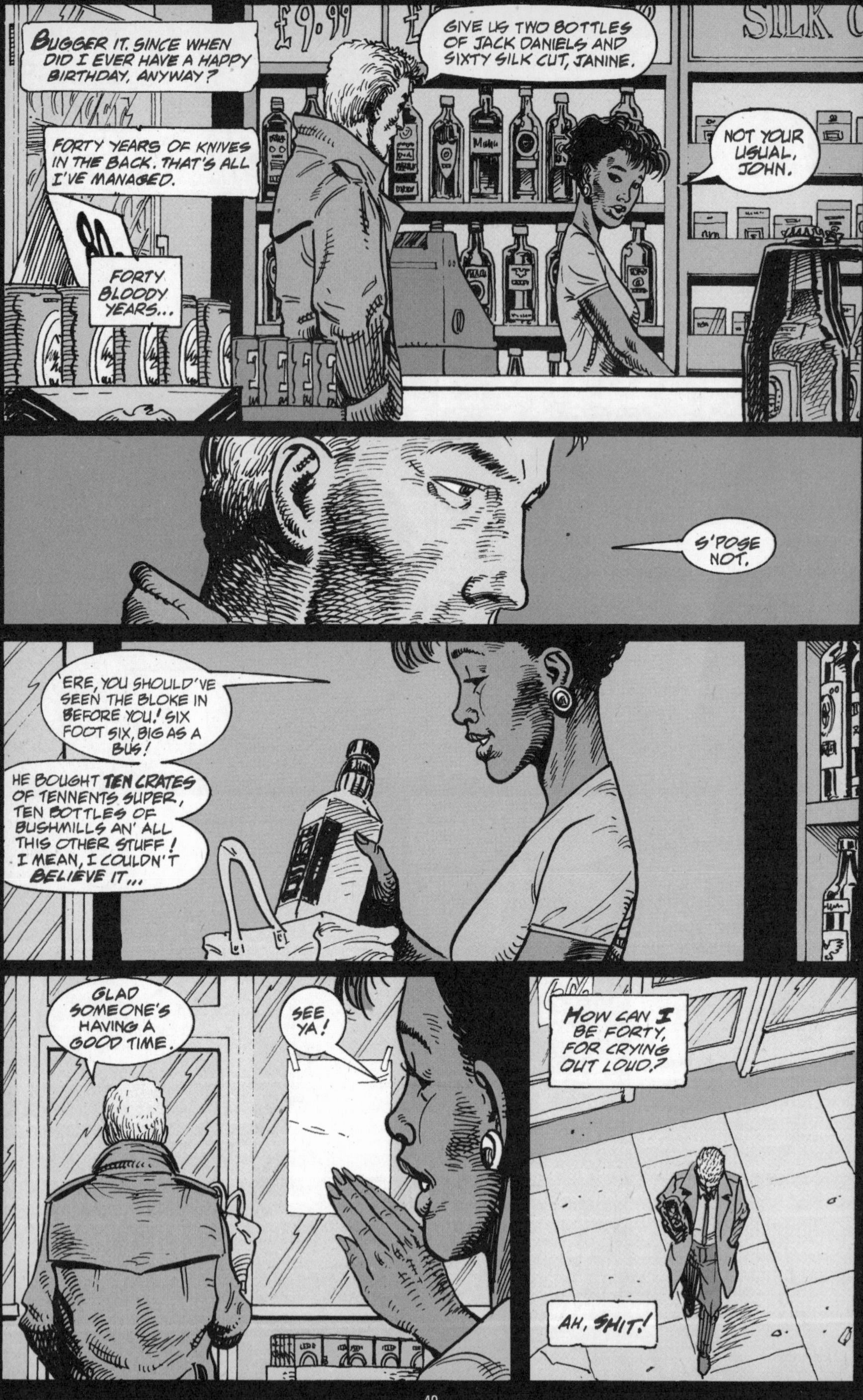

BUGGER IT. SINCE WHEN DID I EVER HAVE A HAPPY BIRTHDAY, ANYWAY?
FORTY YEARS OF KNIVES IN THE BACK. THAT'S ALL I'VE MANAGED.
FORTY BLOODY YEARS...
GIVE US TWO BOTTLES OF JACK DANIELS AND SIXTY SILK CUT, JANINE.
NOT YOUR USUAL, JOHN.
S'POSE NOT.
'ERE, YOU SHOULD'VE SEEN THE BLOKE IN BEFORE YOU! SIX FOOT SIX, BIG AS A BUS!
HE BOUGHT TEN CRATES OF TENNENTS SUPER, TEN BOTTLES OF BUSHMILLS AN' ALL THIS OTHER STUFF! I MEAN, I COULDN'T BELIEVE IT...
GLAD SOMEONE'S HAVING A GOOD TIME.
SEE YA!
HOW CAN I BE FORTY, FOR CRYING OUT LOUD?
AH, SHIT!

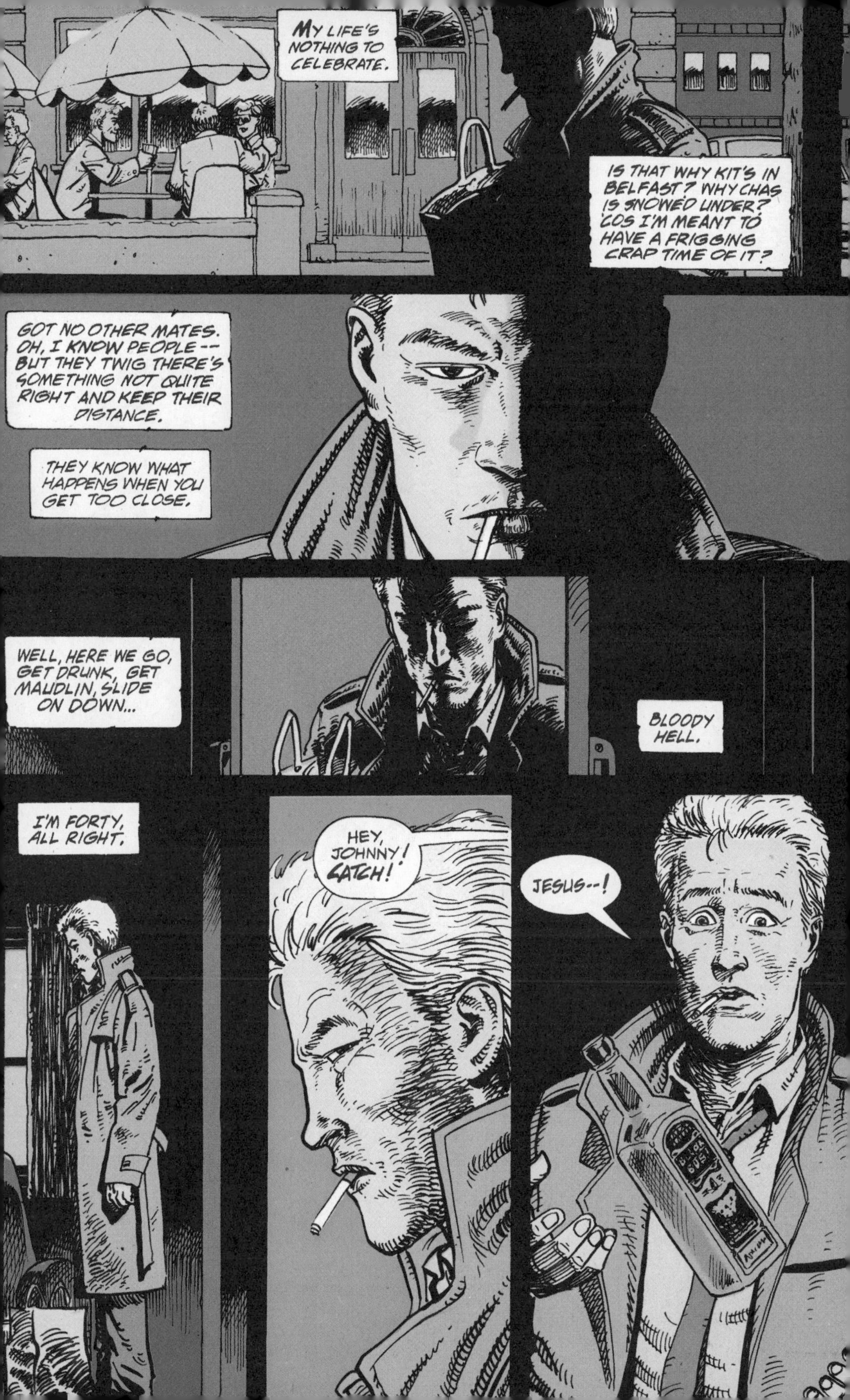
MY LIFE'S NOTHING TO CELEBRATE.
IS THAT WHY KIT'S IN BELFAST? WHY CHAS IS SNOWED UNDER? 'COS I'M MEANT TO HAVE A FRIGGING CRAP TIME OF IT?
GOT NO OTHER MATES. OH, I KNOW PEOPLE -- BUT THEY TWIG THERE'S SOMETHING NOT QUITE RIGHT AND KEEP THEIR DISTANCE.
THEY KNOW WHAT HAPPENS WHEN YOU GET TOO CLOSE.
WELL, HERE WE GO, GET DRUNK, GET MAUDLIN, SLIDE ON DOWN...
BLOODY HELL.
I'M FORTY, ALL RIGHT.
HEY, JOHNNY! CATCH!
JESUS--!

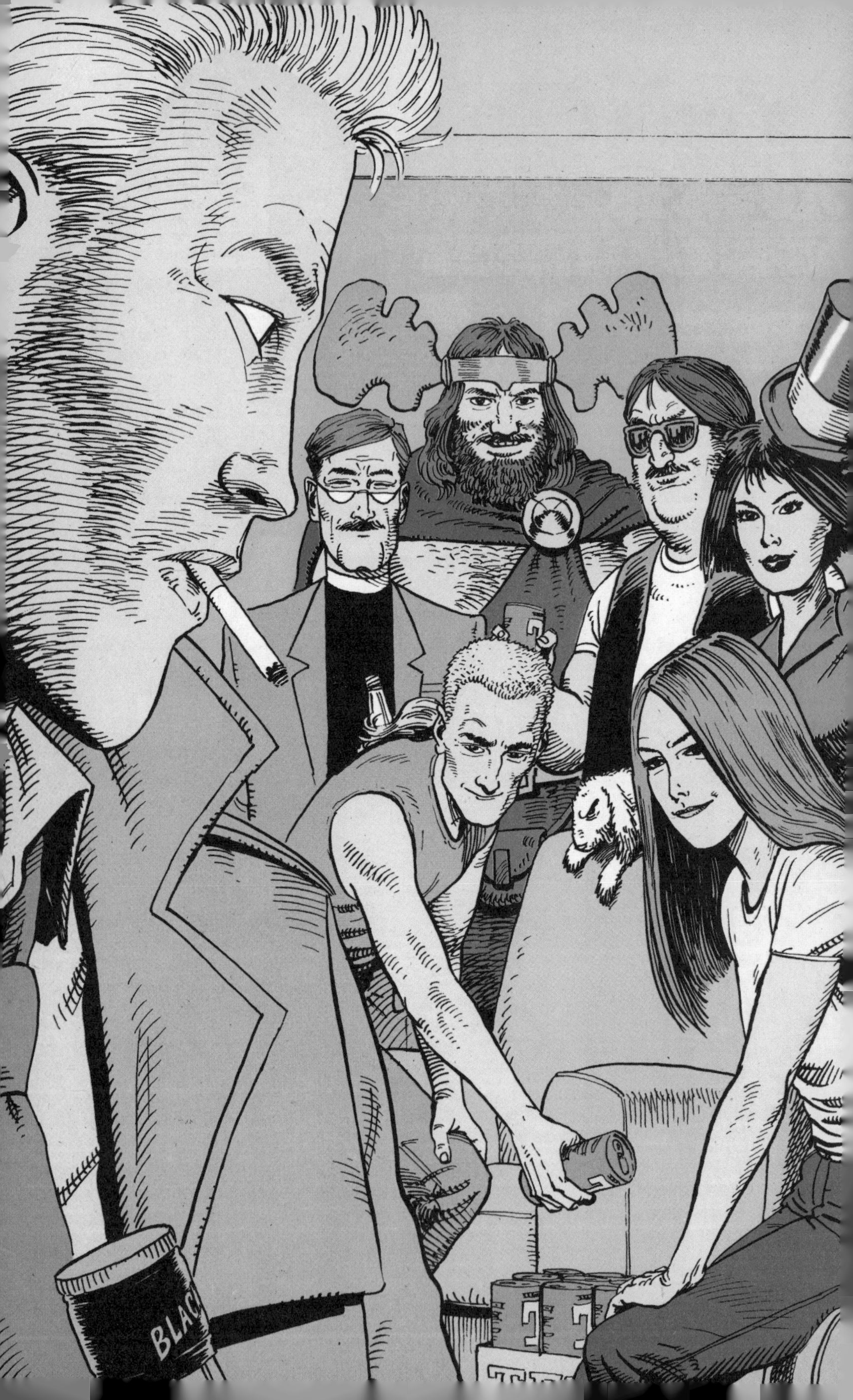

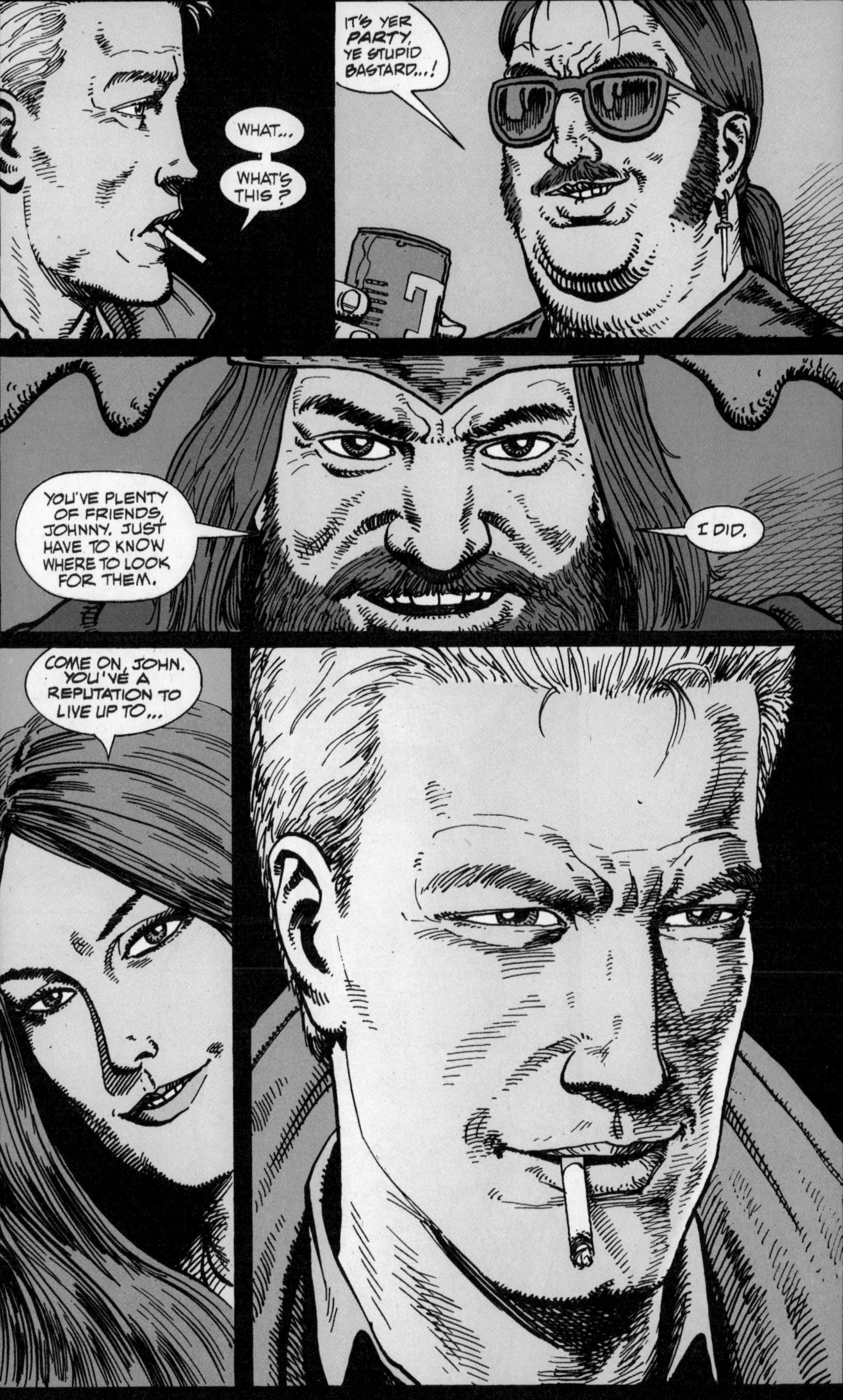
WHAT...
WHAT'S THIS ?
IT'S YER PARTY, YE STUPID BASTARD...!
YOU'VE PLENTY OF FRIENDS, JOHNNY. JUST HAVE TO KNOW WHERE TO LOOK FOR THEM.
I DID.
COME ON, JOHN. YOU'VE A REPUTATION TO LIVE UP TO...

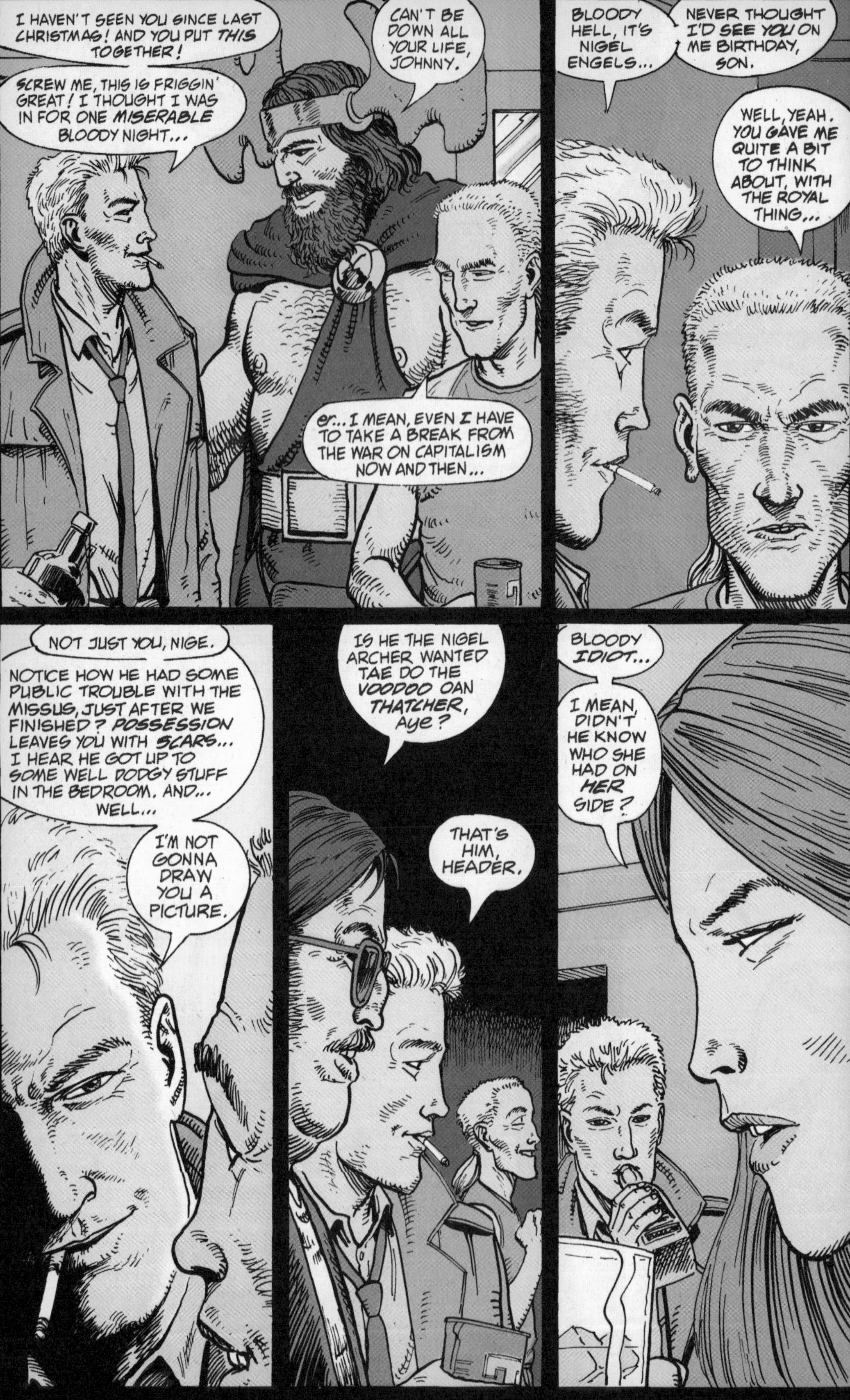
I HAVEN'T SEEN YOU SINCE LAST CHRISTMAS! AND YOU PUT THIS TOGETHER!
SCREW ME, THIS IS FRIGGIN' GREAT! I THOUGHT I WAS IN FOR ONE MISERABLE BLOODY NIGHT...
CAN'T BE DOWN ALL YOUR LIFE, JOHNNY.
er... I MEAN, EVEN I HAVE TO TAKE A BREAK FROM THE WAR ON CAPITALISM NOW AND THEN...
BLOODY HELL, IT'S NIGEL ENGELS...
NEVER THOUGHT I'D SEE YOU ON ME BIRTHDAY, SON.
WELL, YEAH. YOU GAVE ME QUITE A BIT TO THINK ABOUT, WITH THE ROYAL THING...
NOT JUST YOU, NIGE.
NOTICE HOW HE HAD SOME PUBLIC TROUBLE WITH THE MISSUS, JUST AFTER WE FINISHED? POSSESSION LEAVES YOU WITH SCARS... I HEAR HE GOT UP TO SOME WELL DODGY STUFF IN THE BEDROOM. AND... WELL...
I'M NOT GONNA DRAW YOU A PICTURE.
IS HE THE NIGEL ARCHER WANTED TAE DO THE VOODOO OAN THATCHER, Aye?
THAT'S HIM, HEADER.
BLOODY IDIOT...
I MEAN, DIDN'T HE KNOW WHO SHE HAD ON HER SIDE?

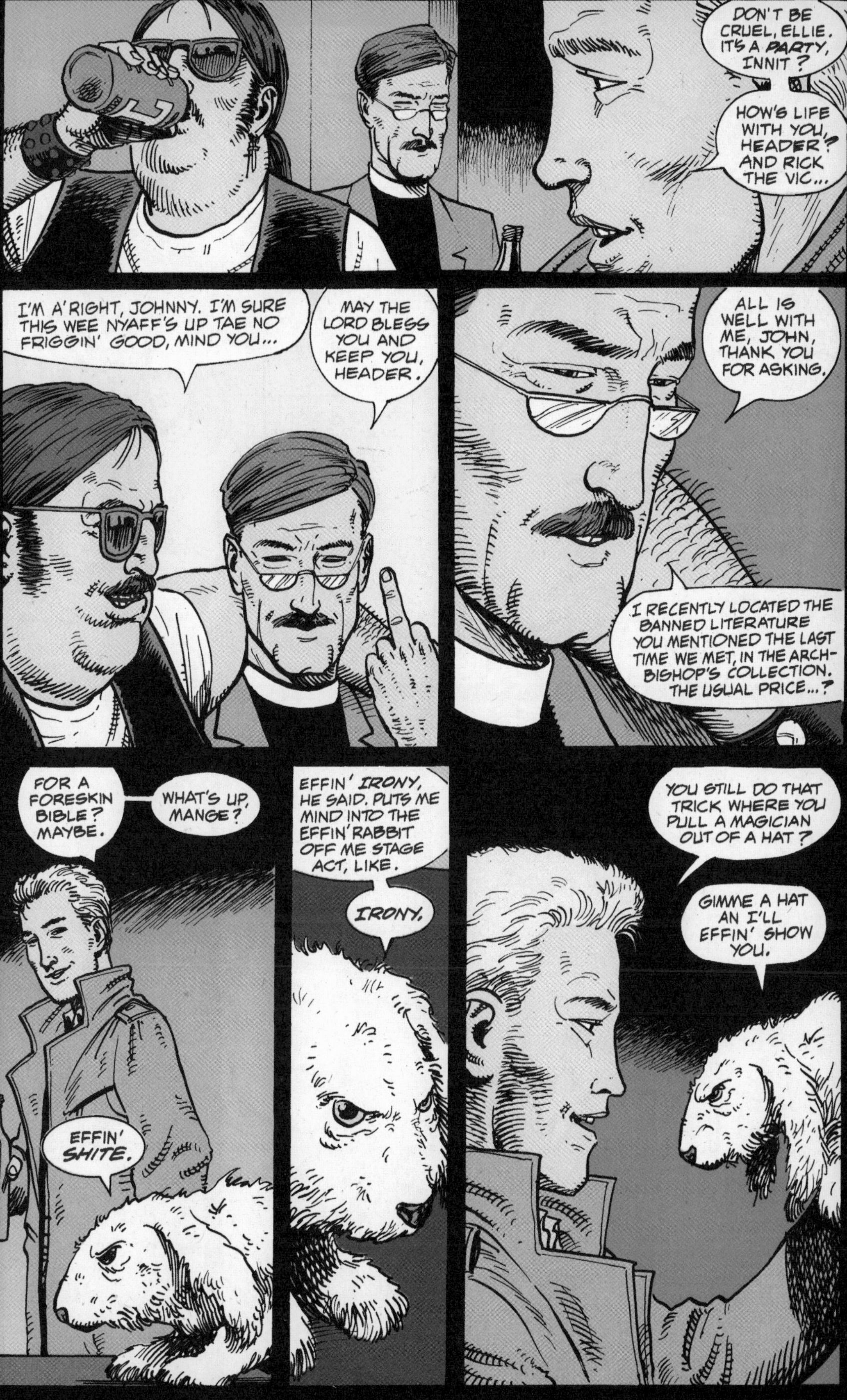

DON'T BE CRUEL, ELLIE. IT'S A PARTY, INNIT?
HOW'S LIFE WITH YOU, HEADER? AND RICK THE VIC...
I'M A'RIGHT, JOHNNY. I'M SURE THIS WEE NYAFF'S UP TAE NO FRIGGIN' GOOD, MIND YOU...
MAY THE LORD BLESS YOU AND KEEP YOU, HEADER.
ALL IS WELL WITH ME, JOHN, THANK YOU FOR ASKING.
I RECENTLY LOCATED THE BANNED LITERATURE YOU MENTIONED THE LAST TIME WE MET, IN THE ARCH-BISHOP'S COLLECTION. THE USUAL PRICE...?
FOR A FORESKIN BIBLE? MAYBE.
WHAT'S UP, MANGE?
EFFIN' SHITE.
EFFIN' IRONY, HE SAID. PUTS ME MIND INTO THE EFFIN' RABBIT OFF ME STAGE ACT, LIKE.
IRONY.
YOU STILL DO THAT TRICK WHERE YOU PULL A MAGICIAN OUT OF A HAT?
GIMME A HAT AN I'LL EFFIN' SHOW YOU.

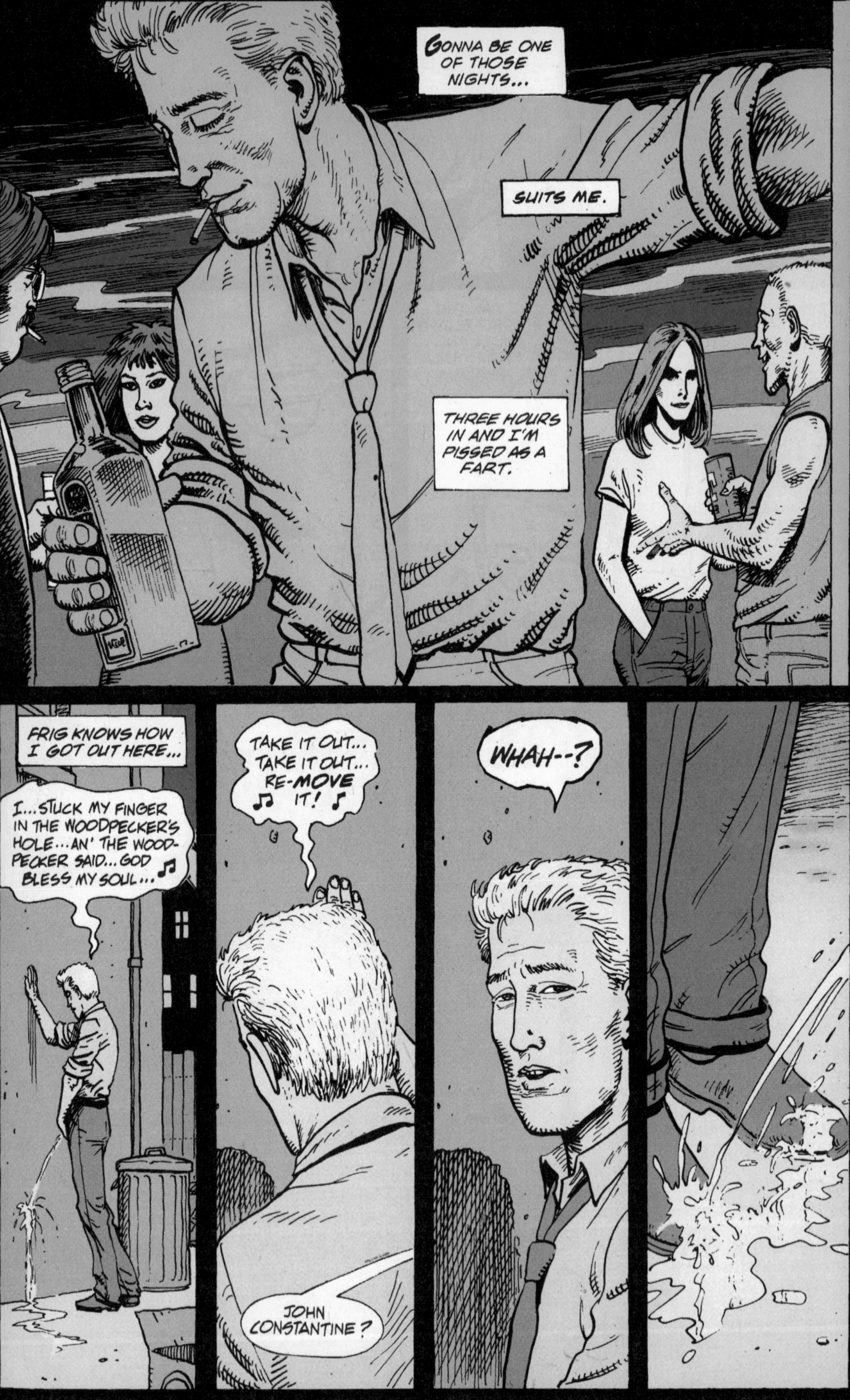
GONNA BE ONE OF THOSE NIGHTS...
SUITS ME.
THREE HOURS IN AND I'M PISSED AS A FART.
FRIG KNOWS HOW I GOT OUT HERE...
I...STUCK MY FINGER IN THE WOODPECKER'S HOLE...AN' THE WOODPECKER SAID...GOD BLESS MY SOUL... ♫
TAKE IT OUT... TAKE IT OUT... RE-MOVE IT! ♫ ♪
JOHN CONSTANTINE?
WHAH--?

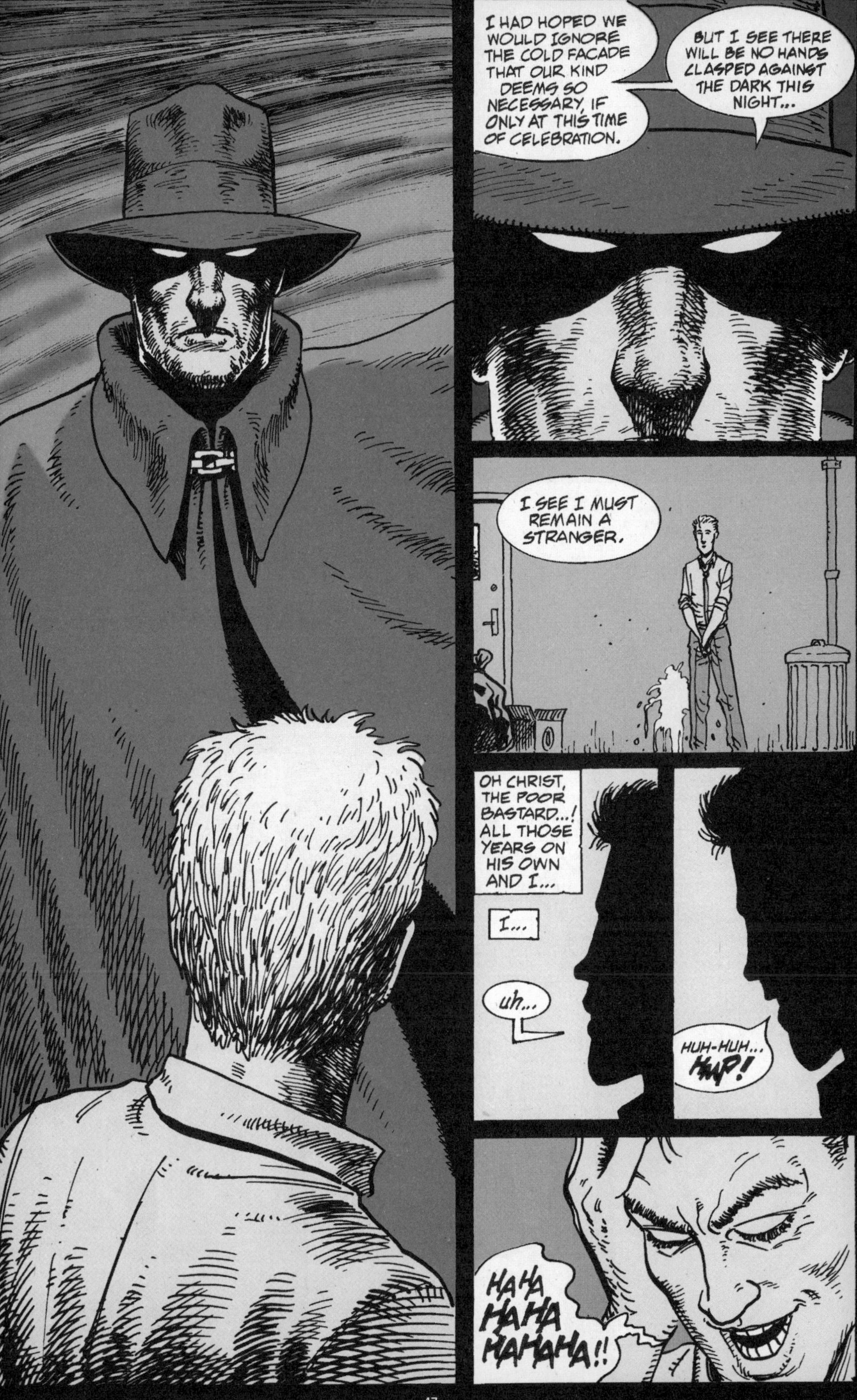
I HAD HOPED WE WOULD IGNORE THE COLD FACADE THAT OUR KIND DEEMS SO NECESSARY, IF ONLY AT THIS TIME OF CELEBRATION.
BUT I SEE THERE WILL BE NO HANDS CLASPED AGAINST THE DARK THIS NIGHT...
I SEE I MUST REMAIN A STRANGER.
OH CHRIST, THE POOR BASTARD...! ALL THOSE YEARS ON HIS OWN AND I...
I...
uh...
HUH-HUH... HWP!
HAHA HAHA HAHAHA!!

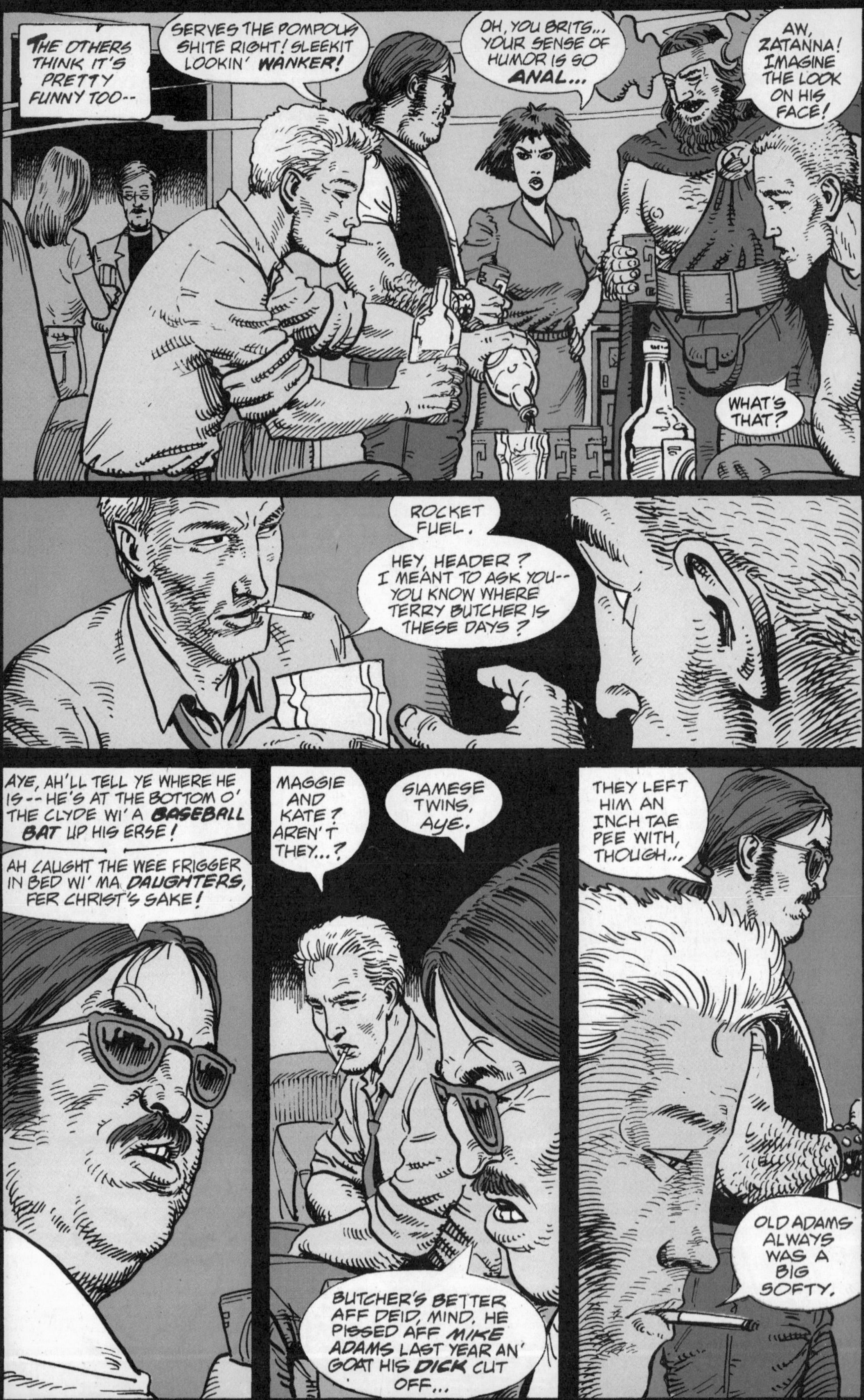
THE OTHERS THINK IT'S PRETTY FUNNY TOO--
SERVES THE POMPOUS SHITE RIGHT! SLEEKIT LOOKIN' WANKER!
OH, YOU BRITS... YOUR SENSE OF HUMOR IS SO ANAL...
AW, ZATANNA! IMAGINE THE LOOK ON HIS FACE!
WHAT'S THAT?
ROCKET FUEL.
HEY, HEADER? I MEANT TO ASK YOU-- YOU KNOW WHERE TERRY BUTCHER IS THESE DAYS?
AYE, AH'LL TELL YE WHERE HE IS-- HE'S AT THE BOTTOM O' THE CLYDE WI' A BASEBALL BAT UP HIS ERSE!
AH CAUGHT THE WEE FRIGGER IN BED WI' MA DAUGHTERS, FER CHRIST'S SAKE!
MAGGIE AND KATE? AREN'T THEY...?
SIAMESE TWINS, AYE.
BUTCHER'S BETTER AFF DEID, MIND. HE PISSED AFF MIKE ADAMS LAST YEAR AN' GOAT HIS DICK CUT OFF...
THEY LEFT HIM AN INCH TAE PEE WITH, THOUGH...
OLD ADAMS ALWAYS WAS A BIG SOFTY.

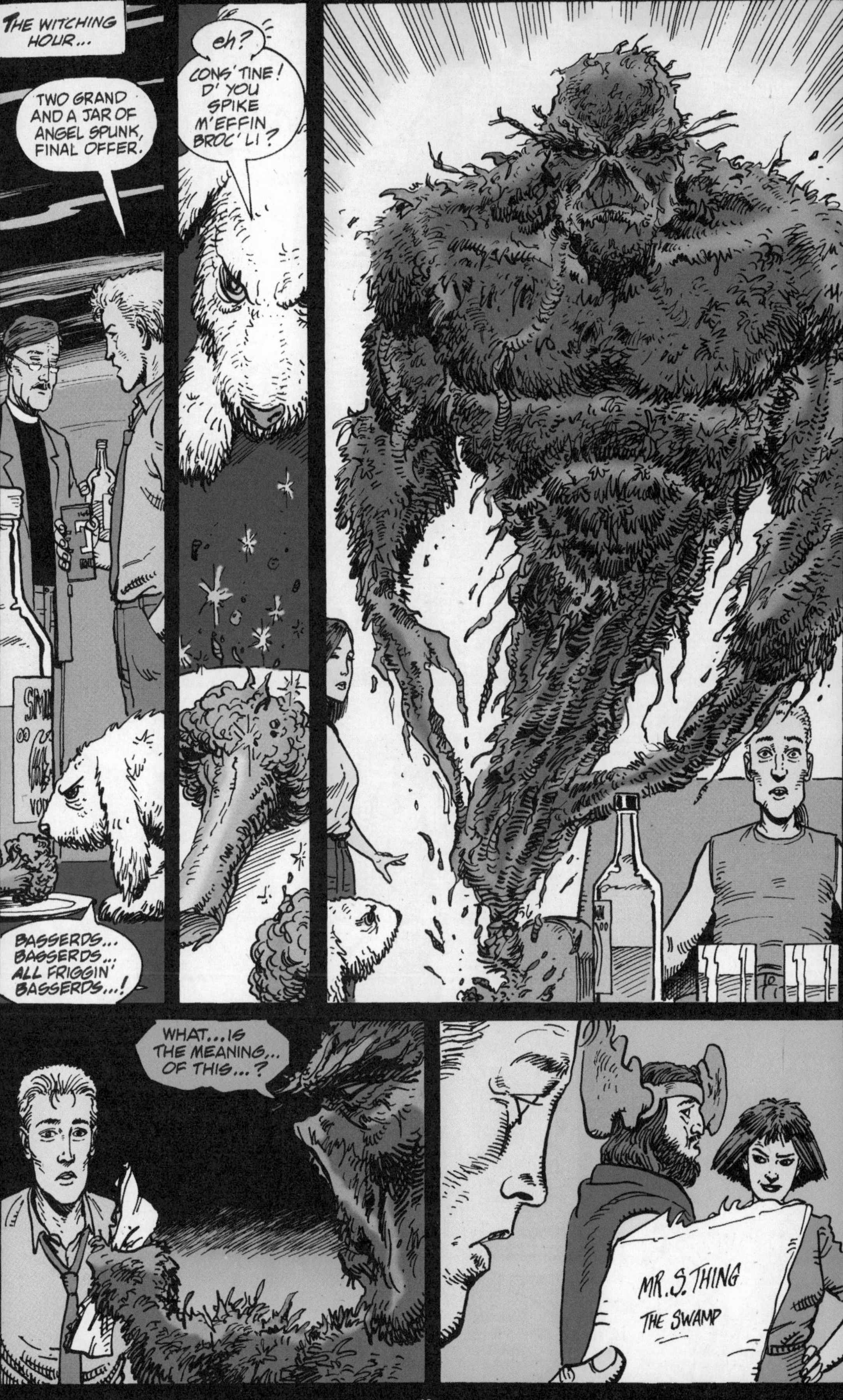
THE WITCHING HOUR...
TWO GRAND AND A JAR OF ANGEL SPUNK, FINAL OFFER.
eh?
CONS'TINE! D' YOU SPIKE M'EFFIN BROC'LI?
BASSERDS... BASSERDS... ALL FRIGGIN' BASSERDS...!
WHAT...IS THE MEANING... OF THIS...?
MR. S. THING
THE SWAMP

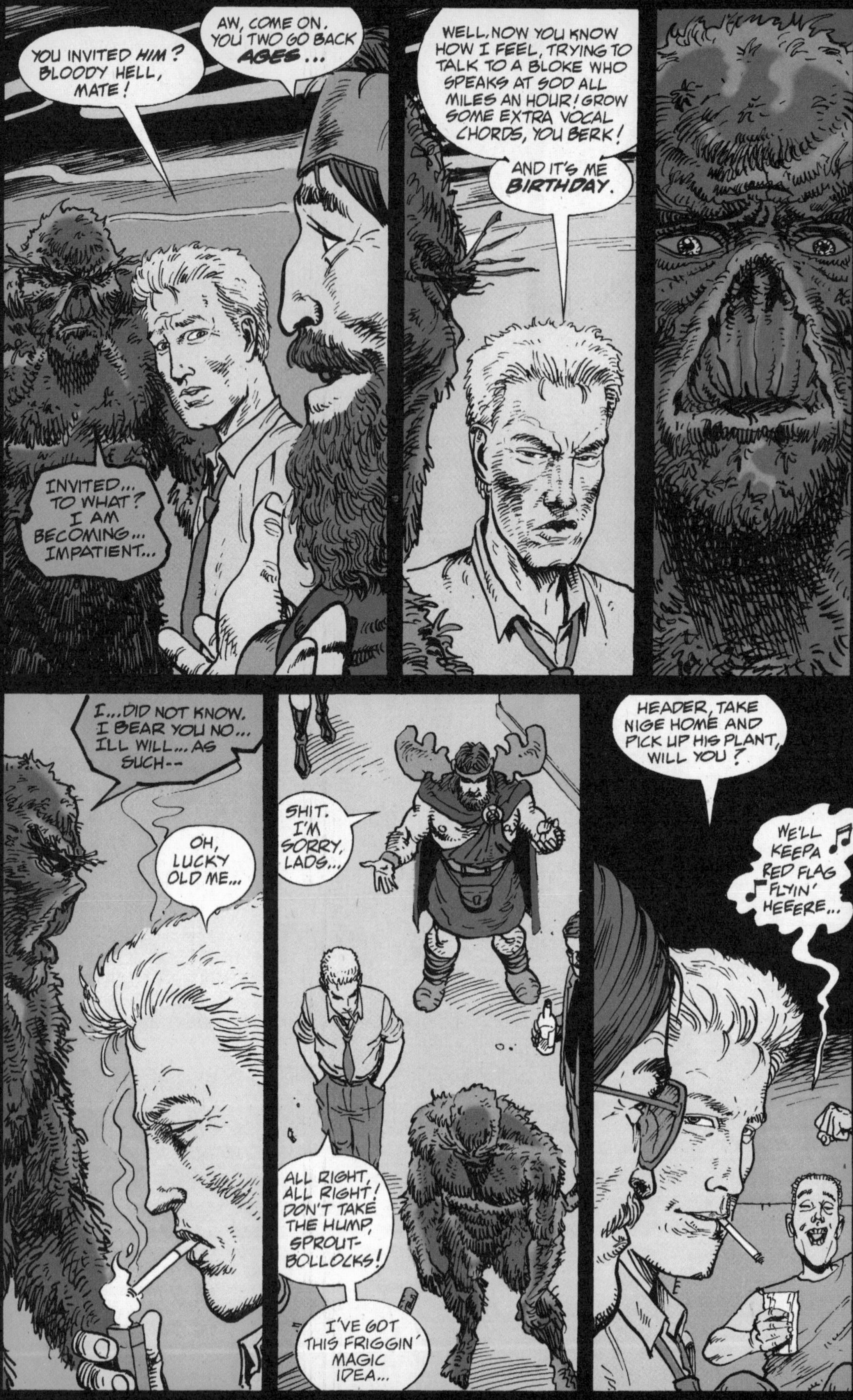
YOU INVITED HIM? BLOODY HELL, MATE!
AW, COME ON. YOU TWO GO BACK AGES...
INVITED... TO WHAT? I AM BECOMING... IMPATIENT...
WELL, NOW YOU KNOW HOW I FEEL, TRYING TO TALK TO A BLOKE WHO SPEAKS AT SOD ALL MILES AN HOUR! GROW SOME EXTRA VOCAL CHORDS, YOU BERK!
AND IT'S ME BIRTHDAY.
I... DID NOT KNOW. I BEAR YOU NO... ILL WILL... AS SUCH--
OH, LUCKY OLD ME...
SHIT. I'M SORRY, LADS...
ALL RIGHT, ALL RIGHT! DON'T TAKE THE HUMP, SPROUT-BOLLOCKS!
I'VE GOT THIS FRIGGIN' MAGIC IDEA...
HEADER, TAKE NIGE HOME AND PICK UP HIS PLANT, WILL YOU?
WE'LL KEEP A RED FLAG FLYIN' HEEERE...

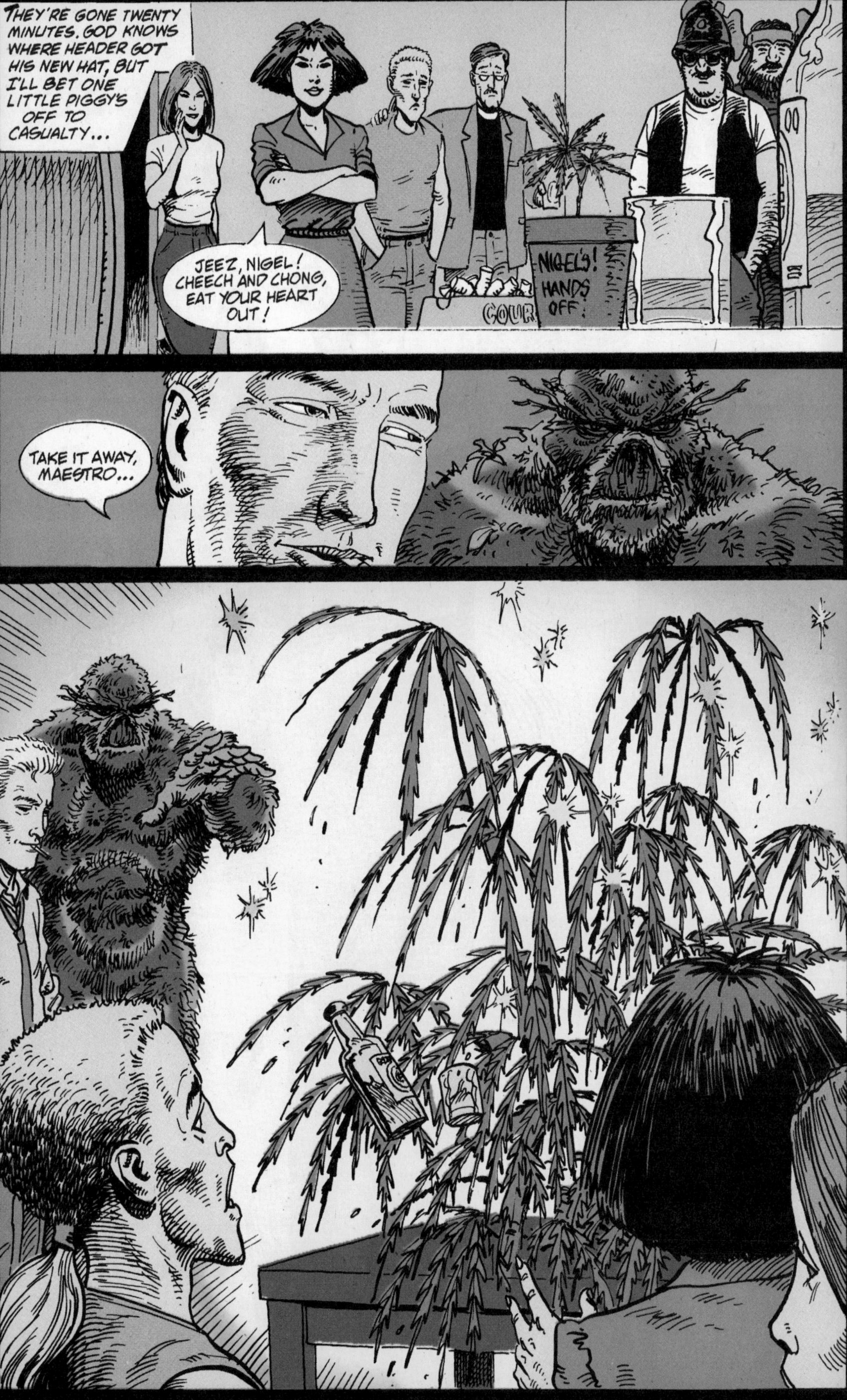
THEY'RE GONE TWENTY MINUTES. GOD KNOWS WHERE HEADER GOT HIS NEW HAT, BUT I'LL BET ONE LITTLE PIGGY'S OFF TO CASUALTY...
JEEZ, NIGEL! CHEECH AND CHONG, EAT YOUR HEART OUT!
NIGEL'S! HANDS OFF!
TAKE IT AWAY, MAESTRO...

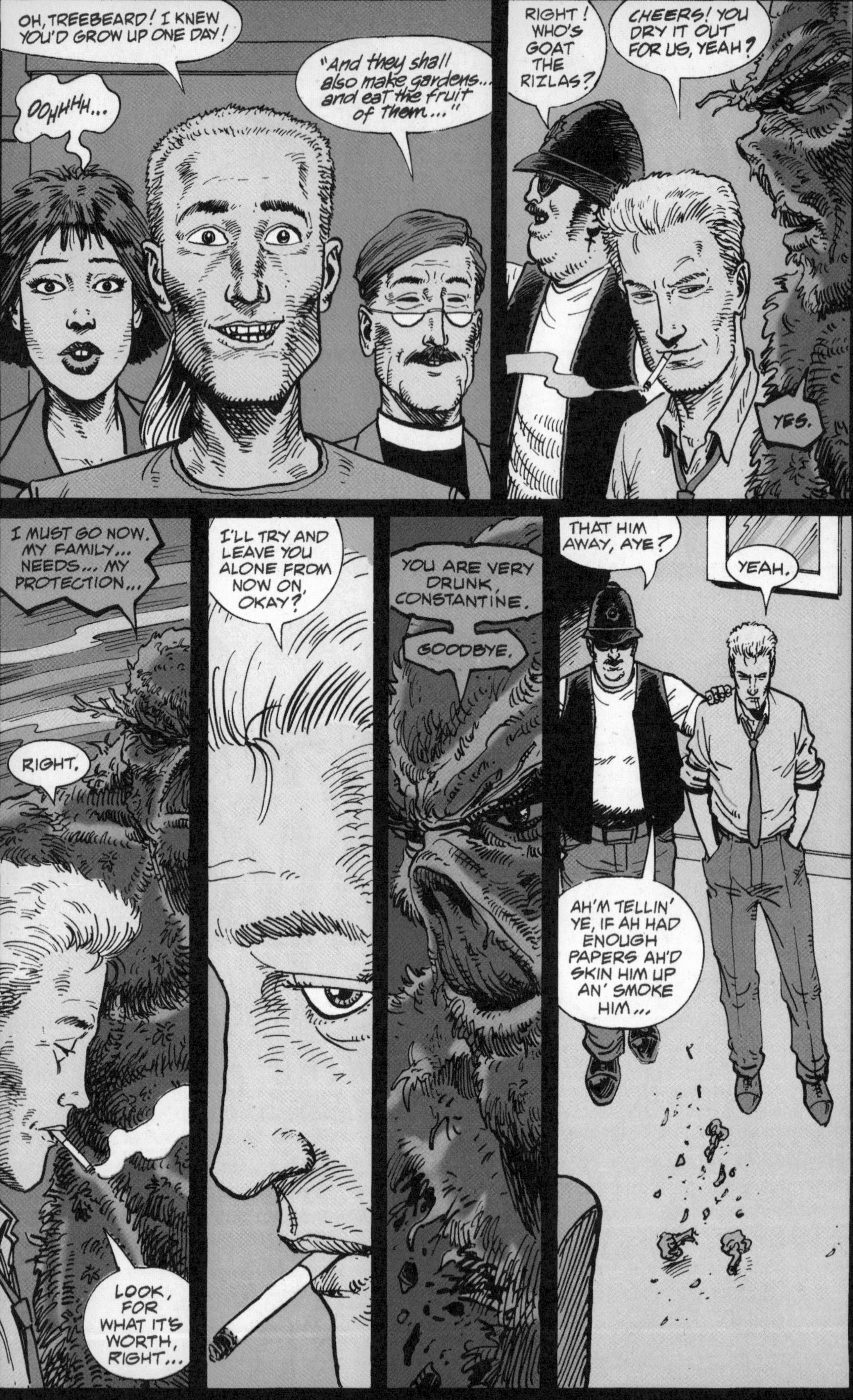

OH, TREEBEARD! I KNEW YOU'D GROW UP ONE DAY!
OOHHHH...
"And they shall also make gardens... and eat the fruit of them..."
RIGHT! WHO'S GOAT THE RIZLAS?
CHEERS! YOU DRY IT OUT FOR US, YEAH?
YES.
I MUST GO NOW. MY FAMILY... NEEDS... MY PROTECTION...
RIGHT.
LOOK, FOR WHAT IT'S WORTH, RIGHT...
I'LL TRY AND LEAVE YOU ALONE FROM NOW ON, OKAY?
YOU ARE VERY DRUNK, CONSTANTINE.
GOODBYE.
THAT HIM AWAY, AYE?
YEAH.
AH'M TELLIN' YE, IF AH HAD ENOUGH PAPERS AH'D SKIN HIM UP AN' SMOKE HIM...

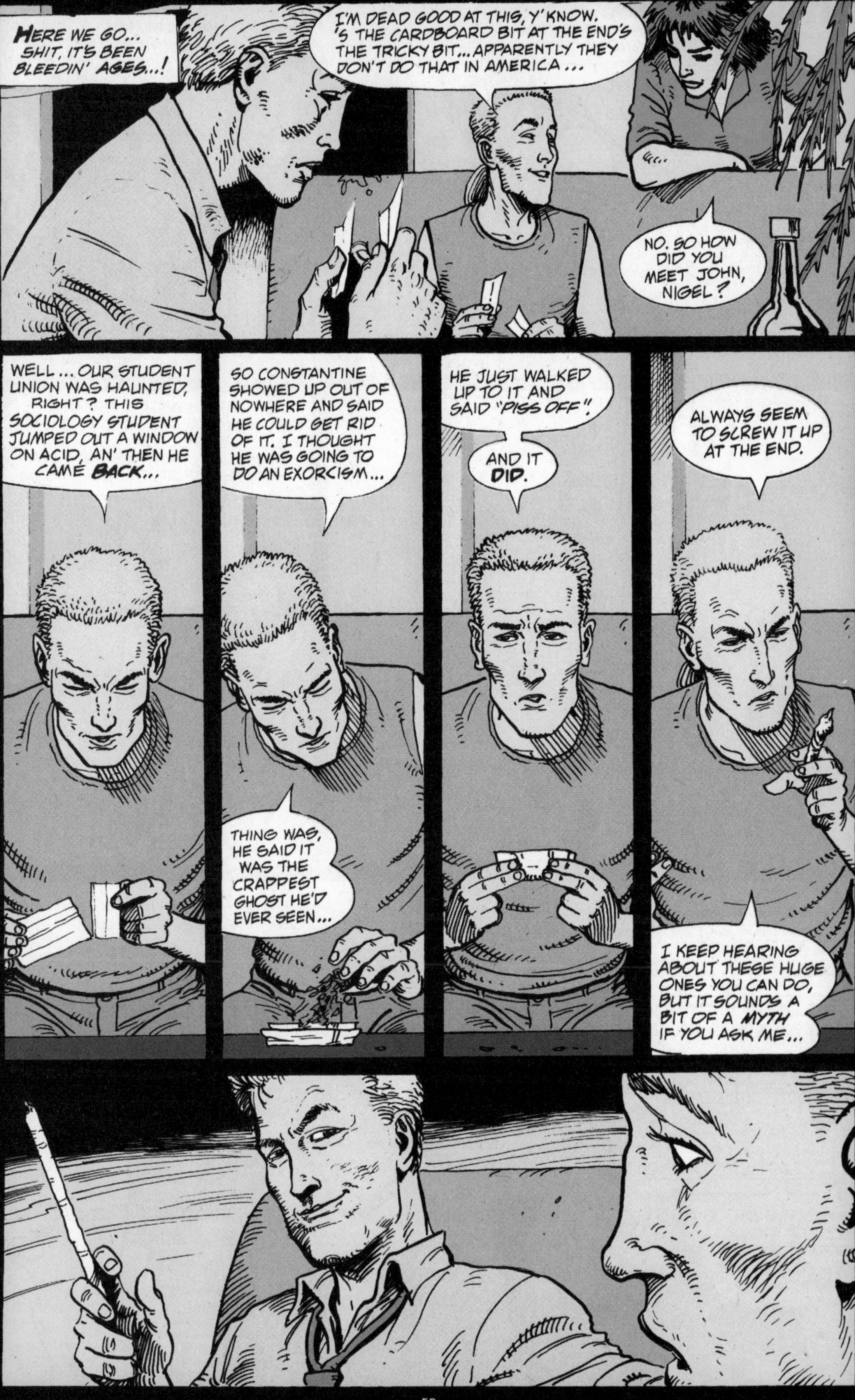
HERE WE GO... SHIT, IT'S BEEN BLEEDIN' AGES...!
I'M DEAD GOOD AT THIS, Y'KNOW. 'S THE CARDBOARD BIT AT THE END'S THE TRICKY BIT... APPARENTLY THEY DON'T DO THAT IN AMERICA...
NO. SO HOW DID YOU MEET JOHN, NIGEL?
WELL... OUR STUDENT UNION WAS HAUNTED, RIGHT? THIS SOCIOLOGY STUDENT JUMPED OUT A WINDOW ON ACID, AN' THEN HE CAME BACK...
SO CONSTANTINE SHOWED UP OUT OF NOWHERE AND SAID HE COULD GET RID OF IT. I THOUGHT HE WAS GOING TO DO AN EXORCISM...
THING WAS, HE SAID IT WAS THE CRAPPEST GHOST HE'D EVER SEEN...
HE JUST WALKED UP TO IT AND SAID "PISS OFF".
AND IT DID.
ALWAYS SEEM TO SCREW IT UP AT THE END.
I KEEP HEARING ABOUT THESE HUGE ONES YOU CAN DO, BUT IT SOUNDS A BIT OF A MYTH IF YOU ASK ME...

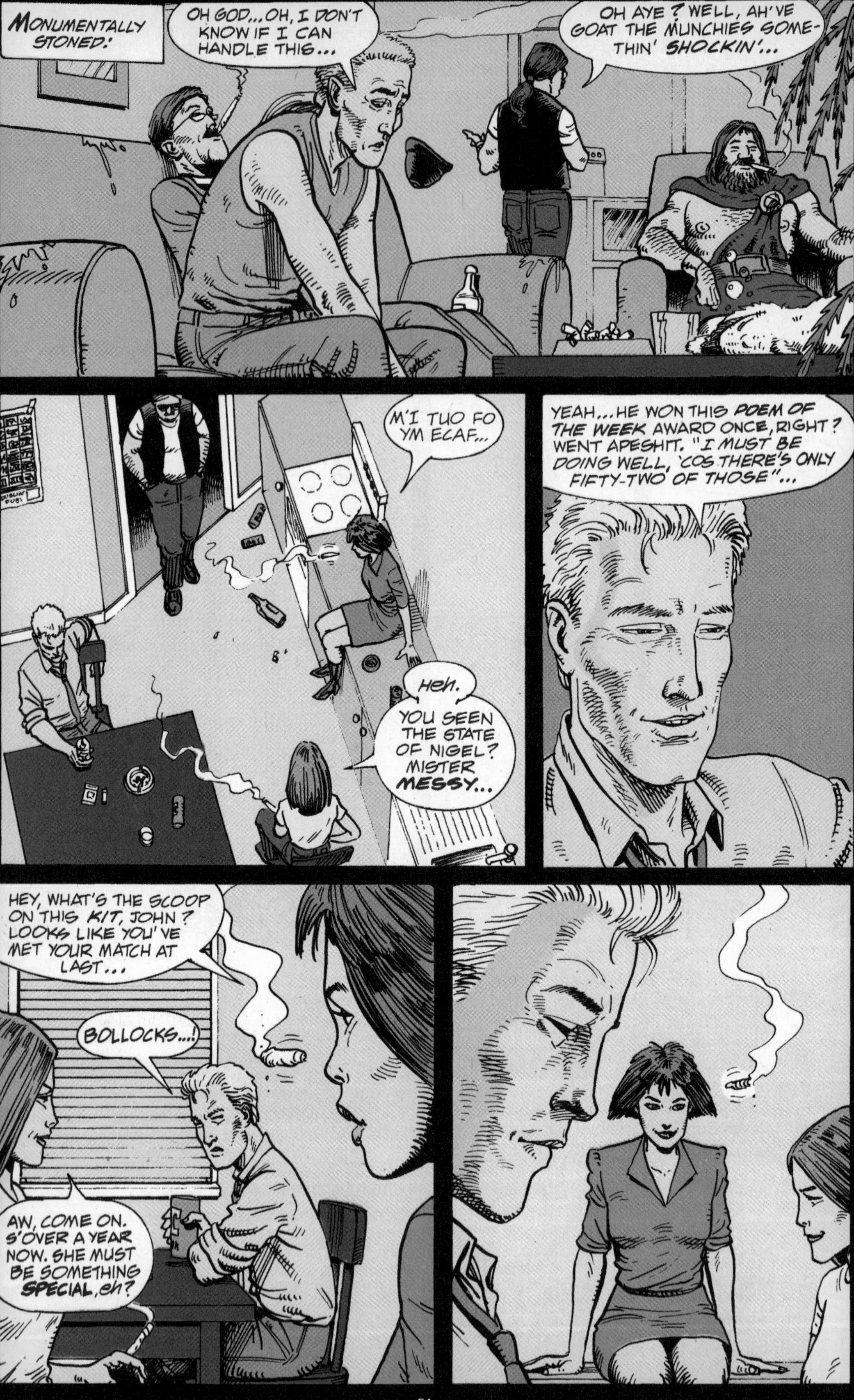
MONUMENTALLY STONED:
OH GOD...OH, I DON'T KNOW IF I CAN HANDLE THIS...
OH AYE? WELL, AH'VE GOAT THE MUNCHIES SOMETHIN' SHOCKIN'...
M'I TUO FO YM ECAF...
Heh.
YOU SEEN THE STATE OF NIGEL? MISTER MESSY...
YEAH...HE WON THIS POEM OF THE WEEK AWARD ONCE, RIGHT? WENT APESHIT. "I MUST BE DOING WELL, 'COS THERE'S ONLY FIFTY-TWO OF THOSE"...
HEY, WHAT'S THE SCOOP ON THIS KIT, JOHN? LOOKS LIKE YOU'VE MET YOUR MATCH AT LAST...
BOLLOCKS...!
AW, COME ON. S'OVER A YEAR NOW. SHE MUST BE SOMETHING SPECIAL, eh?

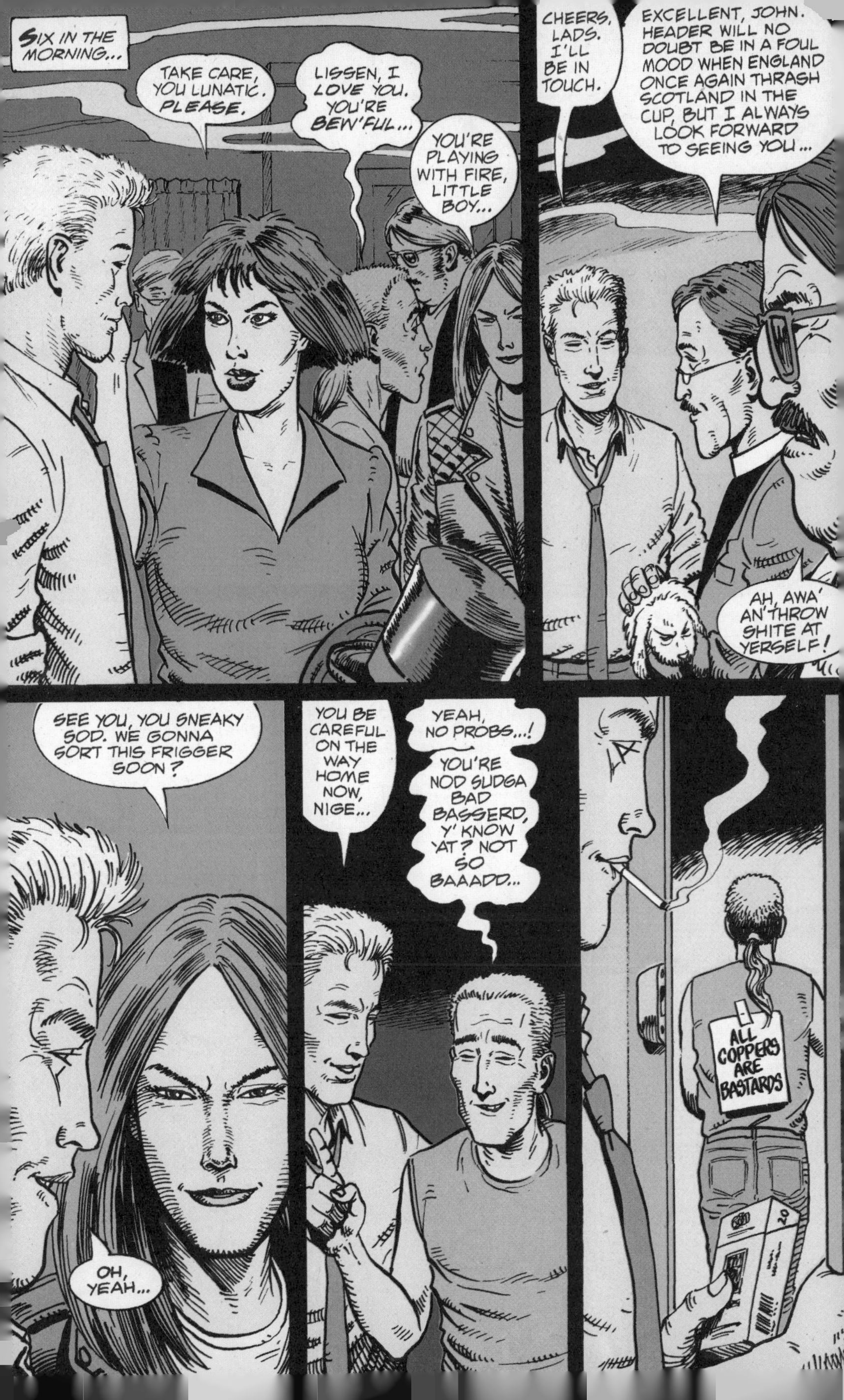

SIX IN THE MORNING...
TAKE CARE, YOU LUNATIC. PLEASE.
LISSEN, I LOVE YOU. YOU'RE BEW'FUL...
YOU'RE PLAYING WITH FIRE, LITTLE BOY...
CHEERS, LADS. I'LL BE IN TOUCH.
EXCELLENT, JOHN. HEADER WILL NO DOUBT BE IN A FOUL MOOD WHEN ENGLAND ONCE AGAIN THRASH SCOTLAND IN THE CUP, BUT I ALWAYS LOOK FORWARD TO SEEING YOU...
AH, AWA' AN' THROW SHITE AT YERSELF!
SEE YOU, YOU SNEAKY SOD. WE GONNA SORT THIS FRIGGER SOON?
OH, YEAH...
YOU BE CAREFUL ON THE WAY HOME NOW, NIGE...
YEAH, NO PROBS...!
YOU'RE NOD SUDGA BAD BASSERD, Y' KNOW 'AT? NOT SO BAAADD...
ALL COPPERS ARE BASTARDS

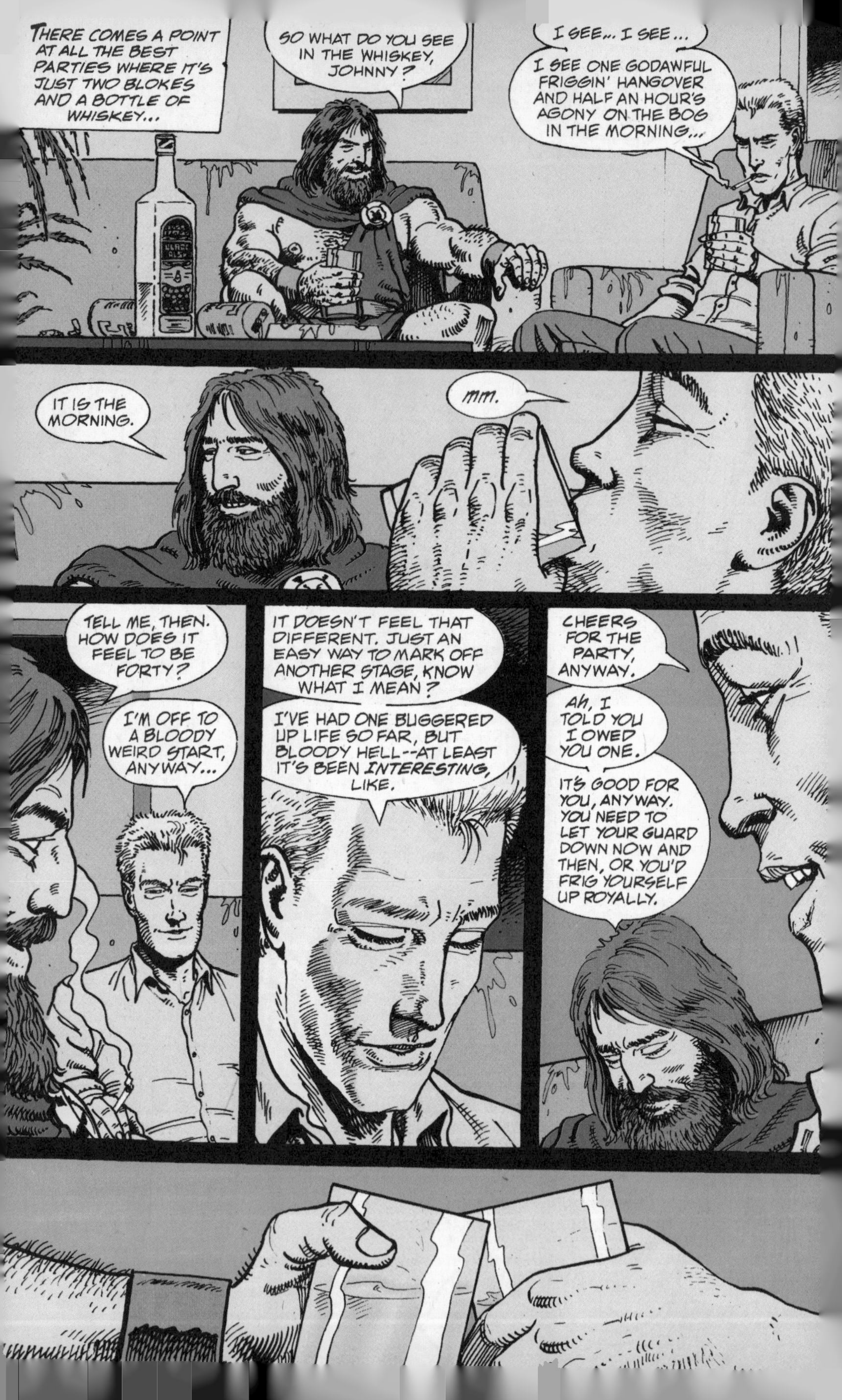
THERE COMES A POINT AT ALL THE BEST PARTIES WHERE IT'S JUST TWO BLOKES AND A BOTTLE OF WHISKEY...
SO WHAT DO YOU SEE IN THE WHISKEY, JOHNNY?
I SEE... I SEE...
I SEE ONE GODAWFUL FRIGGIN' HANGOVER AND HALF AN HOUR'S AGONY ON THE BOG IN THE MORNING...
IT IS THE MORNING.
MM.
TELL ME, THEN. HOW DOES IT FEEL TO BE FORTY?
I'M OFF TO A BLOODY WEIRD START, ANYWAY...
IT DOESN'T FEEL THAT DIFFERENT. JUST AN EASY WAY TO MARK OFF ANOTHER STAGE, KNOW WHAT I MEAN?
I'VE HAD ONE BUGGERED UP LIFE SO FAR, BUT BLOODY HELL--AT LEAST IT'S BEEN *INTERESTING*, LIKE.
CHEERS FOR THE PARTY, ANYWAY.
AH, I TOLD YOU I OWED YOU ONE.
IT'S GOOD FOR YOU, ANYWAY. YOU NEED TO LET YOUR GUARD DOWN NOW AND THEN, OR YOU'D FRIG YOURSELF UP ROYALLY.

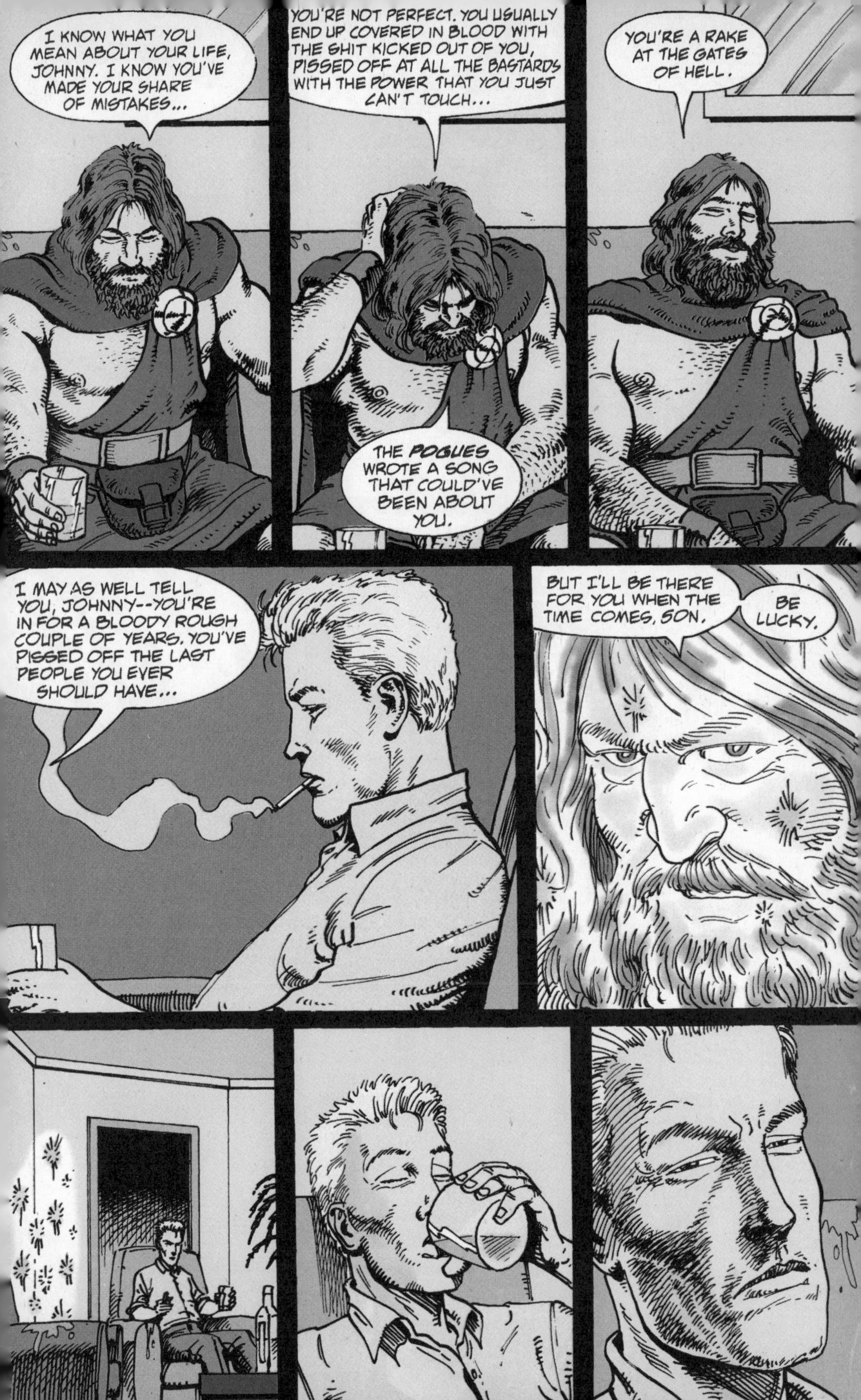
I KNOW WHAT YOU MEAN ABOUT YOUR LIFE, JOHNNY. I KNOW YOU'VE MADE YOUR SHARE OF MISTAKES...
YOU'RE NOT PERFECT. YOU USUALLY END UP COVERED IN BLOOD WITH THE SHIT KICKED OUT OF YOU, PISSED OFF AT ALL THE BASTARDS WITH THE POWER THAT YOU JUST CAN'T TOUCH...
THE POGUES WROTE A SONG THAT COULD'VE BEEN ABOUT YOU.
YOU'RE A RAKE AT THE GATES OF HELL.
I MAY AS WELL TELL YOU, JOHNNY--YOU'RE IN FOR A BLOODY ROUGH COUPLE OF YEARS. YOU'VE PISSED OFF THE LAST PEOPLE YOU EVER SHOULD HAVE...
BUT I'LL BE THERE FOR YOU WHEN THE TIME COMES, SON.
BE LUCKY.

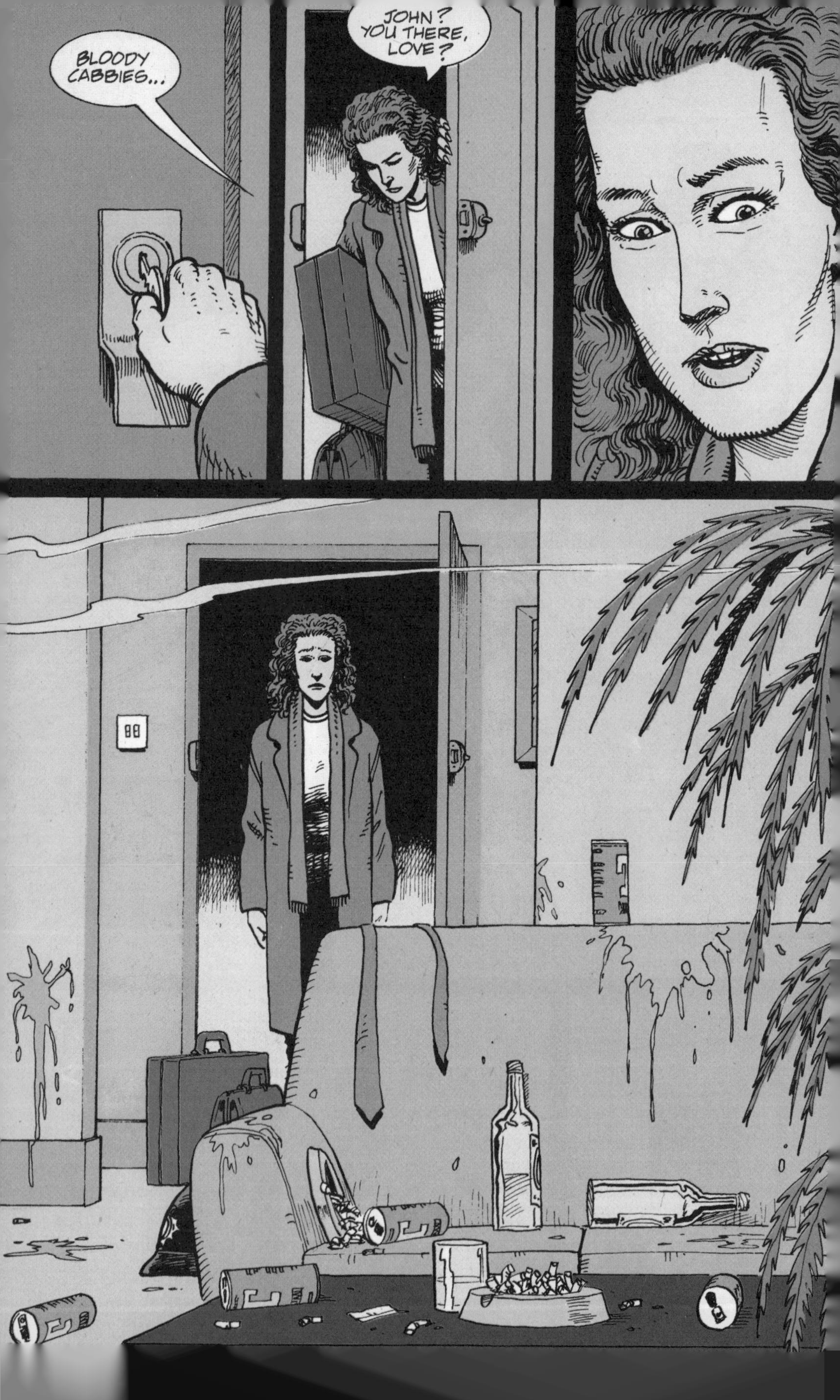
BLOODY CABBIES...
JOHN? YOU THERE, LOVE?

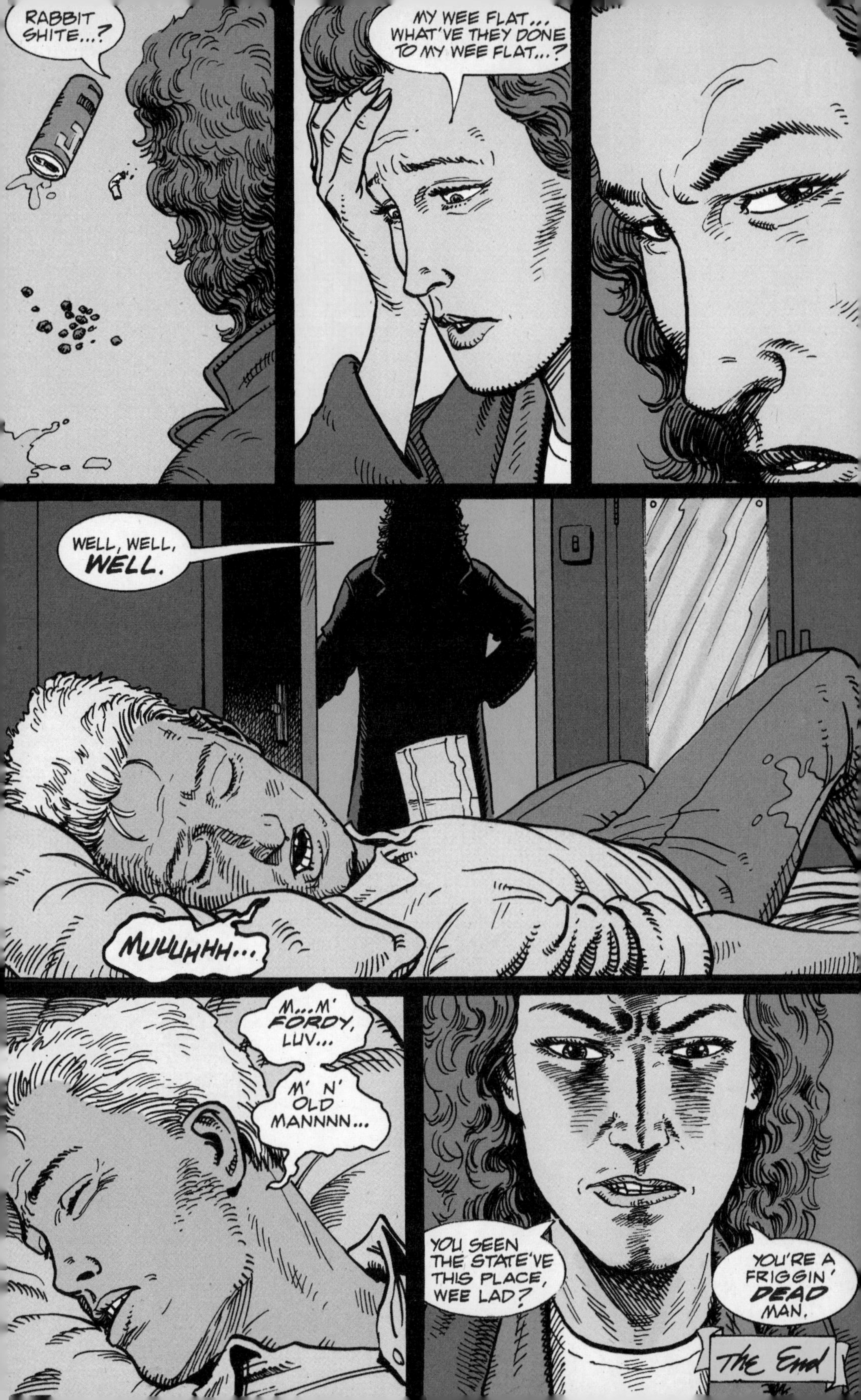
RABBIT SHITE...?
MY WEE FLAT... WHAT'VE THEY DONE TO MY WEE FLAT...?
WELL, WELL, WELL.
MUUUHHH...
M...M' FORDY, LUV...
M' N' OLD MANNNN...
YOU SEEN THE STATE'VE THIS PLACE, WEE LAD?
YOU'RE A FRIGGIN' DEAD MAN.
The End

JOHN CONSTANTINE
HELLBLAZER
DC
VERTIGO
NO. 64
APR 93
$1.75 US
$2.25 CAN
£1.00 UK
SUGGESTED FOR MATURE READERS
My Eng
Fabry '92
GARTH ENNIS
STEVE DILLON

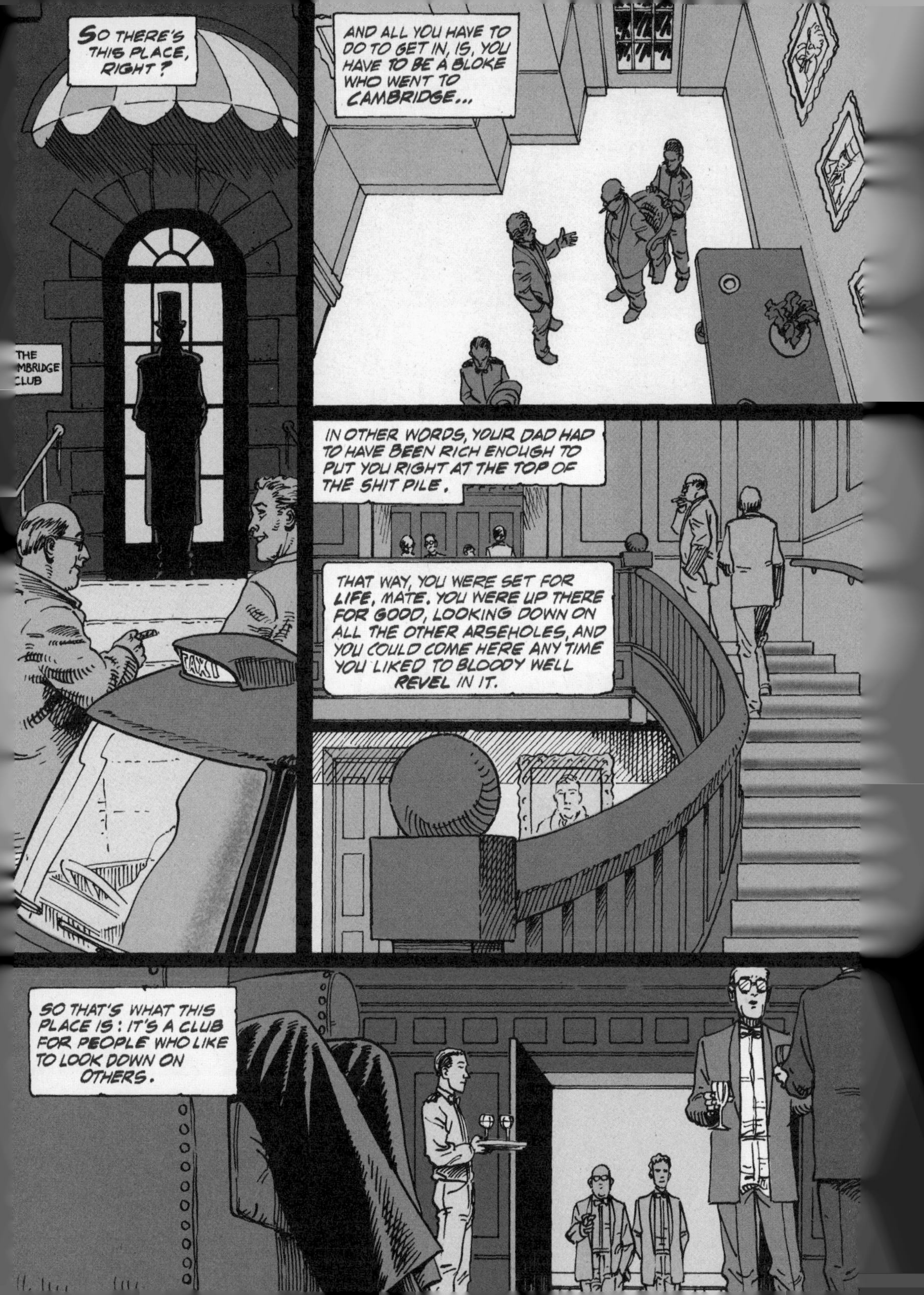
SO THERE'S THIS PLACE, RIGHT?
THE CAMBRIDGE CLUB
TAXI
AND ALL YOU HAVE TO DO TO GET IN, IS, YOU HAVE TO BE A BLOKE WHO WENT TO CAMBRIDGE...
IN OTHER WORDS, YOUR DAD HAD TO HAVE BEEN RICH ENOUGH TO PUT YOU RIGHT AT THE TOP OF THE SHIT PILE.
THAT WAY, YOU WERE SET FOR LIFE, MATE. YOU WERE UP THERE FOR GOOD, LOOKING DOWN ON ALL THE OTHER ARSEHOLES, AND YOU COULD COME HERE ANY TIME YOU LIKED TO BLOODY WELL REVEL IN IT.
SO THAT'S WHAT THIS PLACE IS: IT'S A CLUB FOR PEOPLE WHO LIKE TO LOOK DOWN ON OTHERS.

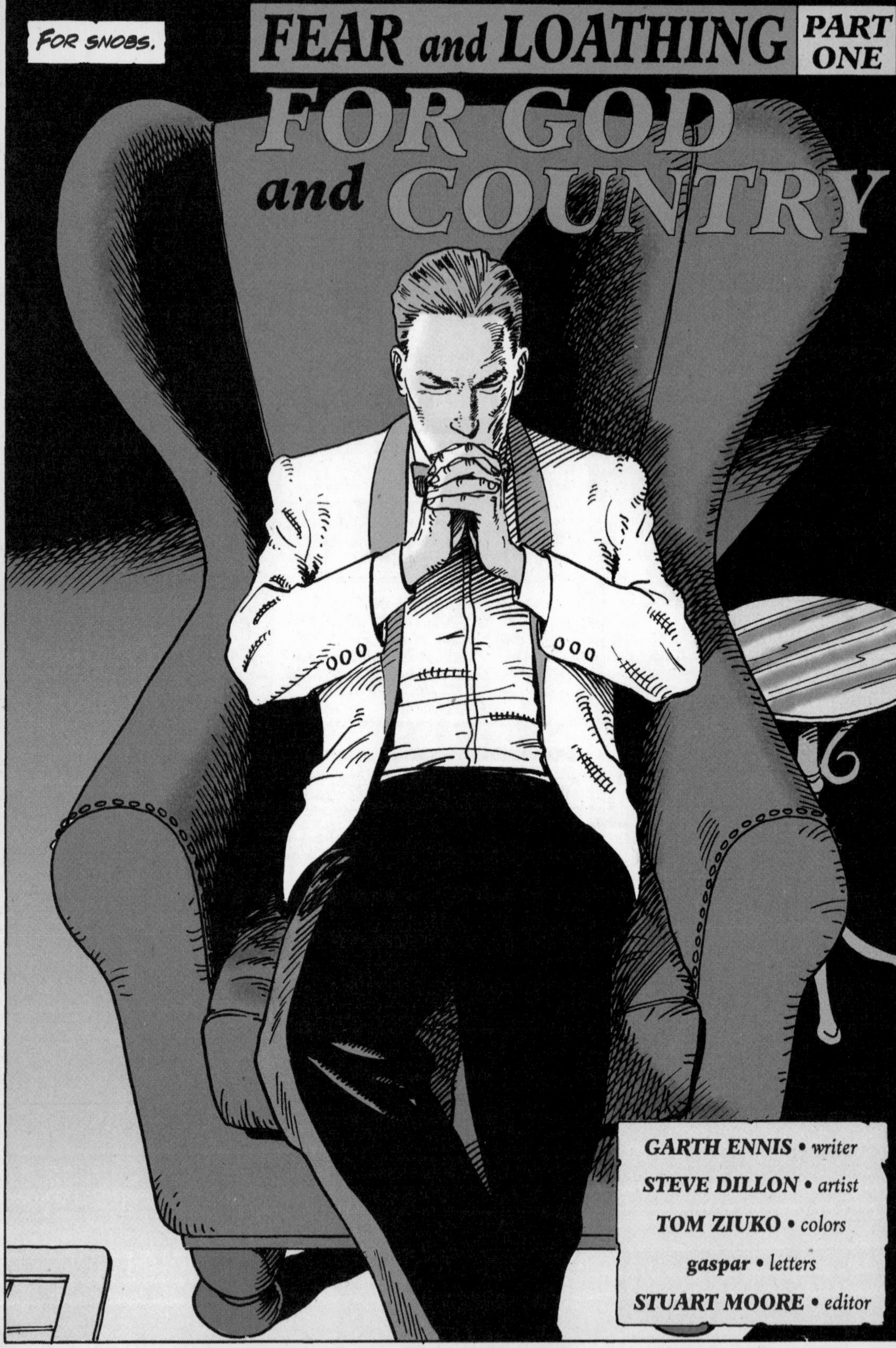

FOR SNOBS.
FEAR and LOATHING
PART ONE
FOR GOD and COUNTRY
GARTH ENNIS • writer
STEVE DILLON • artist
TOM ZIUKO • colors
gaspar • letters
STUART MOORE • editor

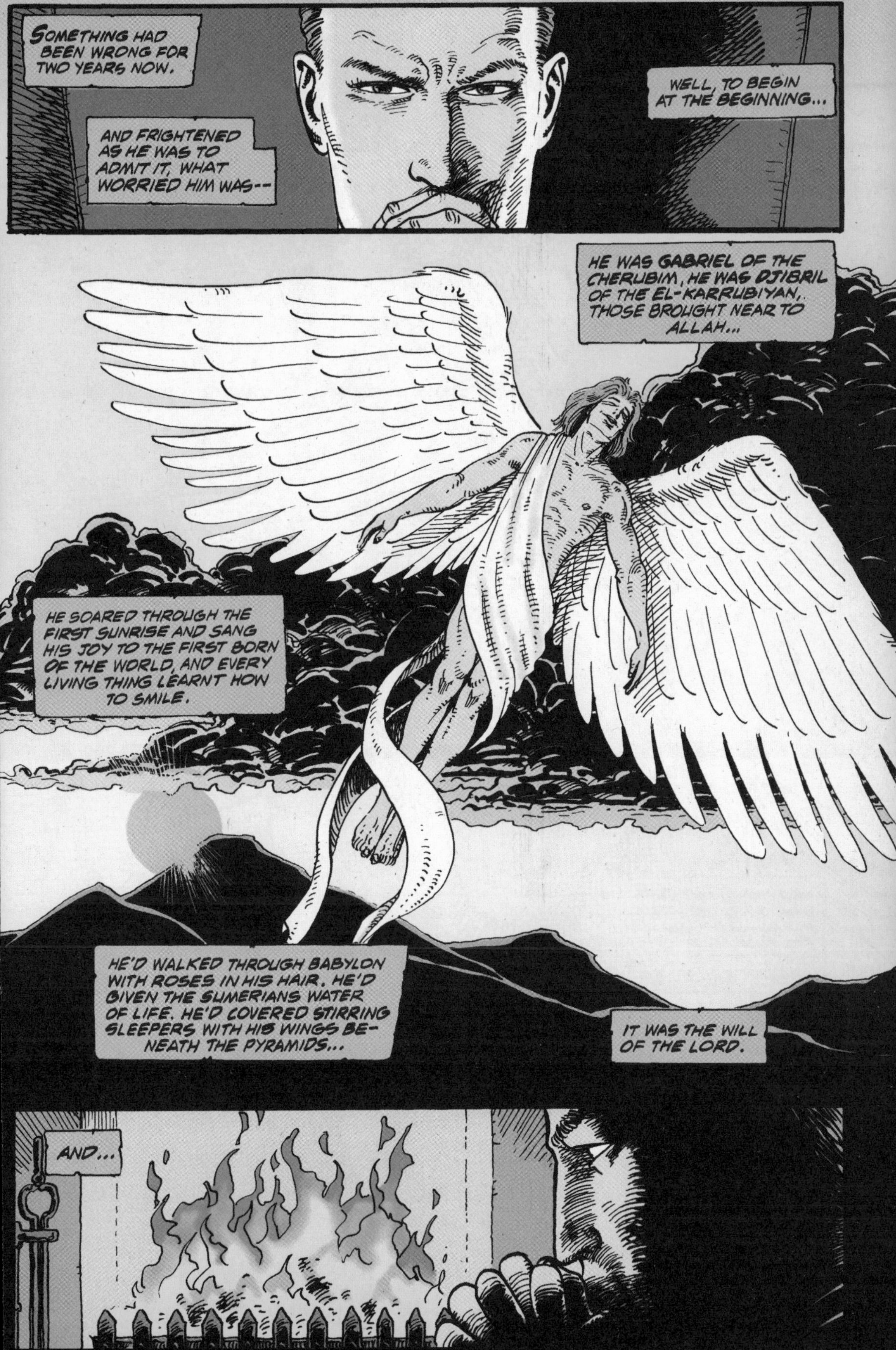
SOMETHING HAD BEEN WRONG FOR TWO YEARS NOW.
AND FRIGHTENED AS HE WAS TO ADMIT IT, WHAT WORRIED HIM WAS--
WELL, TO BEGIN AT THE BEGINNING...
HE WAS GABRIEL OF THE CHERUBIM, HE WAS DJIBRIL OF THE EL-KARRUBIYAN, THOSE BROUGHT NEAR TO ALLAH...
HE SOARED THROUGH THE FIRST SUNRISE AND SANG HIS JOY TO THE FIRST BORN OF THE WORLD, AND EVERY LIVING THING LEARNT HOW TO SMILE.
HE'D WALKED THROUGH BABYLON WITH ROSES IN HIS HAIR. HE'D GIVEN THE SUMERIANS WATER OF LIFE. HE'D COVERED STIRRING SLEEPERS WITH HIS WINGS BE-NEATH THE PYRAMIDS...
IT WAS THE WILL OF THE LORD.
AND...

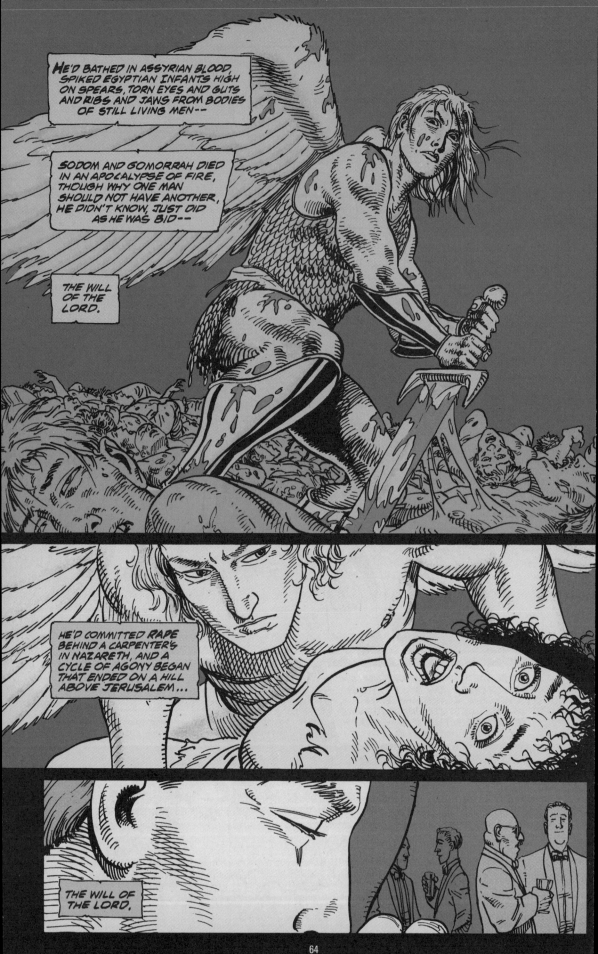

HE'D BATHED IN ASSYRIAN BLOOD, SPIKED EGYPTIAN INFANTS HIGH ON SPEARS, TORN EYES AND GUTS AND RIBS AND JAWS FROM BODIES OF STILL LIVING MEN--

SODOM AND GOMORRAH DIED IN AN APOCALYPSE OF FIRE, THOUGH WHY ONE MAN SHOULD NOT HAVE ANOTHER, HE DIDN'T KNOW, JUST DID AS HE WAS BID--

THE WILL OF THE LORD.

HE'D COMMITTED RAPE BEHIND A CARPENTER'S IN NAZARETH, AND A CYCLE OF AGONY BEGAN THAT ENDED ON A HILL ABOVE JERUSALEM...

THE WILL OF THE LORD.

IT WAS NOT FOR HIM TO DOUBT. EVERYTHING THAT HAPPENED WAS THE CREATOR'S WILL. NOTHING SURPRISED THE LORD OF HOSTS.

SO...

SO CONSTANTINE WAS RIGHT. THE MAN HE'D SPOKEN TO-- CHARLES PATTERSON--WAS A BULLY AND A RACIST THUG. A SINNER.

SO WHY HAD HE, GABRIEL, EVEN BEEN ALLOWED TO TALK TO HIM? WHY HADN'T HE AT LEAST BEEN REPRIMANDED?

THE WILL OF THE LORD?

AND WHAT WAS WILLED FOR HIM NOW, THEN? WHY WAS HE SUDDENLY HEADED IN THIS STRANGEST OF DIRECTIONS?

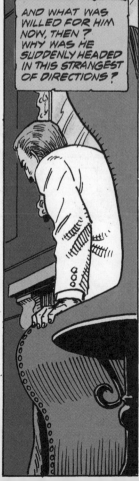

HIS HEART FULL OF TROUBLES, THE ARCHANGEL DECIDED TO TAKE THE AIR.

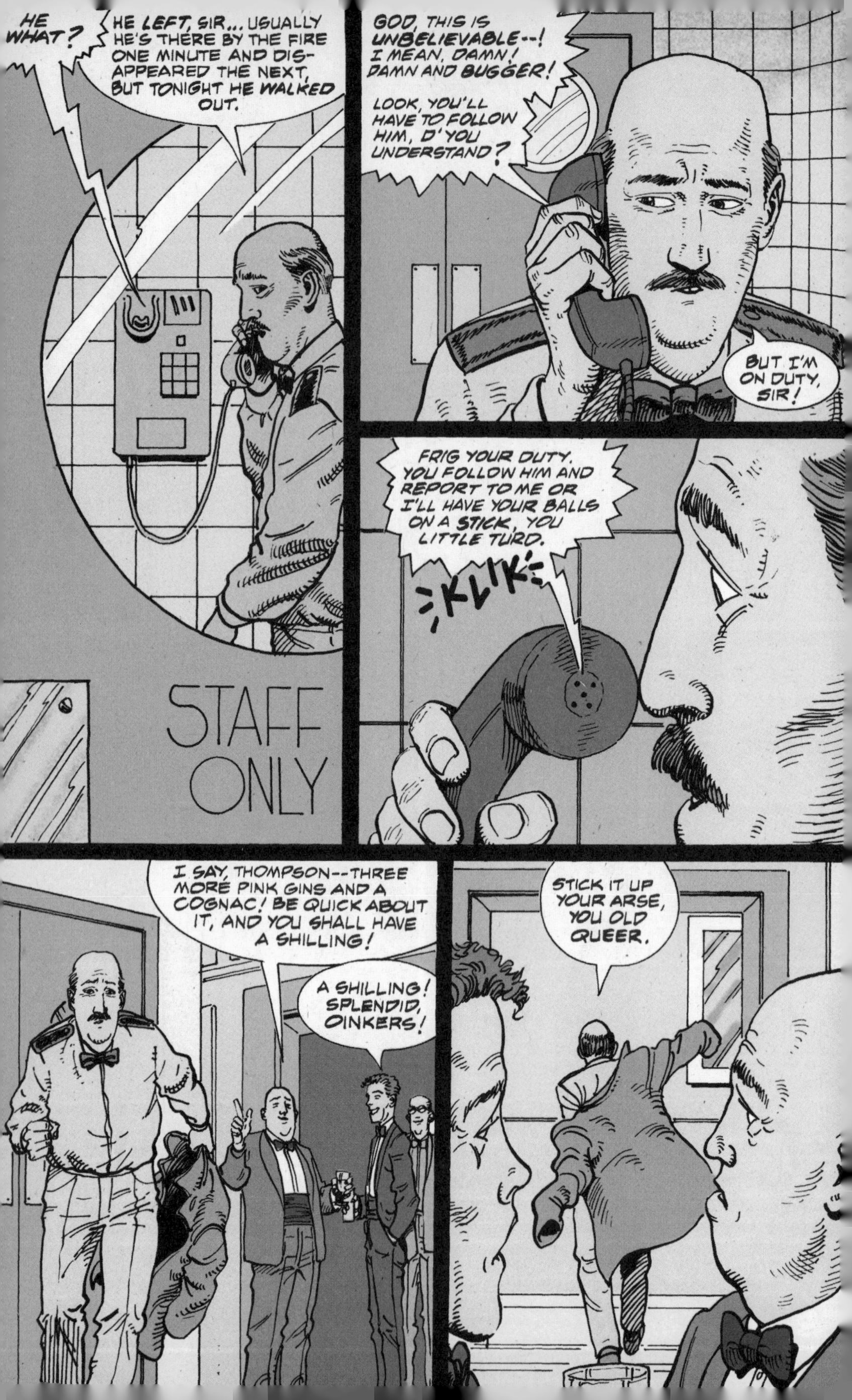
HE WHAT?
HE LEFT, SIR... USUALLY HE'S THERE BY THE FIRE ONE MINUTE AND DISAPPEARED THE NEXT, BUT TONIGHT HE WALKED OUT.
GOD, THIS IS UNBELIEVABLE--! I MEAN, DAMN! DAMN AND BUGGER!
LOOK, YOU'LL HAVE TO FOLLOW HIM, D'YOU UNDERSTAND?
BUT I'M ON DUTY, SIR!
STAFF ONLY
FRIG YOUR DUTY. YOU FOLLOW HIM AND REPORT TO ME OR I'LL HAVE YOUR BALLS ON A STICK, YOU LITTLE TURD.
KLIK
I SAY, THOMPSON--THREE MORE PINK GINS AND A COGNAC! BE QUICK ABOUT IT, AND YOU SHALL HAVE A SHILLING!
A SHILLING! SPLENDID, OINKERS!
STICK IT UP YOUR ARSE, YOU OLD QUEER.

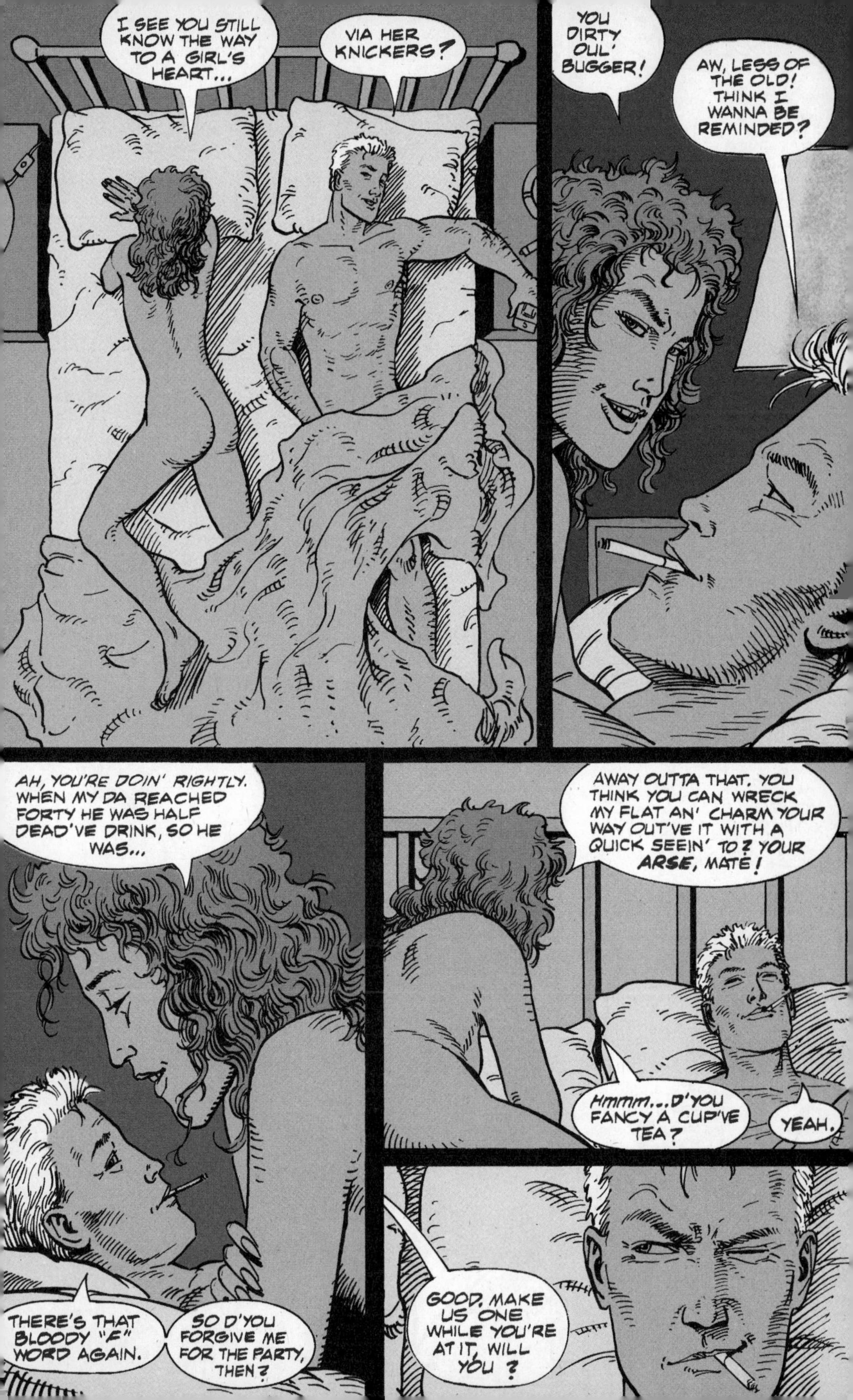
I SEE YOU STILL KNOW THE WAY TO A GIRL'S HEART...
VIA HER KNICKERS?
YOU DIRTY OUL' BUGGER!
AW, LESS OF THE OLD! THINK I WANNA BE REMINDED?
AH, YOU'RE DOIN' RIGHTLY. WHEN MY DA REACHED FORTY HE WAS HALF DEAD'VE DRINK, SO HE WAS...
THERE'S THAT BLOODY "F" WORD AGAIN.
SO D'YOU FORGIVE ME FOR THE PARTY, THEN?
AWAY OUTTA THAT. YOU THINK YOU CAN WRECK MY FLAT AN' CHARM YOUR WAY OUT'VE IT WITH A QUICK SEEIN' TO? YOUR **ARSE**, MATE!
Hmmm...D'YOU FANCY A CUP'VE TEA?
YEAH.
GOOD. MAKE US ONE WHILE YOU'RE AT IT, WILL YOU?

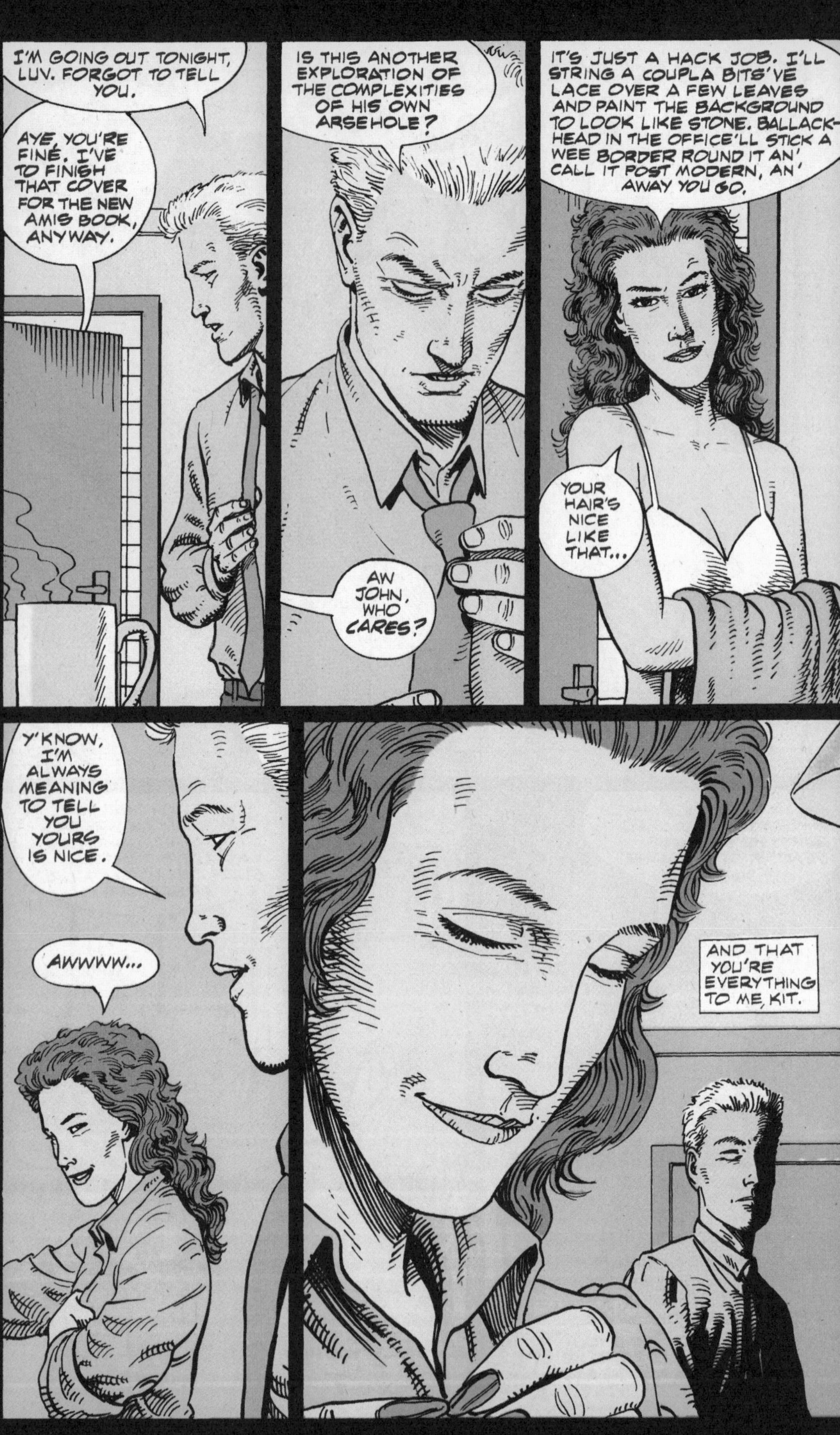
I'M GOING OUT TONIGHT, LUV. FORGOT TO TELL YOU.
AYE, YOU'RE FINE. I'VE TO FINISH THAT COVER FOR THE NEW AMIS BOOK, ANYWAY.
IS THIS ANOTHER EXPLORATION OF THE COMPLEXITIES OF HIS OWN ARSEHOLE?
AW JOHN, WHO CARES?
IT'S JUST A HACK JOB. I'LL STRING A COUPLA BITS'VE LACE OVER A FEW LEAVES AND PAINT THE BACKGROUND TO LOOK LIKE STONE. BALLACK-HEAD IN THE OFFICE'LL STICK A WEE BORDER ROUND IT AN' CALL IT POST MODERN, AN' AWAY YOU GO.
YOUR HAIR'S NICE LIKE THAT...
Y'KNOW, I'M ALWAYS MEANING TO TELL YOU YOURS IS NICE.
AWWWW...
AND THAT YOU'RE EVERYTHING TO ME, KIT.

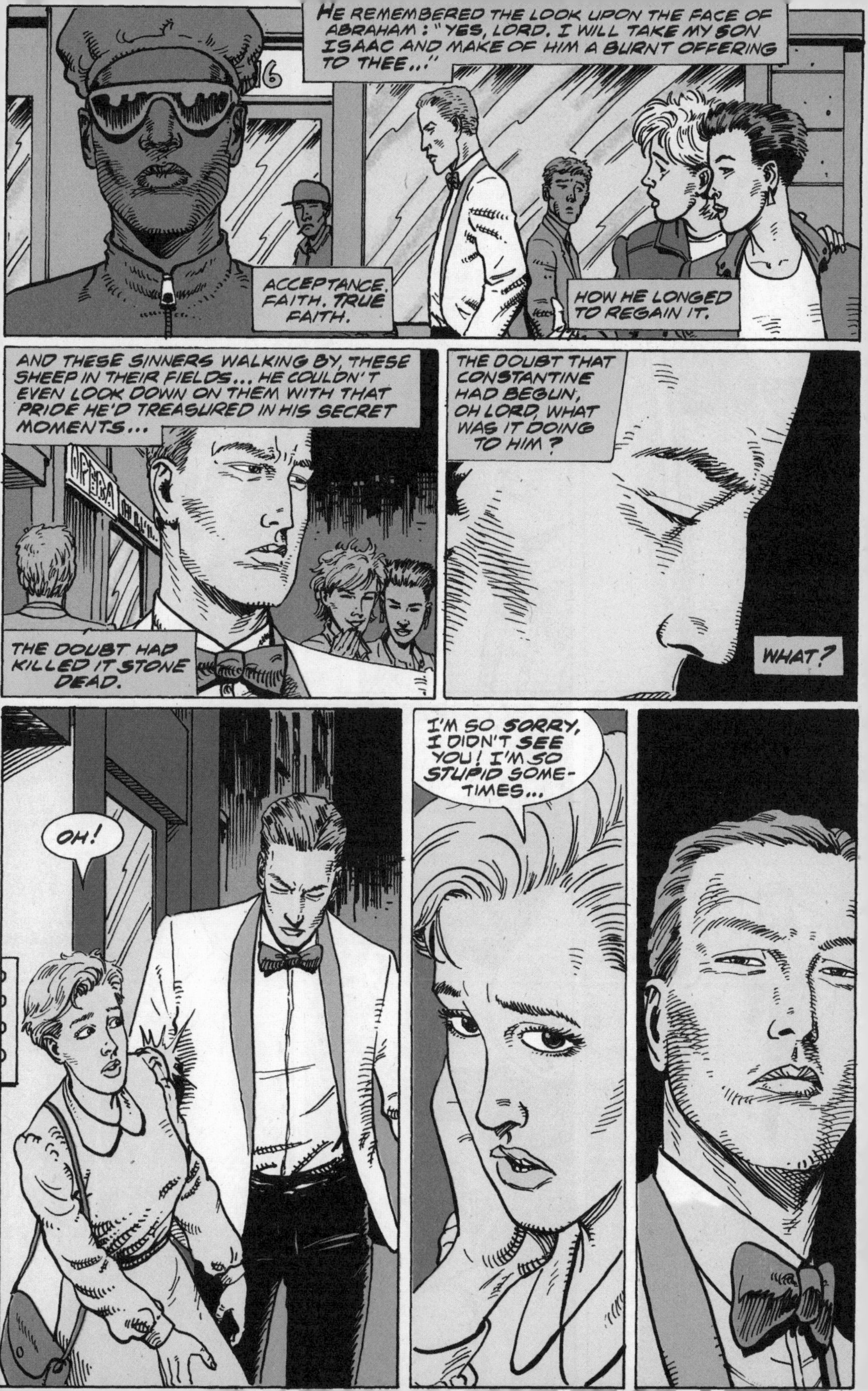
HE REMEMBERED THE LOOK UPON THE FACE OF ABRAHAM: "YES, LORD. I WILL TAKE MY SON ISAAC AND MAKE OF HIM A BURNT OFFERING TO THEE..."
ACCEPTANCE. FAITH. TRUE FAITH.
HOW HE LONGED TO REGAIN IT.
AND THESE SINNERS WALKING BY, THESE SHEEP IN THEIR FIELDS... HE COULDN'T EVEN LOOK DOWN ON THEM WITH THAT PRIDE HE'D TREASURED IN HIS SECRET MOMENTS...
THE DOUBT HAD KILLED IT STONE DEAD.
THE DOUBT THAT CONSTANTINE HAD BEGUN, OH LORD, WHAT WAS IT DOING TO HIM?
WHAT?
OH!
I'M SO SORRY, I DIDN'T SEE YOU! I'M SO STUPID SOME-TIMES...

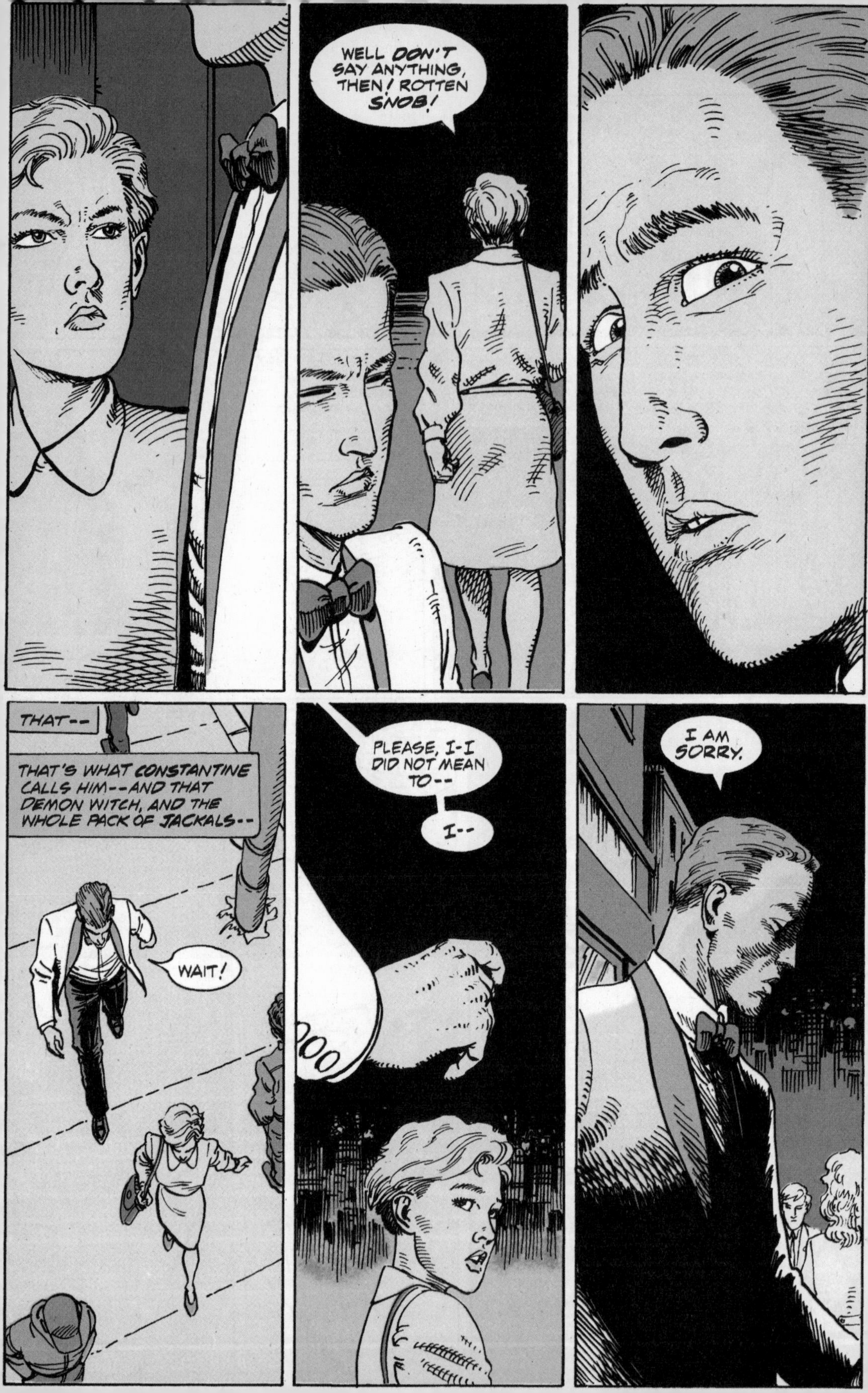

WELL DON'T SAY ANYTHING, THEN! ROTTEN SNOB!
THAT--
THAT'S WHAT CONSTANTINE CALLS HIM--AND THAT DEMON WITCH, AND THE WHOLE PACK OF JACKALS--
WAIT!
PLEASE, I-I DID NOT MEAN TO--
I--
I AM SORRY.

WELL, THAT'S...

THAT'S OKAY...

I, *ah*, I SHOULD NOT HAVE BEEN SO HAUGHTY. I WAS DIS-TRACTED...

I CAN ONLY BEG FOR-GIVENESS.

OH, YOU DON'T HAVE TO SAY *THAT*... LOOK, ARE YOU ALL RIGHT?

I MEAN, D'YOU WANT TO TALK, OR SOMETHING? BECAUSE YOU SEEM AWFULLY WOUND *UP*...

I... I BELIEVE I WOULD LIKE THAT...

OKAY.

I'M JULIE, BY THE WAY.

GABRIEL.

THAT'S REALLY *NICE*... LIKE THE ANGEL, YOU MEAN? IN THE BIBLE?

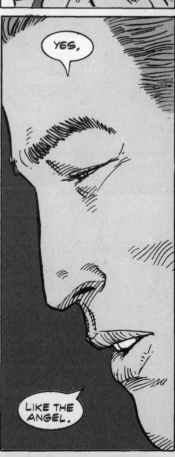

YES,

LIKE THE ANGEL.

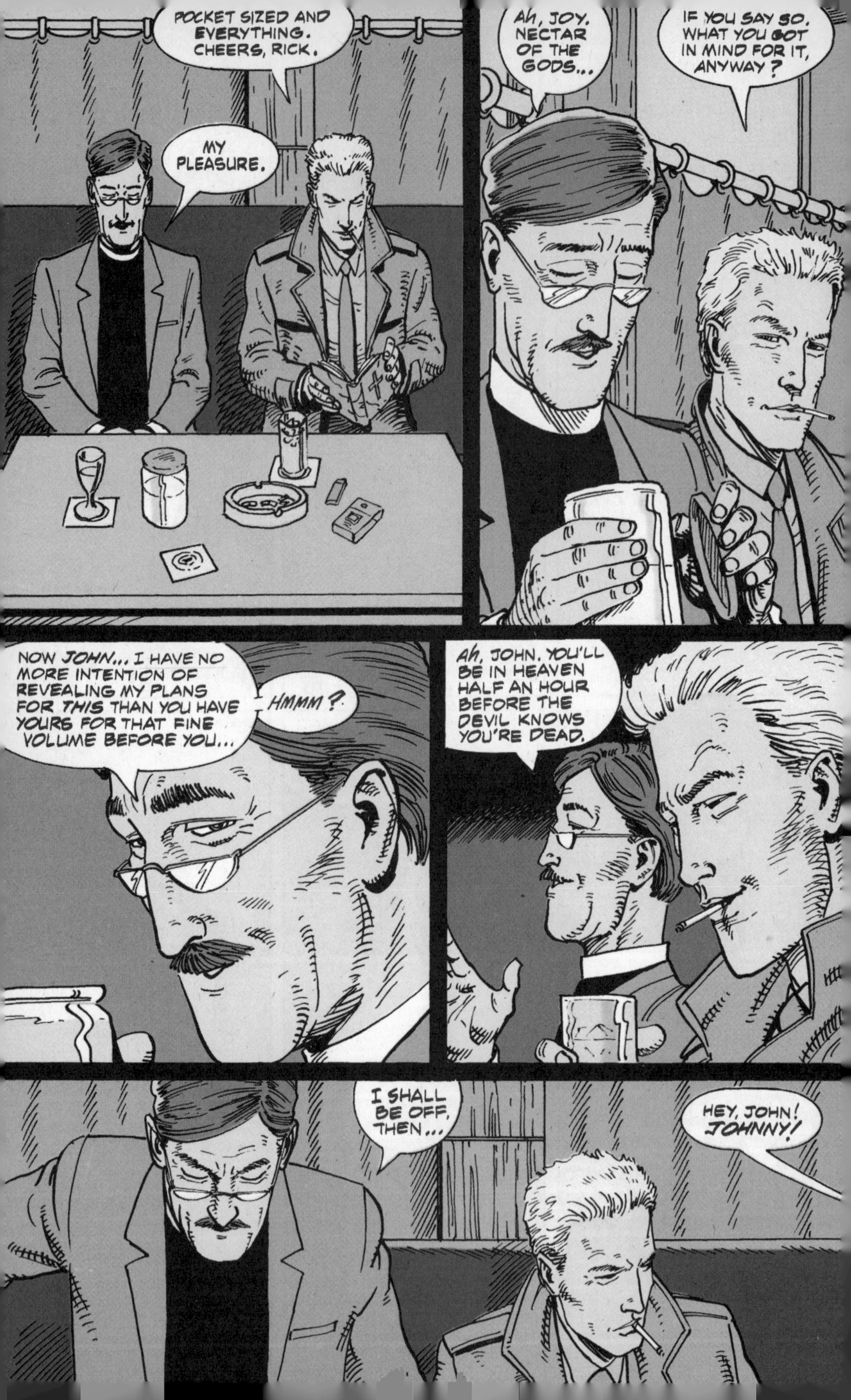
POCKET SIZED AND EVERYTHING. CHEERS, RICK.
MY PLEASURE.
AH, JOY. NECTAR OF THE GODS...
IF YOU SAY SO. WHAT YOU GOT IN MIND FOR IT, ANYWAY?
NOW JOHN... I HAVE NO MORE INTENTION OF REVEALING MY PLANS FOR THIS THAN YOU HAVE YOURS FOR THAT FINE VOLUME BEFORE YOU...
HMMM?
AH, JOHN. YOU'LL BE IN HEAVEN HALF AN HOUR BEFORE THE DEVIL KNOWS YOU'RE DEAD.
I SHALL BE OFF, THEN...
HEY, JOHN! JOHNNY!

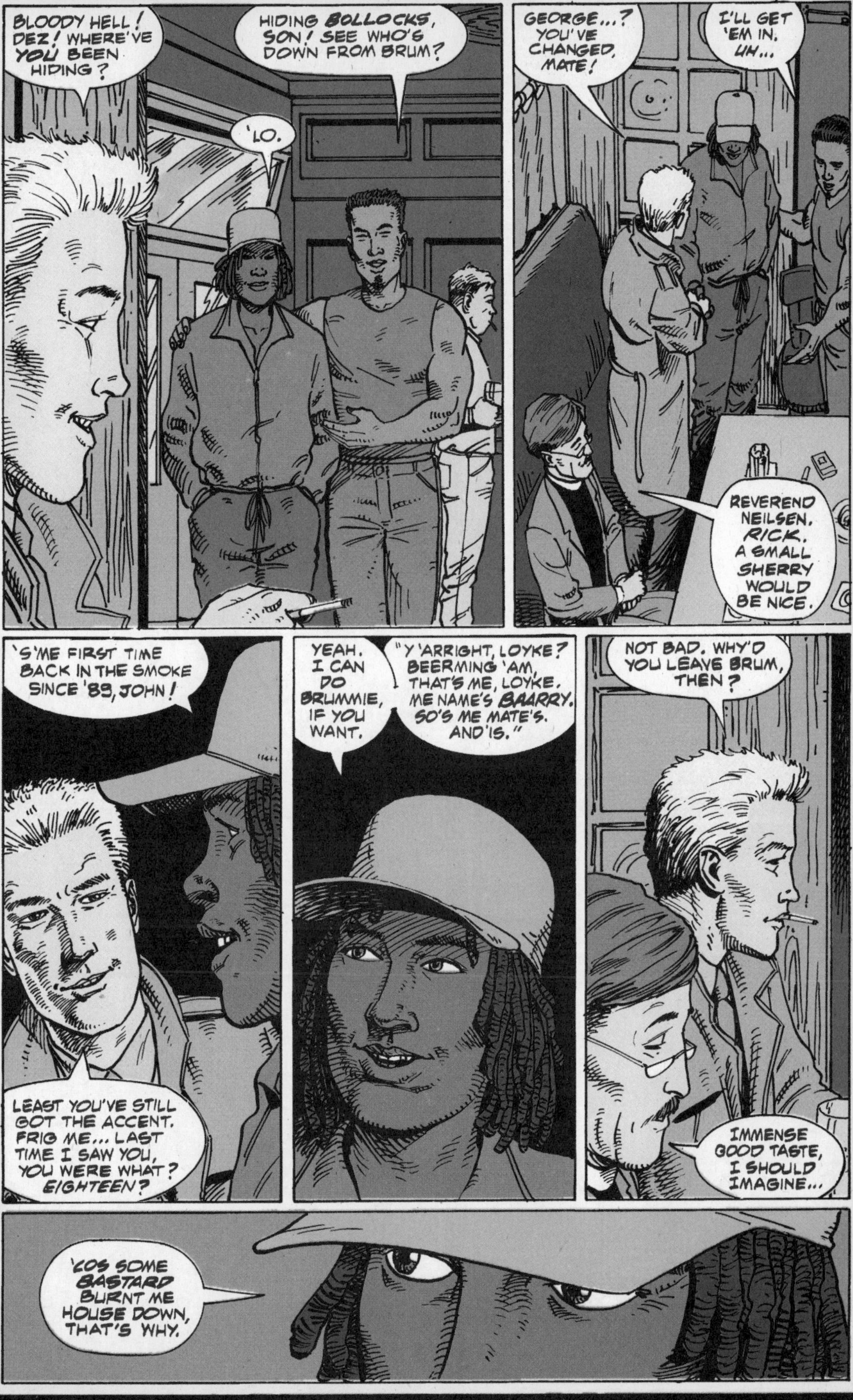
BLOODY HELL! DEZ! WHERE'VE YOU BEEN HIDING?
HIDING BOLLOCKS, SON! SEE WHO'S DOWN FROM BRUM?
'LO.
GEORGE...? YOU'VE CHANGED, MATE!
I'LL GET 'EM IN. UH...
REVEREND NEILSEN. RICK. A SMALL SHERRY WOULD BE NICE.
'S'ME FIRST TIME BACK IN THE SMOKE SINCE '89, JOHN!
LEAST YOU'VE STILL GOT THE ACCENT. FRIG ME... LAST TIME I SAW YOU, YOU WERE WHAT? EIGHTEEN?
YEAH. I CAN DO BRUMMIE, IF YOU WANT.
"Y'ARRIGHT, LOYKE? BEERMING 'AM, THAT'S ME, LOYKE. ME NAME'S BAARRY. SO'S ME MATE'S. AND'IS."
NOT BAD. WHY'D YOU LEAVE BRUM, THEN?
IMMENSE GOOD TASTE, I SHOULD IMAGINE...
'COS SOME BASTARD BURNT ME HOUSE DOWN, THAT'S WHY.

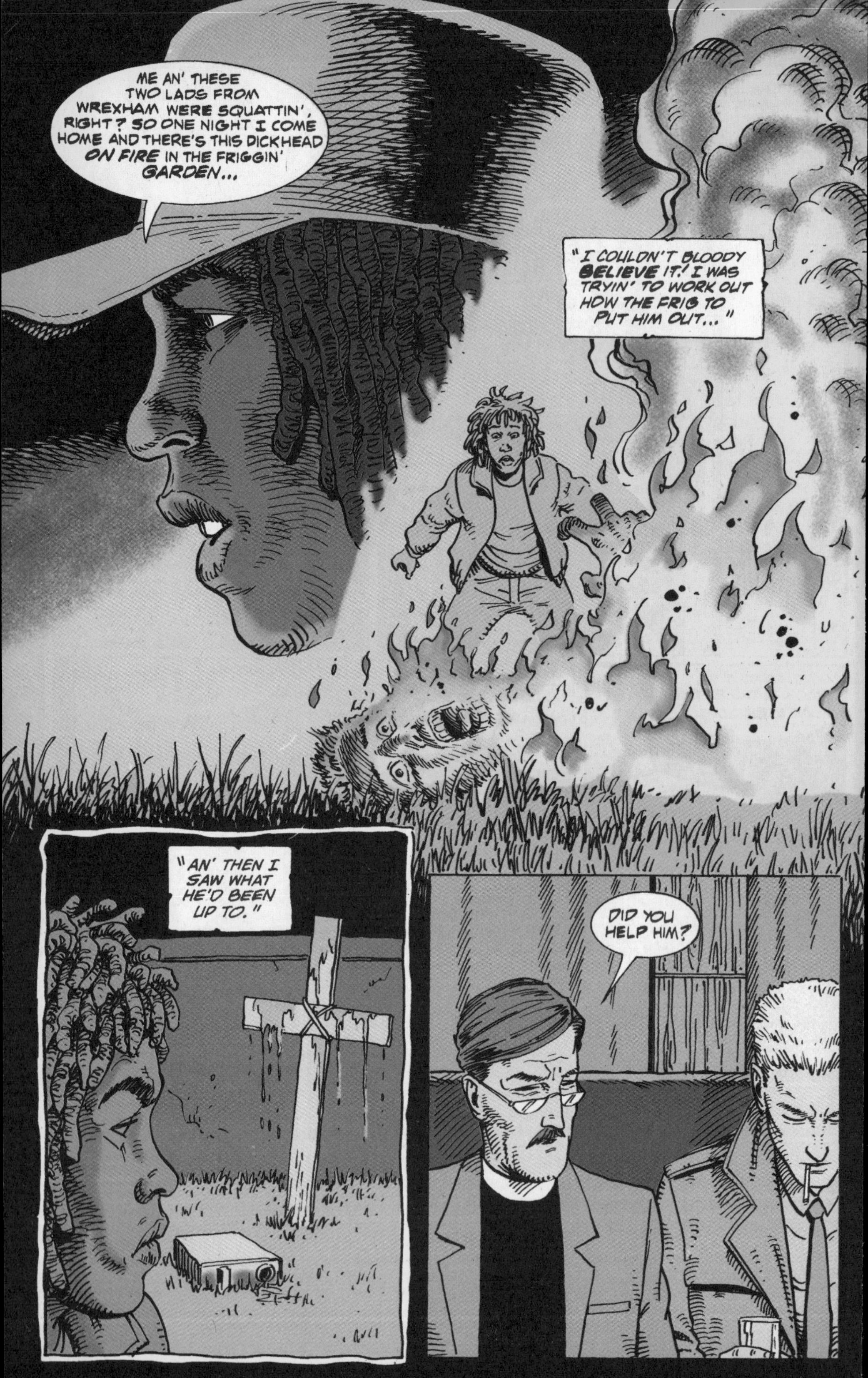
ME AN' THESE TWO LADS FROM WREXHAM WERE SQUATTIN', RIGHT? SO ONE NIGHT I COME HOME AND THERE'S THIS DICKHEAD ON FIRE IN THE FRIGGIN' GARDEN...
"I COULDN'T BLOODY BELIEVE IT! I WAS TRYIN' TO WORK OUT HOW THE FRIG TO PUT HIM OUT..."
"AN' THEN I SAW WHAT HE'D BEEN UP TO."
DID YOU HELP HIM?

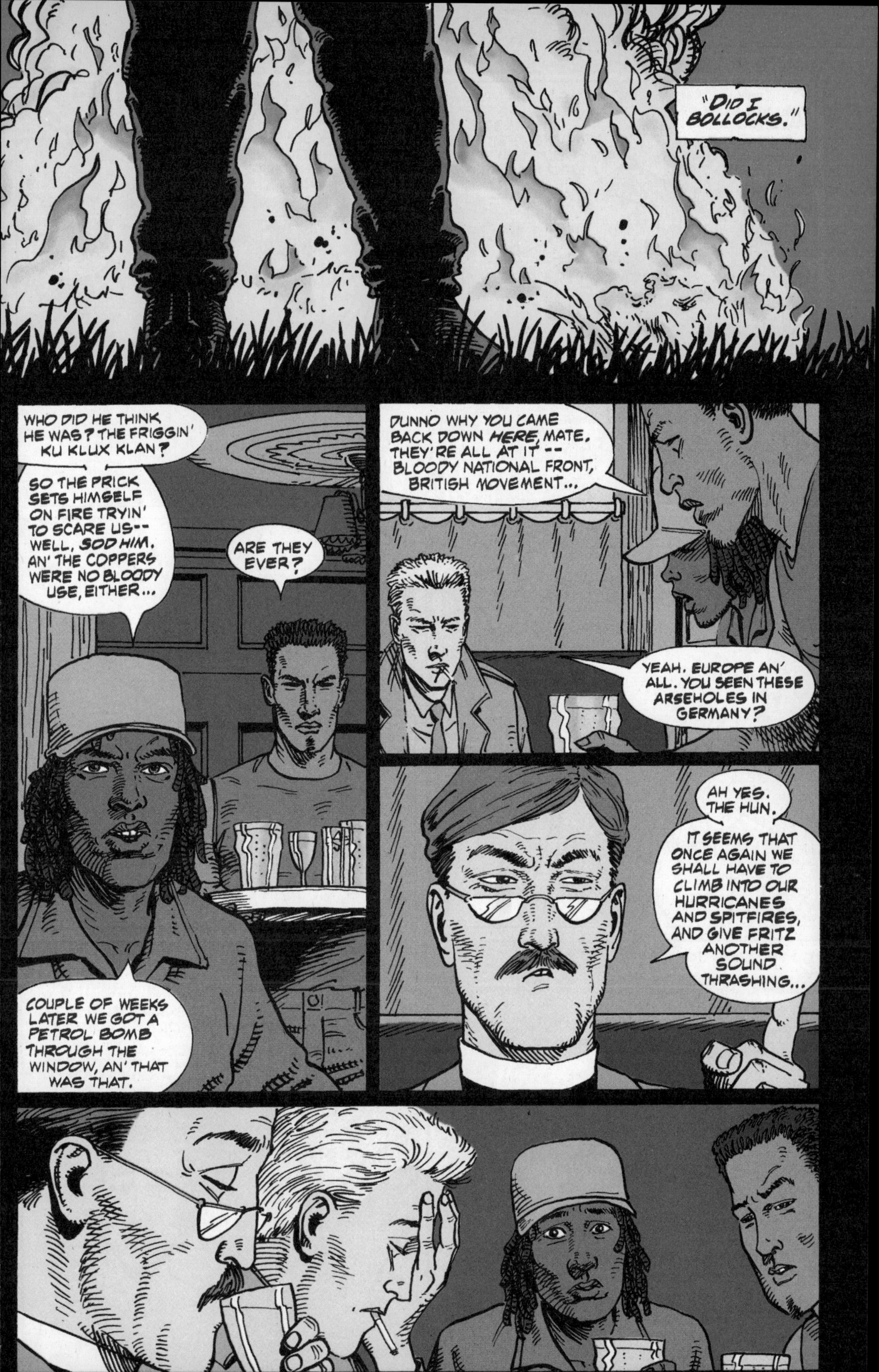
"DID I BOLLOCKS."
WHO DID HE THINK HE WAS? THE FRIGGIN' KU KLUX KLAN?
SO THE PRICK SETS HIMSELF ON FIRE TRYIN' TO SCARE US-- WELL, SOD HIM. AN' THE COPPERS WERE NO BLOODY USE, EITHER...
ARE THEY EVER?
COUPLE OF WEEKS LATER WE GOT A PETROL BOMB THROUGH THE WINDOW, AN' THAT WAS THAT.
DUNNO WHY YOU CAME BACK DOWN HERE, MATE. THEY'RE ALL AT IT -- BLOODY NATIONAL FRONT, BRITISH MOVEMENT...
YEAH. EUROPE AN' ALL. YOU SEEN THESE ARSEHOLES IN GERMANY?
AH YES. THE HUN.
IT SEEMS THAT ONCE AGAIN WE SHALL HAVE TO CLIMB INTO OUR HURRICANES AND SPITFIRES, AND GIVE FRITZ ANOTHER SOUND THRASHING...

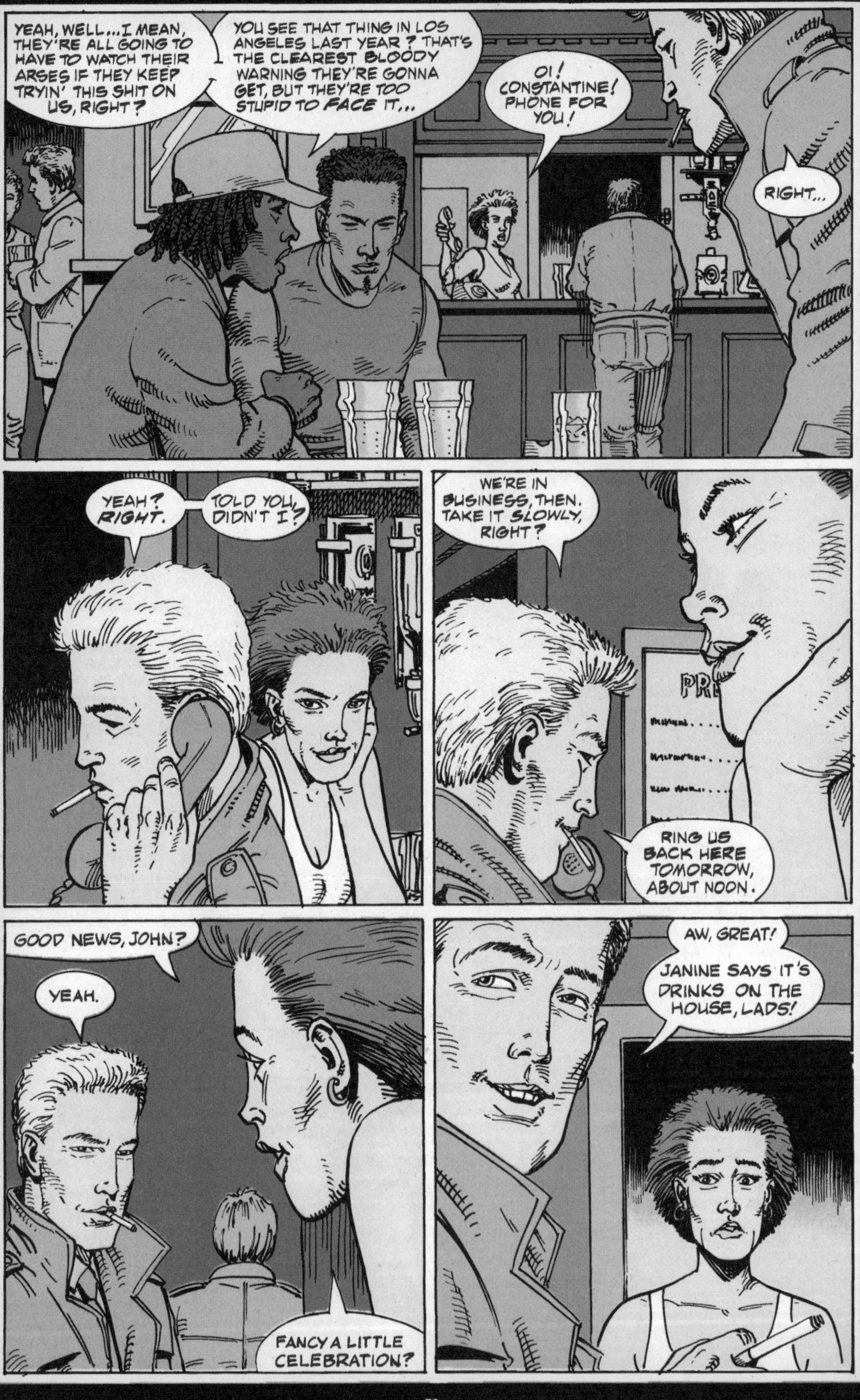

YEAH, WELL... I MEAN, THEY'RE ALL GOING TO HAVE TO WATCH THEIR ARSES IF THEY KEEP TRYIN' THIS SHIT ON US, RIGHT?
YOU SEE THAT THING IN LOS ANGELES LAST YEAR? THAT'S THE CLEAREST BLOODY WARNING THEY'RE GONNA GET, BUT THEY'RE TOO STUPID TO FACE IT...
OI! CONSTANTINE! PHONE FOR YOU!
RIGHT...
YEAH? RIGHT.
TOLD YOU, DIDN'T I?
WE'RE IN BUSINESS, THEN. TAKE IT SLOWLY, RIGHT?
RING US BACK HERE TOMORROW, ABOUT NOON.
GOOD NEWS, JOHN?
YEAH.
FANCY A LITTLE CELEBRATION?
AW, GREAT!
JANINE SAYS IT'S DRINKS ON THE HOUSE, LADS!

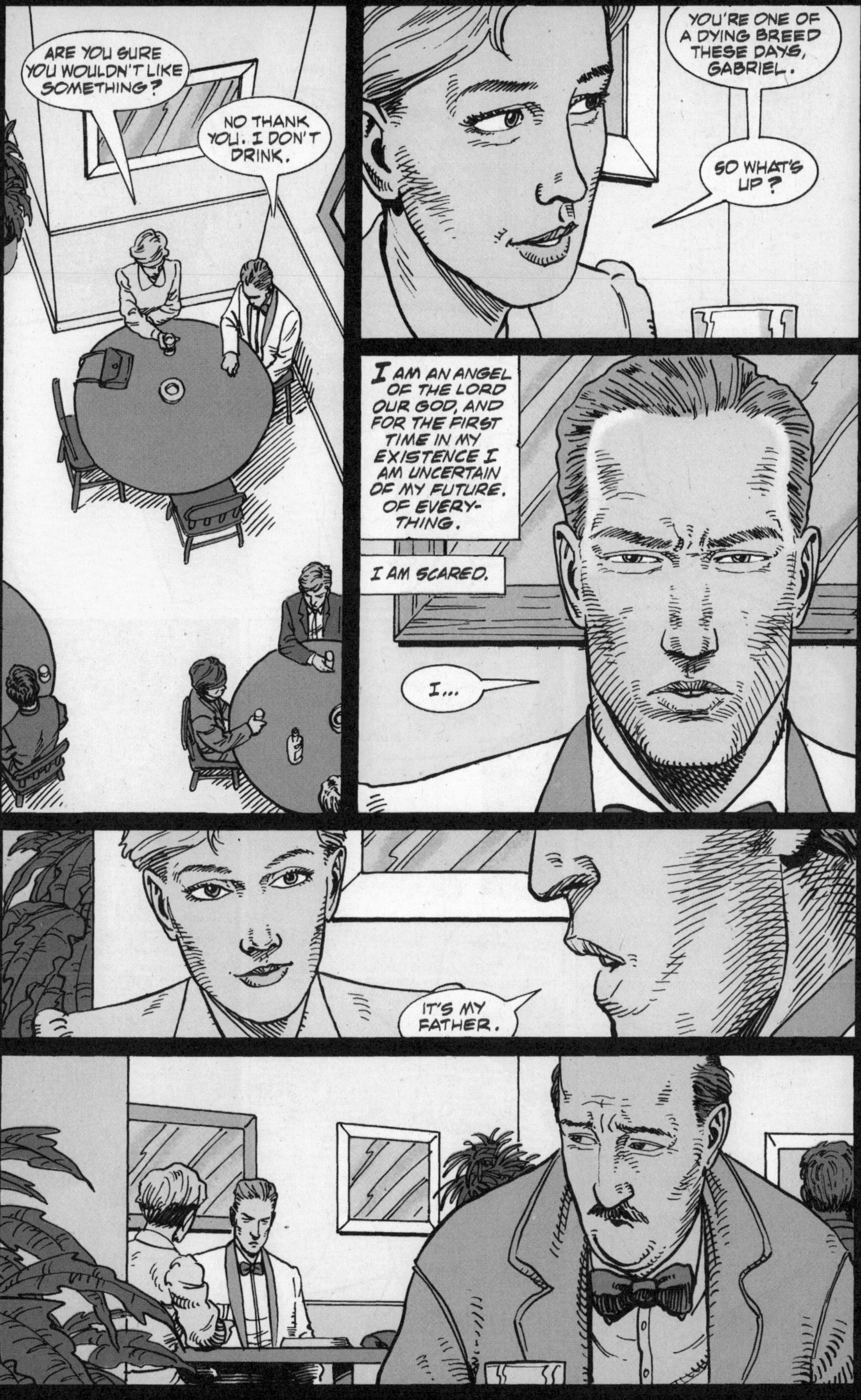
ARE YOU SURE YOU WOULDN'T LIKE SOMETHING?
NO THANK YOU. I DON'T DRINK.
YOU'RE ONE OF A DYING BREED THESE DAYS, GABRIEL.
SO WHAT'S UP?
I AM AN ANGEL OF THE LORD OUR GOD, AND FOR THE FIRST TIME IN MY EXISTENCE I AM UNCERTAIN OF MY FUTURE. OF EVERY-THING.
I AM SCARED.
I...
IT'S MY FATHER.

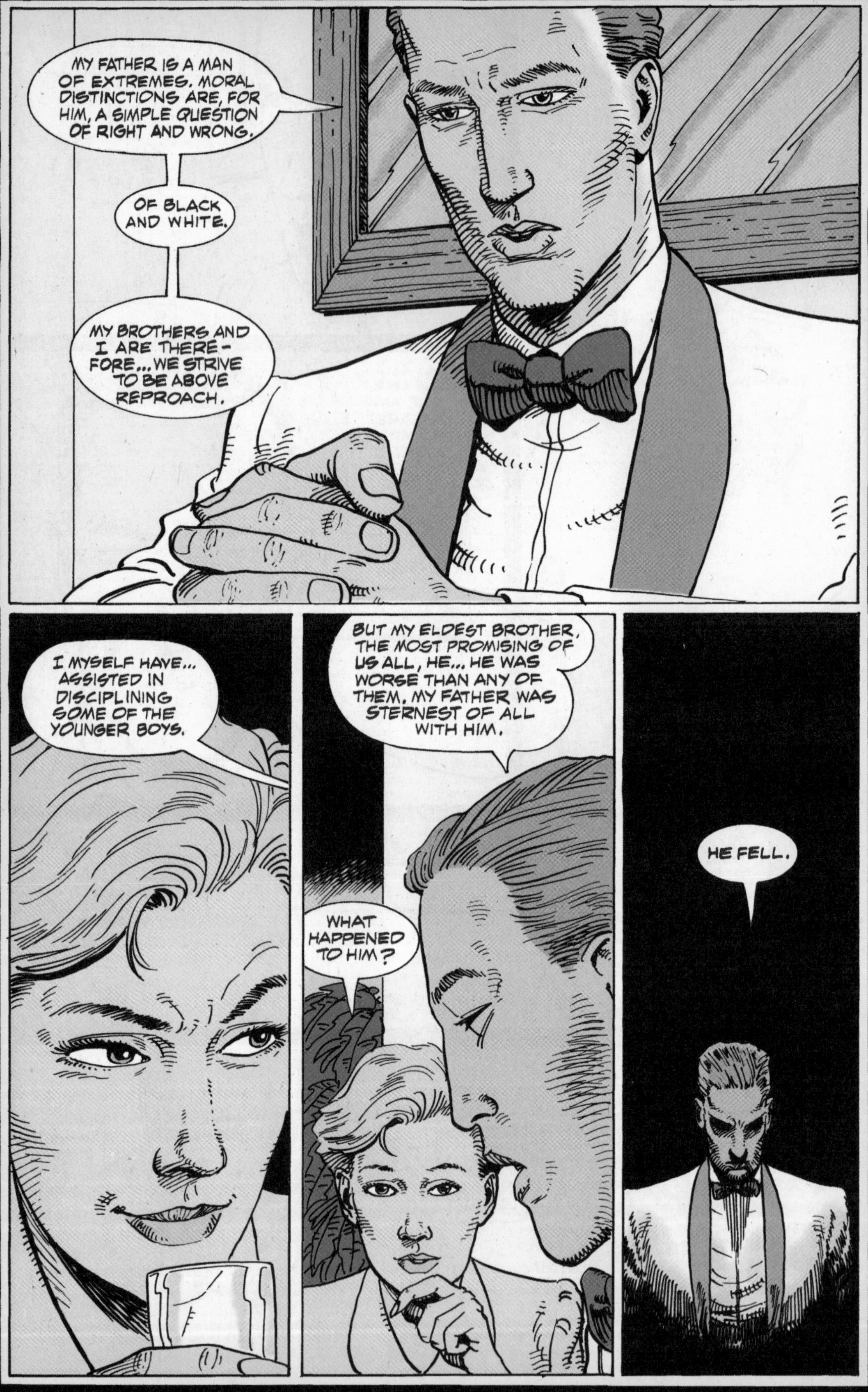
MY FATHER IS A MAN OF EXTREMES. MORAL DISTINCTIONS ARE, FOR HIM, A SIMPLE QUESTION OF RIGHT AND WRONG.
OF BLACK AND WHITE.
MY BROTHERS AND I ARE THERE-FORE... WE STRIVE TO BE ABOVE REPROACH.
I MYSELF HAVE... ASSISTED IN DISCIPLINING SOME OF THE YOUNGER BOYS.
BUT MY ELDEST BROTHER, THE MOST PROMISING OF US ALL, HE... HE WAS WORSE THAN ANY OF THEM. MY FATHER WAS STERNEST OF ALL WITH HIM.
WHAT HAPPENED TO HIM?
HE FELL.

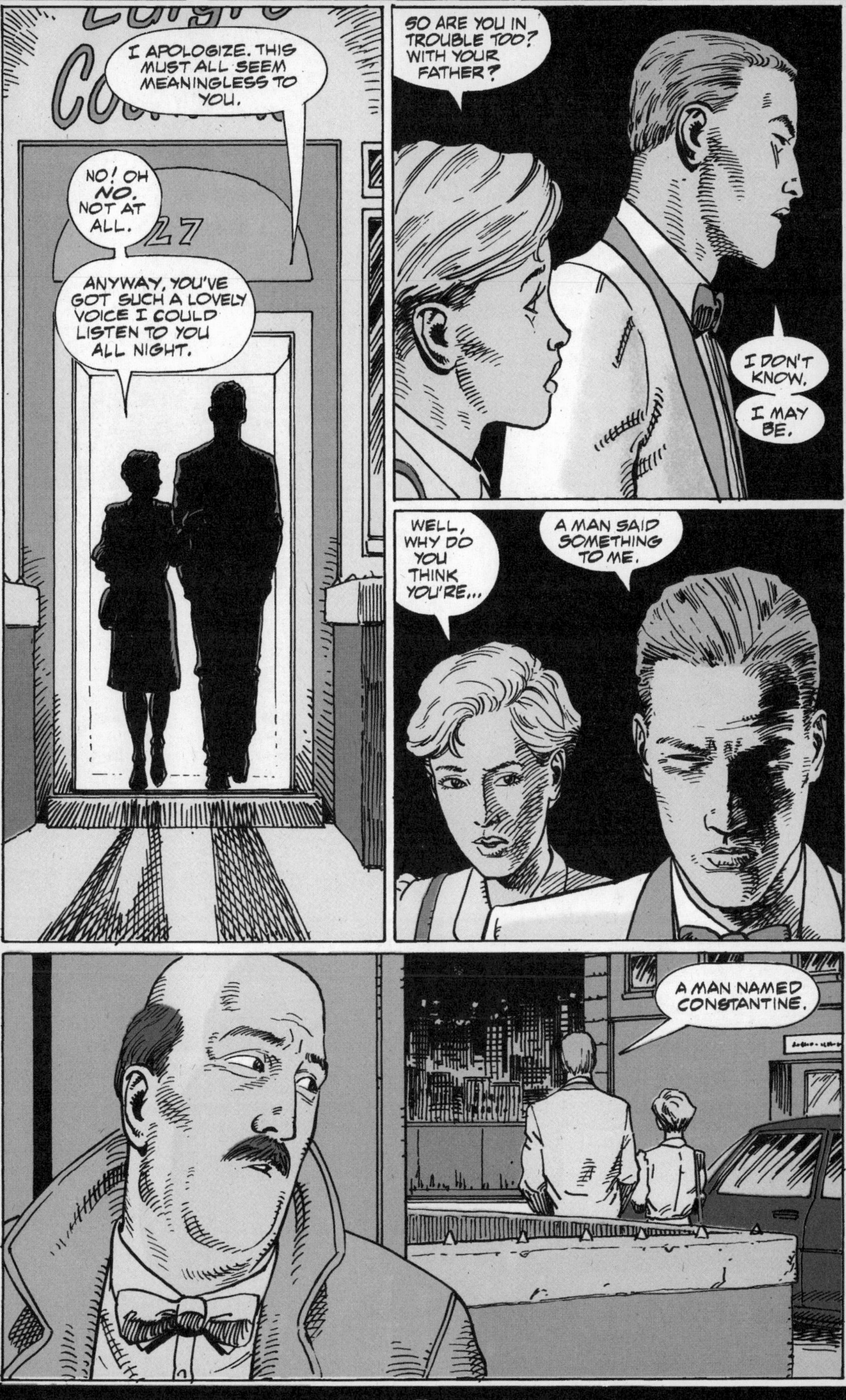
I APOLOGIZE. THIS MUST ALL SEEM MEANINGLESS TO YOU.
NO! OH NO. NOT AT ALL.
ANYWAY, YOU'VE GOT SUCH A LOVELY VOICE I COULD LISTEN TO YOU ALL NIGHT.
27
SO ARE YOU IN TROUBLE TOO? WITH YOUR FATHER?
I DON'T KNOW.
I MAY BE.
WELL, WHY DO YOU THINK YOU'RE...
A MAN SAID SOMETHING TO ME.
A MAN NAMED CONSTANTINE.

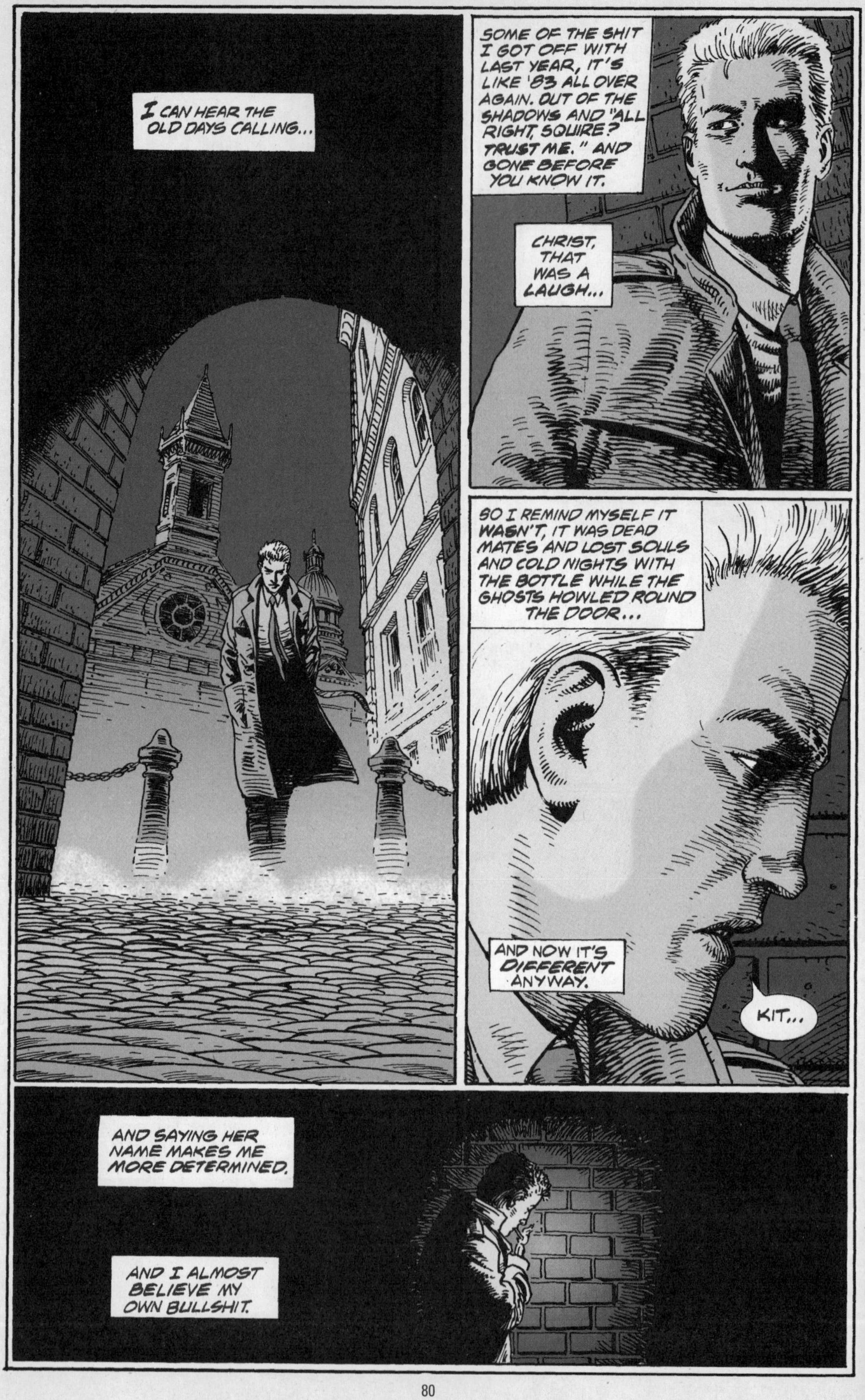
I CAN HEAR THE OLD DAYS CALLING...
SOME OF THE SHIT I GOT OFF WITH LAST YEAR, IT'S LIKE '83 ALL OVER AGAIN. OUT OF THE SHADOWS AND "ALL RIGHT, SQUIRE? TRUST ME." AND GONE BEFORE YOU KNOW IT.
CHRIST, THAT WAS A LAUGH...
SO I REMIND MYSELF IT WASN'T, IT WAS DEAD MATES AND LOST SOULS AND COLD NIGHTS WITH THE BOTTLE WHILE THE GHOSTS HOWLED ROUND THE DOOR...
AND NOW IT'S DIFFERENT ANYWAY.
KIT...
AND SAYING HER NAME MAKES ME MORE DETERMINED.
AND I ALMOST BELIEVE MY OWN BULLSHIT.

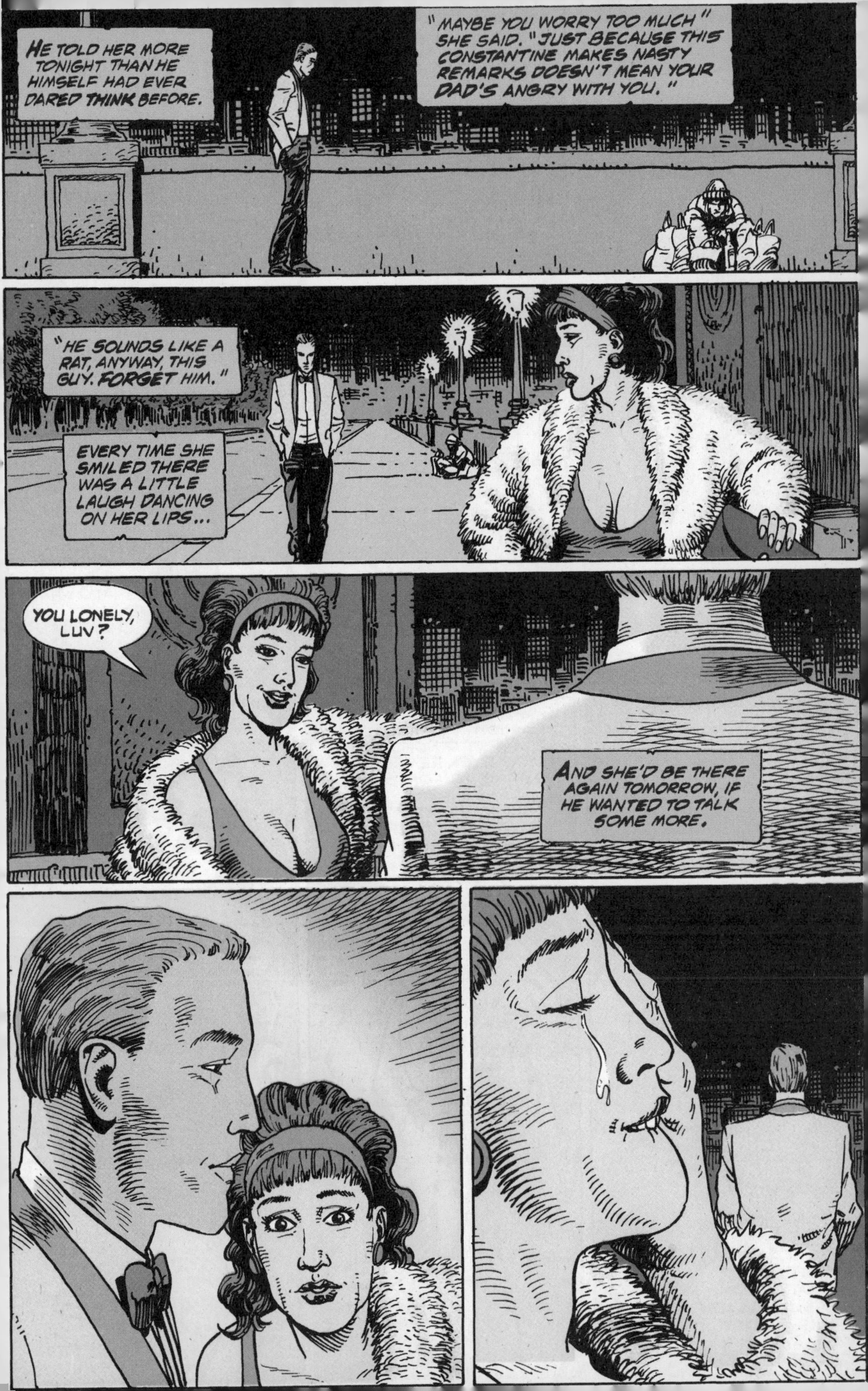
HE TOLD HER MORE TONIGHT THAN HE HIMSELF HAD EVER DARED THINK BEFORE.
"MAYBE YOU WORRY TOO MUCH" SHE SAID. "JUST BECAUSE THIS CONSTANTINE MAKES NASTY REMARKS DOESN'T MEAN YOUR DAD'S ANGRY WITH YOU."
"HE SOUNDS LIKE A RAT, ANYWAY, THIS GUY. FORGET HIM."
EVERY TIME SHE SMILED THERE WAS A LITTLE LAUGH DANCING ON HER LIPS...
YOU LONELY, LUV?
AND SHE'D BE THERE AGAIN TOMORROW, IF HE WANTED TO TALK SOME MORE.

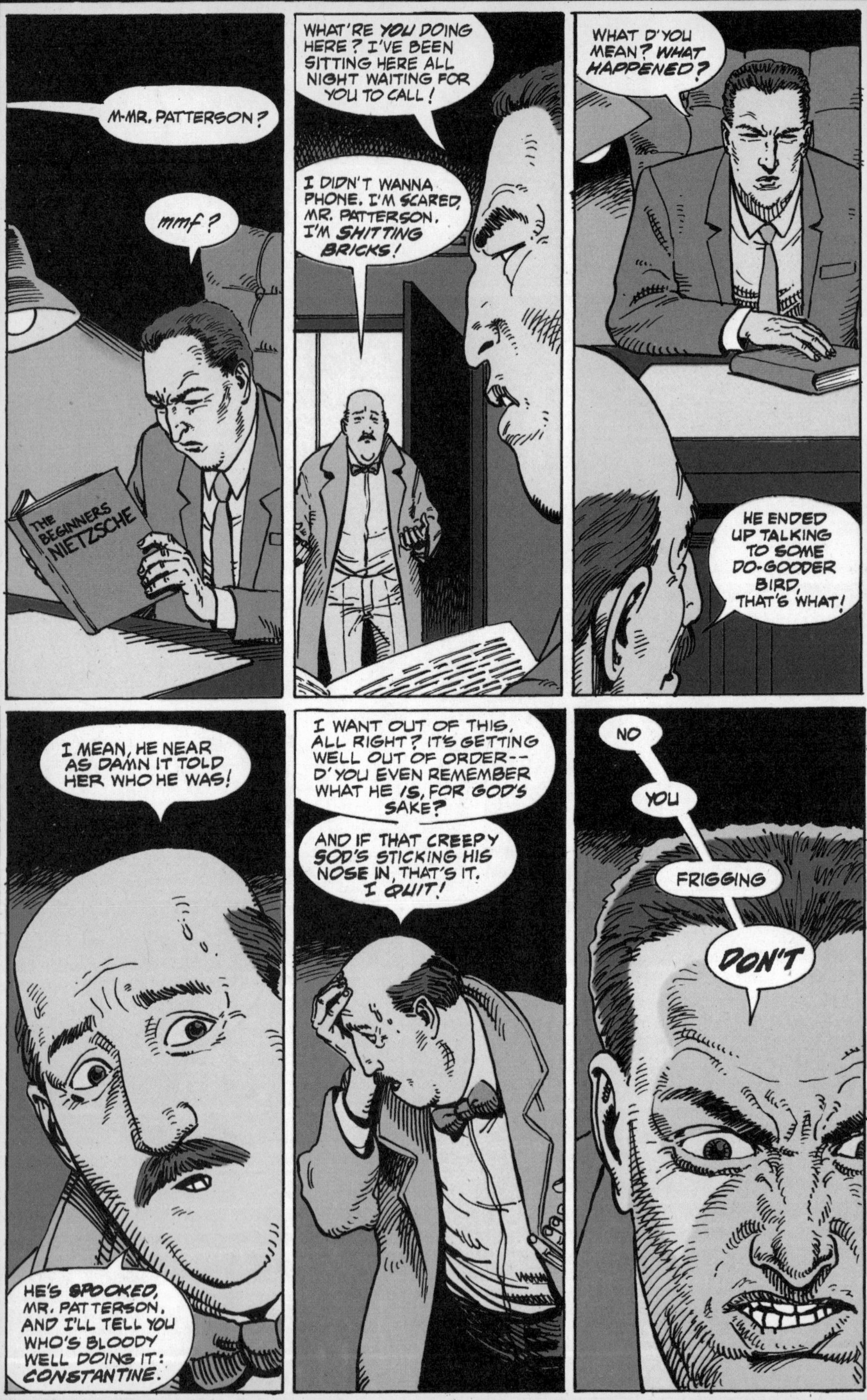
M-MR. PATTERSON?
mmf?
THE BEGINNERS NIETZSCHE
WHAT'RE YOU DOING HERE? I'VE BEEN SITTING HERE ALL NIGHT WAITING FOR YOU TO CALL!
I DIDN'T WANNA PHONE. I'M SCARED, MR. PATTERSON. I'M SHITTING BRICKS!
WHAT D'YOU MEAN? WHAT HAPPENED?
HE ENDED UP TALKING TO SOME DO-GOODER BIRD, THAT'S WHAT!
I MEAN, HE NEAR AS DAMN IT TOLD HER WHO HE WAS!
HE'S SPOOKED, MR. PATTERSON. AND I'LL TELL YOU WHO'S BLOODY WELL DOING IT: CONSTANTINE.
I WANT OUT OF THIS, ALL RIGHT? IT'S GETTING WELL OUT OF ORDER-- D'YOU EVEN REMEMBER WHAT HE IS, FOR GOD'S SAKE?
AND IF THAT CREEPY SOD'S STICKING HIS NOSE IN, THAT'S IT. I QUIT!
NO
YOU
FRIGGING
DON'T

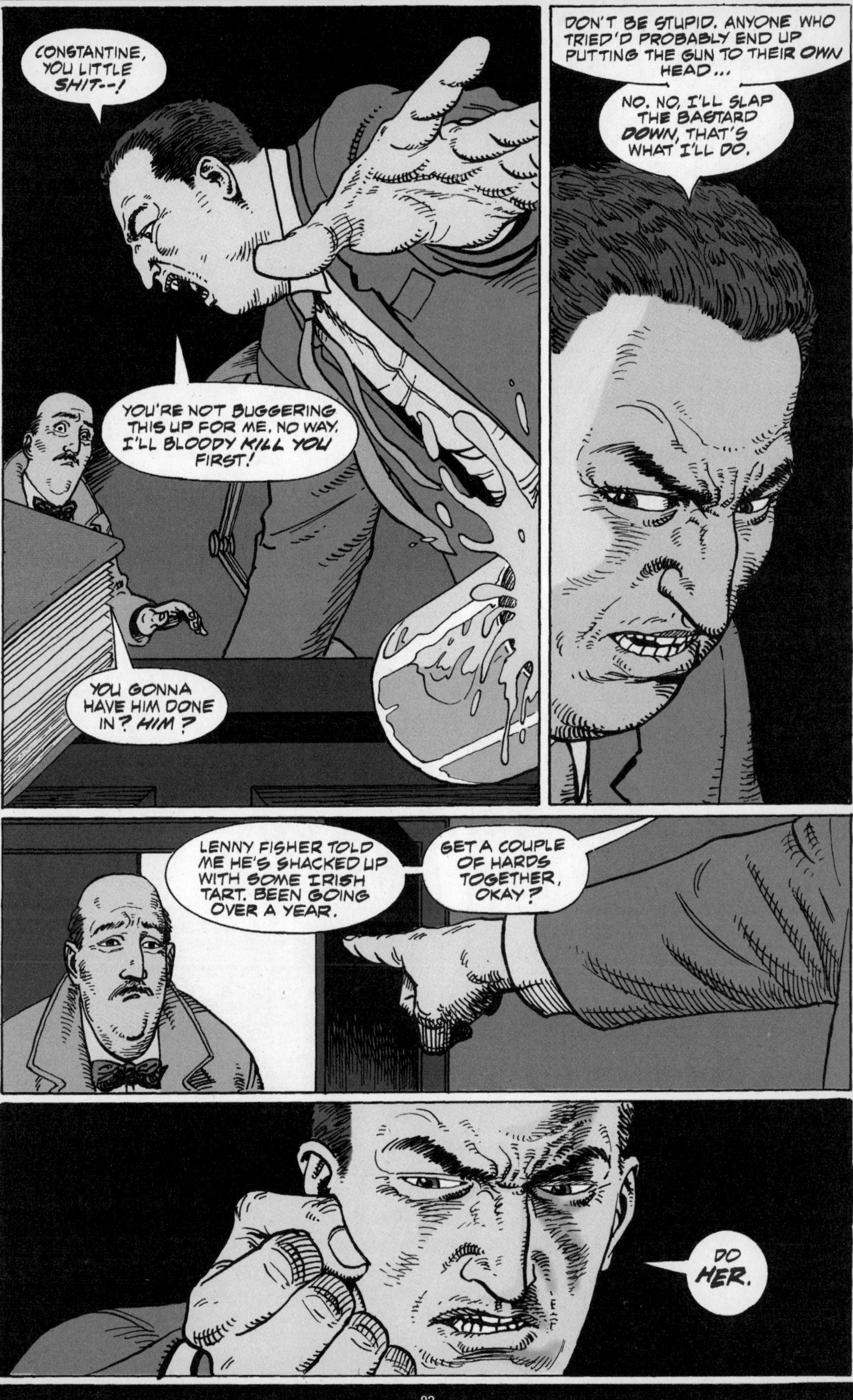
CONSTANTINE, YOU LITTLE SHIT--!
YOU'RE NOT BUGGERING THIS UP FOR ME. NO WAY. I'LL BLOODY KILL YOU FIRST!
YOU GONNA HAVE HIM DONE IN? HIM?
DON'T BE STUPID. ANYONE WHO TRIED'D PROBABLY END UP PUTTING THE GUN TO THEIR OWN HEAD...
NO. NO, I'LL SLAP THE BASTARD DOWN, THAT'S WHAT I'LL DO.
LENNY FISHER TOLD ME HE'S SHACKED UP WITH SOME IRISH TART. BEEN GOING OVER A YEAR.
GET A COUPLE OF HARDS TOGETHER, OKAY?
DO HER.

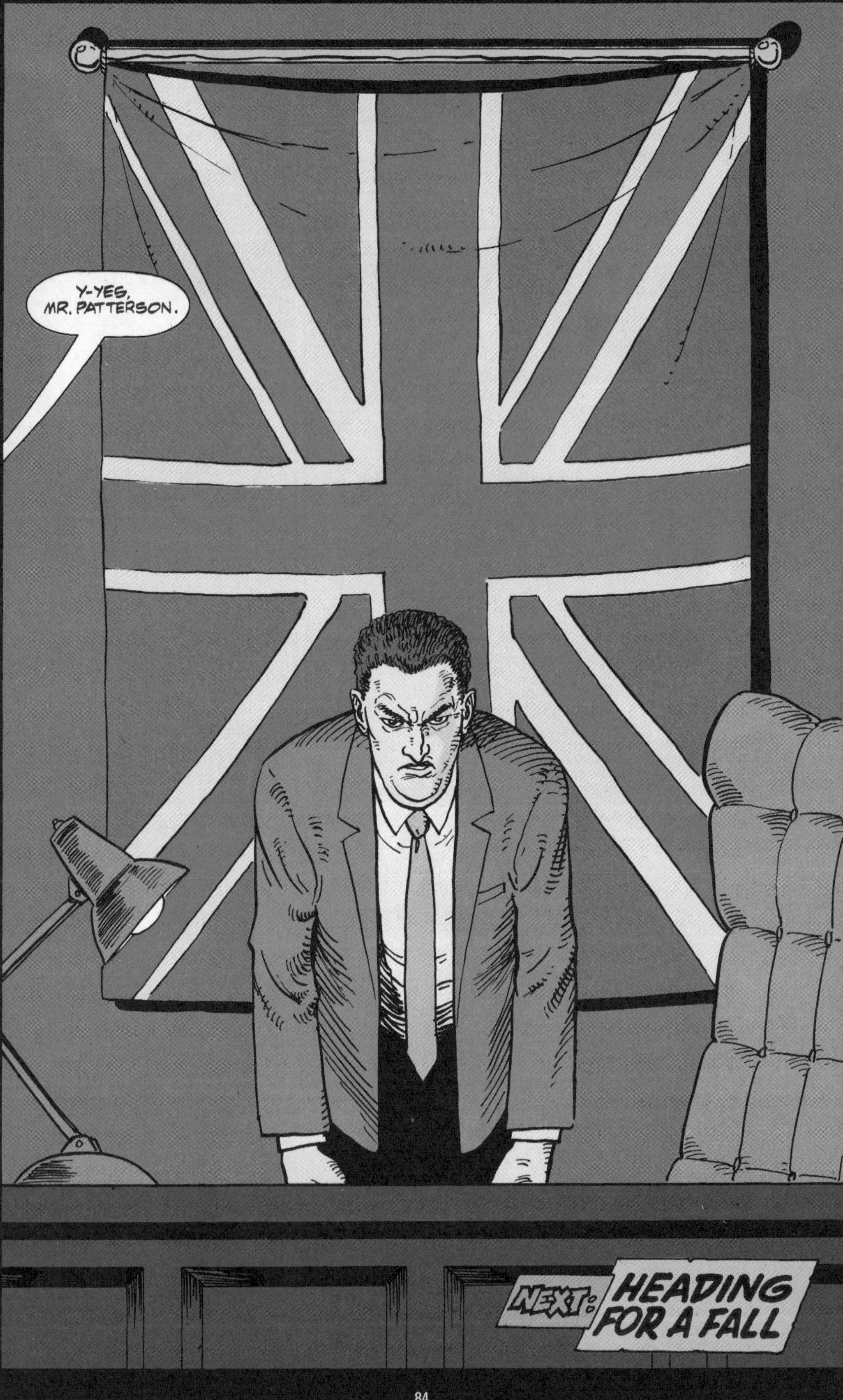

Y-YES, MR. PATTERSON.
NEXT: HEADING FOR A FALL

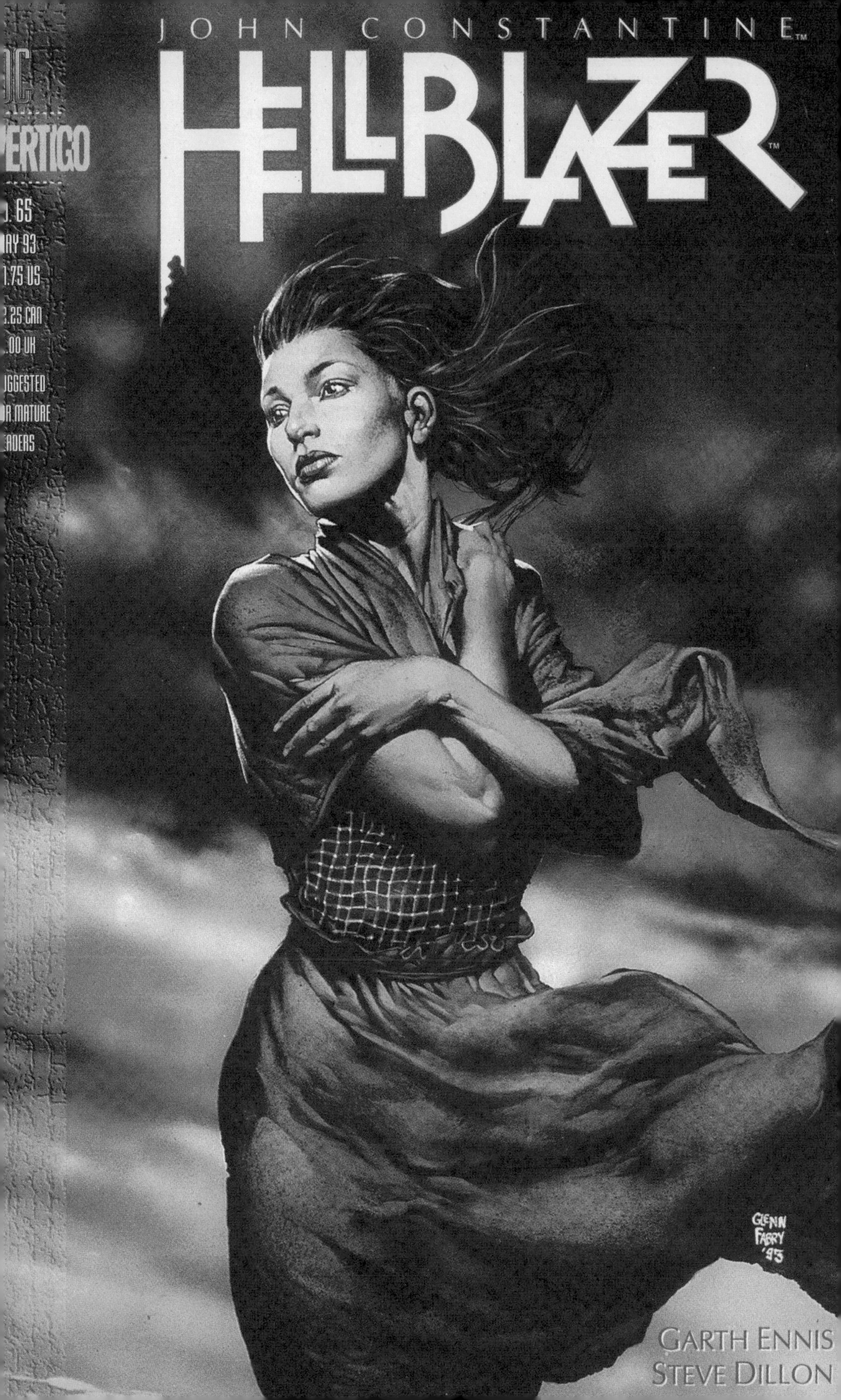

JOHN CONSTANTINE
HELLBLAZER
DC
VERTIGO
.65
AY 93
1.75 US
2.25 CAN
.00 UK
UGGESTED
R MATURE
EADERS
GLENN FABRY '93
GARTH ENNIS
STEVE DILLON

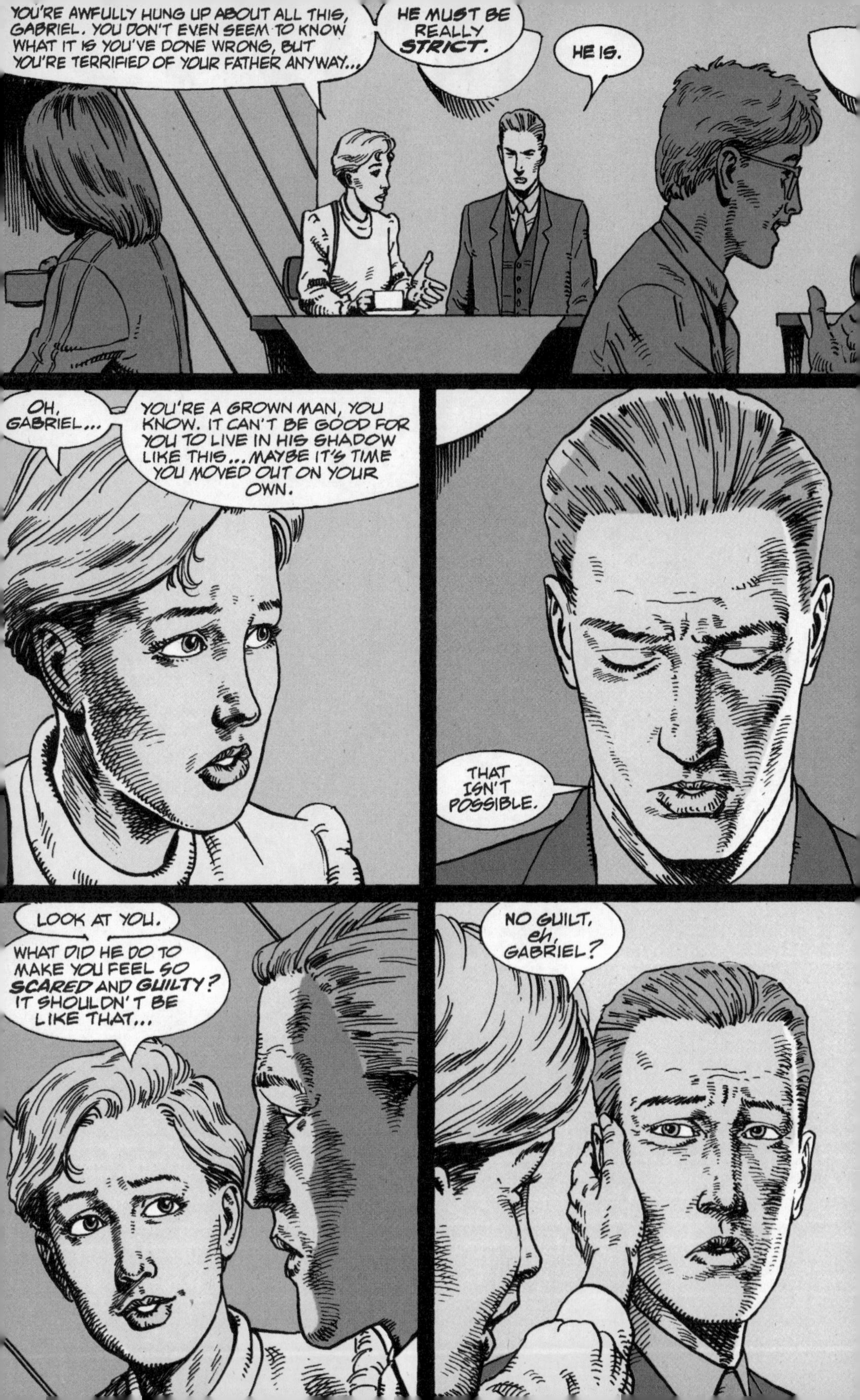
YOU'RE AWFULLY HUNG UP ABOUT ALL THIS, GABRIEL. YOU DON'T EVEN SEEM TO KNOW WHAT IT IS YOU'VE DONE WRONG, BUT YOU'RE TERRIFIED OF YOUR FATHER ANYWAY...
HE MUST BE REALLY STRICT.
HE IS.
OH, GABRIEL...
YOU'RE A GROWN MAN, YOU KNOW. IT CAN'T BE GOOD FOR YOU TO LIVE IN HIS SHADOW LIKE THIS... MAYBE IT'S TIME YOU MOVED OUT ON YOUR OWN.
THAT ISN'T POSSIBLE.
LOOK AT YOU.
WHAT DID HE DO TO MAKE YOU FEEL SO SCARED AND GUILTY? IT SHOULDN'T BE LIKE THAT...
NO GUILT, eh, GABRIEL?

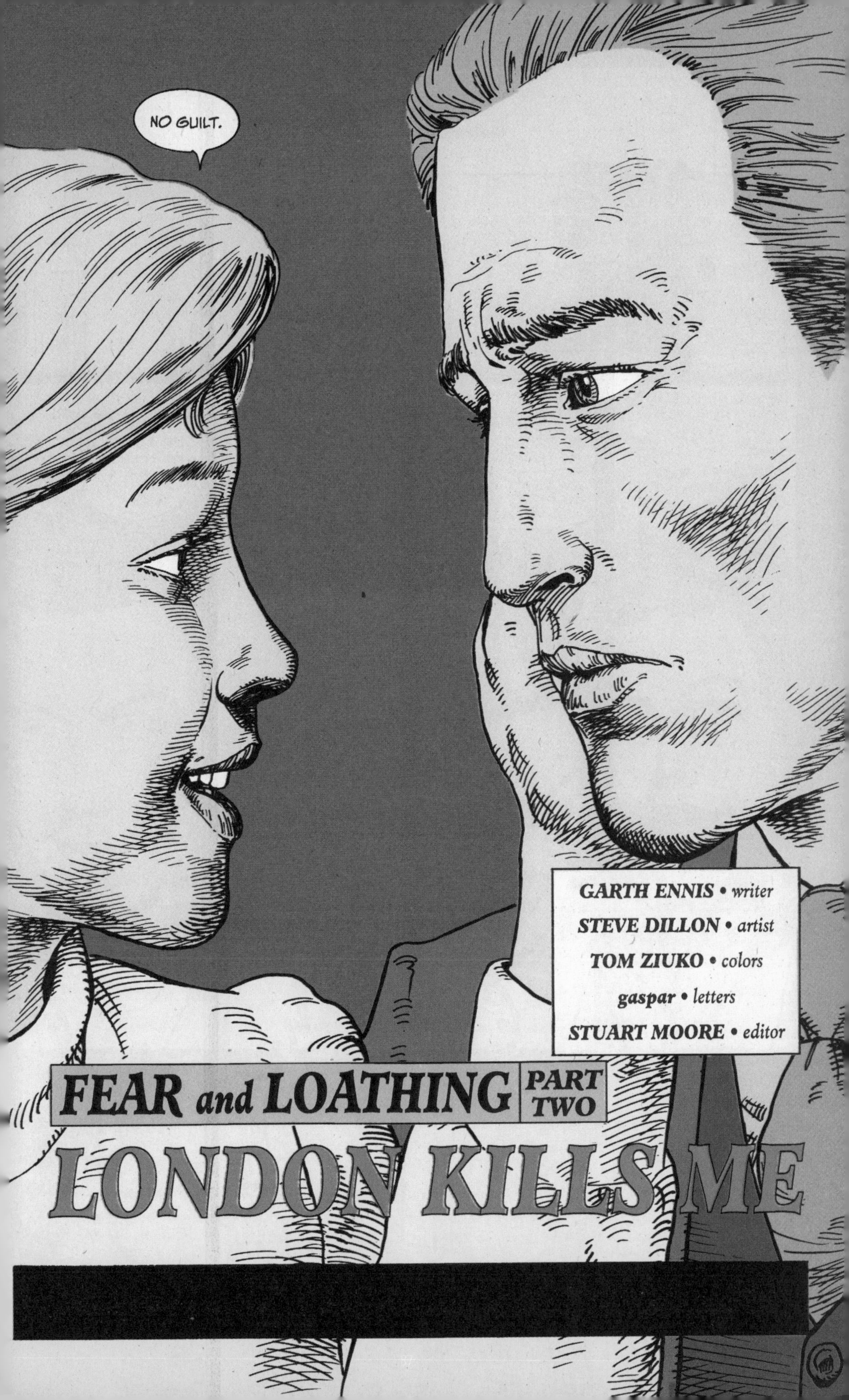

NO GUILT.
GARTH ENNIS • writer
STEVE DILLON • artist
TOM ZIUKO • colors
gaspar • letters
STUART MOORE • editor
FEAR and LOATHING PART TWO
LONDON KILLS ME
[redacted]

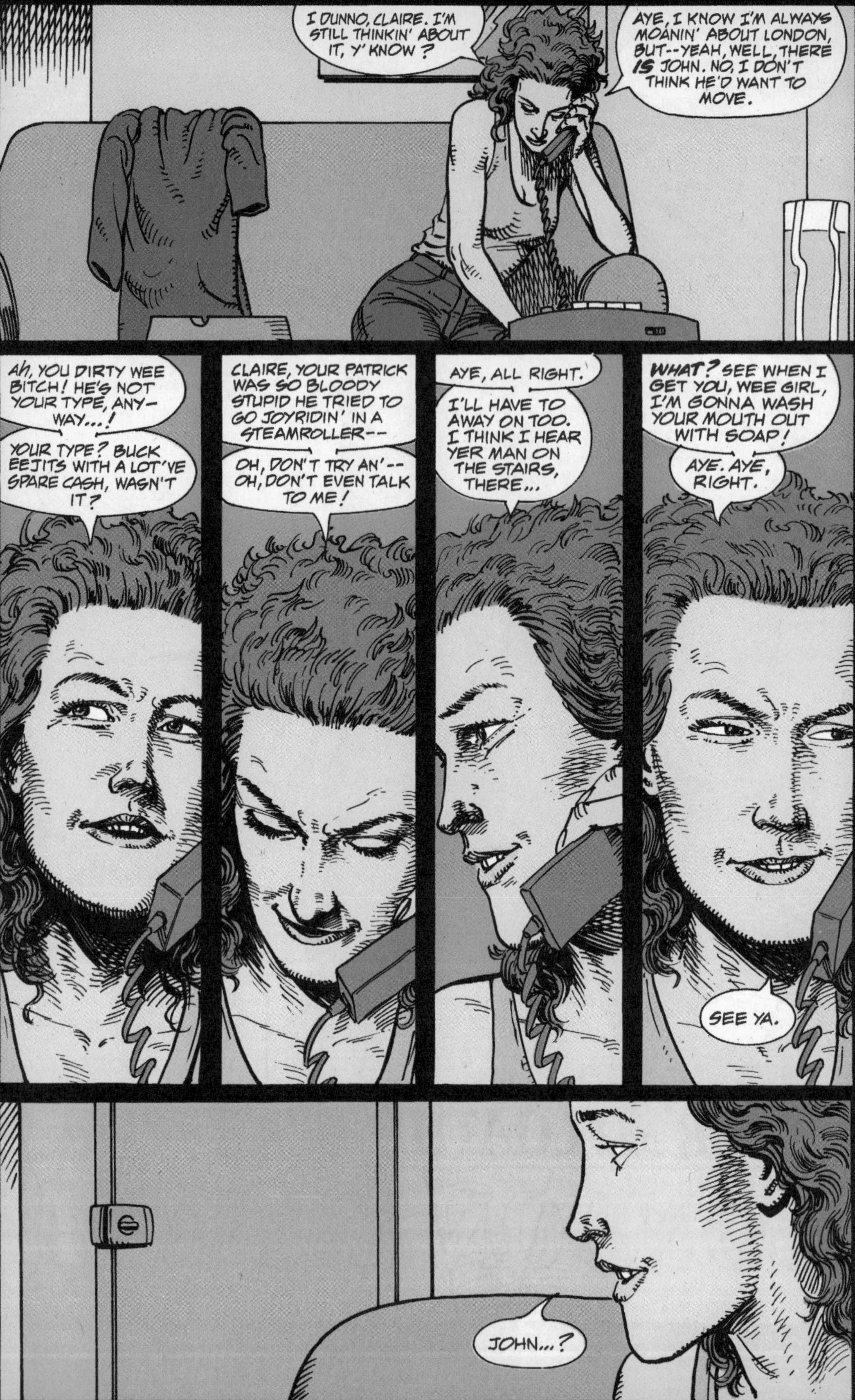
I DUNNO, CLAIRE. I'M STILL THINKIN' ABOUT IT, Y' KNOW?
AYE, I KNOW I'M ALWAYS MOANIN' ABOUT LONDON, BUT--YEAH, WELL, THERE *IS* JOHN. NO, I DON'T THINK HE'D WANT TO MOVE.
AH, YOU DIRTY WEE BITCH! HE'S NOT YOUR TYPE, ANYWAY...!
YOUR TYPE? BUCK EEJITS WITH A LOT'VE SPARE CASH, WASN'T IT?
CLAIRE, YOUR PATRICK WAS SO BLOODY STUPID HE TRIED TO GO JOYRIDIN' IN A STEAMROLLER--
OH, DON'T TRY AN'-- OH, DON'T EVEN TALK TO ME!
AYE, ALL RIGHT.
I'LL HAVE TO AWAY ON TOO. I THINK I HEAR YER MAN ON THE STAIRS, THERE...
WHAT? SEE WHEN I GET YOU, WEE GIRL, I'M GONNA WASH YOUR MOUTH OUT WITH SOAP!
AYE. AYE, RIGHT.
SEE YA.
JOHN...?

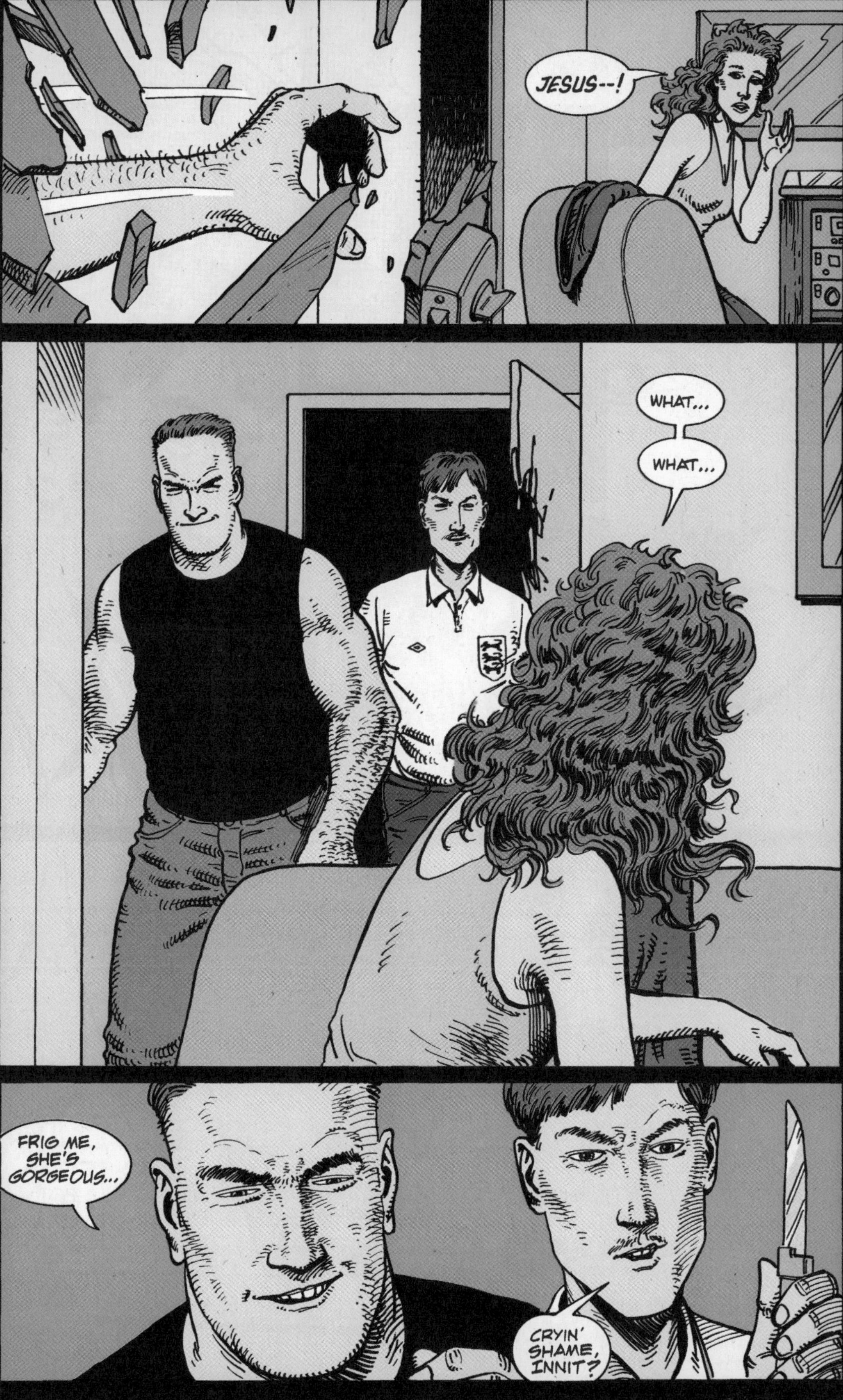
JESUS--!
WHAT...
WHAT...
FRIG ME, SHE'S GORGEOUS...
CRYIN' SHAME, INNIT?

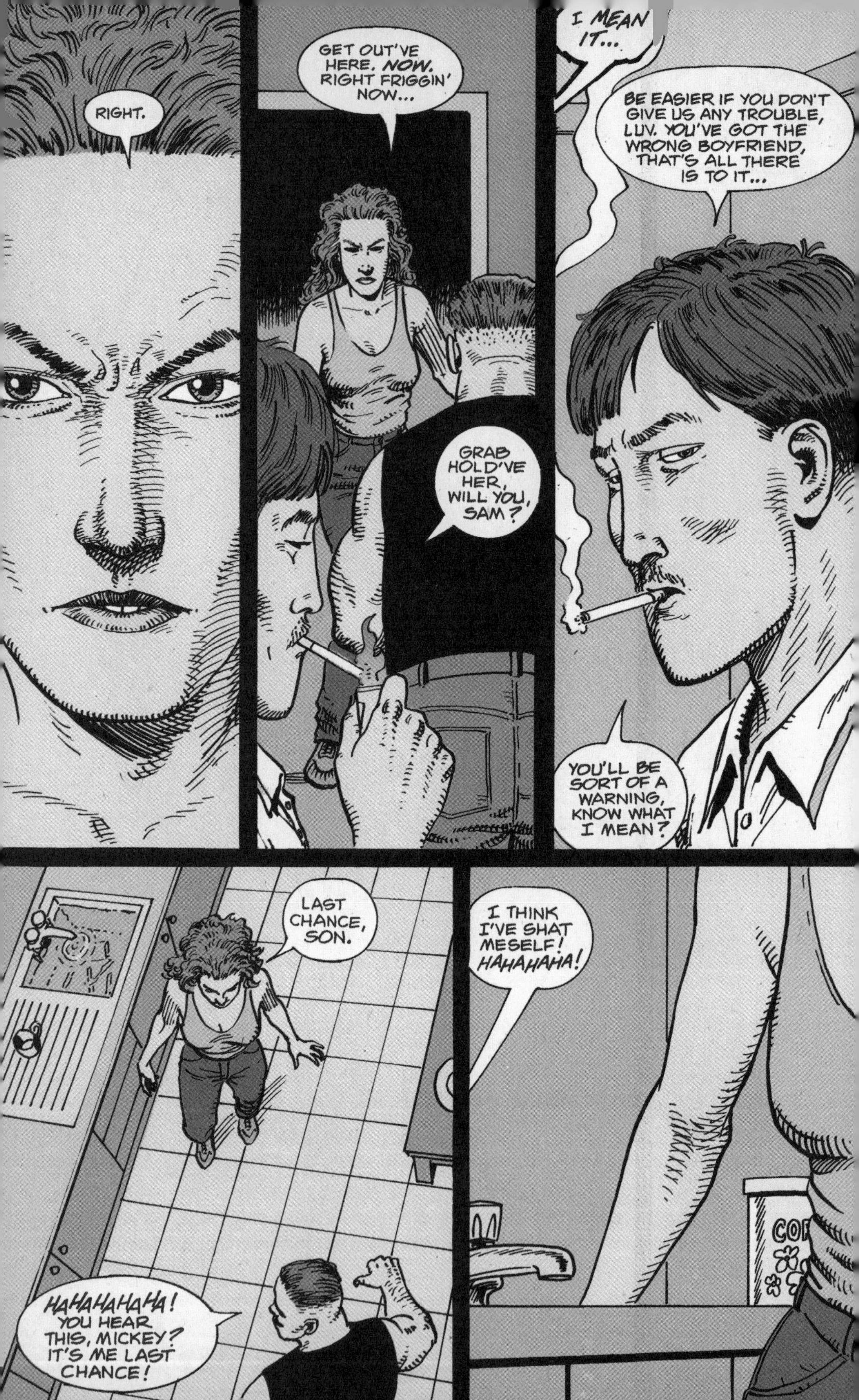
RIGHT.
GET OUT'VE HERE. NOW. RIGHT FRIGGIN' NOW...
GRAB HOLD'VE HER, WILL YOU, SAM?
I MEAN IT...
BE EASIER IF YOU DON'T GIVE US ANY TROUBLE, LUV. YOU'VE GOT THE WRONG BOYFRIEND, THAT'S ALL THERE IS TO IT...
YOU'LL BE SORT OF A WARNING, KNOW WHAT I MEAN?
LAST CHANCE, SON.
HAHAHAHAHA! YOU HEAR THIS, MICKEY? IT'S ME LAST CHANCE!
I THINK I'VE SHAT MESELF! HAHAHAHA!

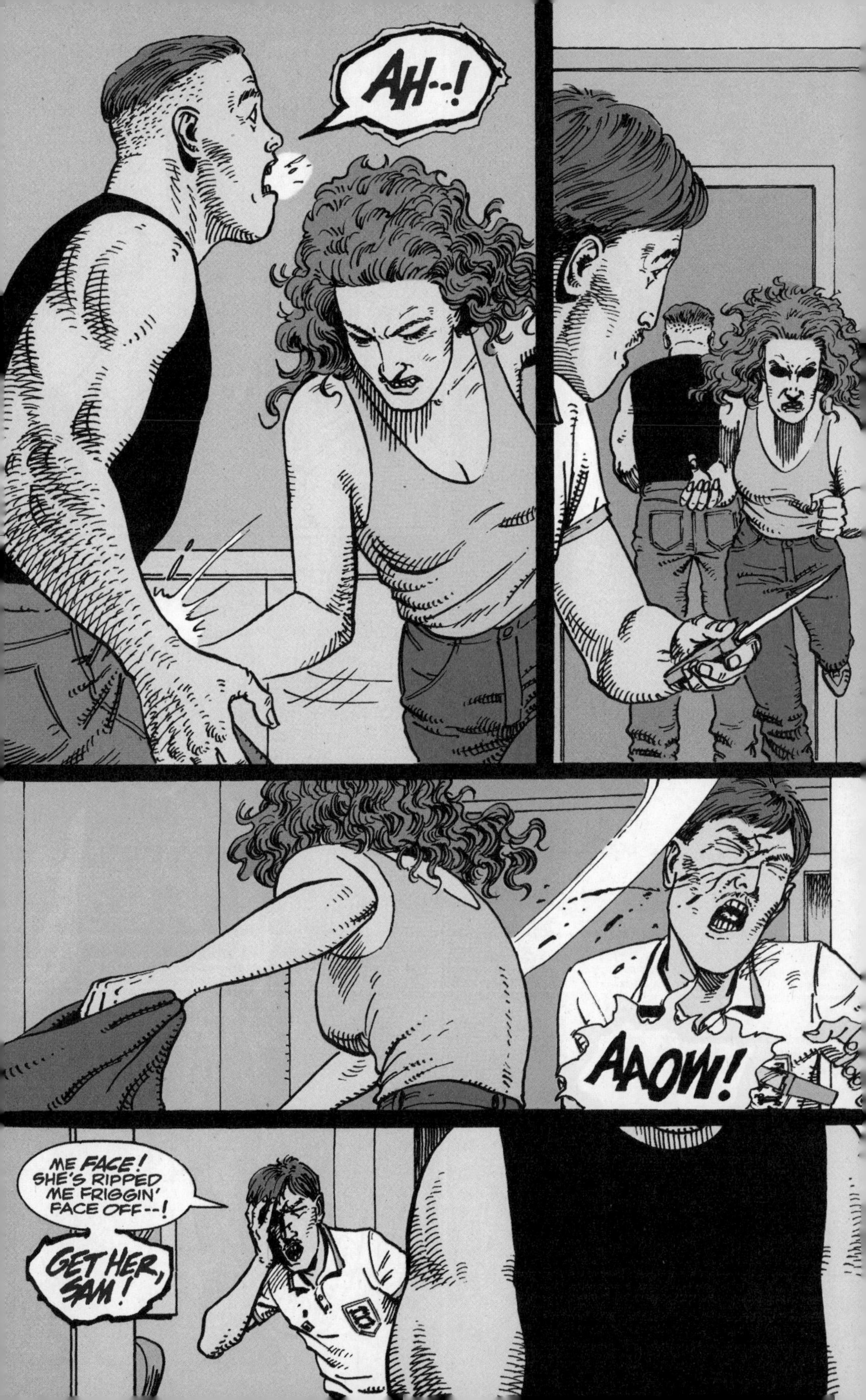
AH--!
AAOW!
ME FACE! SHE'S RIPPED ME FRIGGIN' FACE OFF--!
GET HER, SAM!

M-M-MICKY?
MIIICKYYY!!

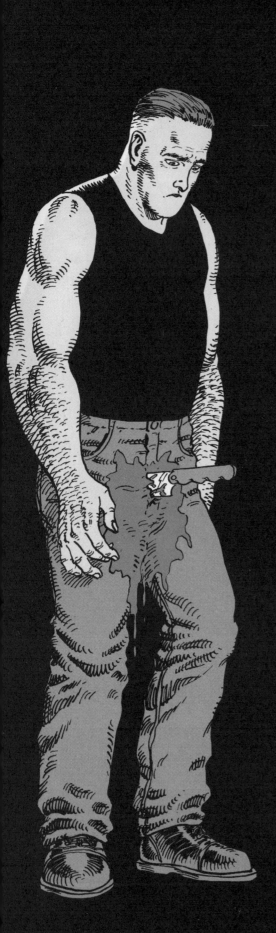

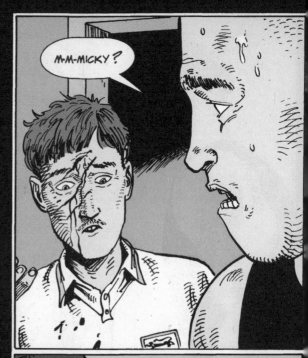

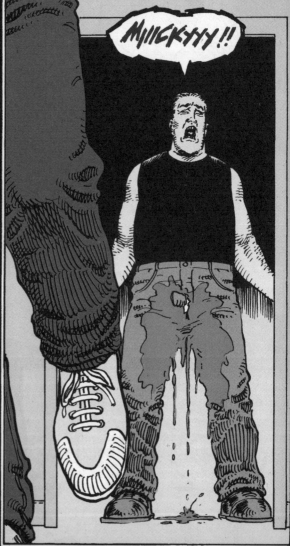

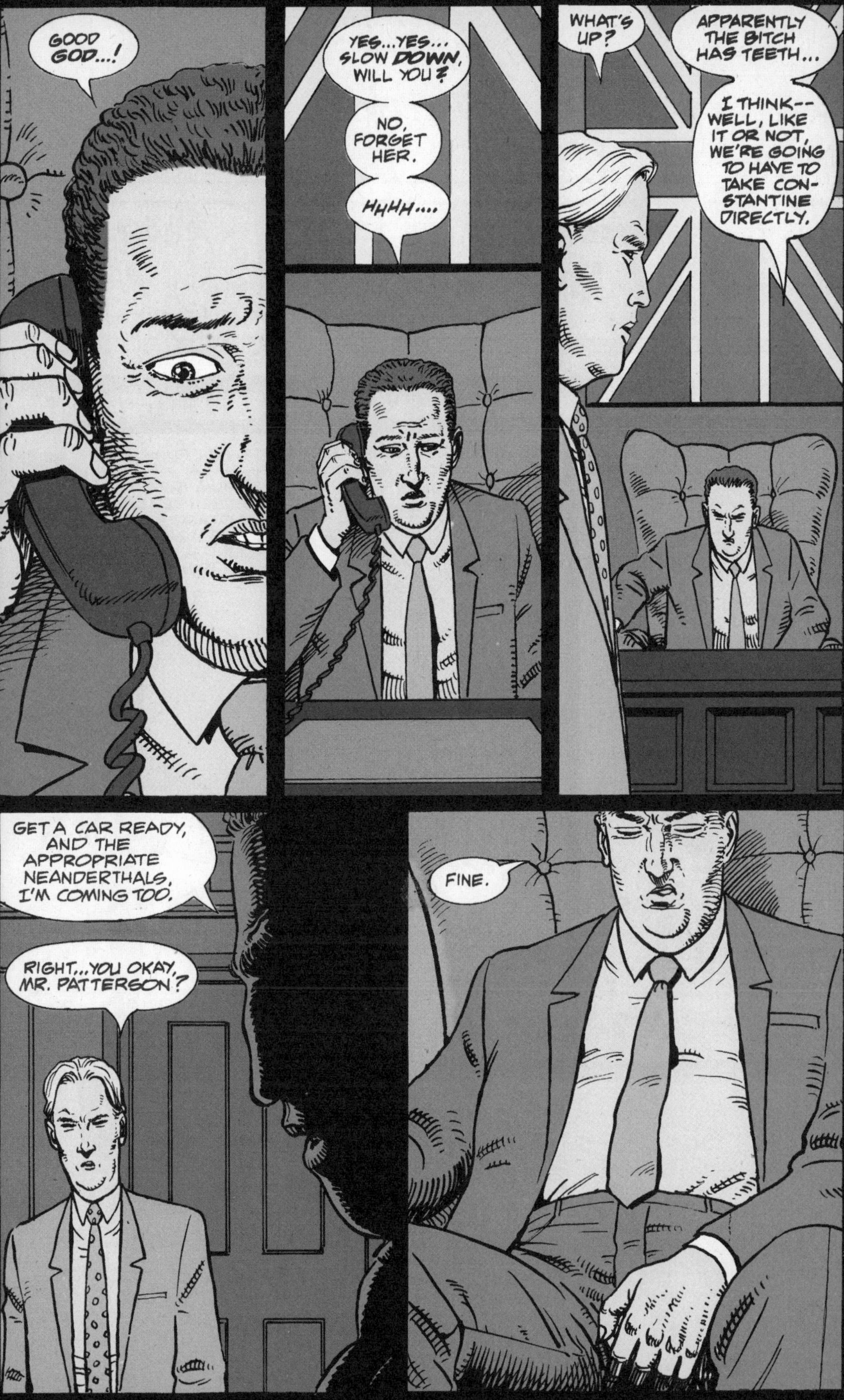

GOOD GOD...!
YES...YES... SLOW DOWN, WILL YOU?
NO, FORGET HER.
HHHH....
WHAT'S UP?
APPARENTLY THE BITCH HAS TEETH...
I THINK-- WELL, LIKE IT OR NOT, WE'RE GOING TO HAVE TO TAKE CONSTANTINE DIRECTLY.
GET A CAR READY, AND THE APPROPRIATE NEANDERTHALS, I'M COMING TOO.
RIGHT...YOU OKAY, MR. PATTERSON?
FINE.

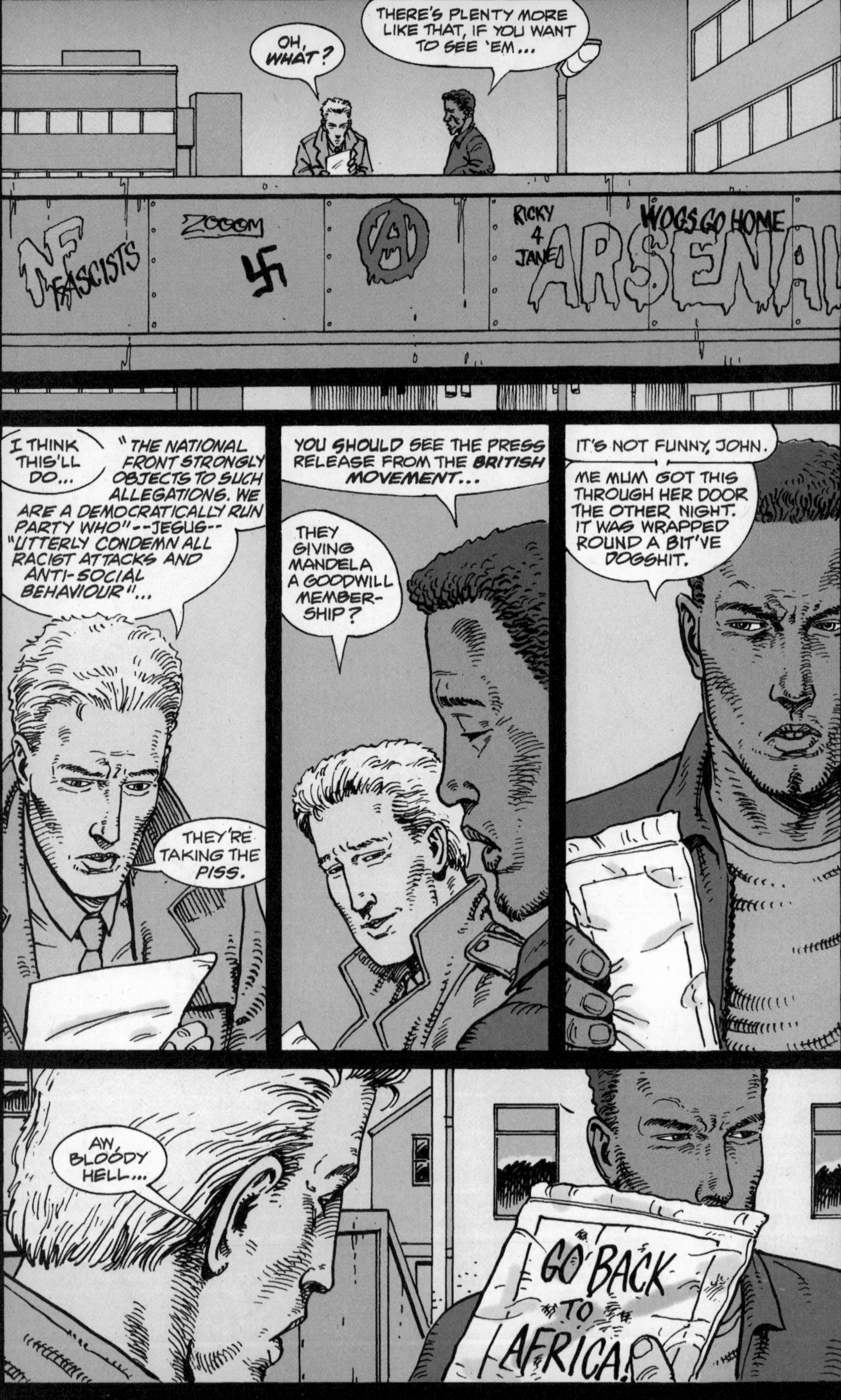

OH, WHAT?
THERE'S PLENTY MORE LIKE THAT, IF YOU WANT TO SEE 'EM...
NF
FASCISTS
ZOOOM
RICKY 4 JANE
WOGS GO HOME
ARSENAL
I THINK THIS'LL DO...
"THE NATIONAL FRONT STRONGLY OBJECTS TO SUCH ALLEGATIONS. WE ARE A DEMOCRATICALLY RUN PARTY WHO"--JESUS--"UTTERLY CONDEMN ALL RACIST ATTACKS AND ANTI-SOCIAL BEHAVIOUR"...
THEY'RE TAKING THE PISS.
YOU SHOULD SEE THE PRESS RELEASE FROM THE BRITISH MOVEMENT...
THEY GIVING MANDELA A GOODWILL MEMBER-SHIP?
IT'S NOT FUNNY, JOHN.
ME MUM GOT THIS THROUGH HER DOOR THE OTHER NIGHT. IT WAS WRAPPED ROUND A BIT'VE DOGSHIT.
AW, BLOODY HELL...
GO BACK TO AFRICA!

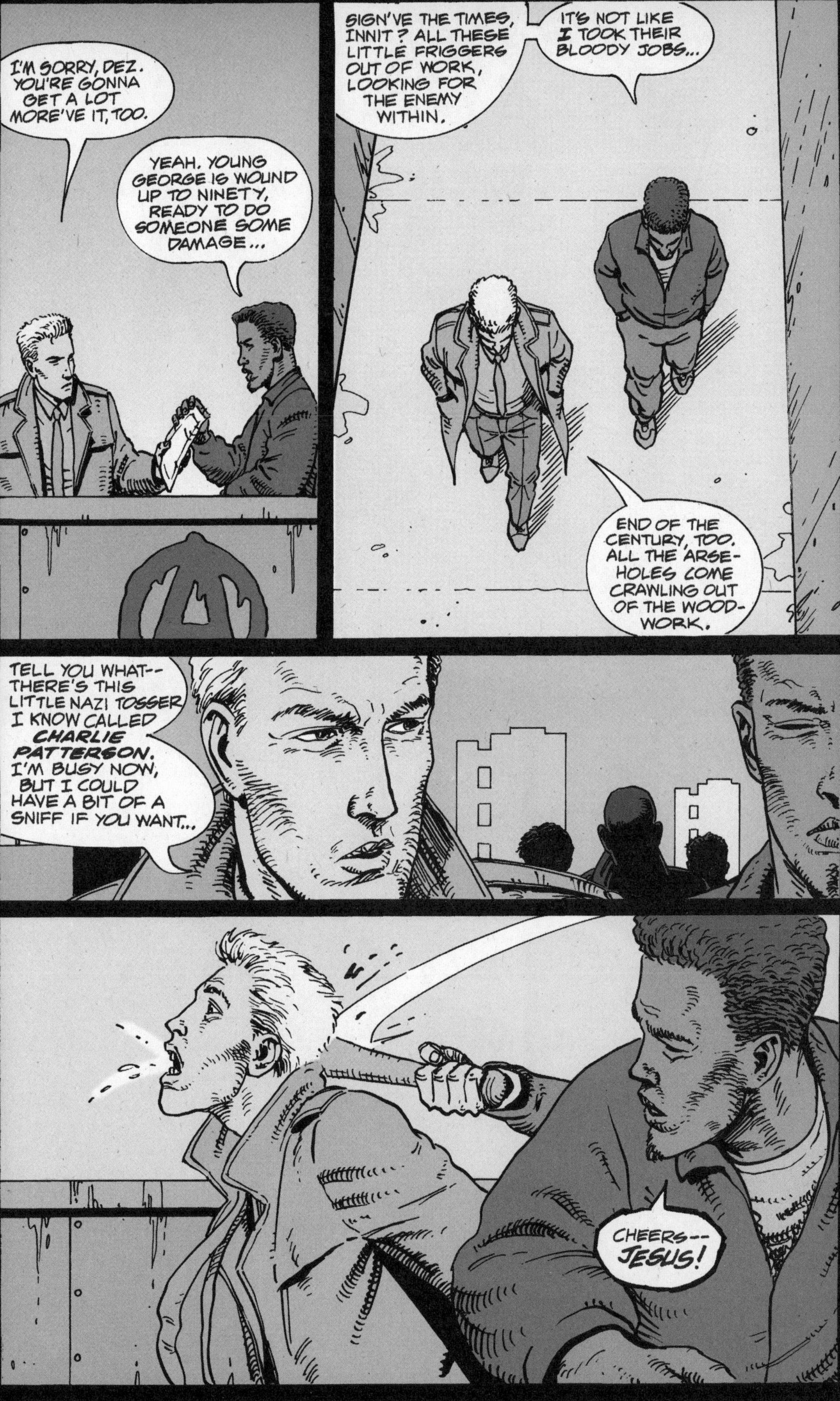
I'M SORRY, DEZ. YOU'RE GONNA GET A LOT MORE'VE IT, TOO.
YEAH. YOUNG GEORGE IS WOUND UP TO NINETY, READY TO DO SOMEONE SOME DAMAGE...
SIGN'VE THE TIMES, INNIT? ALL THESE LITTLE FRIGGERS OUT OF WORK, LOOKING FOR THE ENEMY WITHIN.
IT'S NOT LIKE I TOOK THEIR BLOODY JOBS...
END OF THE CENTURY, TOO. ALL THE ARSE-HOLES COME CRAWLING OUT OF THE WOOD-WORK.
TELL YOU WHAT-- THERE'S THIS LITTLE NAZI TOSSER I KNOW CALLED CHARLIE PATTERSON. I'M BUSY NOW, BUT I COULD HAVE A BIT OF A SNIFF IF YOU WANT...
CHEERS-- JESUS!

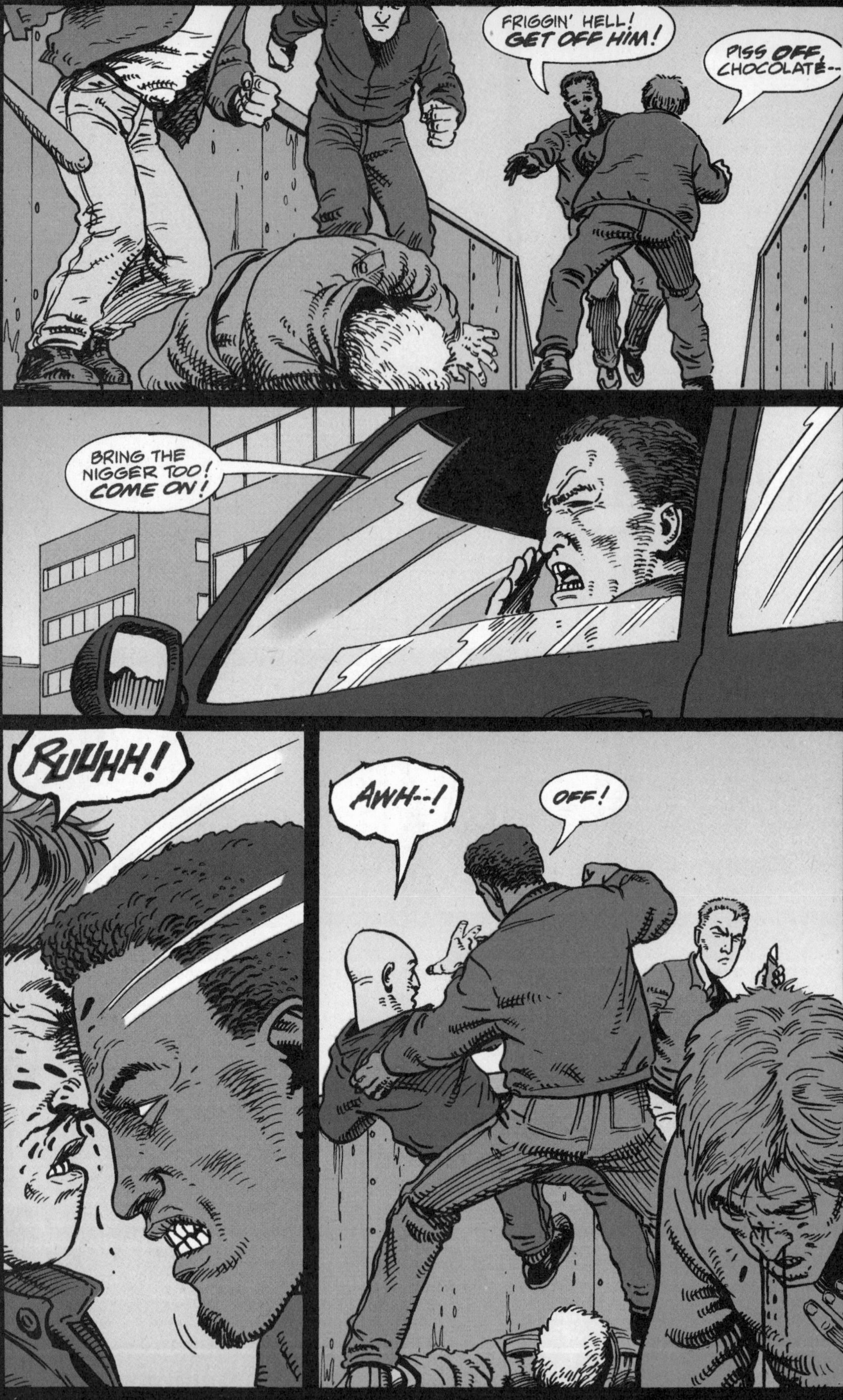
FRIGGIN' HELL! GET OFF HIM!
PISS OFF, CHOCOLATE--
BRING THE NIGGER TOO! COME ON!
RUUHH!
AWH--!
OFF!

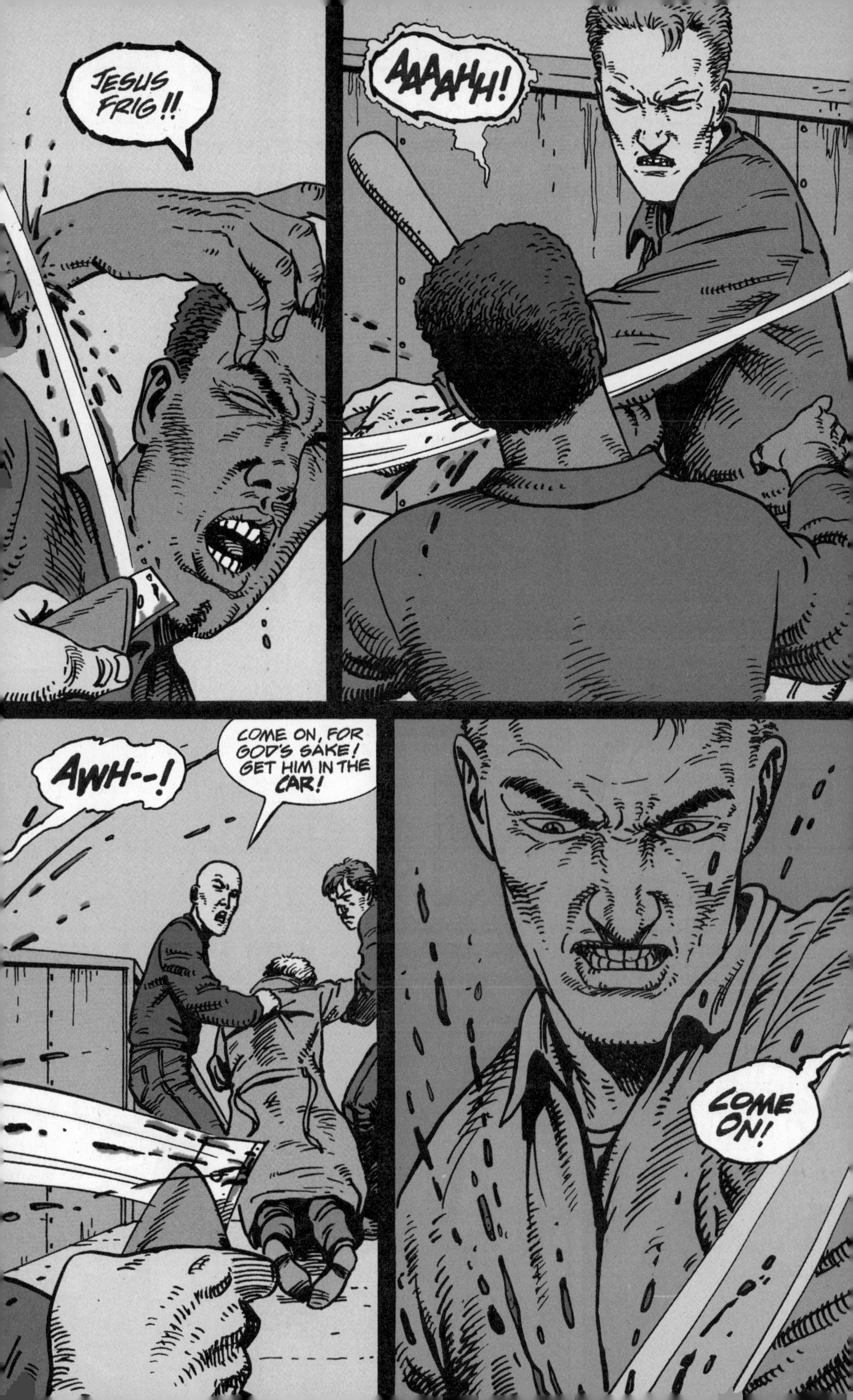
JESUS FRIG!!
AAAAHH!
AWH--!
COME ON, FOR GOD'S SAKE! GET HIM IN THE CAR!
COME ON!

...WELL, LOOK, CHAS: IF YOU SEE HIM, TELL HIM NOT TO GO HOME. TELL HIM I'M IN THE **GREEN MAN** UP NEAR MUSWELL HILL AND I WANT TO SEE HIM **NOW**, RIGHT?

AYE, I KNOW IT'S A LONG WAY--NO, I'M NOT IN TROUBLE--

CHAS, WOULD YOU JUST **DO** IT FOR US, **PLEASE?**

AW, I'M SORRY. OKAY. AYE.

'BYE.

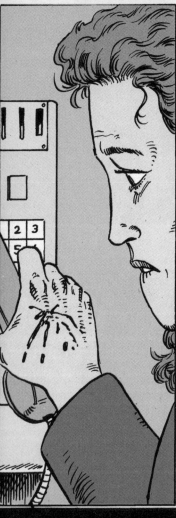

SHE'D BEEN DOING PRETTY WELL, SHE THOUGHT. KNOCK THE BADDIES' SHITE IN, GET TO SOMEWHERE SAFE, SWITCH ON THE OUL' ICE WOMAN BIT AND GET READY TO GIVE CONSTANTINE THE BALLACKIN' OF HIS LIFE--

AYE, WELL. NOBODY'S PERFECT.

LADIE

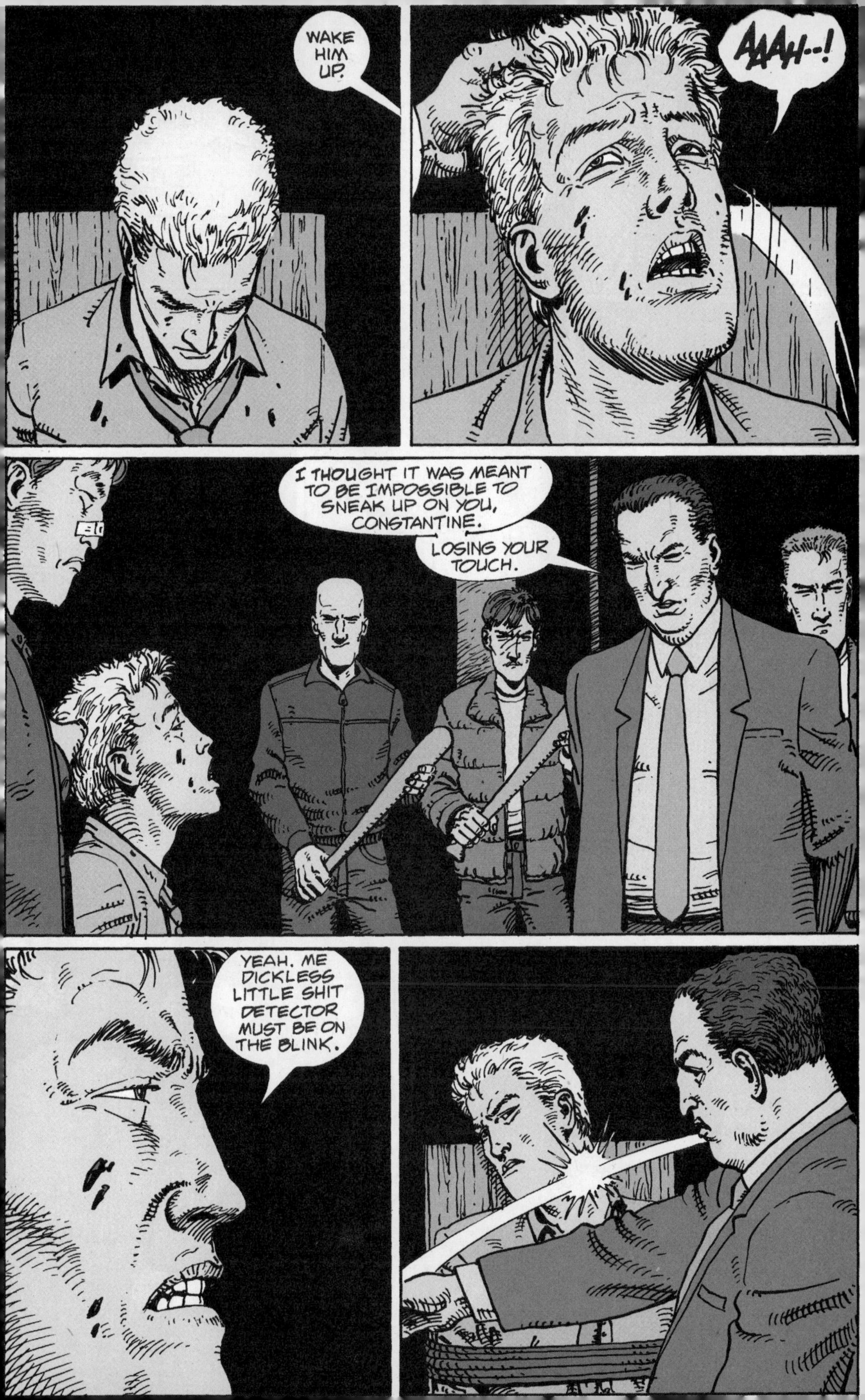
WAKE HIM UP.
AAAH--!
I THOUGHT IT WAS MEANT TO BE IMPOSSIBLE TO SNEAK UP ON YOU, CONSTANTINE.
LOSING YOUR TOUCH.
YEAH. ME DICKLESS LITTLE SHIT DETECTOR MUST BE ON THE BLINK.

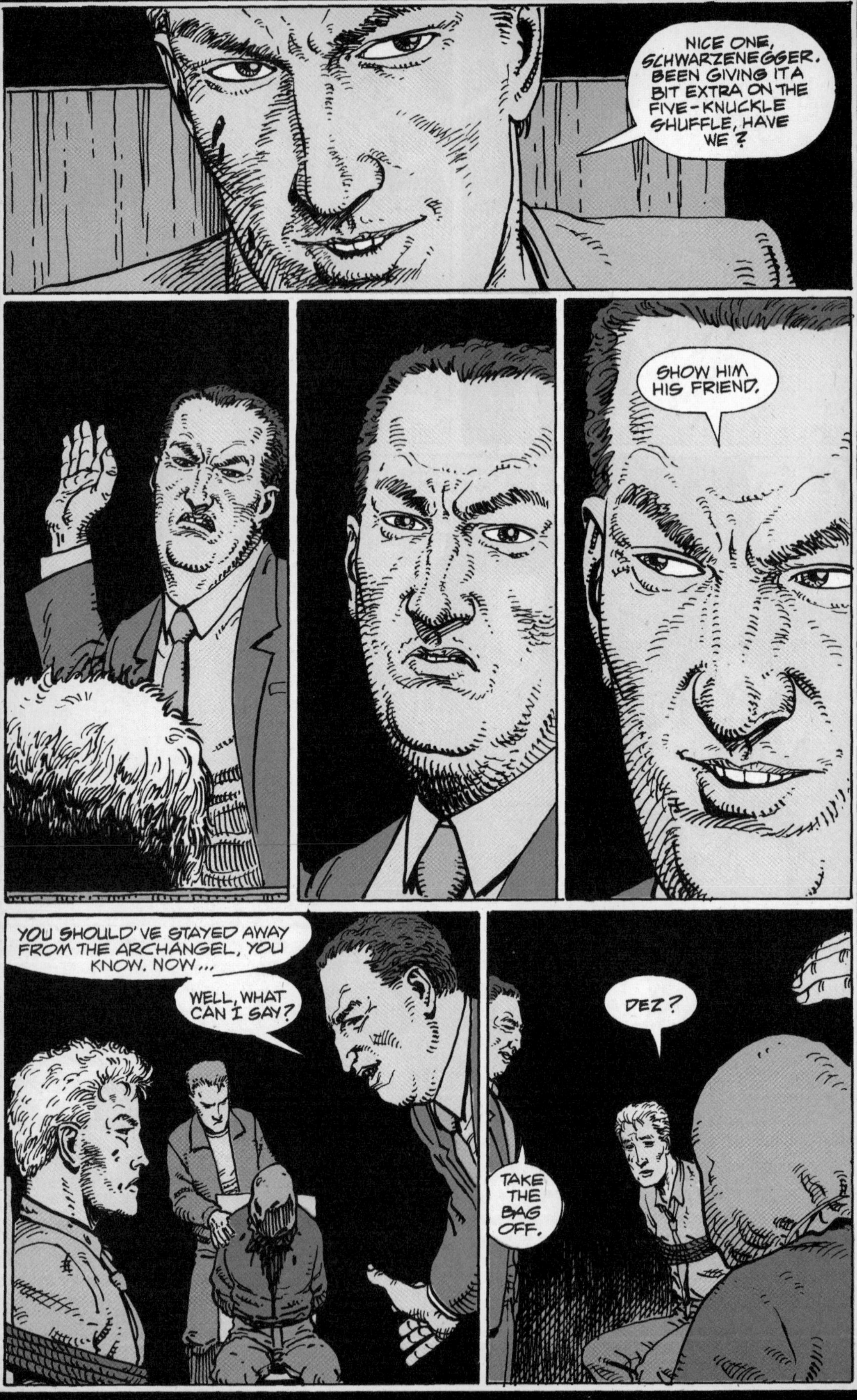
NICE ONE, SCHWARZENEGGER. BEEN GIVING IT A BIT EXTRA ON THE FIVE-KNUCKLE SHUFFLE, HAVE WE?
SHOW HIM HIS FRIEND.
YOU SHOULD'VE STAYED AWAY FROM THE ARCHANGEL, YOU KNOW. NOW...
WELL, WHAT CAN I SAY?
TAKE THE BAG OFF.
DEZ?

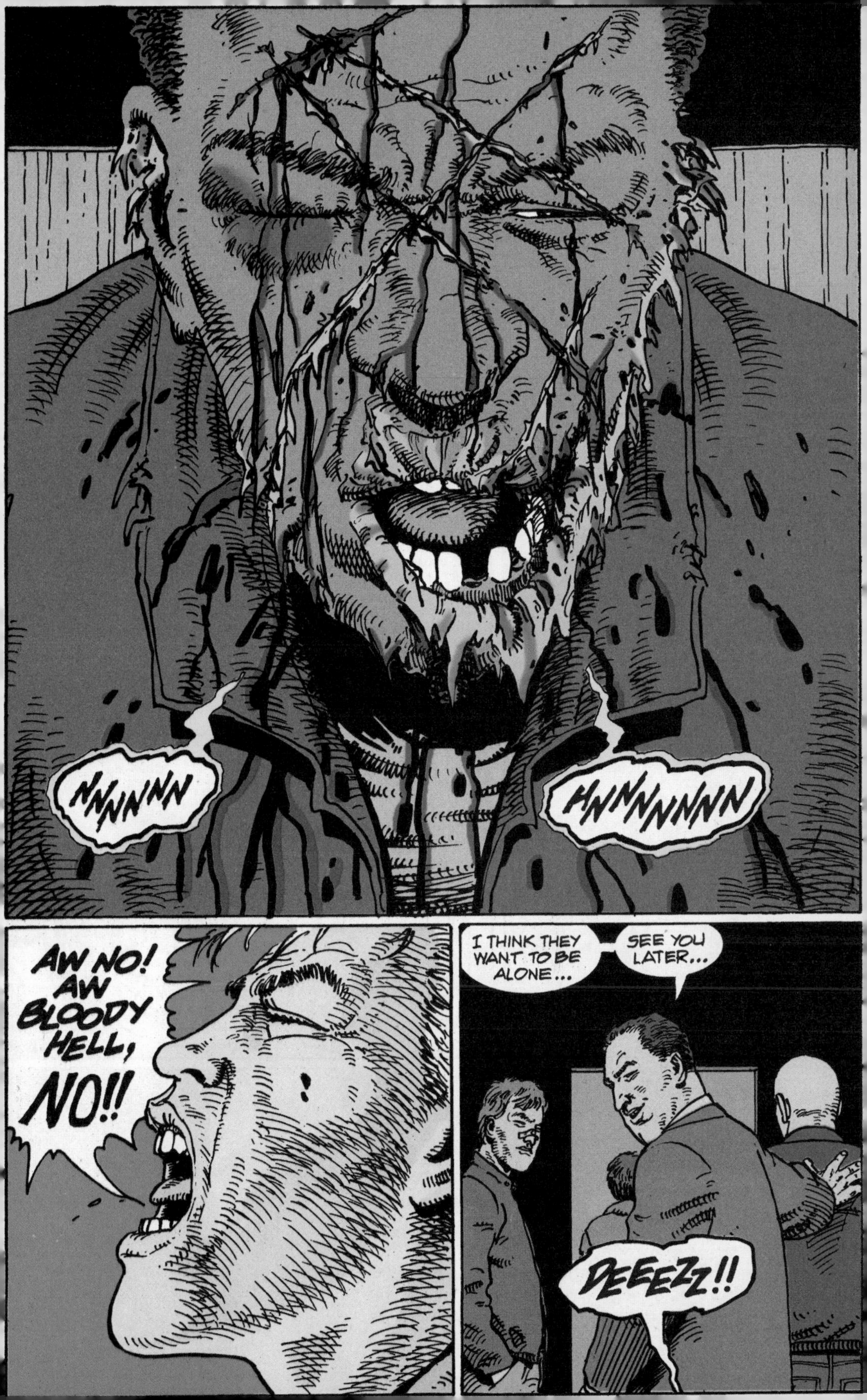
HNNNNN
HNNNNNNNN
AW NO! AW BLOODY HELL, NO!!
I THINK THEY WANT TO BE ALONE...
SEE YOU LATER...
DEEEZZ!!

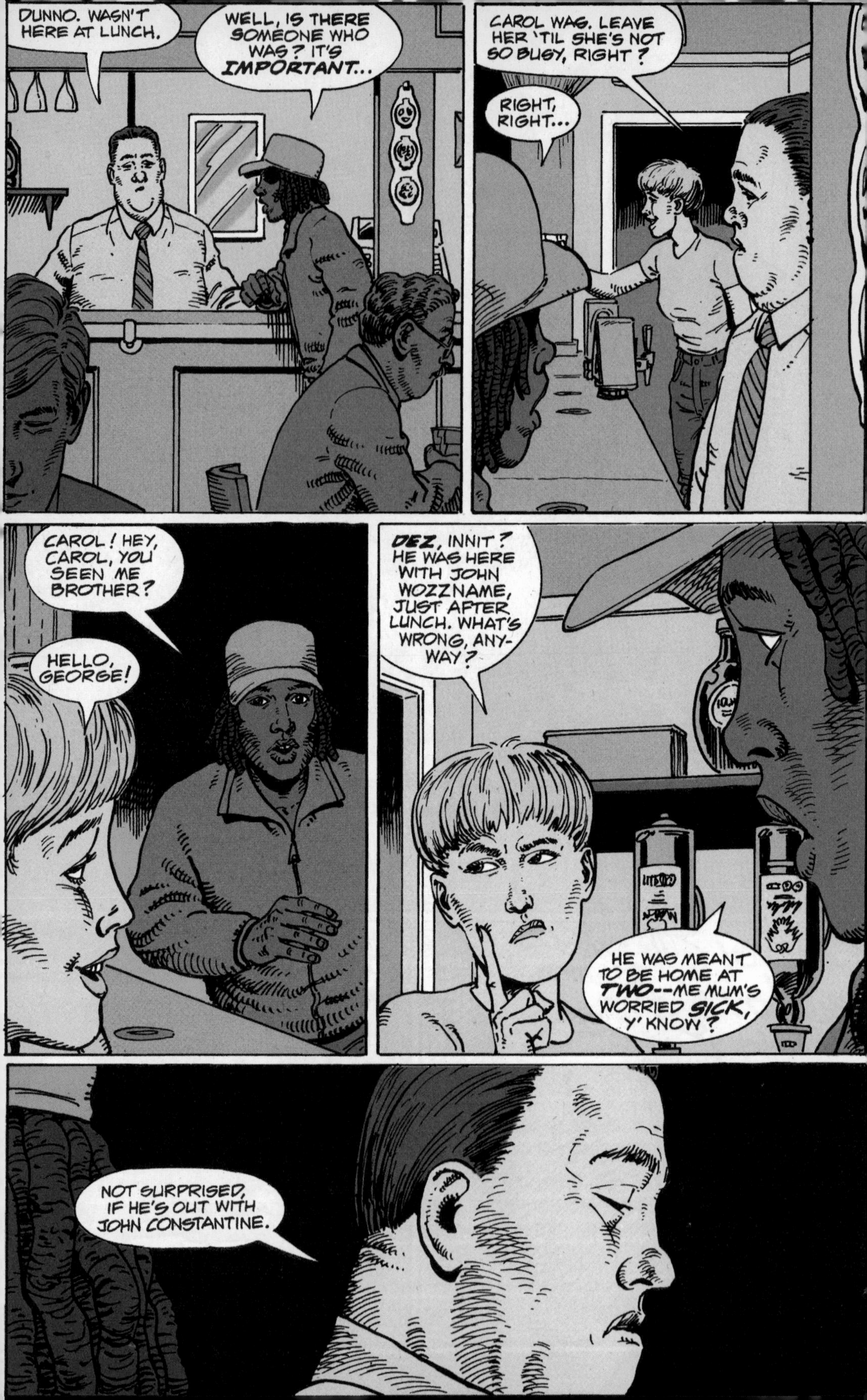
DUNNO. WASN'T HERE AT LUNCH.
WELL, IS THERE SOMEONE WHO WAS? IT'S IMPORTANT...
CAROL WAG. LEAVE HER 'TIL SHE'S NOT SO BUSY, RIGHT?
RIGHT, RIGHT...
CAROL! HEY, CAROL, YOU SEEN ME BROTHER?
HELLO, GEORGE!
DEZ, INNIT? HE WAS HERE WITH JOHN WOZZNAME, JUST AFTER LUNCH. WHAT'S WRONG, ANYWAY?
HE WAS MEANT TO BE HOME AT TWO--ME MUM'S WORRIED SICK, Y' KNOW?
NOT SURPRISED, IF HE'S OUT WITH JOHN CONSTANTINE.

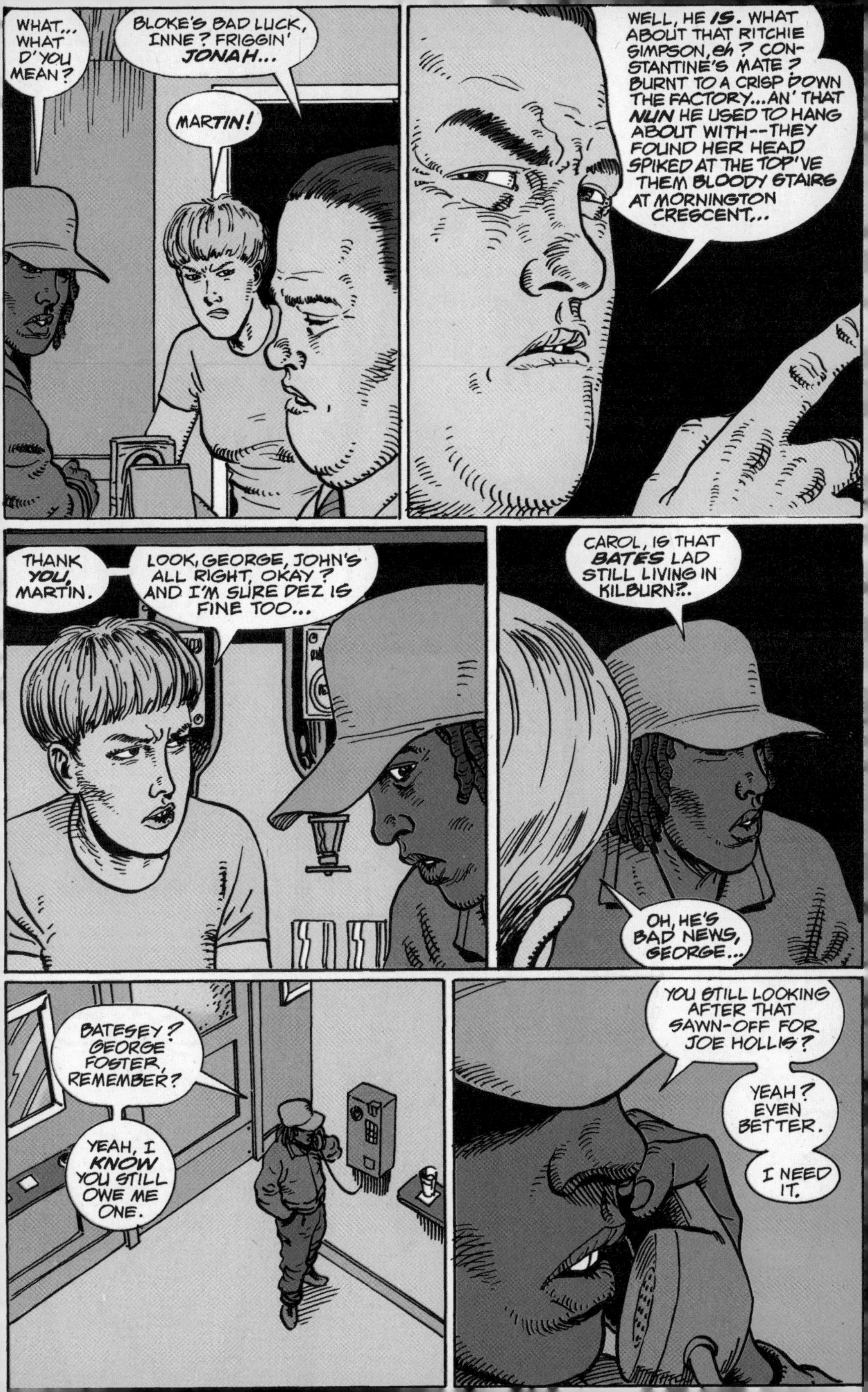
WHAT... WHAT D'YOU MEAN?
BLOKE'S BAD LUCK, INNE? FRIGGIN' JONAH...
MARTIN!
WELL, HE IS. WHAT ABOUT THAT RITCHIE SIMPSON, eh? CONSTANTINE'S MATE? BURNT TO A CRISP DOWN THE FACTORY... AN' THAT NUN HE USED TO HANG ABOUT WITH--THEY FOUND HER HEAD SPIKED AT THE TOP'VE THEM BLOODY STAIRS AT MORNINGTON CRESCENT...
THANK YOU, MARTIN.
LOOK, GEORGE, JOHN'S ALL RIGHT, OKAY? AND I'M SURE DEZ IS FINE TOO...
CAROL, IS THAT BATES LAD STILL LIVING IN KILBURN?..
OH, HE'S BAD NEWS, GEORGE...
BATESEY? GEORGE FOSTER, REMEMBER?
YEAH, I KNOW YOU STILL OWE ME ONE.
YOU STILL LOOKING AFTER THAT SAWN-OFF FOR JOE HOLLIS?
YEAH? EVEN BETTER.
I NEED IT.

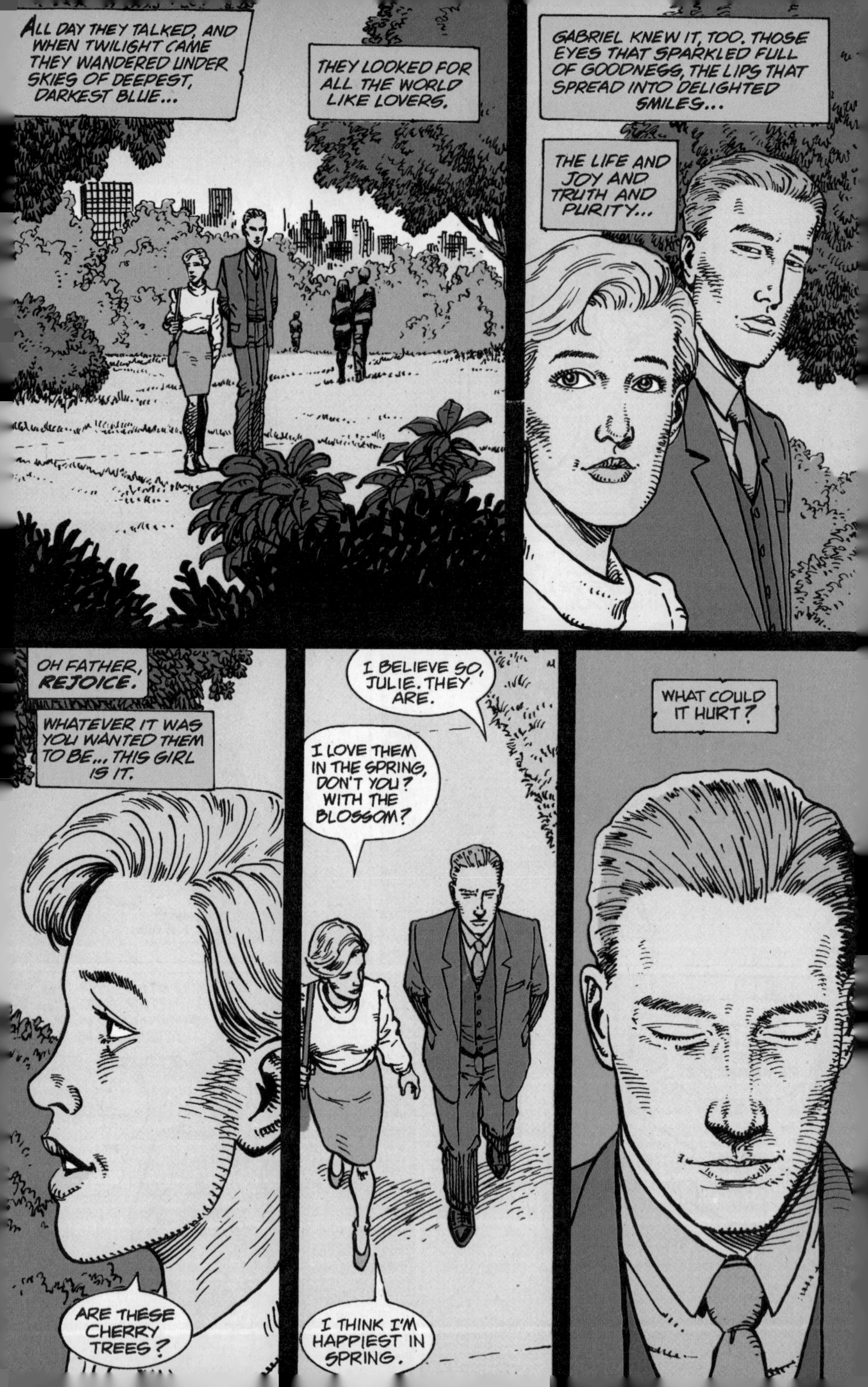

ALL DAY THEY TALKED, AND WHEN TWILIGHT CAME THEY WANDERED UNDER SKIES OF DEEPEST, DARKEST BLUE...
THEY LOOKED FOR ALL THE WORLD LIKE LOVERS.
GABRIEL KNEW IT, TOO. THOSE EYES THAT SPARKLED FULL OF GOODNESS, THE LIPS THAT SPREAD INTO DELIGHTED SMILES...
THE LIFE AND JOY AND TRUTH AND PURITY...
OH FATHER, REJOICE.
WHATEVER IT WAS YOU WANTED THEM TO BE.., THIS GIRL IS IT.
ARE THESE CHERRY TREES?
I BELIEVE SO, JULIE. THEY ARE.
I LOVE THEM IN THE SPRING, DON'T YOU? WITH THE BLOSSOM?
I THINK I'M HAPPIEST IN SPRING.
WHAT COULD IT HURT?

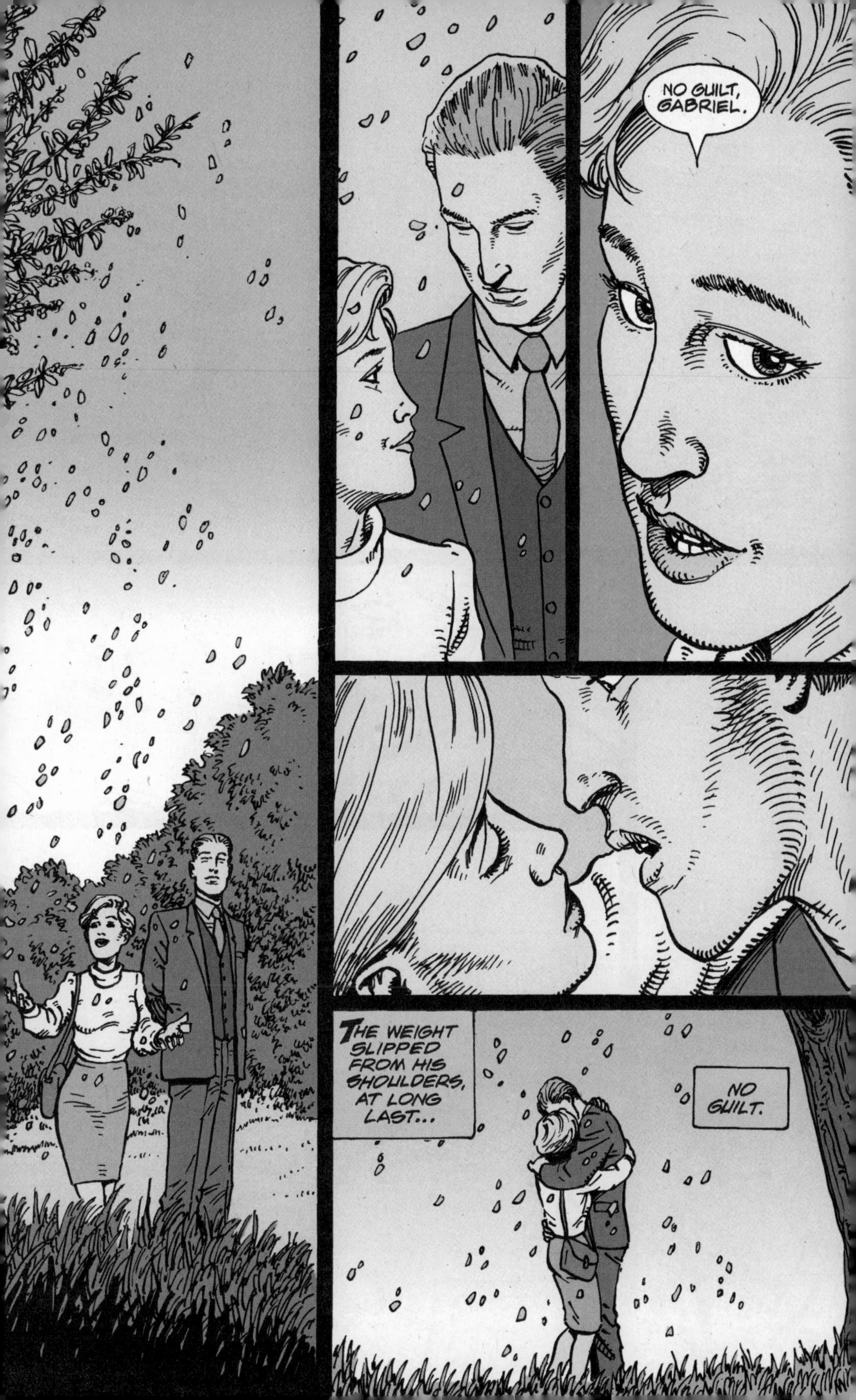
NO GUILT, GABRIEL.
THE WEIGHT SLIPPED FROM HIS SHOULDERS, AT LONG LAST...
NO GUILT.

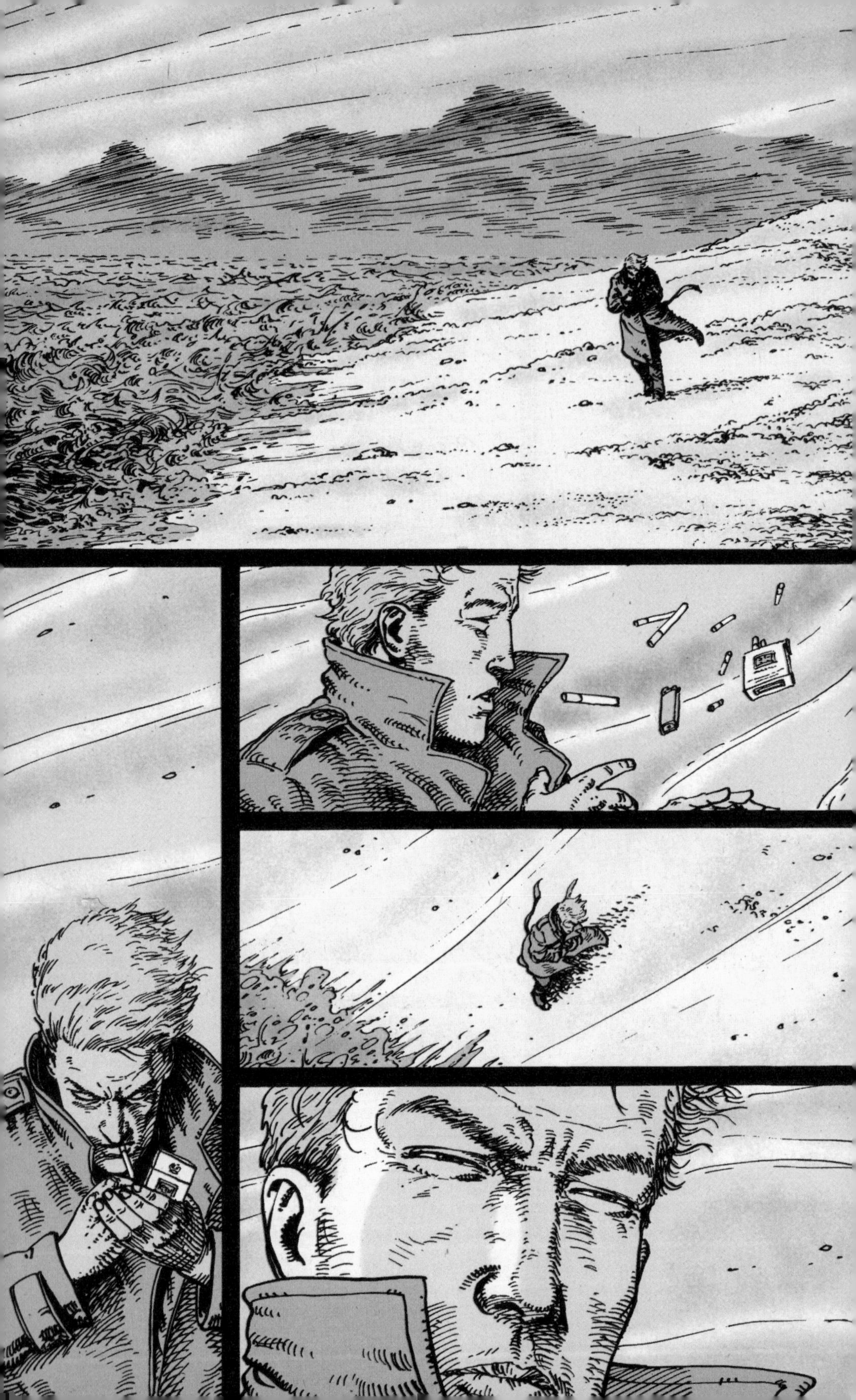

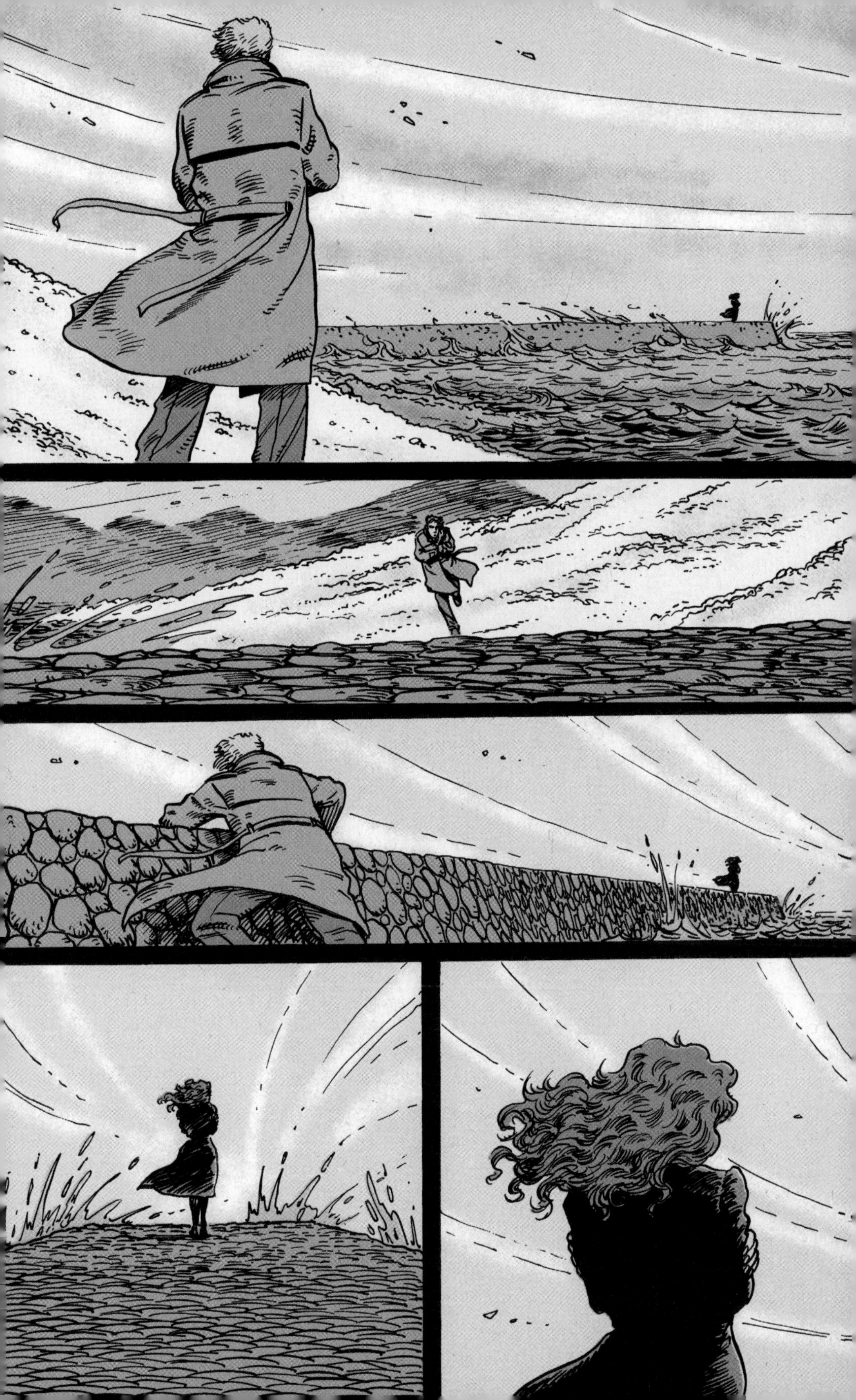

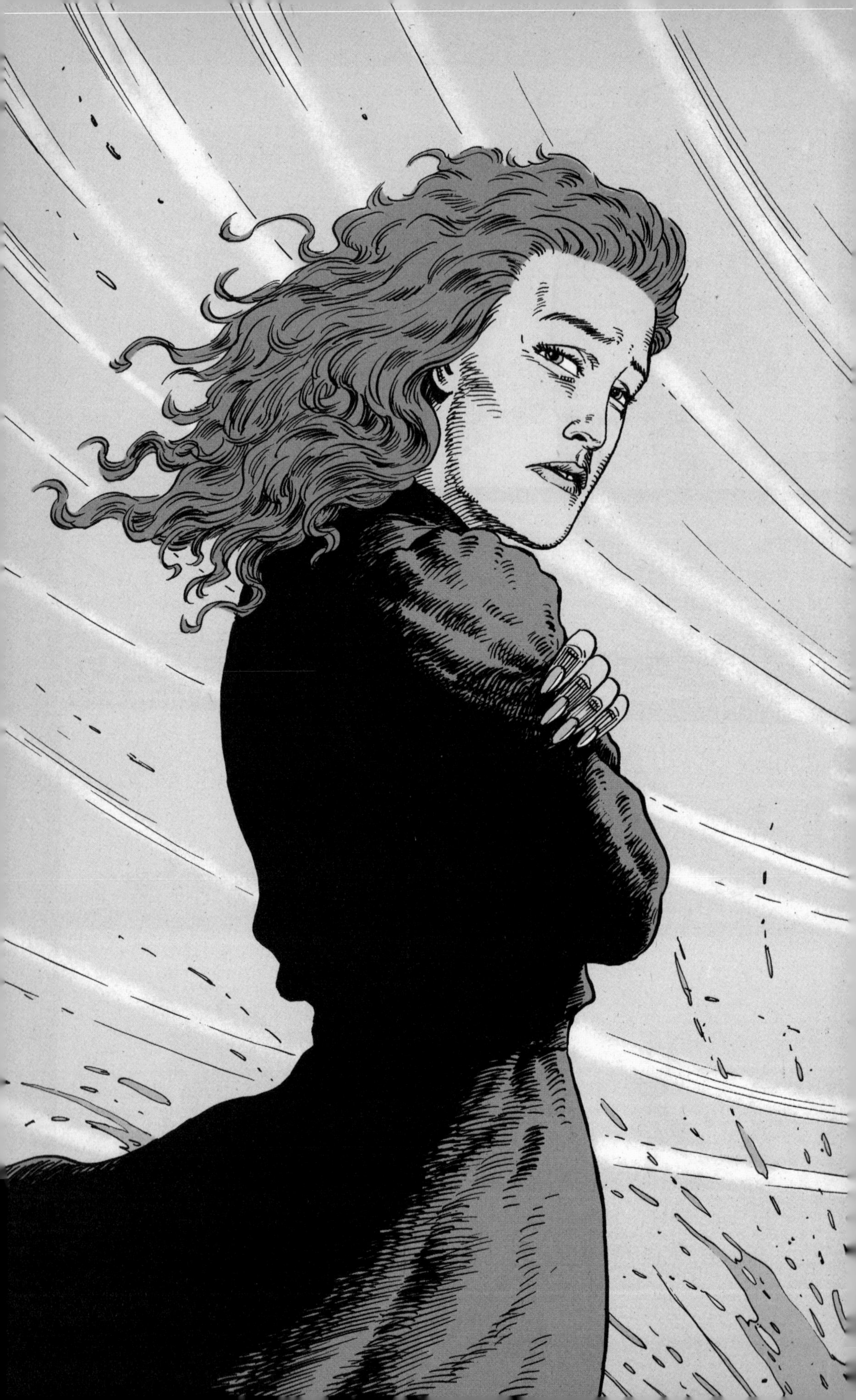

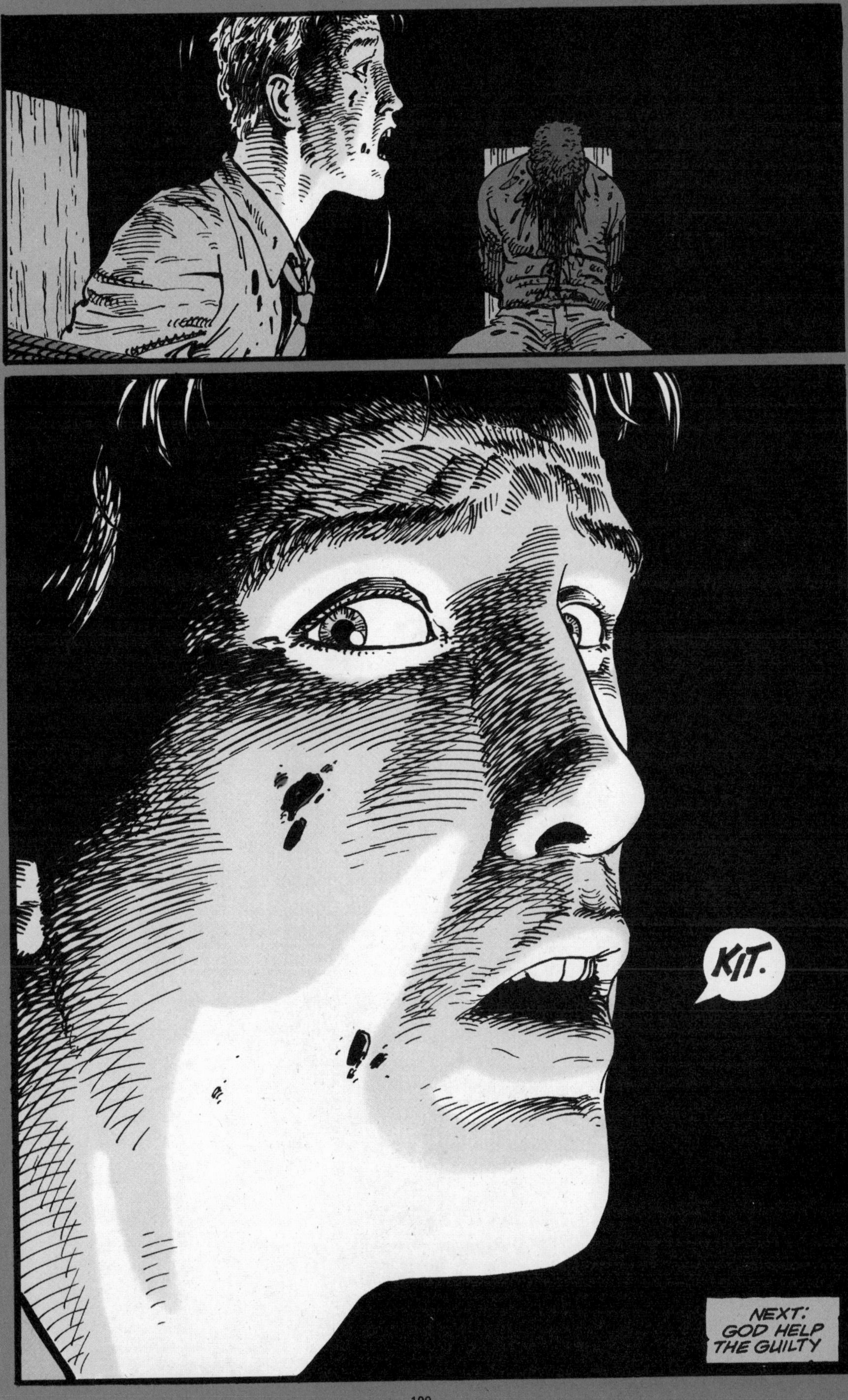
KIT.
NEXT: GOD HELP THE GUILTY

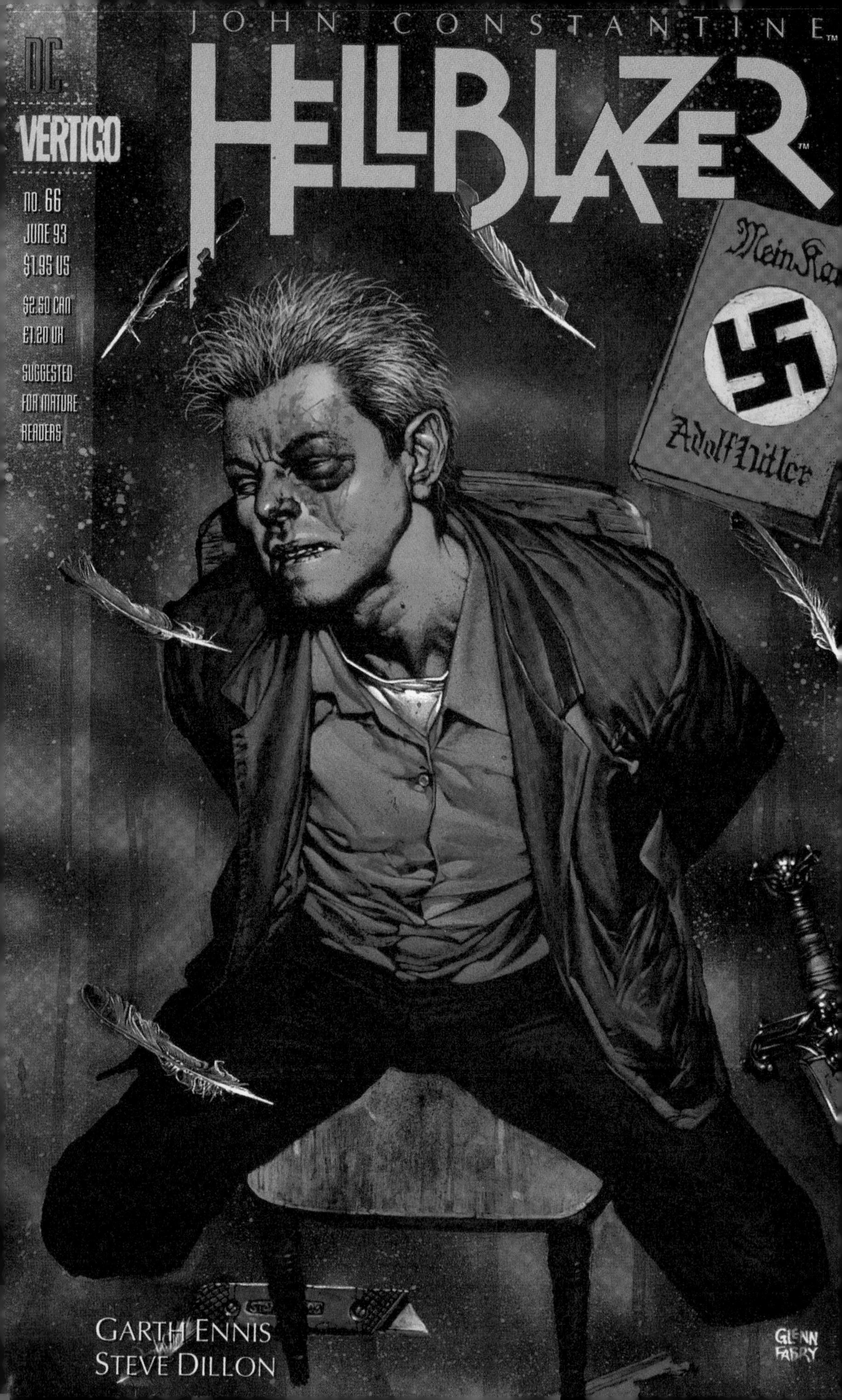

JOHN CONSTANTINE
HELLBLAZER
DC
VERTIGO
NO. 66
JUNE 93
$1.95 US
$2.50 CAN
£1.20 UK
SUGGESTED FOR MATURE READERS
Mein Kampf
Adolf Hitler
GARTH ENNIS
STEVE DILLON
GLENN FABRY

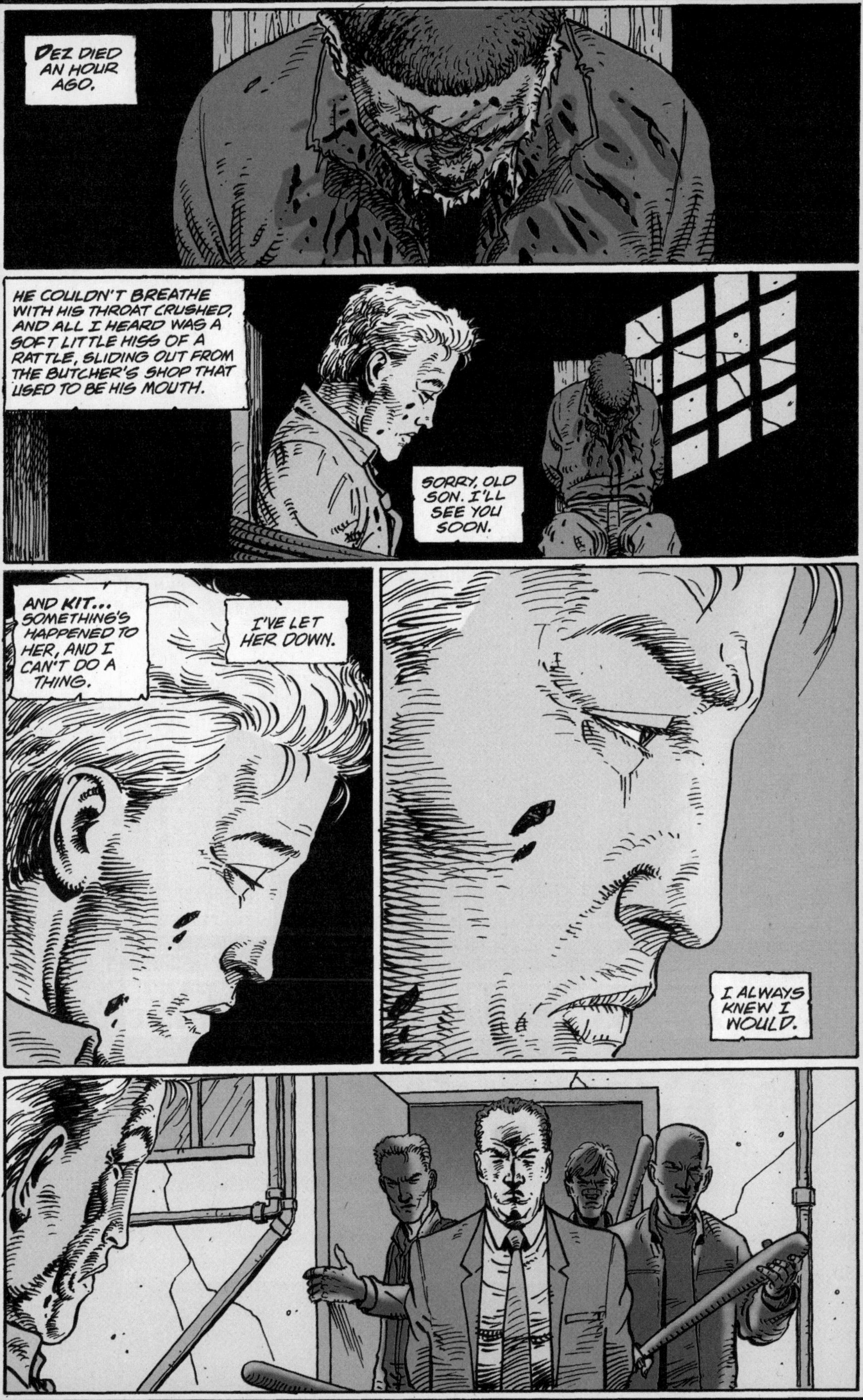
DEZ DIED AN HOUR AGO.
HE COULDN'T BREATHE WITH HIS THROAT CRUSHED, AND ALL I HEARD WAS A SOFT LITTLE HISS OF A RATTLE, SLIDING OUT FROM THE BUTCHER'S SHOP THAT USED TO BE HIS MOUTH.
SORRY, OLD SON. I'LL SEE YOU SOON.
AND KIT... SOMETHING'S HAPPENED TO HER, AND I CAN'T DO A THING.
I'VE LET HER DOWN.
I ALWAYS KNEW I WOULD.

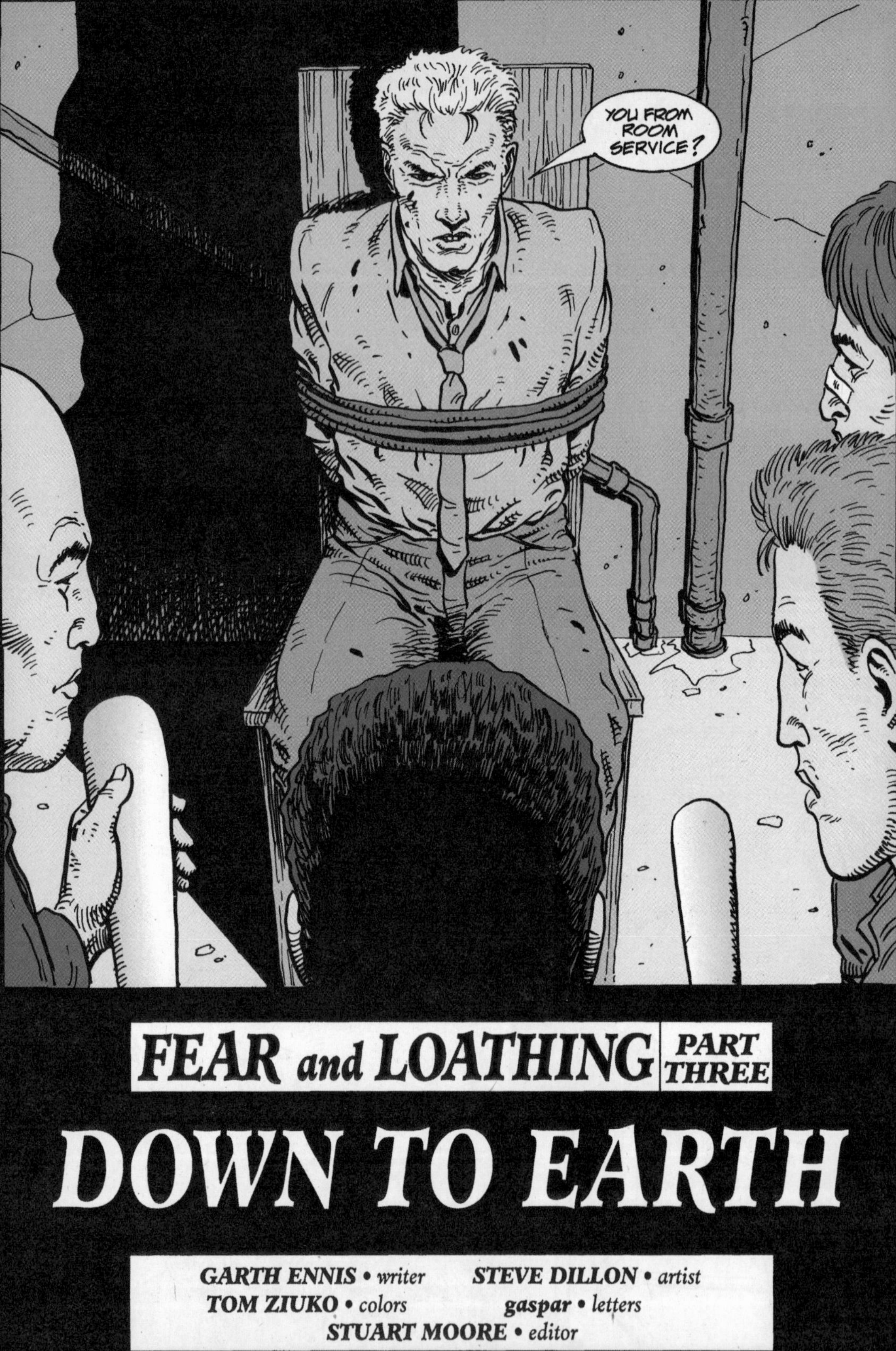
YOU FROM ROOM SERVICE?

FEAR and LOATHING PART THREE

DOWN TO EARTH

GARTH ENNIS • *writer* **STEVE DILLON** • *artist*
TOM ZIUKO • *colors* **gaspar** • *letters*
STUART MOORE • *editor*

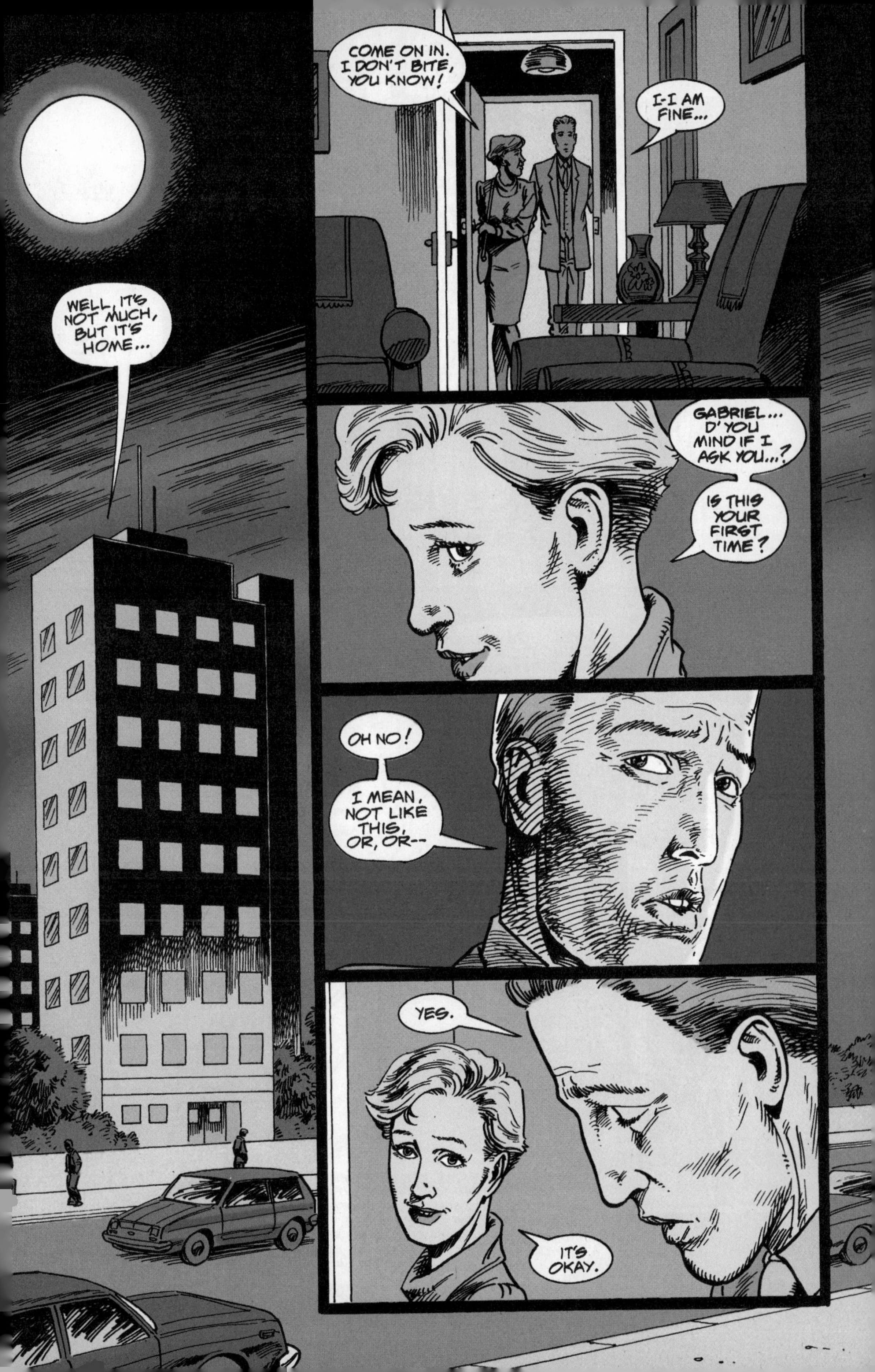

WELL, IT'S NOT MUCH, BUT IT'S HOME...
COME ON IN. I DON'T BITE, YOU KNOW!
I-I AM FINE...
GABRIEL... D'YOU MIND IF I ASK YOU...?
IS THIS YOUR FIRST TIME?
OH NO!
I MEAN, NOT LIKE THIS, OR, OR--
YES.
IT'S OKAY.

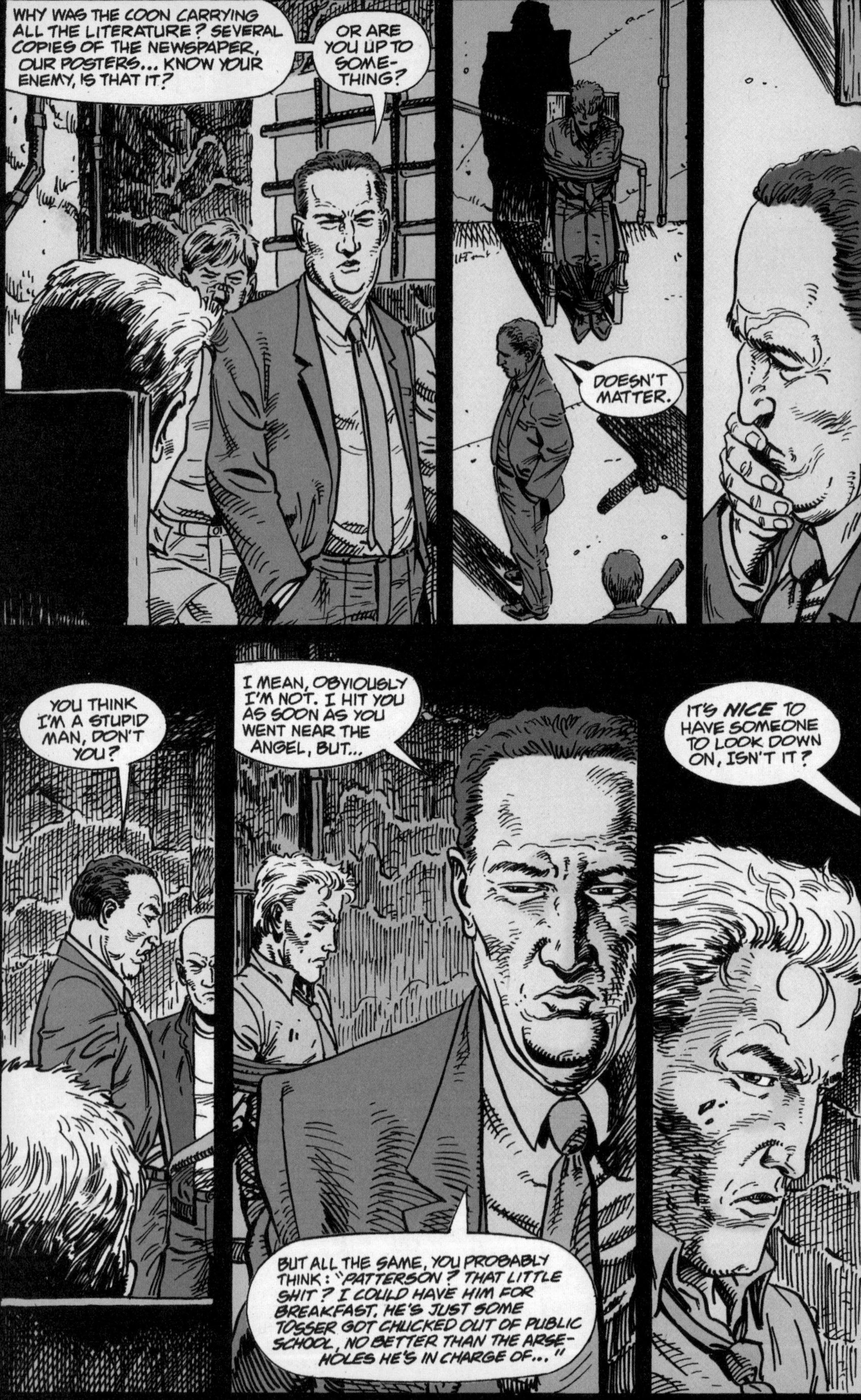
WHY WAS THE COON CARRYING ALL THE LITERATURE? SEVERAL COPIES OF THE NEWSPAPER, OUR POSTERS... KNOW YOUR ENEMY, IS THAT IT?
OR ARE YOU UP TO SOME-THING?
DOESN'T MATTER.
YOU THINK I'M A STUPID MAN, DON'T YOU?
I MEAN, OBVIOUSLY I'M NOT. I HIT YOU AS SOON AS YOU WENT NEAR THE ANGEL, BUT...
BUT ALL THE SAME, YOU PROBABLY THINK: "PATTERSON? THAT LITTLE SHIT? I COULD HAVE HIM FOR BREAKFAST. HE'S JUST SOME TOSSER GOT CHUCKED OUT OF PUBLIC SCHOOL, NO BETTER THAN THE ARSE-HOLES HE'S IN CHARGE OF..."
IT'S NICE TO HAVE SOMEONE TO LOOK DOWN ON, ISN'T IT?

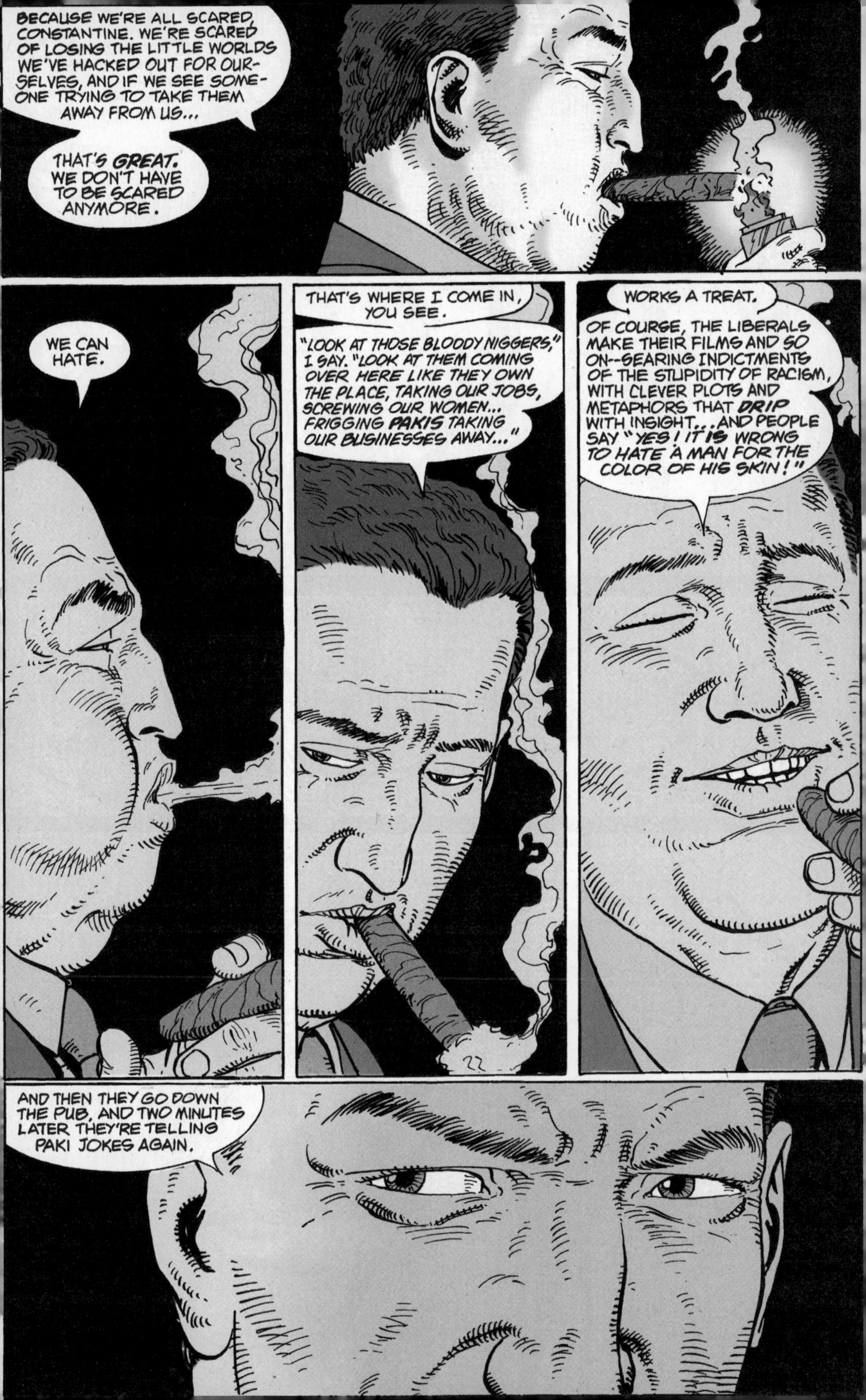
BECAUSE WE'RE ALL SCARED, CONSTANTINE. WE'RE SCARED OF LOSING THE LITTLE WORLDS WE'VE HACKED OUT FOR OURSELVES, AND IF WE SEE SOMEONE TRYING TO TAKE THEM AWAY FROM US...
THAT'S GREAT. WE DON'T HAVE TO BE SCARED ANYMORE.
WE CAN HATE.
THAT'S WHERE I COME IN, YOU SEE.
"LOOK AT THOSE BLOODY NIGGERS," I SAY. "LOOK AT THEM COMING OVER HERE LIKE THEY OWN THE PLACE, TAKING OUR JOBS, SCREWING OUR WOMEN... FRIGGING PAKIS TAKING OUR BUSINESSES AWAY..."
WORKS A TREAT.
OF COURSE, THE LIBERALS MAKE THEIR FILMS AND SO ON--SEARING INDICTMENTS OF THE STUPIDITY OF RACISM, WITH CLEVER PLOTS AND METAPHORS THAT DRIP WITH INSIGHT... AND PEOPLE SAY "YES! IT IS WRONG TO HATE A MAN FOR THE COLOR OF HIS SKIN!"
AND THEN THEY GO DOWN THE PUB, AND TWO MINUTES LATER THEY'RE TELLING PAKI JOKES AGAIN.

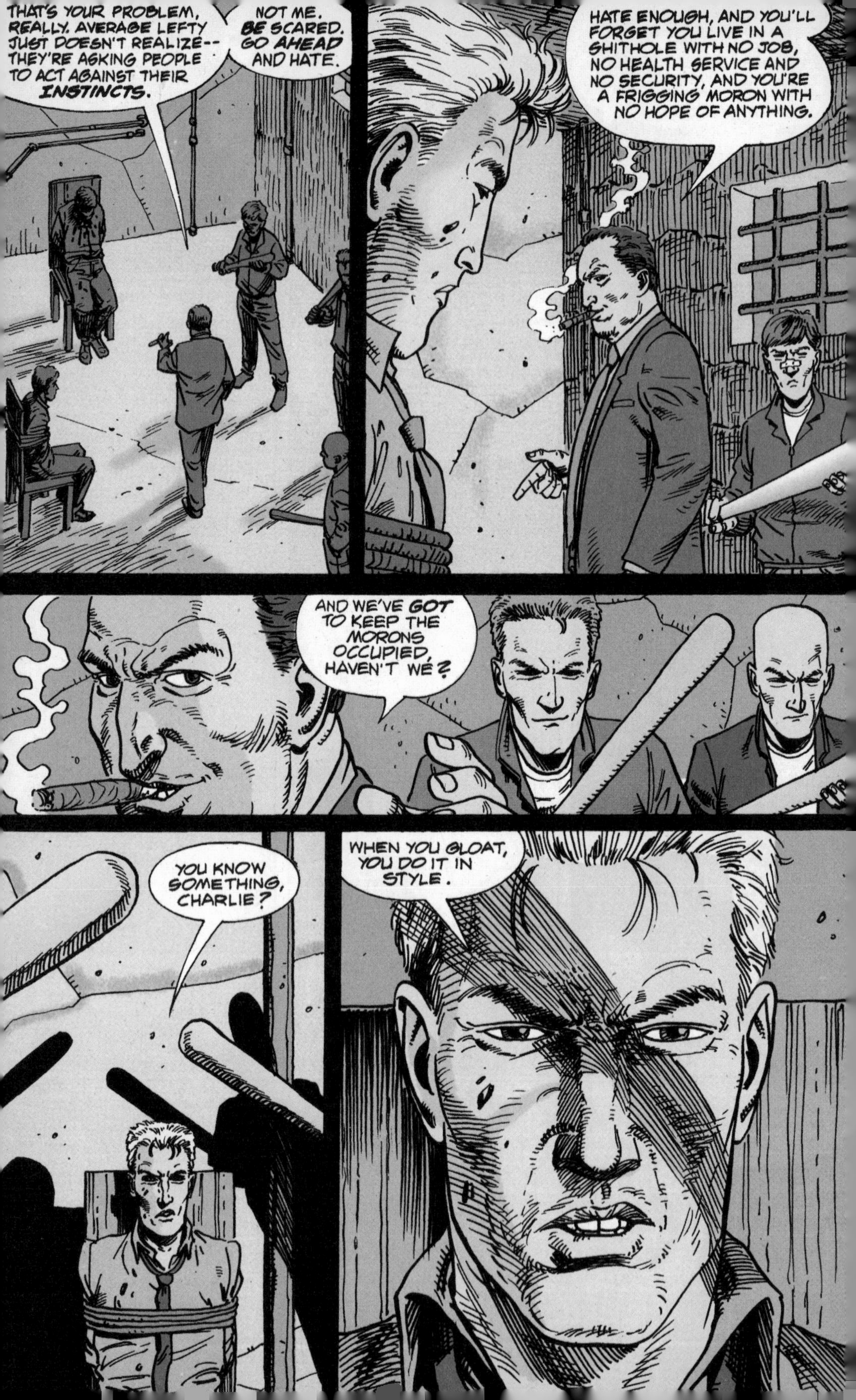
THAT'S YOUR PROBLEM, REALLY. AVERAGE LEFTY JUST DOESN'T REALIZE-- THEY'RE ASKING PEOPLE TO ACT AGAINST THEIR INSTINCTS.
NOT ME. BE SCARED. GO AHEAD AND HATE.
HATE ENOUGH, AND YOU'LL FORGET YOU LIVE IN A SHITHOLE WITH NO JOB, NO HEALTH SERVICE AND NO SECURITY, AND YOU'RE A FRIGGING MORON WITH NO HOPE OF ANYTHING.
AND WE'VE GOT TO KEEP THE MORONS OCCUPIED, HAVEN'T WE?
YOU KNOW SOMETHING, CHARLIE?
WHEN YOU GLOAT, YOU DO IT IN STYLE.

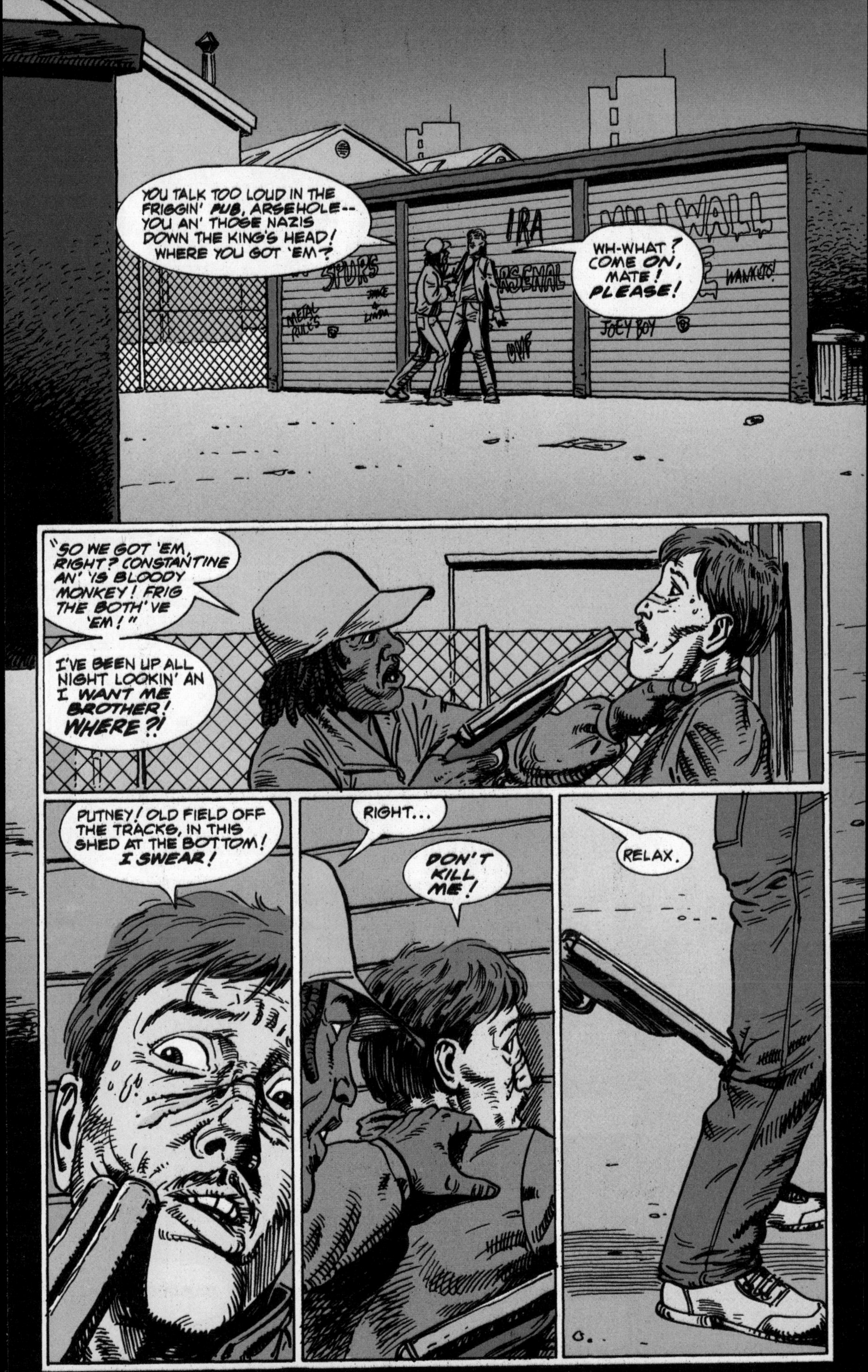
YOU TALK TOO LOUD IN THE FRIGGIN' PUB, ARSEHOLE-- YOU AN' THOSE NAZIS DOWN THE KING'S HEAD! WHERE YOU GOT 'EM?
IRA
MILLWALL
SPURS
ARSENAL
WANKERS!
JAKE & LINDA
METAL RULES
JOEY BOY
WH-WHAT? COME ON, MATE! PLEASE!
"SO WE GOT 'EM, RIGHT? CONSTANTINE AN' 'IS BLOODY MONKEY! FRIG THE BOTH'VE 'EM!"
I'VE BEEN UP ALL NIGHT LOOKIN' AN I WANT ME BROTHER! WHERE?!
PUTNEY! OLD FIELD OFF THE TRACKS, IN THIS SHED AT THE BOTTOM! I SWEAR!
RIGHT...
DON'T KILL ME!
RELAX.

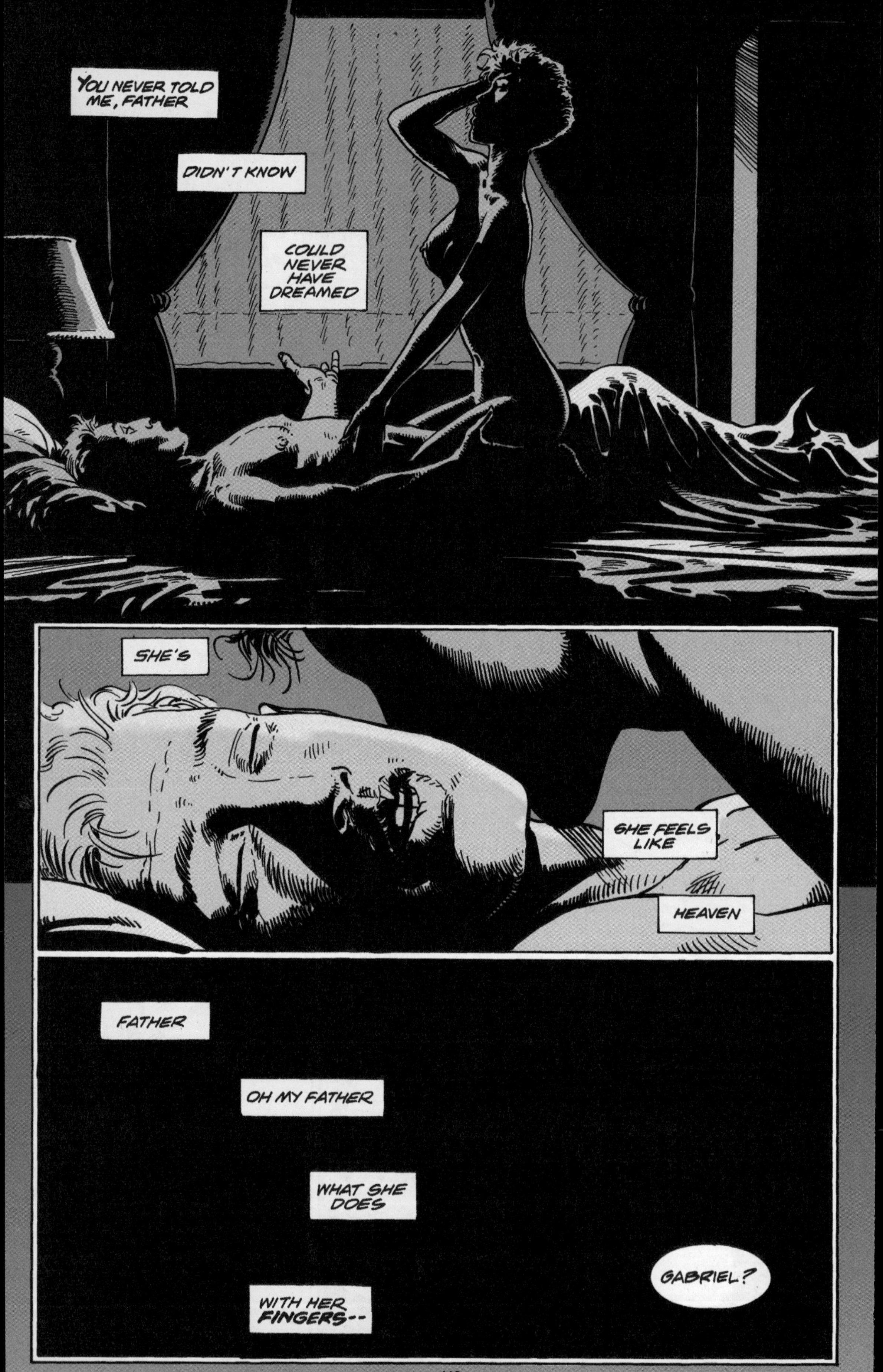
YOU NEVER TOLD ME, FATHER
DIDN'T KNOW
COULD NEVER HAVE DREAMED
SHE'S
SHE FEELS LIKE
HEAVEN
FATHER
OH MY FATHER
WHAT SHE DOES
WITH HER FINGERS--
GABRIEL?

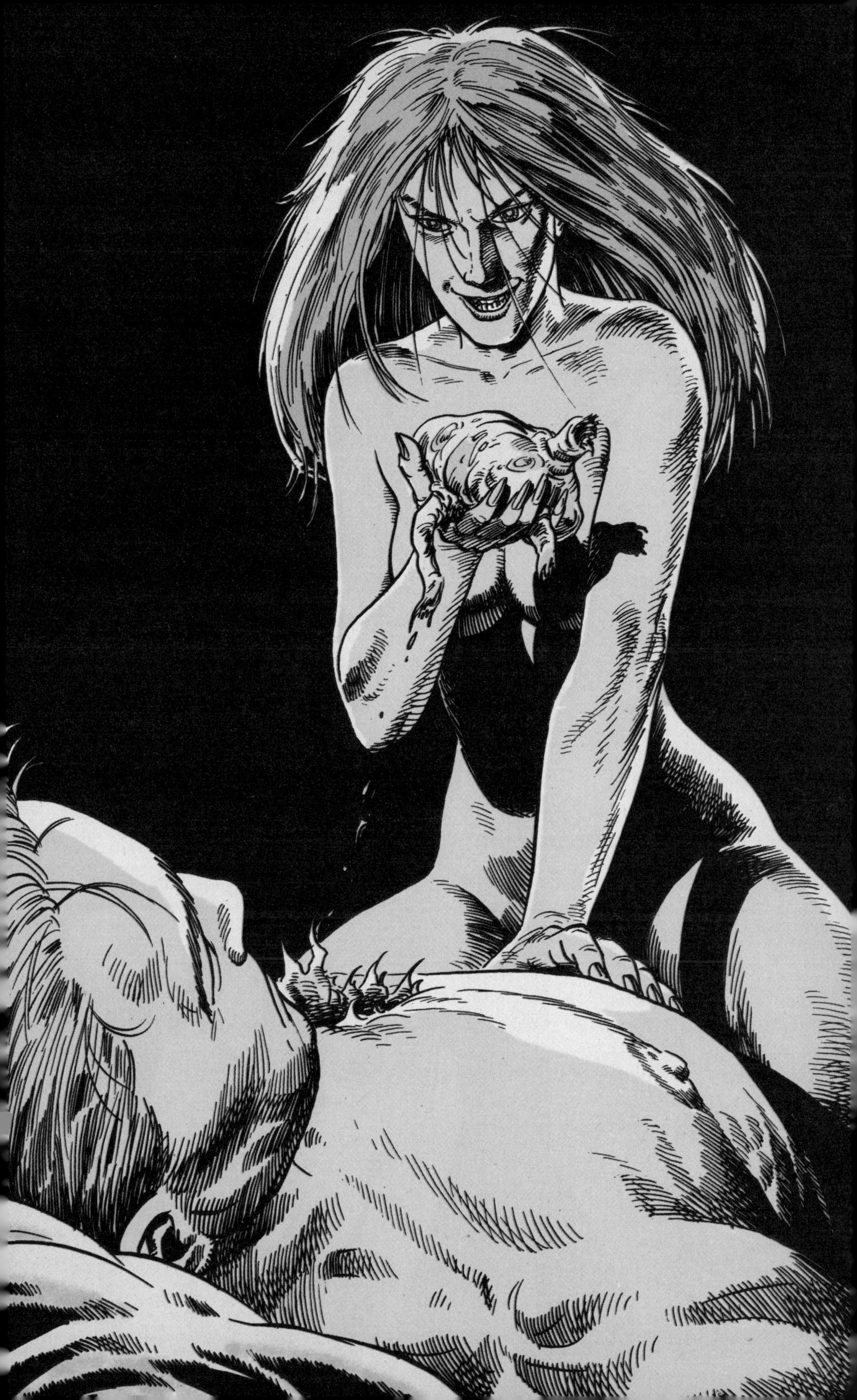

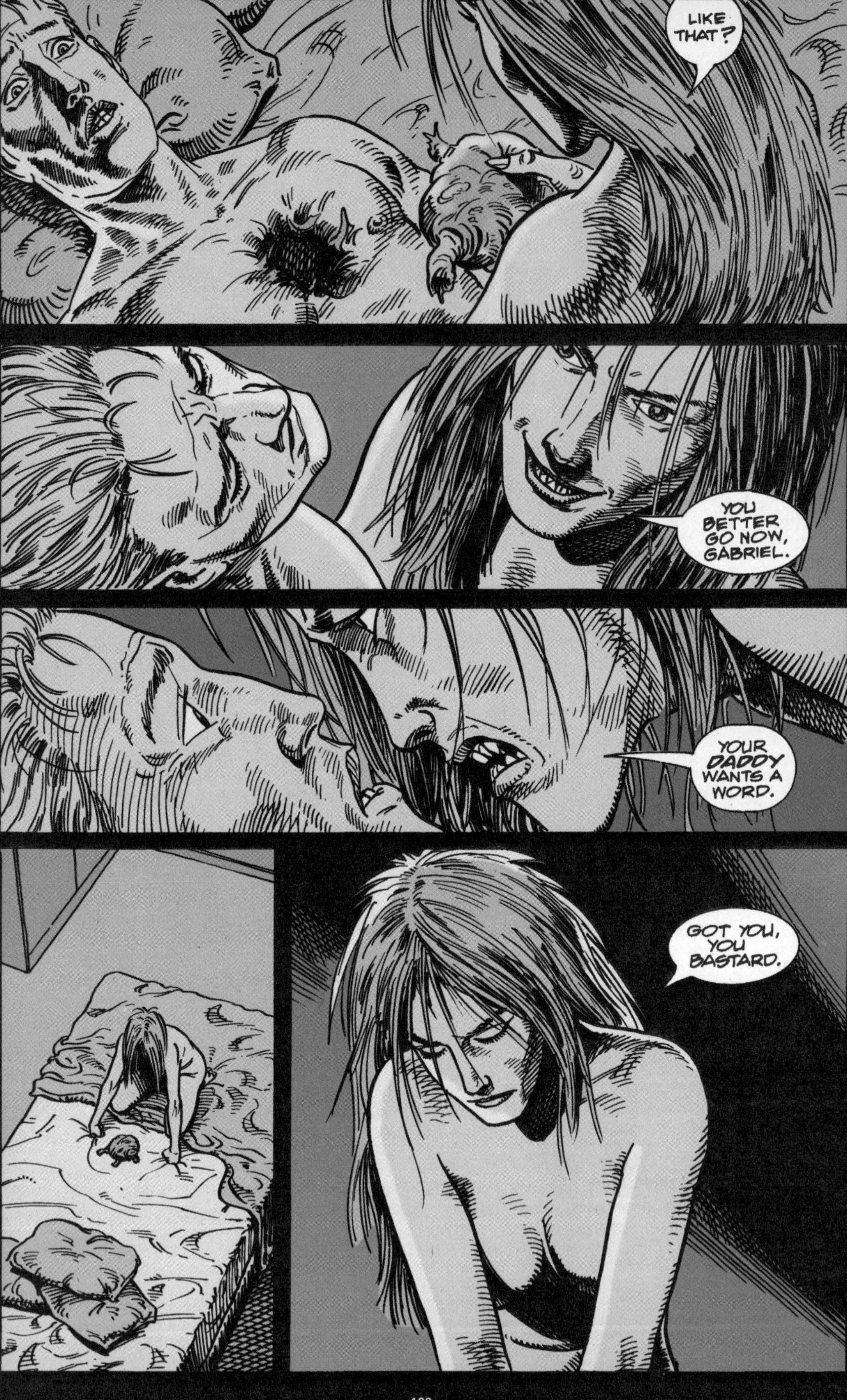
LIKE THAT?
YOU BETTER GO NOW, GABRIEL.
YOUR DADDY WANTS A WORD.
GOT YOU, YOU BASTARD.

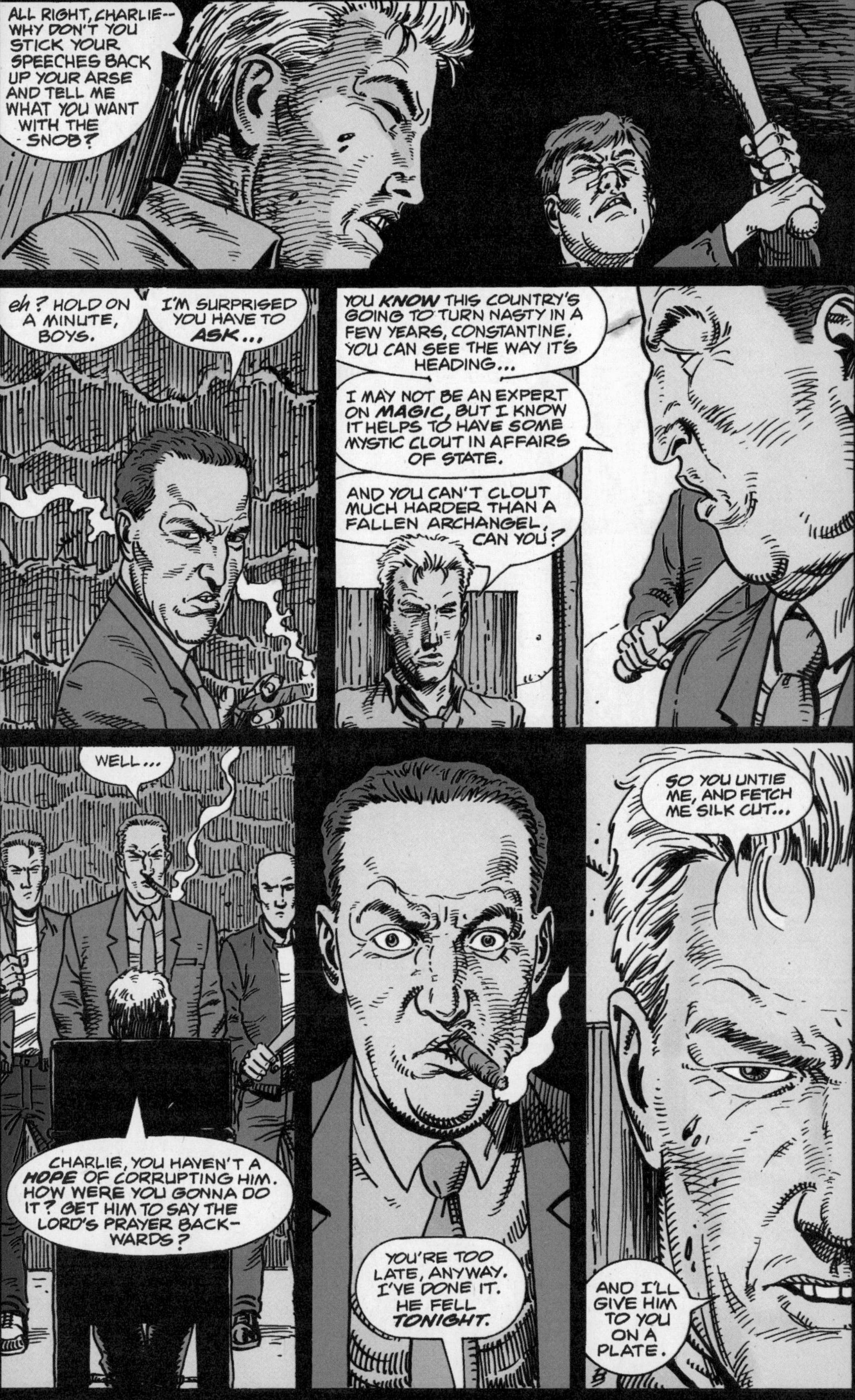
ALL RIGHT, CHARLIE--WHY DON'T YOU STICK YOUR SPEECHES BACK UP YOUR ARSE AND TELL ME WHAT YOU WANT WITH THE SNOB?
eh? HOLD ON A MINUTE, BOYS.
I'M SURPRISED YOU HAVE TO ASK...
YOU KNOW THIS COUNTRY'S GOING TO TURN NASTY IN A FEW YEARS, CONSTANTINE. YOU CAN SEE THE WAY IT'S HEADING...
I MAY NOT BE AN EXPERT ON MAGIC, BUT I KNOW IT HELPS TO HAVE SOME MYSTIC CLOUT IN AFFAIRS OF STATE.
AND YOU CAN'T CLOUT MUCH HARDER THAN A FALLEN ARCHANGEL, CAN YOU?
WELL...
CHARLIE, YOU HAVEN'T A HOPE OF CORRUPTING HIM. HOW WERE YOU GONNA DO IT? GET HIM TO SAY THE LORD'S PRAYER BACKWARDS?
YOU'RE TOO LATE, ANYWAY. I'VE DONE IT. HE FELL TONIGHT.
SO YOU UNTIE ME, AND FETCH ME SILK CUT...
AND I'LL GIVE HIM TO YOU ON A PLATE.

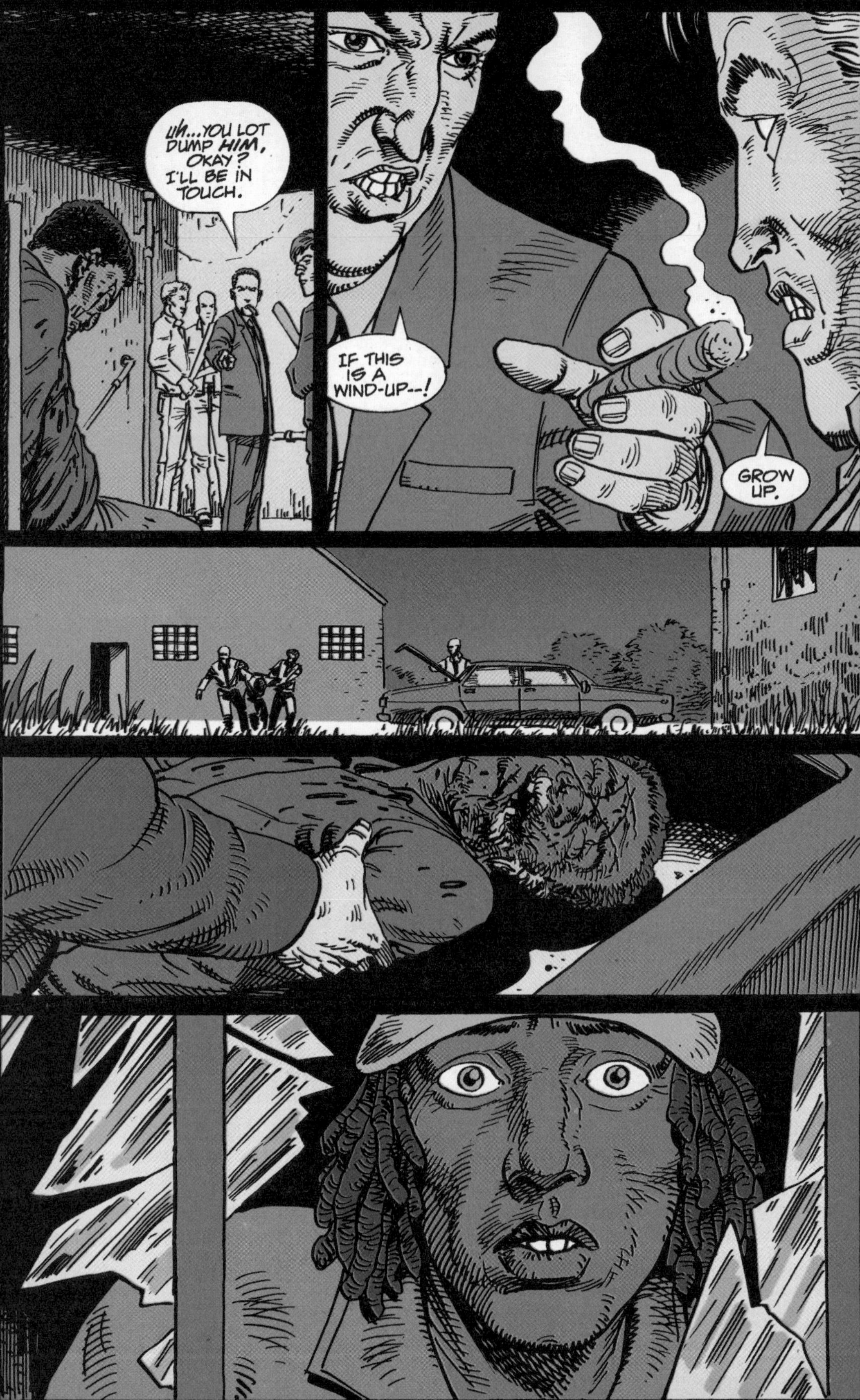
uh...YOU LOT DUMP HIM, OKAY? I'LL BE IN TOUCH.
IF THIS IS A WIND-UP--!
GROW UP.

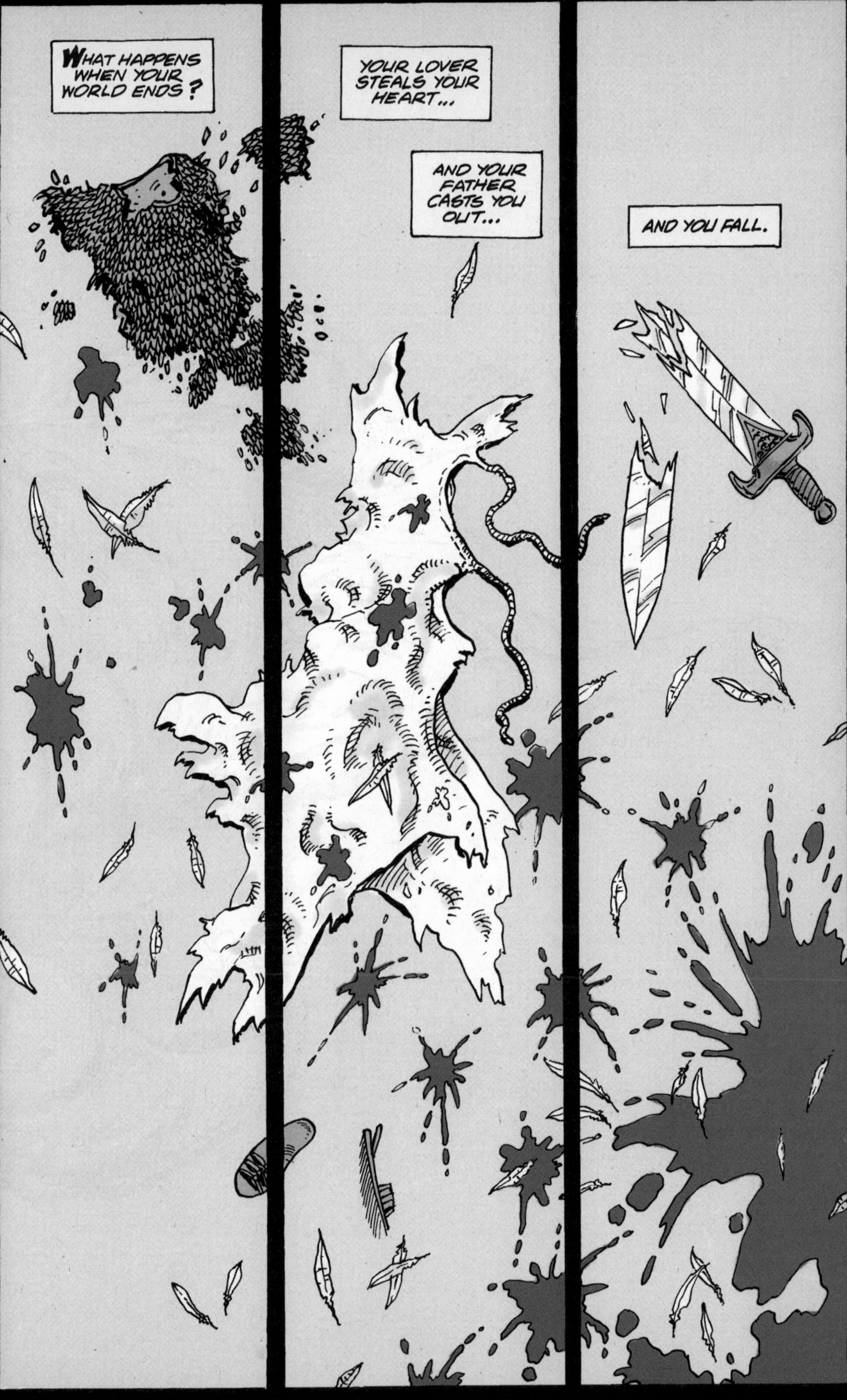
WHAT HAPPENS WHEN YOUR WORLD ENDS?
YOUR LOVER STEALS YOUR HEART...
AND YOUR FATHER CASTS YOU OUT...
AND YOU FALL.

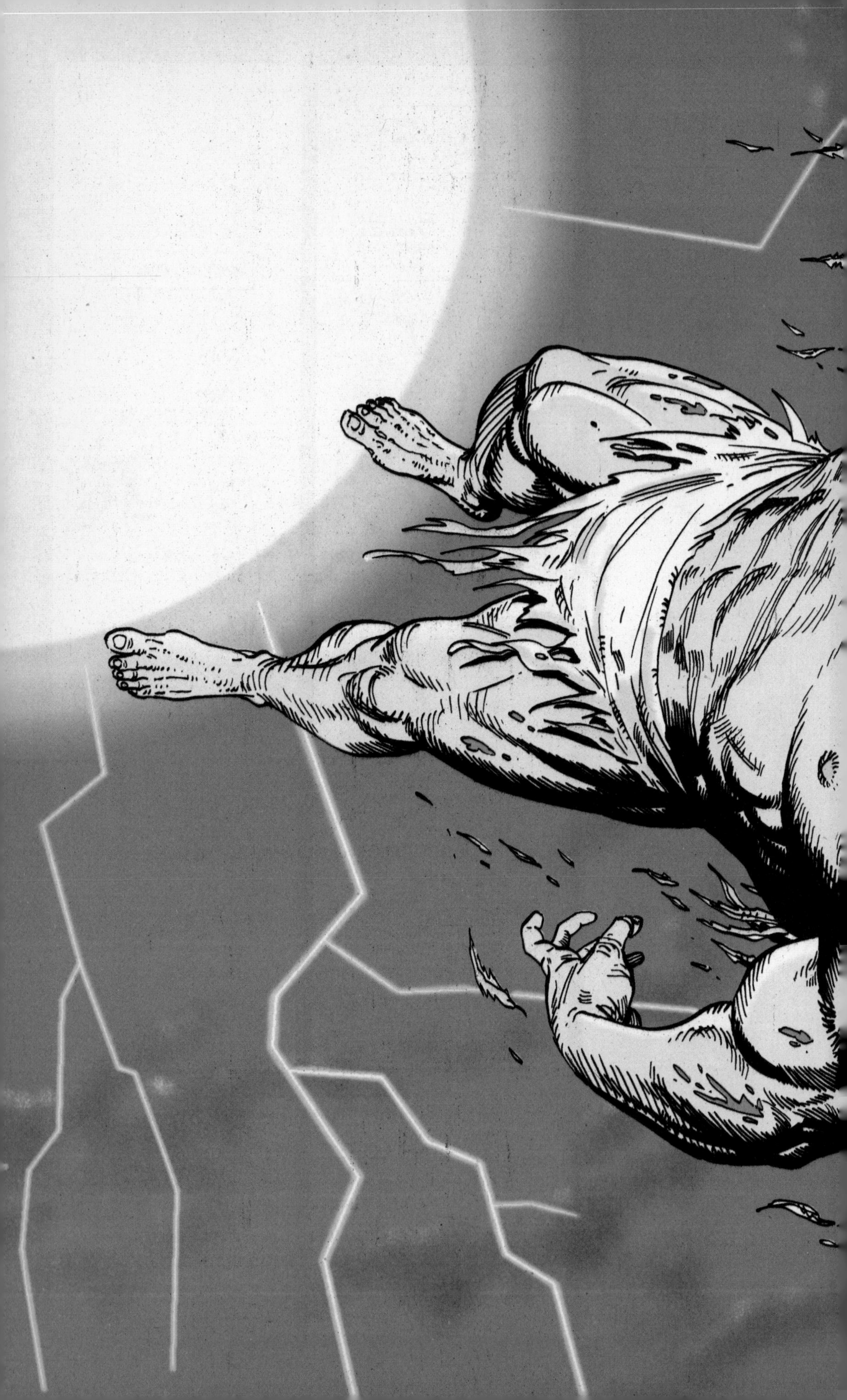

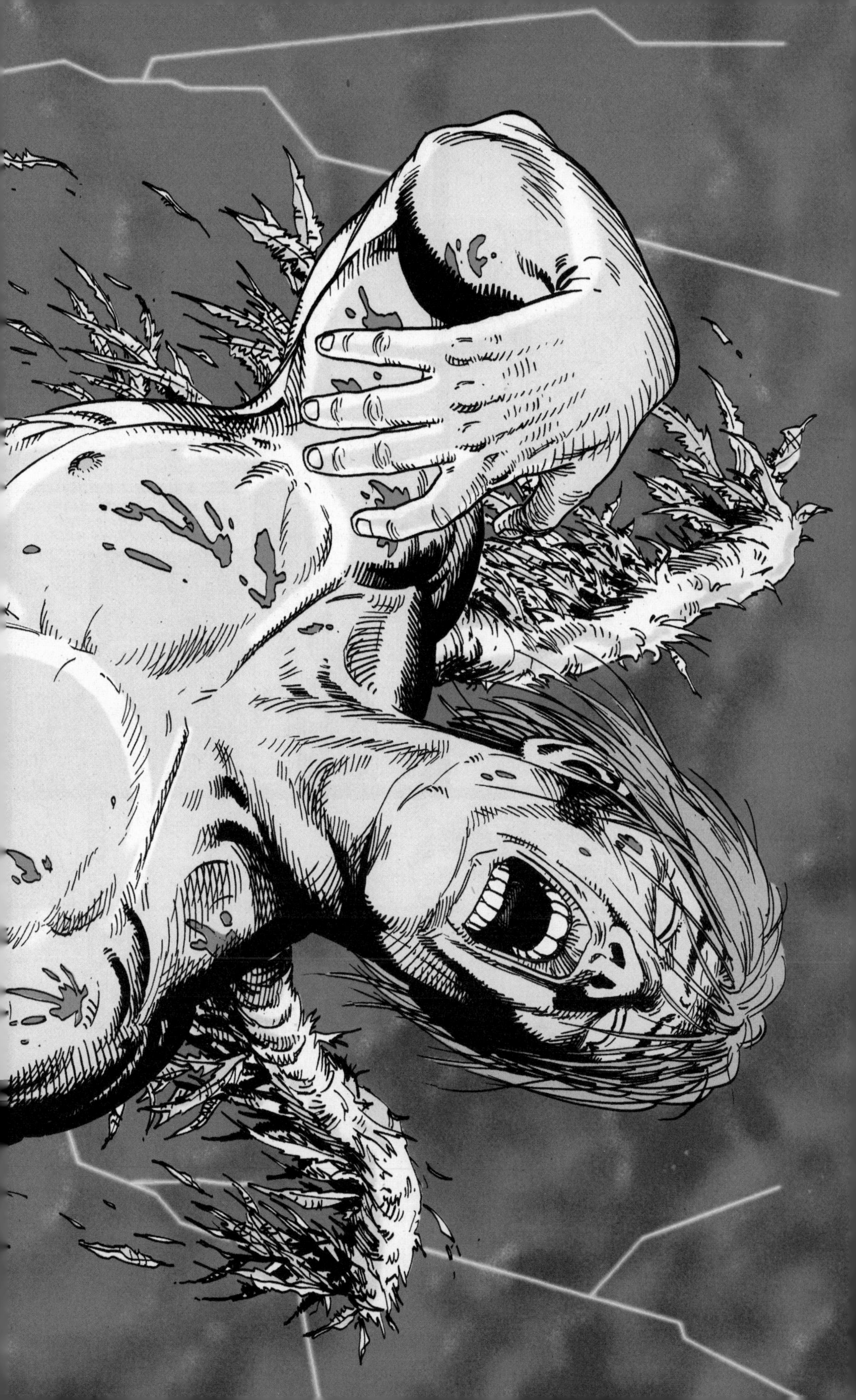

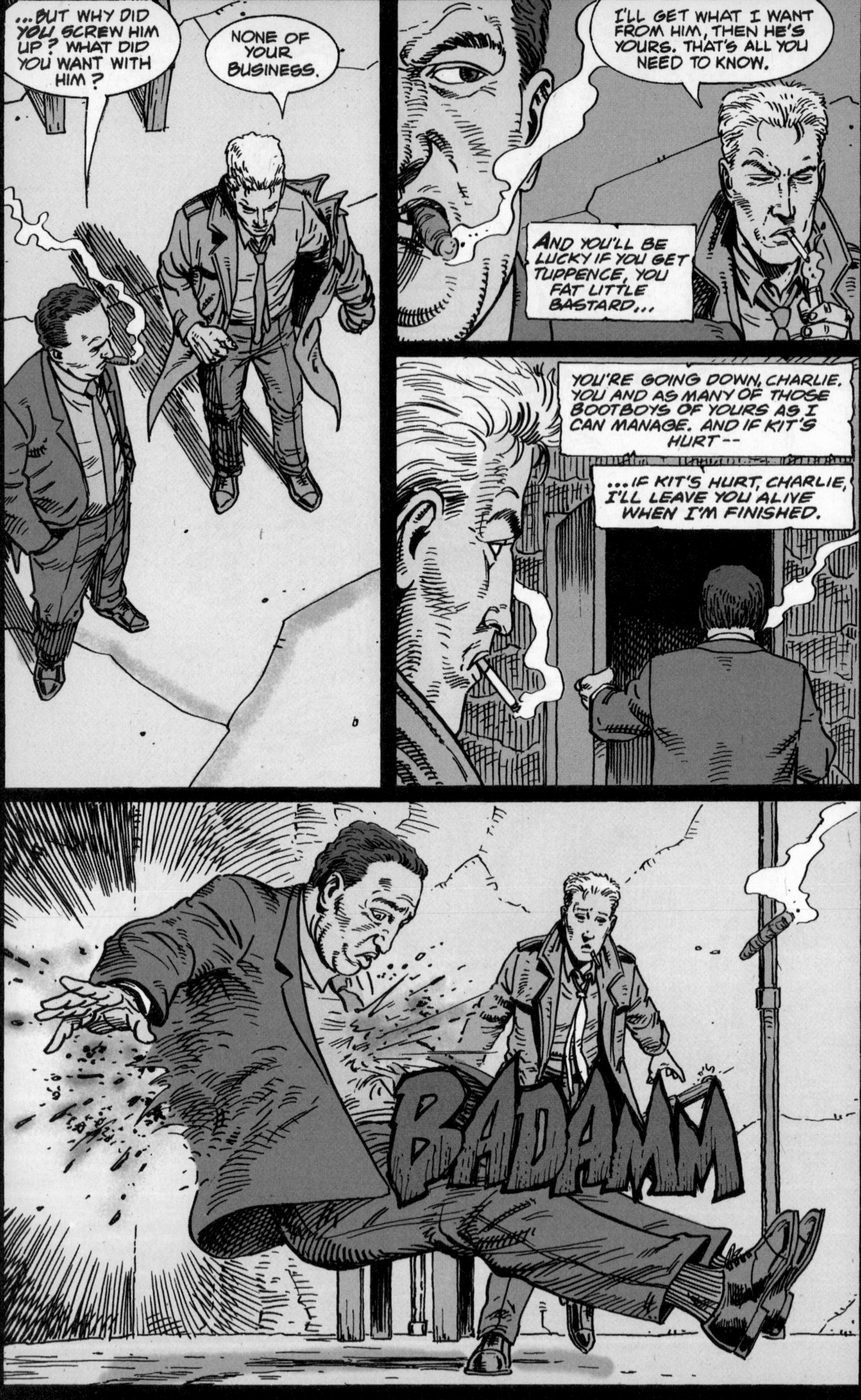
...BUT WHY DID YOU SCREW HIM UP? WHAT DID YOU WANT WITH HIM?
NONE OF YOUR BUSINESS.
I'LL GET WHAT I WANT FROM HIM, THEN HE'S YOURS. THAT'S ALL YOU NEED TO KNOW.
AND YOU'LL BE LUCKY IF YOU GET TUPPENCE, YOU FAT LITTLE BASTARD...
YOU'RE GOING DOWN, CHARLIE. YOU AND AS MANY OF THOSE BOOTBOYS OF YOURS AS I CAN MANAGE. AND IF KIT'S HURT--
...IF KIT'S HURT, CHARLIE, I'LL LEAVE YOU ALIVE WHEN I'M FINISHED.
BADAMM

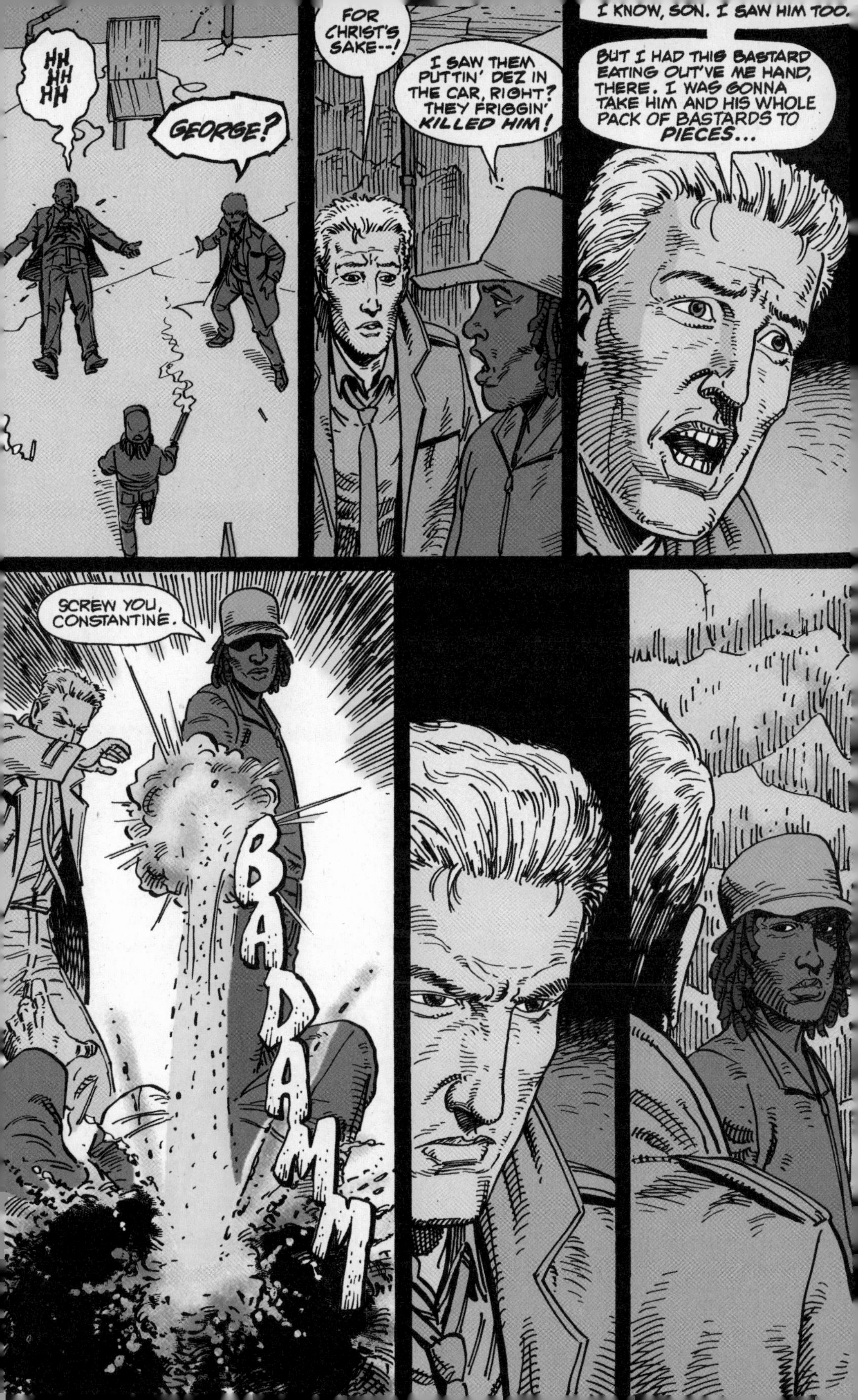
HH HH HH
GEORGE?
FOR CHRIST'S SAKE--!
I SAW THEM PUTTIN' DEZ IN THE CAR, RIGHT? THEY FRIGGIN' KILLED HIM!
I KNOW, SON. I SAW HIM TOO.
BUT I HAD THIS BASTARD EATING OUT'VE ME HAND, THERE. I WAS GONNA TAKE HIM AND HIS WHOLE PACK OF BASTARDS TO PIECES...
SCREW YOU, CONSTANTINE.
BADAMM

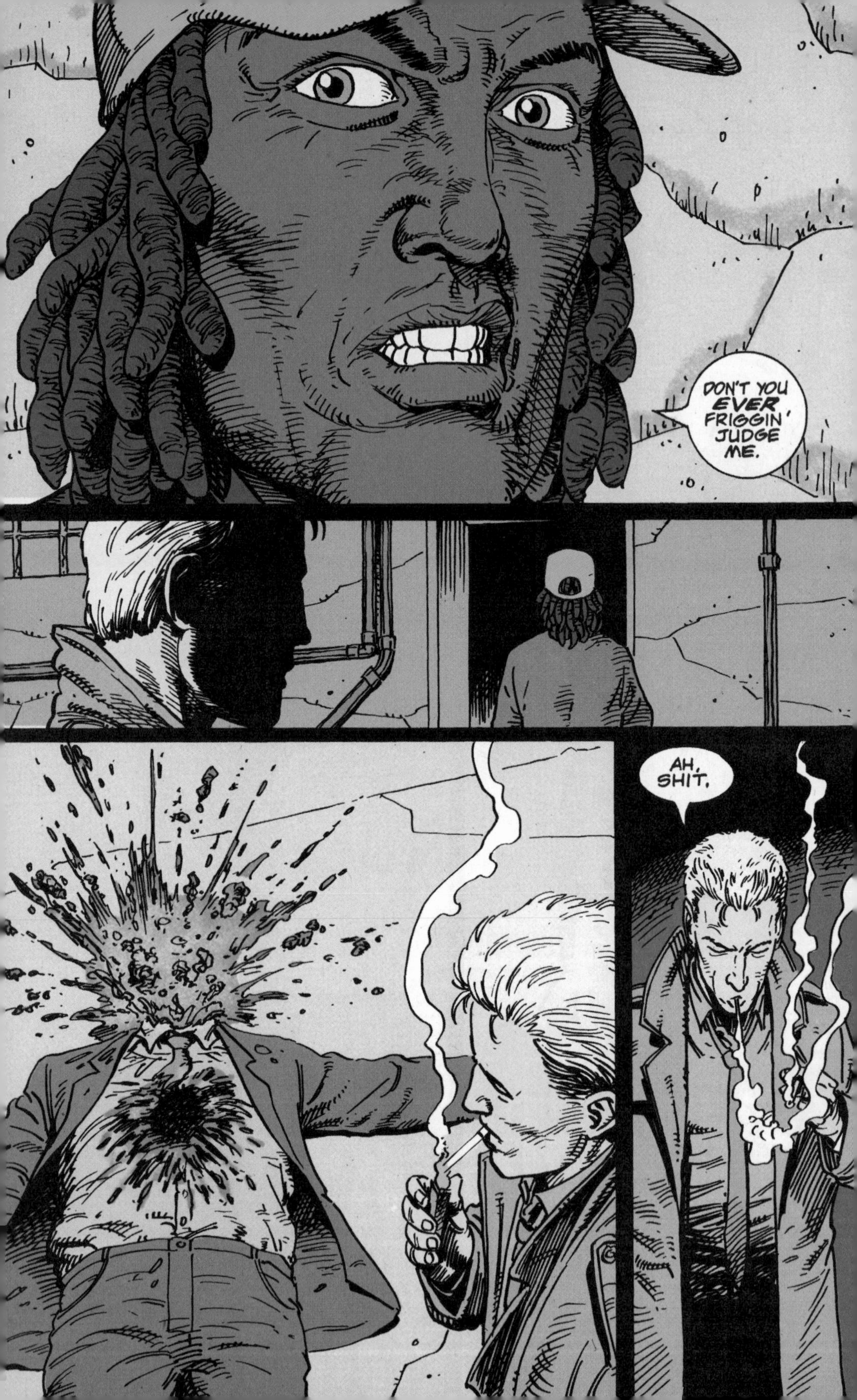
DON'T YOU EVER, FRIGGIN' JUDGE ME.
AH, SHIT.

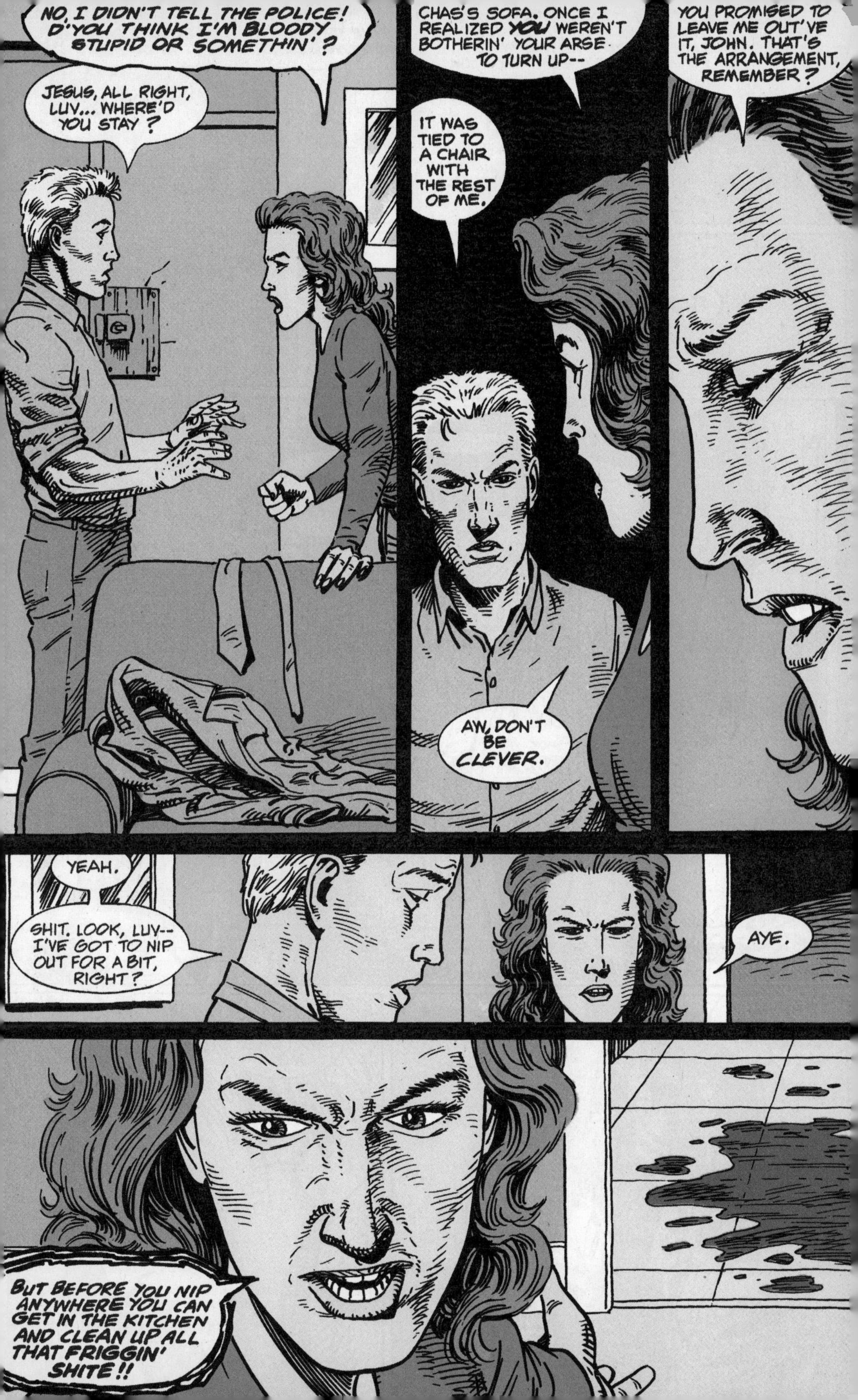
NO, I DIDN'T TELL THE POLICE! D'YOU THINK I'M BLOODY STUPID OR SOMETHIN' ?
JESUS, ALL RIGHT, LUV... WHERE'D YOU STAY ?
CHAS'S SOFA. ONCE I REALIZED YOU WEREN'T BOTHERIN' YOUR ARSE TO TURN UP--
IT WAS TIED TO A CHAIR WITH THE REST OF ME.
AW, DON'T BE CLEVER.
YOU PROMISED TO LEAVE ME OUT'VE IT, JOHN. THAT'S THE ARRANGEMENT, REMEMBER ?
YEAH.
SHIT. LOOK, LUV-- I'VE GOT TO NIP OUT FOR A BIT, RIGHT?
AYE.
BUT BEFORE YOU NIP ANYWHERE YOU CAN GET IN THE KITCHEN AND CLEAN UP ALL THAT FRIGGIN' SHITE!!

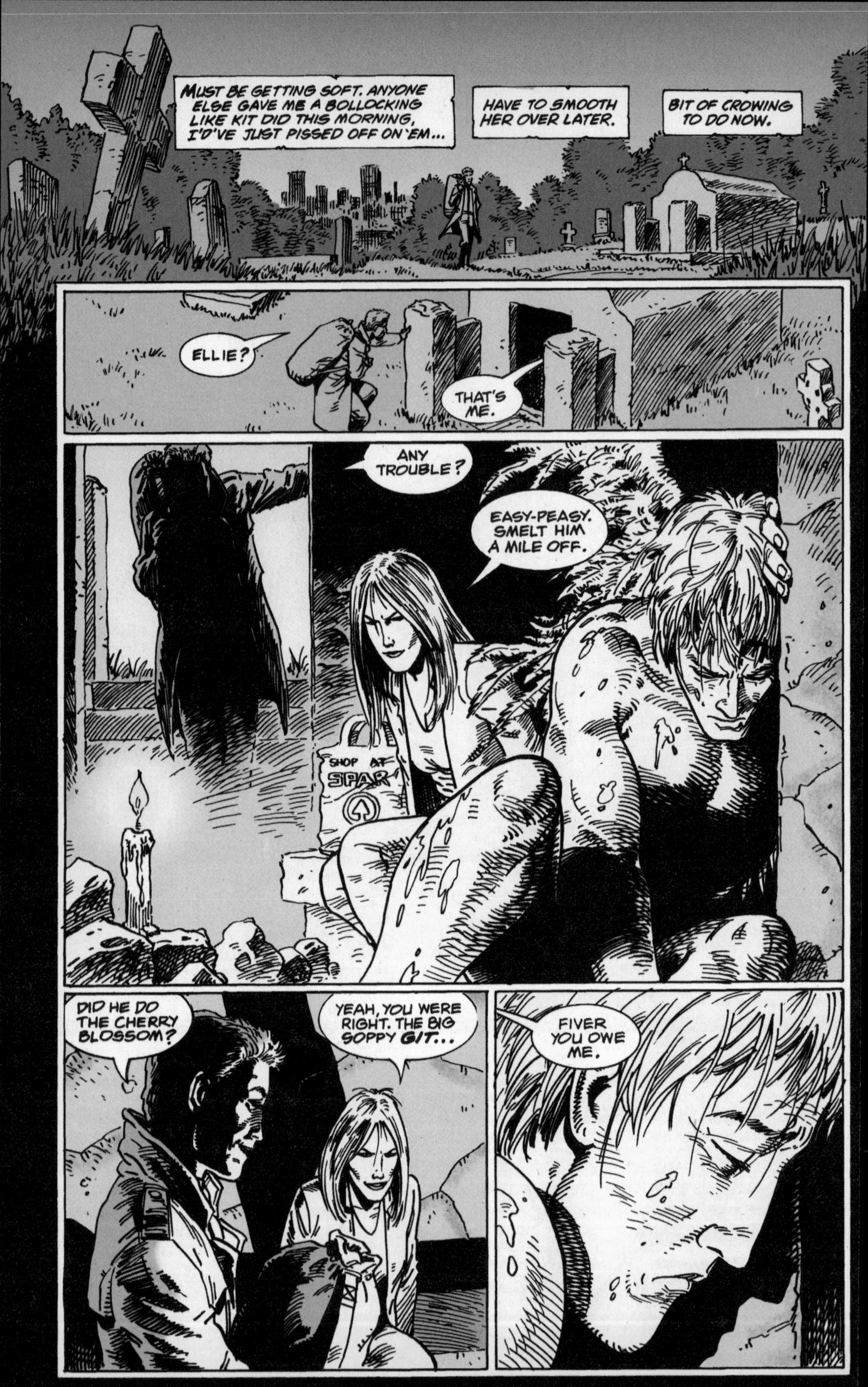

MUST BE GETTING SOFT. ANYONE ELSE GAVE ME A BOLLOCKING LIKE KIT DID THIS MORNING, I'D'VE JUST PISSED OFF ON 'EM...
HAVE TO SMOOTH HER OVER LATER.
BIT OF CROWING TO DO NOW.
ELLIE?
THAT'S ME.
ANY TROUBLE?
EASY-PEASY. SMELT HIM A MILE OFF.
SHOP AT SPAR
DID HE DO THE CHERRY BLOSSOM?
YEAH, YOU WERE RIGHT. THE BIG SOPPY GIT...
FIVER YOU OWE ME.

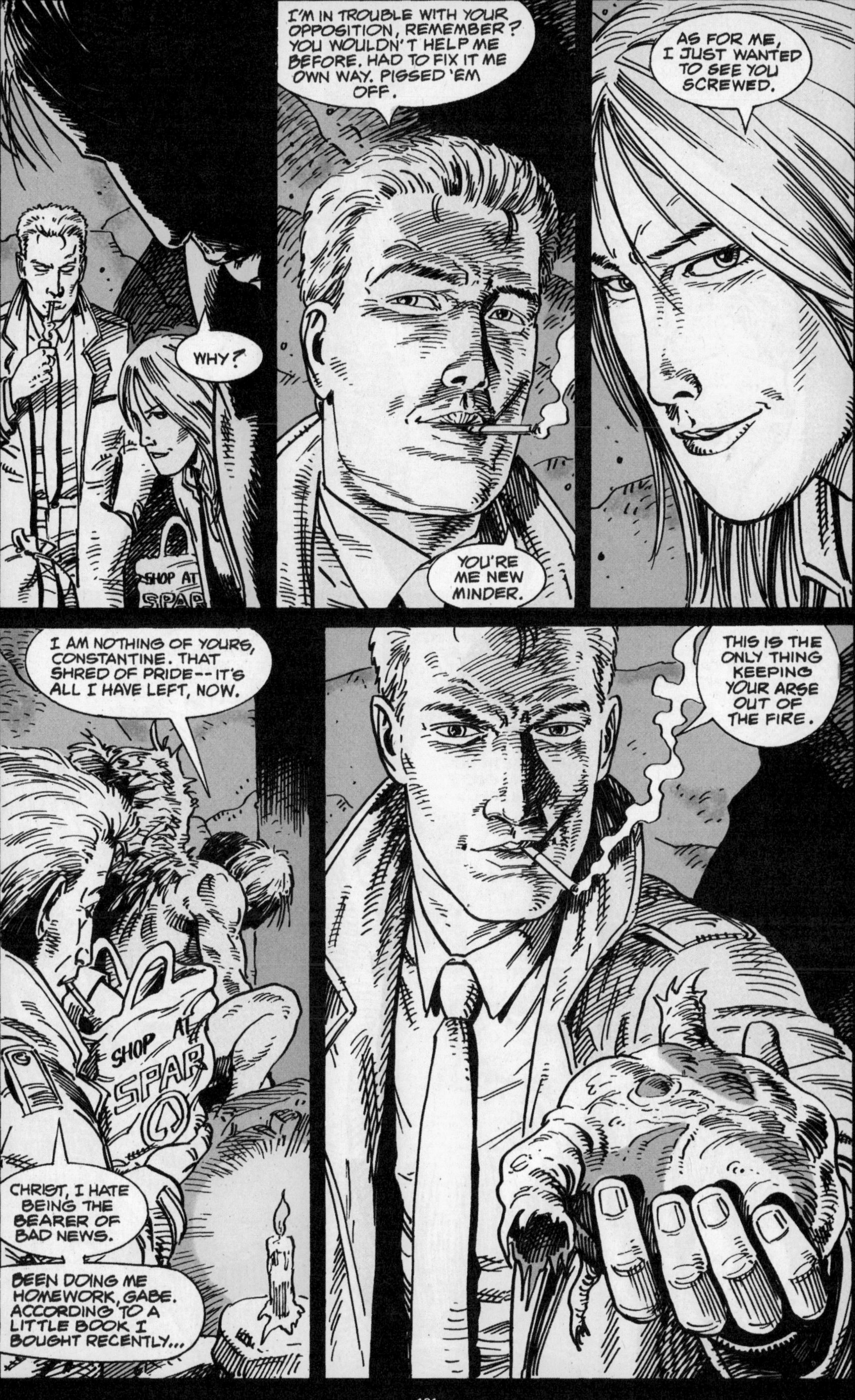
WHY?
I'M IN TROUBLE WITH YOUR OPPOSITION, REMEMBER? YOU WOULDN'T HELP ME BEFORE. HAD TO FIX IT ME OWN WAY. PISSED 'EM OFF.
YOU'RE ME NEW MINDER.
AS FOR ME, I JUST WANTED TO SEE YOU SCREWED.
SHOP AT SPAR
I AM NOTHING OF YOURS, CONSTANTINE. THAT SHRED OF PRIDE--IT'S ALL I HAVE LEFT, NOW.
CHRIST, I HATE BEING THE BEARER OF BAD NEWS.
BEEN DOING ME HOMEWORK, GABE. ACCORDING TO A LITTLE BOOK I BOUGHT RECENTLY...
SHOP AT SPAR
THIS IS THE ONLY THING KEEPING YOUR ARSE OUT OF THE FIRE.

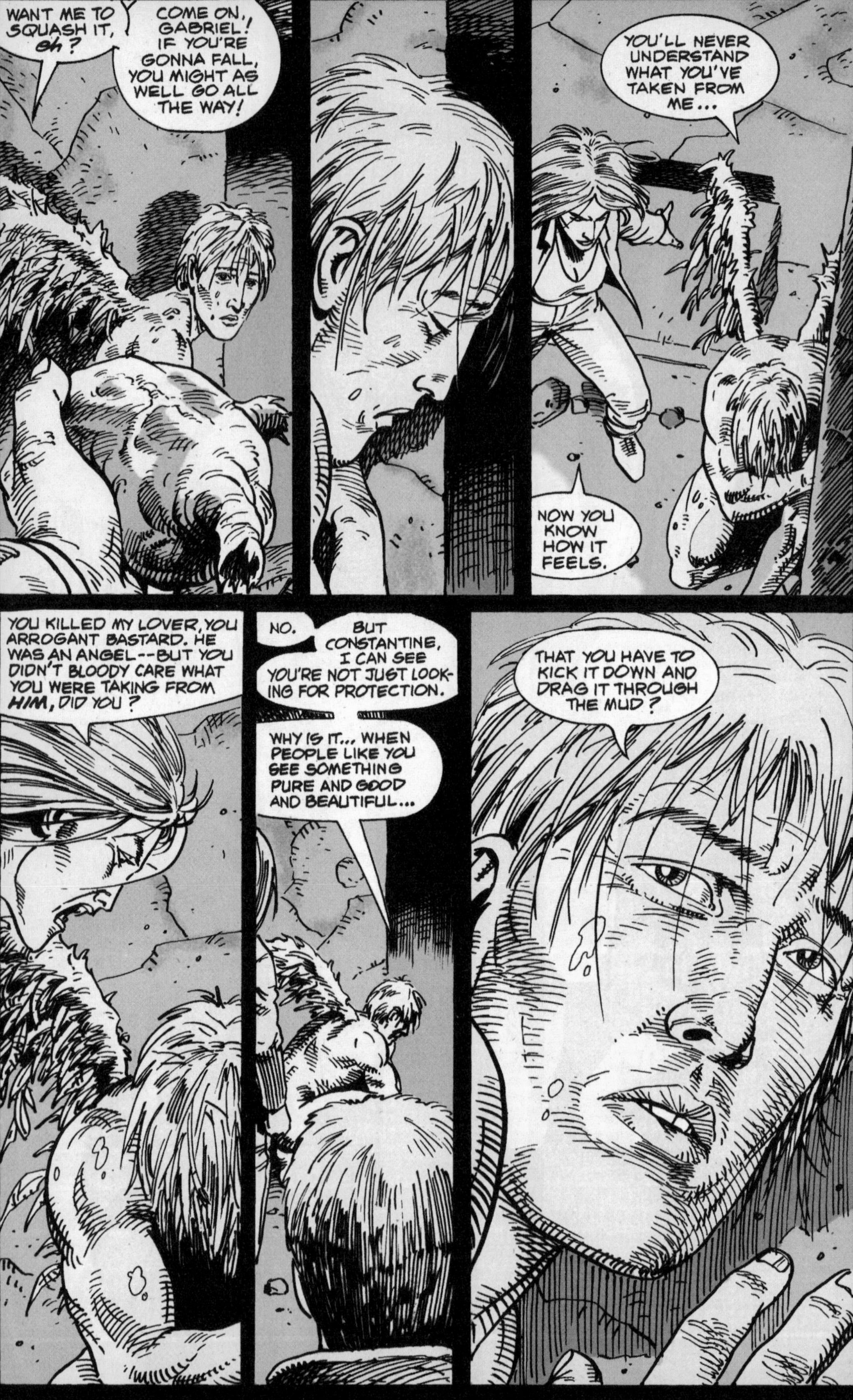
WANT ME TO SQUASH IT, eh ?
COME ON, GABRIEL! IF YOU'RE GONNA FALL, YOU MIGHT AS WELL GO ALL THE WAY!
YOU'LL NEVER UNDERSTAND WHAT YOU'VE TAKEN FROM ME...
NOW YOU KNOW HOW IT FEELS.
YOU KILLED MY LOVER, YOU ARROGANT BASTARD. HE WAS AN ANGEL--BUT YOU DIDN'T BLOODY CARE WHAT YOU WERE TAKING FROM HIM, DID YOU ?
NO.
BUT CONSTANTINE, I CAN SEE YOU'RE NOT JUST LOOKING FOR PROTECTION.
WHY IS IT... WHEN PEOPLE LIKE YOU SEE SOMETHING PURE AND GOOD AND BEAUTIFUL...
THAT YOU HAVE TO KICK IT DOWN AND DRAG IT THROUGH THE MUD ?

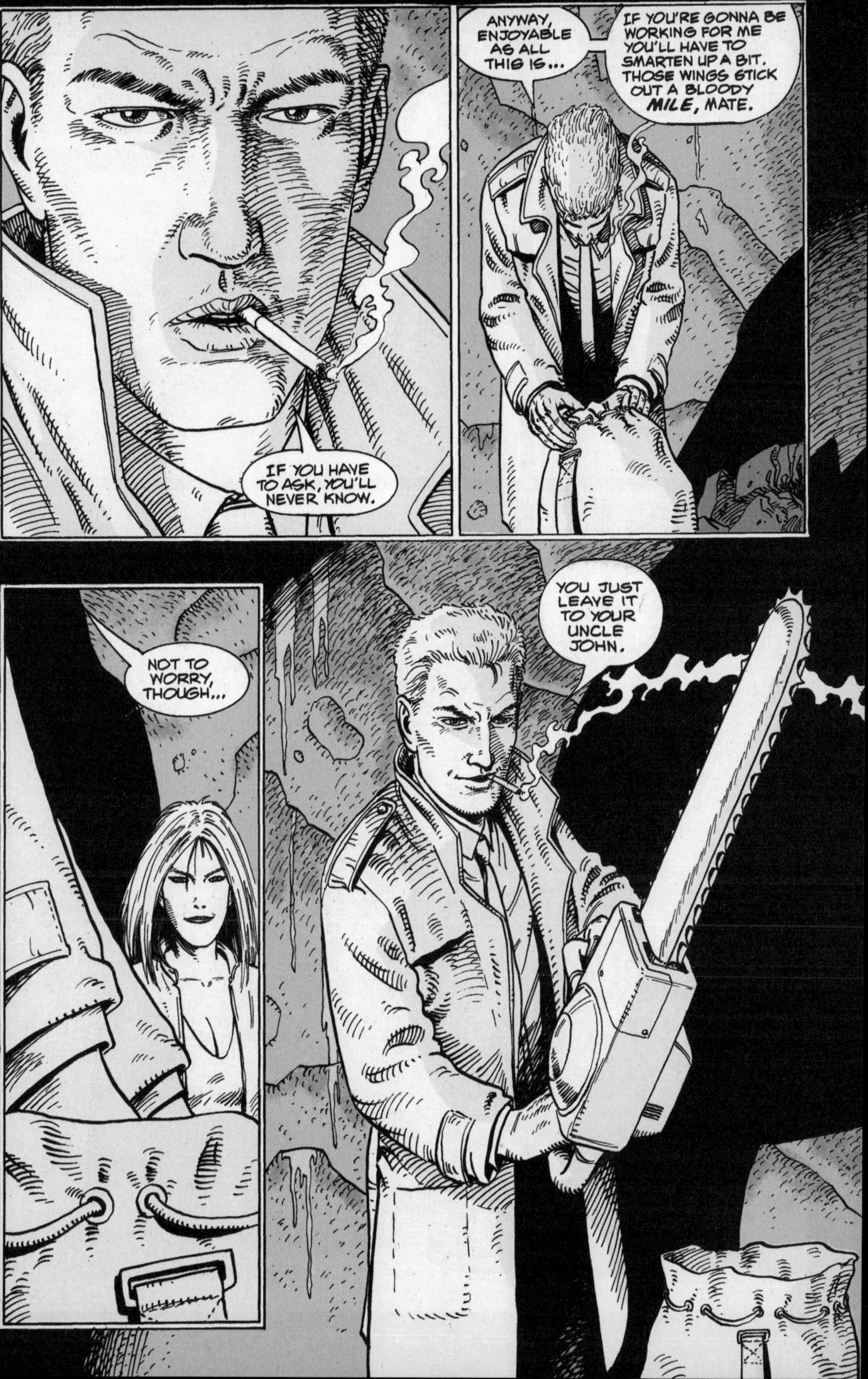
IF YOU HAVE TO ASK, YOU'LL NEVER KNOW.
ANYWAY, ENJOYABLE AS ALL THIS IS...
IF YOU'RE GONNA BE WORKING FOR ME YOU'LL HAVE TO SMARTEN UP A BIT. THOSE WINGS STICK OUT A BLOODY MILE, MATE.
NOT TO WORRY, THOUGH...
YOU JUST LEAVE IT TO YOUR UNCLE JOHN.

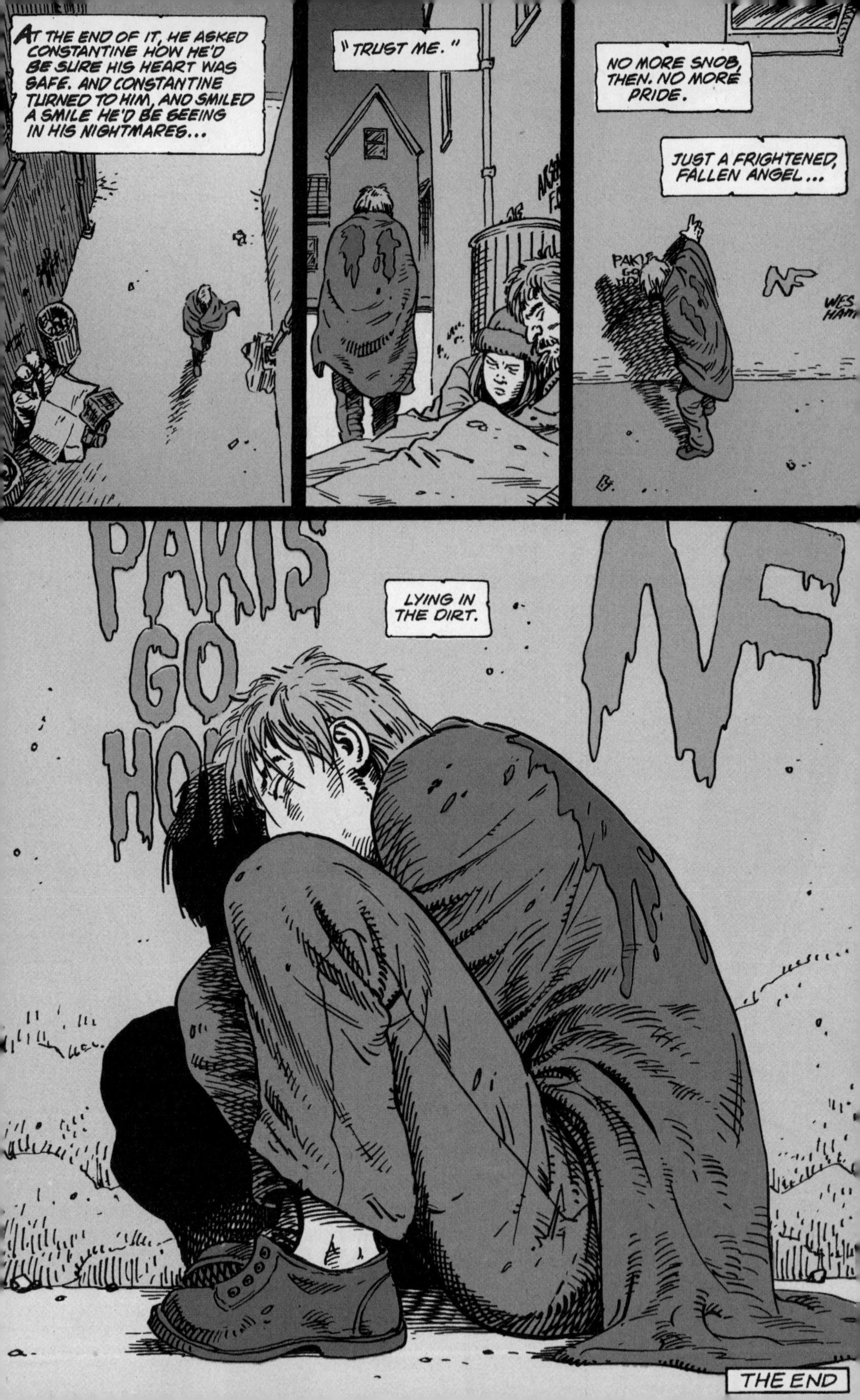
AT THE END OF IT, HE ASKED CONSTANTINE HOW HE'D BE SURE HIS HEART WAS SAFE. AND CONSTANTINE TURNED TO HIM, AND SMILED A SMILE HE'D BE SEEING IN HIS NIGHTMARES...
"TRUST ME."
NO MORE SNOB, THEN. NO MORE PRIDE.
JUST A FRIGHTENED, FALLEN ANGEL...
NF
PAKIS GO HO
NF
LYING IN THE DIRT.
THE END

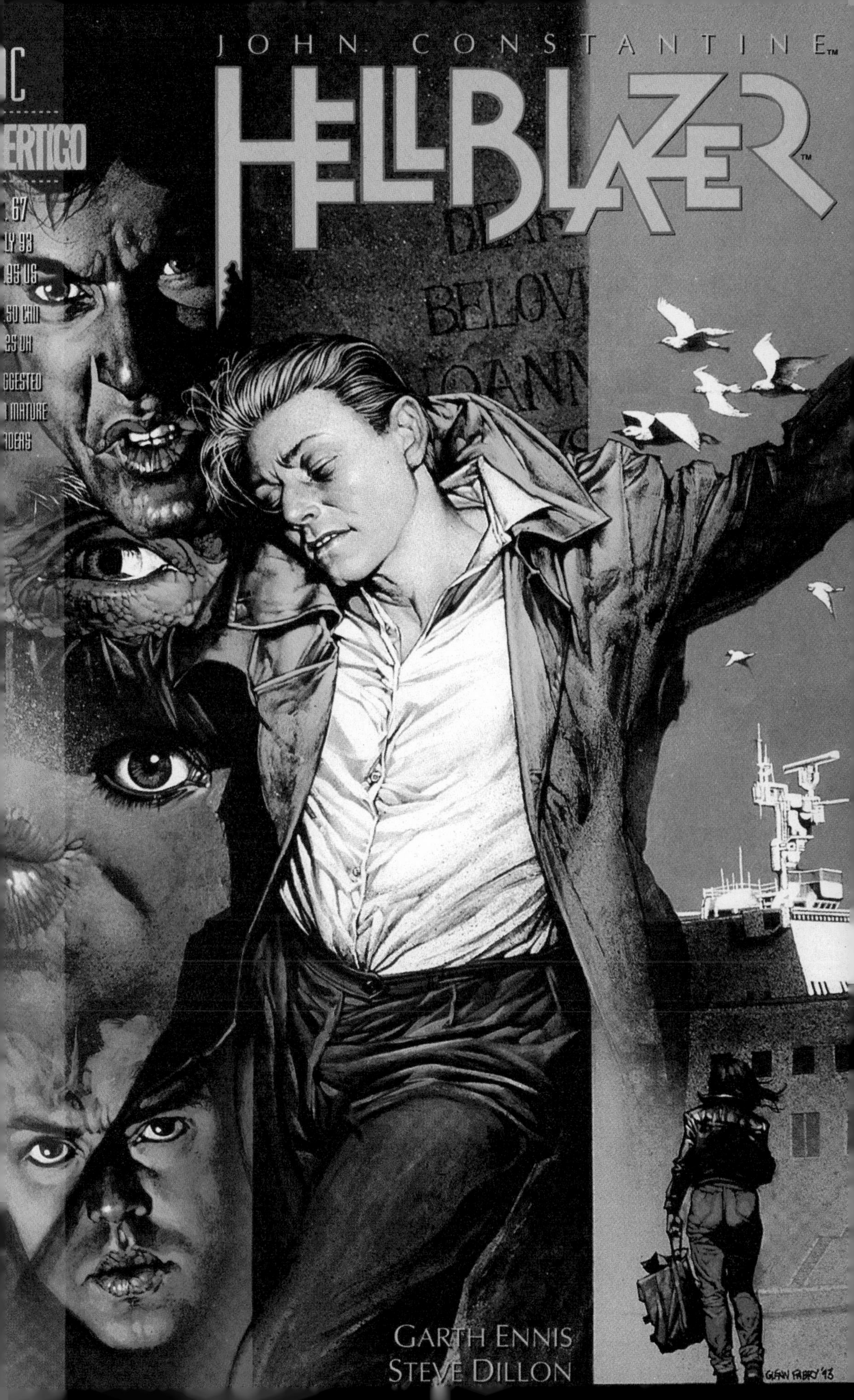

JOHN CONSTANTINE
HELLBLAZER
GARTH ENNIS
STEVE DILLON
GLENN FABRY '93

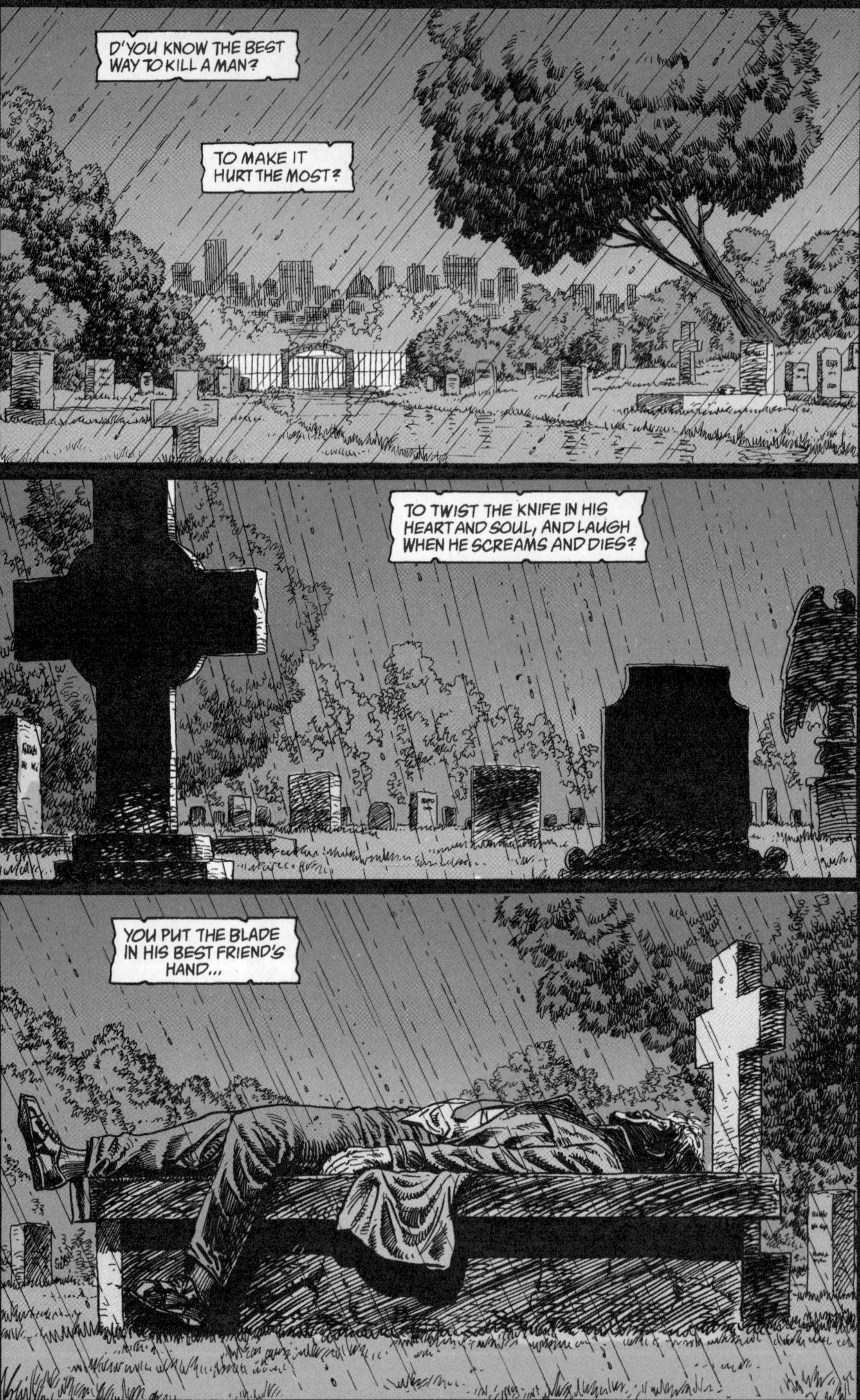
D'YOU KNOW THE BEST WAY TO KILL A MAN?
TO MAKE IT HURT THE MOST?
TO TWIST THE KNIFE IN HIS HEART AND SOUL, AND LAUGH WHEN HE SCREAMS AND DIES?
YOU PUT THE BLADE IN HIS BEST FRIEND'S HAND...

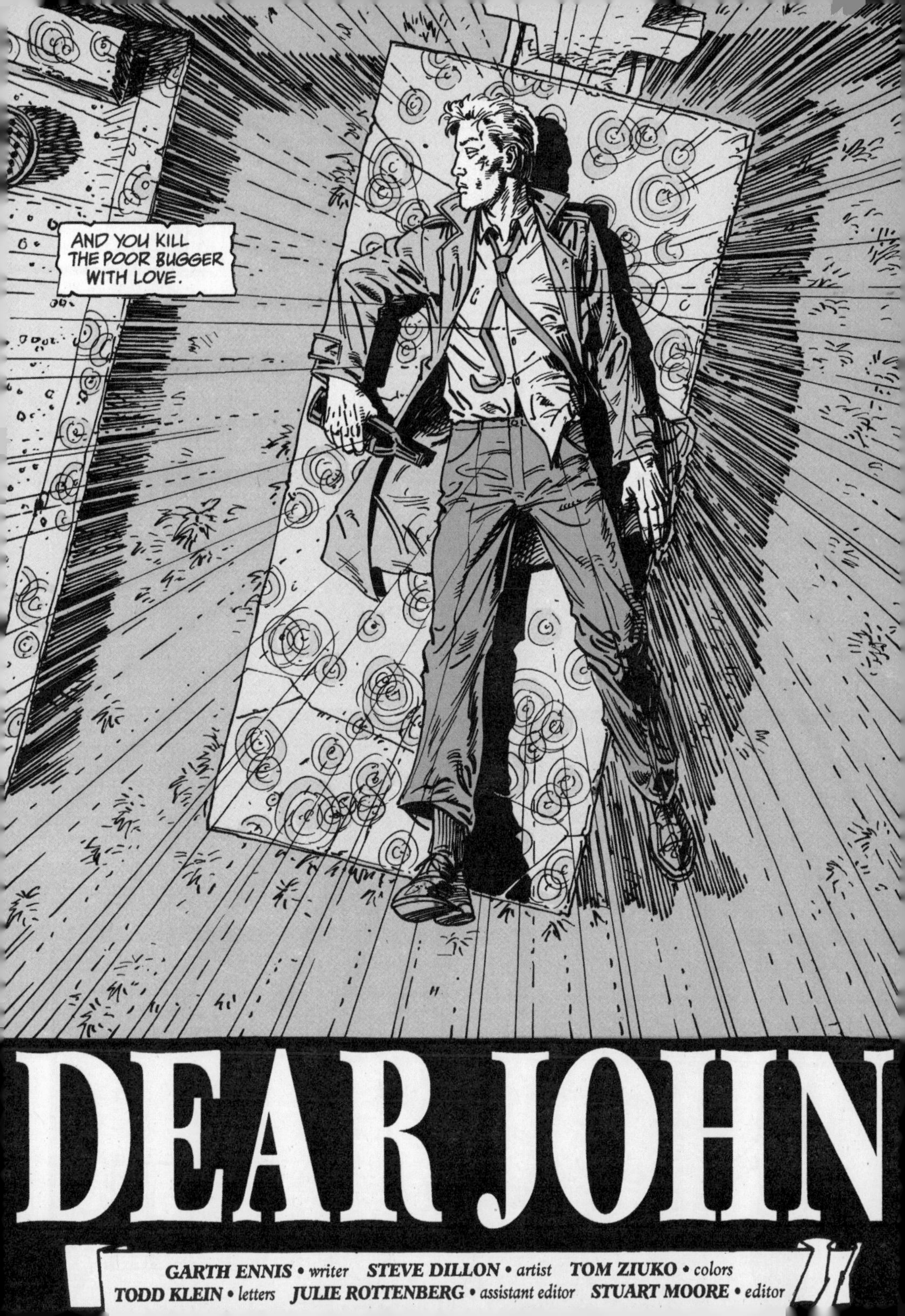
AND YOU KILL THE POOR BUGGER WITH LOVE.

DEAR JOHN

GARTH ENNIS • *writer* **STEVE DILLON** • *artist* **TOM ZIUKO** • *colors*
TODD KLEIN • *letters* **JULIE ROTTENBERG** • *assistant editor* **STUART MOORE** • *editor*

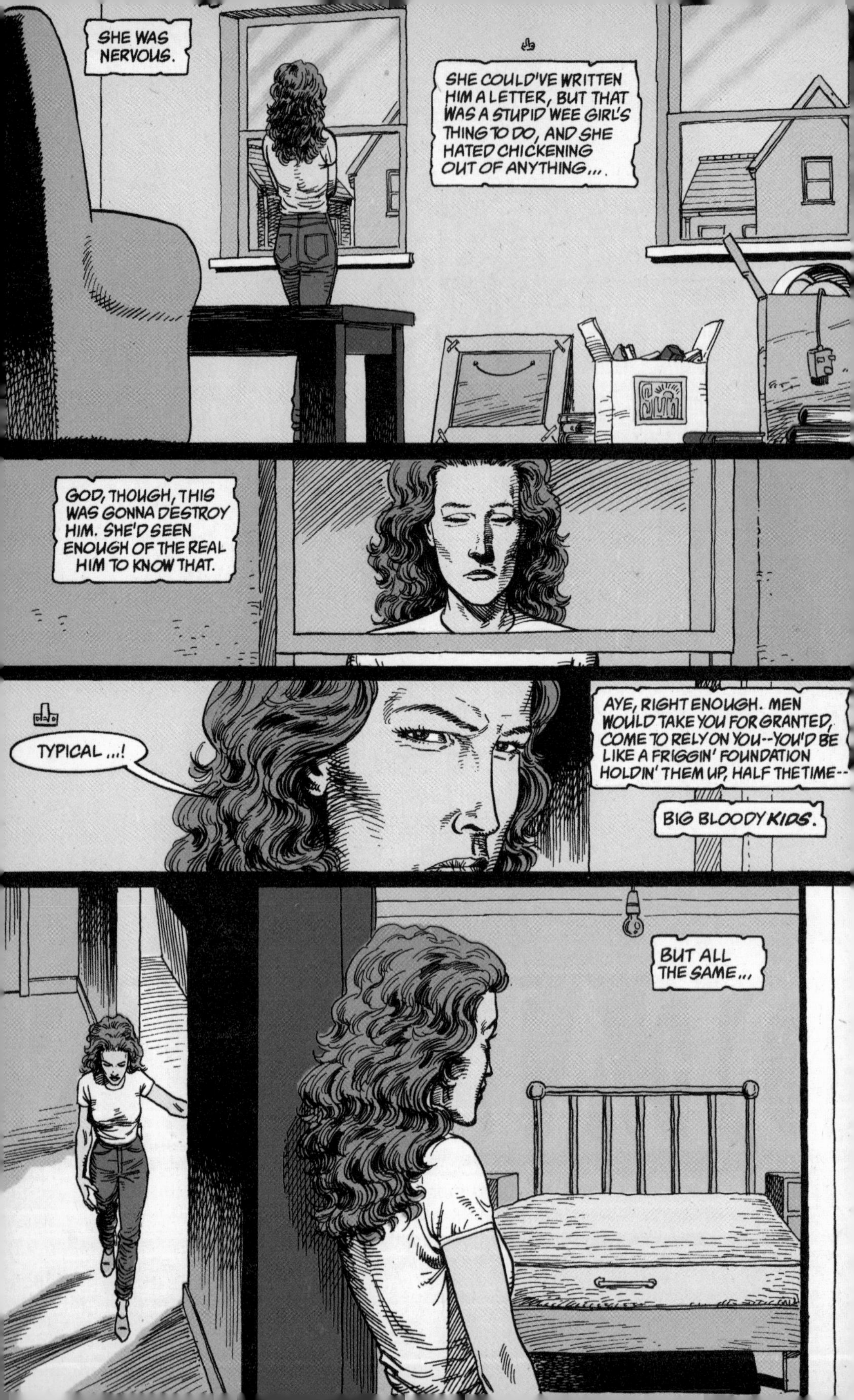

SHE WAS NERVOUS.
SHE COULD'VE WRITTEN HIM A LETTER, BUT THAT WAS A STUPID WEE GIRL'S THING TO DO, AND SHE HATED CHICKENING OUT OF ANYTHING....
GOD, THOUGH, THIS WAS GONNA DESTROY HIM. SHE'D SEEN ENOUGH OF THE REAL HIM TO KNOW THAT.
TYPICAL...!
AYE, RIGHT ENOUGH. MEN WOULD TAKE YOU FOR GRANTED, COME TO RELY ON YOU--YOU'D BE LIKE A FRIGGIN' FOUNDATION HOLDIN' THEM UP, HALF THE TIME--
BIG BLOODY KIDS.
BUT ALL THE SAME...

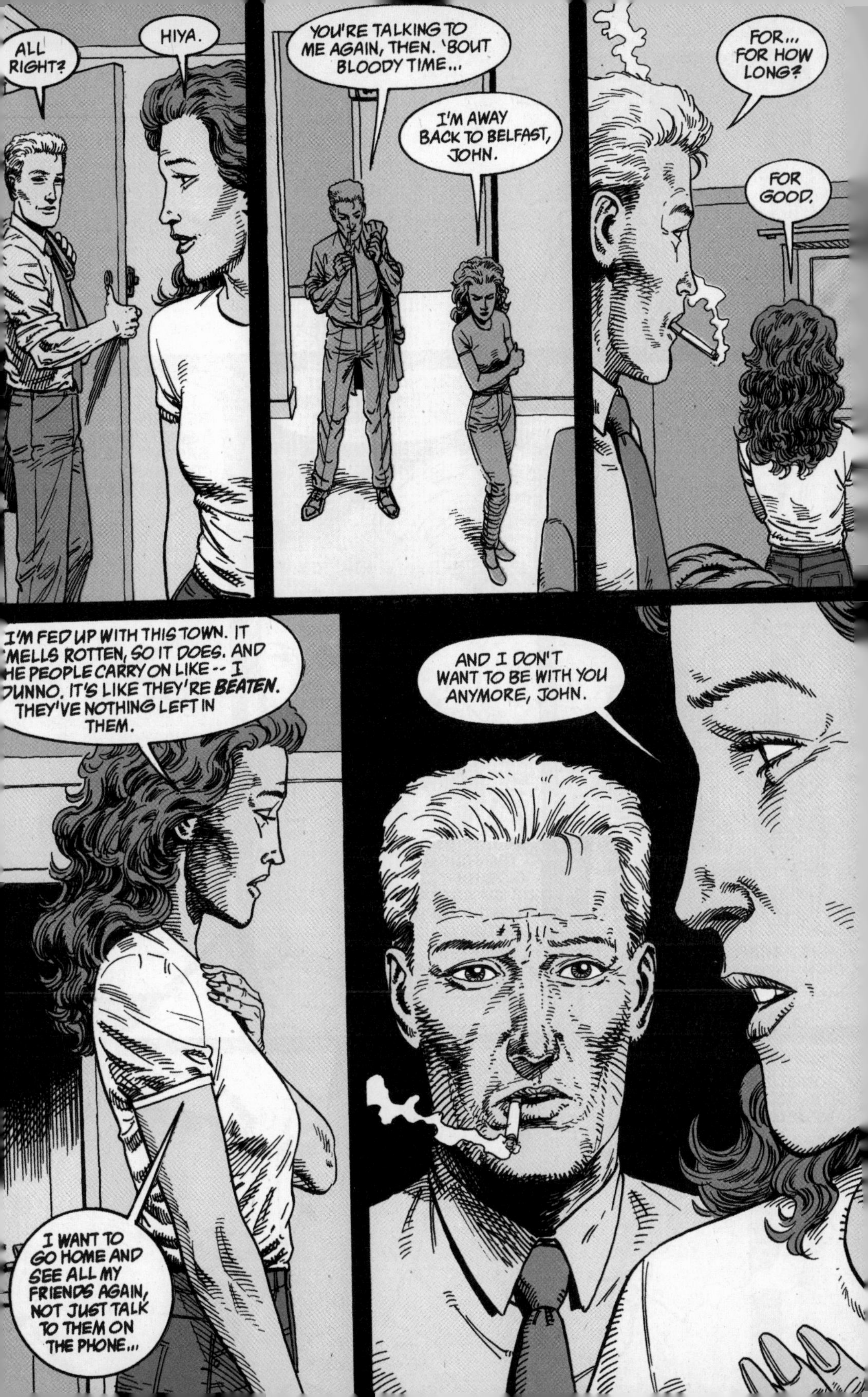
ALL RIGHT?
HIYA.
YOU'RE TALKING TO ME AGAIN, THEN. 'BOUT BLOODY TIME...
I'M AWAY BACK TO BELFAST, JOHN.
FOR... FOR HOW LONG?
FOR GOOD.
I'M FED UP WITH THIS TOWN. IT SMELLS ROTTEN, SO IT DOES. AND THE PEOPLE CARRY ON LIKE -- I DUNNO. IT'S LIKE THEY'RE BEATEN. THEY'VE NOTHING LEFT IN THEM.
I WANT TO GO HOME AND SEE ALL MY FRIENDS AGAIN, NOT JUST TALK TO THEM ON THE PHONE...
AND I DON'T WANT TO BE WITH YOU ANYMORE, JOHN.

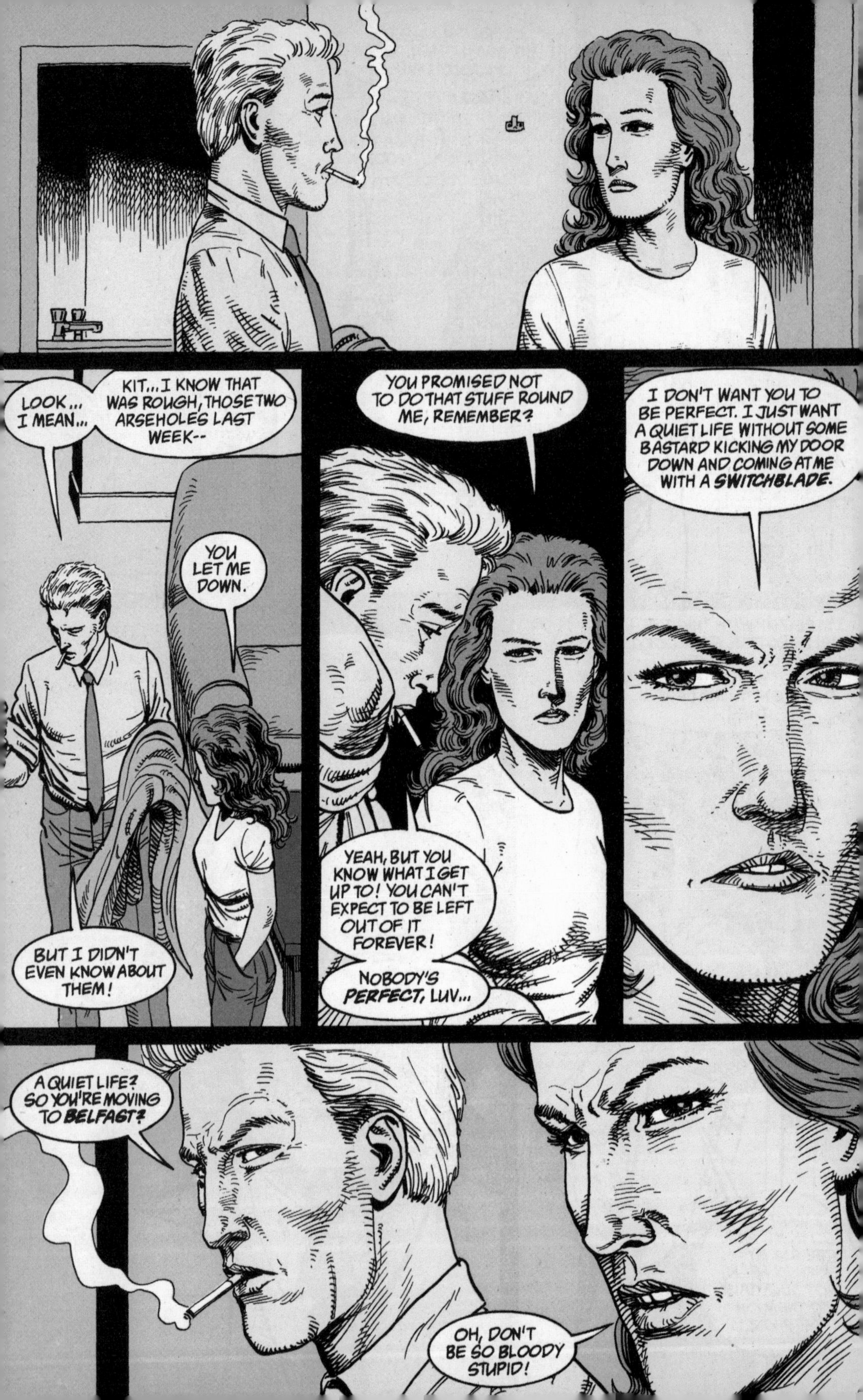
LOOK... I MEAN...
KIT... I KNOW THAT WAS ROUGH, THOSE TWO ARSEHOLES LAST WEEK--
YOU LET ME DOWN.
BUT I DIDN'T EVEN KNOW ABOUT THEM!
YOU PROMISED NOT TO DO THAT STUFF ROUND ME, REMEMBER?
YEAH, BUT YOU KNOW WHAT I GET UP TO! YOU CAN'T EXPECT TO BE LEFT OUT OF IT FOREVER!
NOBODY'S PERFECT, LUV...
I DON'T WANT YOU TO BE PERFECT. I JUST WANT A QUIET LIFE WITHOUT SOME BASTARD KICKING MY DOOR DOWN AND COMING AT ME WITH A SWITCHBLADE.
A QUIET LIFE? SO YOU'RE MOVING TO BELFAST?
OH, DON'T BE SO BLOODY STUPID!

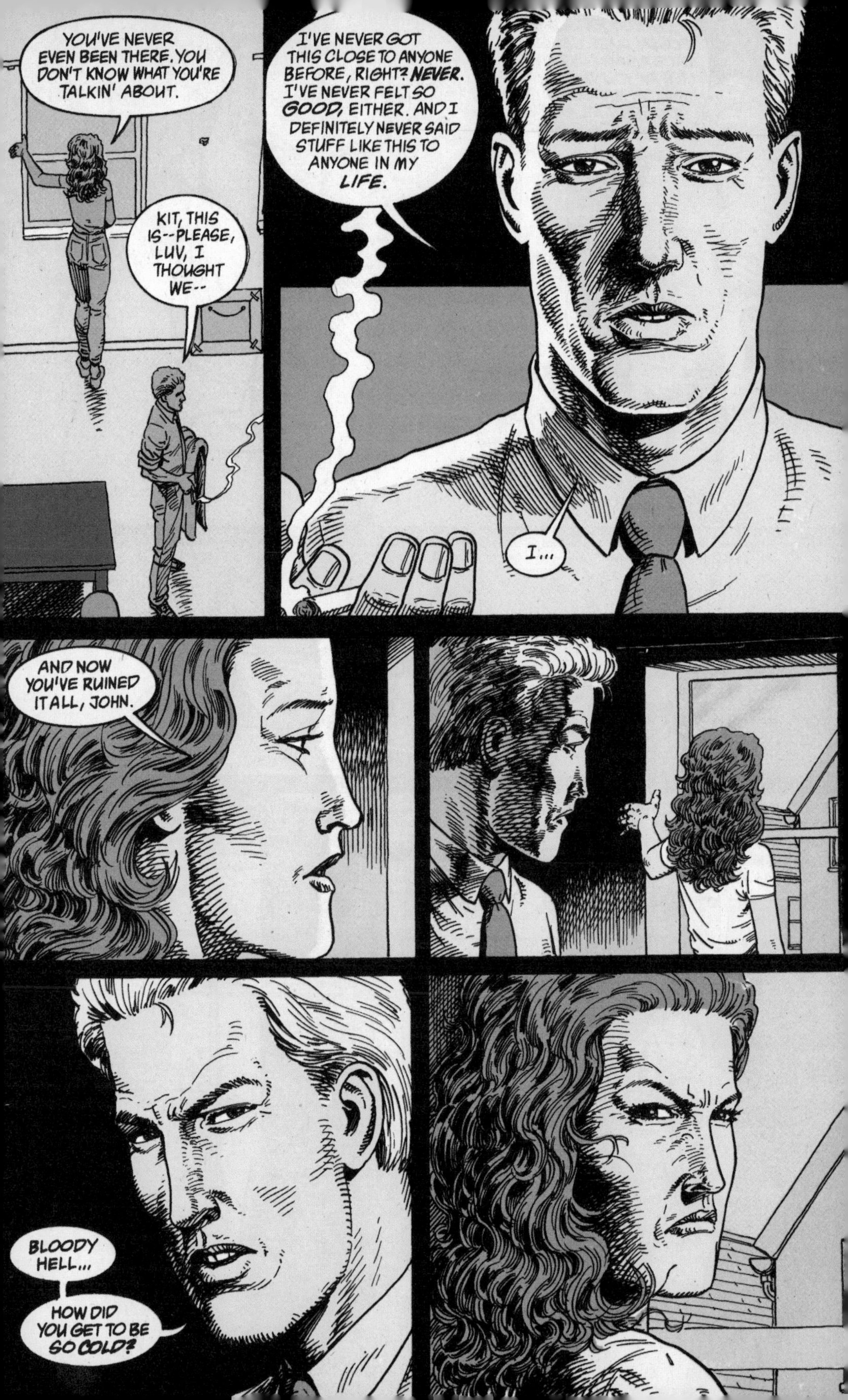
YOU'VE NEVER EVEN BEEN THERE. YOU DON'T KNOW WHAT YOU'RE TALKIN' ABOUT.
KIT, THIS IS--PLEASE, LUV, I THOUGHT WE--
I'VE NEVER GOT THIS CLOSE TO ANYONE BEFORE, RIGHT? NEVER. I'VE NEVER FELT SO GOOD, EITHER. AND I DEFINITELY NEVER SAID STUFF LIKE THIS TO ANYONE IN MY LIFE.
I...
AND NOW YOU'VE RUINED IT ALL, JOHN.
BLOODY HELL...
HOW DID YOU GET TO BE SO COLD?

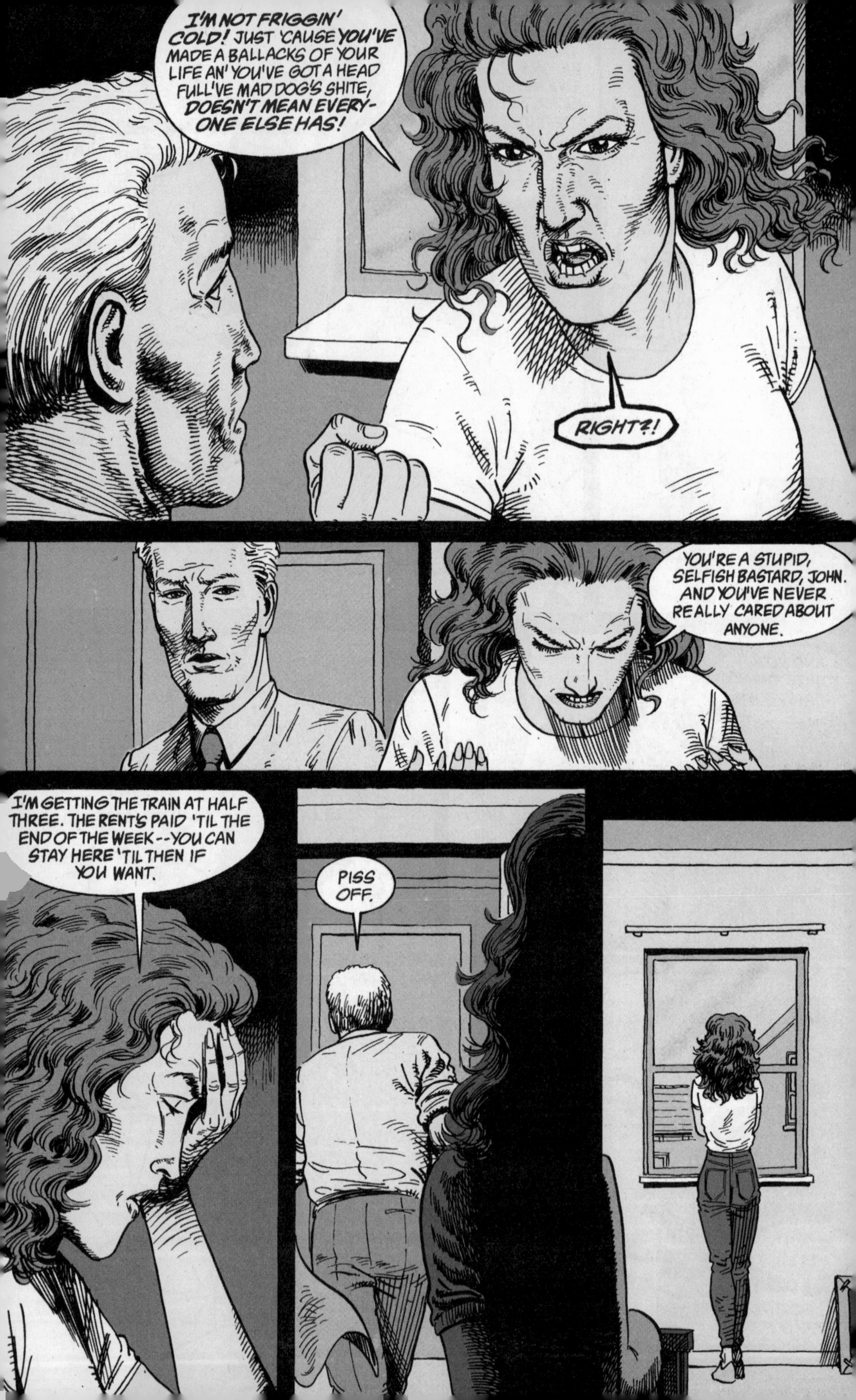
I'M NOT FRIGGIN' COLD! JUST 'CAUSE YOU'VE MADE A BALLACKS OF YOUR LIFE AN' YOU'VE GOT A HEAD FULL'VE MAD DOG'S SHITE, DOESN'T MEAN EVERY-ONE ELSE HAS!
RIGHT?!
YOU'RE A STUPID, SELFISH BASTARD, JOHN. AND YOU'VE NEVER REALLY CARED ABOUT ANYONE.
I'M GETTING THE TRAIN AT HALF THREE. THE RENT'S PAID 'TIL THE END OF THE WEEK--YOU CAN STAY HERE 'TIL THEN IF YOU WANT.
PISS OFF.

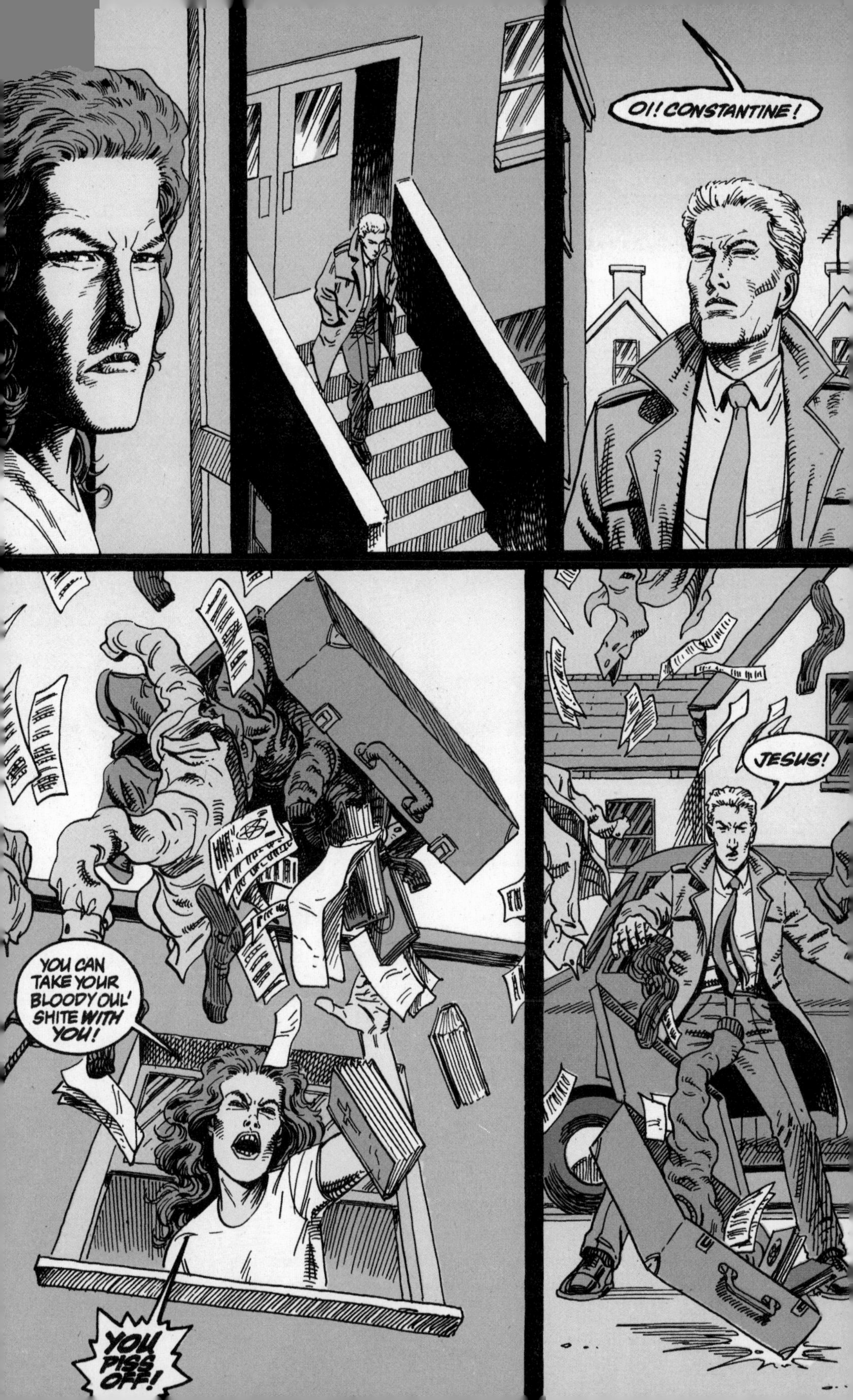
OI! CONSTANTINE!
YOU CAN TAKE YOUR BLOODY OUL' SHITE WITH YOU!
YOU PISS OFF!
JESUS!

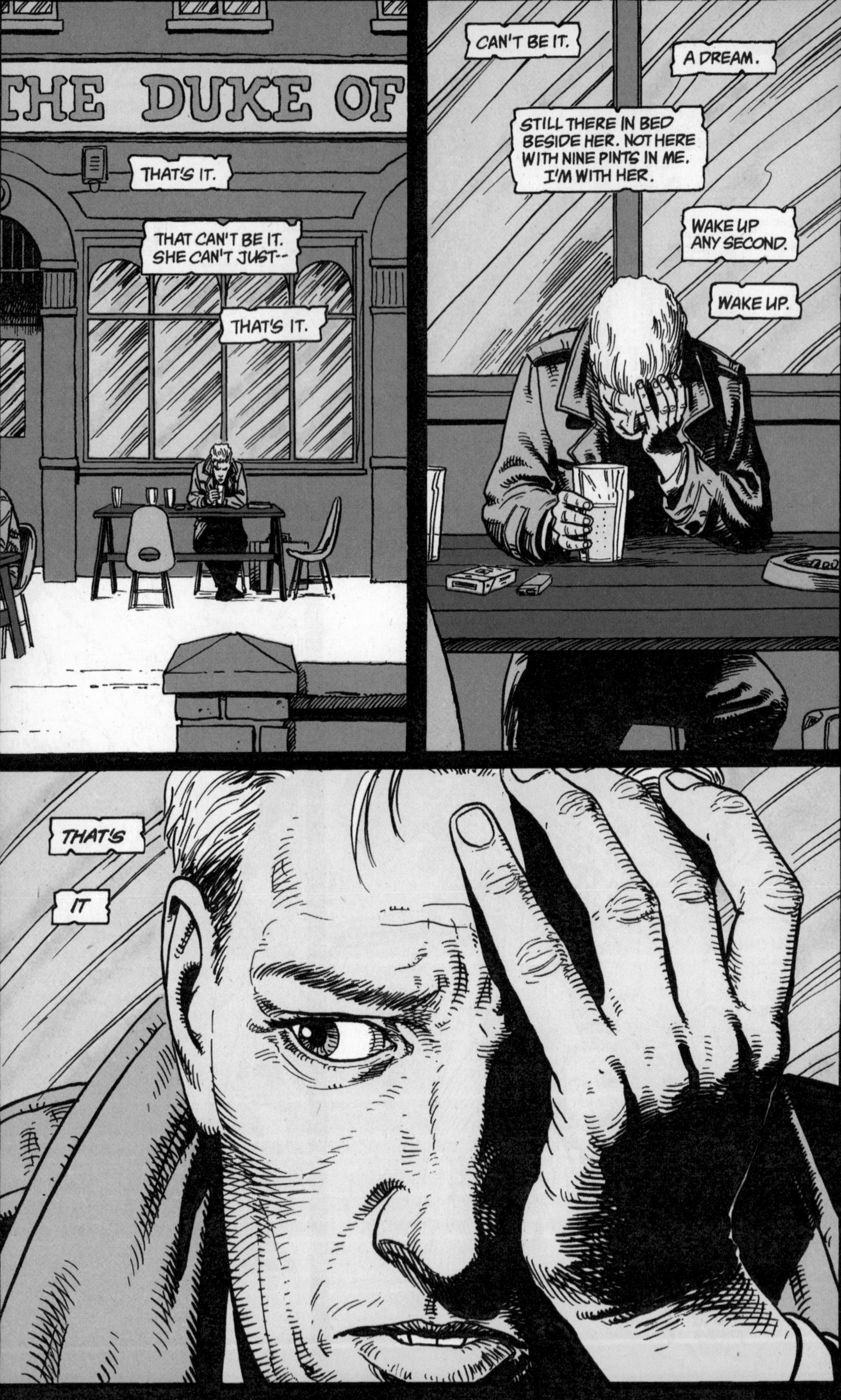
THE DUKE OF
THAT'S IT.
THAT CAN'T BE IT. SHE CAN'T JUST--
THAT'S IT.
CAN'T BE IT.
A DREAM.
STILL THERE IN BED BESIDE HER. NOT HERE WITH NINE PINTS IN ME. I'M WITH HER.
WAKE UP ANY SECOND.
WAKE UP.
THAT'S
IT

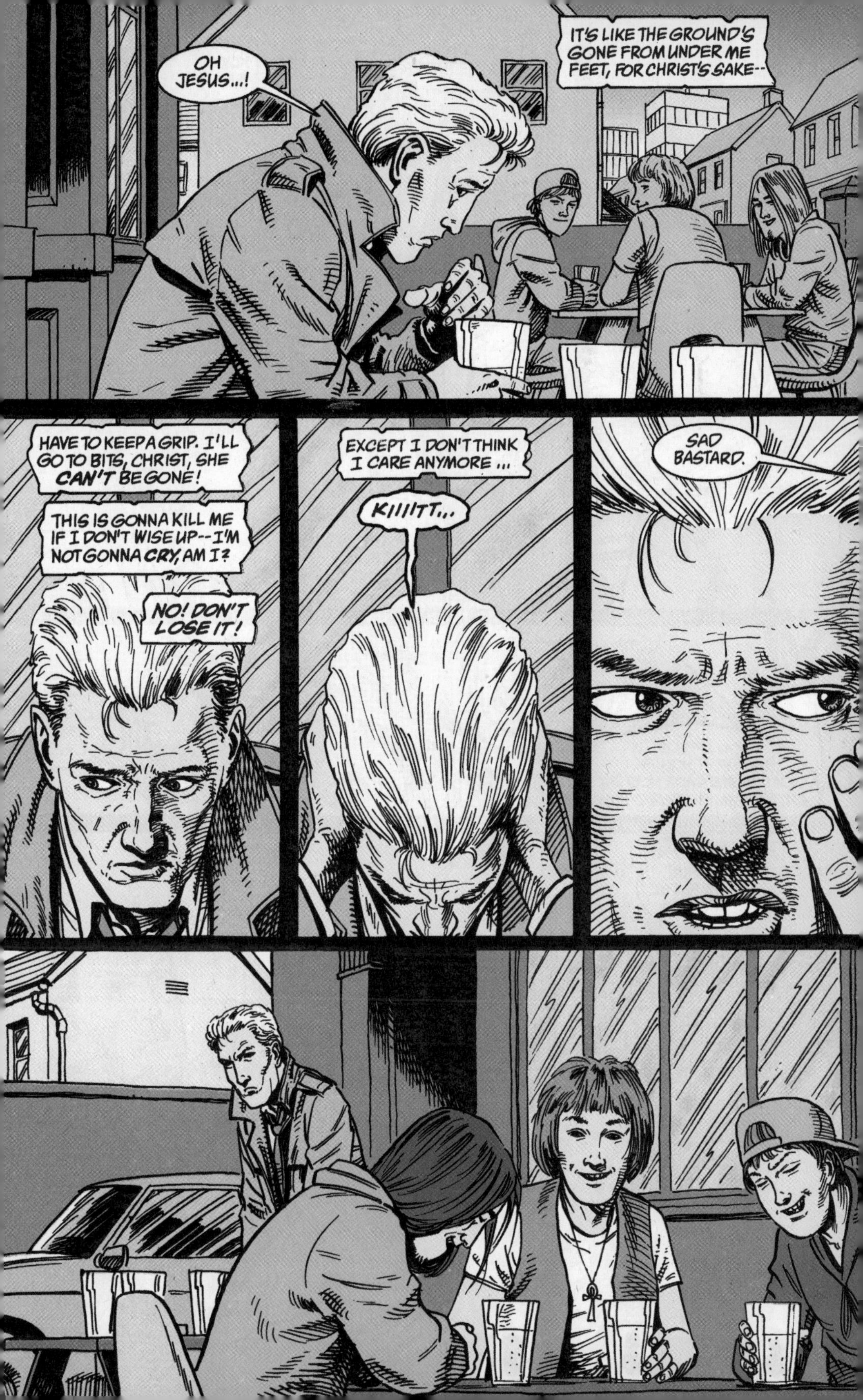
OH JESUS...!
IT'S LIKE THE GROUND'S GONE FROM UNDER ME FEET, FOR CHRIST'S SAKE--
HAVE TO KEEP A GRIP. I'LL GO TO BITS, CHRIST, SHE CAN'T BE GONE!
THIS IS GONNA KILL ME IF I DON'T WISE UP--I'M NOT GONNA CRY, AM I?
NO! DON'T LOSE IT!
EXCEPT I DON'T THINK I CARE ANYMORE...
KIIIITT...
SAD BASTARD.

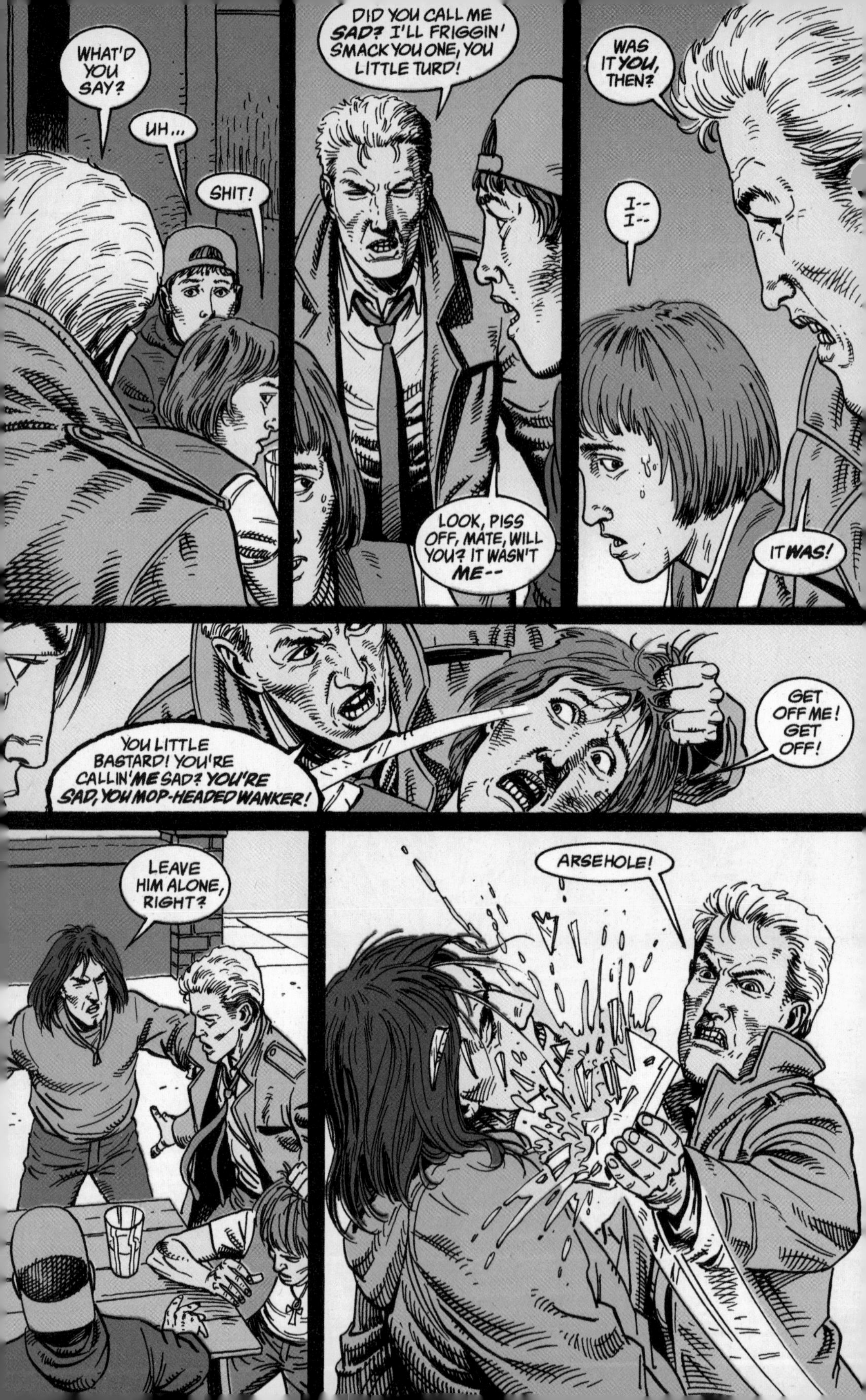
WHAT'D YOU SAY?
UH...
SHIT!
DID YOU CALL ME SAD? I'LL FRIGGIN' SMACK YOU ONE, YOU LITTLE TURD!
LOOK, PISS OFF, MATE, WILL YOU? IT WASN'T ME--
WAS IT YOU, THEN?
I-- I--
IT WAS!
YOU LITTLE BASTARD! YOU'RE CALLIN' ME SAD? YOU'RE SAD, YOU MOP-HEADED WANKER!
GET OFF ME! GET OFF!
LEAVE HIM ALONE, RIGHT?
ARSEHOLE!

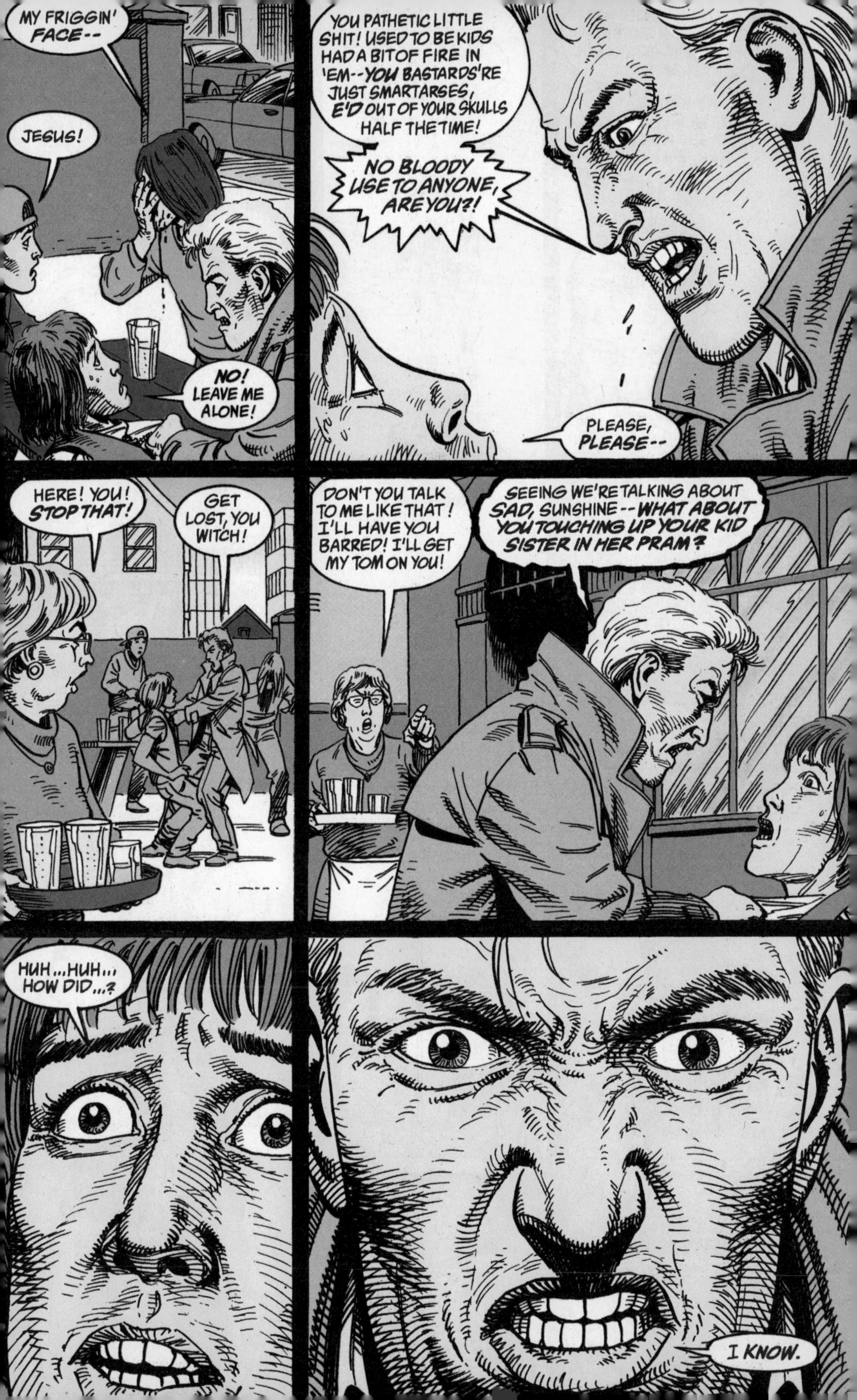
MY FRIGGIN' FACE--
JESUS!
NO! LEAVE ME ALONE!
YOU PATHETIC LITTLE SHIT! USED TO BE KIDS HAD A BIT OF FIRE IN 'EM--YOU BASTARDS'RE JUST SMARTARSES, E'D OUT OF YOUR SKULLS HALF THE TIME!
NO BLOODY USE TO ANYONE, ARE YOU?!
PLEASE, PLEASE--
HERE! YOU! STOP THAT!
GET LOST, YOU WITCH!
DON'T YOU TALK TO ME LIKE THAT! I'LL HAVE YOU BARRED! I'LL GET MY TOM ON YOU!
SEEING WE'RE TALKING ABOUT SAD, SUNSHINE--WHAT ABOUT YOU TOUCHING UP YOUR KID SISTER IN HER PRAM?
HUH...HUH... HOW DID...?
I KNOW.

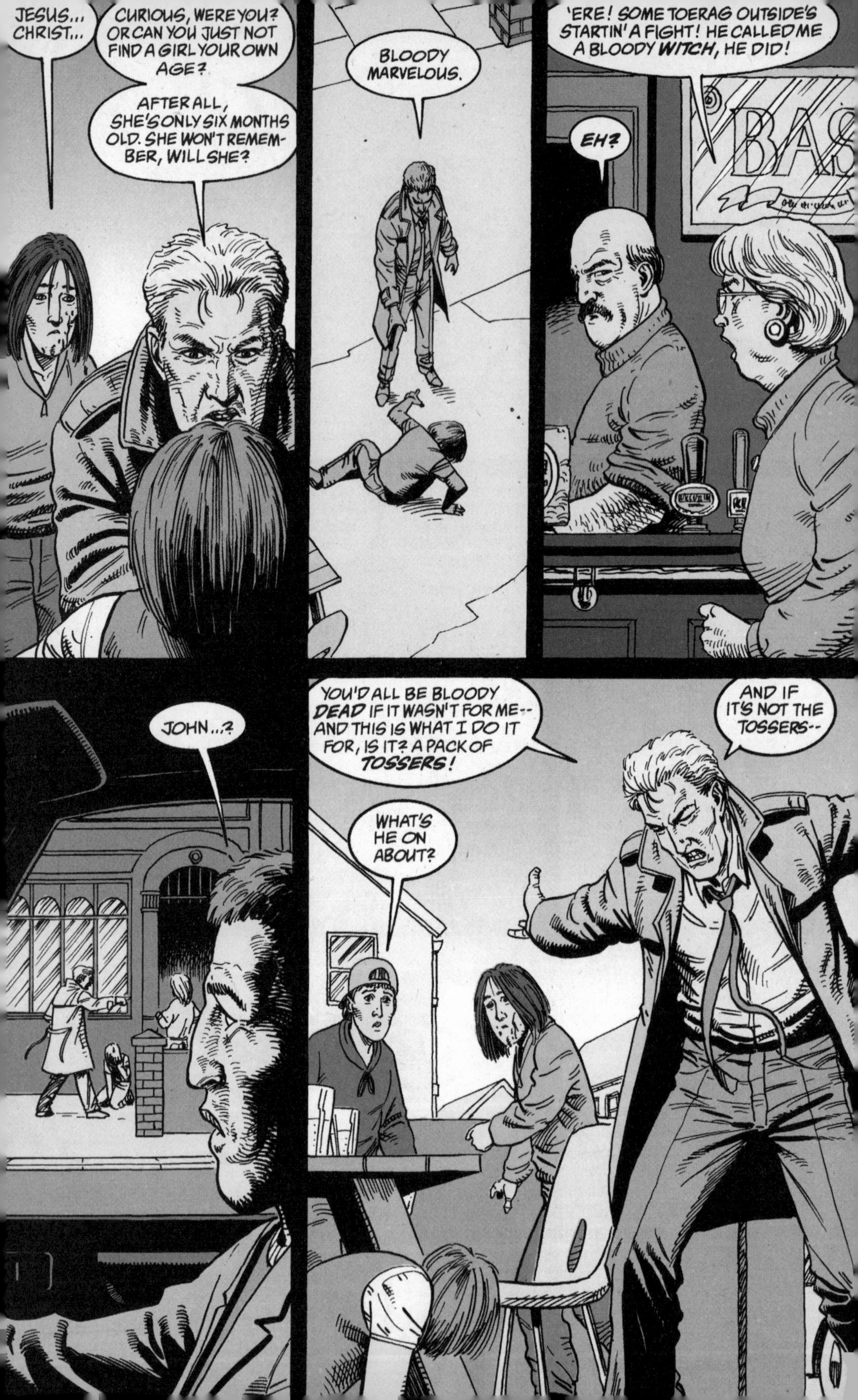
JESUS... CHRIST...
CURIOUS, WERE YOU? OR CAN YOU JUST NOT FIND A GIRL YOUR OWN AGE?
AFTER ALL, SHE'S ONLY SIX MONTHS OLD. SHE WON'T REMEMBER, WILL SHE?
BLOODY MARVELOUS.
'ERE! SOME TOERAG OUTSIDE'S STARTIN' A FIGHT! HE CALLED ME A BLOODY WITCH, HE DID!
EH?
JOHN...?
YOU'D ALL BE BLOODY DEAD IF IT WASN'T FOR ME-- AND THIS IS WHAT I DO IT FOR, IS IT? A PACK OF TOSSERS!
AND IF IT'S NOT THE TOSSERS--
WHAT'S HE ON ABOUT?

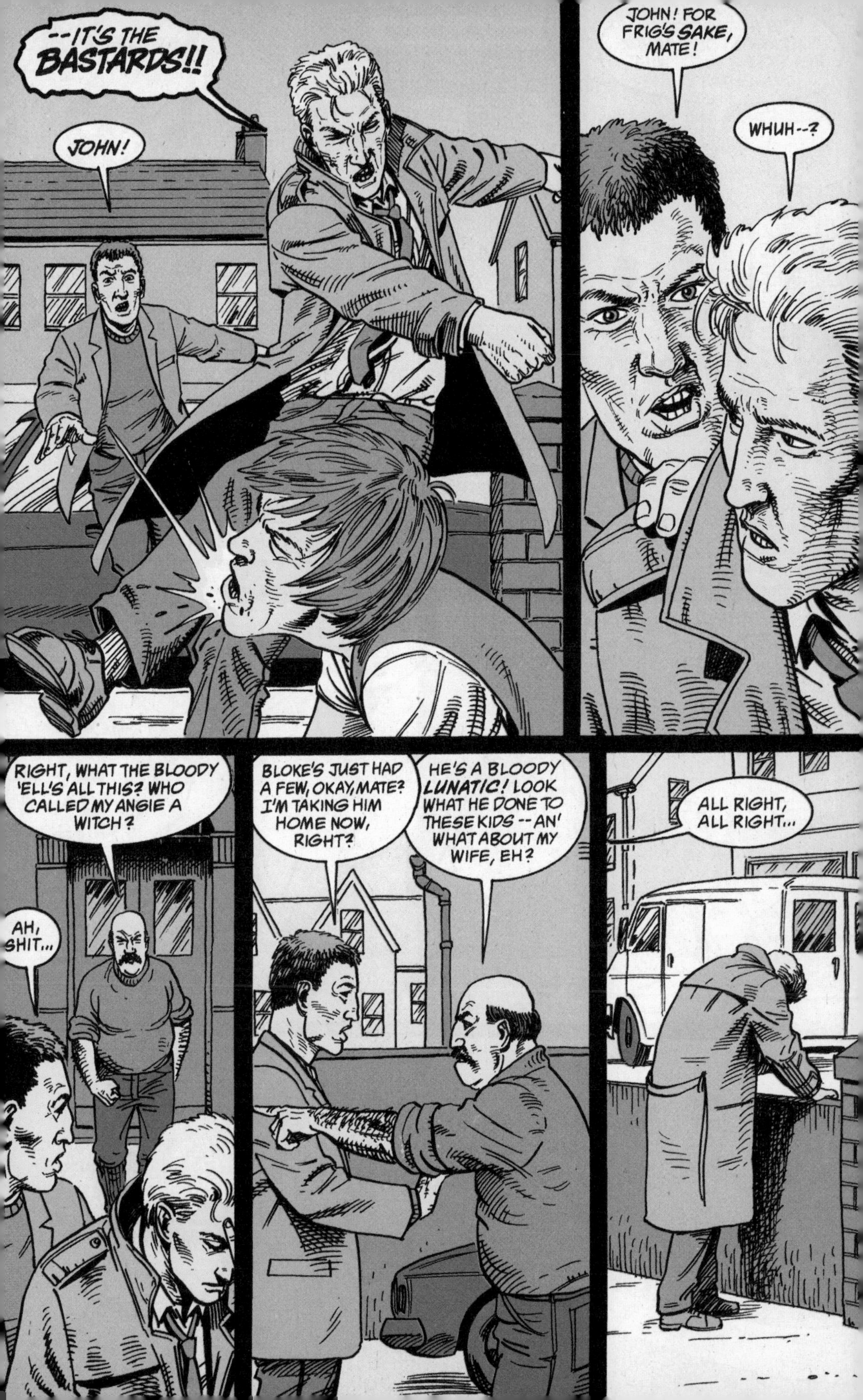
--IT'S THE BASTARDS!!
JOHN!
JOHN! FOR FRIG'S SAKE, MATE!
WHUH--?
RIGHT, WHAT THE BLOODY 'ELL'S ALL THIS? WHO CALLED MY ANGIE A WITCH?
AH, SHIT...
BLOKE'S JUST HAD A FEW, OKAY, MATE? I'M TAKING HIM HOME NOW, RIGHT?
HE'S A BLOODY LUNATIC! LOOK WHAT HE DONE TO THESE KIDS--AN' WHAT ABOUT MY WIFE, EH?
ALL RIGHT, ALL RIGHT...

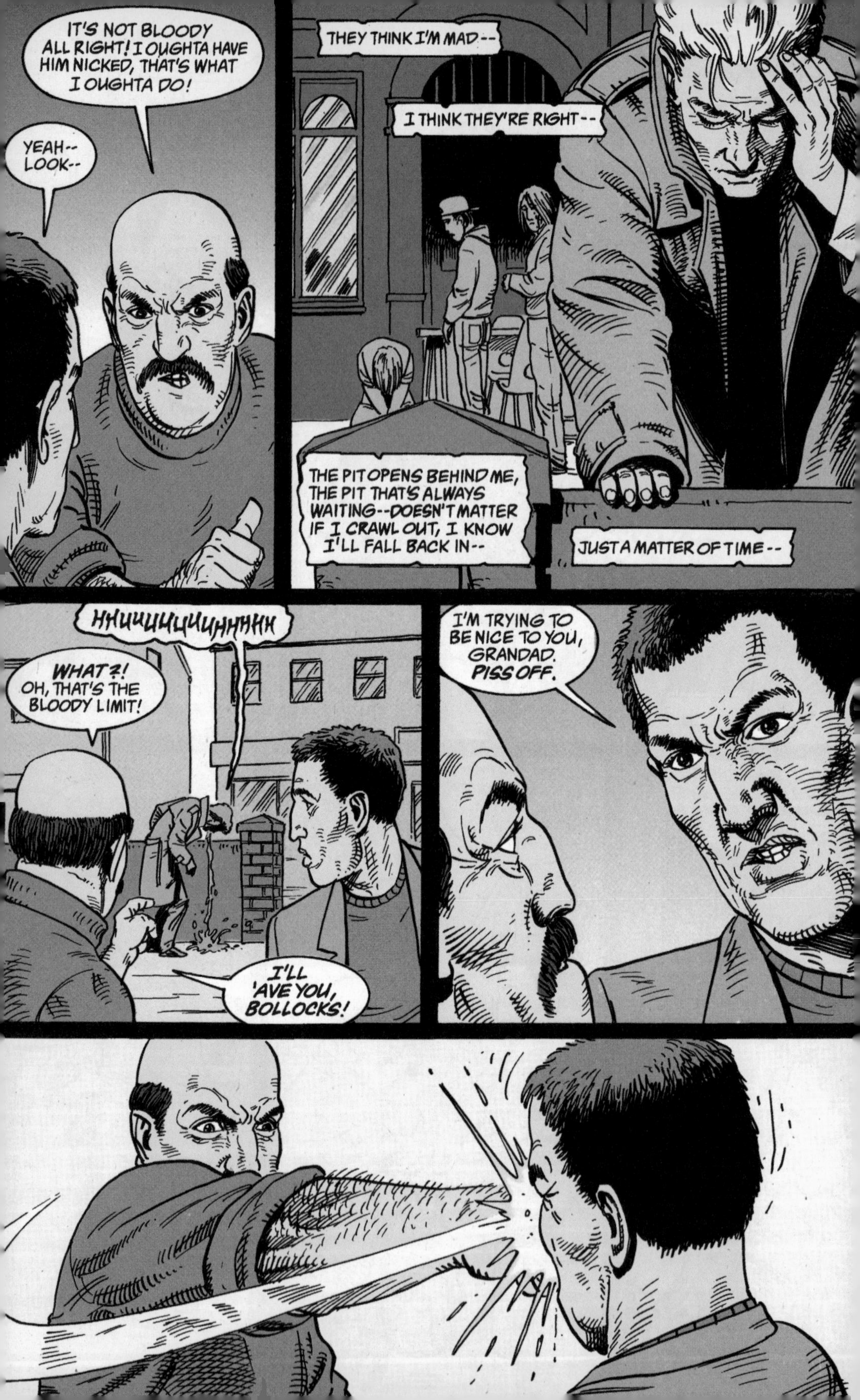
IT'S NOT BLOODY ALL RIGHT! I OUGHTA HAVE HIM NICKED, THAT'S WHAT I OUGHTA DO!
YEAH-- LOOK--
THEY THINK I'M MAD--
I THINK THEY'RE RIGHT--
THE PIT OPENS BEHIND ME, THE PIT THAT'S ALWAYS WAITING--DOESN'T MATTER IF I CRAWL OUT, I KNOW I'LL FALL BACK IN--
JUST A MATTER OF TIME--
HHUUUUUUUHHHHH
WHAT?! OH, THAT'S THE BLOODY LIMIT!
I'LL 'AVE YOU, BOLLOCKS!
I'M TRYING TO BE NICE TO YOU, GRANDAD. PISS OFF.

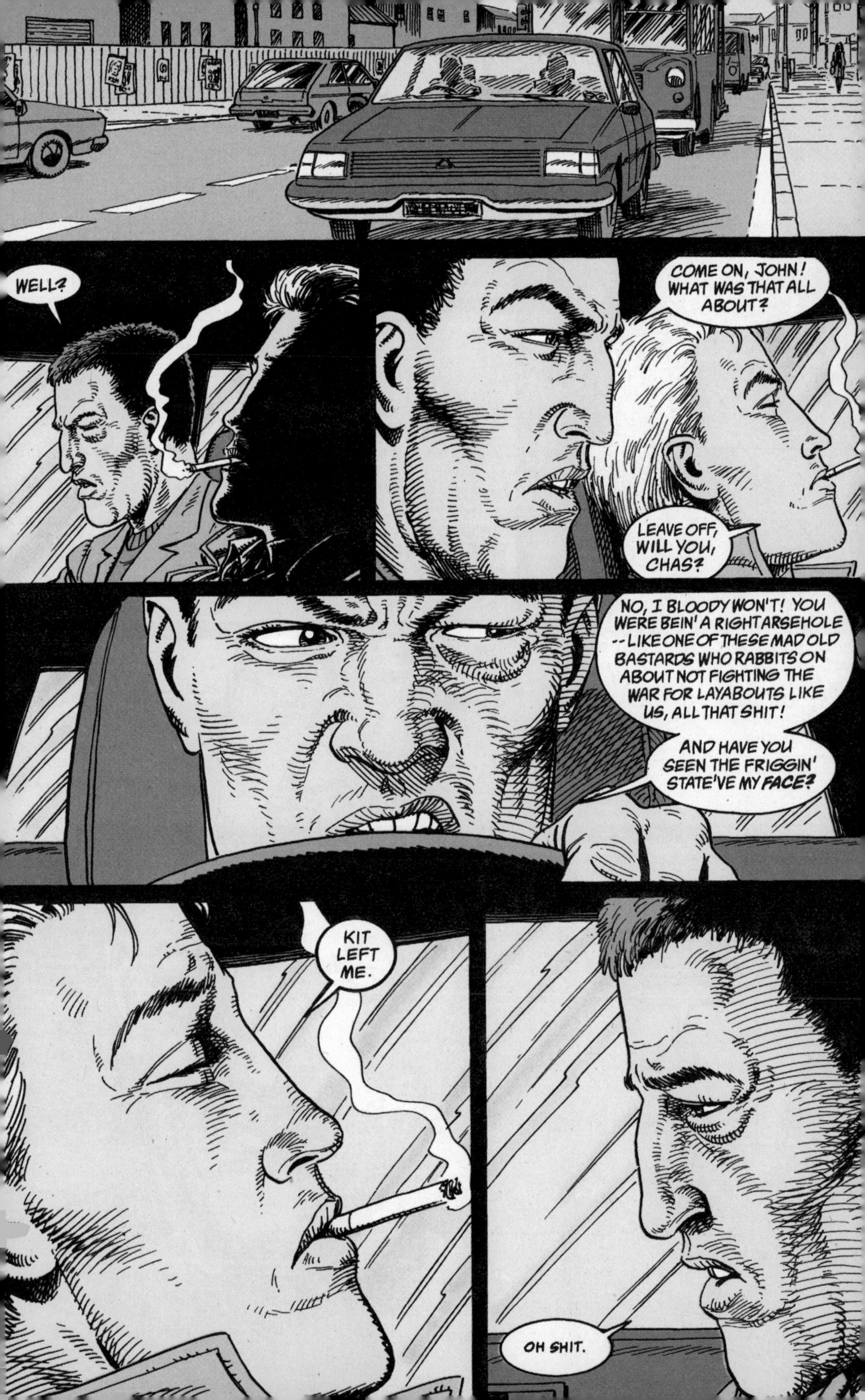
WELL?
COME ON, JOHN! WHAT WAS THAT ALL ABOUT?
LEAVE OFF, WILL YOU, CHAS?
NO, I BLOODY WON'T! YOU WERE BEIN' A RIGHT ARSEHOLE -- LIKE ONE OF THESE MAD OLD BASTARDS WHO RABBITS ON ABOUT NOT FIGHTING THE WAR FOR LAYABOUTS LIKE US, ALL THAT SHIT!
AND HAVE YOU SEEN THE FRIGGIN' STATE'VE MY FACE?
KIT LEFT ME.
OH SHIT.

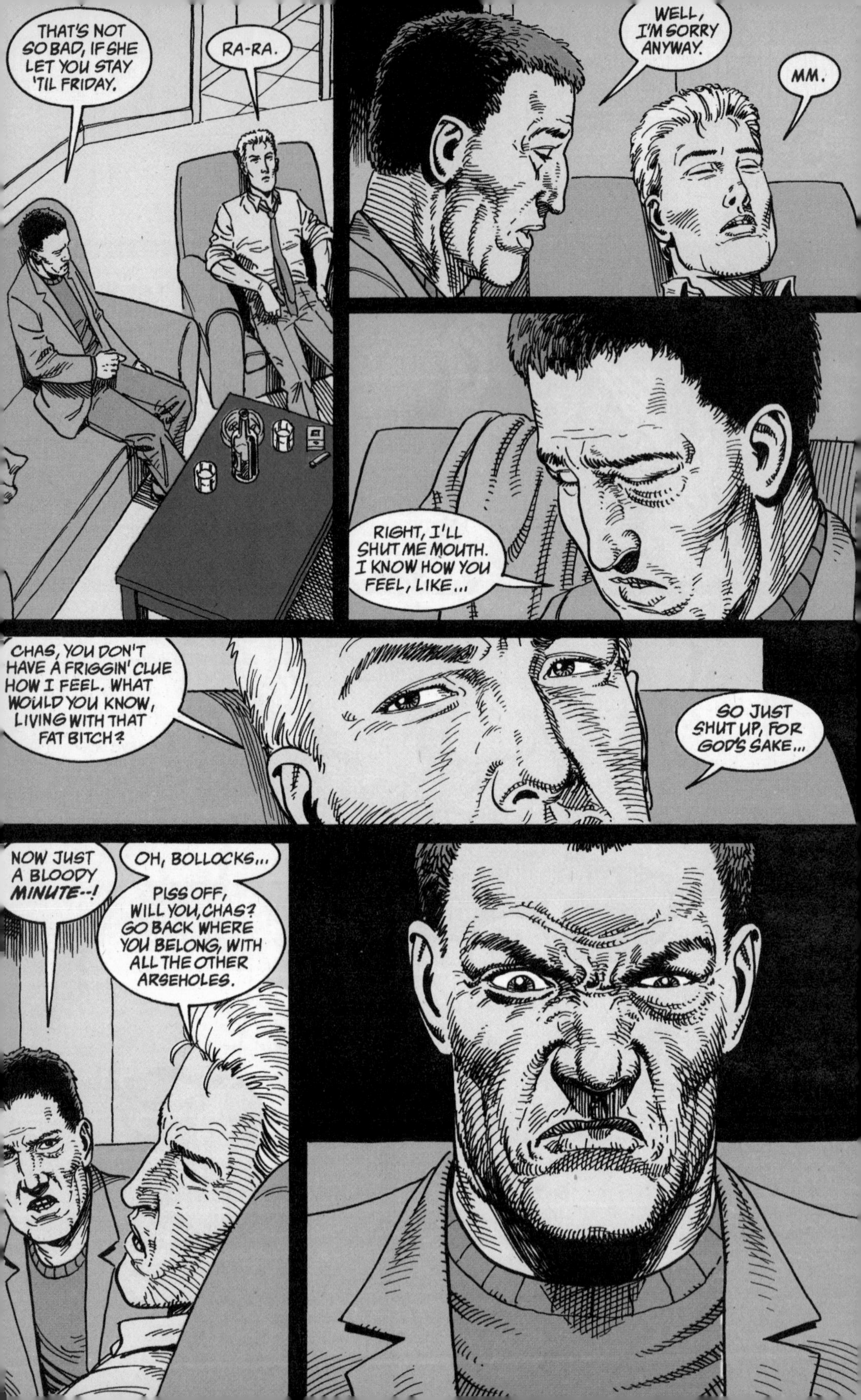
THAT'S NOT SO BAD, IF SHE LET YOU STAY 'TIL FRIDAY.
RA-RA.
WELL, I'M SORRY ANYWAY.
MM.
RIGHT, I'LL SHUT ME MOUTH. I KNOW HOW YOU FEEL, LIKE...
CHAS, YOU DON'T HAVE A FRIGGIN' CLUE HOW I FEEL. WHAT WOULD YOU KNOW, LIVING WITH THAT FAT BITCH?
SO JUST SHUT UP, FOR GOD'S SAKE...
NOW JUST A BLOODY MINUTE--!
OH, BOLLOCKS...
PISS OFF, WILL YOU, CHAS? GO BACK WHERE YOU BELONG, WITH ALL THE OTHER ARSEHOLES.

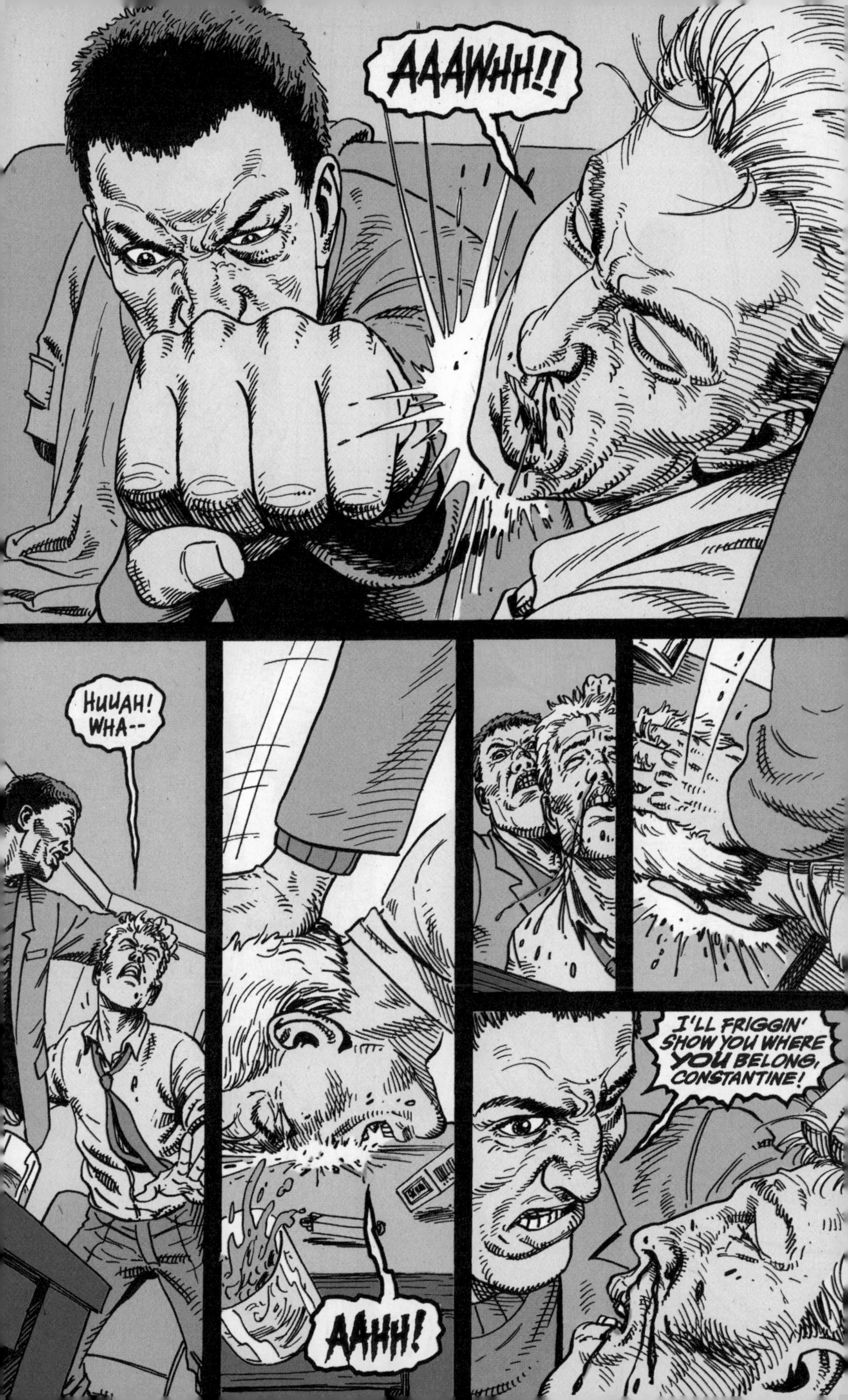
AAAWHH!!
HUUAH! WHA--
AAHH!
I'LL FRIGGIN' SHOW YOU WHERE YOU BELONG, CONSTANTINE!

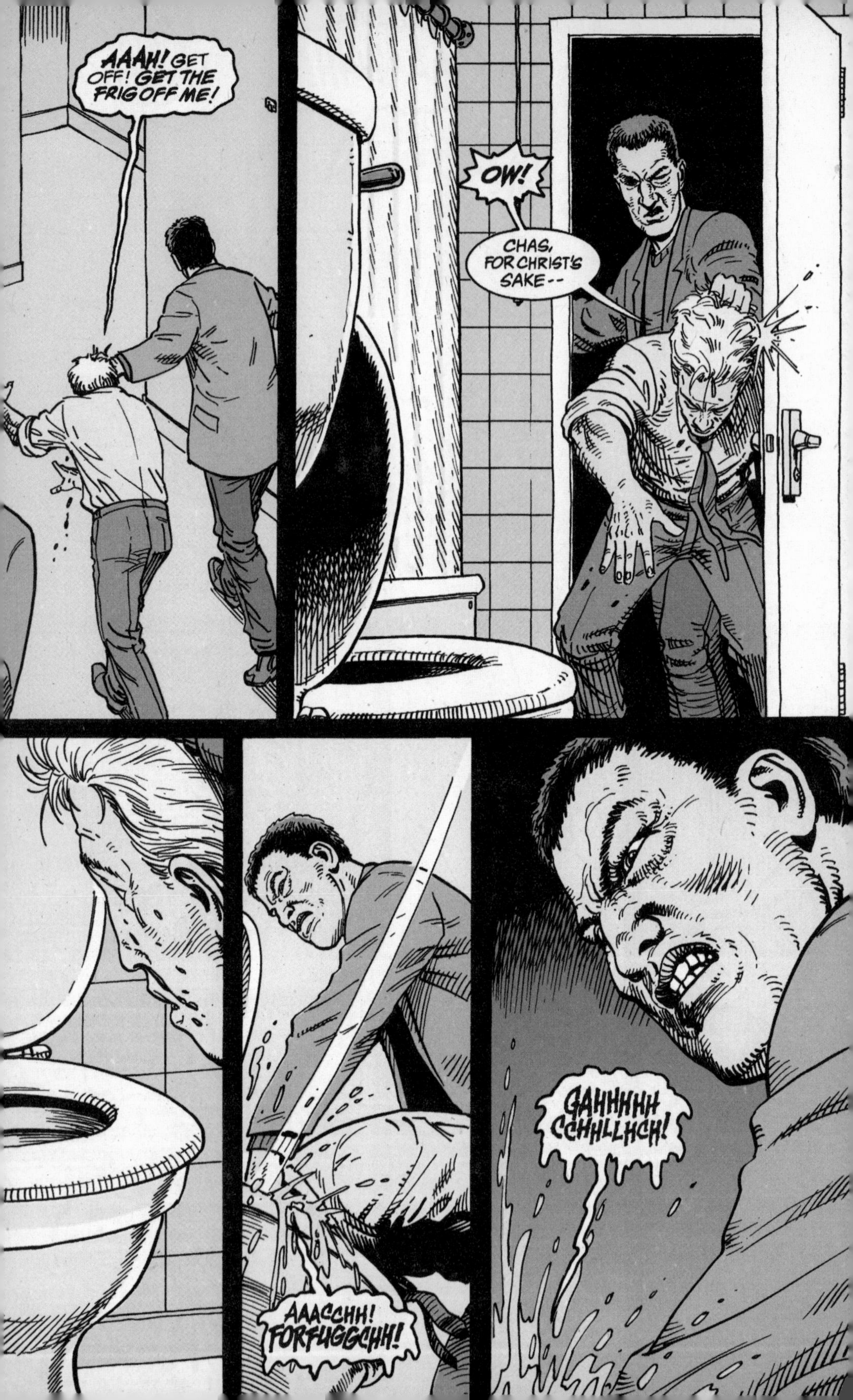
AAAH! GET OFF! GET THE FRIG OFF ME!
OW!
CHAS, FOR CHRIST'S SAKE--
AAACCHH! FORFUGGCHH!
GAHHHHH CCHHLLHCH!

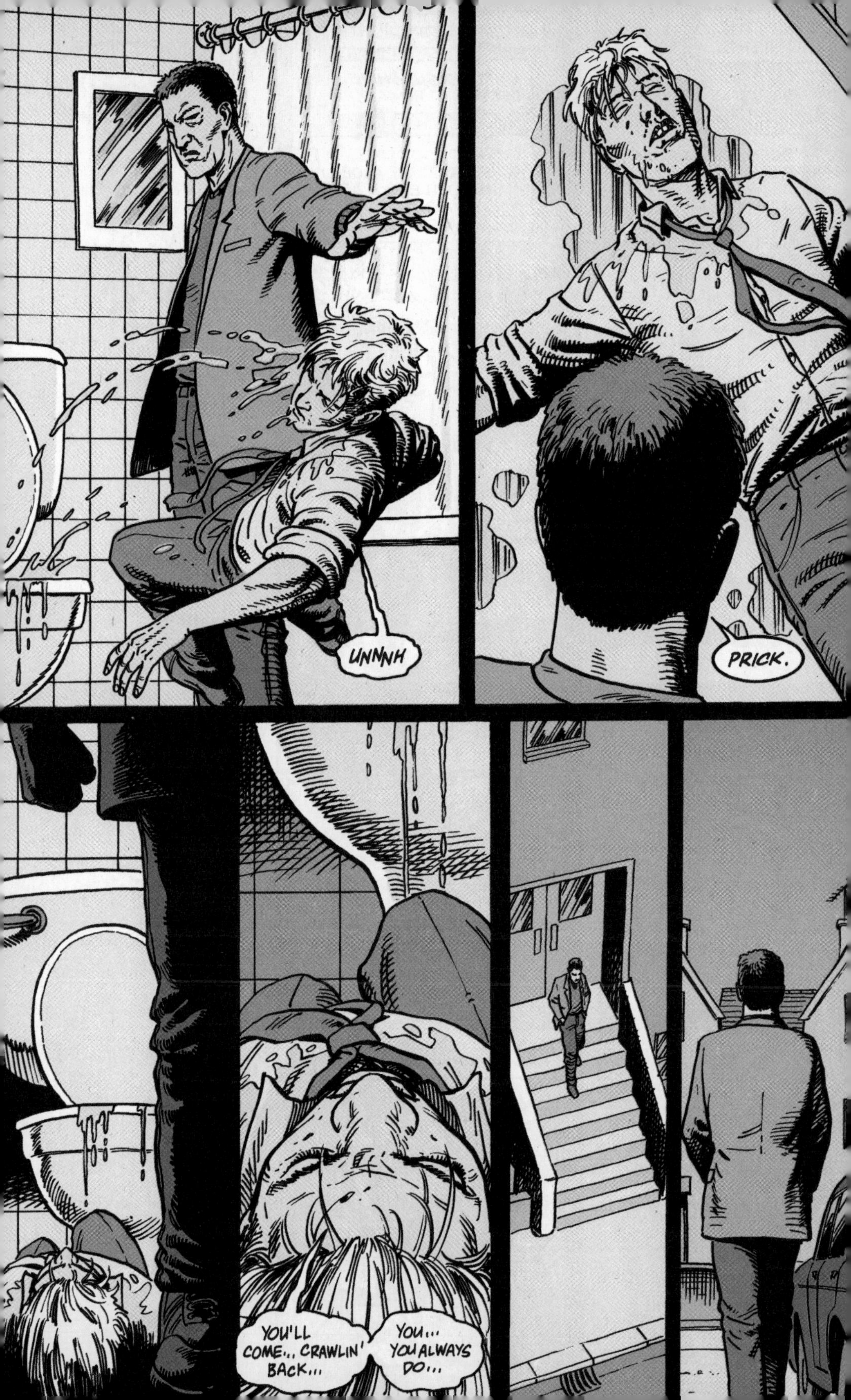
UNNNH
PRICK.
YOU'LL COME... CRAWLIN' BACK...
YOU... YOU ALWAYS DO...

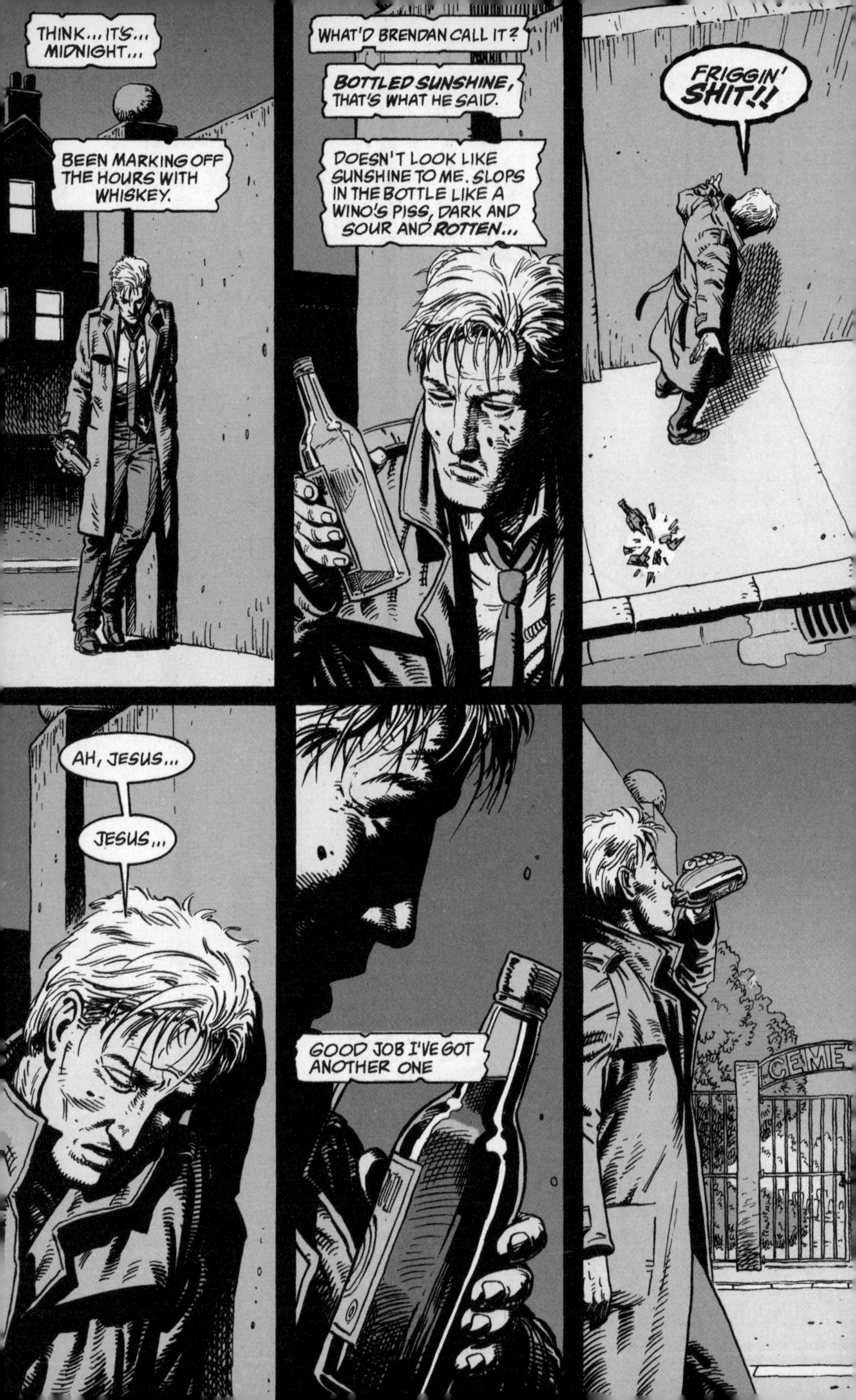
THINK... IT'S... MIDNIGHT...
BEEN MARKING OFF THE HOURS WITH WHISKEY.
WHAT'D BRENDAN CALL IT?
BOTTLED SUNSHINE, THAT'S WHAT HE SAID.
DOESN'T LOOK LIKE SUNSHINE TO ME. SLOPS IN THE BOTTLE LIKE A WINO'S PISS, DARK AND SOUR AND ROTTEN...
FRIGGIN' SHIT!!
AH, JESUS...
JESUS...
GOOD JOB I'VE GOT ANOTHER ONE
CEME

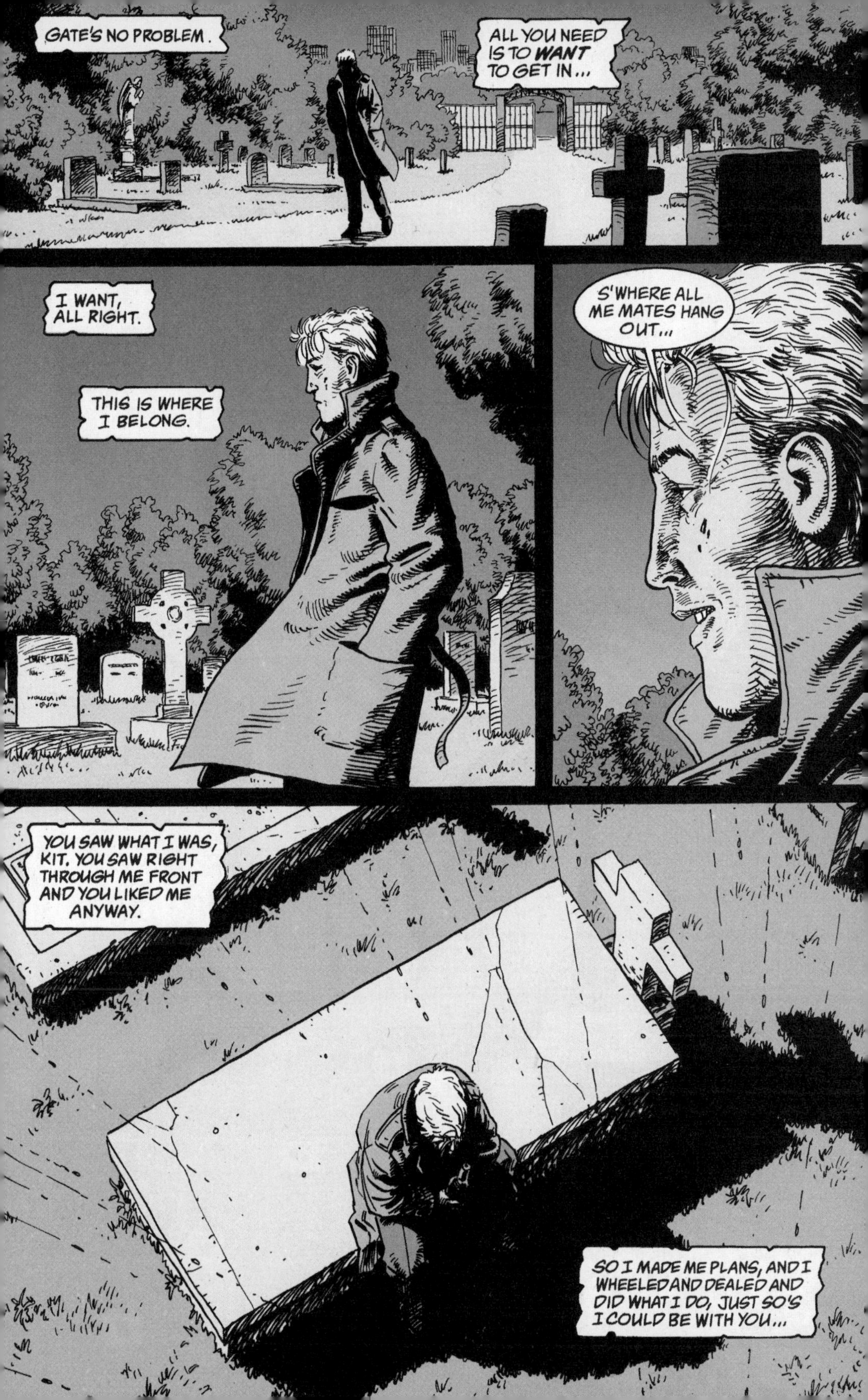
GATE'S NO PROBLEM.
ALL YOU NEED IS TO **WANT** TO GET IN...
I WANT, ALL RIGHT.
THIS IS WHERE I BELONG.
S'WHERE ALL ME MATES HANG OUT...
YOU SAW WHAT I WAS, KIT. YOU SAW RIGHT THROUGH ME FRONT AND YOU LIKED ME ANYWAY.
SO I MADE ME PLANS, AND I WHEELED AND DEALED AND DID WHAT I DO, JUST SO'S I COULD BE WITH YOU...

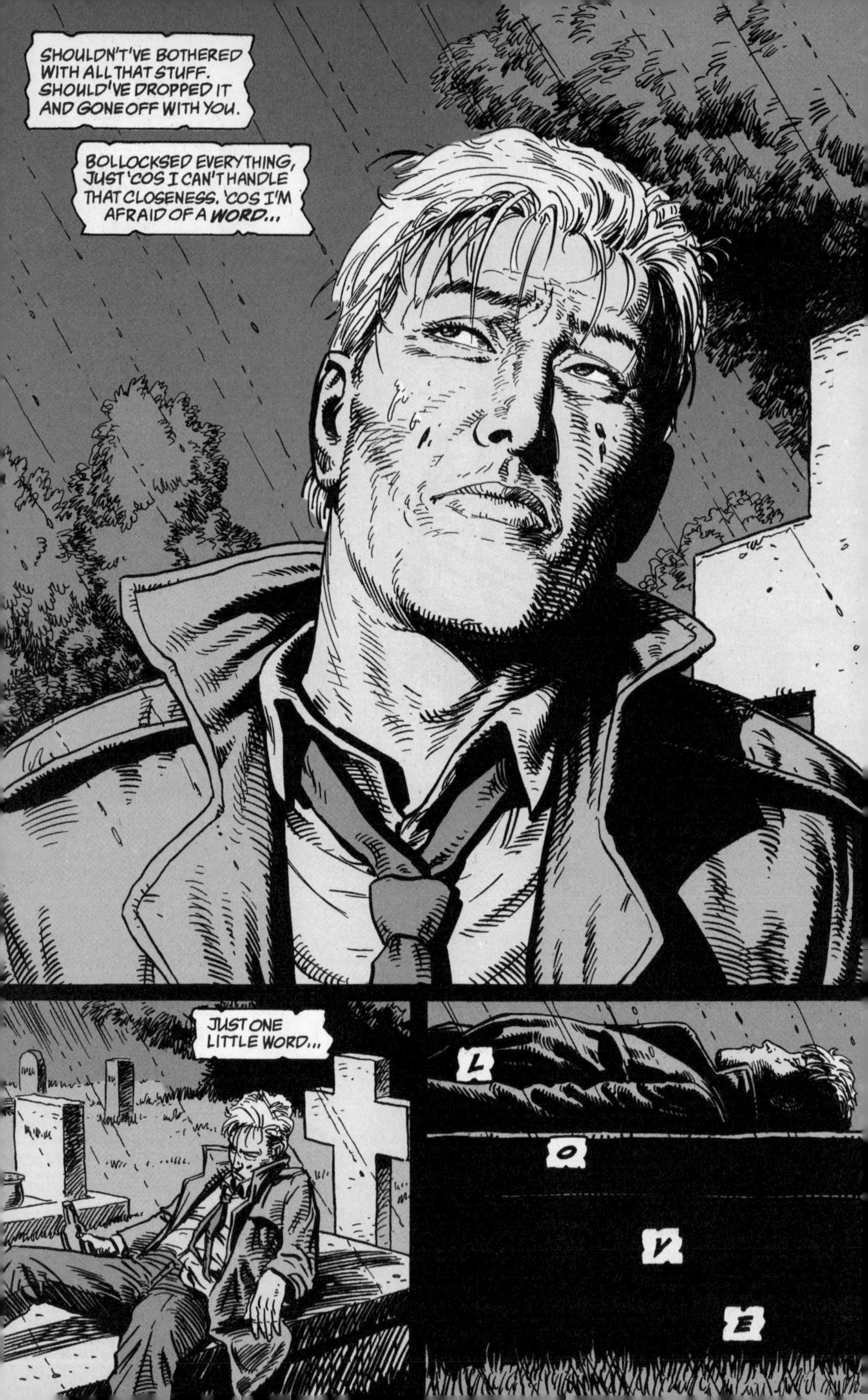
SHOULDN'T'VE BOTHERED WITH ALL THAT STUFF. SHOULD'VE DROPPED IT AND GONE OFF WITH YOU.
BOLLOCKSED EVERYTHING, JUST 'COS I CAN'T HANDLE THAT CLOSENESS. 'COS I'M AFRAID OF A WORD...
JUST ONE LITTLE WORD...
L
O
V
E

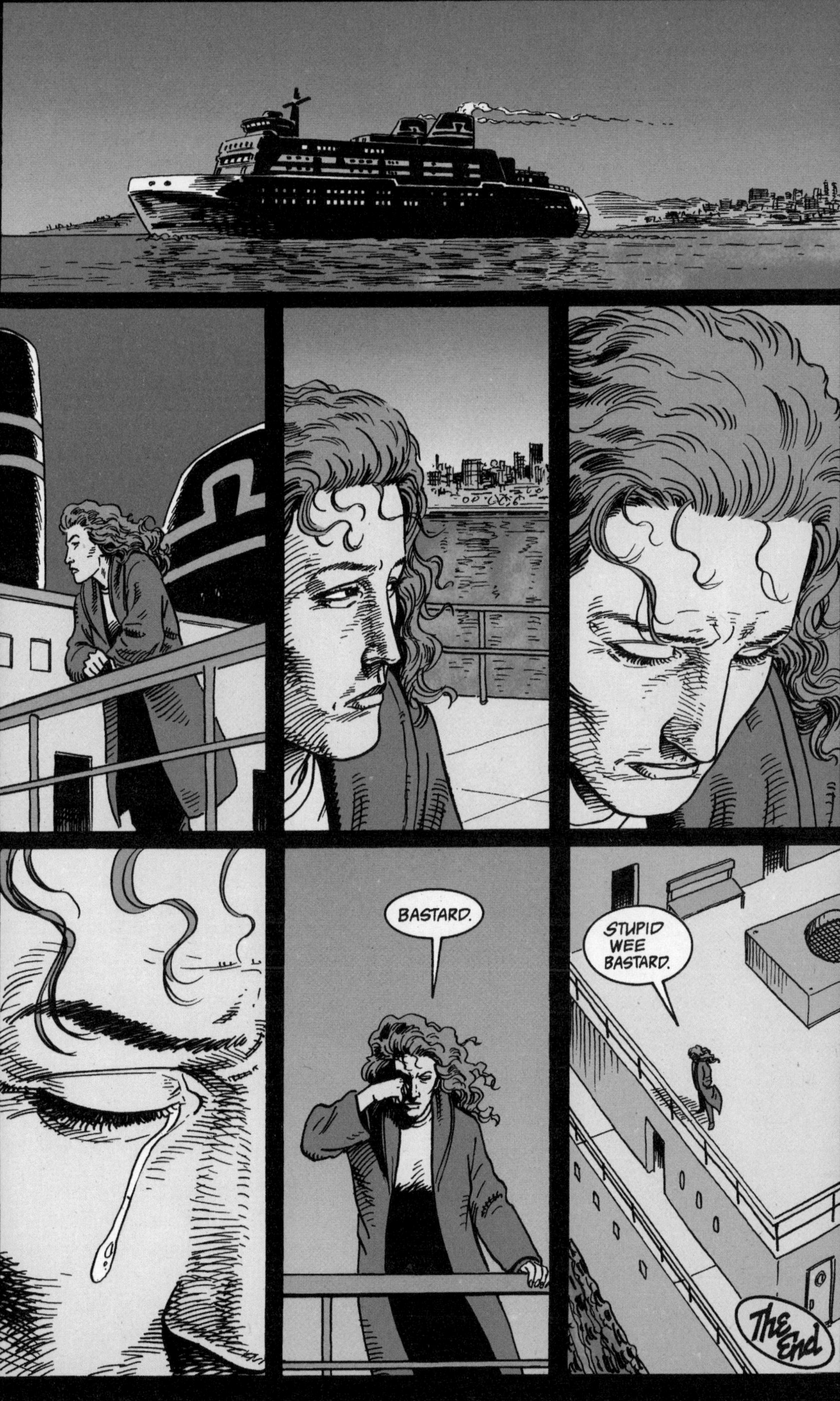
BASTARD.
STUPID WEE BASTARD.
THE End

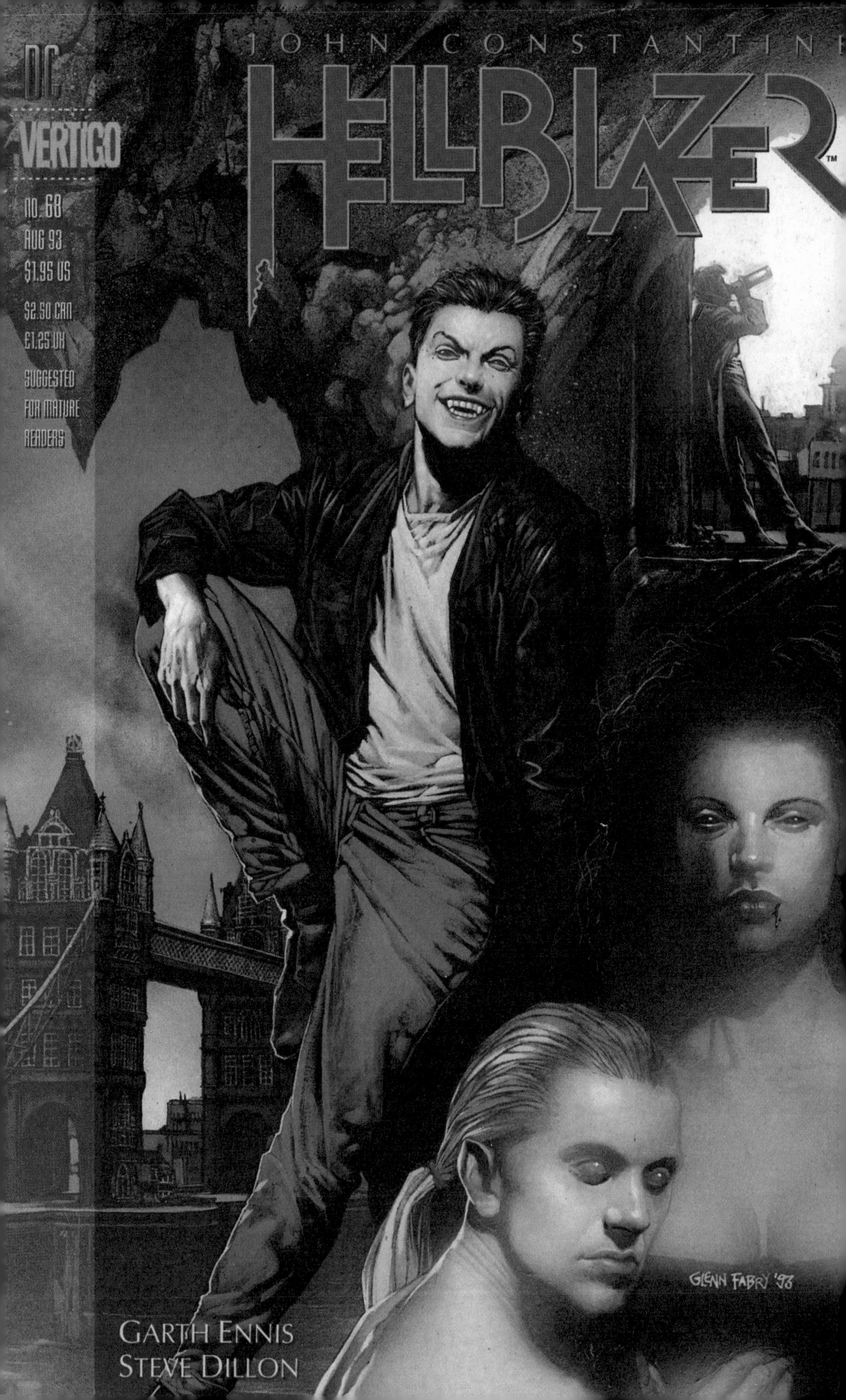
DC
VERTIGO
NO. 68
AUG 93
$1.95 US
$2.50 CAN
£1.25 UK
SUGGESTED FOR MATURE READERS
JOHN CONSTANTINE
HELLBLAZER
GLENN FABRY '93
GARTH ENNIS
STEVE DILLON

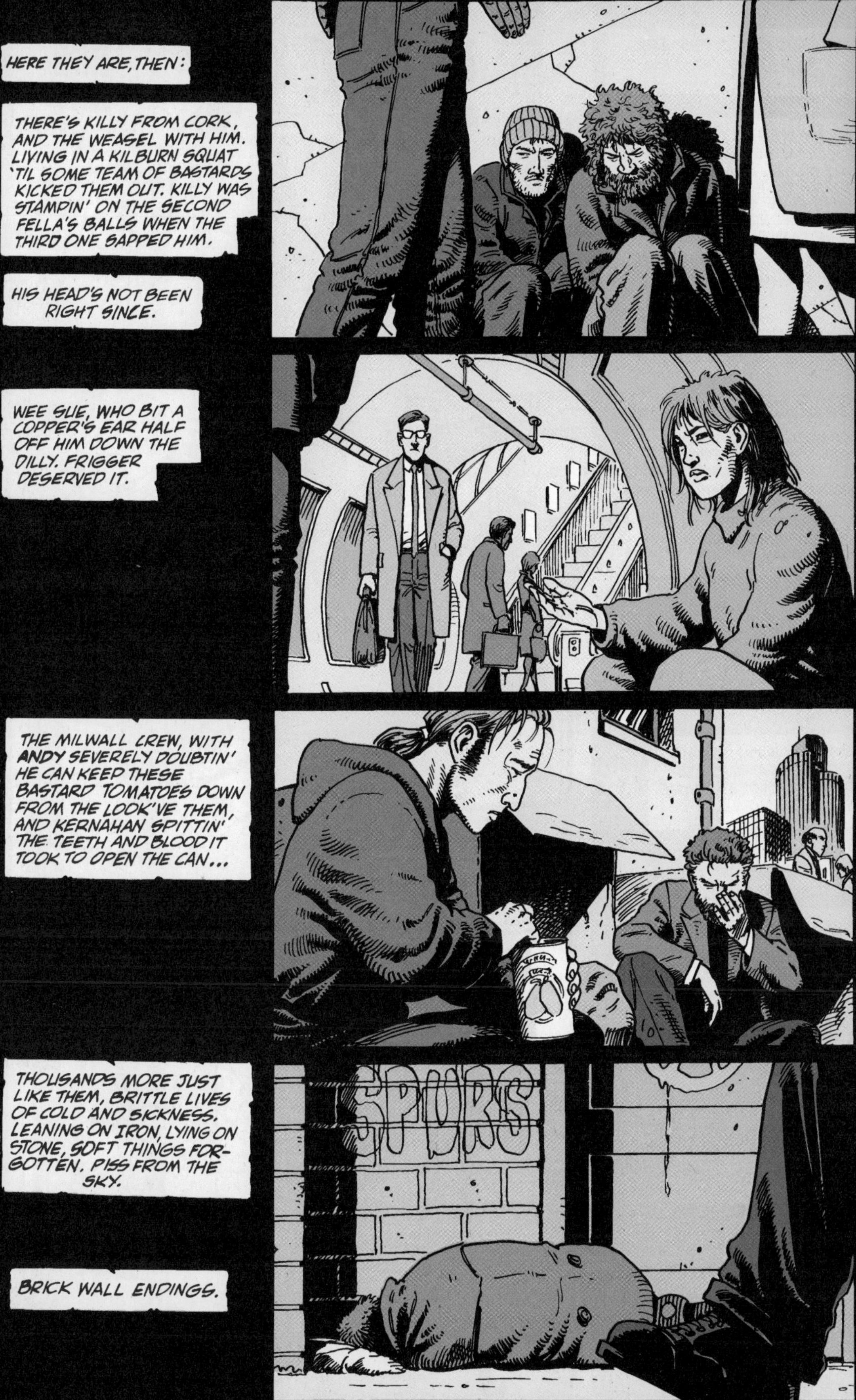
HERE THEY ARE, THEN:
THERE'S KILLY FROM CORK, AND THE WEASEL WITH HIM. LIVING IN A KILBURN SQUAT 'TIL SOME TEAM OF BASTARDS KICKED THEM OUT. KILLY WAS STAMPIN' ON THE SECOND FELLA'S BALLS WHEN THE THIRD ONE SAPPED HIM.
HIS HEAD'S NOT BEEN RIGHT SINCE.
WEE SUE, WHO BIT A COPPER'S EAR HALF OFF HIM DOWN THE DILLY. FRIGGER DESERVED IT.
THE MILWALL CREW, WITH ANDY SEVERELY DOUBTIN' HE CAN KEEP THESE BASTARD TOMATOES DOWN FROM THE LOOK'VE THEM, AND KERNAHAN SPITTIN' THE TEETH AND BLOOD IT TOOK TO OPEN THE CAN...
THOUSANDS MORE JUST LIKE THEM, BRITTLE LIVES OF COLD AND SICKNESS. LEANING ON IRON, LYING ON STONE, SOFT THINGS FORGOTTEN. PISS FROM THE SKY.
BRICK WALL ENDINGS.
SPURS

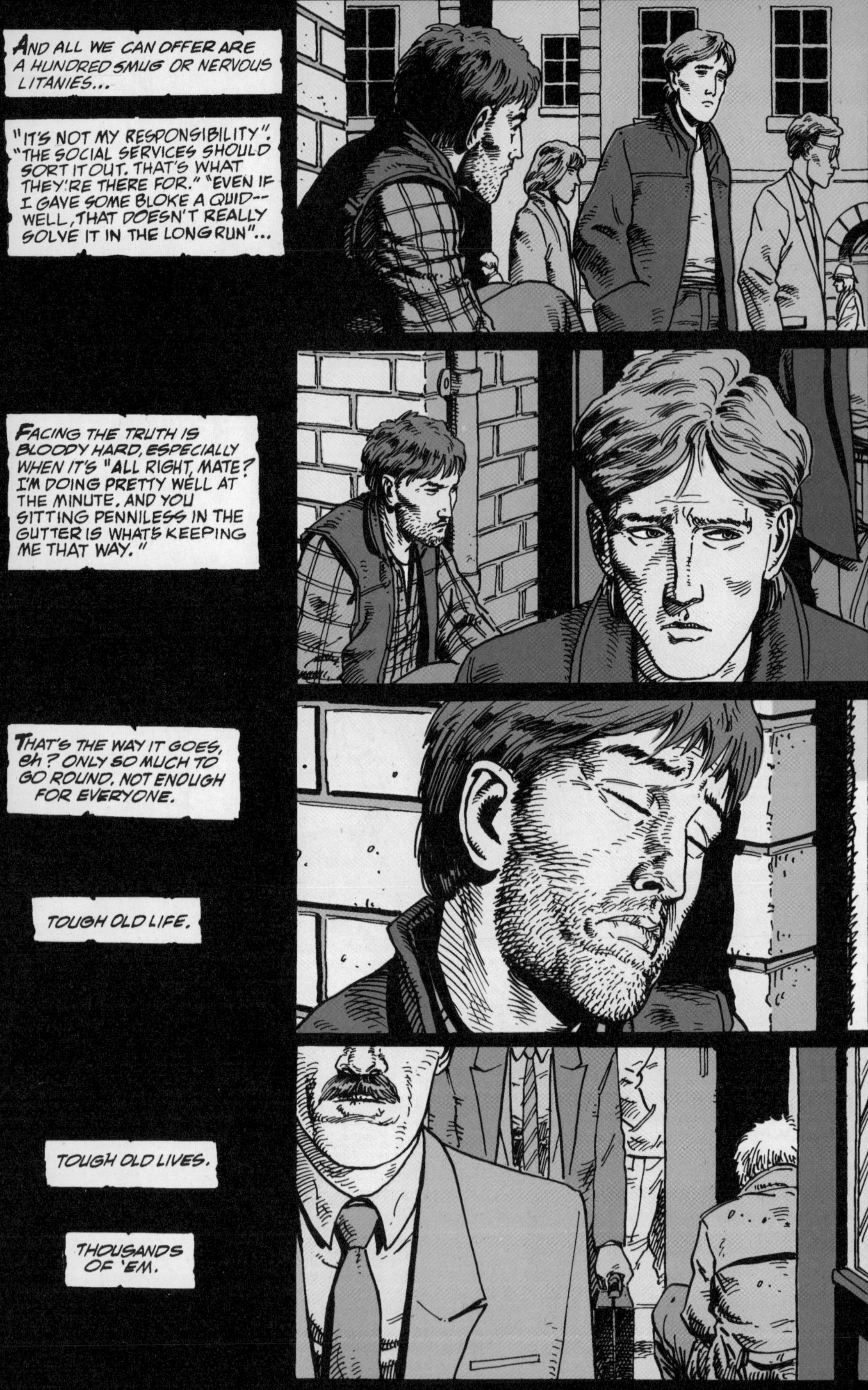
AND ALL WE CAN OFFER ARE A HUNDRED SMUG OR NERVOUS LITANIES...
"IT'S NOT MY RESPONSIBILITY". "THE SOCIAL SERVICES SHOULD SORT IT OUT. THAT'S WHAT THEY'RE THERE FOR." "EVEN IF I GAVE SOME BLOKE A QUID-- WELL, THAT DOESN'T REALLY SOLVE IT IN THE LONG RUN"...
FACING THE TRUTH IS BLOODY HARD, ESPECIALLY WHEN IT'S "ALL RIGHT, MATE? I'M DOING PRETTY WELL AT THE MINUTE. AND YOU SITTING PENNILESS IN THE GUTTER IS WHAT'S KEEPING ME THAT WAY."
THAT'S THE WAY IT GOES, EH? ONLY SO MUCH TO GO ROUND. NOT ENOUGH FOR EVERYONE.
TOUGH OLD LIFE.
TOUGH OLD LIVES.
THOUSANDS OF 'EM.

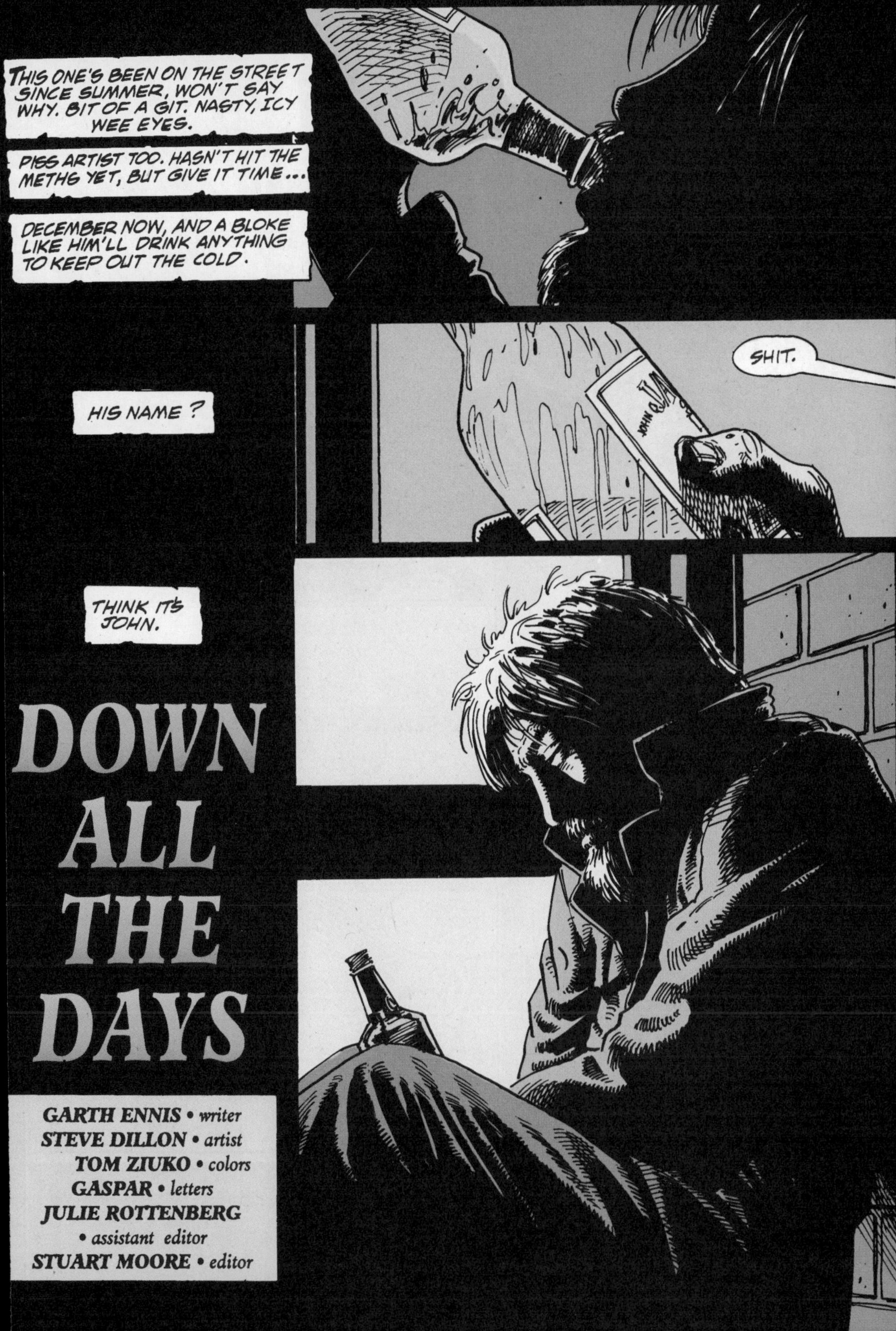
THIS ONE'S BEEN ON THE STREET SINCE SUMMER, WON'T SAY WHY. BIT OF A GIT. NASTY, ICY WEE EYES.
PISS ARTIST TOO. HASN'T HIT THE METHS YET, BUT GIVE IT TIME...
DECEMBER NOW, AND A BLOKE LIKE HIM'LL DRINK ANYTHING TO KEEP OUT THE COLD.
HIS NAME?
SHIT.
THINK IT'S JOHN.
DOWN ALL THE DAYS
GARTH ENNIS • writer
STEVE DILLON • artist
TOM ZIUKO • colors
GASPAR • letters
JULIE ROTTENBERG • assistant editor
STUART MOORE • editor

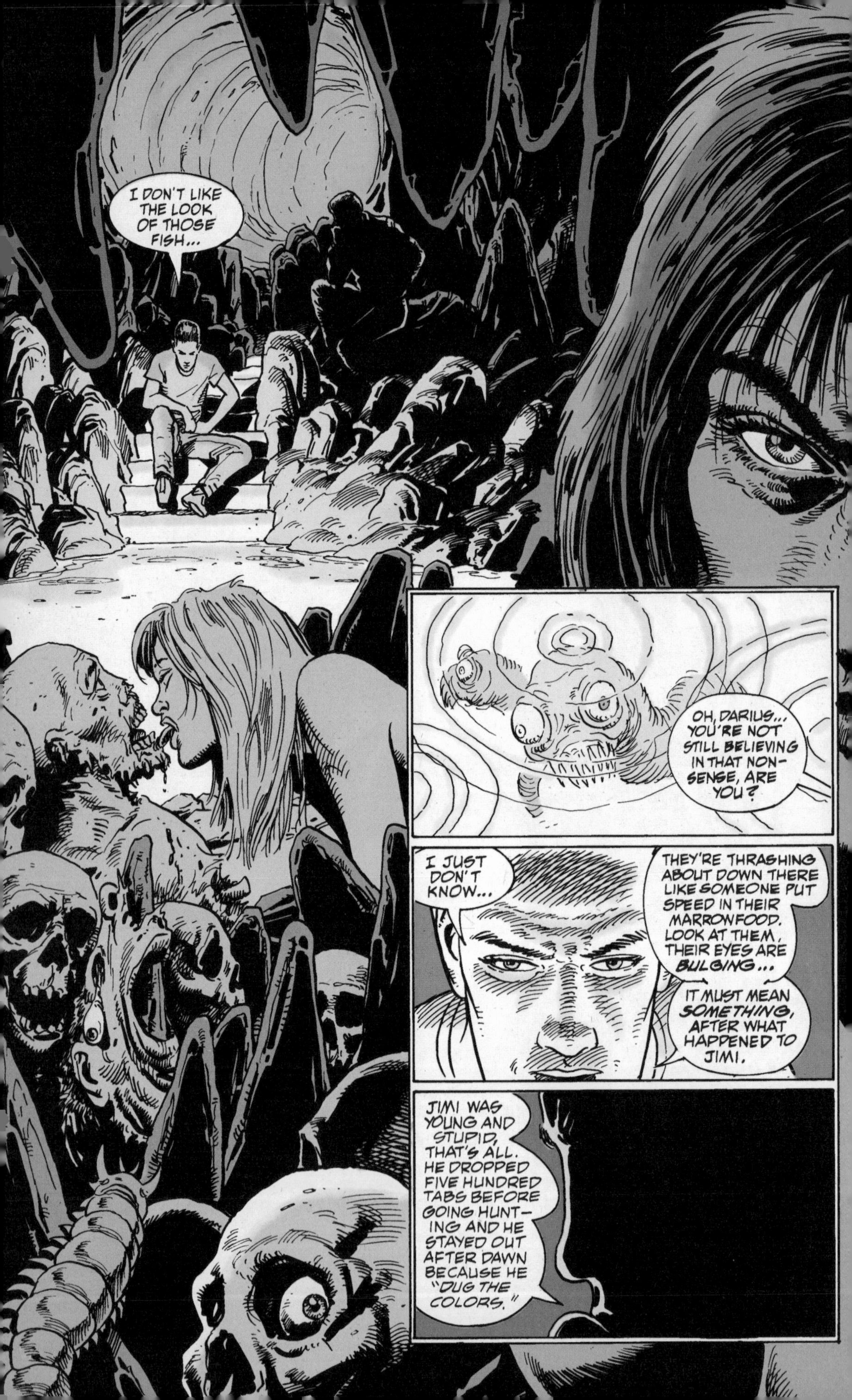
I DON'T LIKE THE LOOK OF THOSE FISH...
OH, DARIUS... YOU'RE NOT STILL BELIEVING IN THAT NON-SENSE, ARE YOU?
I JUST DON'T KNOW...
THEY'RE THRASHING ABOUT DOWN THERE LIKE SOMEONE PUT SPEED IN THEIR MARROWFOOD. LOOK AT THEM, THEIR EYES ARE BULGING...
IT MUST MEAN SOMETHING, AFTER WHAT HAPPENED TO JIMI.
JIMI WAS YOUNG AND STUPID, THAT'S ALL. HE DROPPED FIVE HUNDRED TABS BEFORE GOING HUNT-ING AND HE STAYED OUT AFTER DAWN BECAUSE HE "DUG THE COLORS."

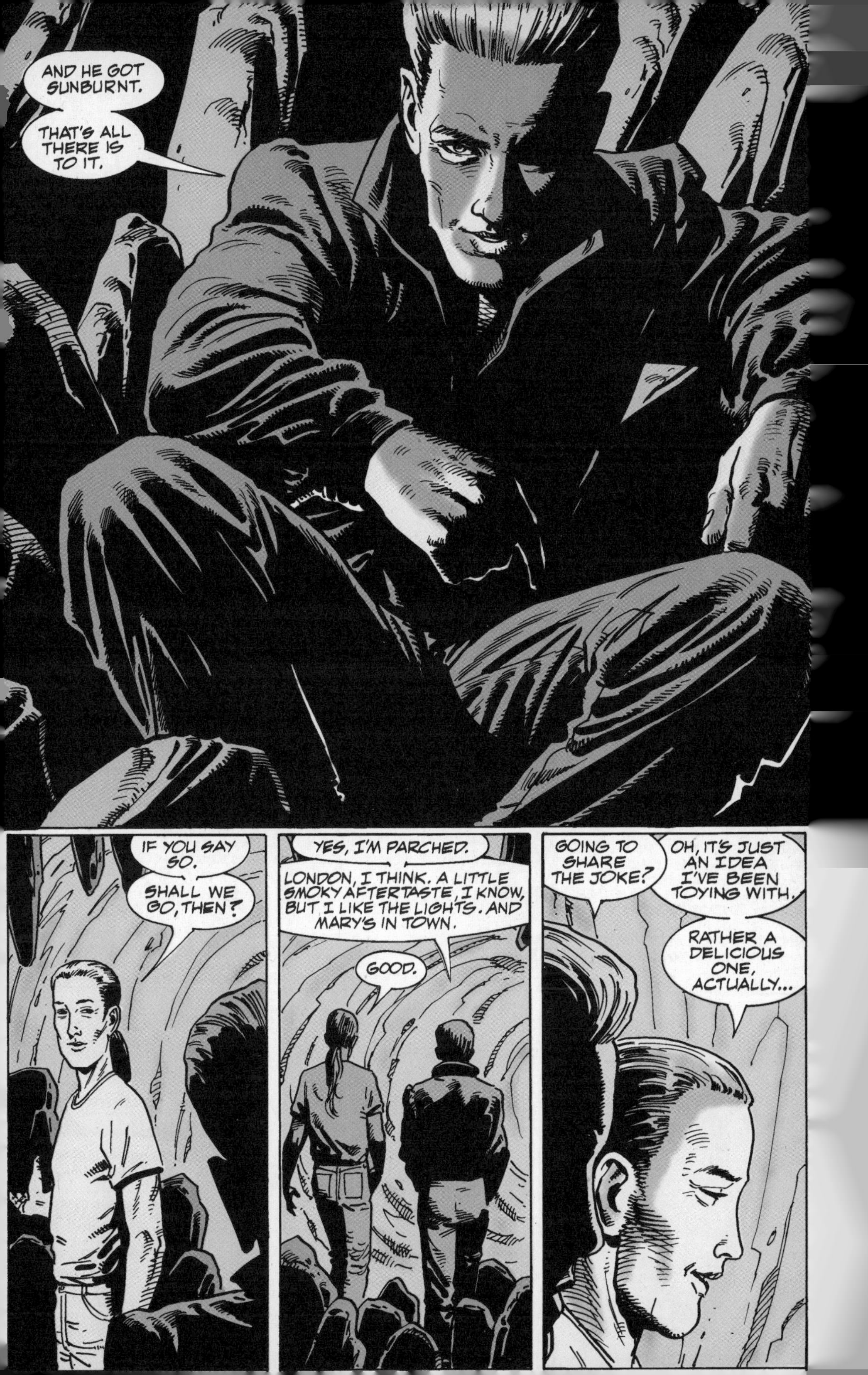
AND HE GOT SUNBURNT.
THAT'S ALL THERE IS TO IT.
IF YOU SAY SO.
SHALL WE GO, THEN?
YES, I'M PARCHED.
LONDON, I THINK. A LITTLE SMOKY AFTERTASTE, I KNOW, BUT I LIKE THE LIGHTS. AND MARY'S IN TOWN.
GOOD.
GOING TO SHARE THE JOKE?
OH, IT'S JUST AN IDEA I'VE BEEN TOYING WITH.
RATHER A DELICIOUS ONE, ACTUALLY...

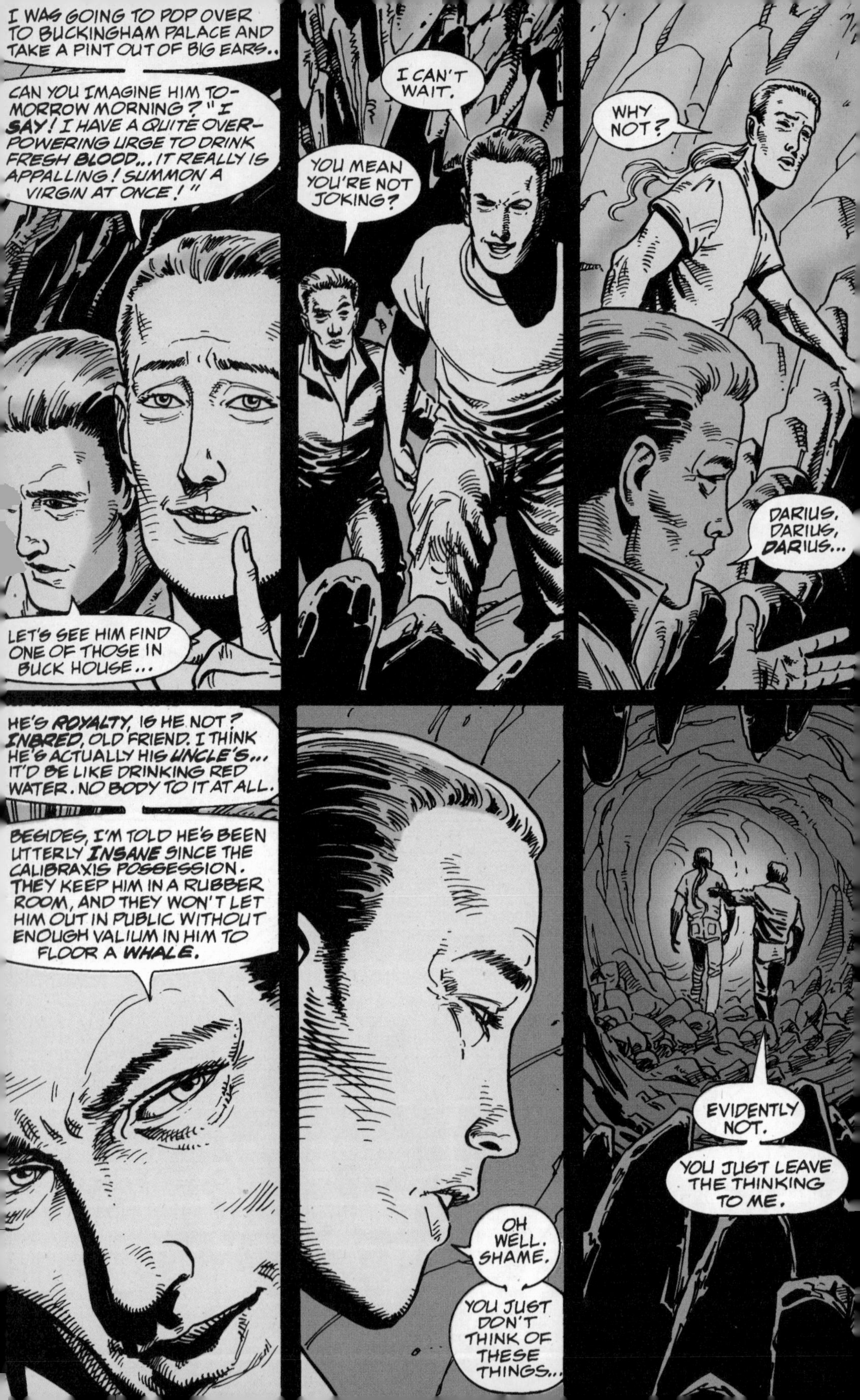
I WAS GOING TO POP OVER TO BUCKINGHAM PALACE AND TAKE A PINT OUT OF BIG EARS..
CAN YOU IMAGINE HIM TO-MORROW MORNING? "I SAY! I HAVE A QUITE OVER-POWERING URGE TO DRINK FRESH BLOOD... IT REALLY IS APPALLING! SUMMON A VIRGIN AT ONCE!"
LET'S SEE HIM FIND ONE OF THOSE IN BUCK HOUSE...
I CAN'T WAIT.
YOU MEAN YOU'RE NOT JOKING?
WHY NOT?
DARIUS, DARIUS, DARIUS...
HE'S ROYALTY, IS HE NOT? INBRED, OLD FRIEND. I THINK HE'S ACTUALLY HIS UNCLE'S... IT'D BE LIKE DRINKING RED WATER. NO BODY TO IT AT ALL.
BESIDES, I'M TOLD HE'S BEEN UTTERLY INSANE SINCE THE CALIBRAXIS POSSESSION. THEY KEEP HIM IN A RUBBER ROOM, AND THEY WON'T LET HIM OUT IN PUBLIC WITHOUT ENOUGH VALIUM IN HIM TO FLOOR A WHALE.
OH WELL. SHAME.
YOU JUST DON'T THINK OF THESE THINGS...
EVIDENTLY NOT.
YOU JUST LEAVE THE THINKING TO ME.

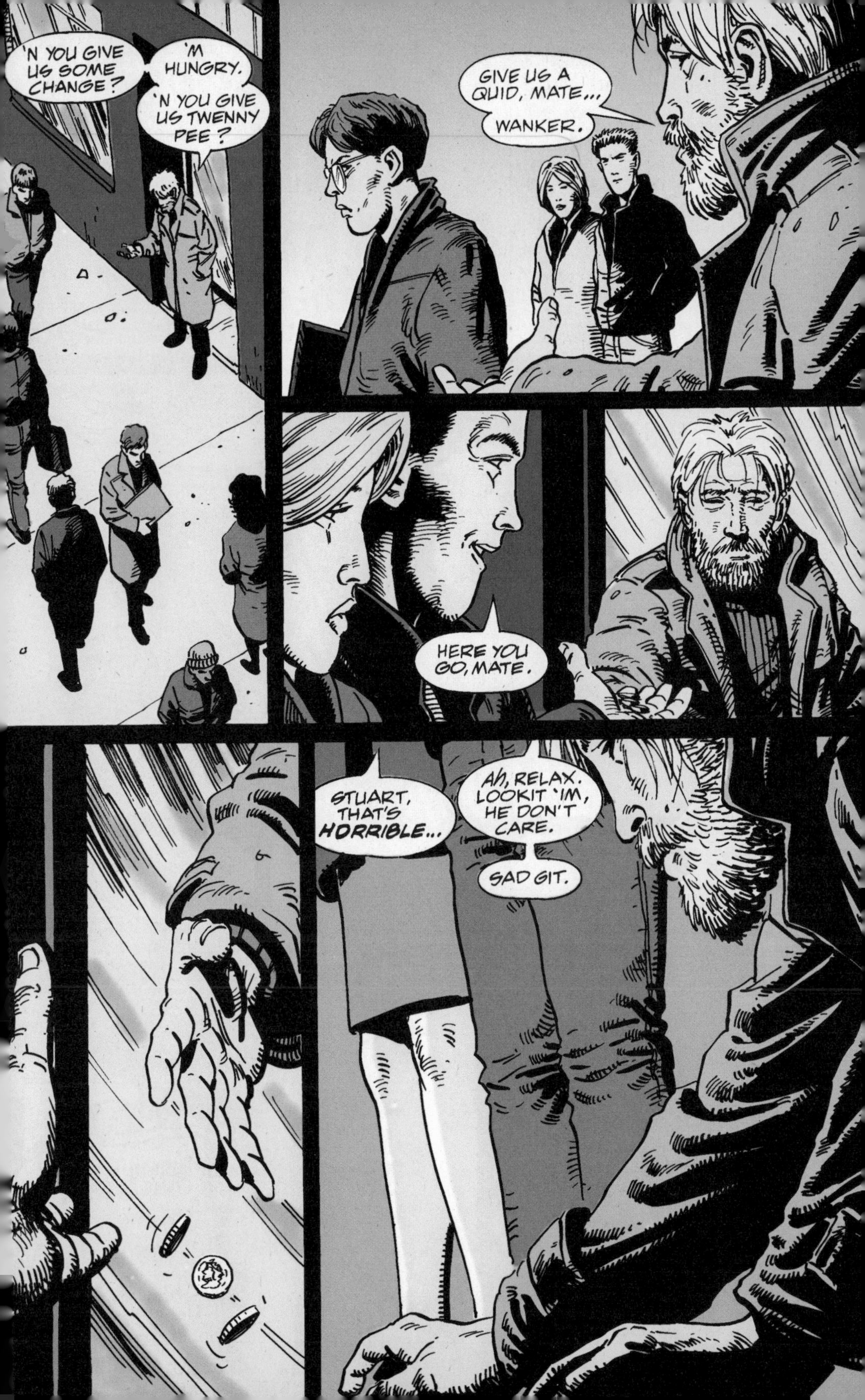
'N YOU GIVE US SOME CHANGE?
'M HUNGRY.
'N YOU GIVE US TWENNY PEE?
GIVE US A QUID, MATE...
WANKER.
HERE YOU GO, MATE.
STUART, THAT'S HORRIBLE...
AH, RELAX. LOOKIT 'IM, HE DON'T CARE.
SAD GIT.

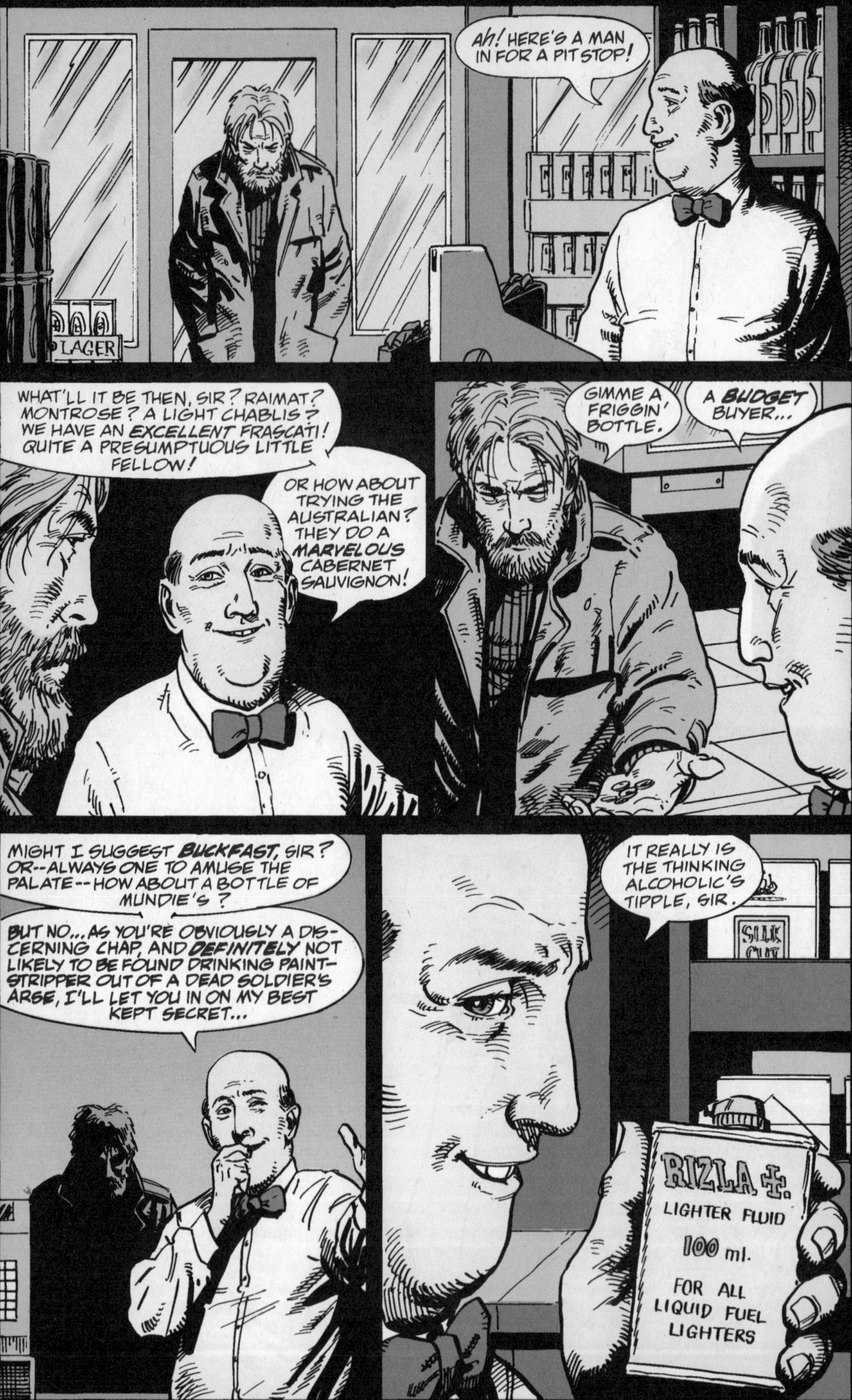

AH! HERE'S A MAN IN FOR A PIT STOP!
LAGER
WHAT'LL IT BE THEN, SIR? RAIMAT? MONTROSE? A LIGHT CHABLIS? WE HAVE AN *EXCELLENT* FRASCATI! QUITE A PRESUMPTUOUS LITTLE FELLOW!
OR HOW ABOUT TRYING THE AUSTRALIAN? THEY DO A *MARVELOUS* CABERNET SAUVIGNON!
GIMME A FRIGGIN' BOTTLE.
A *BUDGET* BUYER...
MIGHT I SUGGEST *BUCKFAST*, SIR? OR--ALWAYS ONE TO AMUSE THE PALATE--HOW ABOUT A BOTTLE OF MUNDIE'S?
BUT NO... AS YOU'RE OBVIOUSLY A DISCERNING CHAP, AND *DEFINITELY* NOT LIKELY TO BE FOUND DRINKING PAINT-STRIPPER OUT OF A DEAD SOLDIER'S ARSE, I'LL LET YOU IN ON MY BEST KEPT SECRET...
IT REALLY IS THE THINKING ALCOHOLIC'S TIPPLE, SIR.
RIZLA +.
LIGHTER FLUID
100 ml.
FOR ALL LIQUID FUEL LIGHTERS

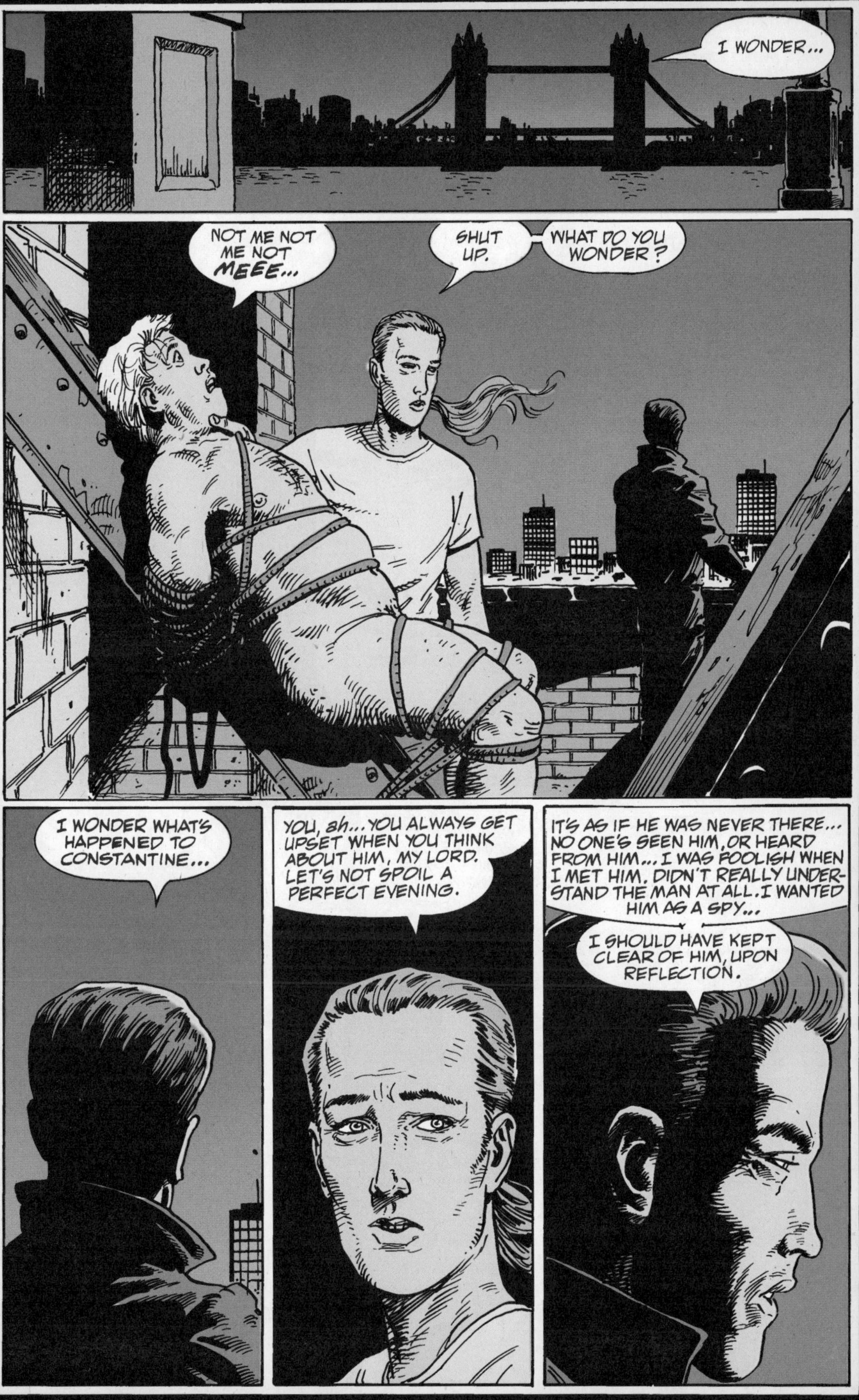
I WONDER...
NOT ME NOT ME NOT MEEE...
SHUT UP.
WHAT DO YOU WONDER?
I WONDER WHAT'S HAPPENED TO CONSTANTINE...
YOU, ah... YOU ALWAYS GET UPSET WHEN YOU THINK ABOUT HIM, MY LORD. LET'S NOT SPOIL A PERFECT EVENING.
IT'S AS IF HE WAS NEVER THERE... NO ONE'S SEEN HIM, OR HEARD FROM HIM... I WAS FOOLISH WHEN I MET HIM. DIDN'T REALLY UNDERSTAND THE MAN AT ALL. I WANTED HIM AS A SPY...
I SHOULD HAVE KEPT CLEAR OF HIM, UPON REFLECTION.

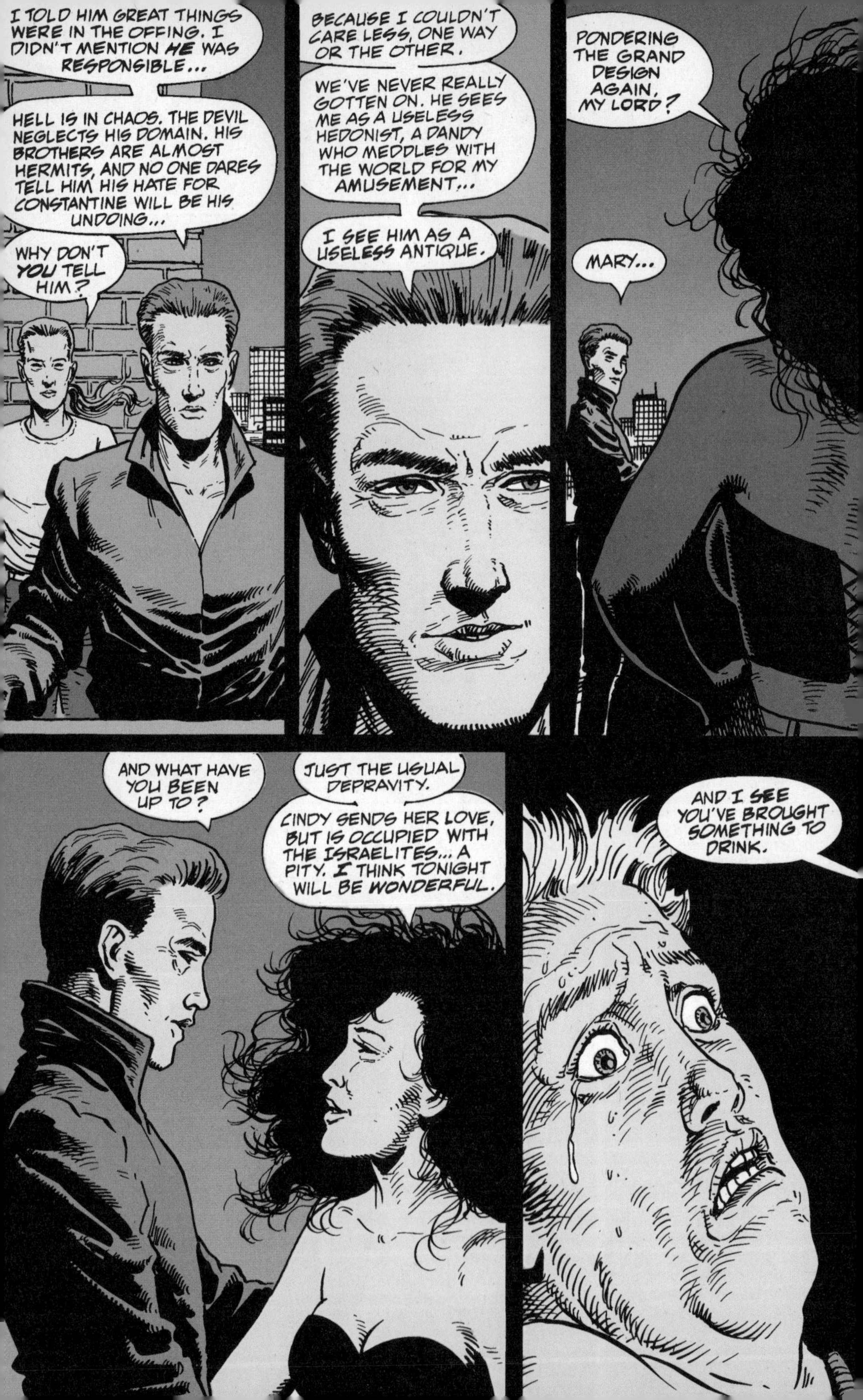
I TOLD HIM GREAT THINGS WERE IN THE OFFING. I DIDN'T MENTION HE WAS RESPONSIBLE...
HELL IS IN CHAOS. THE DEVIL NEGLECTS HIS DOMAIN. HIS BROTHERS ARE ALMOST HERMITS, AND NO ONE DARES TELL HIM HIS HATE FOR CONSTANTINE WILL BE HIS UNDOING...
WHY DON'T YOU TELL HIM?
BECAUSE I COULDN'T CARE LESS, ONE WAY OR THE OTHER.
WE'VE NEVER REALLY GOTTEN ON. HE SEES ME AS A USELESS HEDONIST, A DANDY WHO MEDDLES WITH THE WORLD FOR MY AMUSEMENT...
I SEE HIM AS A USELESS ANTIQUE.
PONDERING THE GRAND DESIGN AGAIN, MY LORD?
MARY...
AND WHAT HAVE YOU BEEN UP TO?
JUST THE USUAL DEPRAVITY.
CINDY SENDS HER LOVE, BUT IS OCCUPIED WITH THE ISRAELITES... A PITY. I THINK TONIGHT WILL BE WONDERFUL.
AND I SEE YOU'VE BROUGHT SOMETHING TO DRINK.

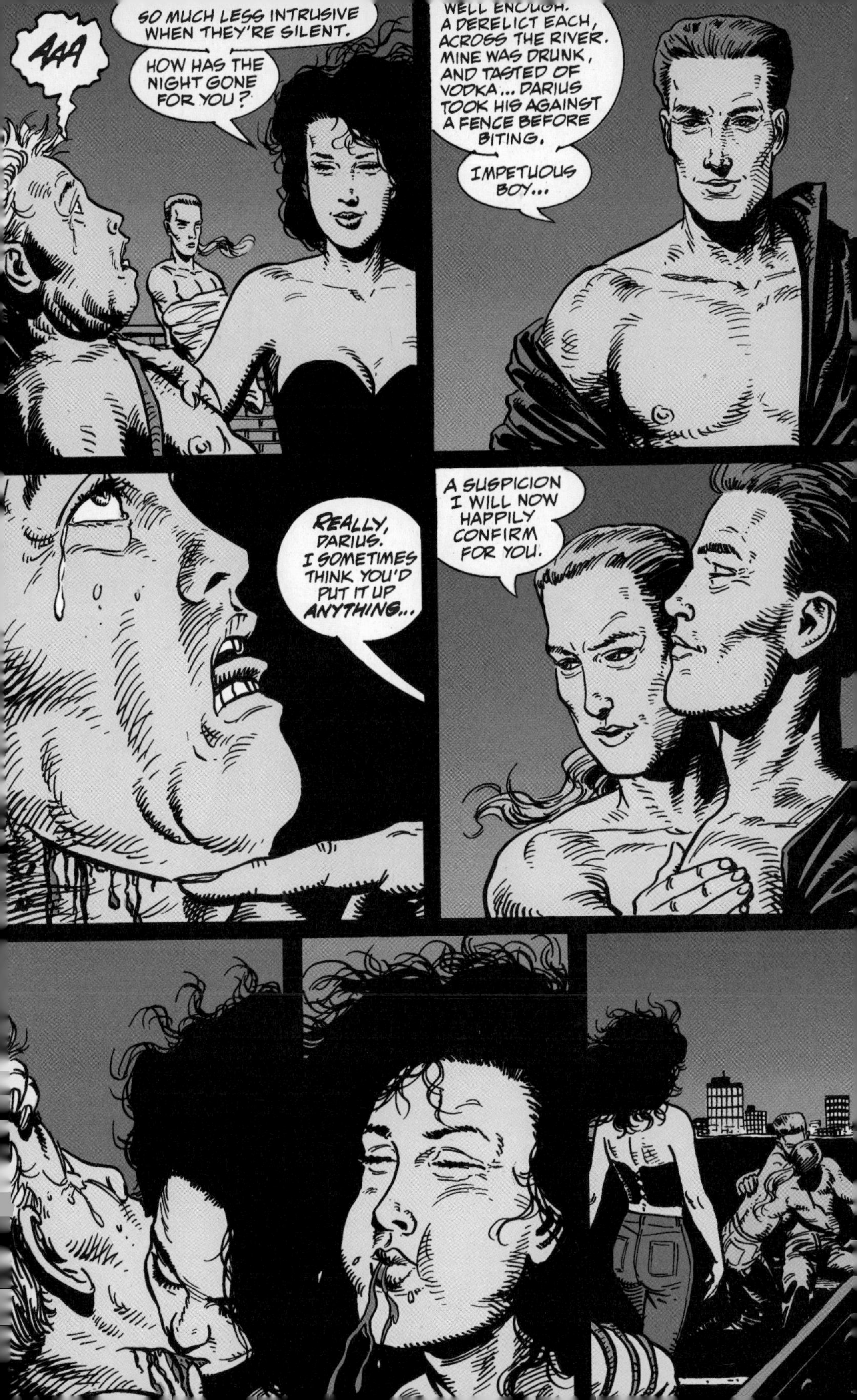
AAA
SO MUCH LESS INTRUSIVE WHEN THEY'RE SILENT.
HOW HAS THE NIGHT GONE FOR YOU?
WELL ENOUGH. A DERELICT EACH, ACROSS THE RIVER. MINE WAS DRUNK, AND TASTED OF VODKA... DARIUS TOOK HIS AGAINST A FENCE BEFORE BITING.
IMPETUOUS BOY...
REALLY, DARIUS. I SOMETIMES THINK YOU'D PUT IT UP ANYTHING...
A SUSPICION I WILL NOW HAPPILY CONFIRM FOR YOU.

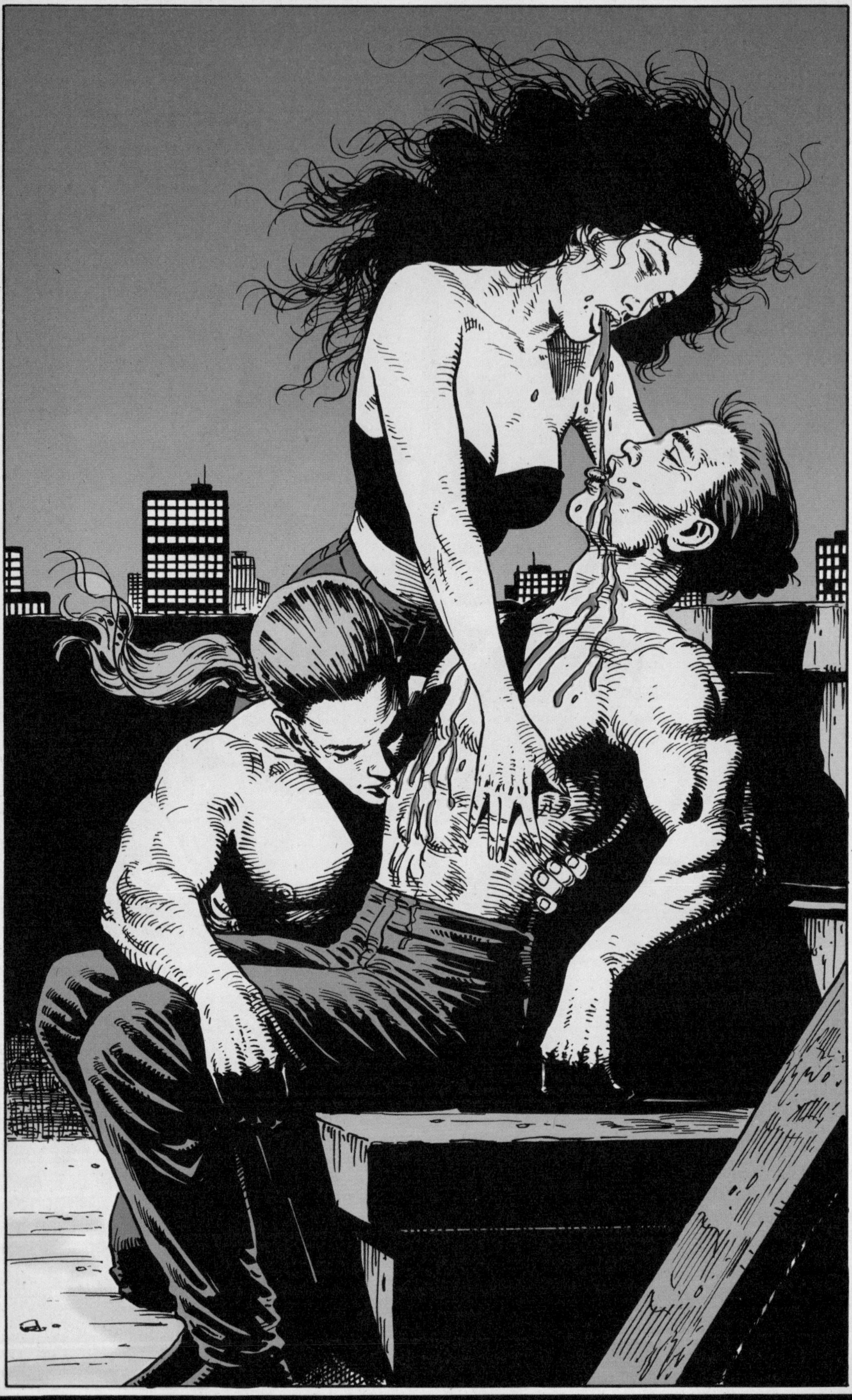

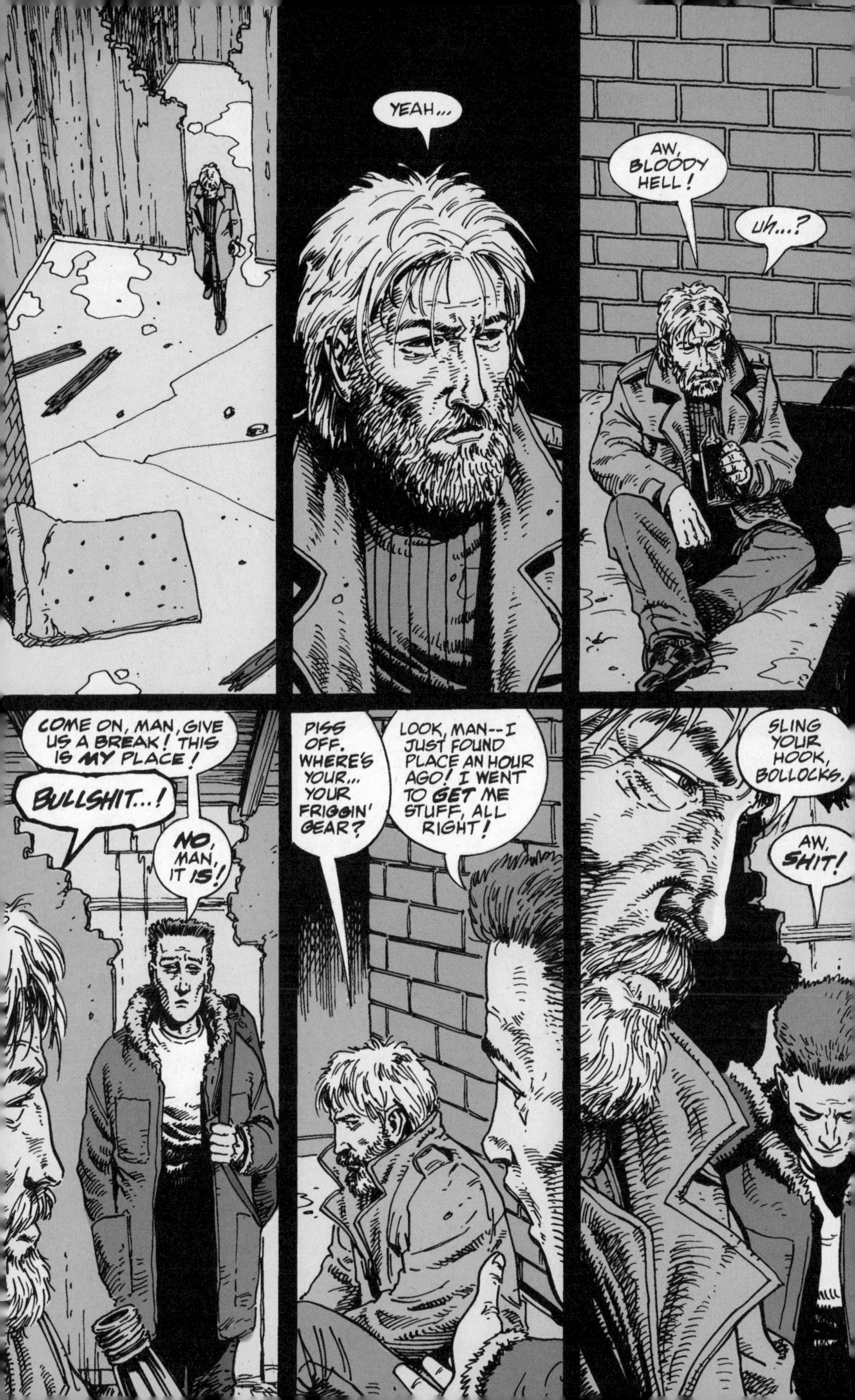
YEAH...
AW, BLOODY HELL!
uh...?
COME ON, MAN, GIVE US A BREAK! THIS IS MY PLACE!
BULLSHIT...!
NO, MAN, IT IS!
PISS OFF. WHERE'S YOUR... YOUR FRIGGIN' GEAR?
LOOK, MAN--I JUST FOUND PLACE AN HOUR AGO! I WENT TO GET ME STUFF, ALL RIGHT!
SLING YOUR HOOK, BOLLOCKS.
AW, SHIT!

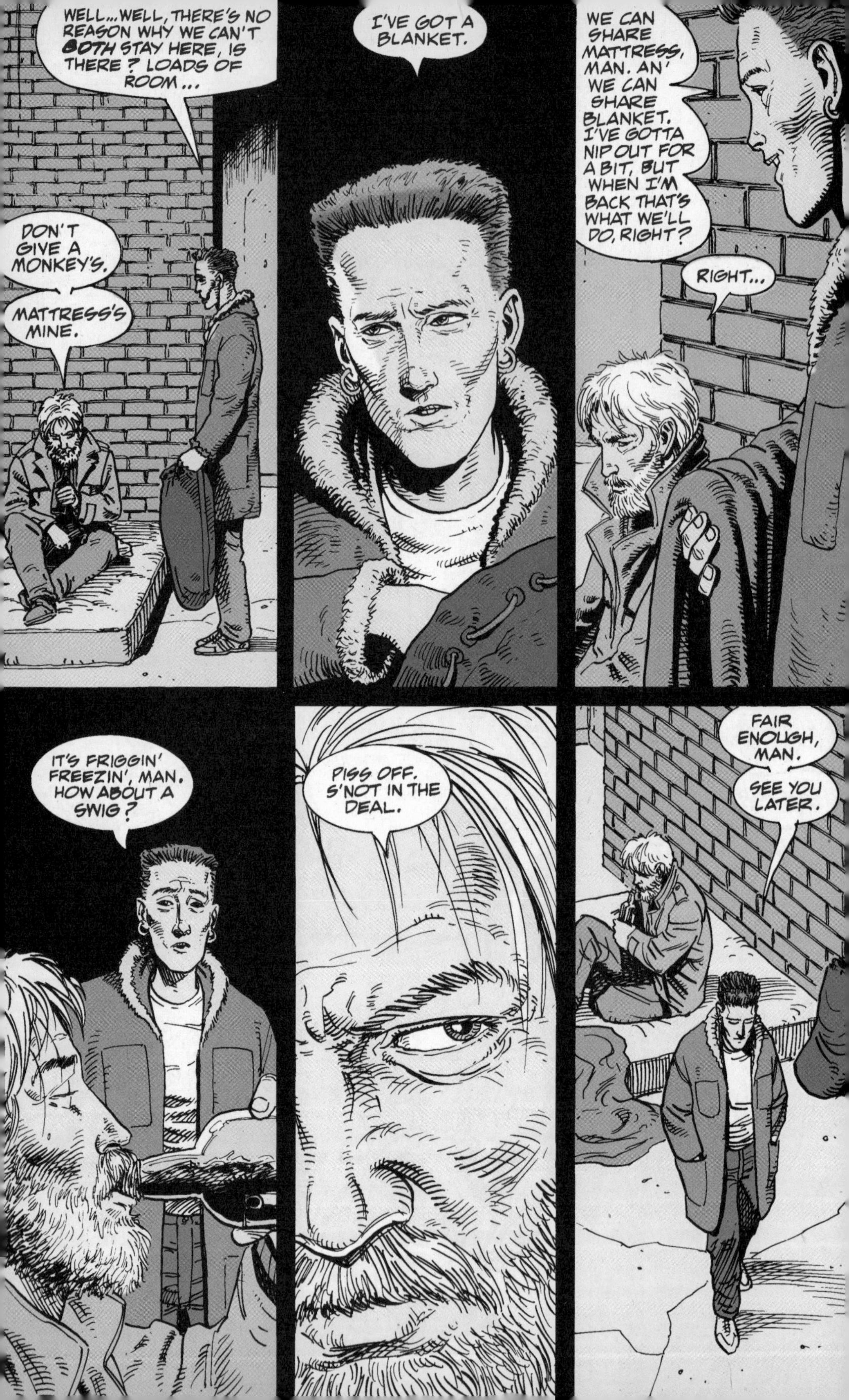
WELL...WELL, THERE'S NO REASON WHY WE CAN'T BOTH STAY HERE, IS THERE? LOADS OF ROOM...
DON'T GIVE A MONKEY'S.
MATTRESS'S MINE.
I'VE GOT A BLANKET.
WE CAN SHARE MATTRESS, MAN. AN' WE CAN SHARE BLANKET. I'VE GOTTA NIP OUT FOR A BIT, BUT WHEN I'M BACK THAT'S WHAT WE'LL DO, RIGHT?
RIGHT...
IT'S FRIGGIN' FREEZIN', MAN. HOW ABOUT A SWIG?
PISS OFF. S'NOT IN THE DEAL.
FAIR ENOUGH, MAN.
SEE YOU LATER.

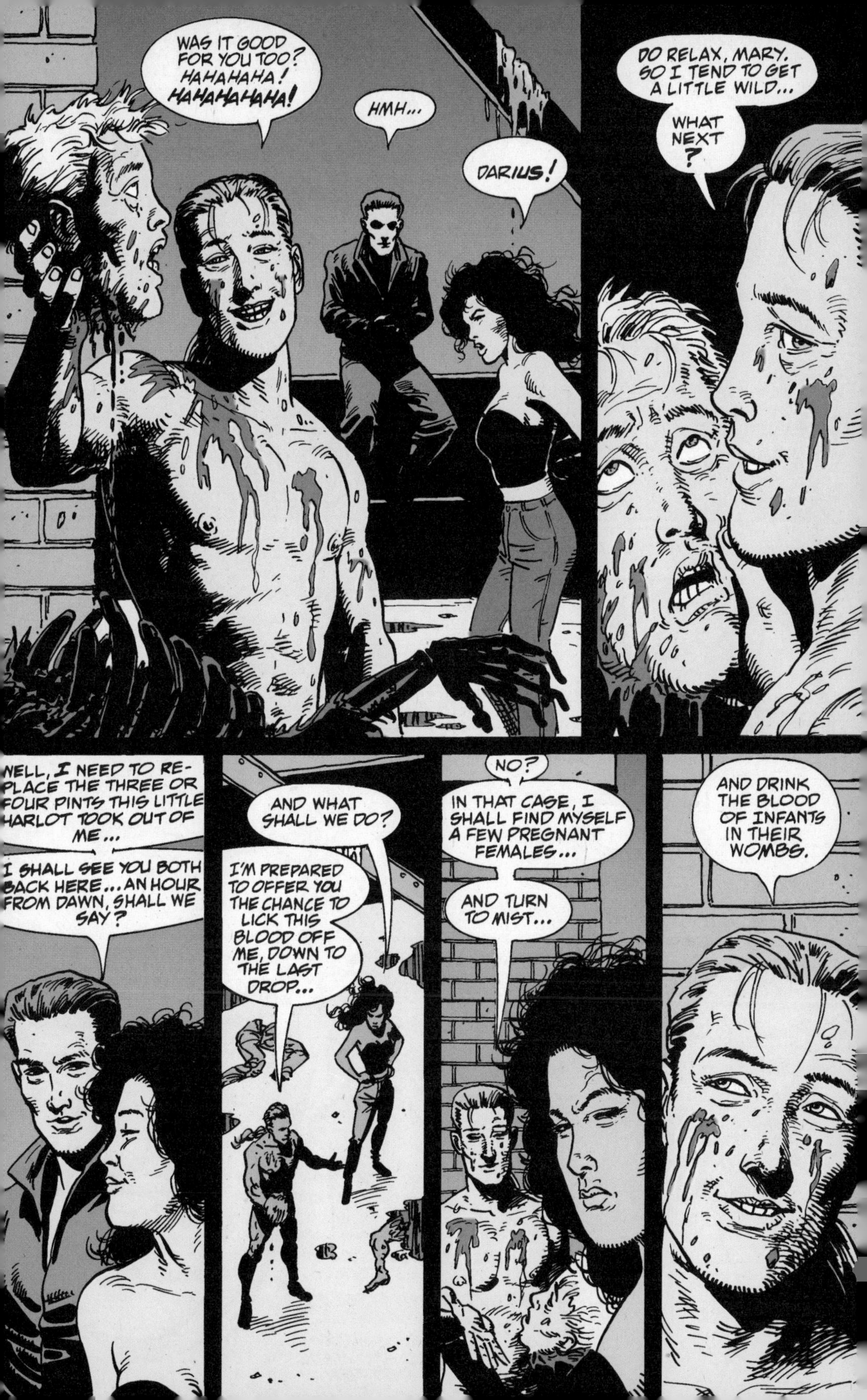
WAS IT GOOD FOR YOU TOO? HAHAHAHA! HAHAHAHAHA!
HMH...
DARIUS!
DO RELAX, MARY. SO I TEND TO GET A LITTLE WILD...
WHAT NEXT ?
WELL, I NEED TO RE-PLACE THE THREE OR FOUR PINTS THIS LITTLE HARLOT TOOK OUT OF ME...
I SHALL SEE YOU BOTH BACK HERE... AN HOUR FROM DAWN, SHALL WE SAY?
AND WHAT SHALL WE DO?
I'M PREPARED TO OFFER YOU THE CHANCE TO LICK THIS BLOOD OFF ME, DOWN TO THE LAST DROP...
NO?
IN THAT CASE, I SHALL FIND MYSELF A FEW PREGNANT FEMALES...
AND TURN TO MIST...
AND DRINK THE BLOOD OF INFANTS IN THEIR WOMBS.

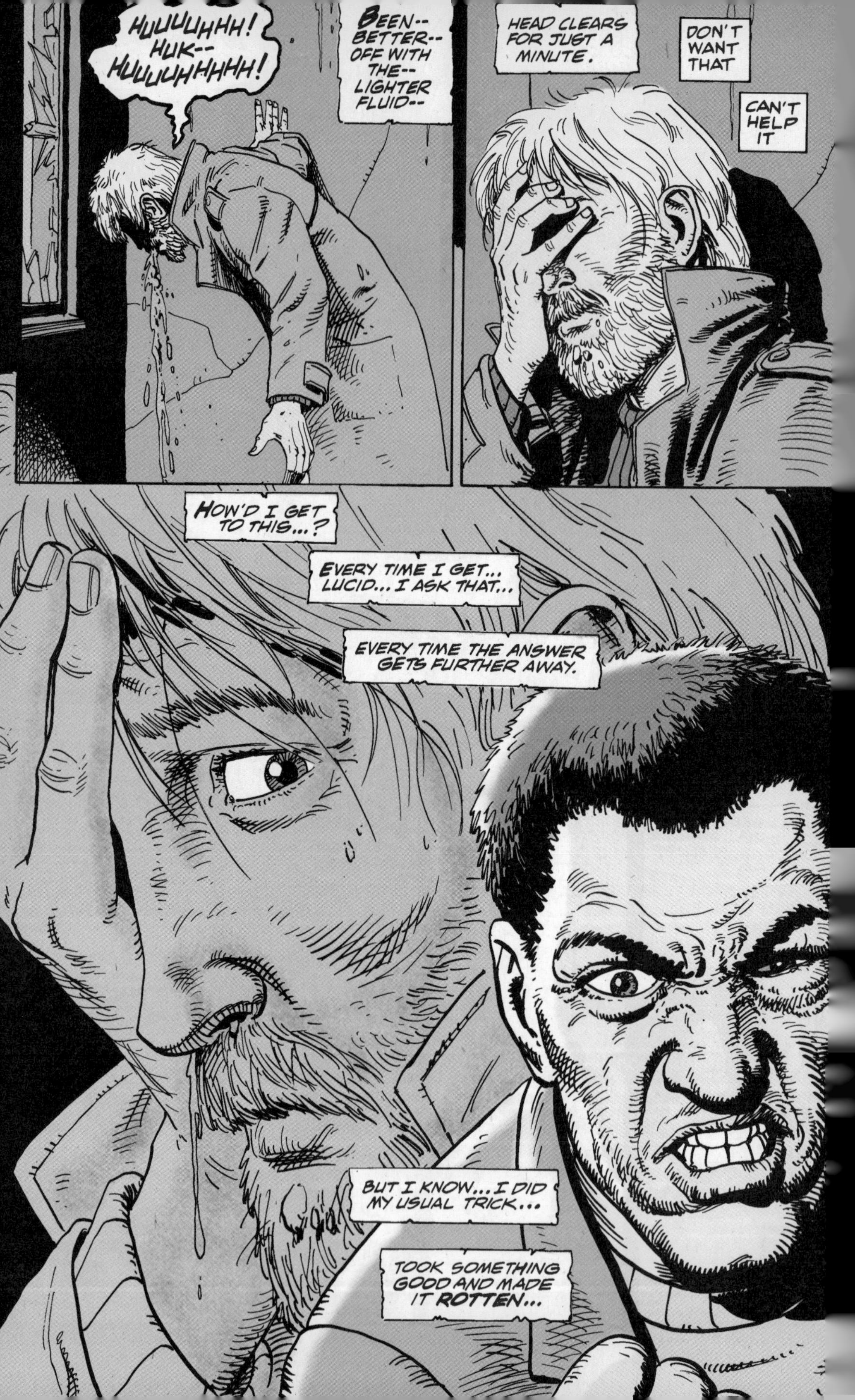
HUUUUHHH! HUK-- HUUUUHHHHH!
BEEN-- BETTER-- OFF WITH THE-- LIGHTER FLUID--
HEAD CLEARS FOR JUST A MINUTE.
DON'T WANT THAT
CAN'T HELP IT
HOW'D I GET TO THIS...?
EVERY TIME I GET... LUCID... I ASK THAT...
EVERY TIME THE ANSWER GETS FURTHER AWAY.
BUT I KNOW... I DID MY USUAL TRICK...
TOOK SOMETHING GOOD AND MADE IT ROTTEN...

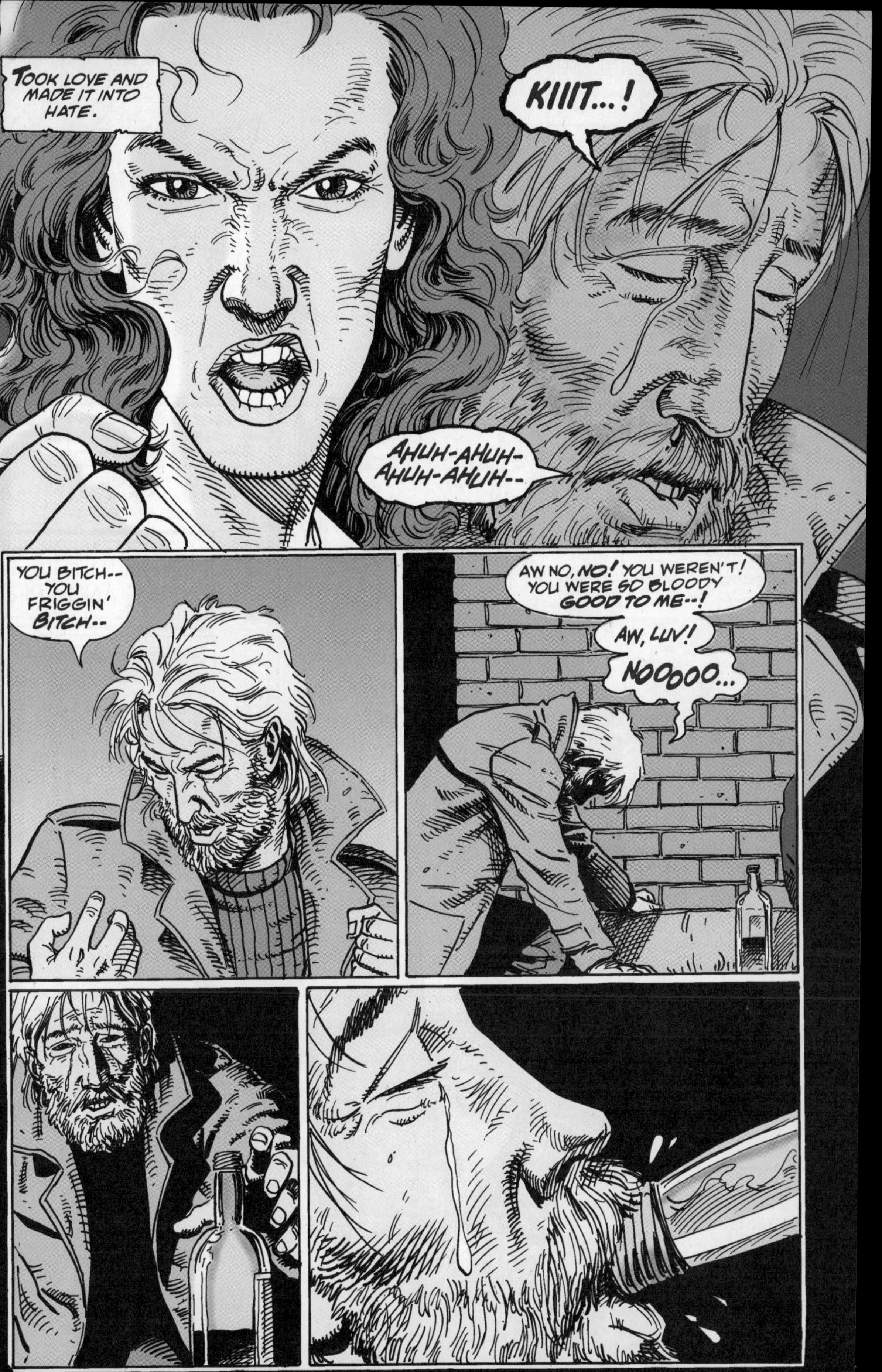
TOOK LOVE AND MADE IT INTO HATE.
KIIIT...!
AHUH-AHUH-AHUH-AHUH--
YOU BITCH--YOU FRIGGIN' BITCH--
AW NO, NO! YOU WEREN'T! YOU WERE SO BLOODY GOOD TO ME--!
AW, LUV!
NOOOOO...

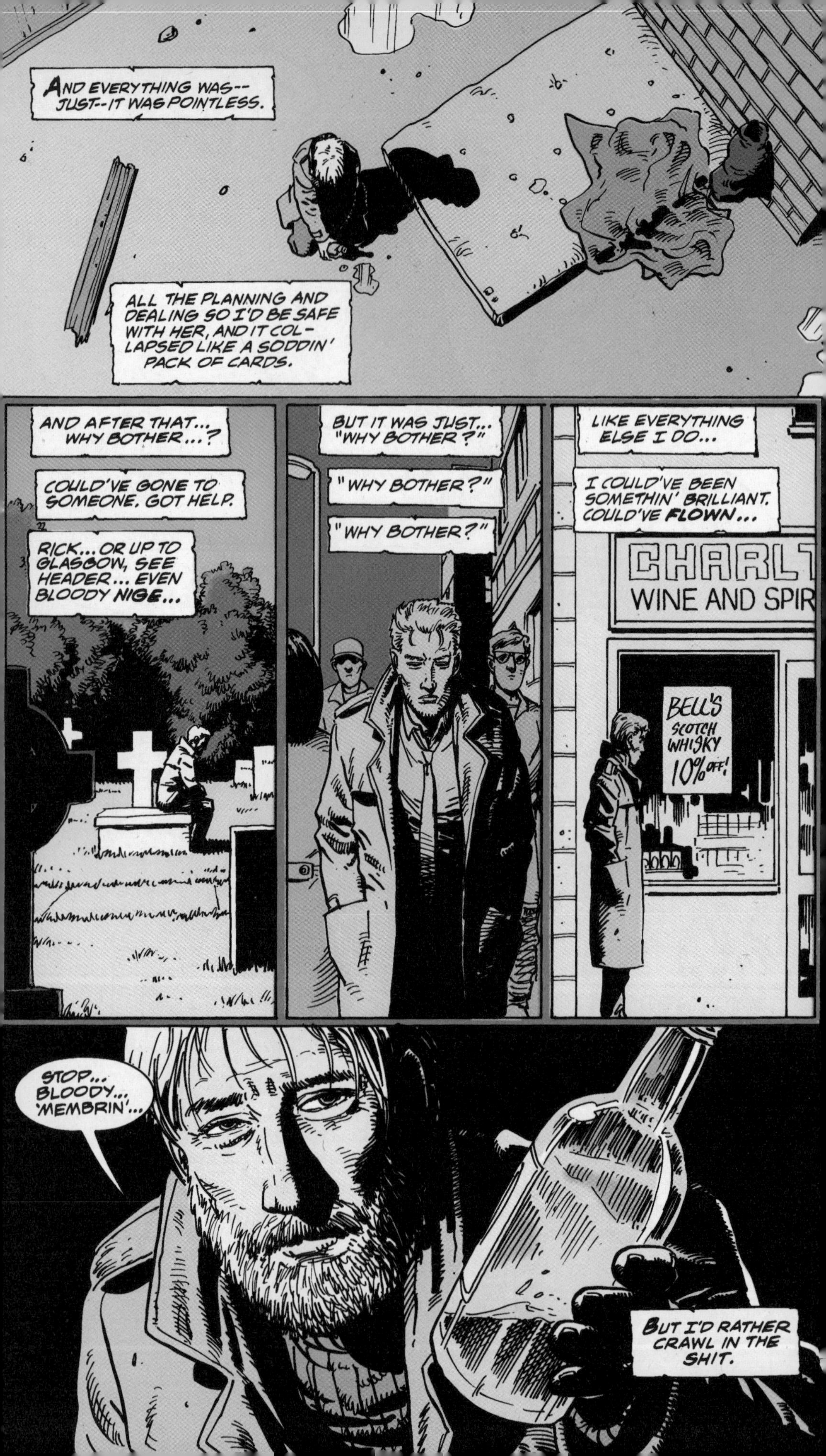
AND EVERYTHING WAS-- JUST--IT WAS POINTLESS.
ALL THE PLANNING AND DEALING SO I'D BE SAFE WITH HER, AND IT COL-LAPSED LIKE A SODDIN' PACK OF CARDS.
AND AFTER THAT... WHY BOTHER...?
COULD'VE GONE TO SOMEONE. GOT HELP.
RICK...OR UP TO GLASGOW, SEE HEADER... EVEN BLOODY NIGE...
BUT IT WAS JUST... "WHY BOTHER?"
"WHY BOTHER?"
"WHY BOTHER?"
LIKE EVERYTHING ELSE I DO...
I COULD'VE BEEN SOMETHIN' BRILLIANT. COULD'VE FLOWN...
CHARLT
WINE AND SPIR
BELL'S SCOTCH WHISKY 10% OFF!
STOP... BLOODY... 'MEMBRIN'...
BUT I'D RATHER CRAWL IN THE SHIT.

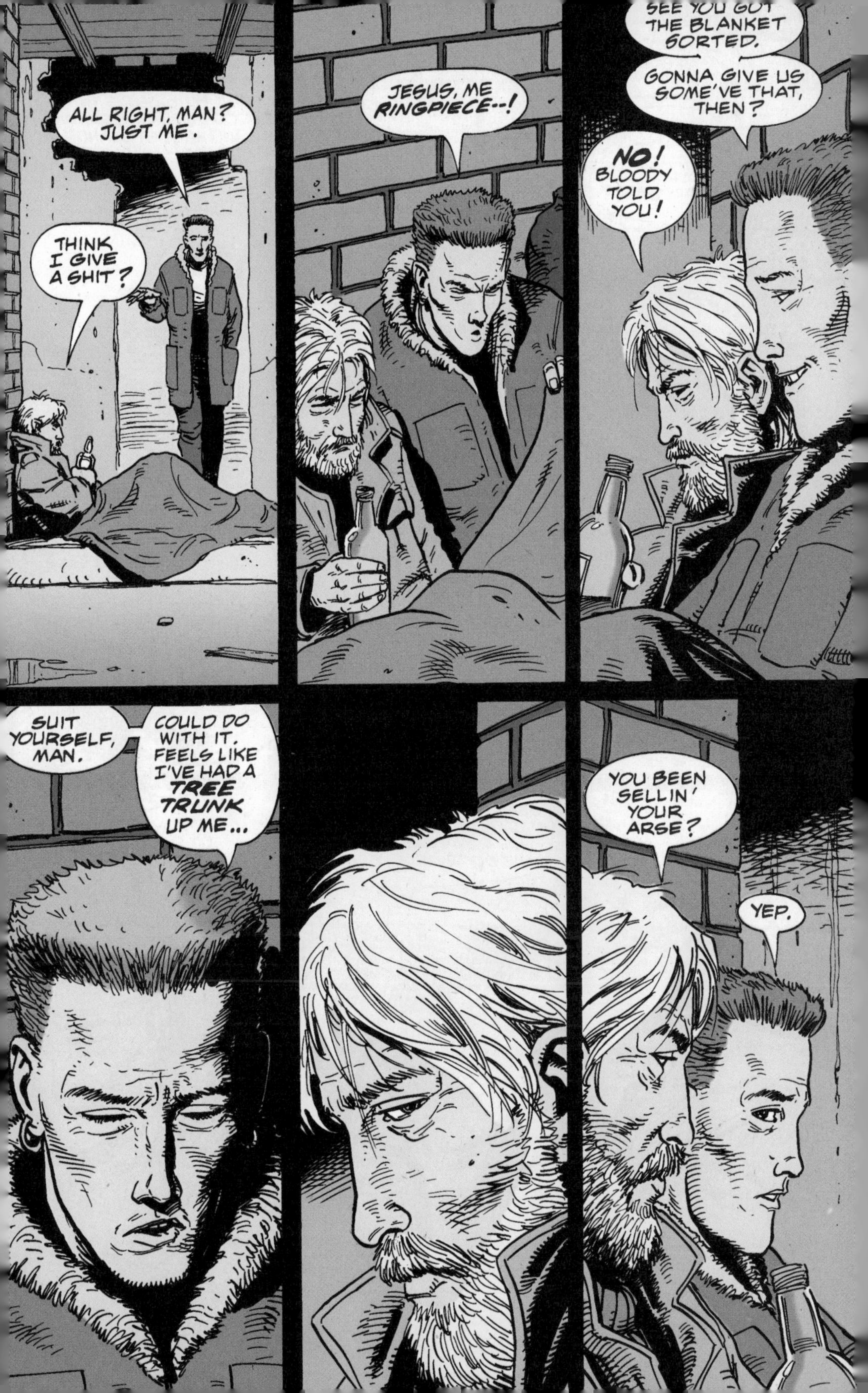
ALL RIGHT, MAN? JUST ME.
THINK I GIVE A SHIT?
JESUS, ME RINGPIECE--!
SEE YOU GOT THE BLANKET SORTED.
GONNA GIVE US SOME'VE THAT, THEN?
NO! BLOODY TOLD YOU!
SUIT YOURSELF, MAN.
COULD DO WITH IT. FEELS LIKE I'VE HAD A TREE TRUNK UP ME...
YOU BEEN SELLIN' YOUR ARSE?
YEP.

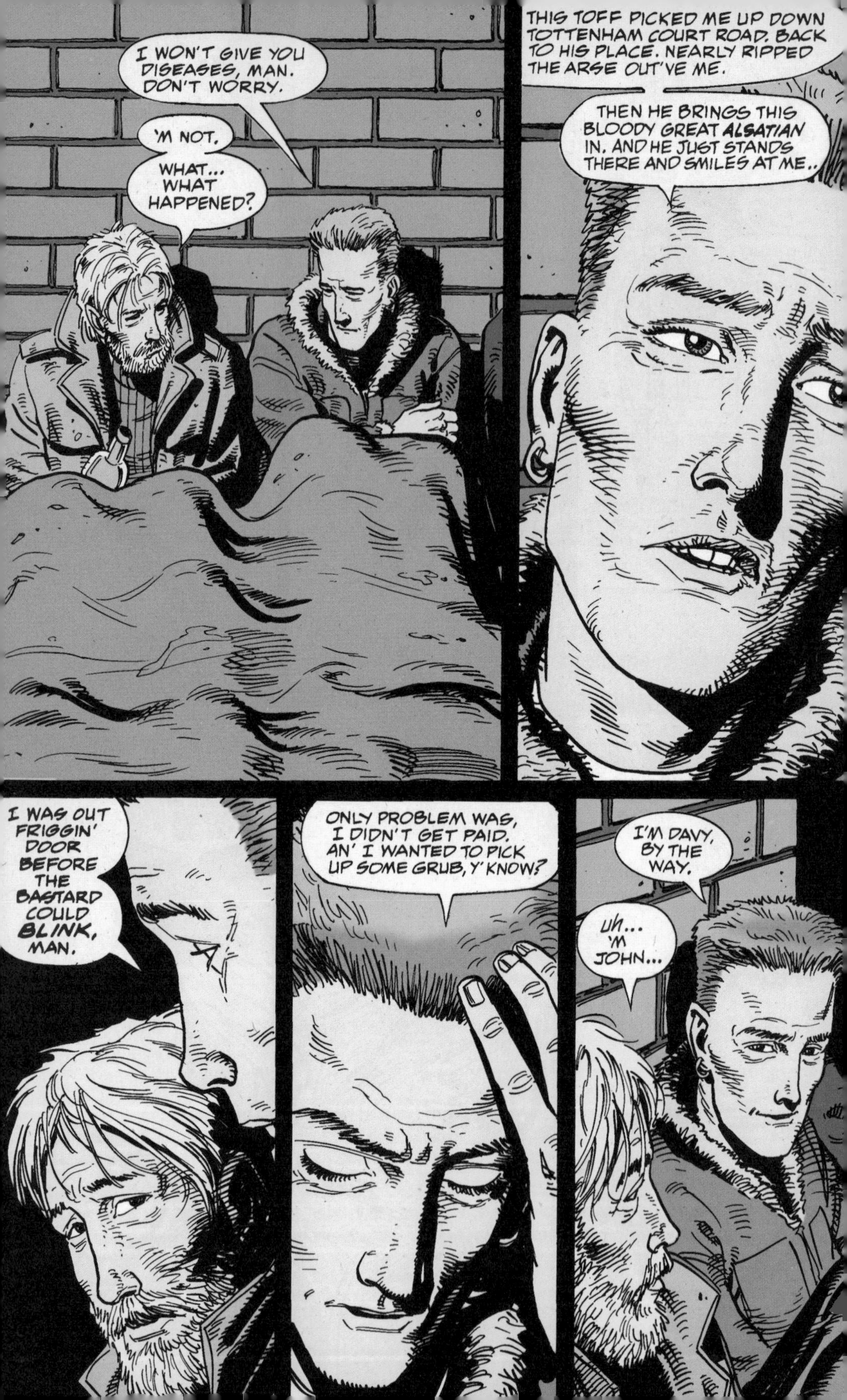
I WON'T GIVE YOU DISEASES, MAN. DON'T WORRY.
'M NOT.
WHAT... WHAT HAPPENED?
THIS TOFF PICKED ME UP DOWN TOTTENHAM COURT ROAD. BACK TO HIS PLACE. NEARLY RIPPED THE ARSE OUT'VE ME.
THEN HE BRINGS THIS BLOODY GREAT ALSATIAN IN. AND HE JUST STANDS THERE AND SMILES AT ME...
I WAS OUT FRIGGIN' DOOR BEFORE THE BASTARD COULD BLINK, MAN.
ONLY PROBLEM WAS, I DIDN'T GET PAID. AN' I WANTED TO PICK UP SOME GRUB, Y'KNOW?
I'M DAVY, BY THE WAY.
uh... 'M JOHN...

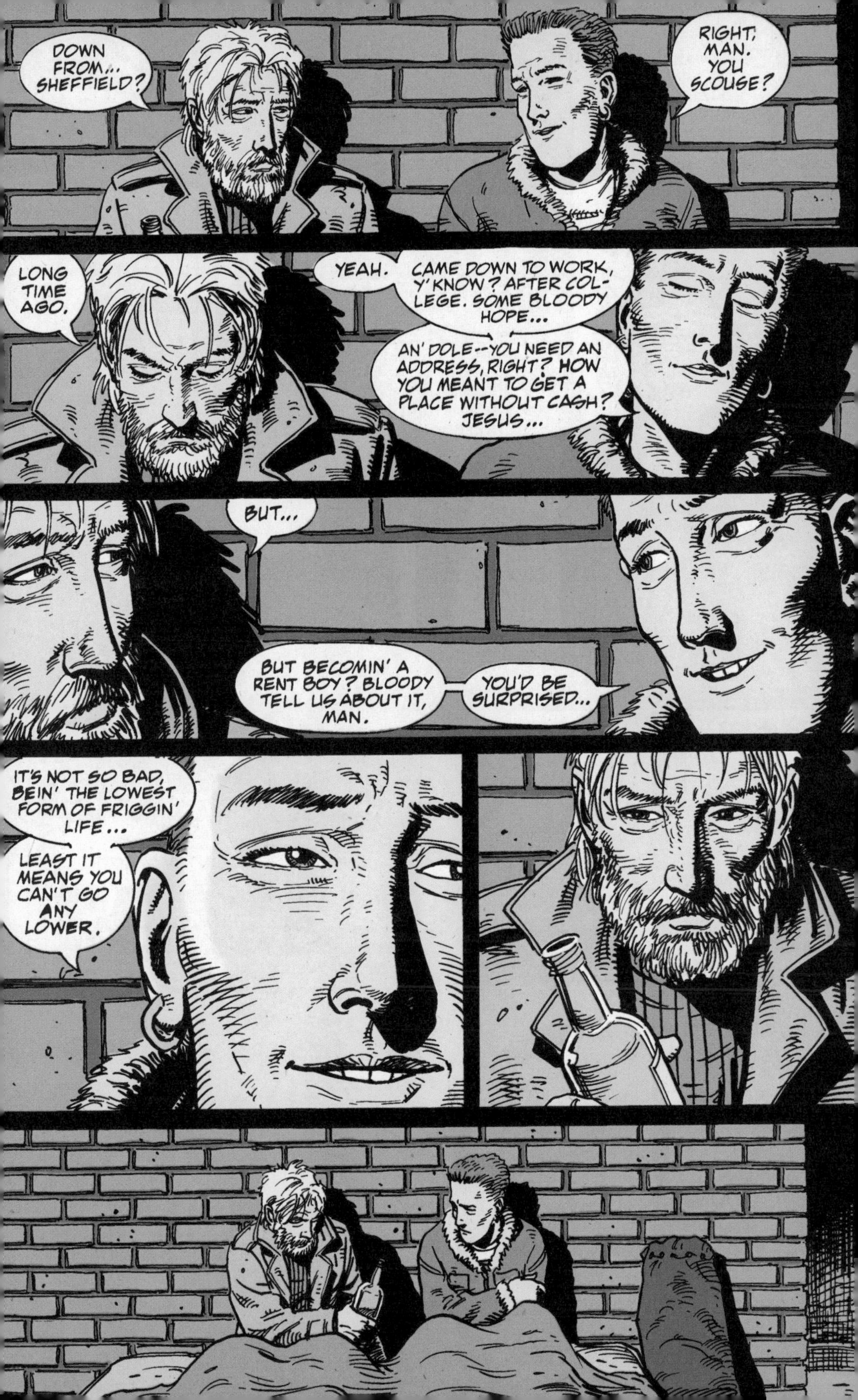
DOWN FROM... SHEFFIELD?
RIGHT, MAN. YOU SCOUSE?
LONG TIME AGO.
YEAH.
CAME DOWN TO WORK, Y'KNOW? AFTER COL-LEGE. SOME BLOODY HOPE...
AN' DOLE--YOU NEED AN ADDRESS, RIGHT? HOW YOU MEANT TO GET A PLACE WITHOUT CASH? JESUS...
BUT...
BUT BECOMIN' A RENT BOY? BLOODY TELL US ABOUT IT, MAN.
YOU'D BE SURPRISED...
IT'S NOT SO BAD, BEIN' THE LOWEST FORM OF FRIGGIN' LIFE...
LEAST IT MEANS YOU CAN'T GO ANY LOWER.

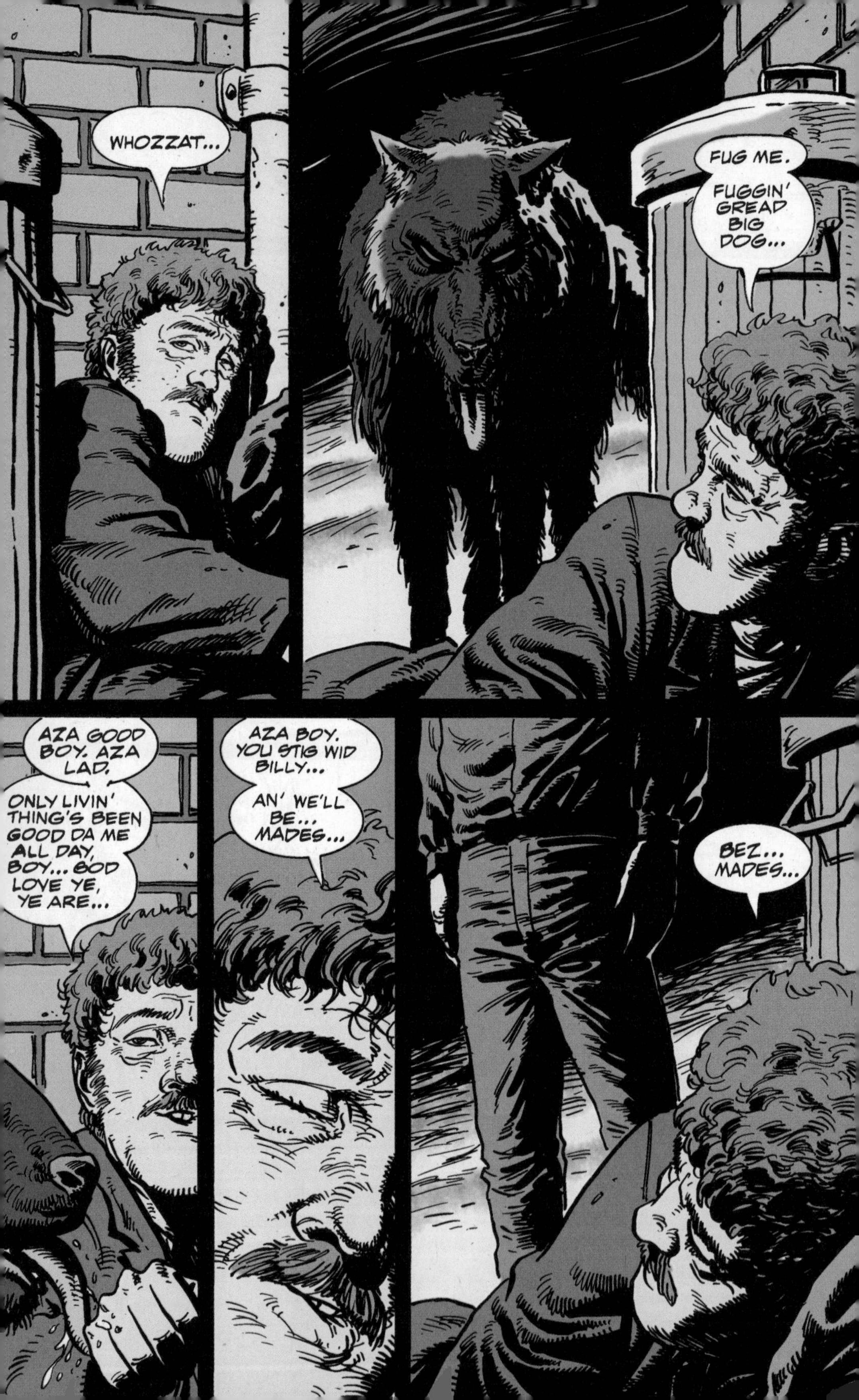
WHOZZAT...
FUG ME.
FUGGIN' GREAD BIG DOG...
AZA GOOD BOY. AZA LAD.
ONLY LIVIN' THING'S BEEN GOOD DA ME ALL DAY, BOY... GOD LOVE YE, YE ARE...
AZA BOY. YOU STIG WID BILLY...
AN' WE'LL BE... MADES...
BEZ... MADES...

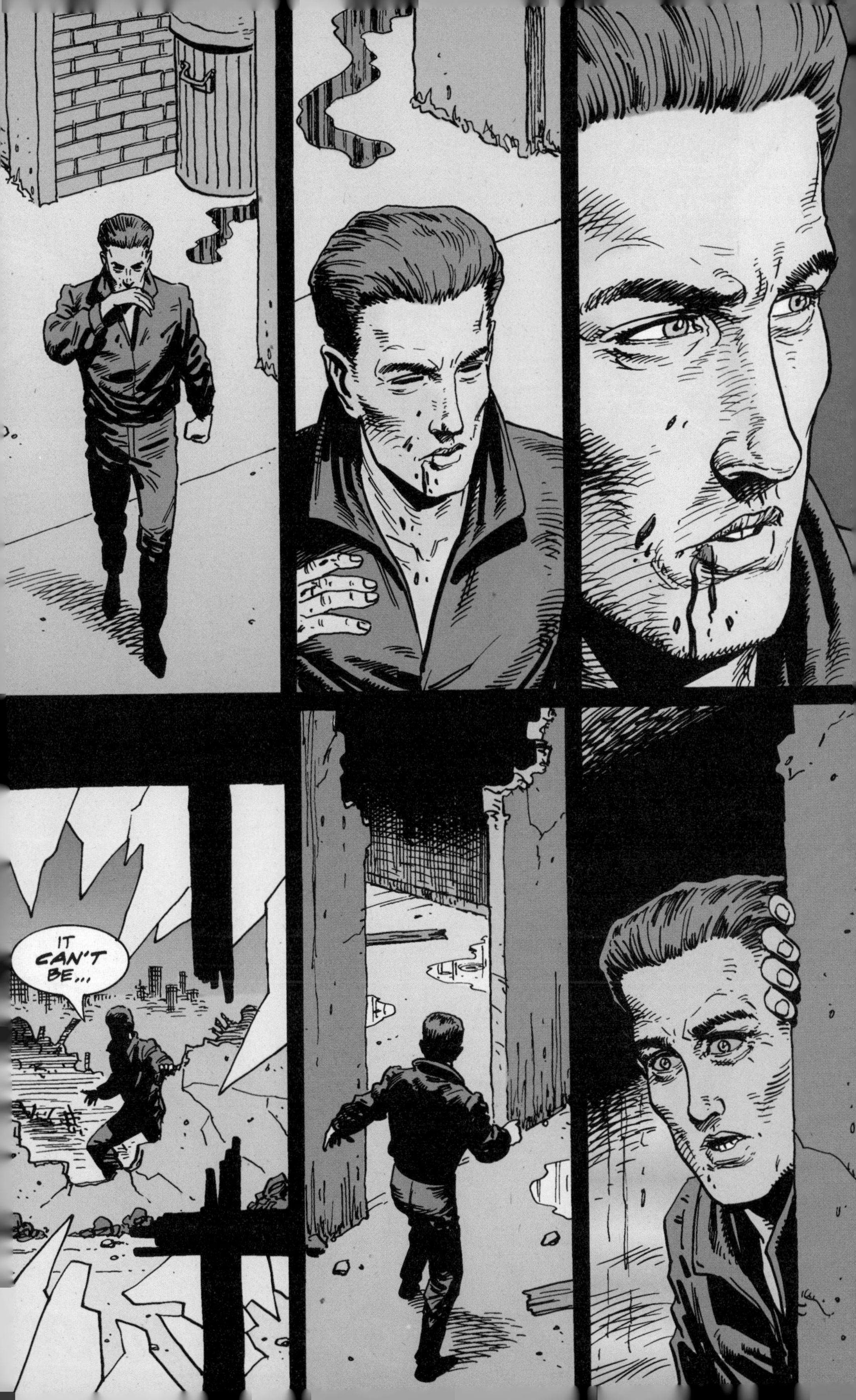
IT CAN'T BE...

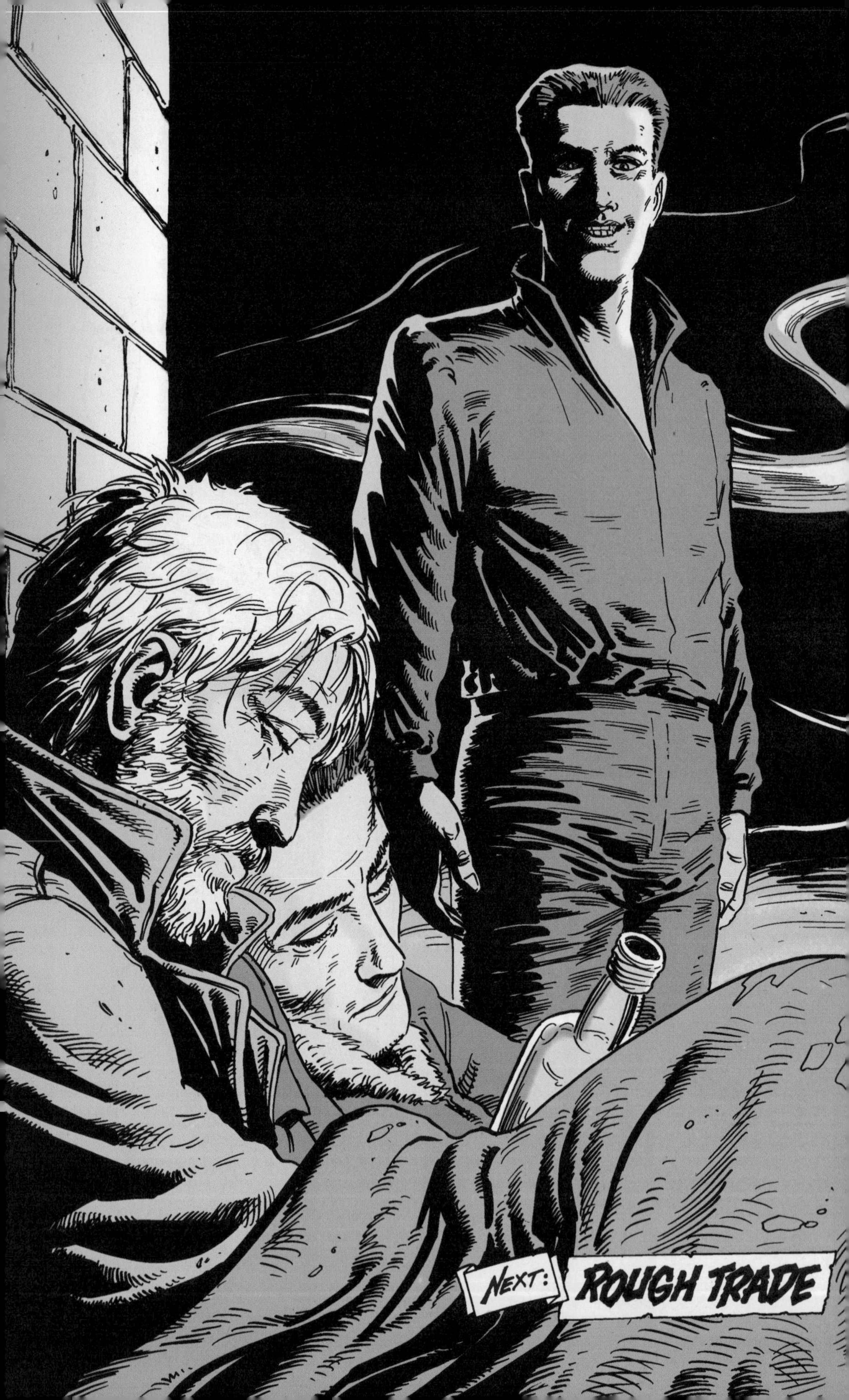
NEXT: ROUGH TRADE

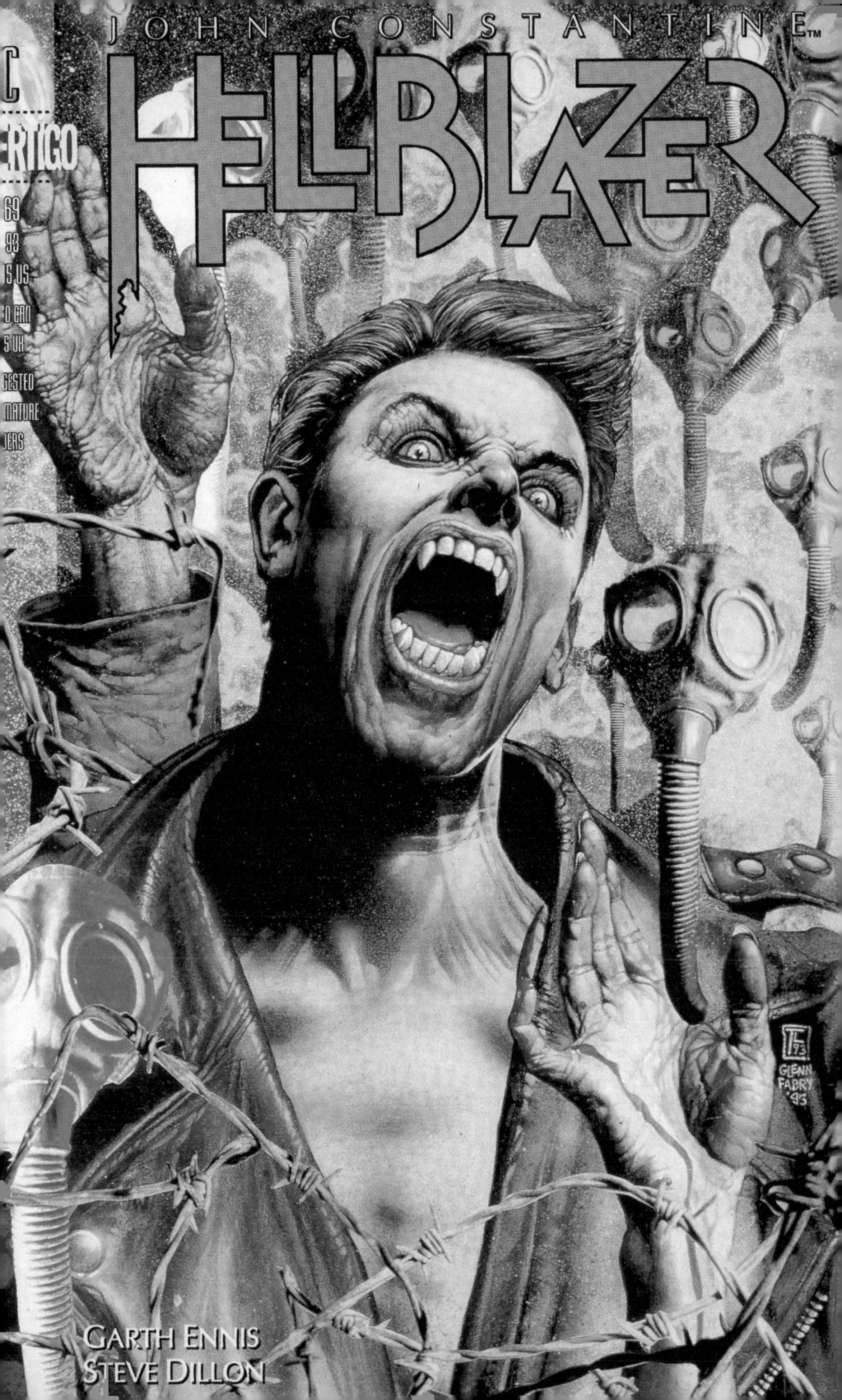
JOHN CONSTANTINE
HELLBLAZER
RTIGO
69
93
GLENN FABRY '93
GARTH ENNIS
STEVE DILLON

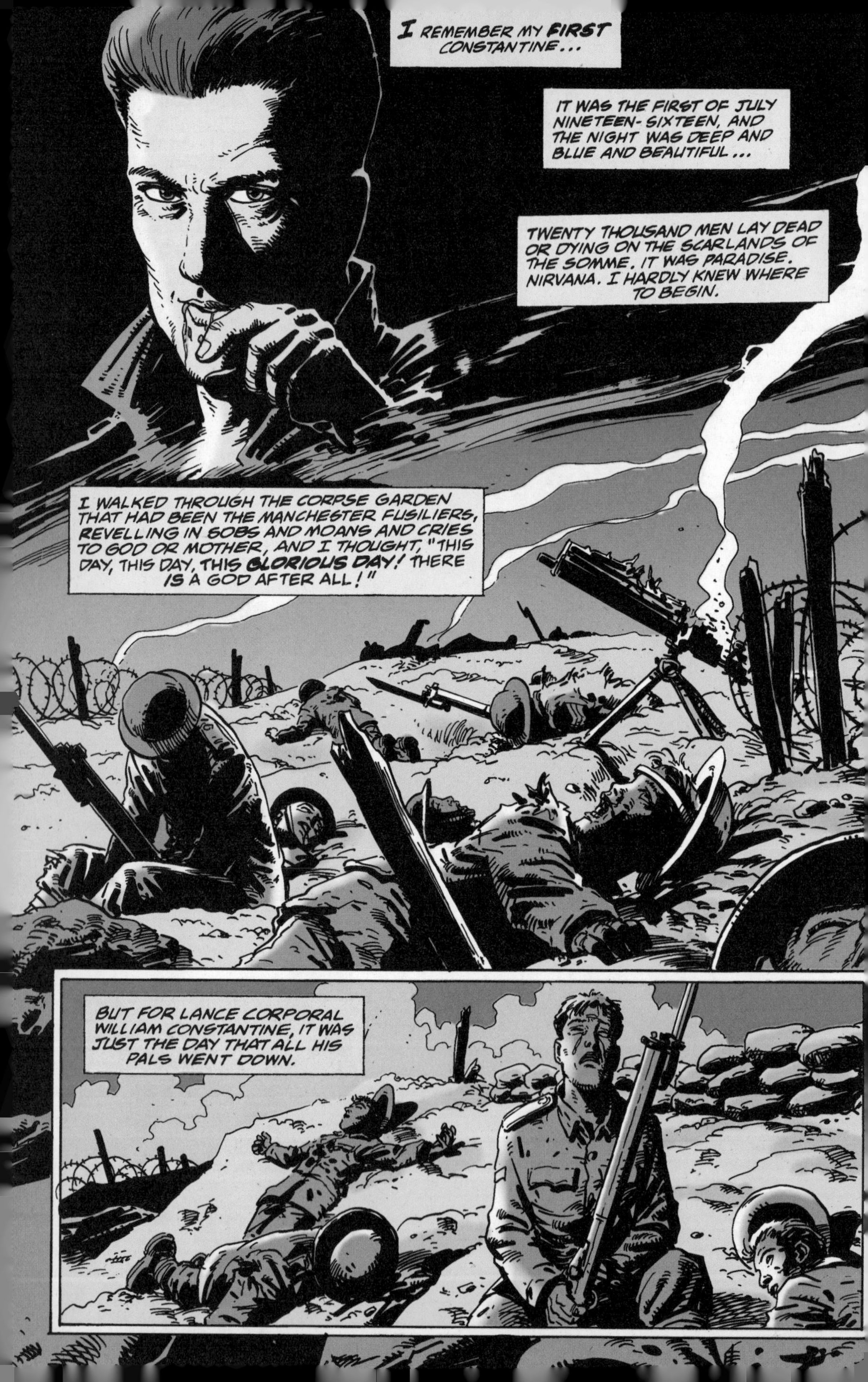
I REMEMBER MY FIRST CONSTANTINE...
IT WAS THE FIRST OF JULY NINETEEN-SIXTEEN, AND THE NIGHT WAS DEEP AND BLUE AND BEAUTIFUL...
TWENTY THOUSAND MEN LAY DEAD OR DYING ON THE SCARLANDS OF THE SOMME. IT WAS PARADISE. NIRVANA. I HARDLY KNEW WHERE TO BEGIN.
I WALKED THROUGH THE CORPSE GARDEN THAT HAD BEEN THE MANCHESTER FUSILIERS, REVELLING IN SOBS AND MOANS AND CRIES TO GOD OR MOTHER, AND I THOUGHT, "THIS DAY, THIS DAY, THIS GLORIOUS DAY! THERE IS A GOD AFTER ALL!"
BUT FOR LANCE CORPORAL WILLIAM CONSTANTINE, IT WAS JUST THE DAY THAT ALL HIS PALS WENT DOWN.

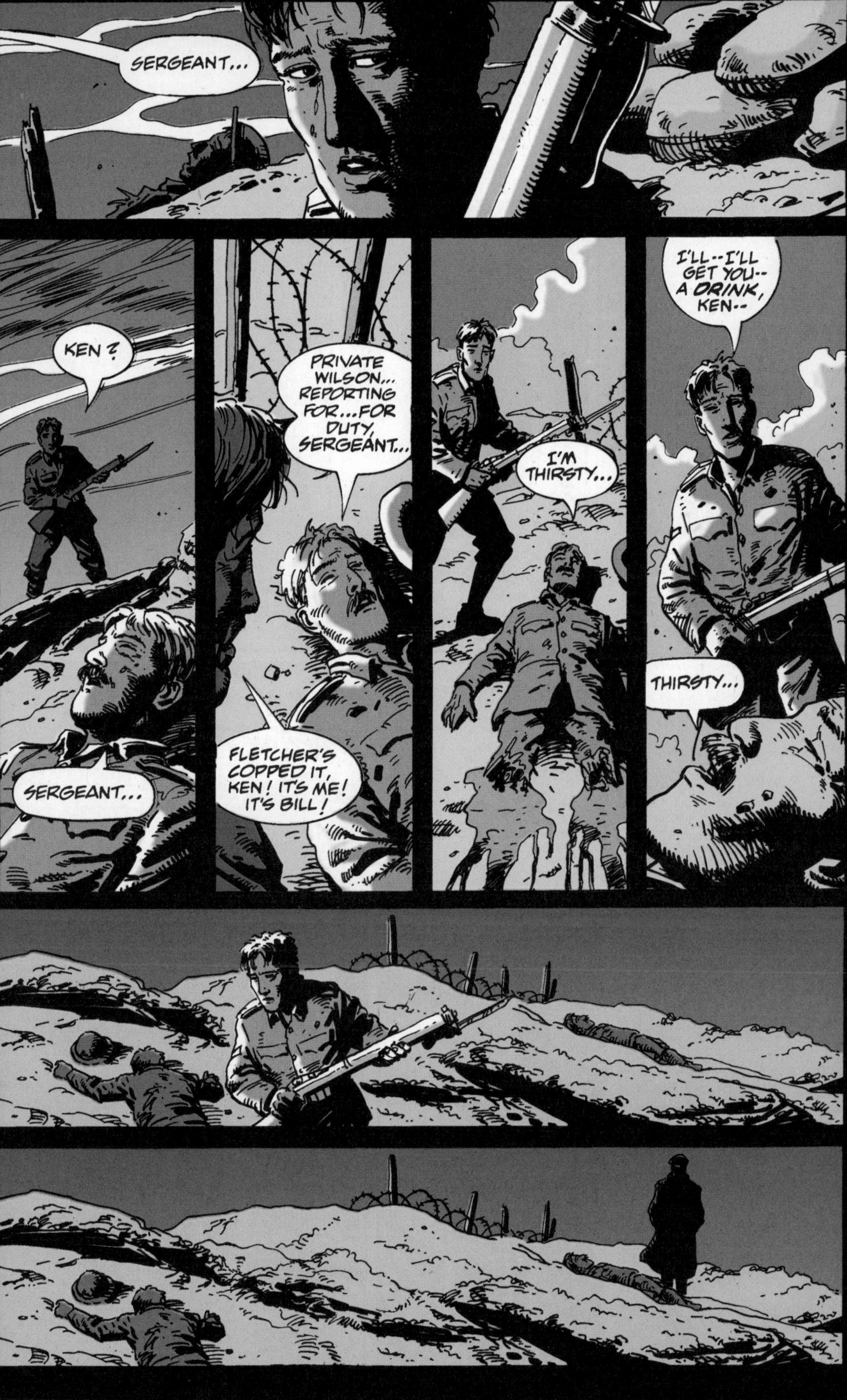
SERGEANT...
KEN ?
SERGEANT...
PRIVATE WILSON... REPORTING FOR...FOR DUTY, SERGEANT...
FLETCHER'S COPPED IT, KEN! IT'S ME! IT'S BILL!
I'M THIRSTY...
I'LL--I'LL GET YOU-- A DRINK, KEN--
THIRSTY...

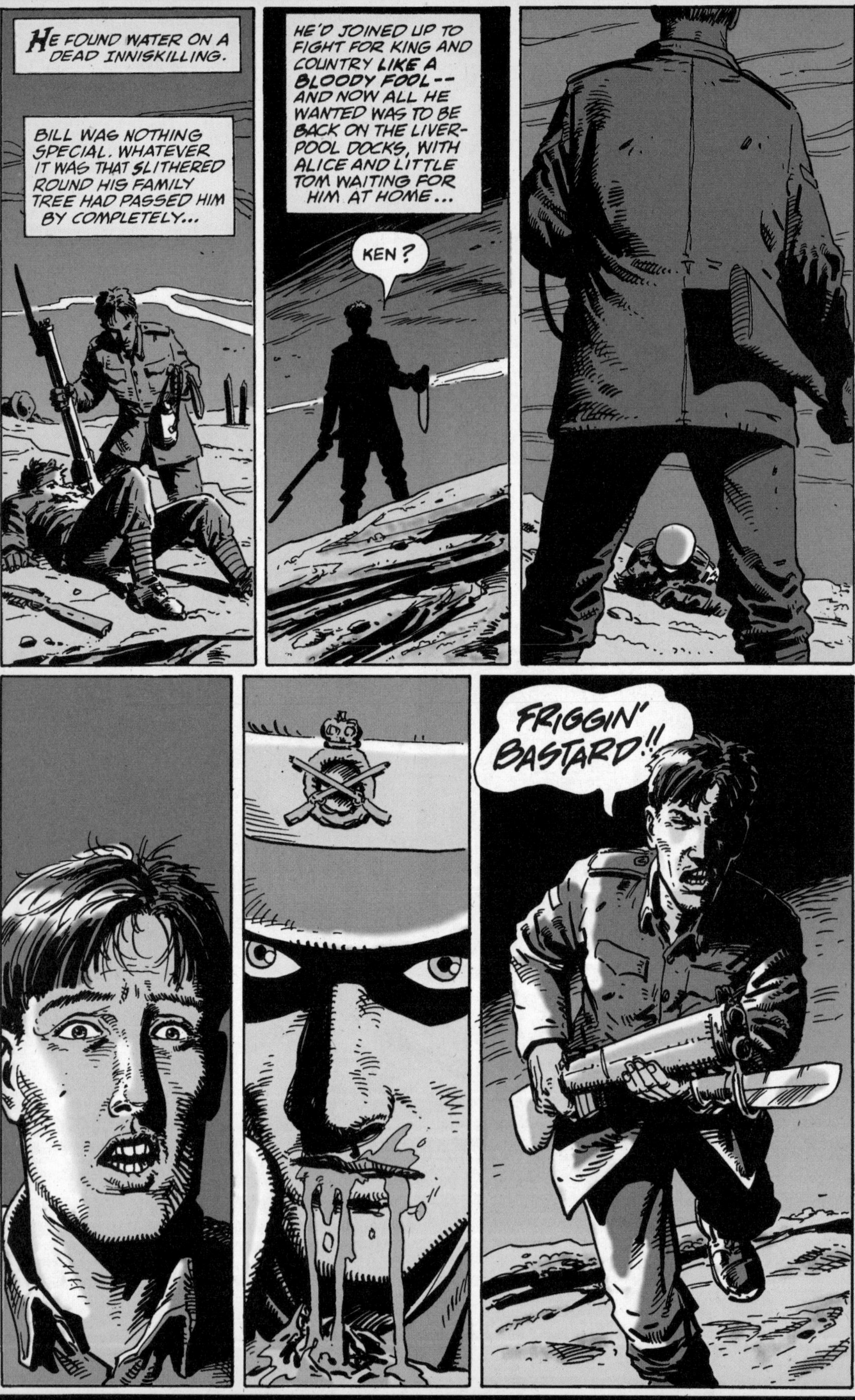
HE FOUND WATER ON A DEAD INNISKILLING.
BILL WAS NOTHING SPECIAL. WHATEVER IT WAS THAT SLITHERED ROUND HIS FAMILY TREE HAD PASSED HIM BY COMPLETELY...
HE'D JOINED UP TO FIGHT FOR KING AND COUNTRY LIKE A BLOODY FOOL -- AND NOW ALL HE WANTED WAS TO BE BACK ON THE LIVERPOOL DOCKS, WITH ALICE AND LITTLE TOM WAITING FOR HIM AT HOME...
KEN?
FRIGGIN' BASTARD!!

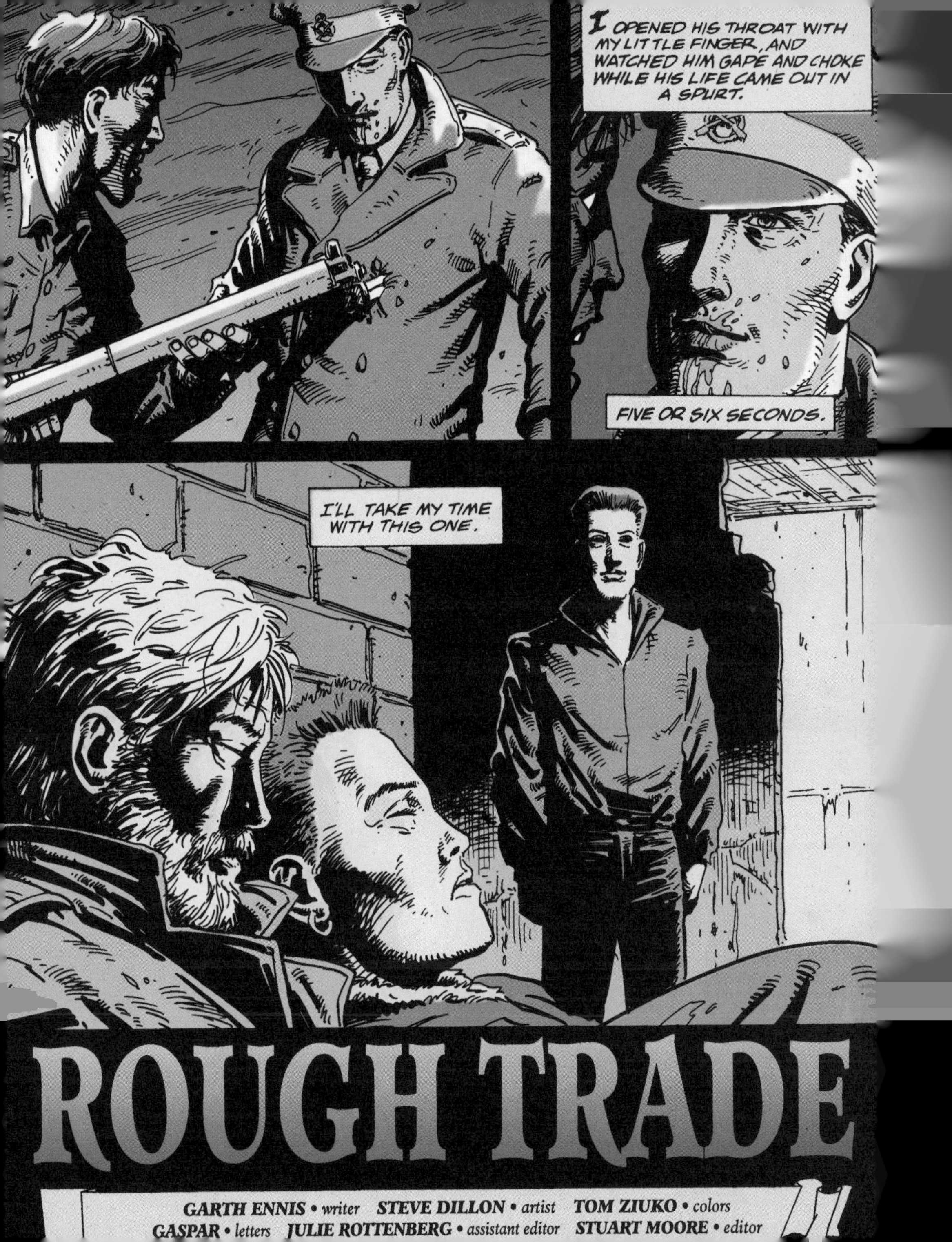
I OPENED HIS THROAT WITH MY LITTLE FINGER, AND WATCHED HIM GAPE AND CHOKE WHILE HIS LIFE CAME OUT IN A SPURT.
FIVE OR SIX SECONDS.
I'LL TAKE MY TIME WITH THIS ONE.

ROUGH TRADE

GARTH ENNIS • *writer* **STEVE DILLON** • *artist* **TOM ZIUKO** • *colors*
GASPAR • *letters* **JULIE ROTTENBERG** • *assistant editor* **STUART MOORE** • *editor*

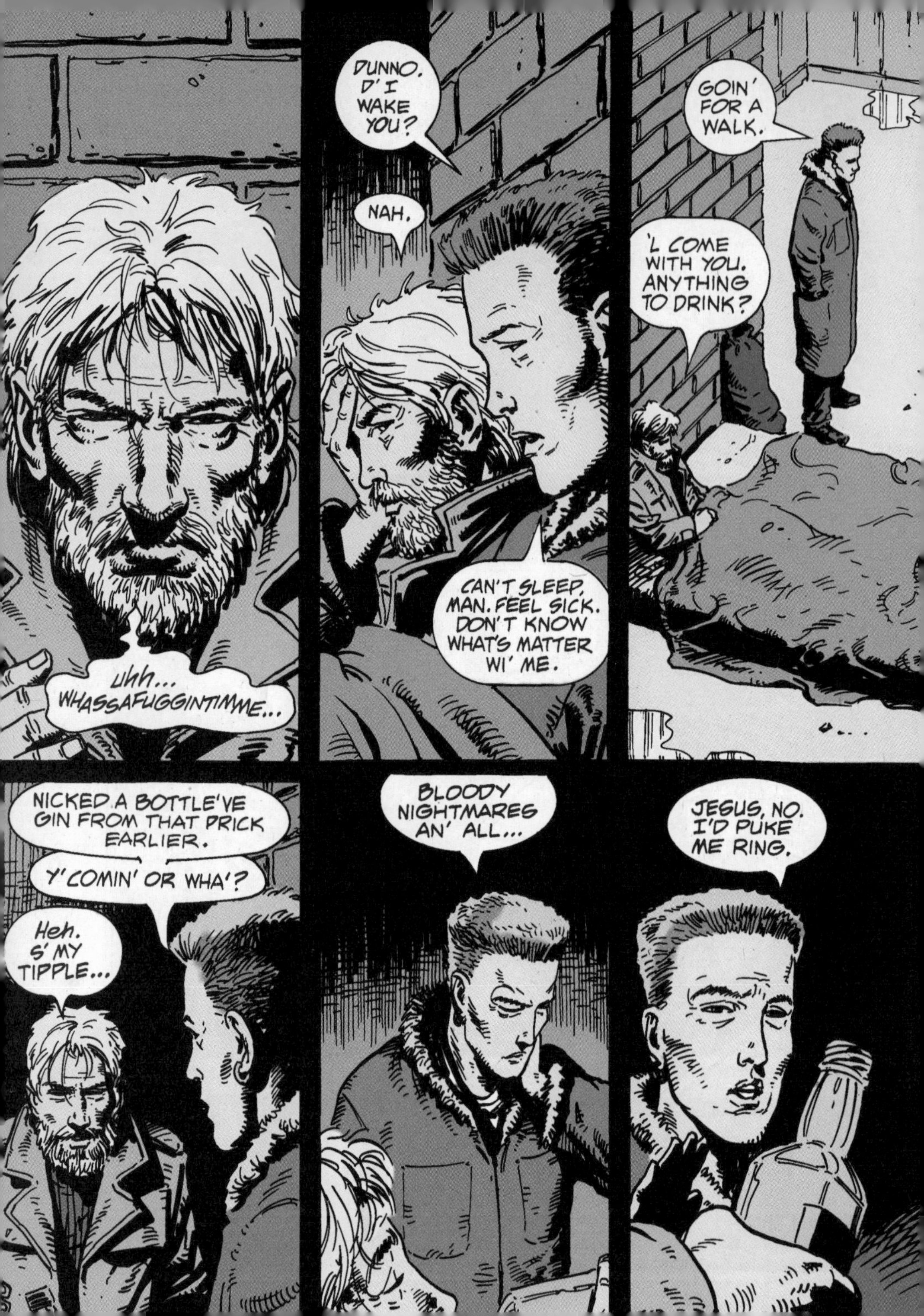

uhh... WHASSAFUGGINTIMME...
DUNNO. D' I WAKE YOU?
NAH.
CAN'T SLEEP, MAN. FEEL SICK. DON'T KNOW WHAT'S MATTER WI' ME.
GOIN' FOR A WALK.
'L COME WITH YOU. ANYTHING TO DRINK?
NICKED A BOTTLE'VE GIN FROM THAT PRICK EARLIER.
Y'COMIN' OR WHA'?
Heh. S' MY TIPPLE...
BLOODY NIGHTMARES AN' ALL...
JESUS, NO. I'D PUKE ME RING.

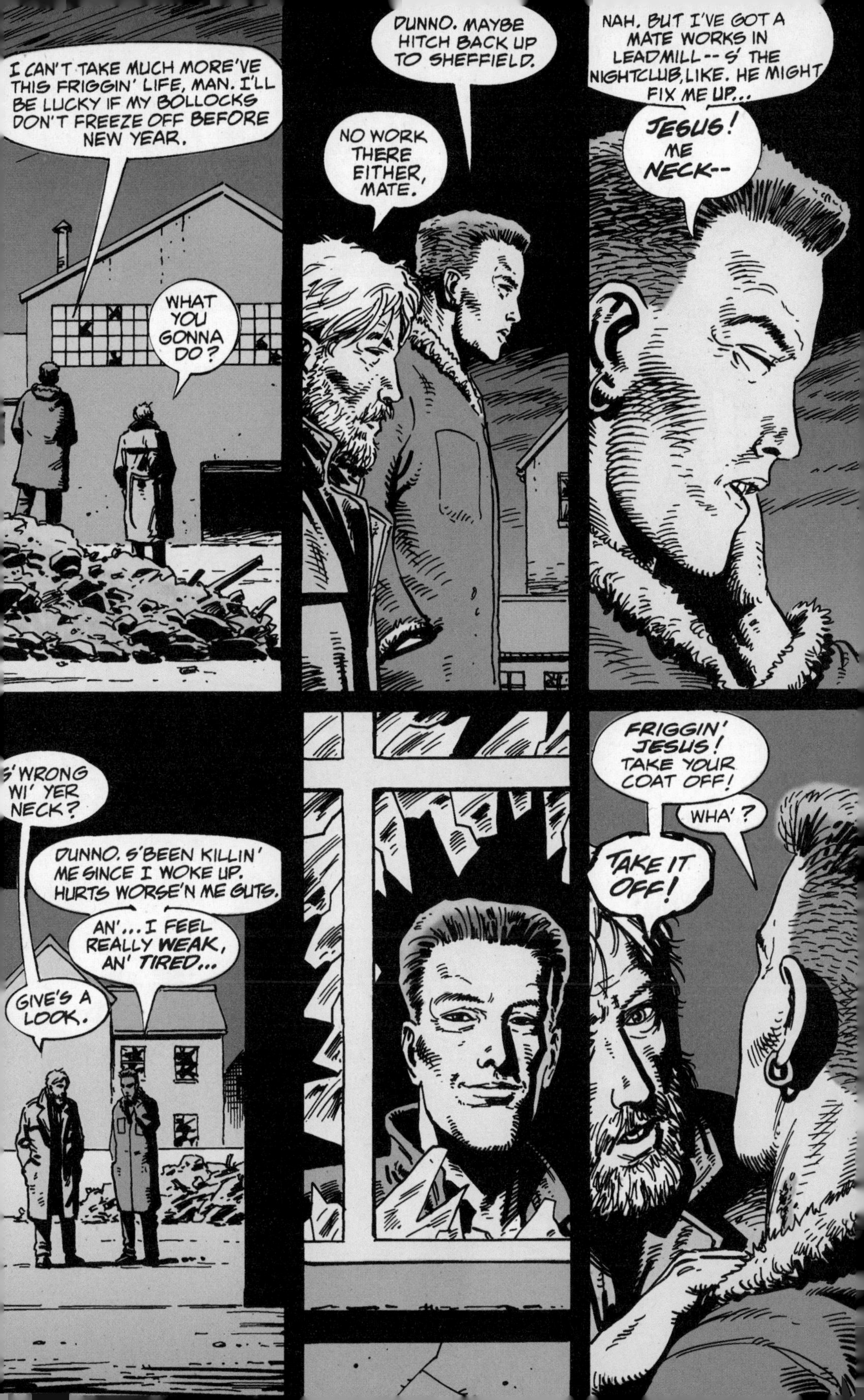
I CAN'T TAKE MUCH MORE'VE THIS FRIGGIN' LIFE, MAN. I'LL BE LUCKY IF MY BOLLOCKS DON'T FREEZE OFF BEFORE NEW YEAR.
WHAT YOU GONNA DO?
DUNNO. MAYBE HITCH BACK UP TO SHEFFIELD.
NO WORK THERE EITHER, MATE.
NAH. BUT I'VE GOT A MATE WORKS IN LEADMILL -- S' THE NIGHTCLUB, LIKE. HE MIGHT FIX ME UP...
JESUS! ME NECK--
S'WRONG WI' YER NECK?
DUNNO. S'BEEN KILLIN' ME SINCE I WOKE UP. HURTS WORSE'N ME GUTS.
AN'... I FEEL REALLY WEAK, AN' TIRED...
GIVE'S A LOOK.
FRIGGIN' JESUS! TAKE YOUR COAT OFF!
WHA'?
TAKE IT OFF!

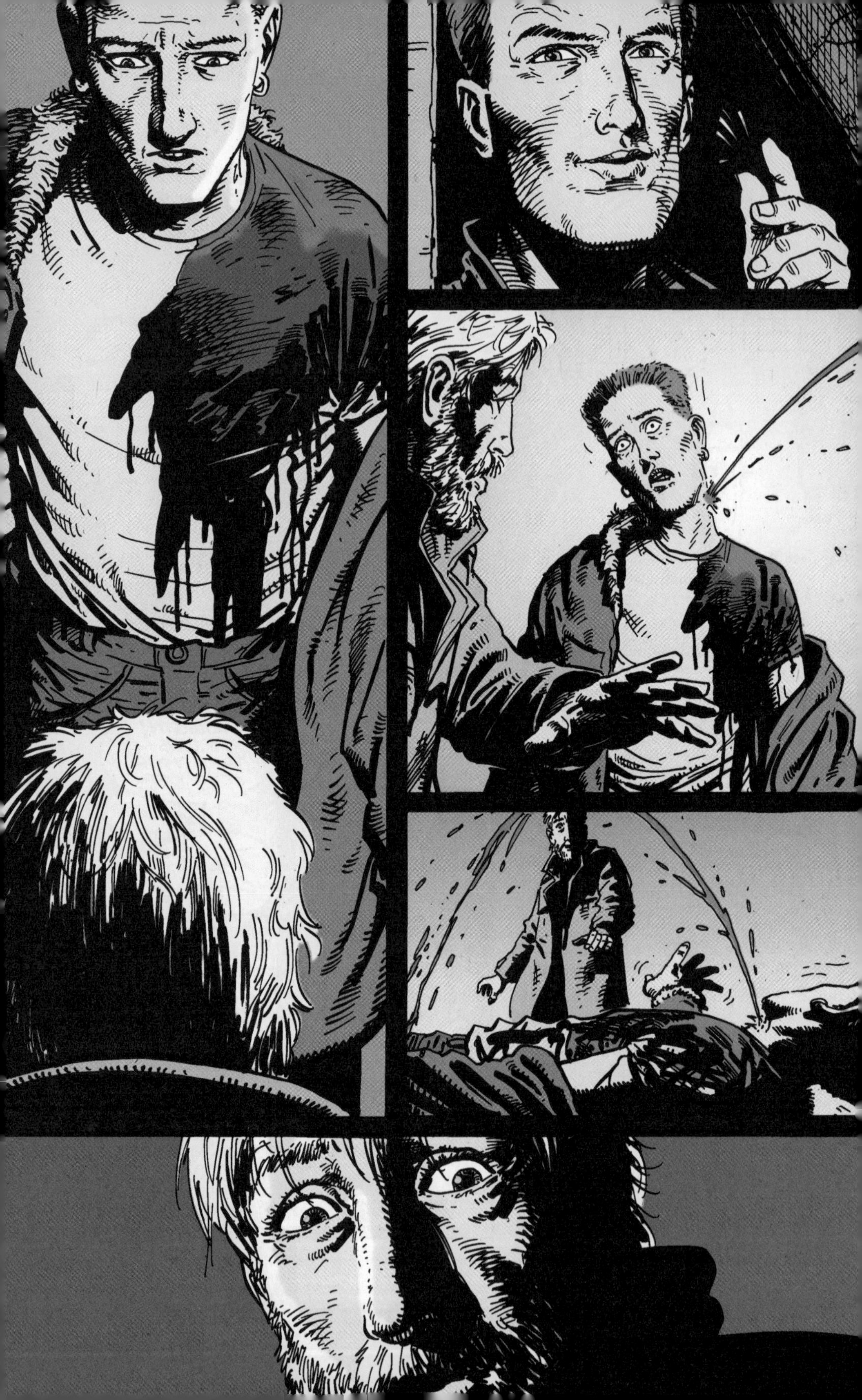

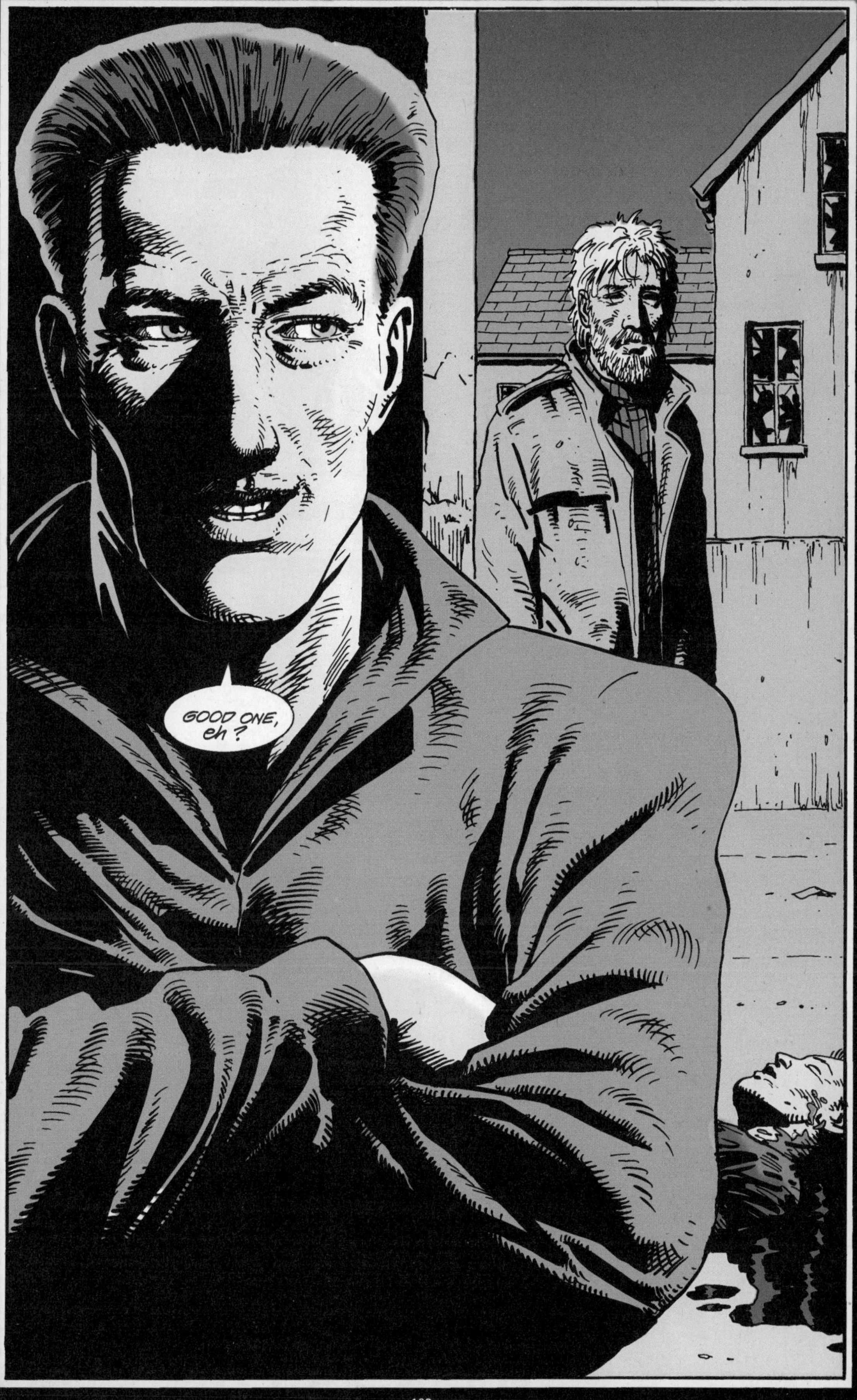
GOOD ONE, eh ?

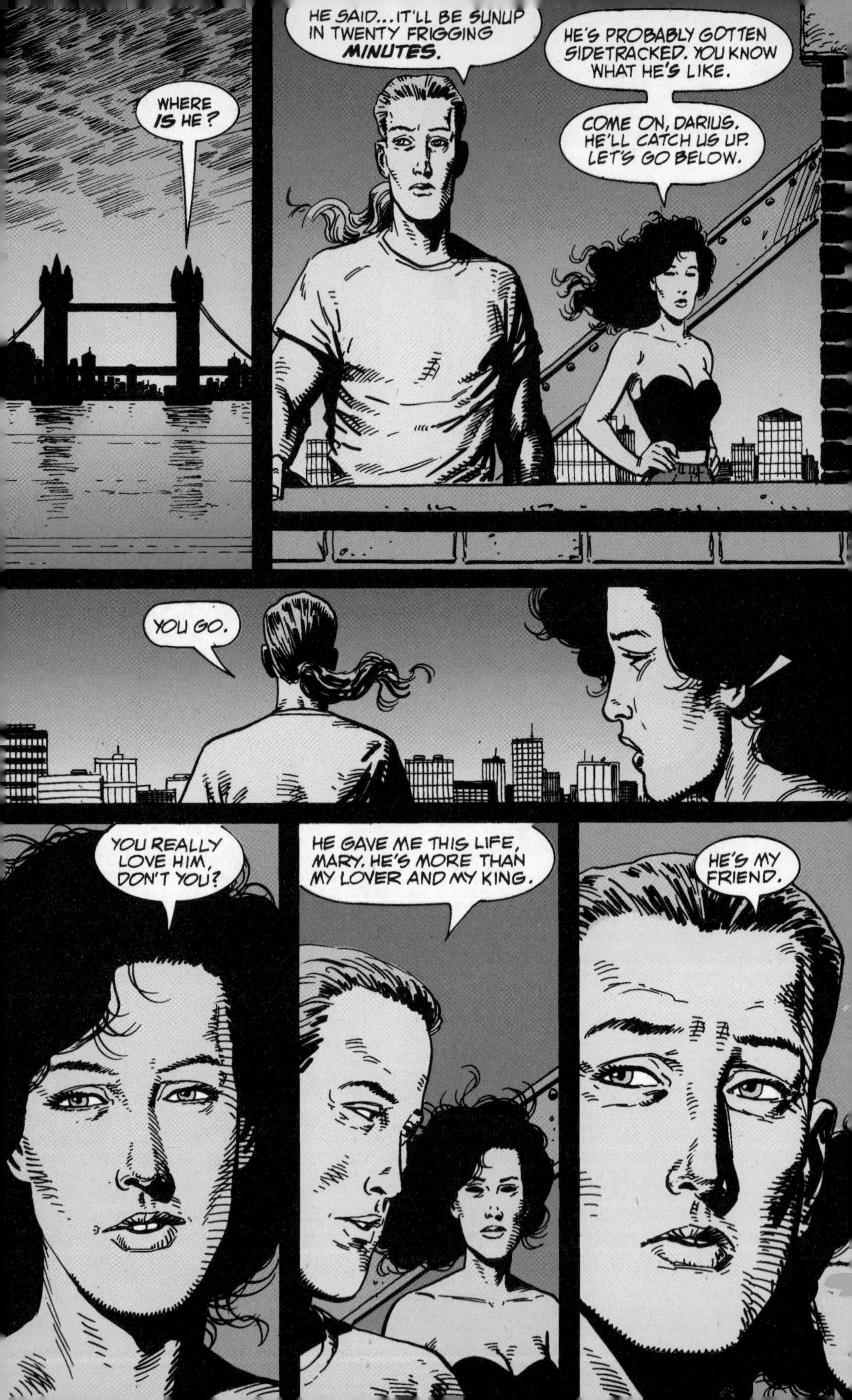
WHERE IS HE?
HE SAID...IT'LL BE SUNUP IN TWENTY FRIGGING MINUTES.
HE'S PROBABLY GOTTEN SIDETRACKED. YOU KNOW WHAT HE'S LIKE.
COME ON, DARIUS. HE'LL CATCH US UP. LET'S GO BELOW.
YOU GO.
YOU REALLY LOVE HIM, DON'T YOU?
HE GAVE ME THIS LIFE, MARY. HE'S MORE THAN MY LOVER AND MY KING.
HE'S MY FRIEND.

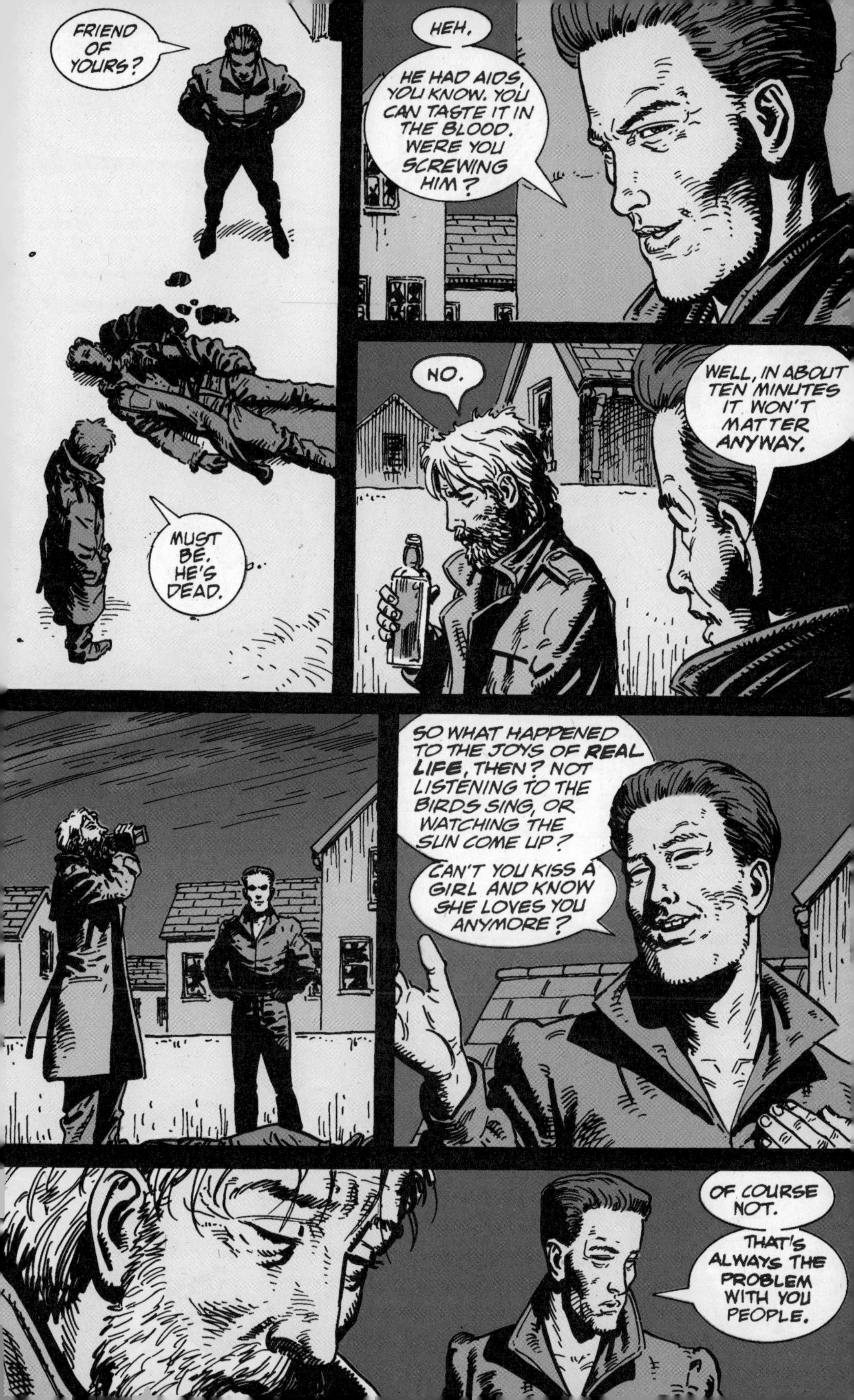

FRIEND OF YOURS?
HEH,
HE HAD AIDS, YOU KNOW. YOU CAN TASTE IT IN THE BLOOD. WERE YOU SCREWING HIM?
MUST BE. HE'S DEAD.
NO.
WELL, IN ABOUT TEN MINUTES IT WON'T MATTER ANYWAY.
SO WHAT HAPPENED TO THE JOYS OF REAL LIFE, THEN? NOT LISTENING TO THE BIRDS SING, OR WATCHING THE SUN COME UP?
CAN'T YOU KISS A GIRL AND KNOW SHE LOVES YOU ANYMORE?
OF COURSE NOT.
THAT'S ALWAYS THE PROBLEM WITH YOU PEOPLE.

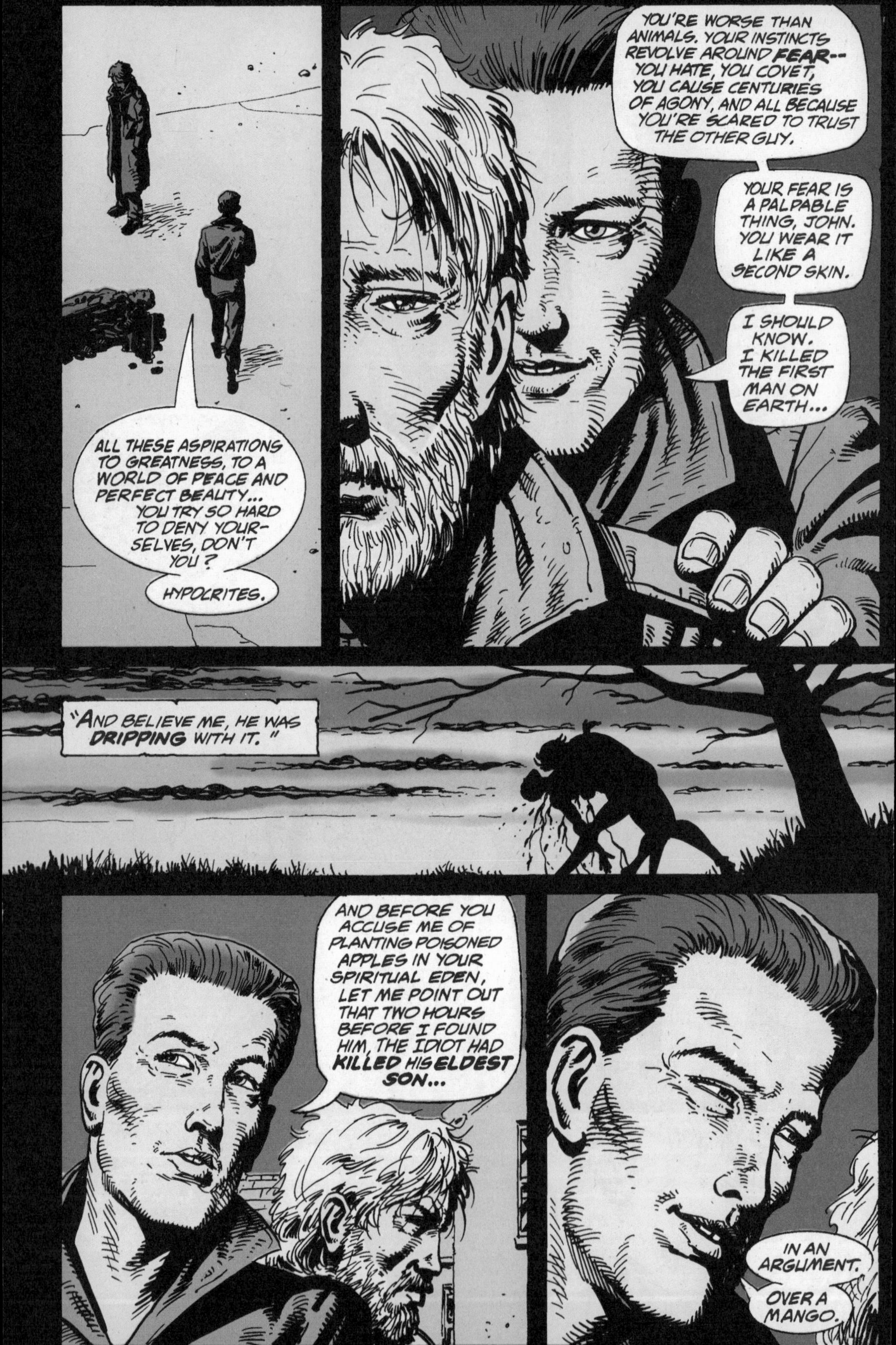
ALL THESE ASPIRATIONS TO GREATNESS, TO A WORLD OF PEACE AND PERFECT BEAUTY... YOU TRY SO HARD TO DENY YOURSELVES, DON'T YOU?
HYPOCRITES.
YOU'RE WORSE THAN ANIMALS. YOUR INSTINCTS REVOLVE AROUND FEAR-- YOU HATE, YOU COVET, YOU CAUSE CENTURIES OF AGONY, AND ALL BECAUSE YOU'RE SCARED TO TRUST THE OTHER GUY.
YOUR FEAR IS A PALPABLE THING, JOHN. YOU WEAR IT LIKE A SECOND SKIN.
I SHOULD KNOW. I KILLED THE FIRST MAN ON EARTH...
"AND BELIEVE ME, HE WAS DRIPPING WITH IT."
AND BEFORE YOU ACCUSE ME OF PLANTING POISONED APPLES IN YOUR SPIRITUAL EDEN, LET ME POINT OUT THAT TWO HOURS BEFORE I FOUND HIM, THE IDIOT HAD KILLED HIS ELDEST SON...
IN AN ARGUMENT.
OVER A MANGO.

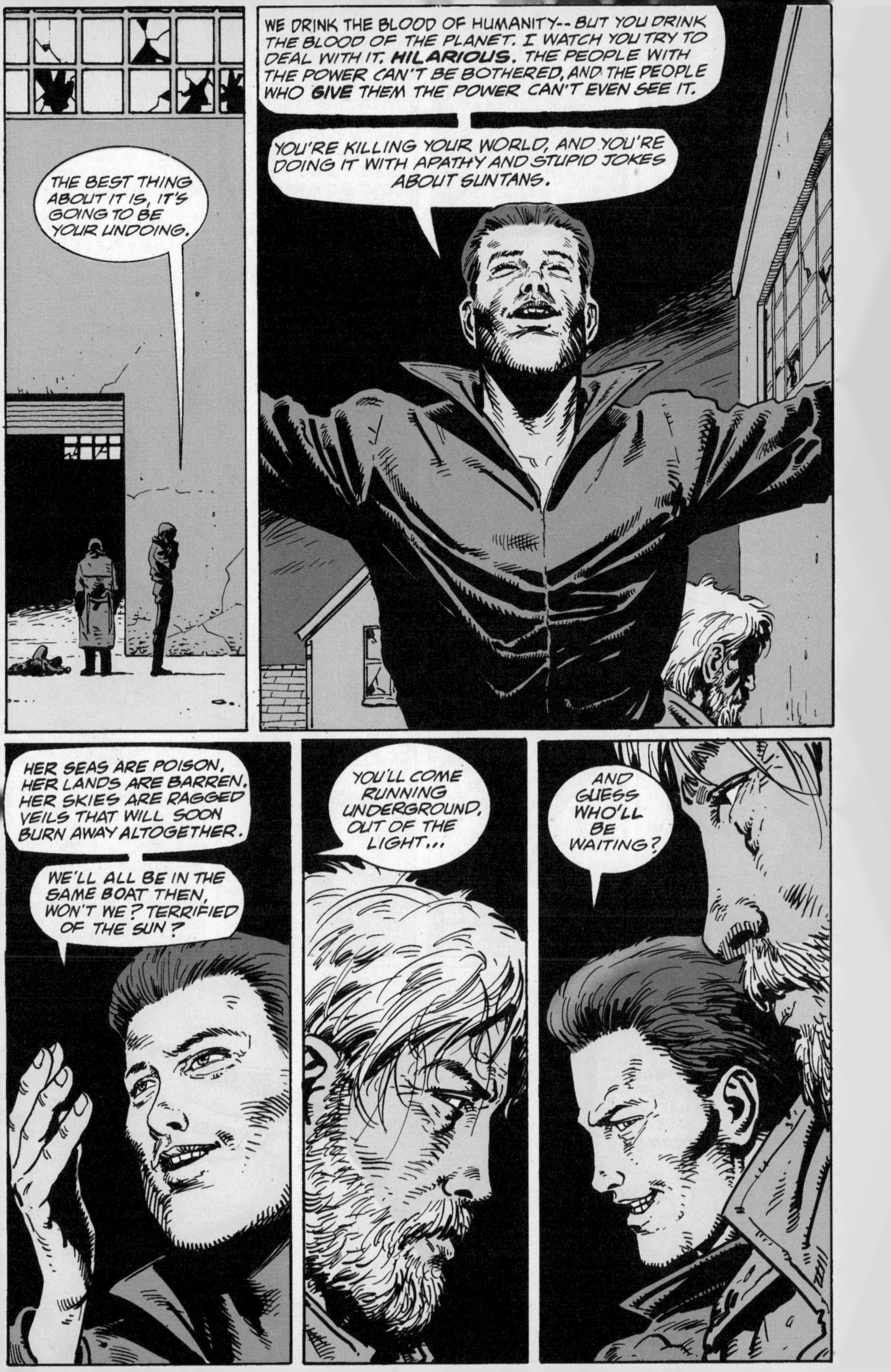
THE BEST THING ABOUT IT IS, IT'S GOING TO BE YOUR UNDOING.
WE DRINK THE BLOOD OF HUMANITY-- BUT YOU DRINK THE BLOOD OF THE PLANET. I WATCH YOU TRY TO DEAL WITH IT. HILARIOUS. THE PEOPLE WITH THE POWER CAN'T BE BOTHERED, AND THE PEOPLE WHO GIVE THEM THE POWER CAN'T EVEN SEE IT.
YOU'RE KILLING YOUR WORLD, AND YOU'RE DOING IT WITH APATHY AND STUPID JOKES ABOUT SUNTANS.
HER SEAS ARE POISON, HER LANDS ARE BARREN. HER SKIES ARE RAGGED VEILS THAT WILL SOON BURN AWAY ALTOGETHER.
WE'LL ALL BE IN THE SAME BOAT THEN, WON'T WE? TERRIFIED OF THE SUN?
YOU'LL COME RUNNING UNDERGROUND, OUT OF THE LIGHT...
AND GUESS WHO'LL BE WAITING?

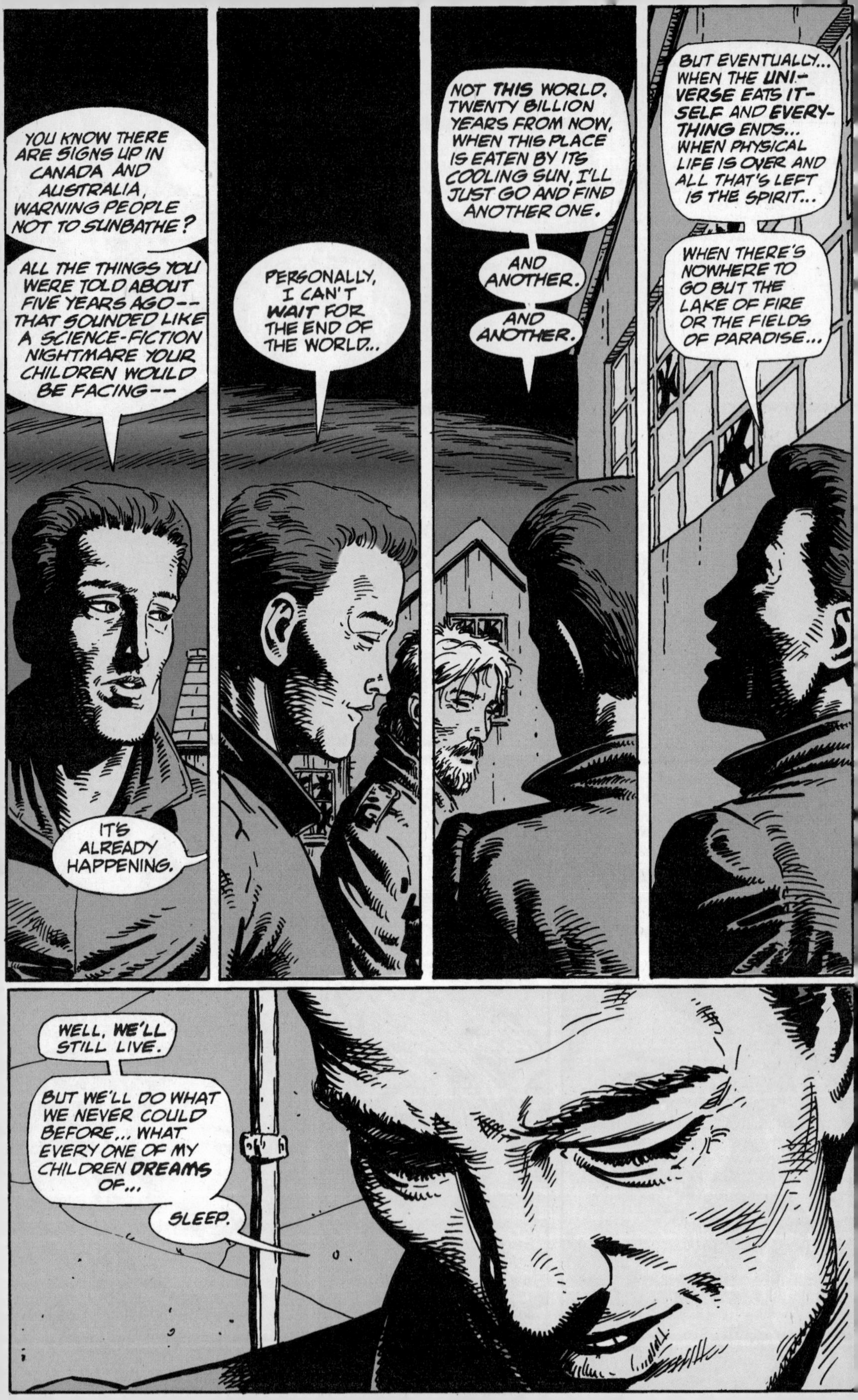
YOU KNOW THERE ARE SIGNS UP IN CANADA AND AUSTRALIA, WARNING PEOPLE NOT TO SUNBATHE?
ALL THE THINGS YOU WERE TOLD ABOUT FIVE YEARS AGO--THAT SOUNDED LIKE A SCIENCE-FICTION NIGHTMARE YOUR CHILDREN WOULD BE FACING--
IT'S ALREADY HAPPENING.
PERSONALLY, I CAN'T WAIT FOR THE END OF THE WORLD...
NOT THIS WORLD. TWENTY BILLION YEARS FROM NOW, WHEN THIS PLACE IS EATEN BY ITS COOLING SUN, I'LL JUST GO AND FIND ANOTHER ONE.
AND ANOTHER.
AND ANOTHER.
BUT EVENTUALLY... WHEN THE UNIVERSE EATS ITSELF AND EVERYTHING ENDS... WHEN PHYSICAL LIFE IS OVER AND ALL THAT'S LEFT IS THE SPIRIT...
WHEN THERE'S NOWHERE TO GO BUT THE LAKE OF FIRE OR THE FIELDS OF PARADISE...
WELL, WE'LL STILL LIVE.
BUT WE'LL DO WHAT WE NEVER COULD BEFORE... WHAT EVERY ONE OF MY CHILDREN DREAMS OF...
SLEEP.

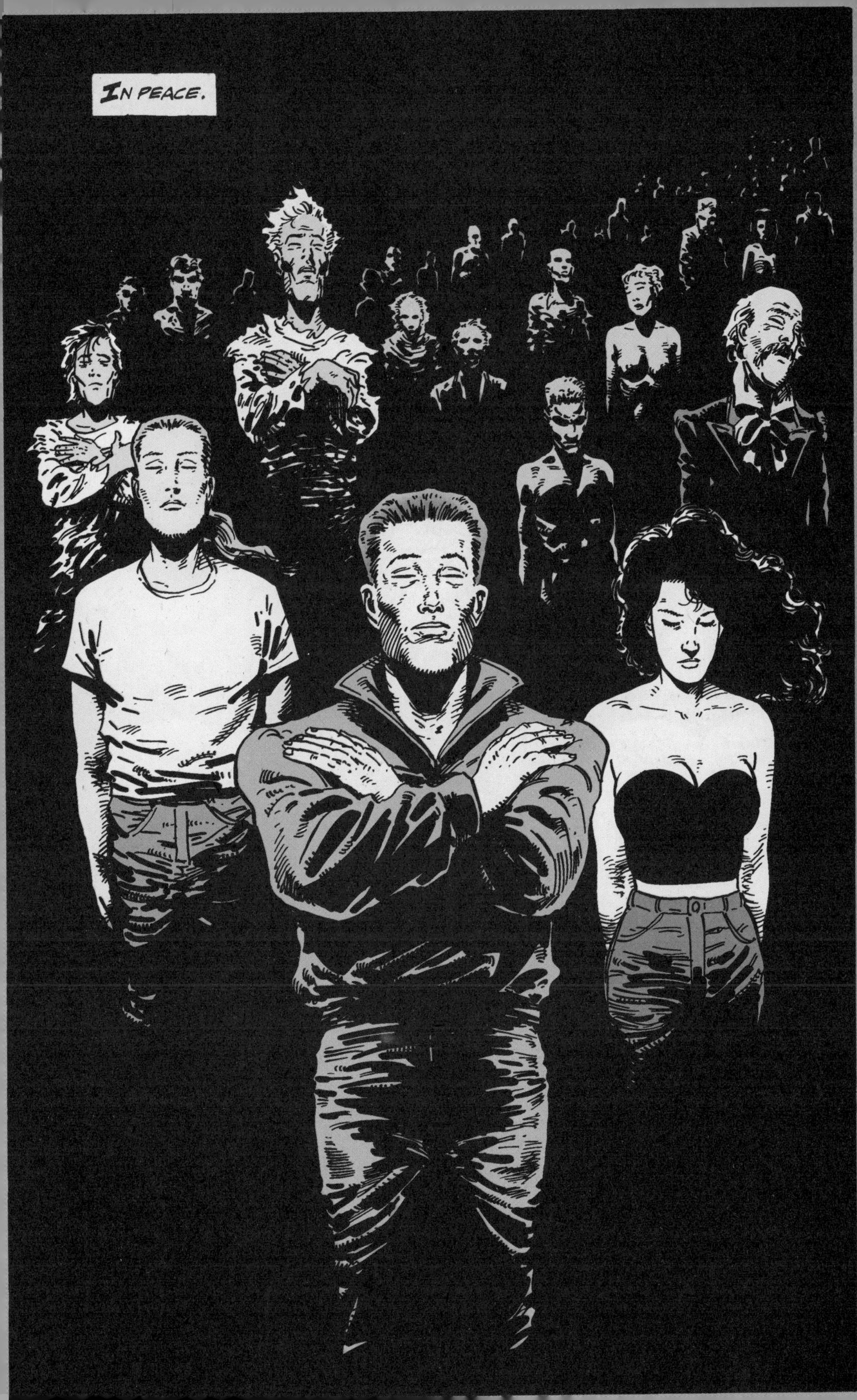
IN PEACE.

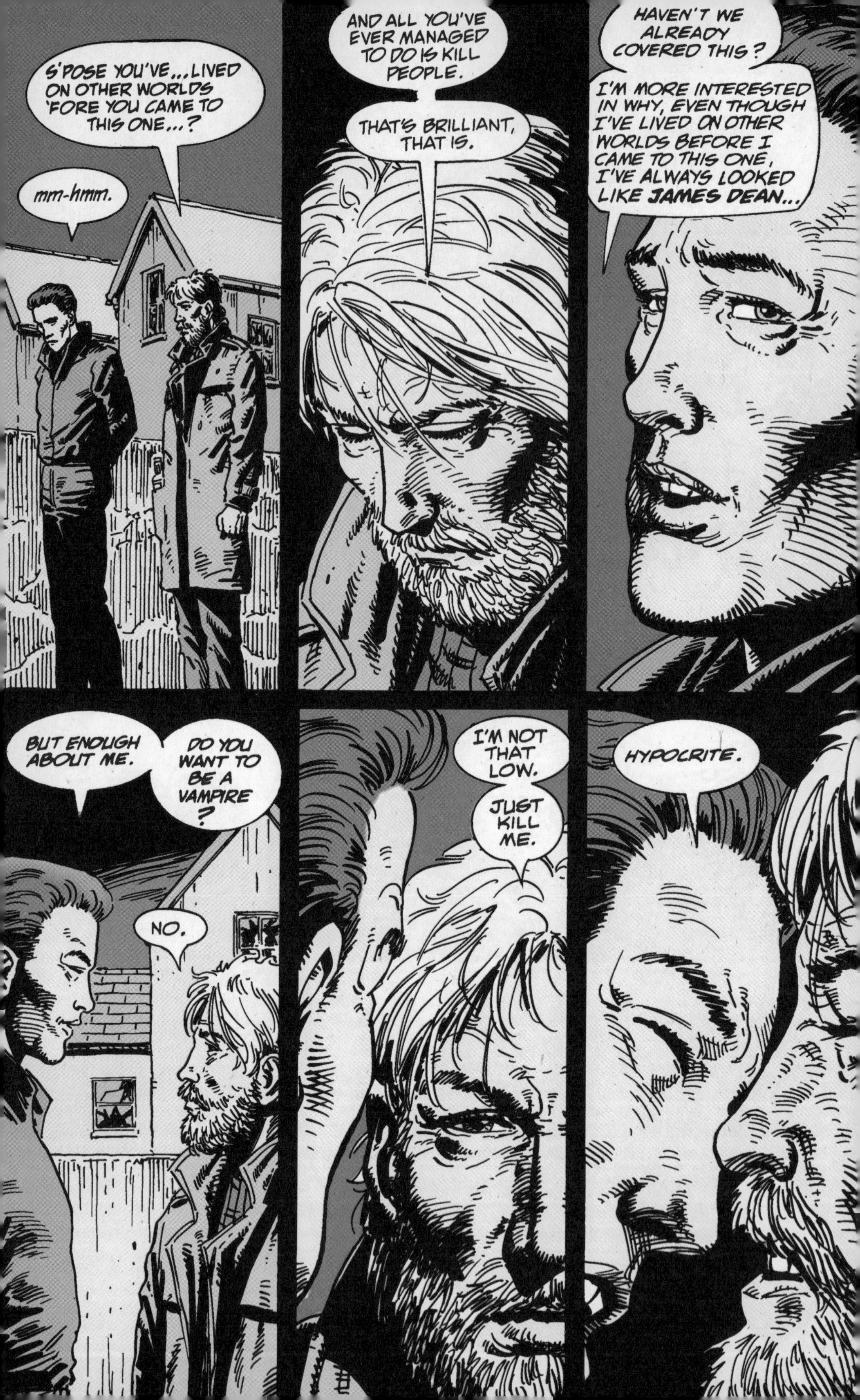

S'POSE YOU'VE... LIVED ON OTHER WORLDS 'FORE YOU CAME TO THIS ONE...?
mm-hmm.
AND ALL YOU'VE EVER MANAGED TO DO IS KILL PEOPLE.
THAT'S BRILLIANT, THAT IS.
HAVEN'T WE ALREADY COVERED THIS?
I'M MORE INTERESTED IN WHY, EVEN THOUGH I'VE LIVED ON OTHER WORLDS BEFORE I CAME TO THIS ONE, I'VE ALWAYS LOOKED LIKE JAMES DEAN...
BUT ENOUGH ABOUT ME.
DO YOU WANT TO BE A VAMPIRE?
NO.
I'M NOT THAT LOW.
JUST KILL ME.
HYPOCRITE.

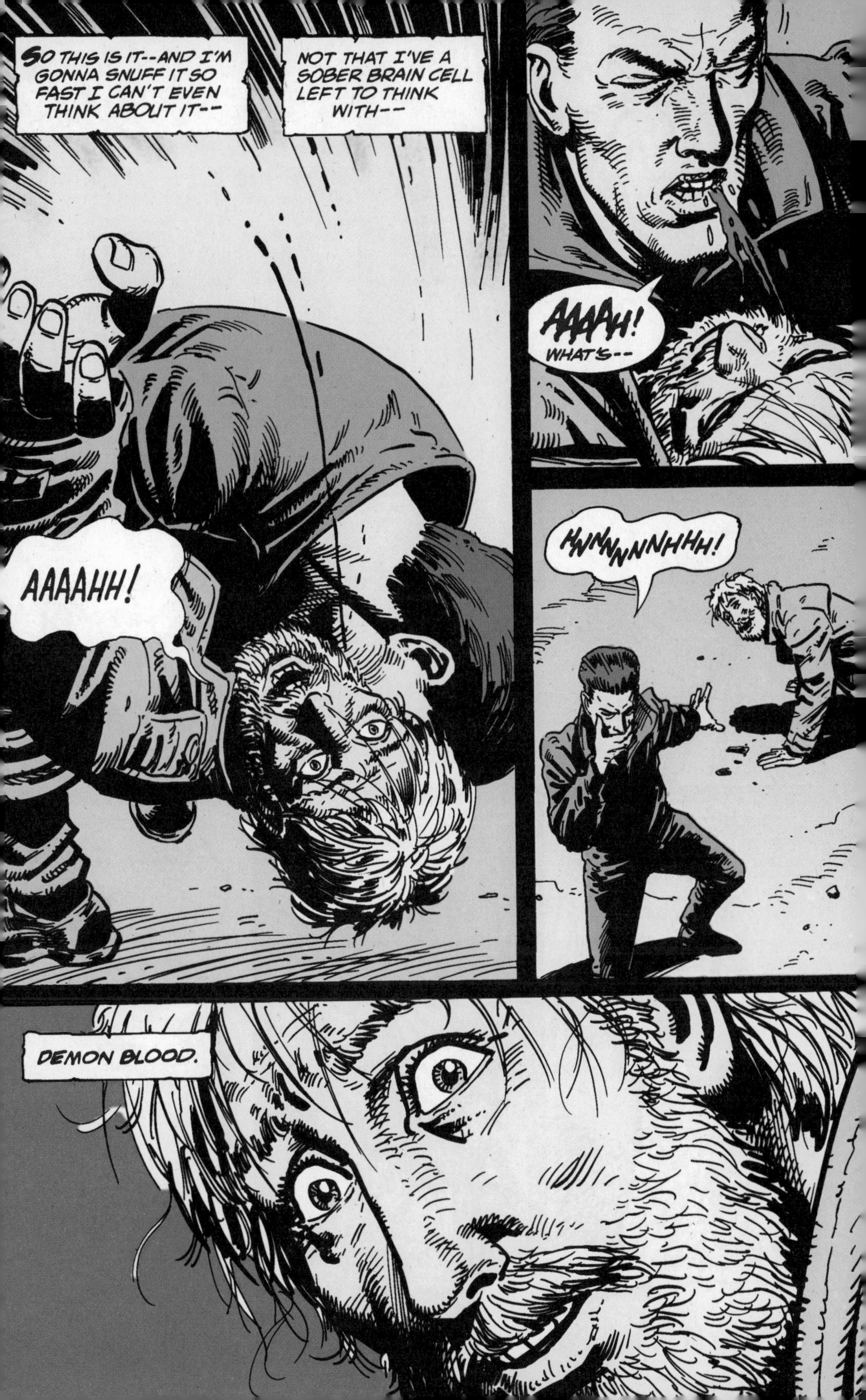
SO THIS IS IT--AND I'M GONNA SNUFF IT SO FAST I CAN'T EVEN THINK ABOUT IT--
NOT THAT I'VE A SOBER BRAIN CELL LEFT TO THINK WITH--
AAAAHH!
AAAAH! WHAT'S--
HNNNNNNHHHH!
DEMON BLOOD.

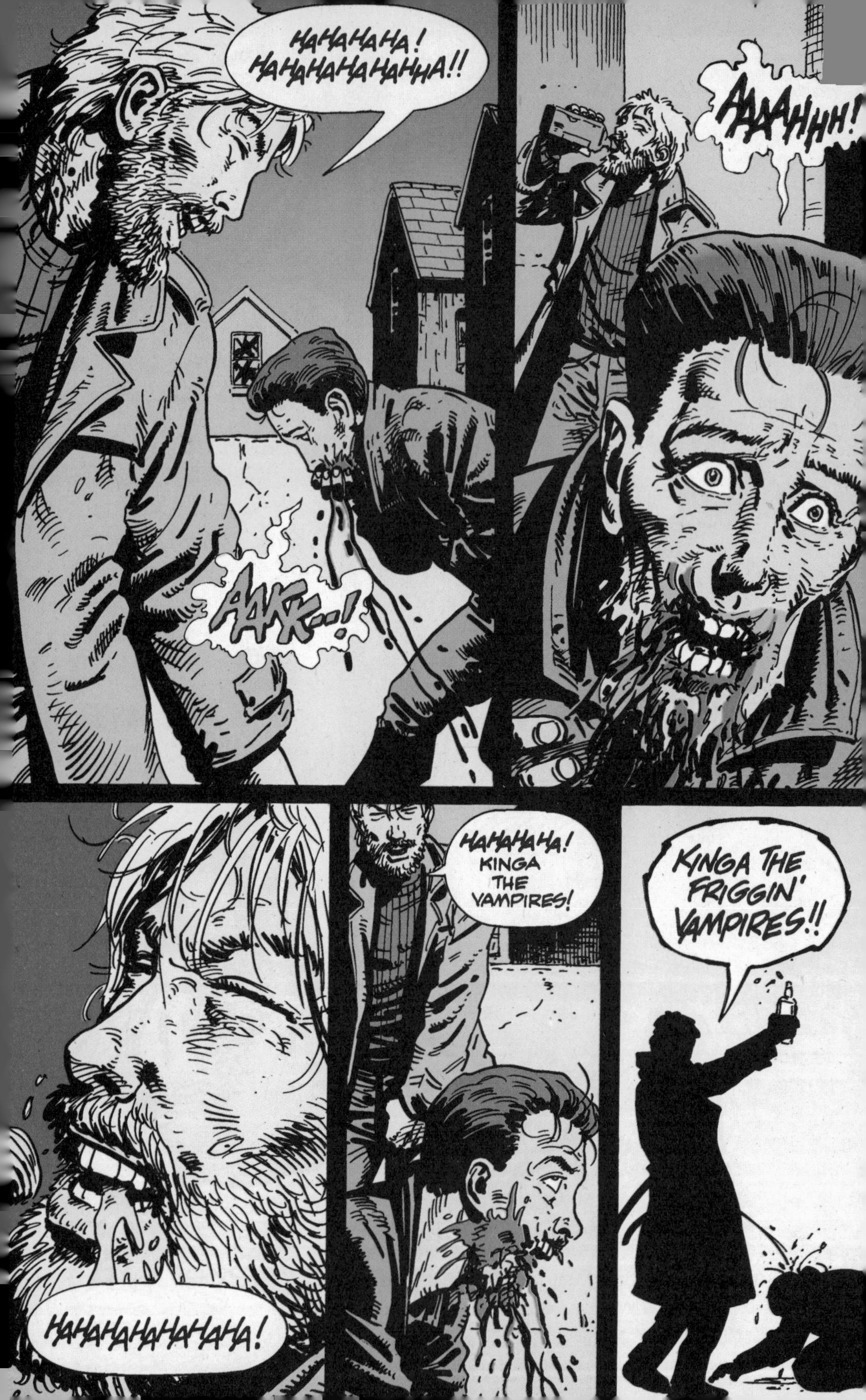

HAHAHAHA!
HAHAHAHAHAHAHHA!!
AAK--!
AAAAHHH!
HAHAHAHAHAHAHAHA!
HAHAHAHA!
KINGA
THE
VAMPIRES!
KINGA THE
FRIGGIN'
VAMPIRES!!

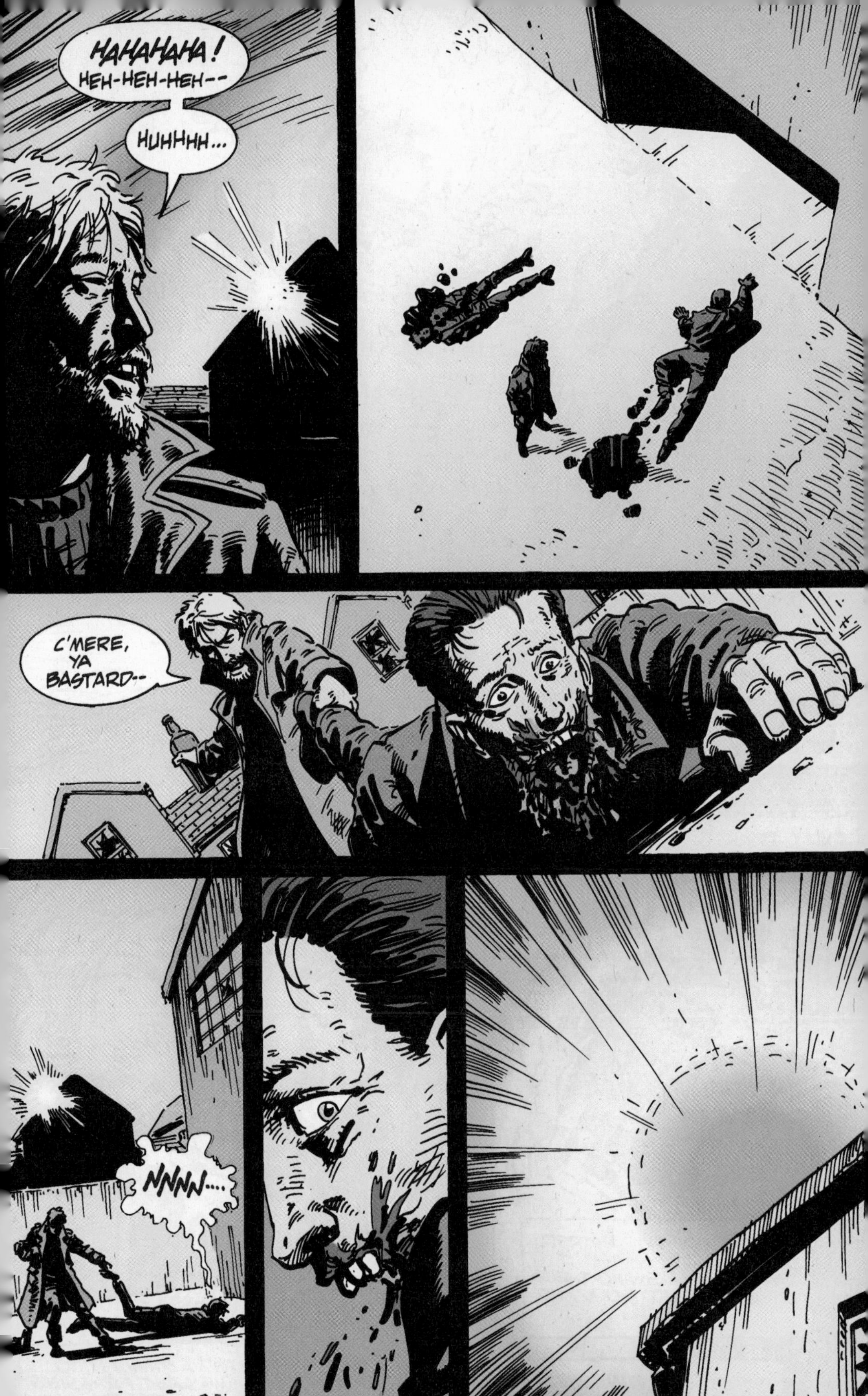
HAHAHAHA! HEH-HEH-HEH--
HUHHHH...
C'MERE, YA BASTARD--
NNNN....

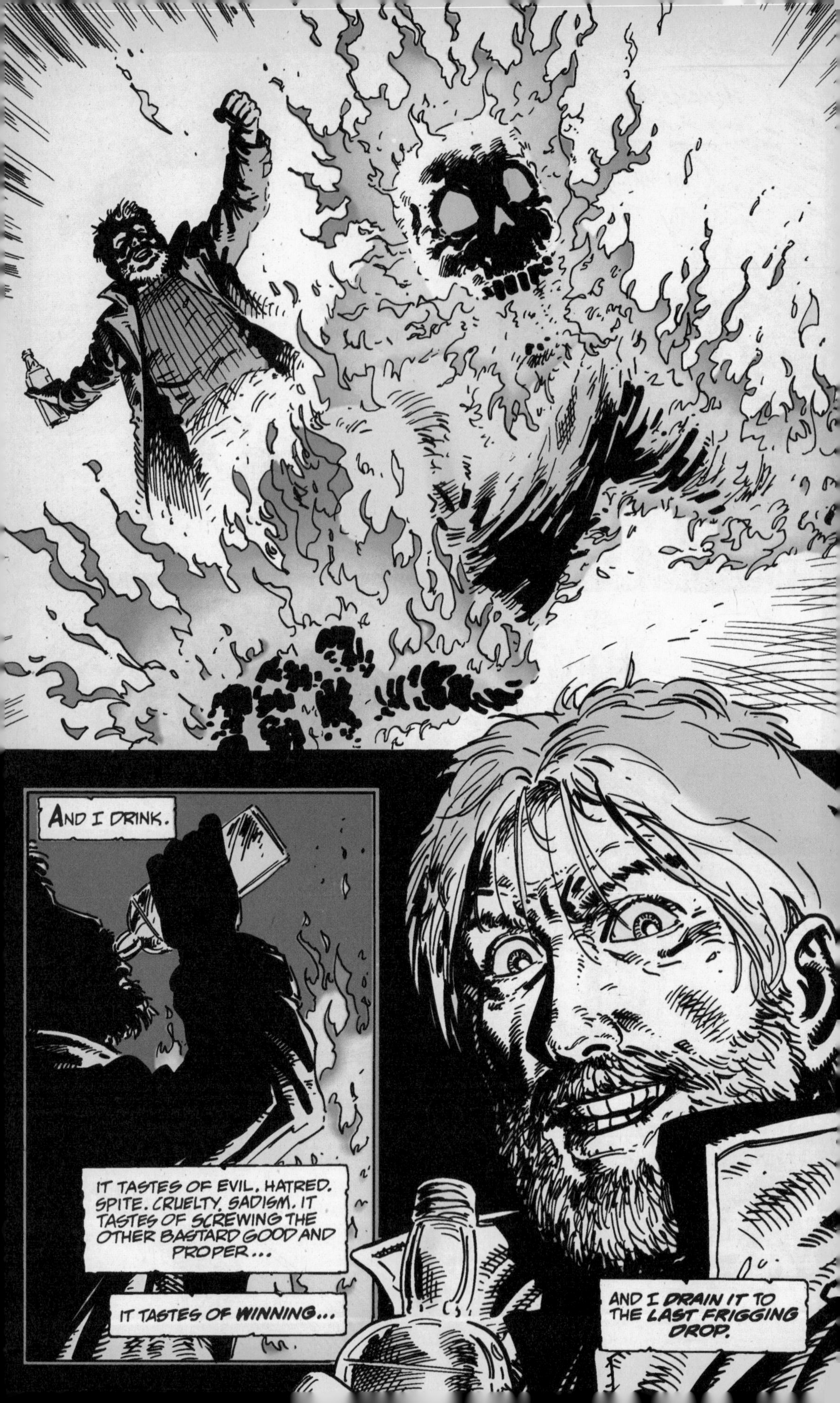
AND I DRINK.
IT TASTES OF EVIL. HATRED. SPITE. CRUELTY. SADISM. IT TASTES OF SCREWING THE OTHER BASTARD GOOD AND PROPER...
IT TASTES OF WINNING...
AND I DRAIN IT TO THE LAST FRIGGING DROP.

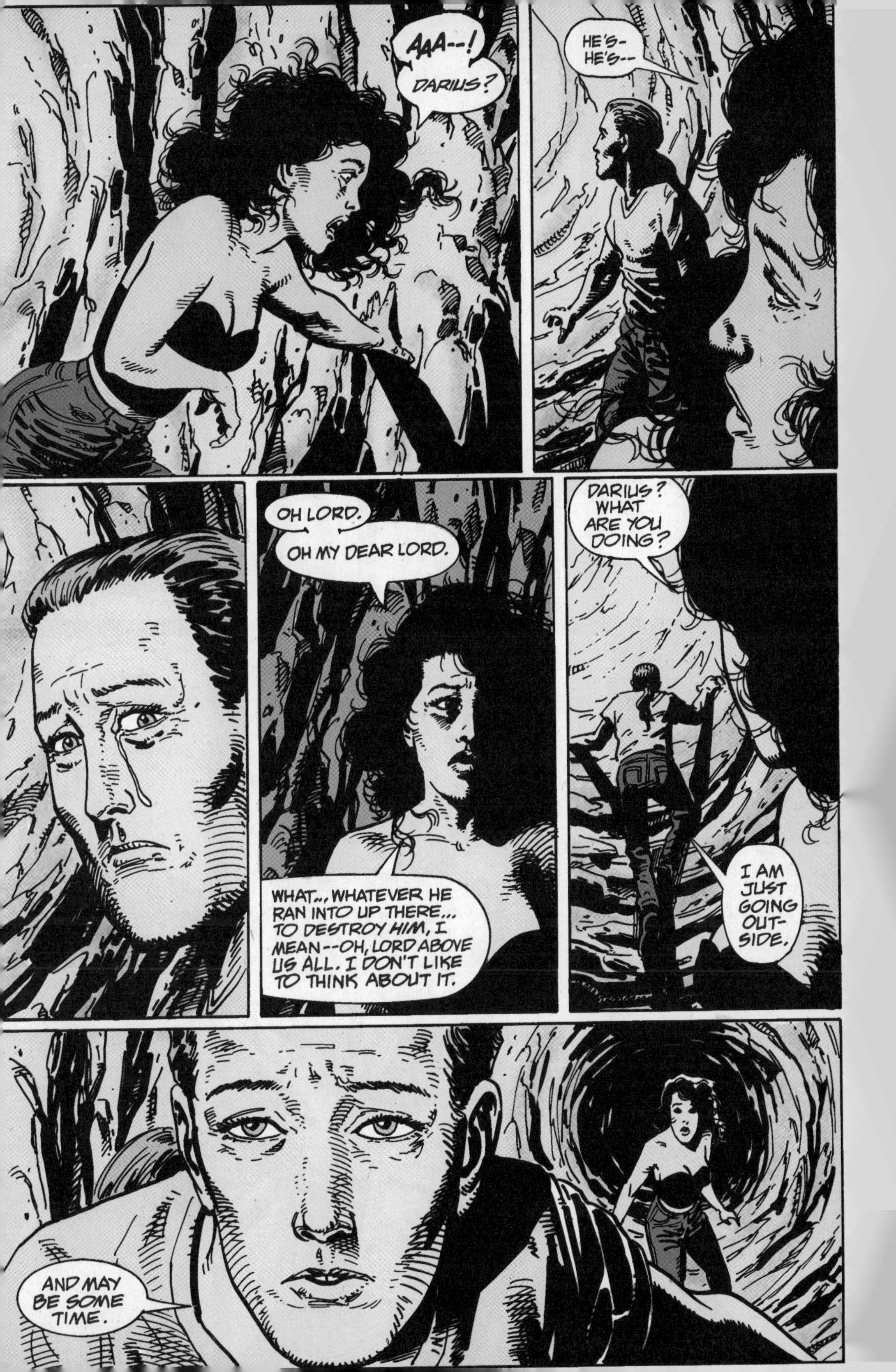
AAA--!
DARIUS?
HE'S-
HE'S--
OH LORD.
OH MY DEAR LORD.
WHAT... WHATEVER HE RAN INTO UP THERE... TO DESTROY HIM, I MEAN--OH, LORD ABOVE US ALL. I DON'T LIKE TO THINK ABOUT IT.
DARIUS? WHAT ARE YOU DOING?
I AM JUST GOING OUT-SIDE.
AND MAY BE SOME TIME.

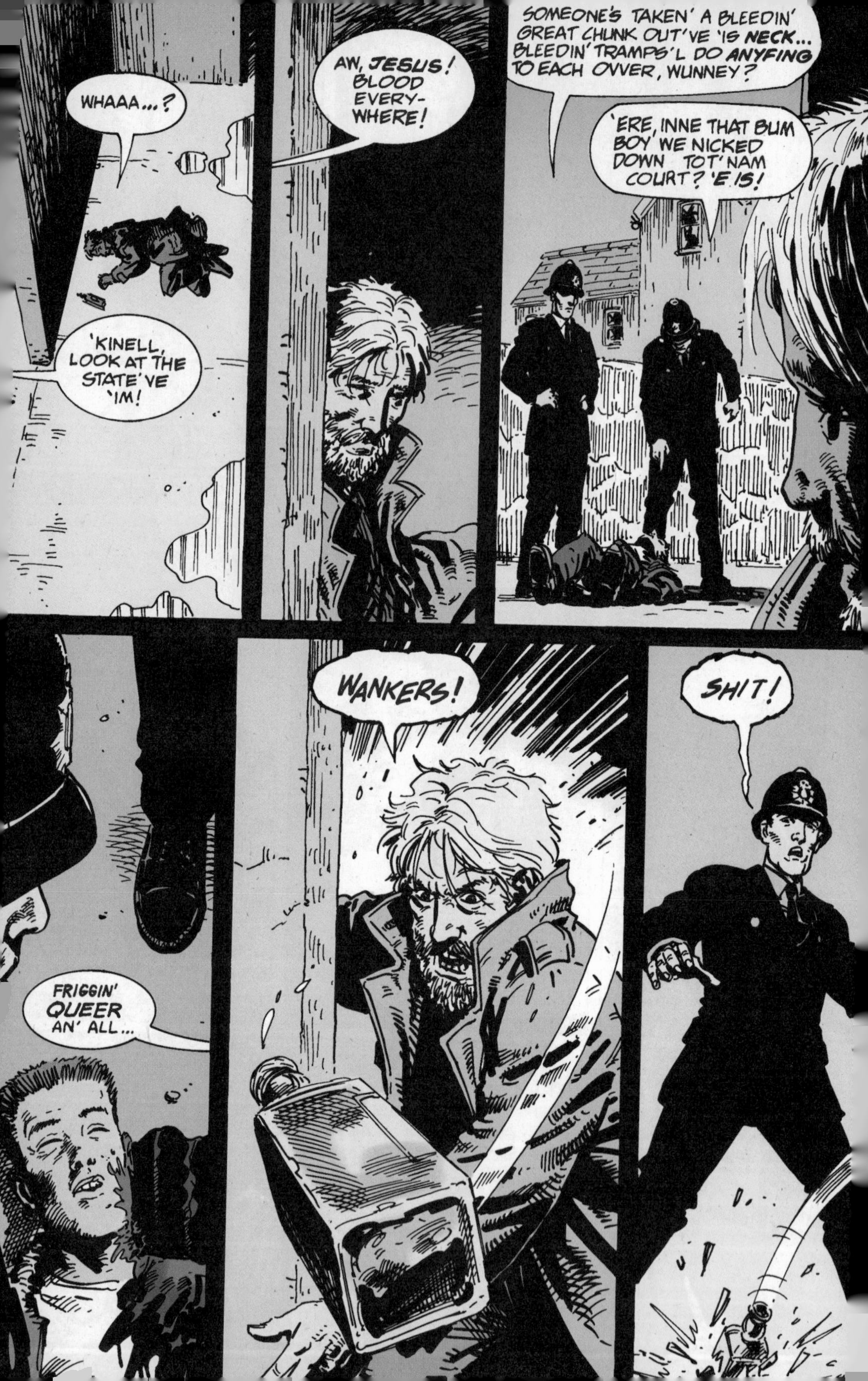
WHAAA...?
'KINELL, LOOK AT THE STATE'VE 'IM!
AW, JESUS! BLOOD EVERY-WHERE!
SOMEONE'S TAKEN' A BLEEDIN' GREAT CHUNK OUT'VE 'IS NECK... BLEEDIN' TRAMPS'L DO ANYFING TO EACH OVVER, WUNNEY?
'ERE, INNE THAT BUM BOY WE NICKED DOWN TOT'NAM COURT? 'E IS!
FRIGGIN' QUEER AN' ALL...
WANKERS!
SHIT!

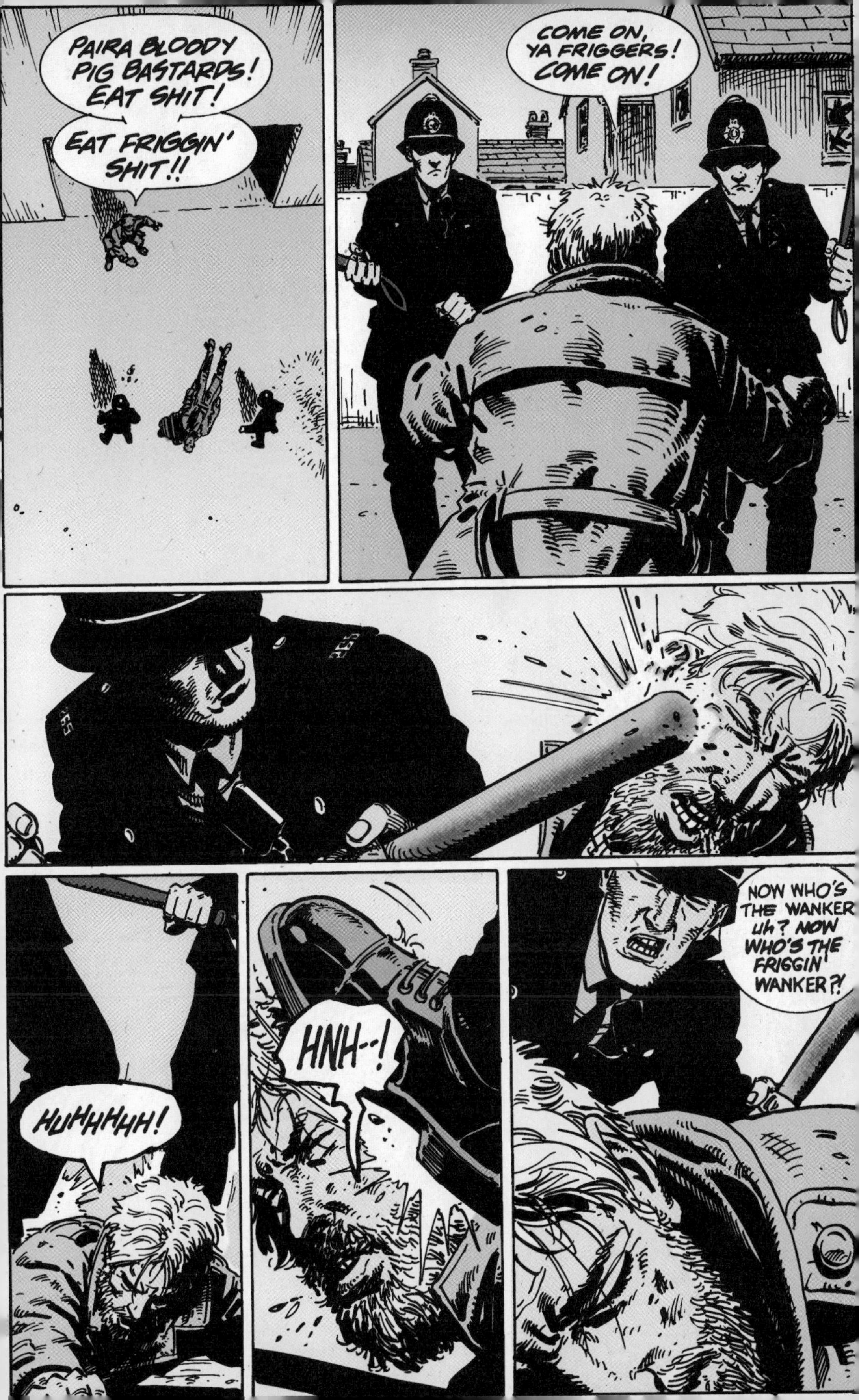
PAIRA BLOODY PIG BASTARDS! EAT SHIT!
EAT FRIGGIN' SHIT!!
COME ON, YA FRIGGERS! COME ON!
HUHHHHH!
HNH--!
NOW WHO'S THE WANKER uh? NOW WHO'S THE FRIGGIN' WANKER?!

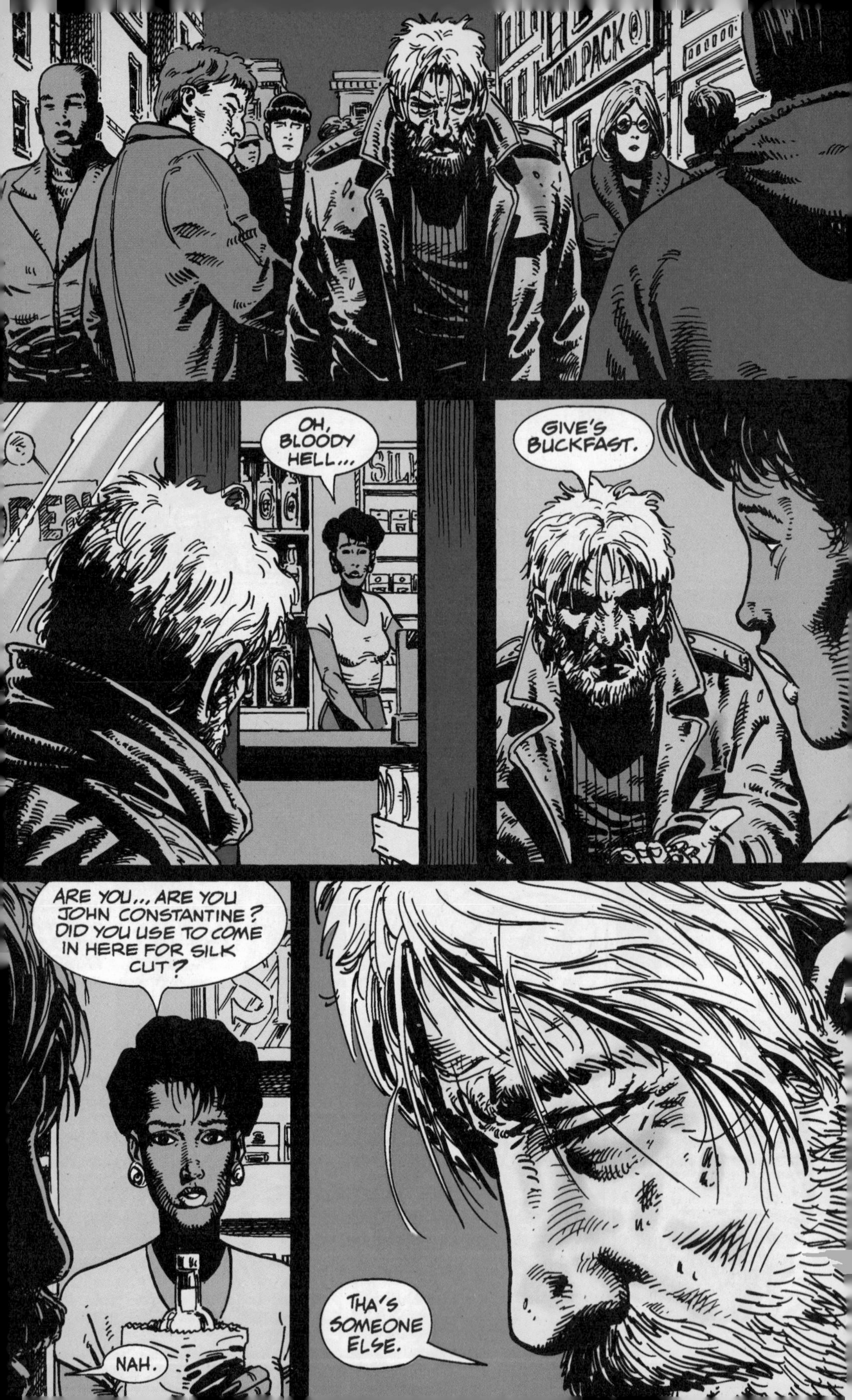
WOOLPACK
OH, BLOODY HELL...
GIVE'S BUCKFAST.
ARE YOU... ARE YOU JOHN CONSTANTINE? DID YOU USE TO COME IN HERE FOR SILK CUT?
NAH.
THA'S SOMEONE ELSE.

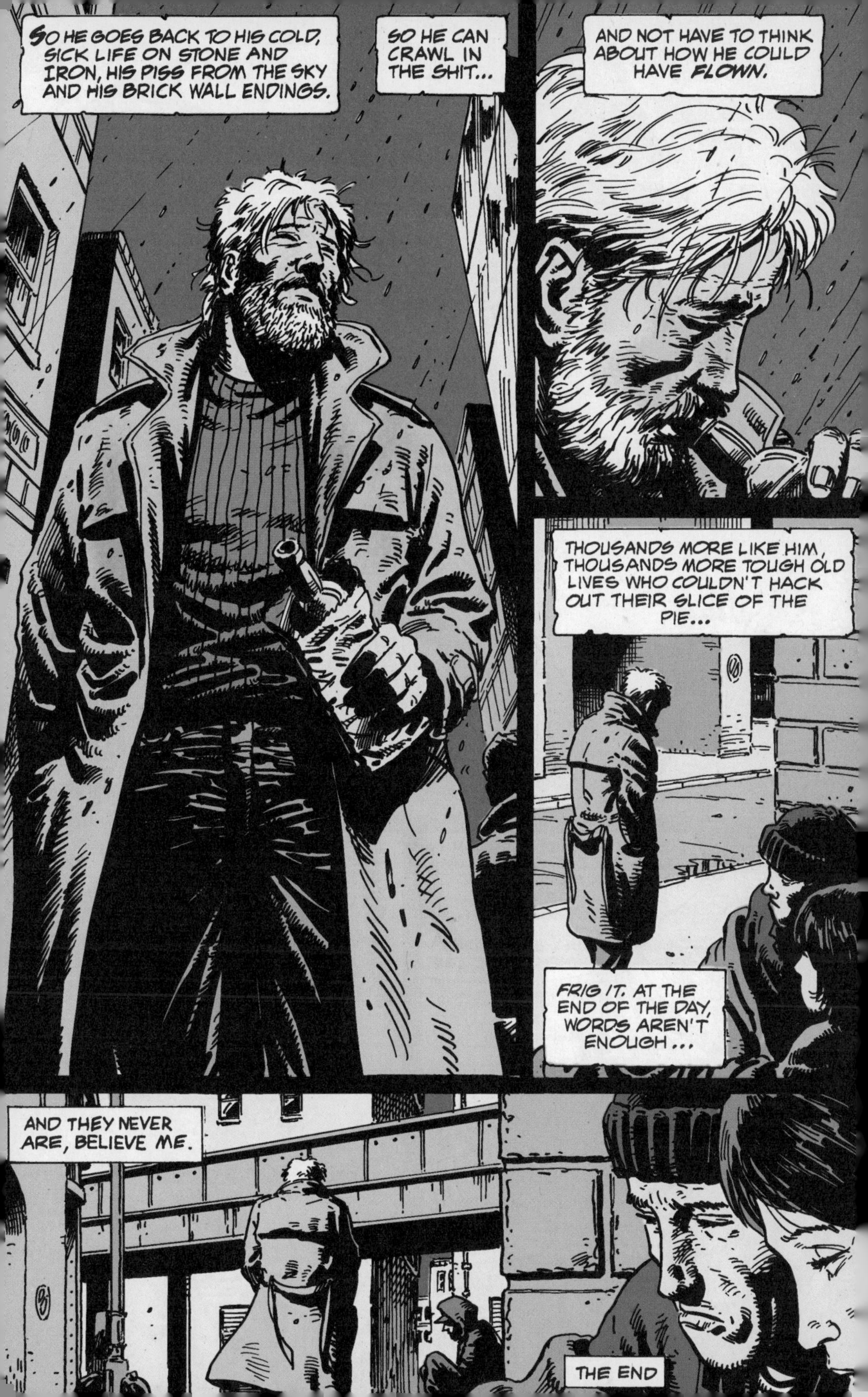
SO HE GOES BACK TO HIS COLD, SICK LIFE ON STONE AND IRON, HIS PISS FROM THE SKY AND HIS BRICK WALL ENDINGS.
SO HE CAN CRAWL IN THE SHIT...
AND NOT HAVE TO THINK ABOUT HOW HE COULD HAVE FLOWN.
THOUSANDS MORE LIKE HIM, THOUSANDS MORE TOUGH OLD LIVES WHO COULDN'T HACK OUT THEIR SLICE OF THE PIE...
FRIG IT. AT THE END OF THE DAY, WORDS AREN'T ENOUGH...
AND THEY NEVER ARE, BELIEVE ME.
THE END

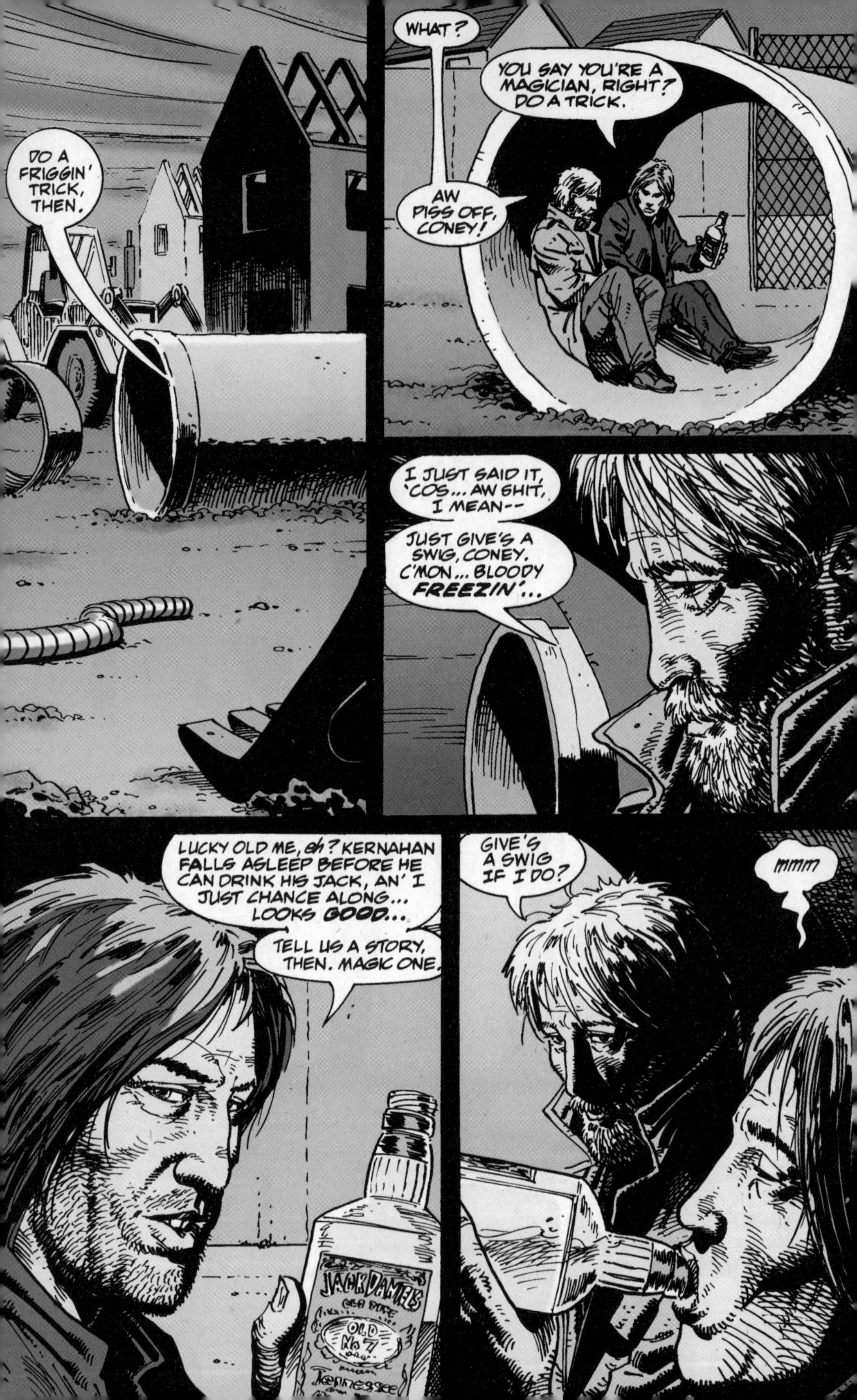
DO A FRIGGIN' TRICK, THEN.
WHAT?
YOU SAY YOU'RE A MAGICIAN, RIGHT? DO A TRICK.
AW PISS OFF, CONEY!
I JUST SAID IT, 'COS... AW SHIT, I MEAN--
JUST GIVE'S A SWIG, CONEY. C'MON... BLOODY FREEZIN'...
LUCKY OLD ME, eh? KERNAHAN FALLS ASLEEP BEFORE HE CAN DRINK HIS JACK, AN' I JUST CHANCE ALONG... LOOKS GOOD...
TELL US A STORY, THEN. MAGIC ONE.
GIVE'S A SWIG IF I DO?
mmm
JACK DANIEL'S
OLD No 7
Tennessee

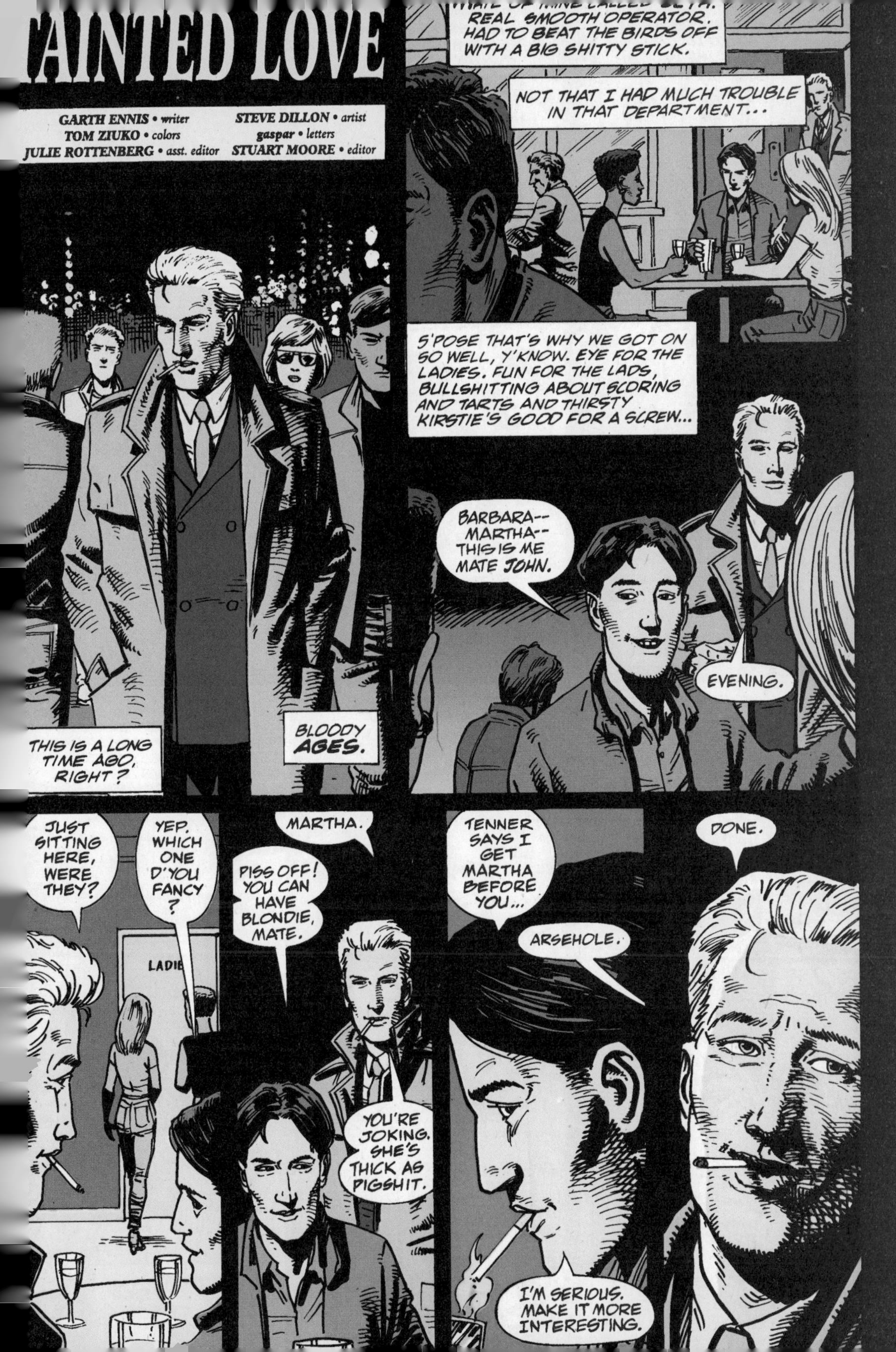

TAINTED LOVE
GARTH ENNIS • writer
STEVE DILLON • artist
TOM ZIUKO • colors
gaspar • letters
JULIE ROTTENBERG • asst. editor
STUART MOORE • editor
THIS IS A LONG TIME AGO, RIGHT?
BLOODY AGES.
REAL SMOOTH OPERATOR. HAD TO BEAT THE BIRDS OFF WITH A BIG SHITTY STICK.
NOT THAT I HAD MUCH TROUBLE IN THAT DEPARTMENT...
S'POSE THAT'S WHY WE GOT ON SO WELL, Y'KNOW. EYE FOR THE LADIES. FUN FOR THE LADS, BULLSHITTING ABOUT SCORING AND TARTS AND THIRSTY KIRSTIE'S GOOD FOR A SCREW...
BARBARA-- MARTHA-- THIS IS ME MATE JOHN.
EVENING.
JUST SITTING HERE, WERE THEY?
YEP. WHICH ONE D'YOU FANCY?
LADIE
MARTHA.
PISS OFF! YOU CAN HAVE BLONDIE, MATE.
YOU'RE JOKING. SHE'S THICK AS PIGSHIT.
TENNER SAYS I GET MARTHA BEFORE YOU...
DONE.
ARSEHOLE.
I'M SERIOUS. MAKE IT MORE INTERESTING.

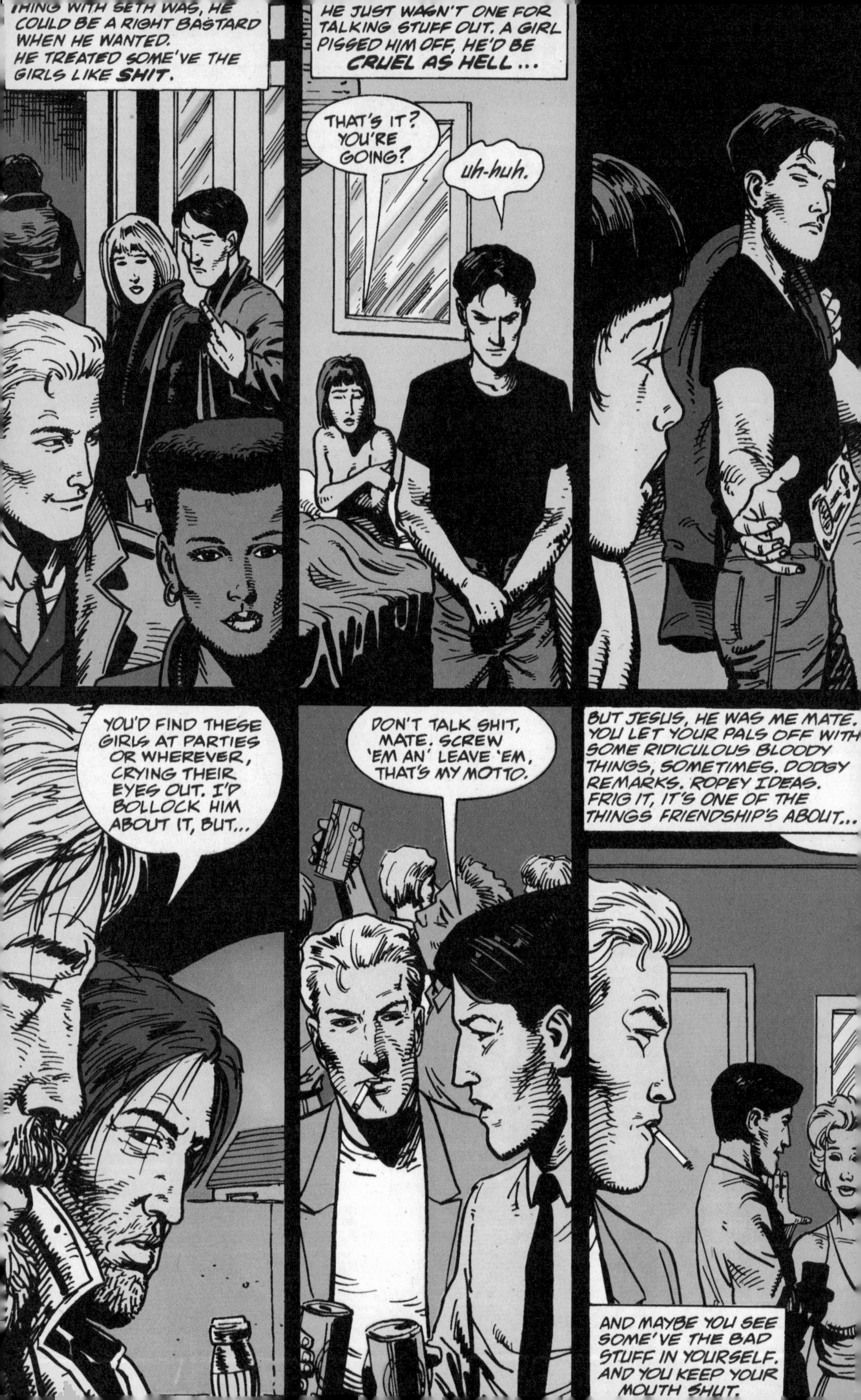
THING WITH SETH WAS, HE COULD BE A RIGHT BASTARD WHEN HE WANTED. HE TREATED SOME'VE THE GIRLS LIKE SHIT.
HE JUST WASN'T ONE FOR TALKING STUFF OUT. A GIRL PISSED HIM OFF, HE'D BE CRUEL AS HELL...
THAT'S IT? YOU'RE GOING?
uh-huh.
YOU'D FIND THESE GIRLS AT PARTIES OR WHEREVER, CRYING THEIR EYES OUT. I'D BOLLOCK HIM ABOUT IT, BUT...
DON'T TALK SHIT, MATE. SCREW 'EM AN' LEAVE 'EM, THAT'S MY MOTTO.
BUT JESUS, HE WAS ME MATE. YOU LET YOUR PALS OFF WITH SOME RIDICULOUS BLOODY THINGS, SOMETIMES. DODGY REMARKS. ROPEY IDEAS. FRIG IT, IT'S ONE OF THE THINGS FRIENDSHIP'S ABOUT...
AND MAYBE YOU SEE SOME'VE THE BAD STUFF IN YOURSELF. AND YOU KEEP YOUR MOUTH SHUT.

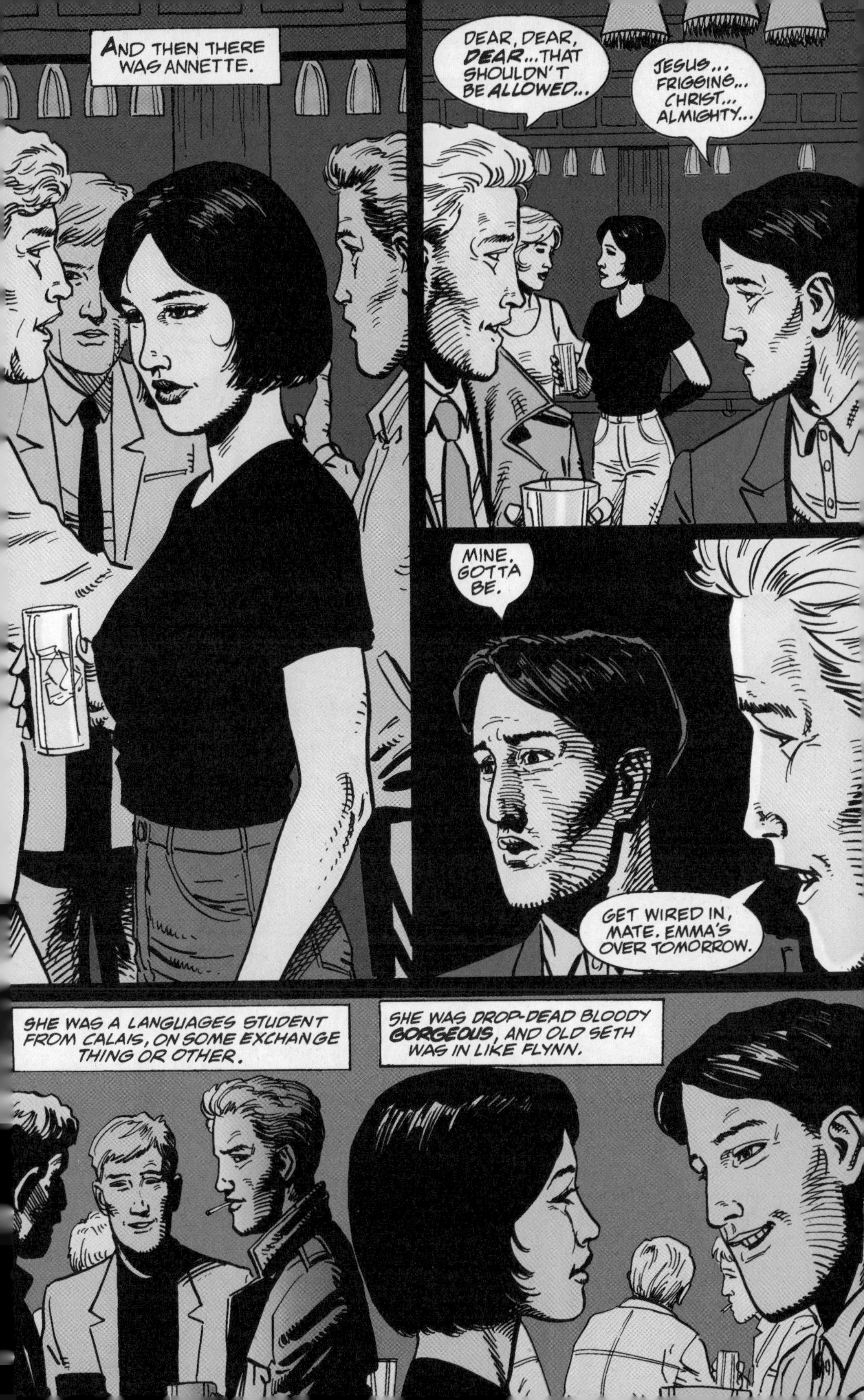

AND THEN THERE WAS ANNETTE.
DEAR, DEAR, DEAR... THAT SHOULDN'T BE ALLOWED...
JESUS... FRIGGING... CHRIST... ALMIGHTY...
MINE. GOTTA BE.
GET WIRED IN, MATE. EMMA'S OVER TOMORROW.
SHE WAS A LANGUAGES STUDENT FROM CALAIS, ON SOME EXCHANGE THING OR OTHER.
SHE WAS DROP-DEAD BLOODY GORGEOUS, AND OLD SETH WAS IN LIKE FLYNN.

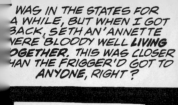

WAS IN THE STATES FOR A WHILE, BUT WHEN I GOT BACK, SETH AN' ANNETTE WERE 'BLOODY WELL *LIVING* TOGETHER. THIS WAS CLOSER THAN THE FRIGGER'D GOT TO ANYONE, RIGHT?

I COULDN'T BELIEVE ME EYES.

SO WHAT HAPPENED TO "SCREW 'EM AN' LEAVE 'EM"?

JESUS, NO, MATE. NOT WITH HER. SHE'S...

LOOK, I GOTTA GO ANYWAY. SHE'S COOKING TONIGHT.

PISS OFF! IT'S NOT LIKE THAT AT ALL!

BLOODY WELL SOUNDS LIKE IT, CHUM.

IT'S NOT, MATE.

SHE'S THE ONE.

SHE WASN'T.

SETH GAVE A PARTY ABOUT A WEEK LATER. HALF WAY THROUGH, THE SHIT HIT THE FAN.

WHAT IS *WRONG* WITH YOU? I WAS ONLY *TALKING* TO HER, FOR GOD'S SAKE! SHE'S AN OLD FRIEND!

YOU WERE *KISSING* HER, SETH! DO YOU THINK I AM STUPID? AM I NOT ENOUGH FOR YOU?

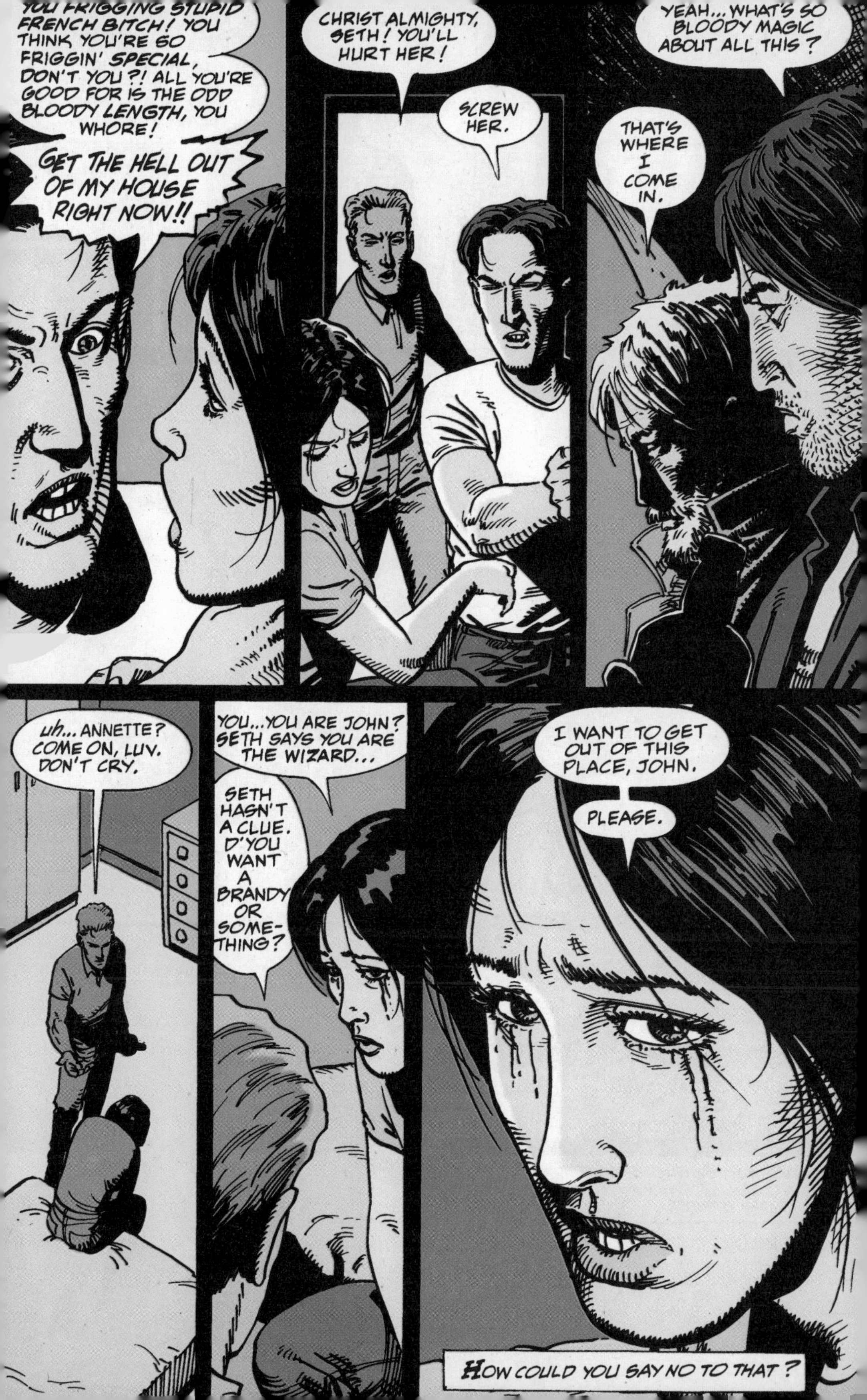
YOU FRIGGING STUPID FRENCH BITCH! YOU THINK YOU'RE SO FRIGGIN' SPECIAL, DON'T YOU?! ALL YOU'RE GOOD FOR IS THE ODD BLOODY LENGTH, YOU WHORE!
GET THE HELL OUT OF MY HOUSE RIGHT NOW!!
CHRIST ALMIGHTY, SETH! YOU'LL HURT HER!
SCREW HER.
YEAH... WHAT'S SO BLOODY MAGIC ABOUT ALL THIS?
THAT'S WHERE I COME IN.
uh... ANNETTE? COME ON, LUV. DON'T CRY.
YOU... YOU ARE JOHN? SETH SAYS YOU ARE THE WIZARD...
SETH HASN'T A CLUE. D'YOU WANT A BRANDY OR SOMETHING?
I WANT TO GET OUT OF THIS PLACE, JOHN.
PLEASE.
HOW COULD YOU SAY NO TO THAT?

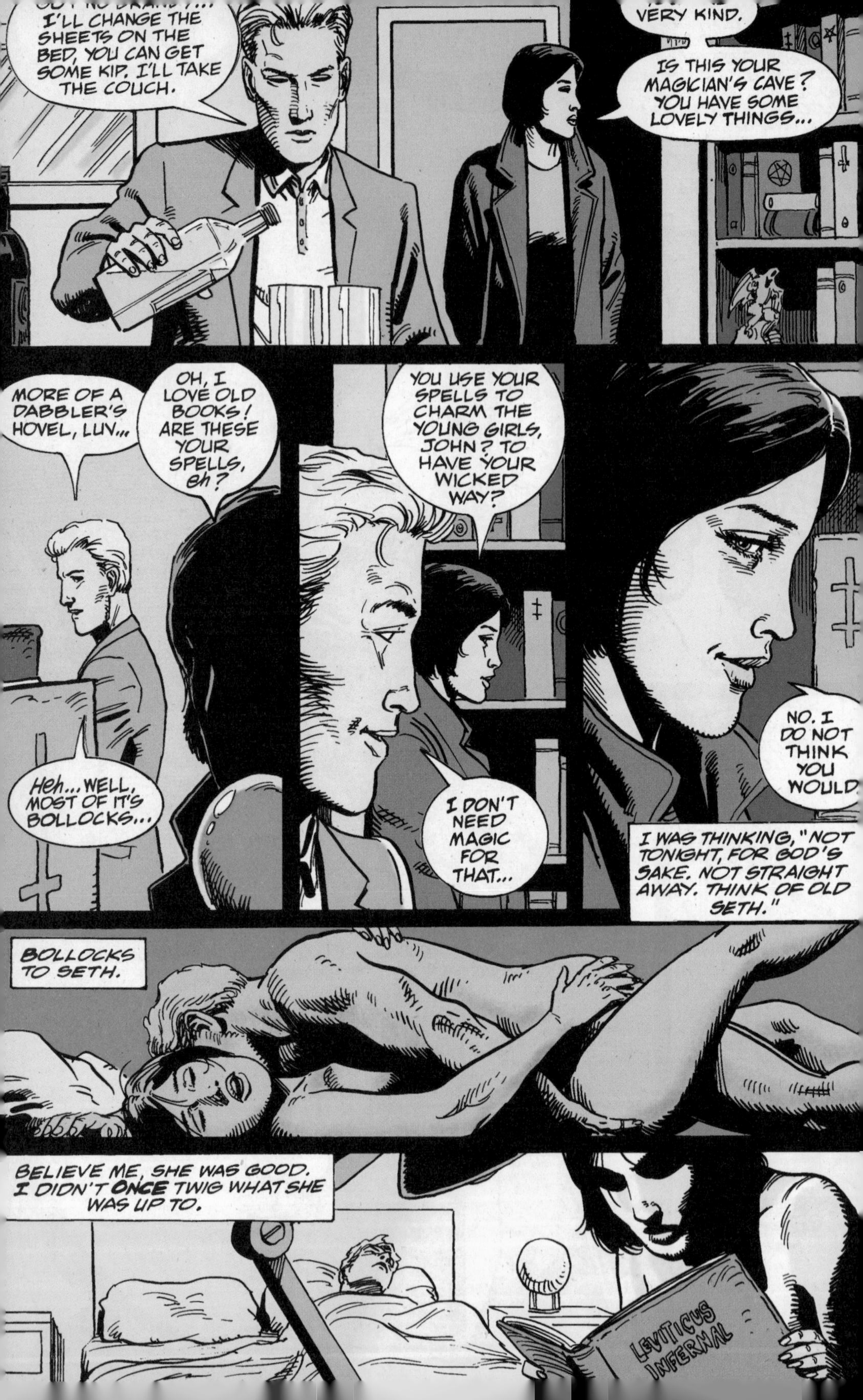
I'LL CHANGE THE SHEETS ON THE BED, YOU CAN GET SOME KIP. I'LL TAKE THE COUCH.
VERY KIND.
IS THIS YOUR MAGICIAN'S CAVE? YOU HAVE SOME LOVELY THINGS...
MORE OF A DABBLER'S HOVEL, LUV...
OH, I LOVE OLD BOOKS! ARE THESE YOUR SPELLS, eh?
Heh... WELL, MOST OF IT'S BOLLOCKS...
YOU USE YOUR SPELLS TO CHARM THE YOUNG GIRLS, JOHN? TO HAVE YOUR WICKED WAY?
I DON'T NEED MAGIC FOR THAT...
NO. I DO NOT THINK YOU WOULD.
I WAS THINKING, "NOT TONIGHT, FOR GOD'S SAKE. NOT STRAIGHT AWAY. THINK OF OLD SETH."
BOLLOCKS TO SETH.
BELIEVE ME, SHE WAS GOOD. I DIDN'T ONCE TWIG WHAT SHE WAS UP TO.
LEVITICUS INFERNAL

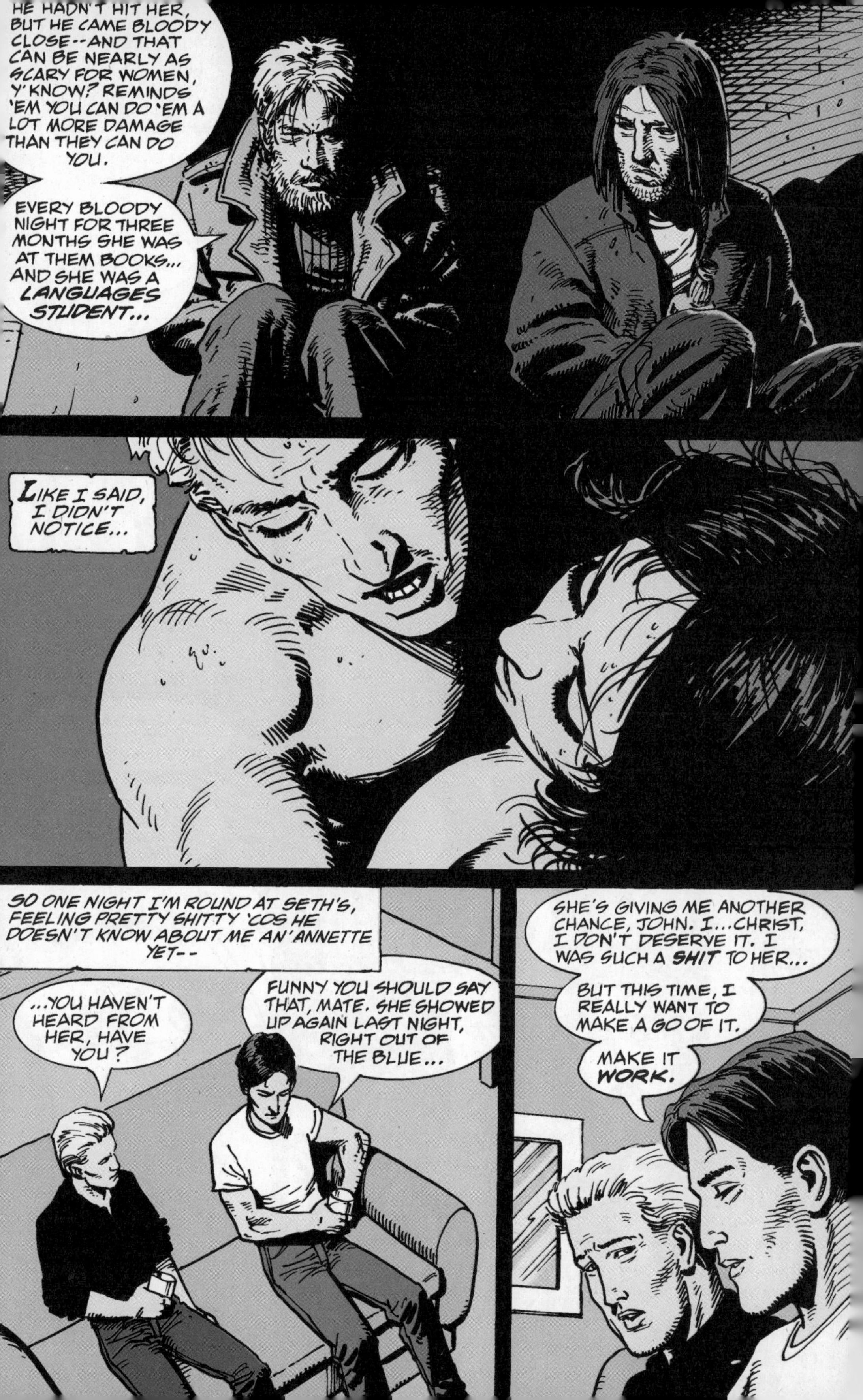
HE HADN'T HIT HER, BUT HE CAME BLOODY CLOSE--AND THAT CAN BE NEARLY AS SCARY FOR WOMEN, Y'KNOW? REMINDS 'EM YOU CAN DO 'EM A LOT MORE DAMAGE THAN THEY CAN DO YOU.
EVERY BLOODY NIGHT FOR THREE MONTHS SHE WAS AT THEM BOOKS... AND SHE WAS A LANGUAGES STUDENT...
LIKE I SAID, I DIDN'T NOTICE...
SO ONE NIGHT I'M ROUND AT SETH'S, FEELING PRETTY SHITTY 'COS HE DOESN'T KNOW ABOUT ME AN' ANNETTE YET--
...YOU HAVEN'T HEARD FROM HER, HAVE YOU?
FUNNY YOU SHOULD SAY THAT, MATE. SHE SHOWED UP AGAIN LAST NIGHT, RIGHT OUT OF THE BLUE...
SHE'S GIVING ME ANOTHER CHANCE, JOHN. I...CHRIST, I DON'T DESERVE IT. I WAS SUCH A SHIT TO HER...
BUT THIS TIME, I REALLY WANT TO MAKE A GO OF IT.
MAKE IT WORK.

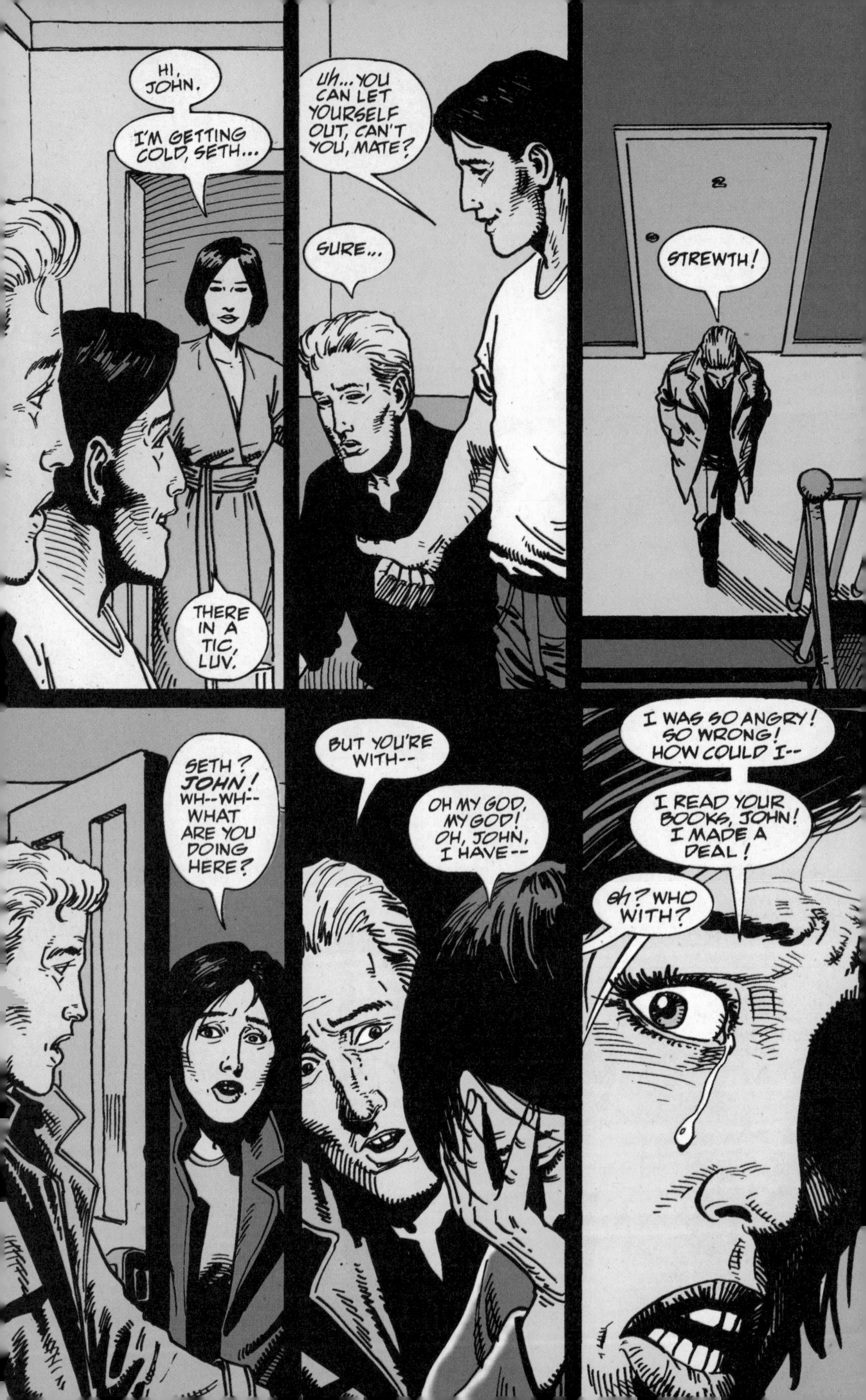
HI, JOHN.
I'M GETTING COLD, SETH...
THERE IN A TIC, LUV.
UH... YOU CAN LET YOURSELF OUT, CAN'T YOU, MATE?
SURE...
STREWTH!
SETH? JOHN! WH--WH-- WHAT ARE YOU DOING HERE?
BUT YOU'RE WITH--
OH MY GOD, MY GOD! OH, JOHN, I HAVE--
I WAS SO ANGRY! SO WRONG! HOW COULD I--
I READ YOUR BOOKS, JOHN! I MADE A DEAL!
OH? WHO WITH?

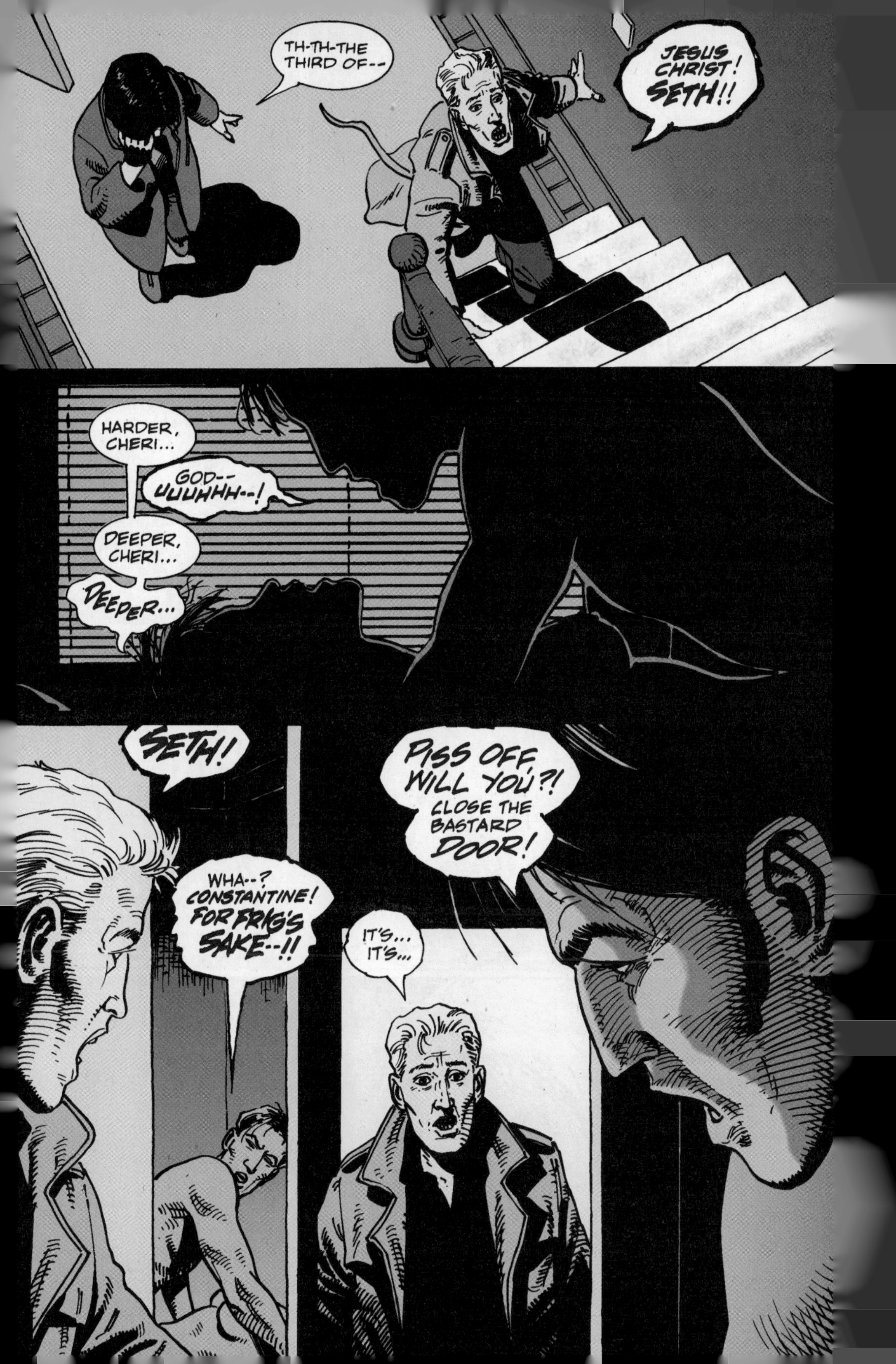
TH-TH-THE THIRD OF--
JESUS CHRIST! SETH!!
HARDER, CHERI...
GOD-- UUUHHH--!
DEEPER, CHERI...
DEEPER...
SETH!
PISS OFF WILL YOU?! CLOSE THE BASTARD DOOR!
WHA--? CONSTANTINE! FOR FRIG'S SAKE--!!
IT'S... IT'S...

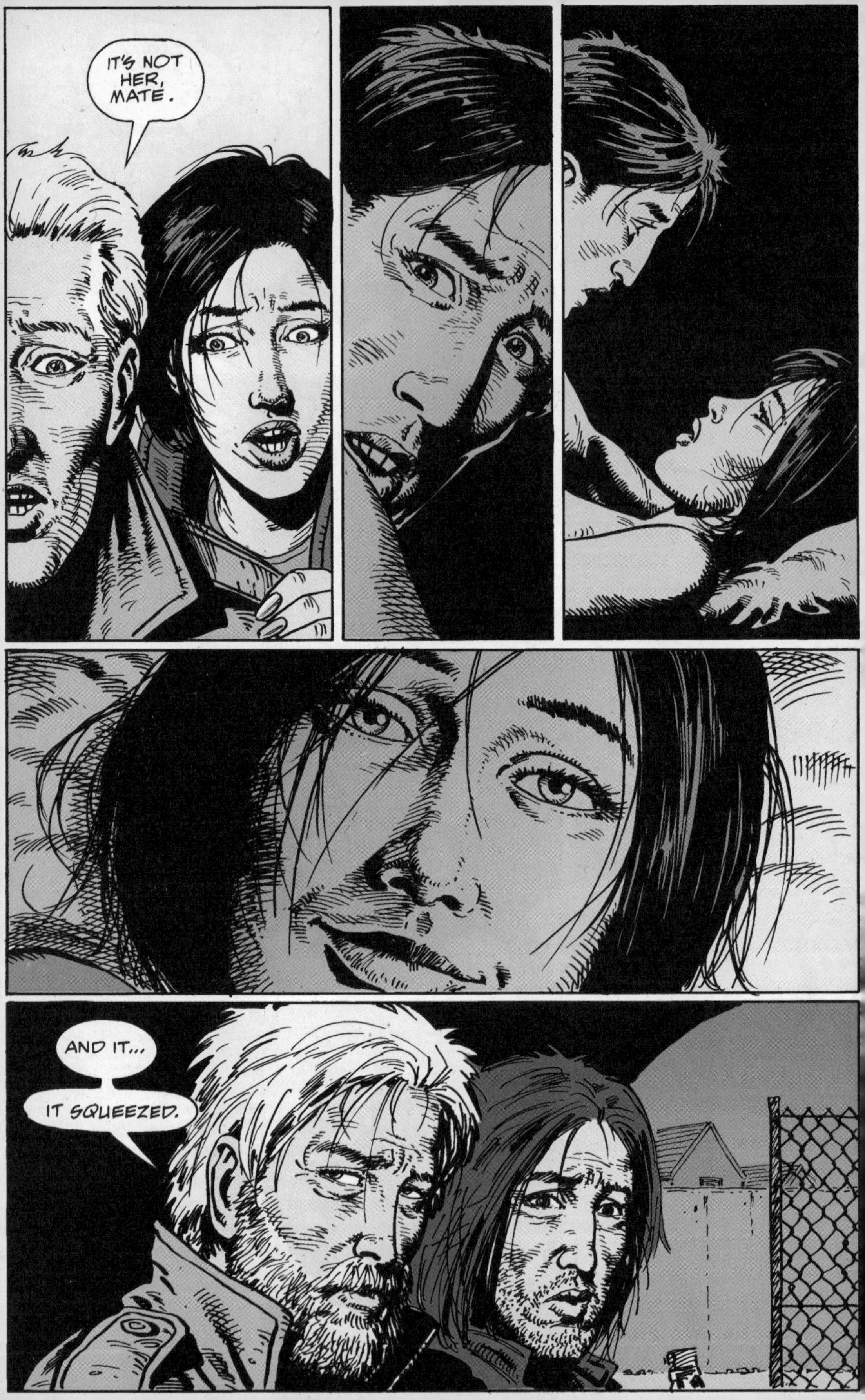
IT'S NOT HER, MATE.
AND IT...
IT SQUEEZED.

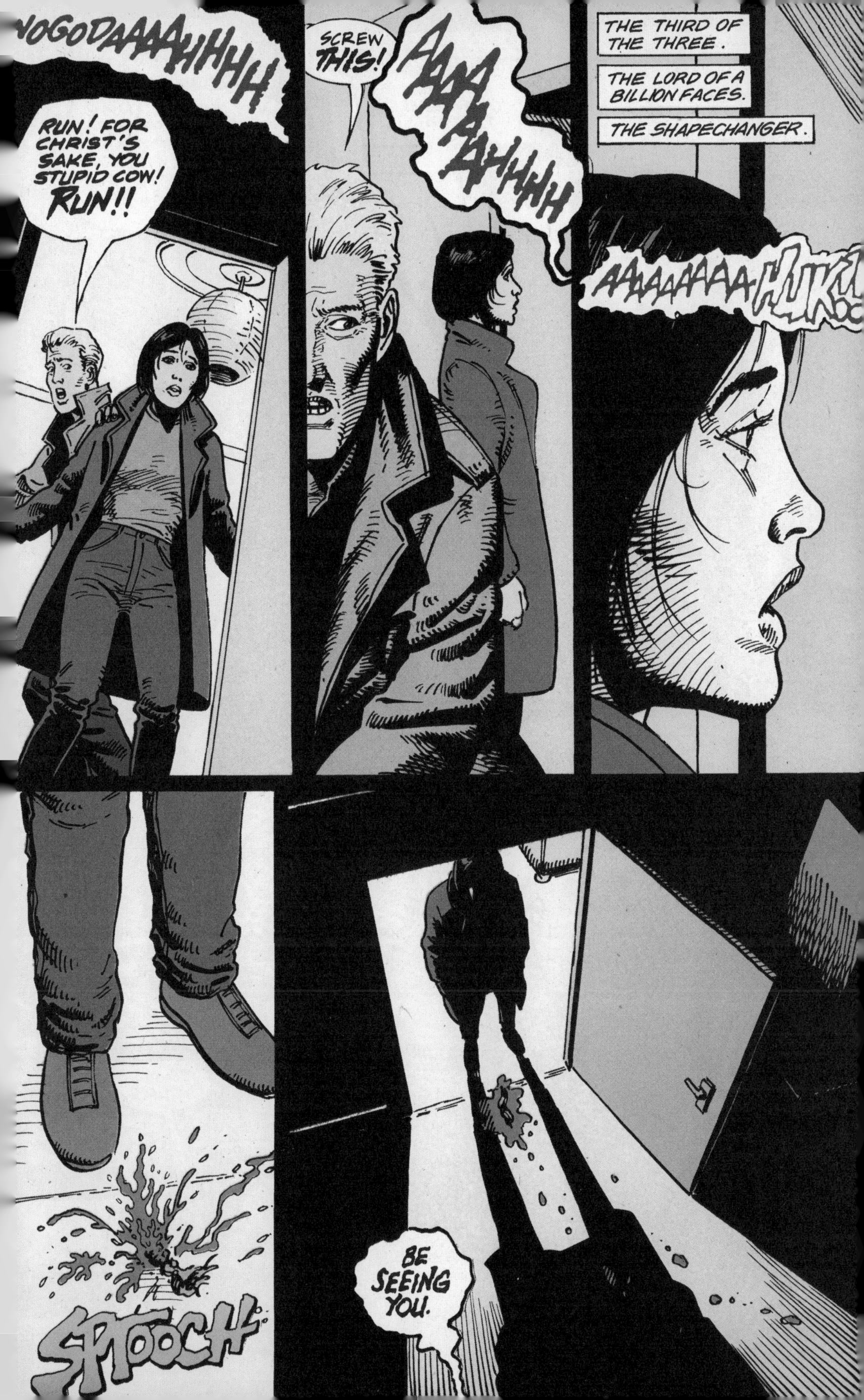
NOGODAAAAAHHHHH
RUN! FOR CHRIST'S SAKE, YOU STUPID COW! RUN!!
SCREW THIS!
AAAAAAAHHHHH
THE THIRD OF THE THREE.
THE LORD OF A BILLION FACES.
THE SHAPECHANGER.
AAAAAAAAAHUK
SPLOOCH
BE SEEING YOU.

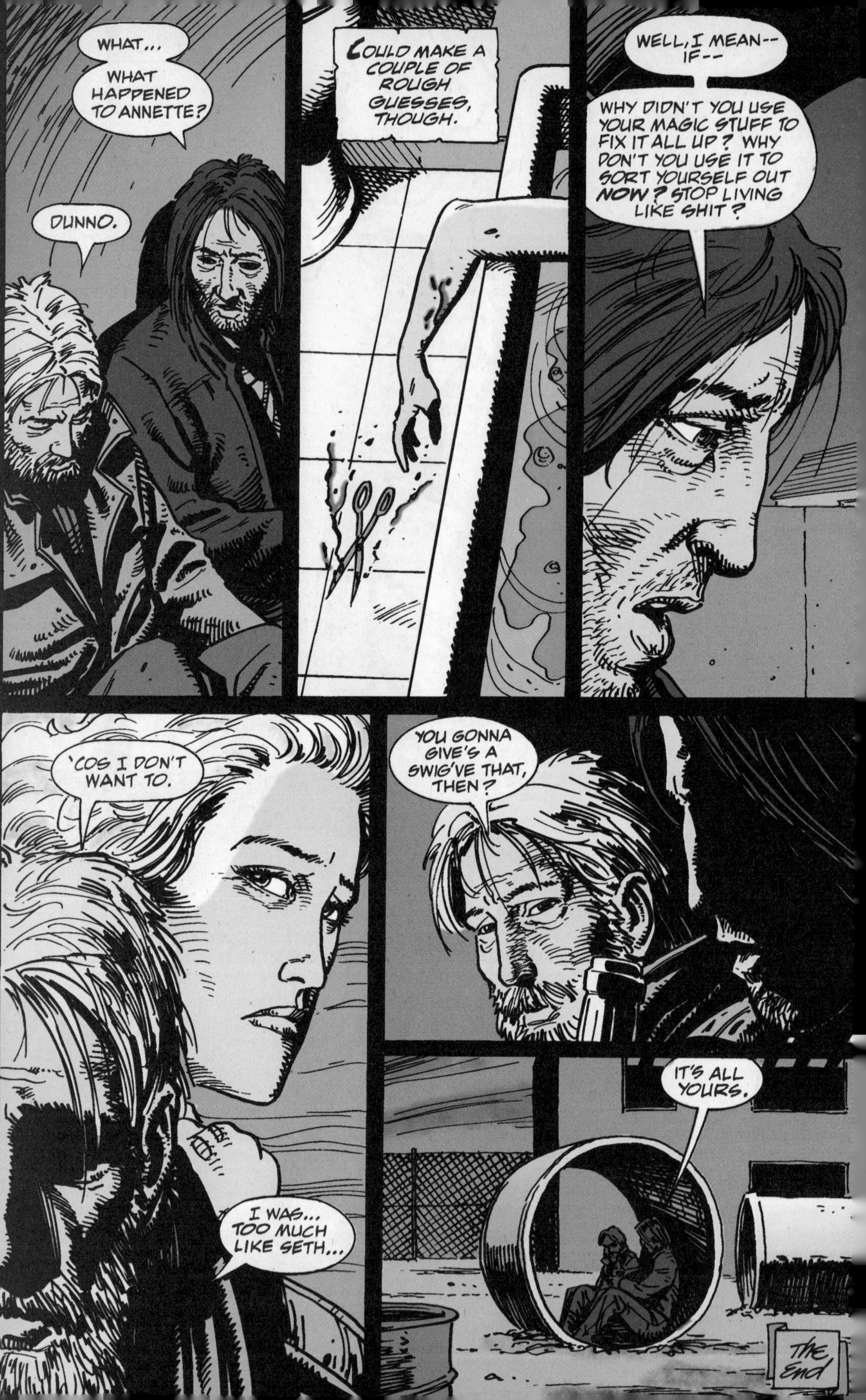
WHAT...
WHAT HAPPENED TO ANNETTE?
DUNNO.
COULD MAKE A COUPLE OF ROUGH GUESSES, THOUGH.
WELL, I MEAN-- IF--
WHY DIDN'T YOU USE YOUR MAGIC STUFF TO FIX IT ALL UP? WHY DON'T YOU USE IT TO SORT YOURSELF OUT NOW? STOP LIVING LIKE SHIT?
'COS I DON'T WANT TO.
I WAS... TOO MUCH LIKE SETH...
YOU GONNA GIVE'S A SWIG'VE THAT, THEN?
IT'S ALL YOURS.
The End

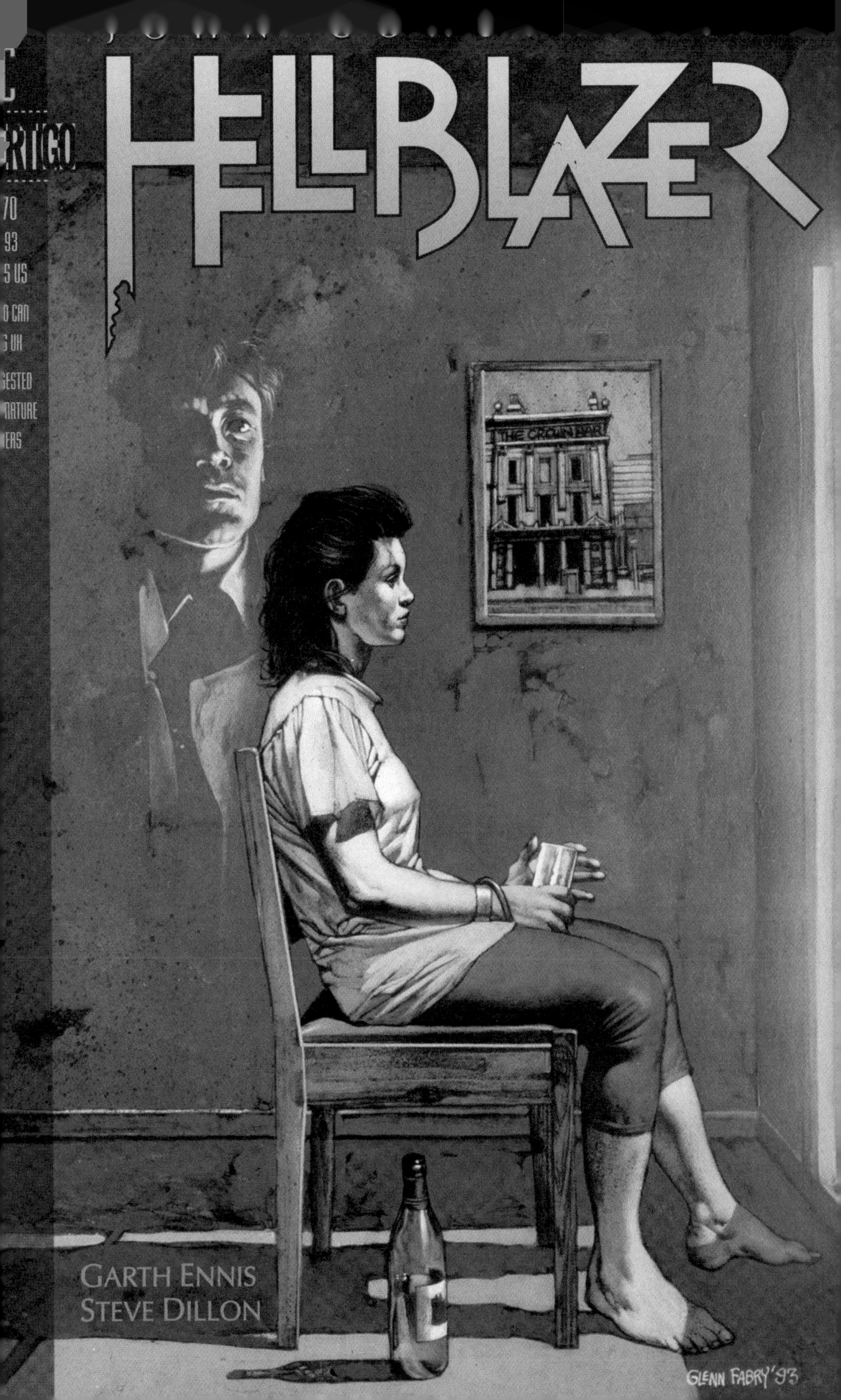
HELLBLAZER
70
93
GARTH ENNIS
STEVE DILLON
THE CROWN BAR
GLENN FABRY '93

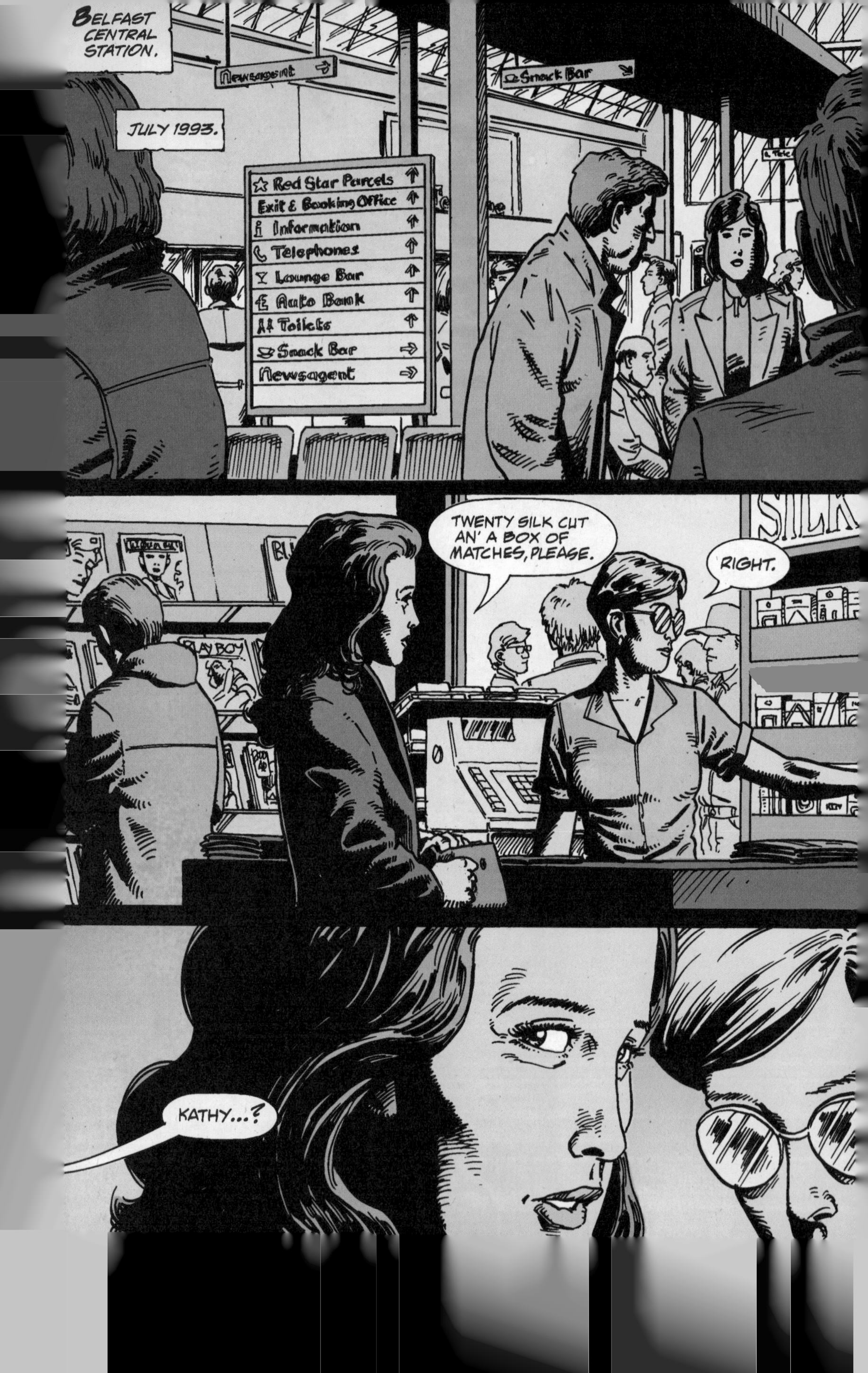
BELFAST CENTRAL STATION.
Newsagent
Snack Bar
JULY 1993.
Red Star Parcels
Exit & Booking Office
Information
Telephones
Lounge Bar
Auto Bank
Toilets
Snack Bar
Newsagent
PLAYBOY
TWENTY SILK CUT AN' A BOX OF MATCHES, PLEASE.
RIGHT.
KATHY...?

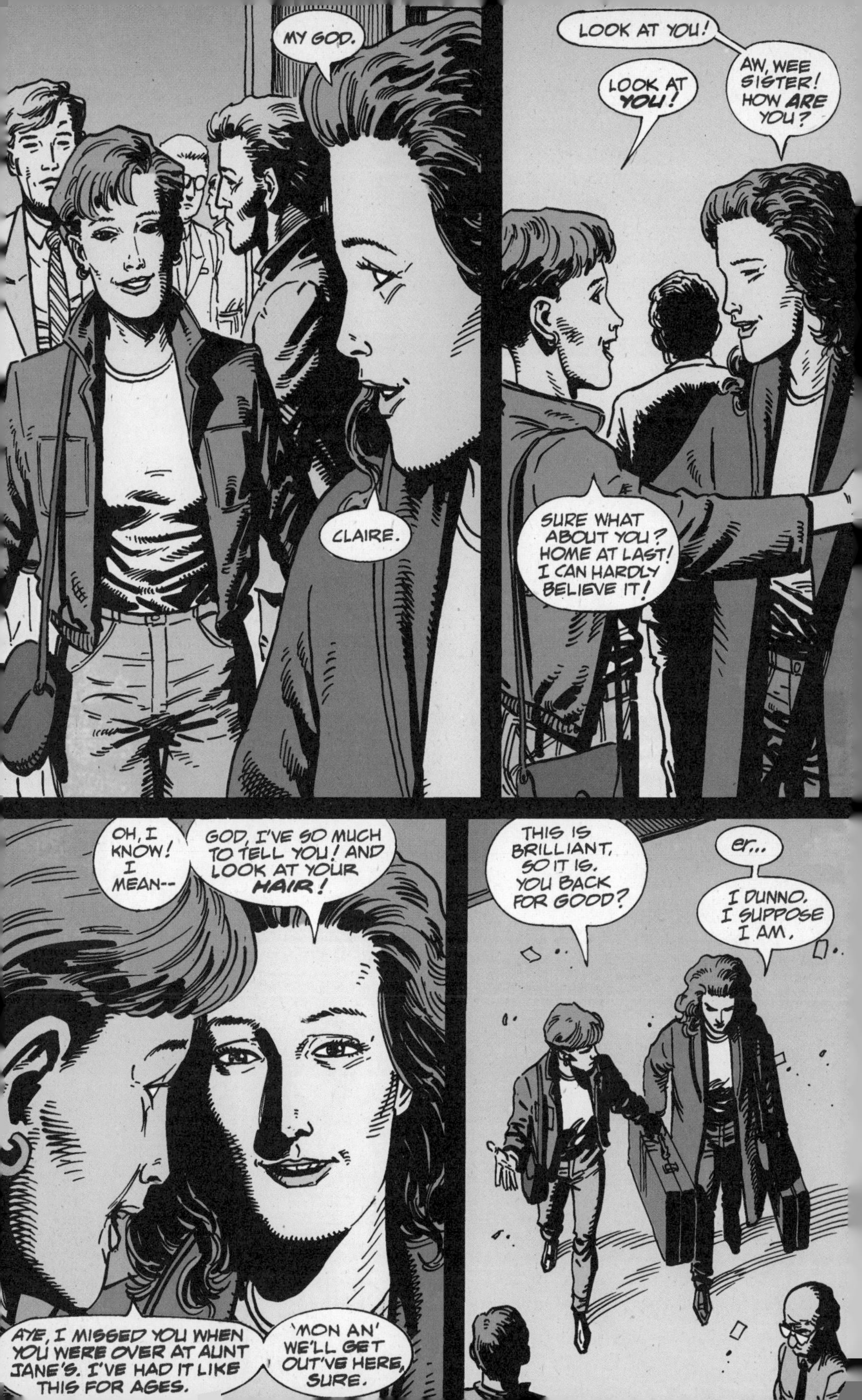
MY GOD.
CLAIRE.
LOOK AT YOU!
LOOK AT YOU!
AW, WEE SISTER! HOW ARE YOU?
SURE WHAT ABOUT YOU? HOME AT LAST! I CAN HARDLY BELIEVE IT!
OH, I KNOW! I MEAN--
GOD, I'VE SO MUCH TO TELL YOU! AND LOOK AT YOUR HAIR!
AYE, I MISSED YOU WHEN YOU WERE OVER AT AUNT JANE'S. I'VE HAD IT LIKE THIS FOR AGES.
'MON AN' WE'LL GET OUT'VE HERE, SURE.
THIS IS BRILLIANT, SO IT IS. YOU BACK FOR GOOD?
er...
I DUNNO. I SUPPOSE I AM.

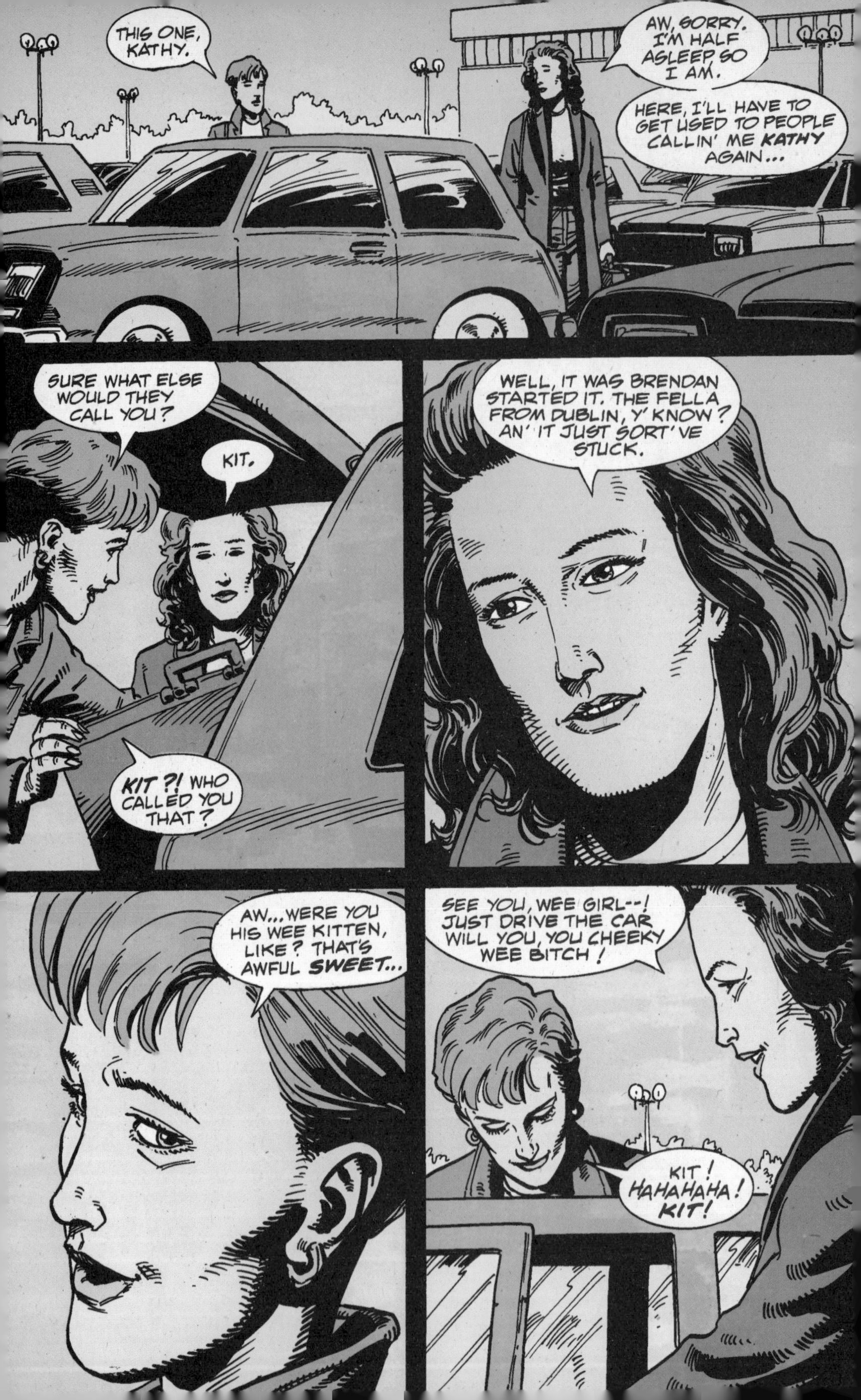
THIS ONE, KATHY.
AW, SORRY. I'M HALF ASLEEP, SO I AM.
HERE, I'LL HAVE TO GET USED TO PEOPLE CALLIN' ME **KATHY** AGAIN...
SURE WHAT ELSE WOULD THEY CALL YOU?
KIT.
KIT?! WHO CALLED YOU THAT?
WELL, IT WAS BRENDAN STARTED IT. THE FELLA FROM DUBLIN, Y' KNOW? AN' IT JUST SORT'VE STUCK.
AW...WERE YOU HIS WEE KITTEN, LIKE? THAT'S AWFUL **SWEET**...
SEE YOU, WEE GIRL--! JUST DRIVE THE CAR WILL YOU, YOU CHEEKY WEE BITCH!
KIT! **HAHAHAHA! KIT!**

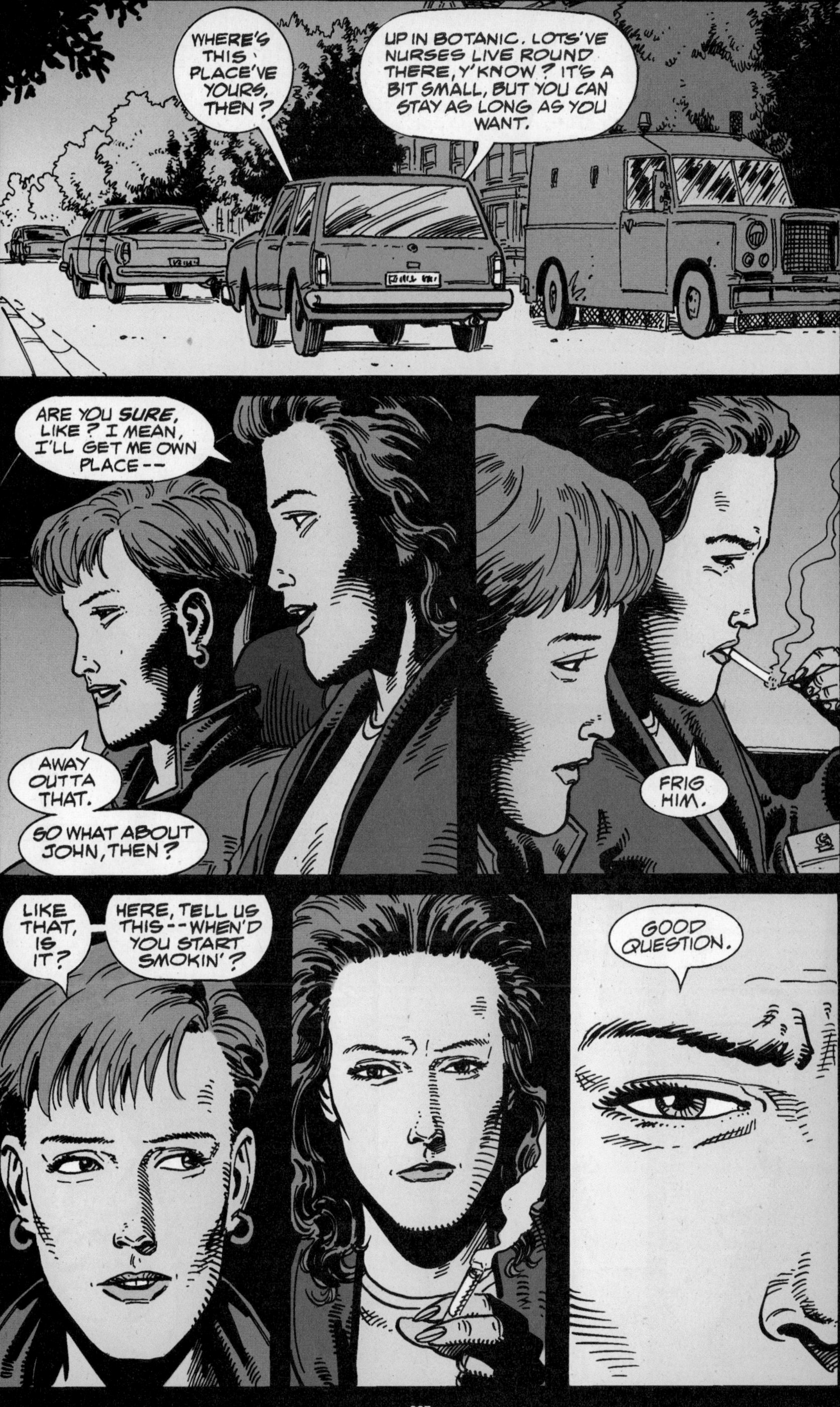
WHERE'S THIS PLACE'VE YOURS, THEN?
UP IN BOTANIC. LOTS'VE NURSES LIVE ROUND THERE, Y'KNOW? IT'S A BIT SMALL, BUT YOU CAN STAY AS LONG AS YOU WANT.
ARE YOU SURE, LIKE? I MEAN, I'LL GET ME OWN PLACE--
AWAY OUTTA THAT.
SO WHAT ABOUT JOHN, THEN?
FRIG HIM.
LIKE THAT, IS IT?
HERE, TELL US THIS--WHEN'D YOU START SMOKIN'?
GOOD QUESTION.

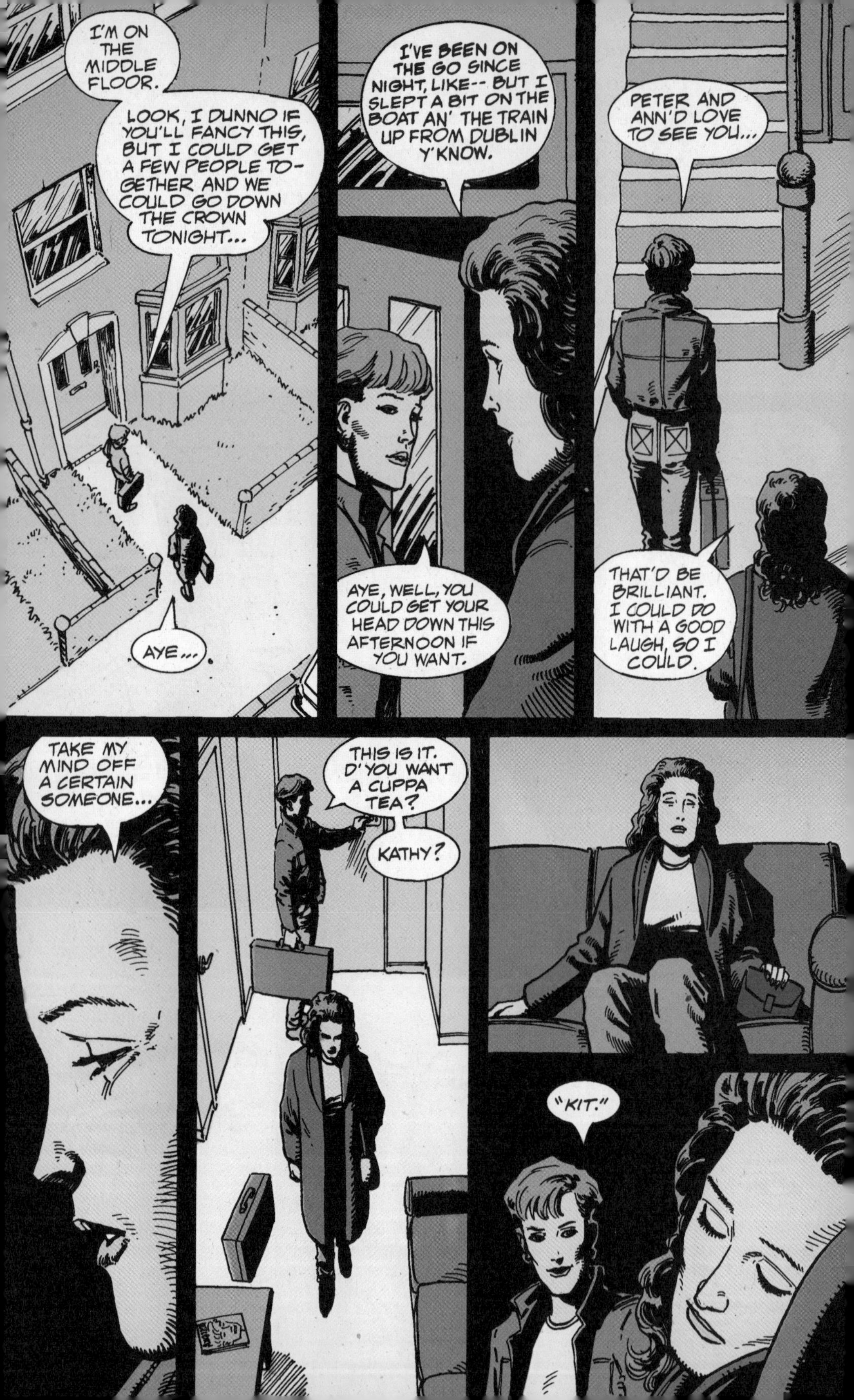
I'M ON THE MIDDLE FLOOR.
LOOK, I DUNNO IF YOU'LL FANCY THIS, BUT I COULD GET A FEW PEOPLE TOGETHER AND WE COULD GO DOWN THE CROWN TONIGHT...
AYE...
I'VE BEEN ON THE GO SINCE NIGHT, LIKE-- BUT I SLEPT A BIT ON THE BOAT AN' THE TRAIN UP FROM DUBLIN Y'KNOW.
AYE, WELL, YOU COULD GET YOUR HEAD DOWN THIS AFTERNOON IF YOU WANT.
PETER AND ANN'D LOVE TO SEE YOU...
THAT'D BE BRILLIANT. I COULD DO WITH A GOOD LAUGH, SO I COULD.
TAKE MY MIND OFF A CERTAIN SOMEONE...
THIS IS IT. D'YOU WANT A CUPPA TEA?
KATHY?
"KIT."

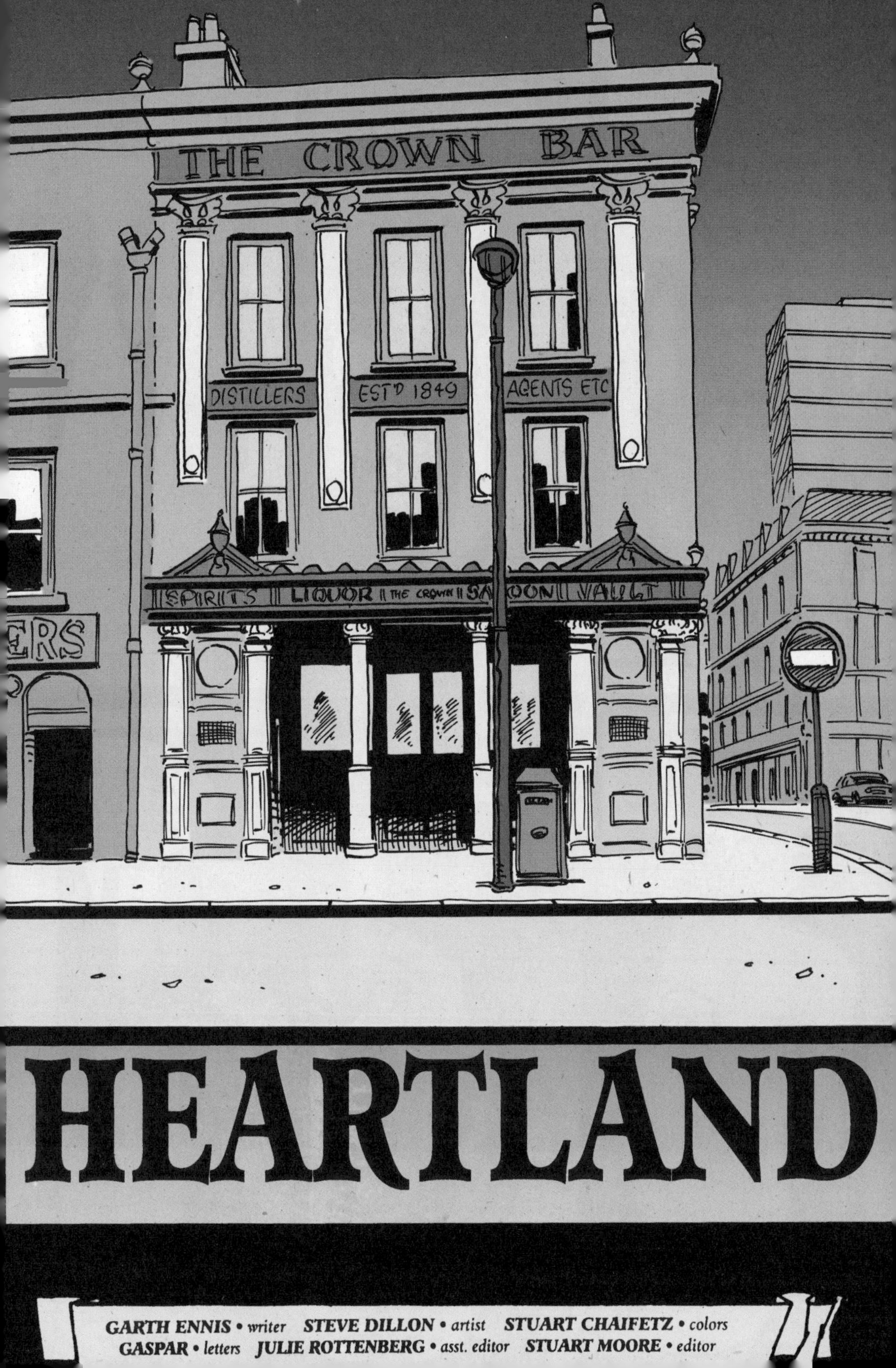
THE CROWN BAR
DISTILLERS
EST'D 1849
AGENTS ETC
SPIRITS
LIQUOR
THE CROWN
SALOON
VAULT

HEARTLAND

GARTH ENNIS • *writer* **STEVE DILLON** • *artist* **STUART CHAIFETZ** • *colors*
GASPAR • *letters* **JULIE ROTTENBERG** • *asst. editor* **STUART MOORE** • *editor*

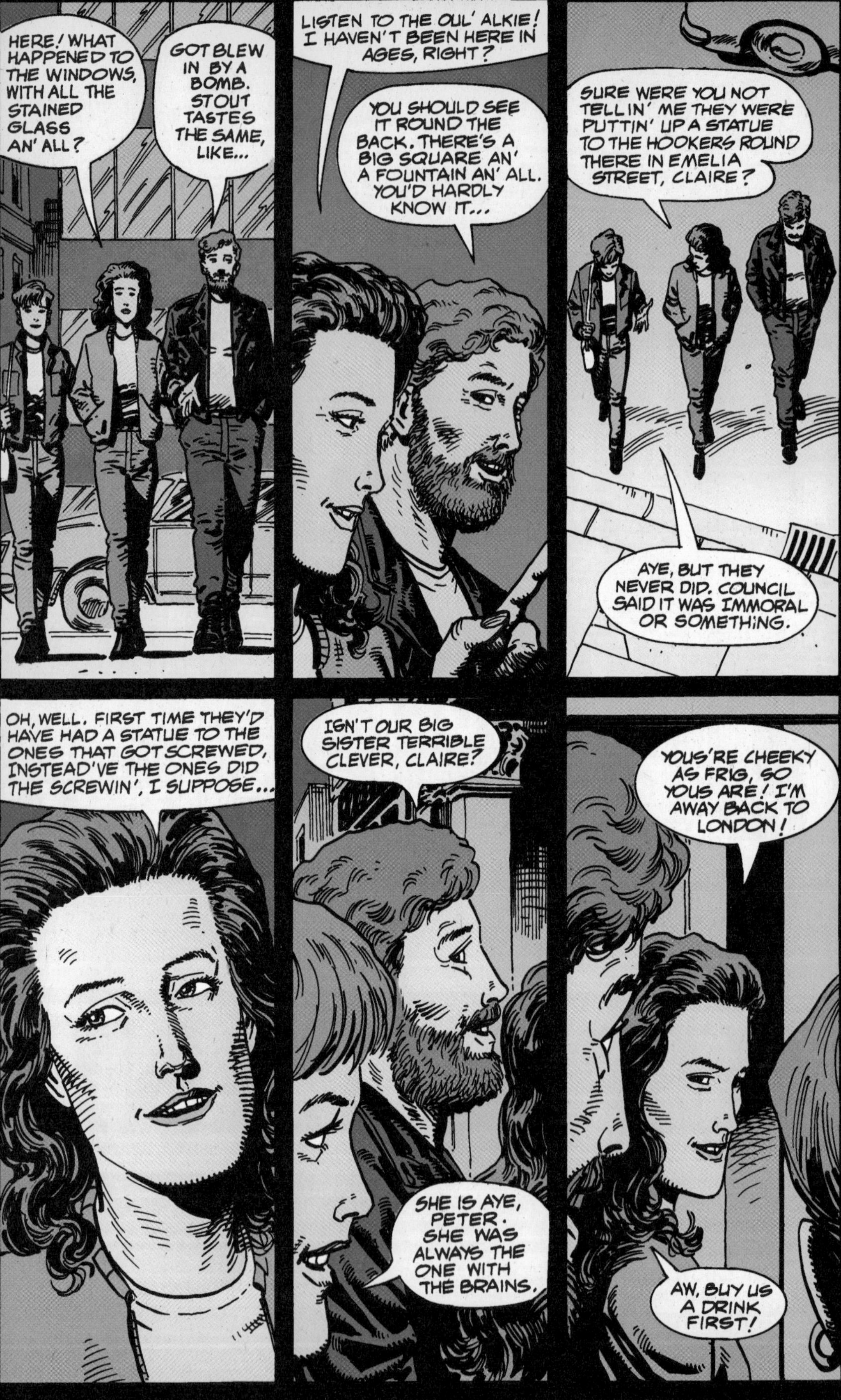
HERE! WHAT HAPPENED TO THE WINDOWS, WITH ALL THE STAINED GLASS AN' ALL?
GOT BLEW IN BY A BOMB. STOUT TASTES THE SAME, LIKE...
LISTEN TO THE OUL' ALKIE! I HAVEN'T BEEN HERE IN AGES, RIGHT?
YOU SHOULD SEE IT ROUND THE BACK. THERE'S A BIG SQUARE AN' A FOUNTAIN AN' ALL. YOU'D HARDLY KNOW IT...
SURE WERE YOU NOT TELLIN' ME THEY WERE PUTTIN' UP A STATUE TO THE HOOKERS ROUND THERE IN EMELIA STREET, CLAIRE?
AYE, BUT THEY NEVER DID. COUNCIL SAID IT WAS IMMORAL OR SOMETHING.
OH, WELL. FIRST TIME THEY'D HAVE HAD A STATUE TO THE ONES THAT GOT SCREWED, INSTEAD'VE THE ONES DID THE SCREWIN', I SUPPOSE...
ISN'T OUR BIG SISTER TERRIBLE CLEVER, CLAIRE?
SHE IS AYE, PETER. SHE WAS ALWAYS THE ONE WITH THE BRAINS.
YOUS'RE CHEEKY AS FRIG, SO YOUS ARE! I'M AWAY BACK TO LONDON!
AW, BUY US A DRINK FIRST!

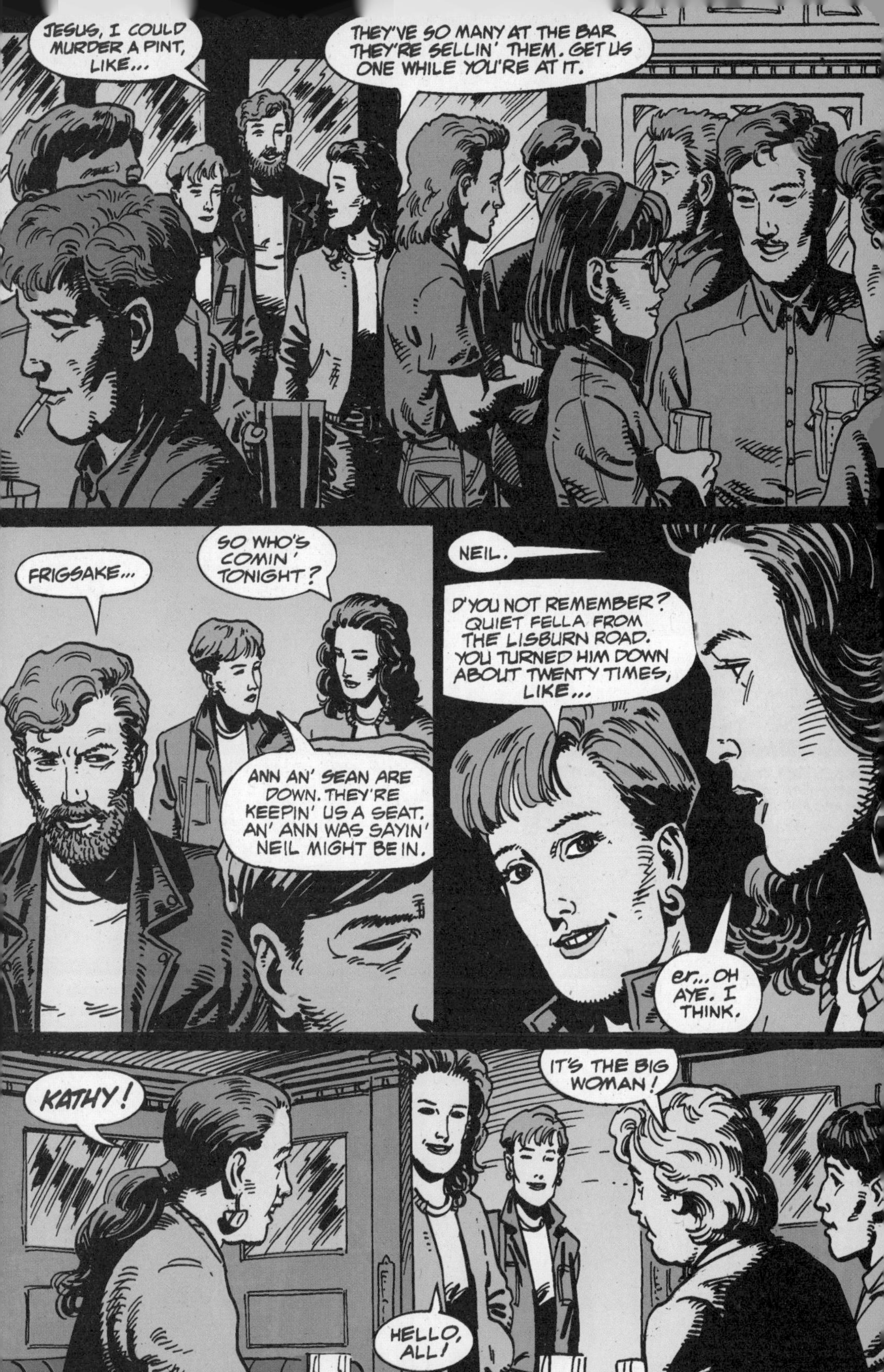
JESUS, I COULD MURDER A PINT, LIKE...
THEY'VE SO MANY AT THE BAR THEY'RE SELLIN' THEM. GET US ONE WHILE YOU'RE AT IT.
FRIGSAKE...
SO WHO'S COMIN' TONIGHT?
ANN AN' SEAN ARE DOWN. THEY'RE KEEPIN' US A SEAT. AN' ANN WAS SAYIN' NEIL MIGHT BE IN.
NEIL.
D'YOU NOT REMEMBER? QUIET FELLA FROM THE LISBURN ROAD. YOU TURNED HIM DOWN ABOUT TWENTY TIMES, LIKE...
er... OH AYE. I THINK.
KATHY!
IT'S THE BIG WOMAN!
HELLO, ALL!

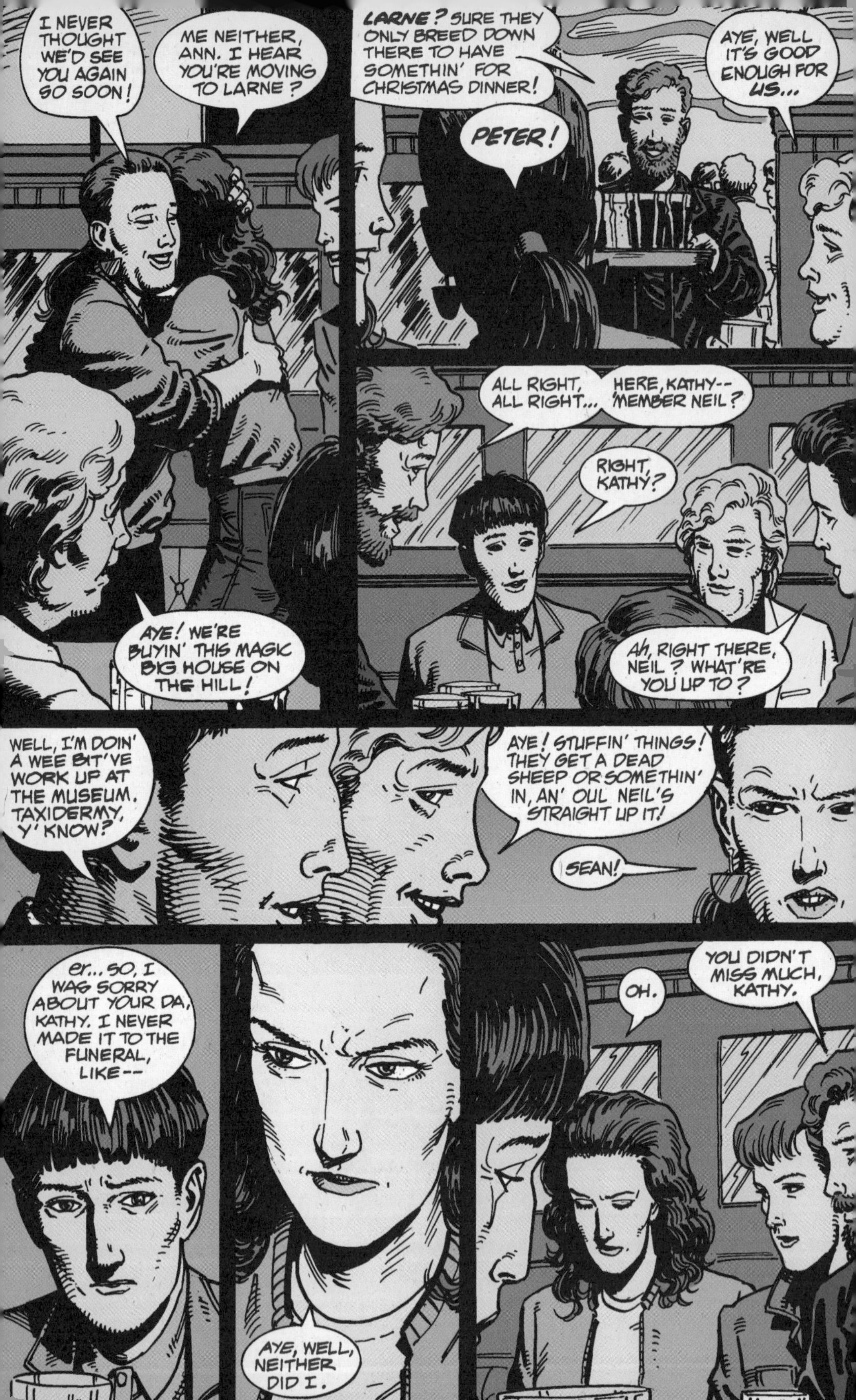

I NEVER THOUGHT WE'D SEE YOU AGAIN SO SOON!
ME NEITHER, ANN. I HEAR YOU'RE MOVING TO LARNE?
LARNE? SURE THEY ONLY BREED DOWN THERE TO HAVE SOMETHIN' FOR CHRISTMAS DINNER!
AYE, WELL IT'S GOOD ENOUGH FOR US...
PETER!
AYE! WE'RE BUYIN' THIS MAGIC BIG HOUSE ON THE HILL!
ALL RIGHT, ALL RIGHT...
HERE, KATHY-- 'MEMBER NEIL?
RIGHT, KATHY?
Ah, RIGHT THERE, NEIL? WHAT'RE YOU UP TO?
WELL, I'M DOIN' A WEE BIT'VE WORK UP AT THE MUSEUM. TAXIDERMY, Y' KNOW?
AYE! STUFFIN' THINGS! THEY GET A DEAD SHEEP OR SOMETHIN' IN, AN' OUL NEIL'S STRAIGHT UP IT!
SEAN!
er... SO, I WAS SORRY ABOUT YOUR DA, KATHY. I NEVER MADE IT TO THE FUNERAL, LIKE--
AYE, WELL, NEITHER DID I.
OH.
YOU DIDN'T MISS MUCH, KATHY.

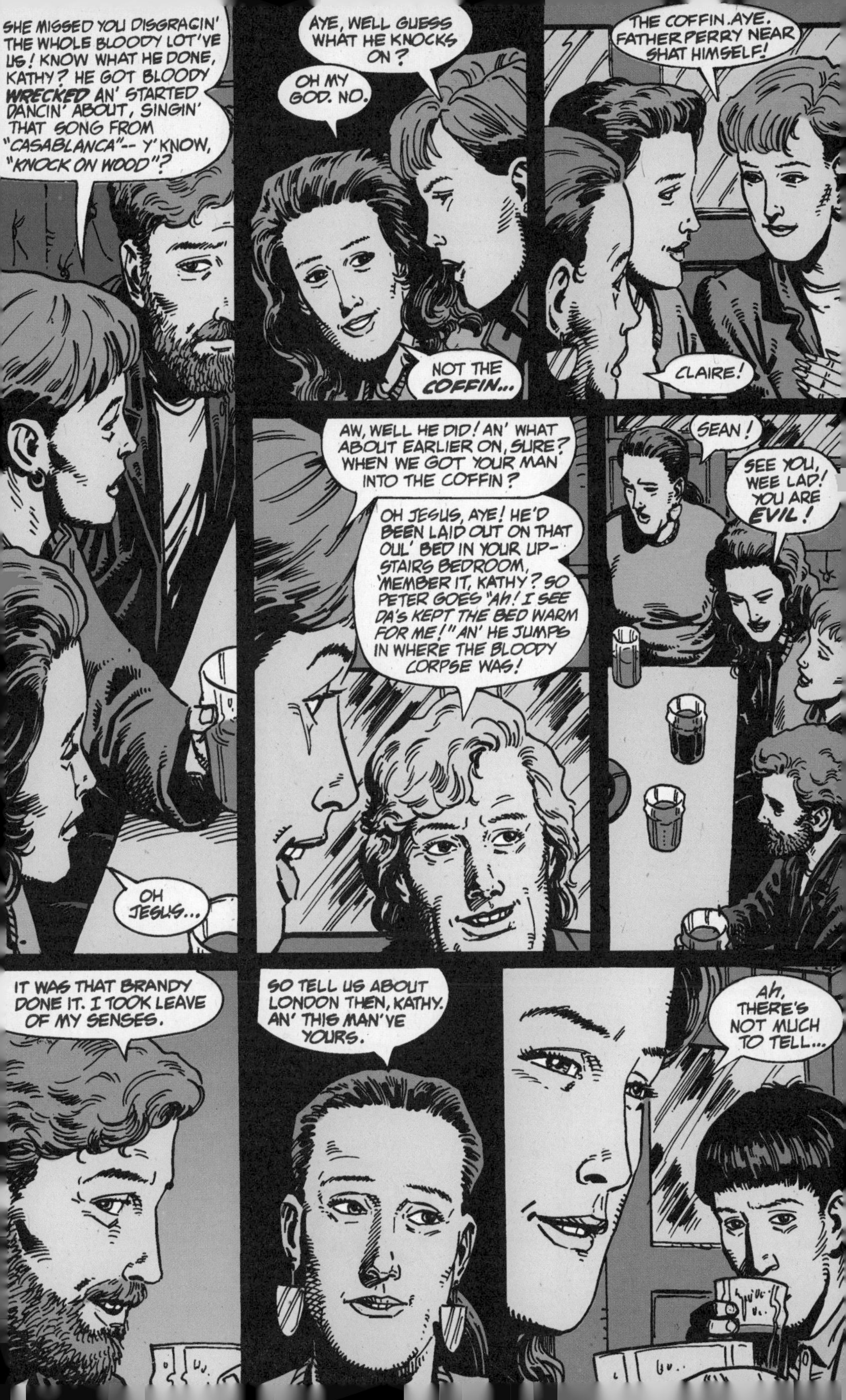

SHE MISSED YOU DISGRACIN' THE WHOLE BLOODY LOT'YE US! KNOW WHAT HE DONE, KATHY? HE GOT BLOODY **WRECKED** AN' STARTED DANCIN' ABOUT, SINGIN' THAT SONG FROM "CASABLANCA"-- Y'KNOW, "KNOCK ON WOOD"?
AYE, WELL GUESS WHAT HE KNOCKS ON?
OH MY GOD. NO.
NOT THE **COFFIN...**
THE COFFIN. AYE. FATHER PERRY NEAR SHAT HIMSELF!
CLAIRE!
AW, WELL HE DID! AN' WHAT ABOUT EARLIER ON, SURE? WHEN WE GOT YOUR MAN INTO THE COFFIN?
OH JESUS, AYE! HE'D BEEN LAID OUT ON THAT OUL' BED IN YOUR UPSTAIRS BEDROOM, 'MEMBER IT, KATHY? SO PETER GOES "*Ah! I SEE DA'S KEPT THE BED WARM FOR ME!*" AN' HE JUMPS IN WHERE THE BLOODY CORPSE WAS!
OH JESUS...
SEAN!
SEE YOU, WEE LAD! YOU ARE **EVIL**!
IT WAS THAT BRANDY DONE IT. I TOOK LEAVE OF MY SENSES.
SO TELL US ABOUT LONDON THEN, KATHY. AN' THIS MAN'YE YOURS.
Ah, THERE'S NOT MUCH TO TELL...

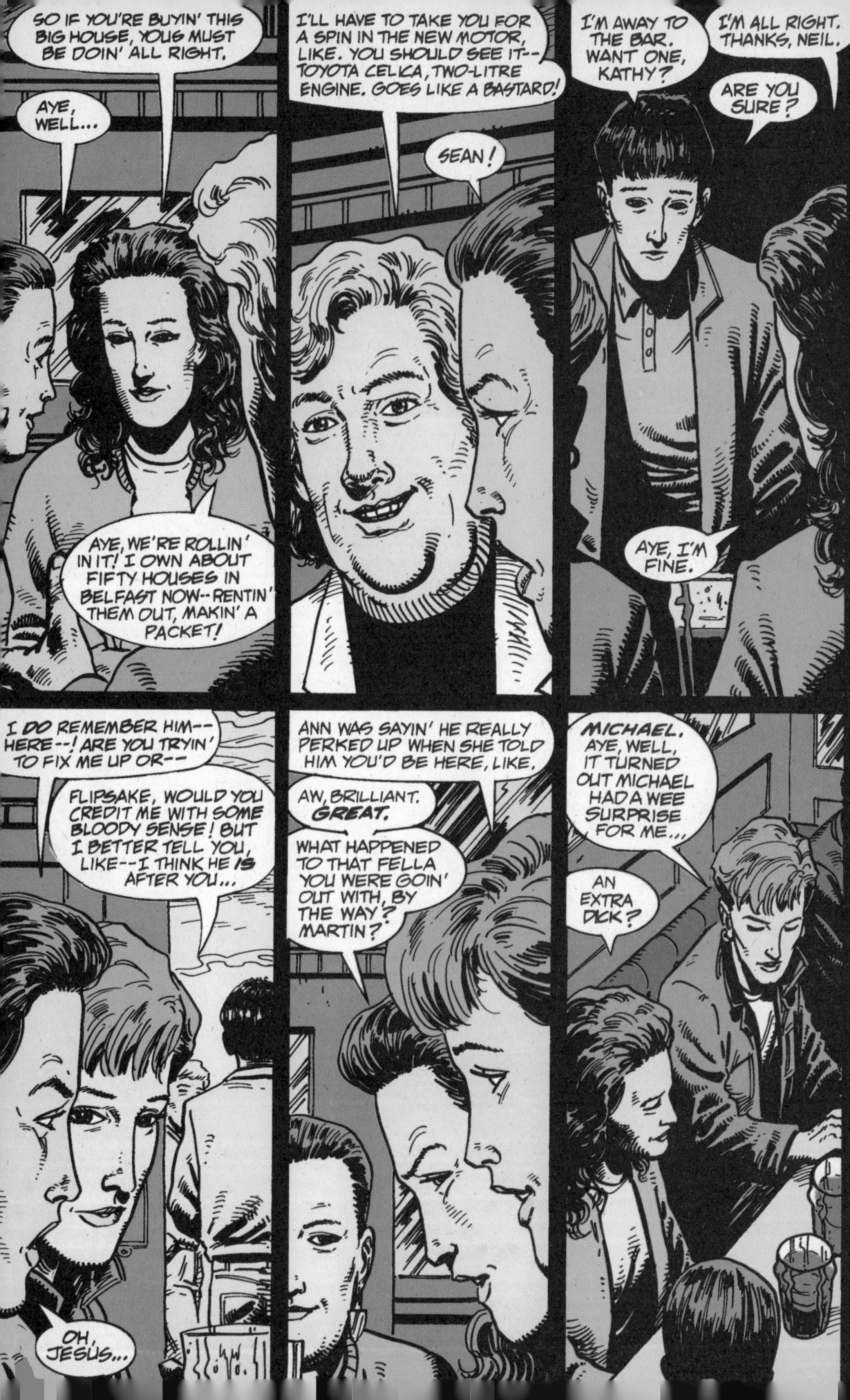
SO IF YOU'RE BUYIN' THIS BIG HOUSE, YOUS MUST BE DOIN' ALL RIGHT.
AYE, WELL...
AYE, WE'RE ROLLIN' IN IT! I OWN ABOUT FIFTY HOUSES IN BELFAST NOW--RENTIN' THEM OUT, MAKIN' A PACKET!
I'LL HAVE TO TAKE YOU FOR A SPIN IN THE NEW MOTOR, LIKE. YOU SHOULD SEE IT--TOYOTA CELICA, TWO-LITRE ENGINE. GOES LIKE A BASTARD!
SEAN!
I'M AWAY TO THE BAR. WANT ONE, KATHY?
I'M ALL RIGHT. THANKS, NEIL.
ARE YOU SURE?
AYE, I'M FINE.
I DO REMEMBER HIM--HERE--! ARE YOU TRYIN' TO FIX ME UP OR--
FLIPSAKE, WOULD YOU CREDIT ME WITH SOME BLOODY SENSE! BUT I BETTER TELL YOU, LIKE--I THINK HE IS AFTER YOU...
OH, JESUS...
ANN WAS SAYIN' HE REALLY PERKED UP WHEN SHE TOLD HIM YOU'D BE HERE, LIKE.
AW, BRILLIANT. GREAT.
WHAT HAPPENED TO THAT FELLA YOU WERE GOIN' OUT WITH, BY THE WAY? MARTIN?
MICHAEL. AYE, WELL, IT TURNED OUT MICHAEL HAD A WEE SURPRISE FOR ME...
AN EXTRA DICK?

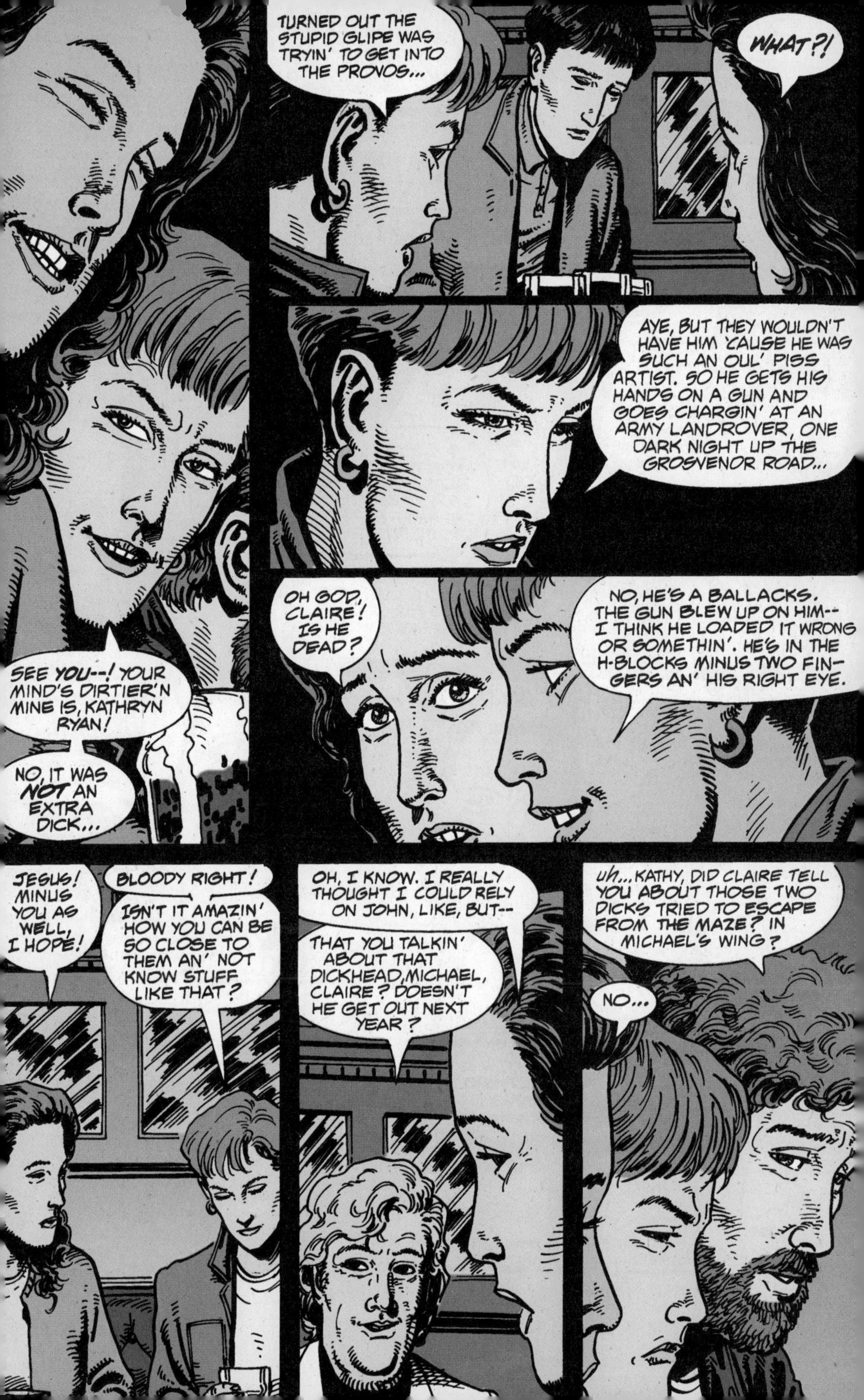
SEE YOU--! YOUR MIND'S DIRTIER'N MINE IS, KATHRYN RYAN!
NO, IT WAS NOT AN EXTRA DICK...
TURNED OUT THE STUPID GLIPE WAS TRYIN' TO GET INTO THE PROVOS...
WHAT?!
AYE, BUT THEY WOULDN'T HAVE HIM 'CAUSE HE WAS SUCH AN OUL' PISS ARTIST. SO HE GETS HIS HANDS ON A GUN AND GOES CHARGIN' AT AN ARMY LANDROVER, ONE DARK NIGHT UP THE GROSVENOR ROAD...
OH GOD, CLAIRE! IS HE DEAD?
NO, HE'S A BALLACKS. THE GUN BLEW UP ON HIM-- I THINK HE LOADED IT WRONG OR SOMETHIN'. HE'S IN THE H-BLOCKS MINUS TWO FINGERS AN' HIS RIGHT EYE.
JESUS! MINUS YOU AS WELL, I HOPE!
BLOODY RIGHT!
ISN'T IT AMAZIN' HOW YOU CAN BE SO CLOSE TO THEM AN' NOT KNOW STUFF LIKE THAT?
OH, I KNOW. I REALLY THOUGHT I COULD RELY ON JOHN, LIKE, BUT--
THAT YOU TALKIN' ABOUT THAT DICKHEAD, MICHAEL, CLAIRE? DOESN'T HE GET OUT NEXT YEAR?
UH... KATHY, DID CLAIRE TELL YOU ABOUT THOSE TWO DICKS TRIED TO ESCAPE FROM THE MAZE? IN MICHAEL'S WING?
NO...

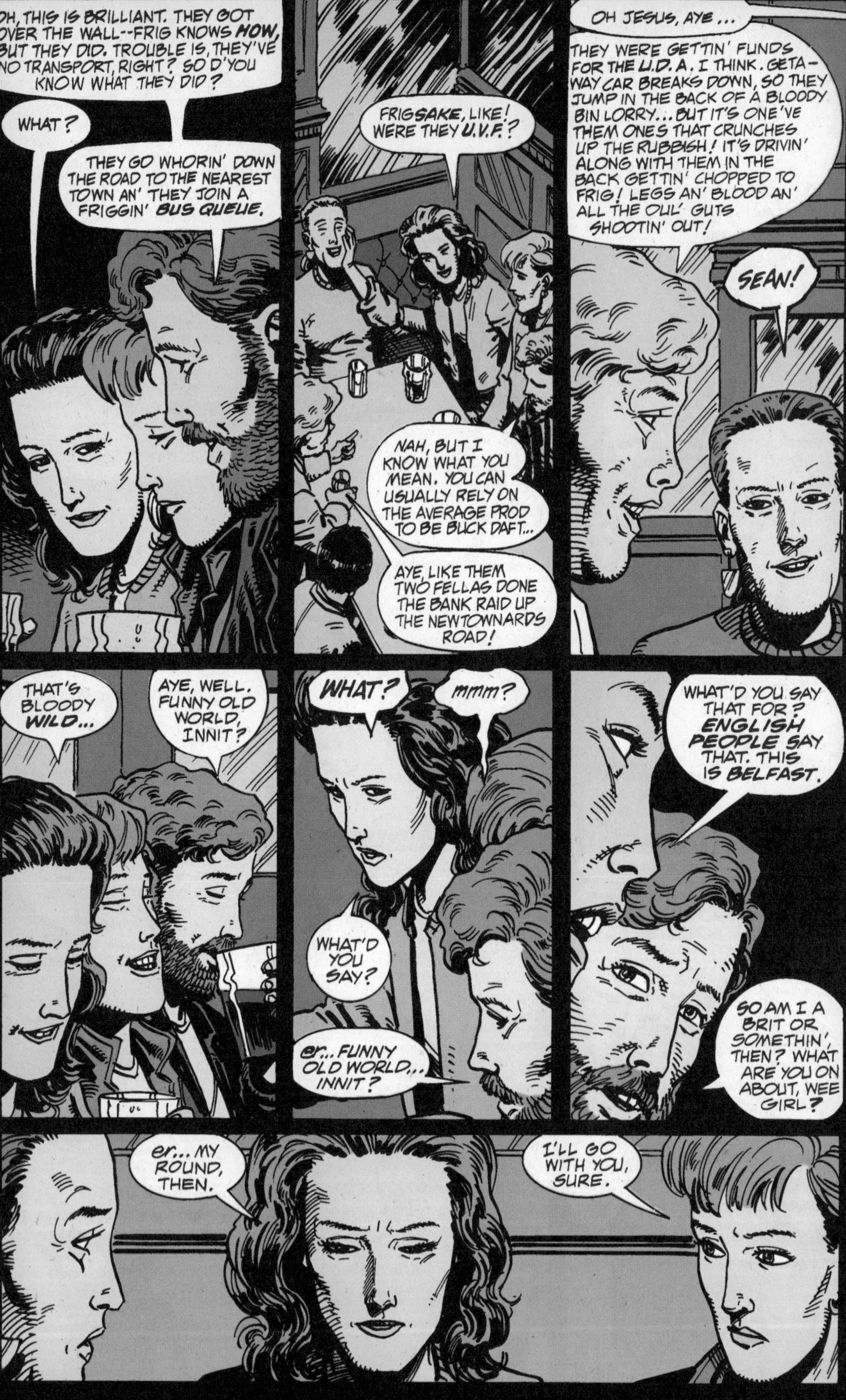

OH, THIS IS BRILLIANT. THEY GOT OVER THE WALL--FRIG KNOWS HOW, BUT THEY DID. TROUBLE IS, THEY'VE NO TRANSPORT, RIGHT? SO D'YOU KNOW WHAT THEY DID?
WHAT?
THEY GO WHORIN' DOWN THE ROAD TO THE NEAREST TOWN AN' THEY JOIN A FRIGGIN' BUS QUEUE.
FRIGSAKE, LIKE! WERE THEY U.V.F.?
NAH, BUT I KNOW WHAT YOU MEAN. YOU CAN USUALLY RELY ON THE AVERAGE PROD TO BE BUCK DAFT...
AYE, LIKE THEM TWO FELLAS DONE THE BANK RAID UP THE NEWTOWNARDS ROAD!
OH JESUS, AYE...
THEY WERE GETTIN' FUNDS FOR THE U.D.A. I THINK. GETAWAY CAR BREAKS DOWN, SO THEY JUMP IN THE BACK OF A BLOODY BIN LORRY... BUT IT'S ONE 'VE THEM ONES THAT CRUNCHES UP THE RUBBISH! IT'S DRIVIN' ALONG WITH THEM IN THE BACK GETTIN' CHOPPED TO FRIG! LEGS AN' BLOOD AN' ALL THE OUL' GUTS SHOOTIN' OUT!
SEAN!
THAT'S BLOODY WILD...
AYE, WELL. FUNNY OLD WORLD, INNIT?
WHAT?
mmm?
WHAT'D YOU SAY?
er... FUNNY OLD WORLD... INNIT?
WHAT'D YOU SAY THAT FOR? ENGLISH PEOPLE SAY THAT. THIS IS BELFAST.
SO AM I A BRIT OR SOMETHIN', THEN? WHAT ARE YOU ON ABOUT, WEE GIRL?
er... MY ROUND, THEN.
I'LL GO WITH YOU, SURE.

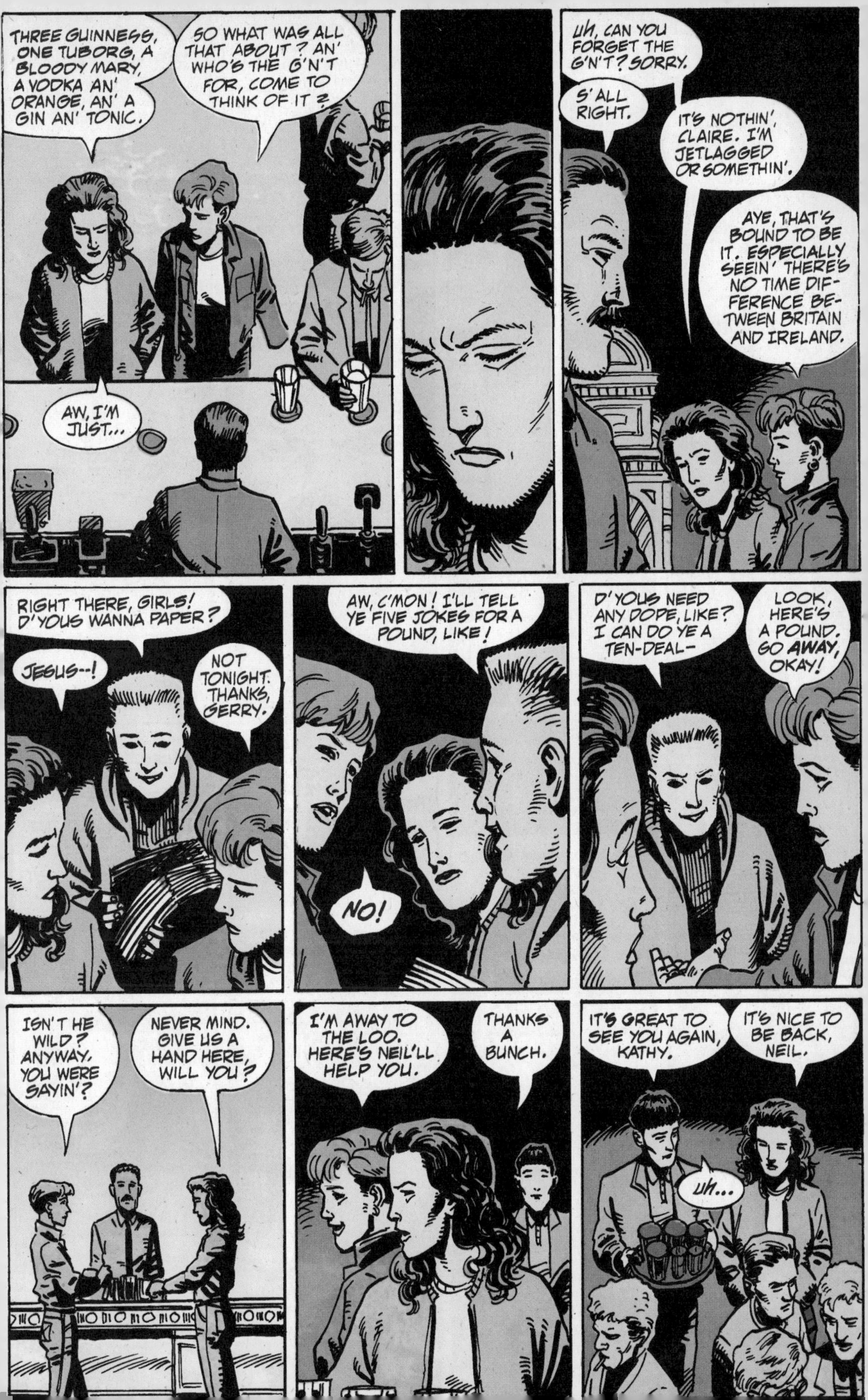
THREE GUINNESS, ONE TUBORG, A BLOODY MARY, A VODKA AN' ORANGE, AN' A GIN AN' TONIC.
SO WHAT WAS ALL THAT ABOUT? AN' WHO'S THE G'N'T FOR, COME TO THINK OF IT?
AW, I'M JUST...
UH, CAN YOU FORGET THE G'N'T? SORRY.
S' ALL RIGHT.
IT'S NOTHIN', CLAIRE. I'M JETLAGGED OR SOMETHIN'.
AYE, THAT'S BOUND TO BE IT. ESPECIALLY SEEIN' THERE'S NO TIME DIFFERENCE BETWEEN BRITAIN AND IRELAND.
RIGHT THERE, GIRLS! D'YOUS WANNA PAPER?
JESUS--!
NOT TONIGHT. THANKS, GERRY.
AW, C'MON! I'LL TELL YE FIVE JOKES FOR A POUND, LIKE!
NO!
D'YOUS NEED ANY DOPE, LIKE? I CAN DO YE A TEN-DEAL-
LOOK, HERE'S A POUND. GO AWAY, OKAY!
ISN'T HE WILD? ANYWAY, YOU WERE SAYIN'?
NEVER MIND. GIVE US A HAND HERE, WILL YOU?
I'M AWAY TO THE LOO. HERE'S NEIL'LL HELP YOU.
THANKS A BUNCH.
IT'S GREAT TO SEE YOU AGAIN, KATHY.
IT'S NICE TO BE BACK, NEIL.
UH...

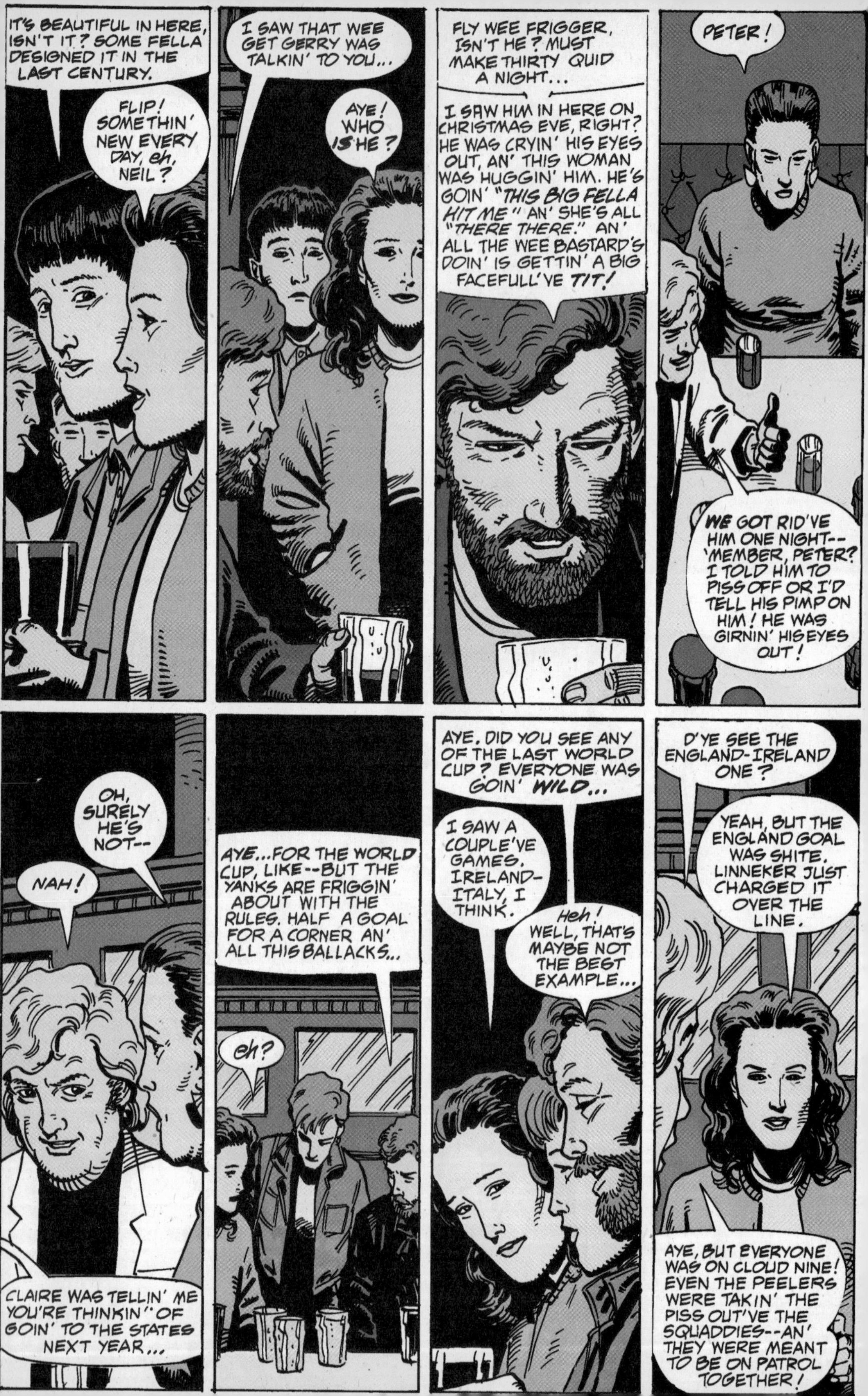
IT'S BEAUTIFUL IN HERE, ISN'T IT? SOME FELLA DESIGNED IT IN THE LAST CENTURY.
FLIP! SOMETHIN' NEW EVERY DAY, eh, NEIL?
I SAW THAT WEE GET GERRY WAS TALKIN' TO YOU...
AYE! WHO IS HE?
FLY WEE FRIGGER, ISN'T HE? MUST MAKE THIRTY QUID A NIGHT...
I SAW HIM IN HERE ON CHRISTMAS EVE, RIGHT? HE WAS CRYIN' HIS EYES OUT, AN' THIS WOMAN WAS HUGGIN' HIM. HE'S GOIN' "THIS BIG FELLA HIT ME" AN' SHE'S ALL "THERE THERE." AN' ALL THE WEE BASTARD'S DOIN' IS GETTIN' A BIG FACEFULL'VE TIT!
PETER!
WE GOT RID'VE HIM ONE NIGHT--'MEMBER, PETER? I TOLD HIM TO PISS OFF OR I'D TELL HIS PIMP ON HIM! HE WAS GIRNIN' HIS EYES OUT!
OH, SURELY HE'S NOT--
NAH!
CLAIRE WAS TELLIN' ME YOU'RE THINKIN' OF GOIN' TO THE STATES NEXT YEAR...
AYE...FOR THE WORLD CUP, LIKE--BUT THE YANKS ARE FRIGGIN' ABOUT WITH THE RULES. HALF A GOAL FOR A CORNER AN' ALL THIS BALLACKS...
eh?
AYE. DID YOU SEE ANY OF THE LAST WORLD CUP? EVERYONE WAS GOIN' WILD...
I SAW A COUPLE'VE GAMES. IRELAND-ITALY, I THINK.
Heh! WELL, THAT'S MAYBE NOT THE BEST EXAMPLE...
D'YE SEE THE ENGLAND-IRELAND ONE?
YEAH, BUT THE ENGLAND GOAL WAS SHITE. LINNEKER JUST CHARGED IT OVER THE LINE.
AYE, BUT EVERYONE WAS ON CLOUD NINE! EVEN THE PEELERS WERE TAKIN' THE PISS OUT'VE THE SQUADDIES--AN' THEY WERE MEANT TO BE ON PATROL TOGETHER!

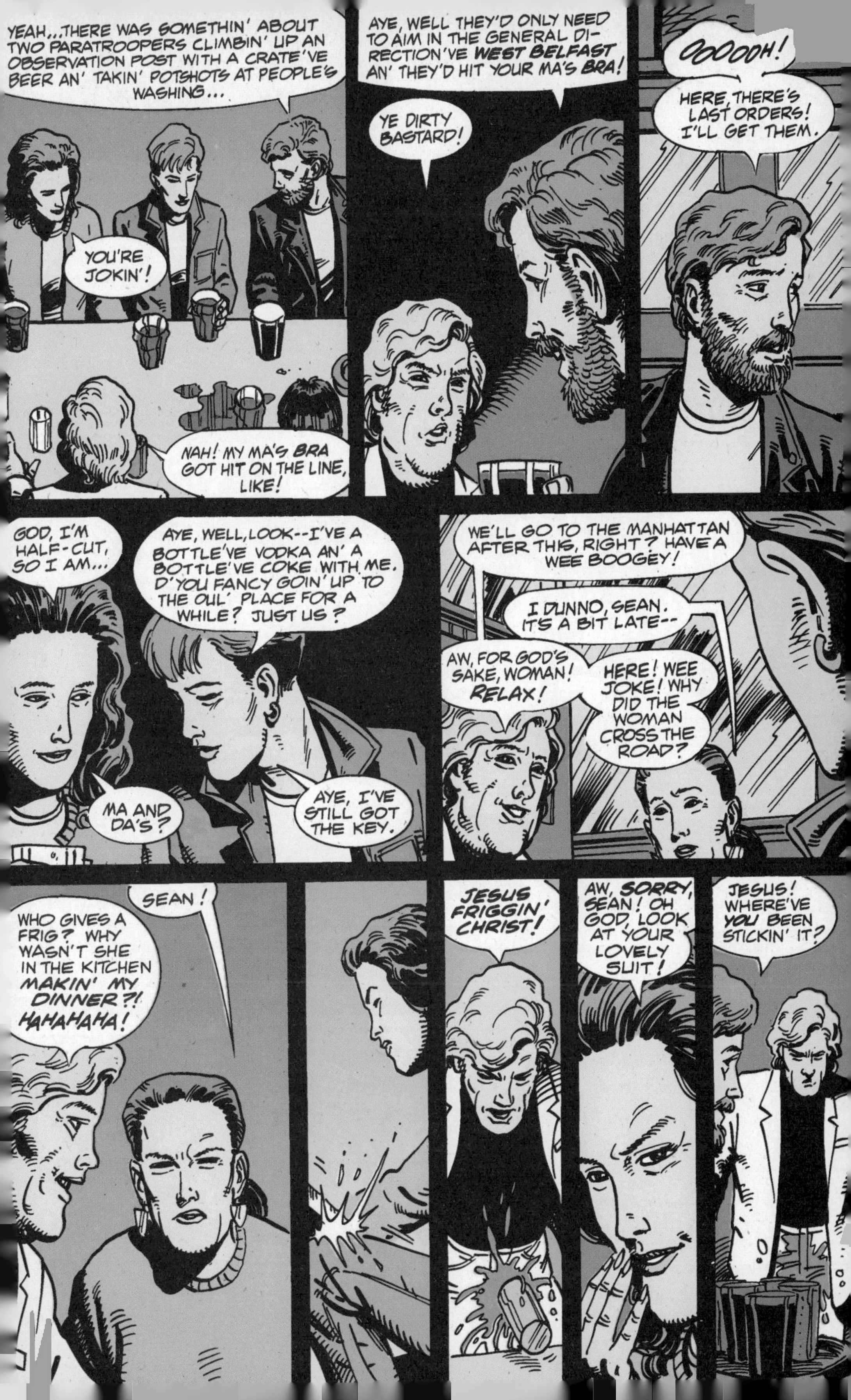

YEAH...THERE WAS SOMETHIN' ABOUT TWO PARATROOPERS CLIMBIN' UP AN OBSERVATION POST WITH A CRATE'VE BEER AN' TAKIN' POTSHOTS AT PEOPLE'S WASHING...
YOU'RE JOKIN'!
NAH! MY MA'S BRA GOT HIT ON THE LINE, LIKE!
AYE, WELL THEY'D ONLY NEED TO AIM IN THE GENERAL DIRECTION'VE WEST BELFAST AN' THEY'D HIT YOUR MA'S BRA!
YE DIRTY BASTARD!
OOOOOH!
HERE, THERE'S LAST ORDERS! I'LL GET THEM.
GOD, I'M HALF-CUT, SO I AM...
AYE, WELL, LOOK--I'VE A BOTTLE'VE VODKA AN' A BOTTLE'VE COKE WITH ME. D'YOU FANCY GOIN' UP TO THE OUL' PLACE FOR A WHILE? JUST US?
MA AND DA'S?
AYE, I'VE STILL GOT THE KEY.
WE'LL GO TO THE MANHATTAN AFTER THIS, RIGHT? HAVE A WEE BOOGEY!
I DUNNO, SEAN. IT'S A BIT LATE--
AW, FOR GOD'S SAKE, WOMAN! RELAX!
HERE! WEE JOKE! WHY DID THE WOMAN CROSS THE ROAD?
WHO GIVES A FRIG? WHY WASN'T SHE IN THE KITCHEN MAKIN' MY DINNER?! HAHAHAHA!
SEAN!
JESUS FRIGGIN' CHRIST!
AW, SORRY, SEAN! OH GOD, LOOK AT YOUR LOVELY SUIT!
JESUS! WHERE'VE YOU BEEN STICKIN' IT?

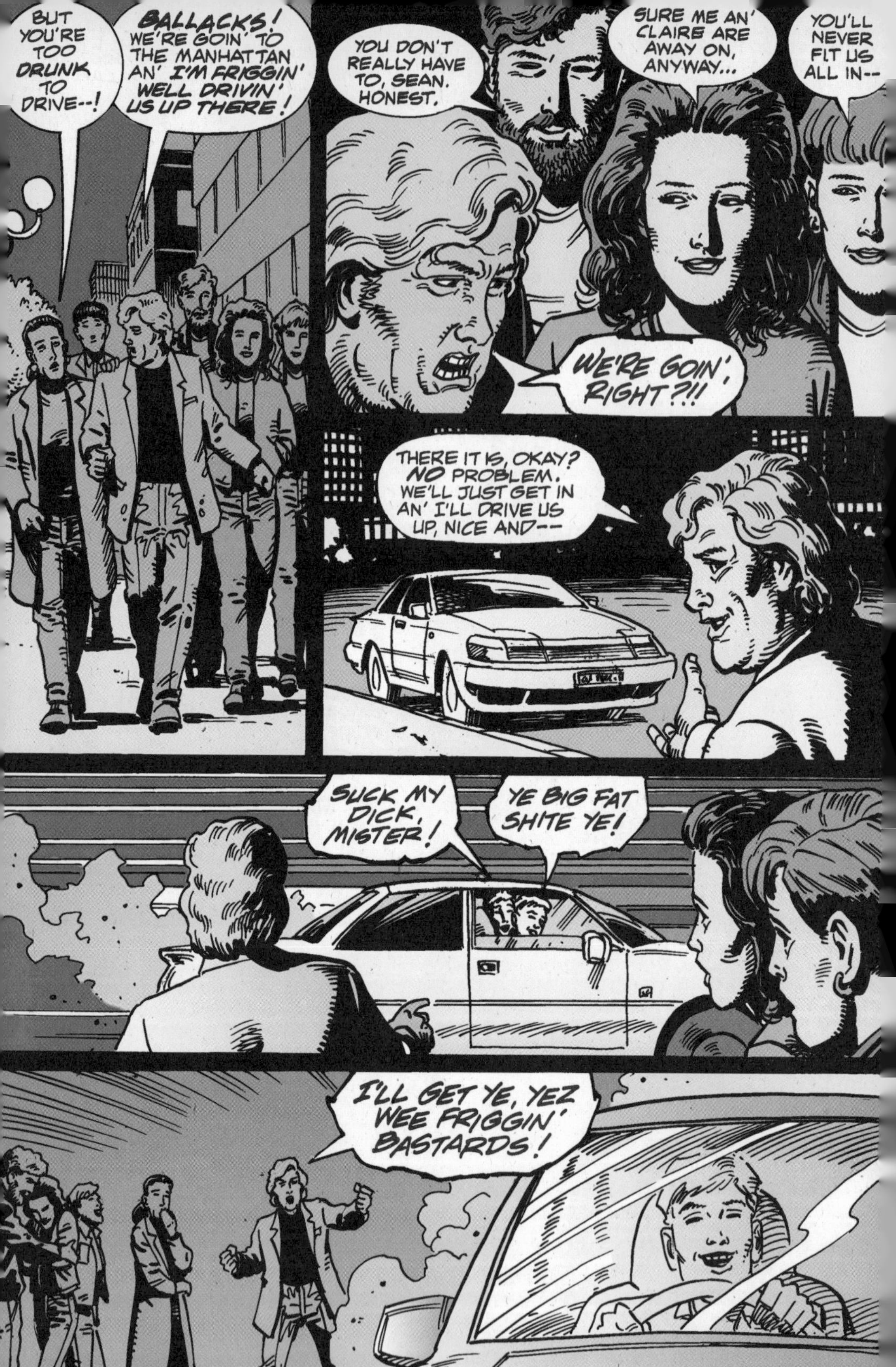
BUT YOU'RE TOO DRUNK TO DRIVE--!
BALLACKS! WE'RE GOIN' TO THE MANHATTAN AN' I'M FRIGGIN' WELL DRIVIN' US UP THERE!
YOU DON'T REALLY HAVE TO, SEAN. HONEST.
SURE ME AN' CLAIRE ARE AWAY ON, ANYWAY...
YOU'LL NEVER FIT US ALL IN--
WE'RE GOIN', RIGHT?!!
THERE IT IS, OKAY? NO PROBLEM. WE'LL JUST GET IN AN' I'LL DRIVE US UP, NICE AND--
SUCK MY DICK, MISTER!
YE BIG FAT SHITE YE!
I'LL GET YE, YEZ WEE FRIGGIN' BASTARDS!

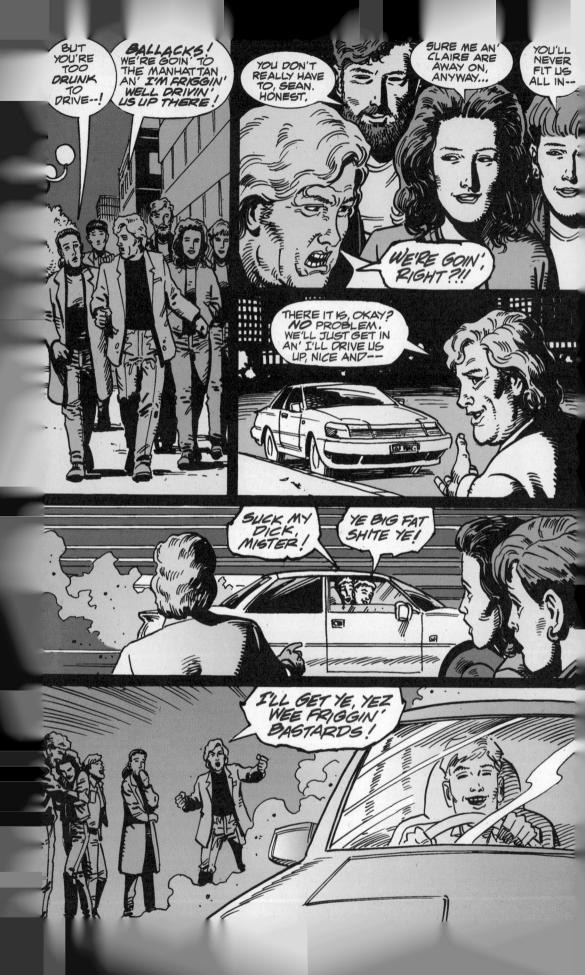

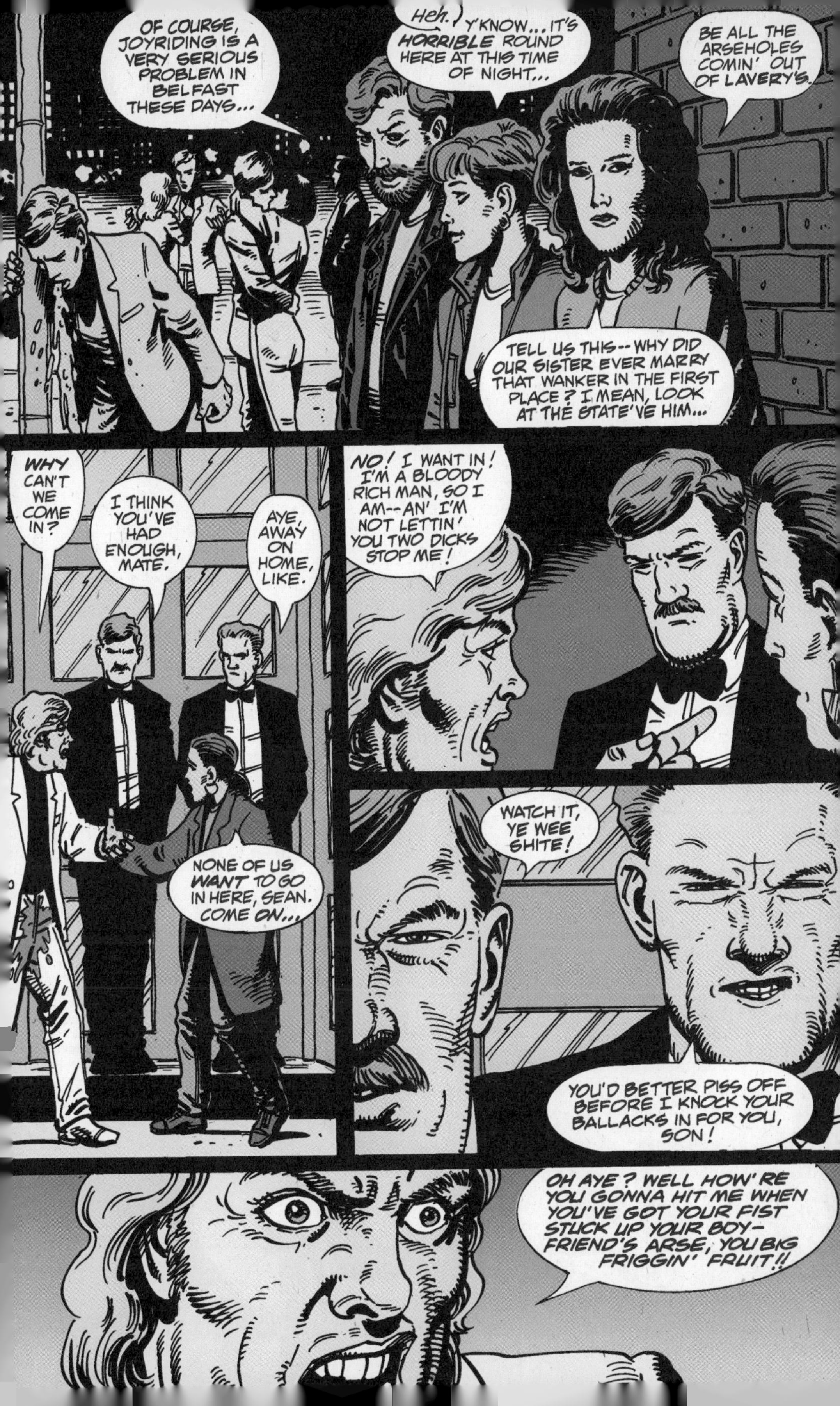
OF COURSE, JOYRIDING IS A VERY SERIOUS PROBLEM IN BELFAST THESE DAYS...
Heh.
Y'KNOW... IT'S HORRIBLE ROUND HERE AT THIS TIME OF NIGHT...
BE ALL THE ARSEHOLES COMIN' OUT OF LAVERY'S.
TELL US THIS-- WHY DID OUR SISTER EVER MARRY THAT WANKER IN THE FIRST PLACE? I MEAN, LOOK AT THE STATE'VE HIM...
WHY CAN'T WE COME IN?
I THINK YOU'VE HAD ENOUGH, MATE.
AYE, AWAY ON HOME, LIKE.
NONE OF US WANT TO GO IN HERE, SEAN. COME ON...
NO! I WANT IN! I'M A BLOODY RICH MAN, SO I AM-- AN' I'M NOT LETTIN' YOU TWO DICKS STOP ME!
WATCH IT, YE WEE SHITE!
YOU'D BETTER PISS OFF BEFORE I KNOCK YOUR BALLACKS IN FOR YOU, SON!
OH AYE? WELL HOW'RE YOU GONNA HIT ME WHEN YOU'VE GOT YOUR FIST STUCK UP YOUR BOY-FRIEND'S ARSE, YOU BIG FRIGGIN' FRUIT!!

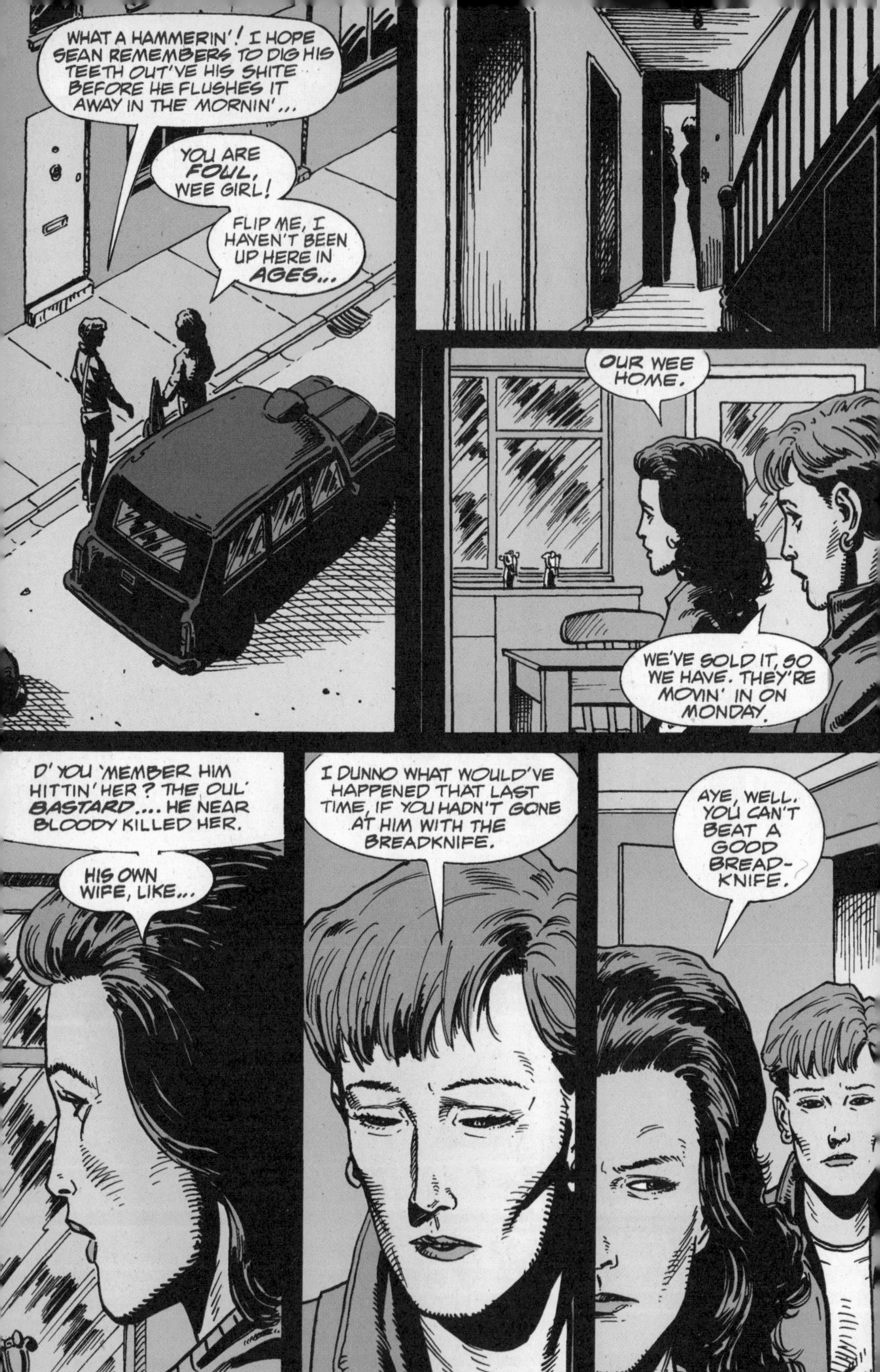

WHAT A HAMMERIN'! I HOPE SEAN REMEMBERS TO DIG HIS TEETH OUT'VE HIS SHITE BEFORE HE FLUSHES IT AWAY IN THE MORNIN'...
YOU ARE FOUL, WEE GIRL!
FLIP ME, I HAVEN'T BEEN UP HERE IN AGES...
OUR WEE HOME.
WE'VE SOLD IT, SO WE HAVE. THEY'RE MOVIN' IN ON MONDAY.
D' YOU 'MEMBER HIM HITTIN' HER? THE OUL' BASTARD.... HE NEAR BLOODY KILLED HER.
HIS OWN WIFE, LIKE...
I DUNNO WHAT WOULD'VE HAPPENED THAT LAST TIME, IF YOU HADN'T GONE AT HIM WITH THE BREADKNIFE.
AYE, WELL. YOU CAN'T BEAT A GOOD BREAD-KNIFE.

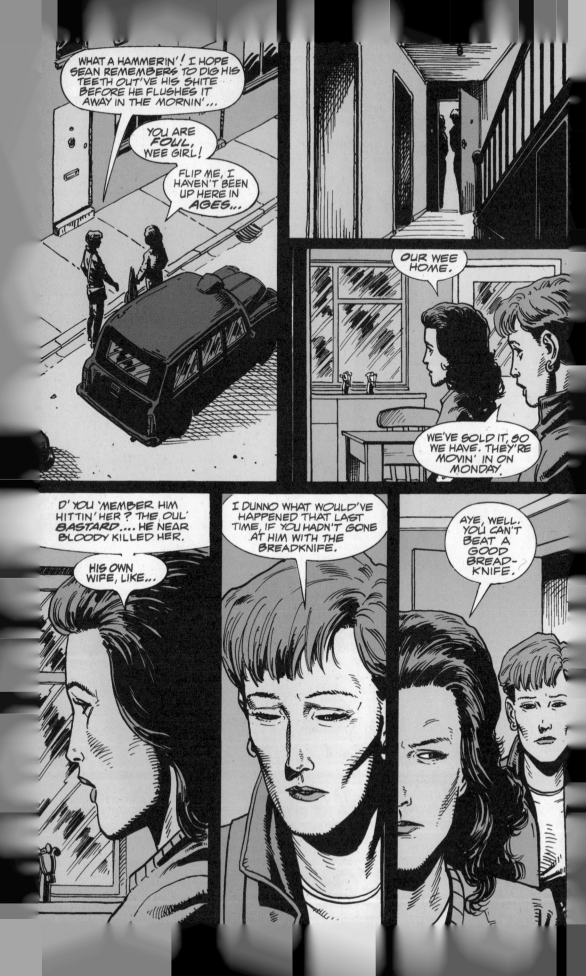

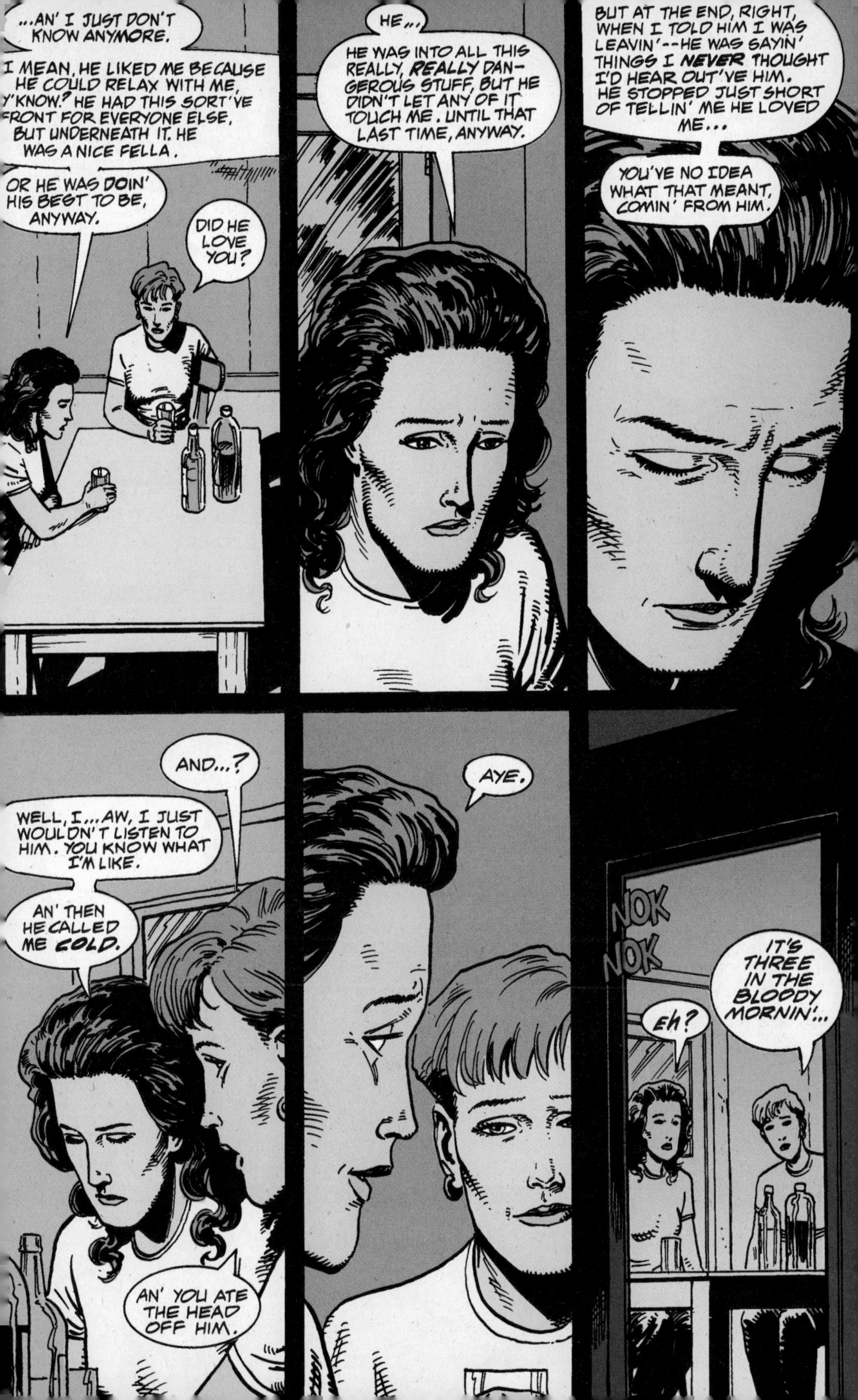
...AN' I JUST DON'T KNOW ANYMORE.
I MEAN, HE LIKED ME BECAUSE HE COULD RELAX WITH ME, Y'KNOW? HE HAD THIS SORT'VE FRONT FOR EVERYONE ELSE, BUT UNDERNEATH IT, HE WAS A NICE FELLA.
OR HE WAS DOIN' HIS BEST TO BE, ANYWAY.
DID HE LOVE YOU?
HE...
HE WAS INTO ALL THIS REALLY, REALLY DANGEROUS STUFF, BUT HE DIDN'T LET ANY OF IT TOUCH ME. UNTIL THAT LAST TIME, ANYWAY.
BUT AT THE END, RIGHT, WHEN I TOLD HIM I WAS LEAVIN'--HE WAS SAYIN' THINGS I NEVER THOUGHT I'D HEAR OUT'VE HIM. HE STOPPED JUST SHORT OF TELLIN' ME HE LOVED ME...
YOU'VE NO IDEA WHAT THAT MEANT, COMIN' FROM HIM.
AND...?
WELL, I...AW, I JUST WOULDN'T LISTEN TO HIM. YOU KNOW WHAT I'M LIKE.
AN' THEN HE CALLED ME COLD.
AN' YOU ATE THE HEAD OFF HIM.
AYE.
NOK
NOK
IT'S THREE IN THE BLOODY MORNIN'...
Eh?

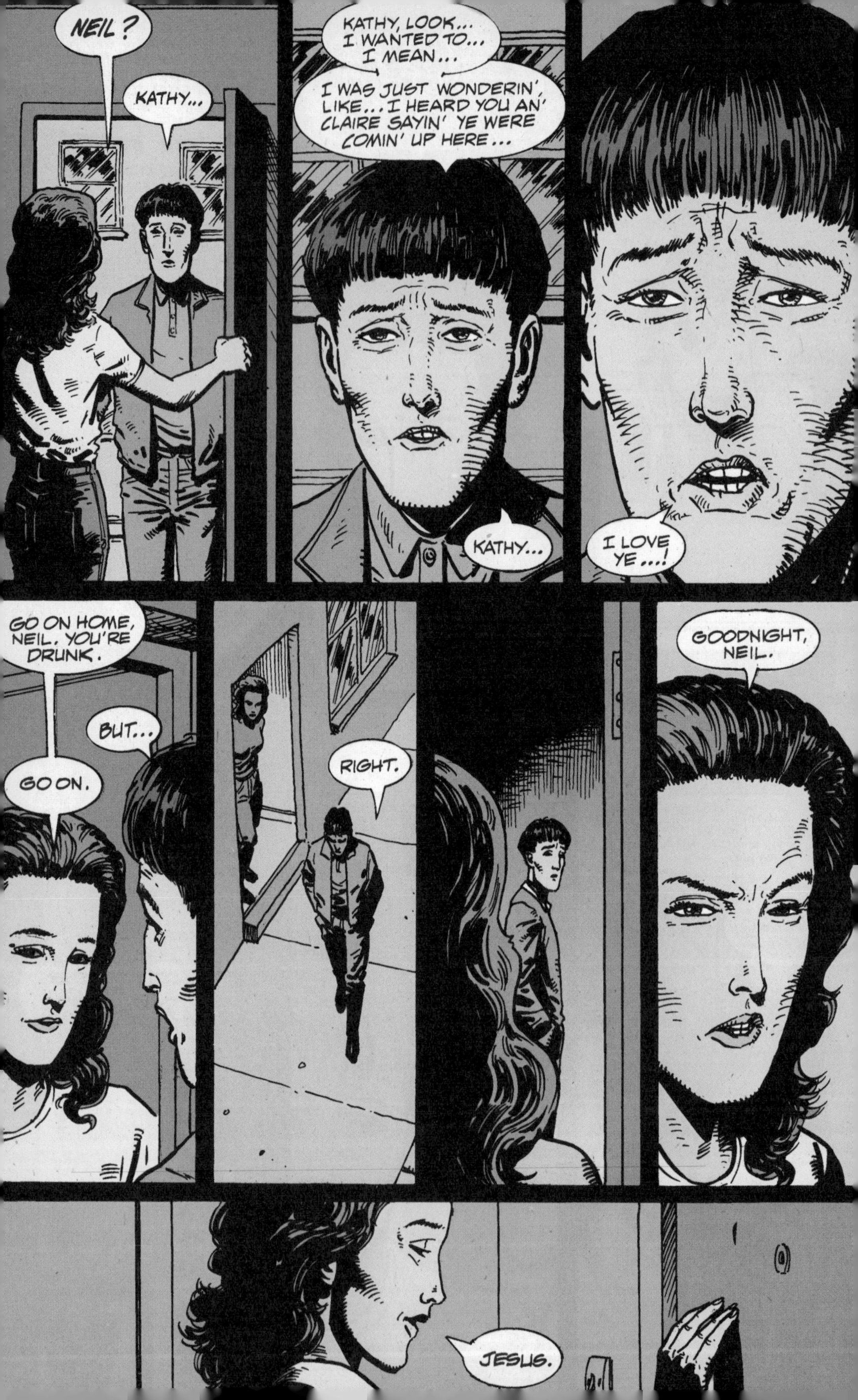
NEIL?
KATHY...
KATHY, LOOK... I WANTED TO... I MEAN...
I WAS JUST WONDERIN', LIKE... I HEARD YOU AN' CLAIRE SAYIN' YE WERE COMIN' UP HERE...
KATHY...
I LOVE YE...!
GO ON HOME, NEIL. YOU'RE DRUNK.
BUT...
GO ON.
RIGHT.
GOODNIGHT, NEIL.
JESUS.

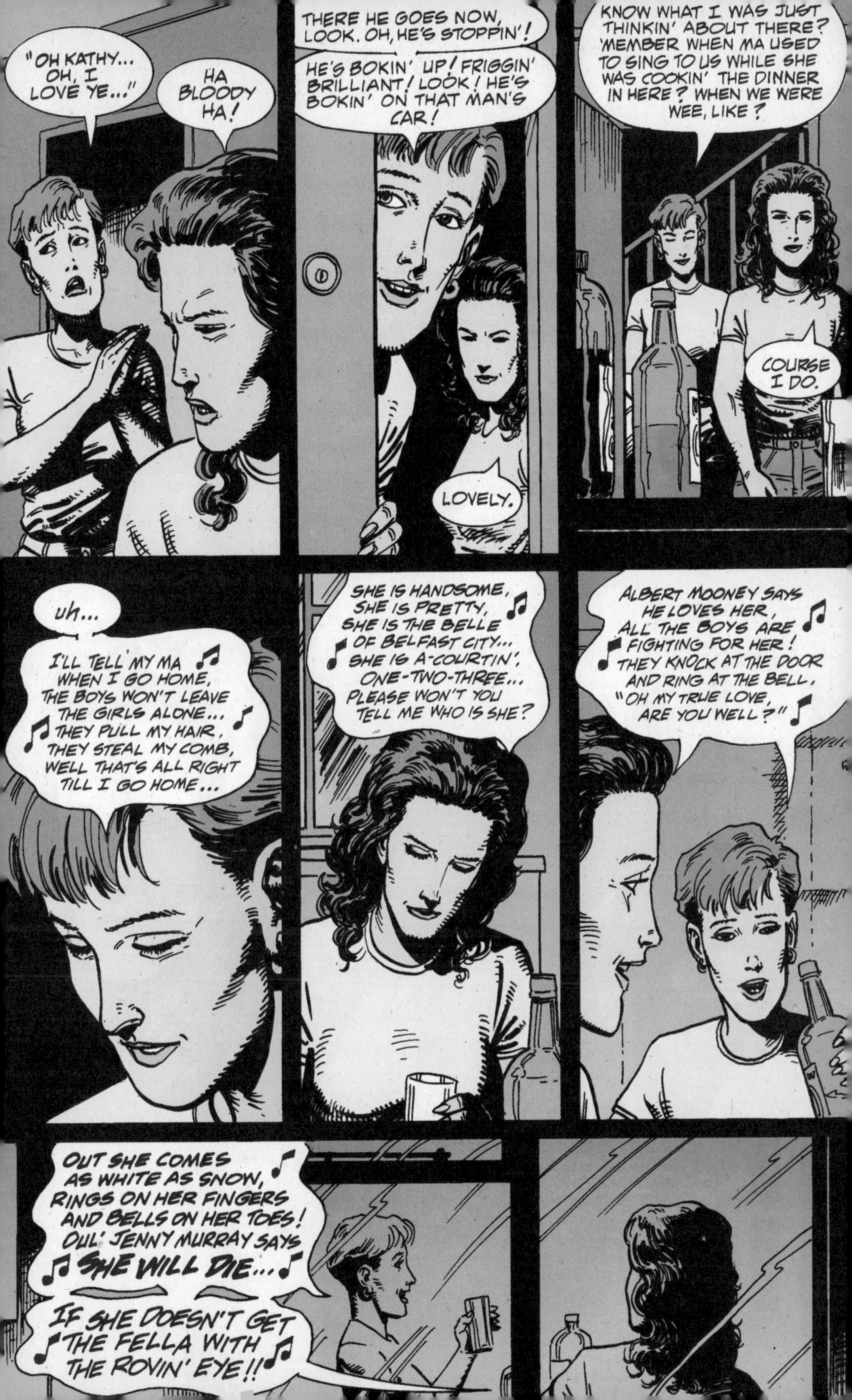
"OH KATHY... OH, I LOVE YE..."
HA BLOODY HA!
THERE HE GOES NOW, LOOK. OH, HE'S STOPPIN'!
HE'S BOKIN' UP! FRIGGIN' BRILLIANT! LOOK! HE'S BOKIN' ON THAT MAN'S CAR!
LOVELY.
KNOW WHAT I WAS JUST THINKIN' ABOUT THERE? 'MEMBER WHEN MA USED TO SING TO US WHILE SHE WAS COOKIN' THE DINNER IN HERE? WHEN WE WERE WEE, LIKE?
COURSE I DO.
uh...
I'LL TELL MY MA WHEN I GO HOME, THE BOYS WON'T LEAVE THE GIRLS ALONE... THEY PULL MY HAIR, THEY STEAL MY COMB, WELL THAT'S ALL RIGHT TILL I GO HOME...
SHE IS HANDSOME, SHE IS PRETTY, SHE IS THE BELLE OF BELFAST CITY... SHE IS A-COURTIN', ONE-TWO-THREE... PLEASE WON'T YOU TELL ME WHO IS SHE?
ALBERT MOONEY SAYS HE LOVES HER, ALL THE BOYS ARE FIGHTING FOR HER! THEY KNOCK AT THE DOOR AND RING AT THE BELL, "OH MY TRUE LOVE, ARE YOU WELL?"
OUT SHE COMES AS WHITE AS SNOW, RINGS ON HER FINGERS AND BELLS ON HER TOES! OUL' JENNY MURRAY SAYS SHE WILL DIE...
IF SHE DOESN'T GET THE FELLA WITH THE ROVIN' EYE!!

MM-HMM-HMM...
HMM-HMM-HMM-HMM...
DEE DEE DEE DEE,
DEE OUM DEE...

"YOU SHOULDN'T EVER
TAKE SHIT OFF ANY-
ONE"

OH, JOHN.

OH, JOHN,
MAYBE I
SHOULD
HAVE.

LET THE WIND...
AN' THE RAIN...
AN THE HAIL
BLOW HIGH...
AN' THE SNOW
COME TUMBLING
FROM THE SKY...

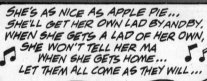

SHE'S AS NICE AS APPLE PIE...
SHE'LL GET HER OWN LAD BY AND BY.
WHEN SHE GETS A LAD OF HER OWN,
SHE WON'T TELL HER MA
WHEN SHE GETS HOME...
LET THEM ALL COME AS THEY WILL...

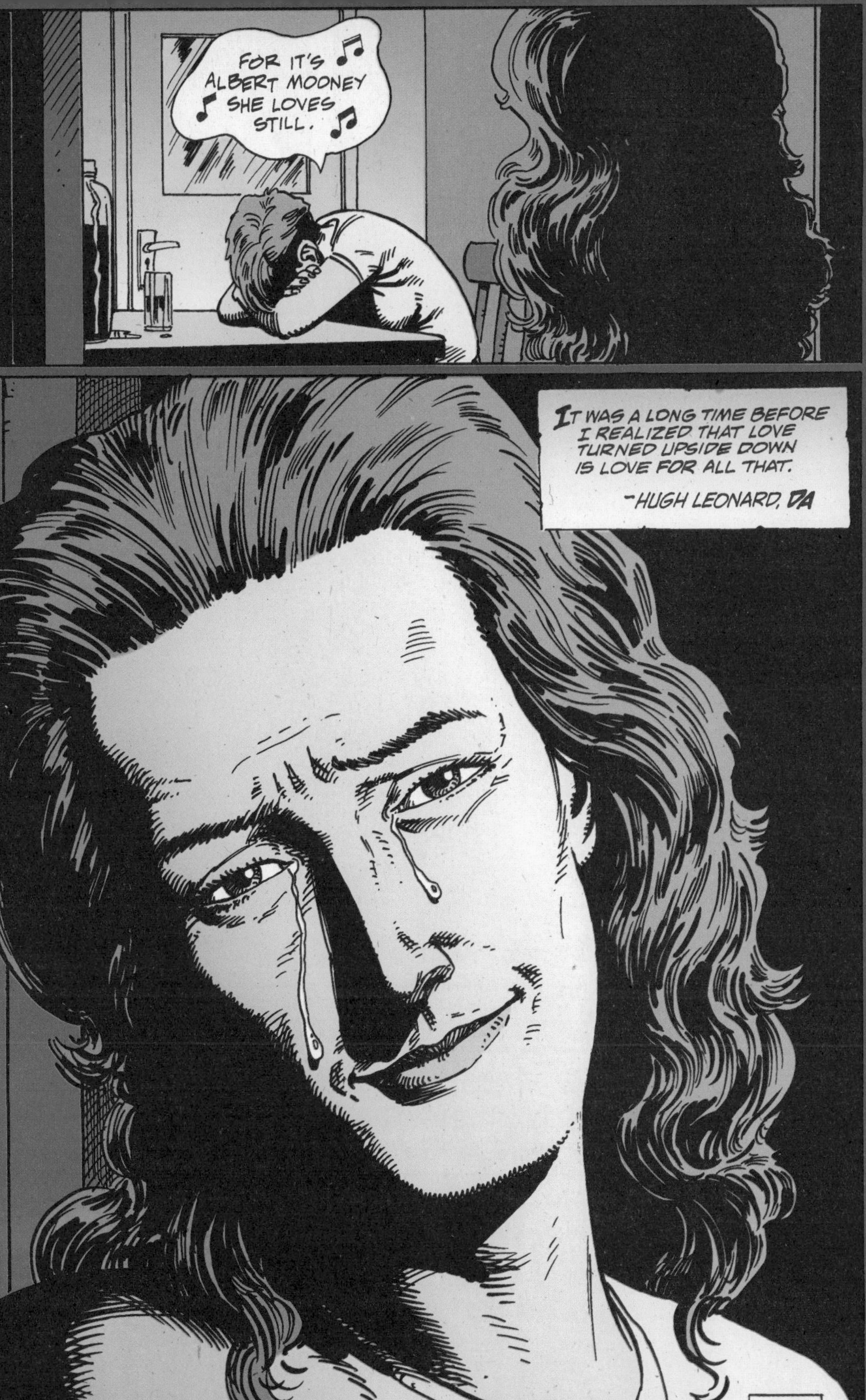
FOR IT'S ALBERT MOONEY SHE LOVES STILL.
IT WAS A LONG TIME BEFORE I REALIZED THAT LOVE TURNED UPSIDE DOWN IS LOVE FOR ALL THAT.
-HUGH LEONARD, DA
THE END

JOHN CONSTANTINE
HELLBLAZER
DC
VERTIGO
NO. 71
NOV 93
$1.95 US
$2.50 CAN
£1.25 UK
SUGGESTED FOR MATURE READERS
GARTH ENNIS
STEVE DILLON

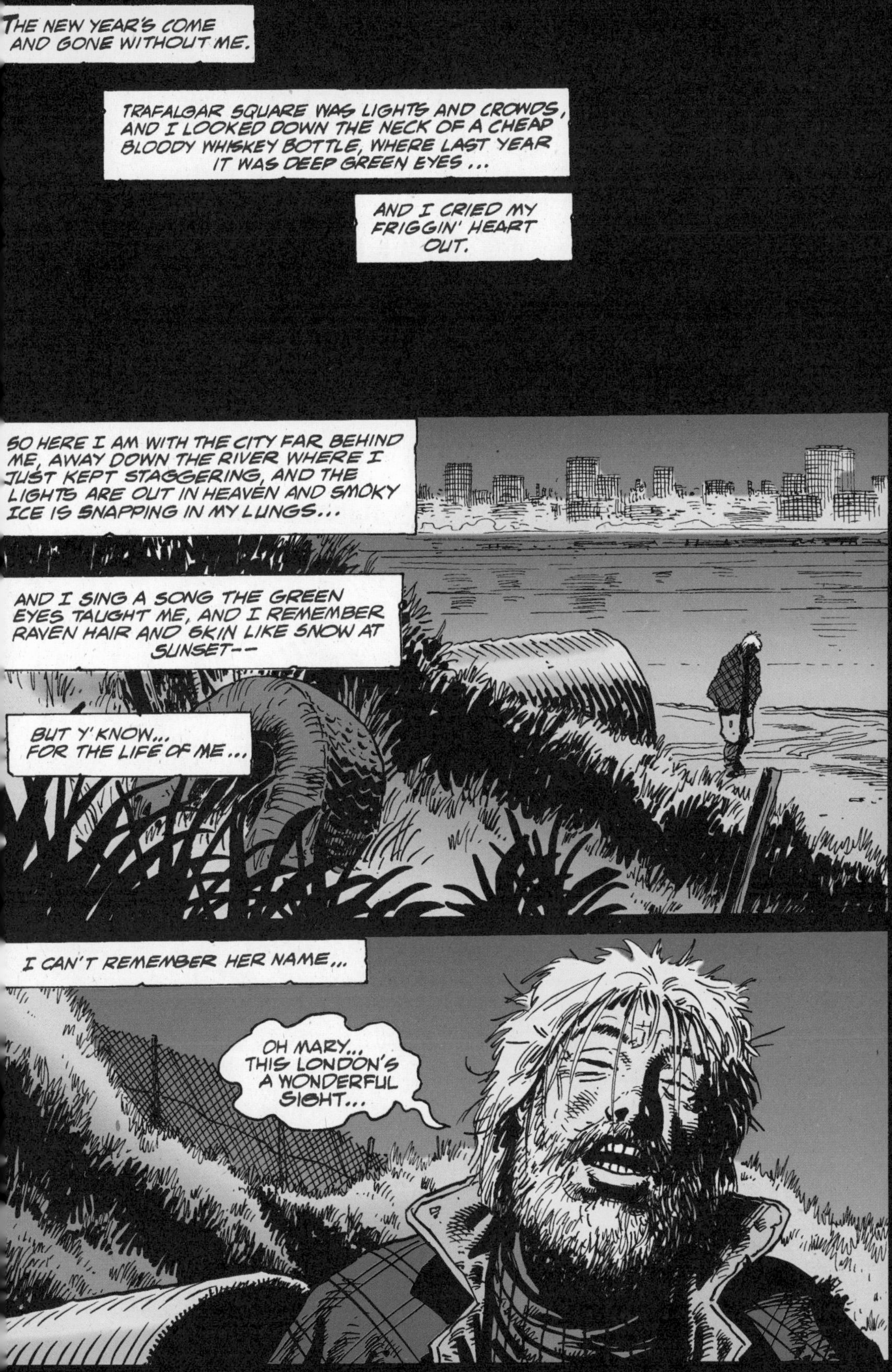
THE NEW YEAR'S COME AND GONE WITHOUT ME.
TRAFALGAR SQUARE WAS LIGHTS AND CROWDS, AND I LOOKED DOWN THE NECK OF A CHEAP BLOODY WHISKEY BOTTLE, WHERE LAST YEAR IT WAS DEEP GREEN EYES ...
AND I CRIED MY FRIGGIN' HEART OUT.
SO HERE I AM WITH THE CITY FAR BEHIND ME, AWAY DOWN THE RIVER WHERE I JUST KEPT STAGGERING, AND THE LIGHTS ARE OUT IN HEAVEN AND SMOKY ICE IS SNAPPING IN MY LUNGS...
AND I SING A SONG THE GREEN EYES TAUGHT ME, AND I REMEMBER RAVEN HAIR AND SKIN LIKE SNOW AT SUNSET--
BUT Y'KNOW... FOR THE LIFE OF ME...
I CAN'T REMEMBER HER NAME...
OH MARY... THIS LONDON'S A WONDERFUL SIGHT...

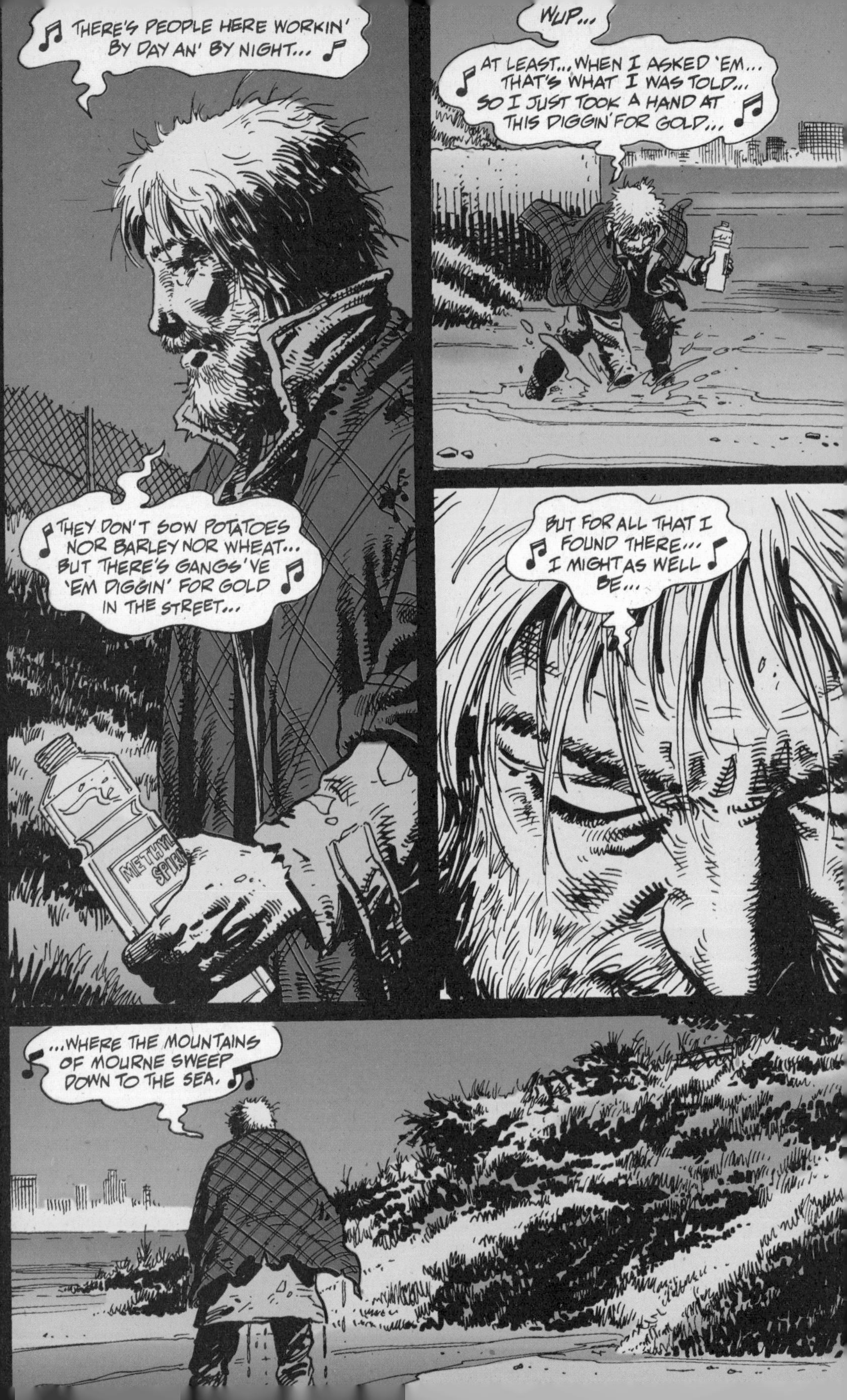
♫ THERE'S PEOPLE HERE WORKIN' BY DAY AN' BY NIGHT... ♫
♫ THEY DON'T SOW POTATOES NOR BARLEY NOR WHEAT... BUT THERE'S GANGS'VE 'EM DIGGIN' FOR GOLD IN THE STREET... ♫
WUP...
♫ AT LEAST... WHEN I ASKED 'EM... THAT'S WHAT I WAS TOLD... SO I JUST TOOK A HAND AT THIS DIGGIN' FOR GOLD... ♫
♫ BUT FOR ALL THAT I FOUND THERE... I MIGHT AS WELL BE... ♫
♫ ...WHERE THE MOUNTAINS OF MOURNE SWEEP DOWN TO THE SEA. ♫

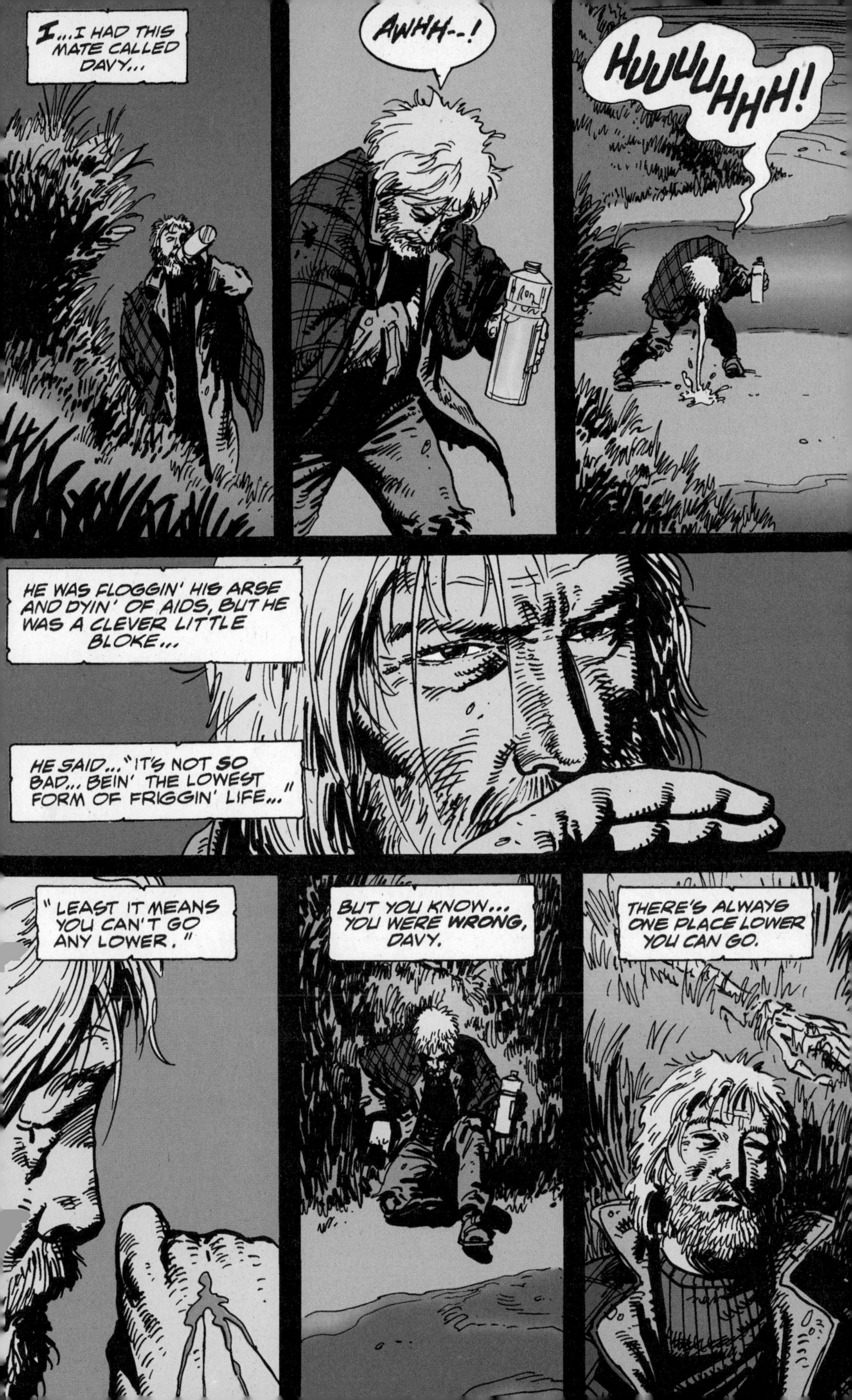
I...I HAD THIS MATE CALLED DAVY...
AWHH--!
HUUUUHHH!
HE WAS FLOGGIN' HIS ARSE AND DYIN' OF AIDS, BUT HE WAS A CLEVER LITTLE BLOKE...
HE SAID... "IT'S NOT SO BAD... BEIN' THE LOWEST FORM OF FRIGGIN' LIFE..."
"LEAST IT MEANS YOU CAN'T GO ANY LOWER."
BUT YOU KNOW... YOU WERE **WRONG**, DAVY.
THERE'S ALWAYS ONE PLACE LOWER YOU CAN GO.

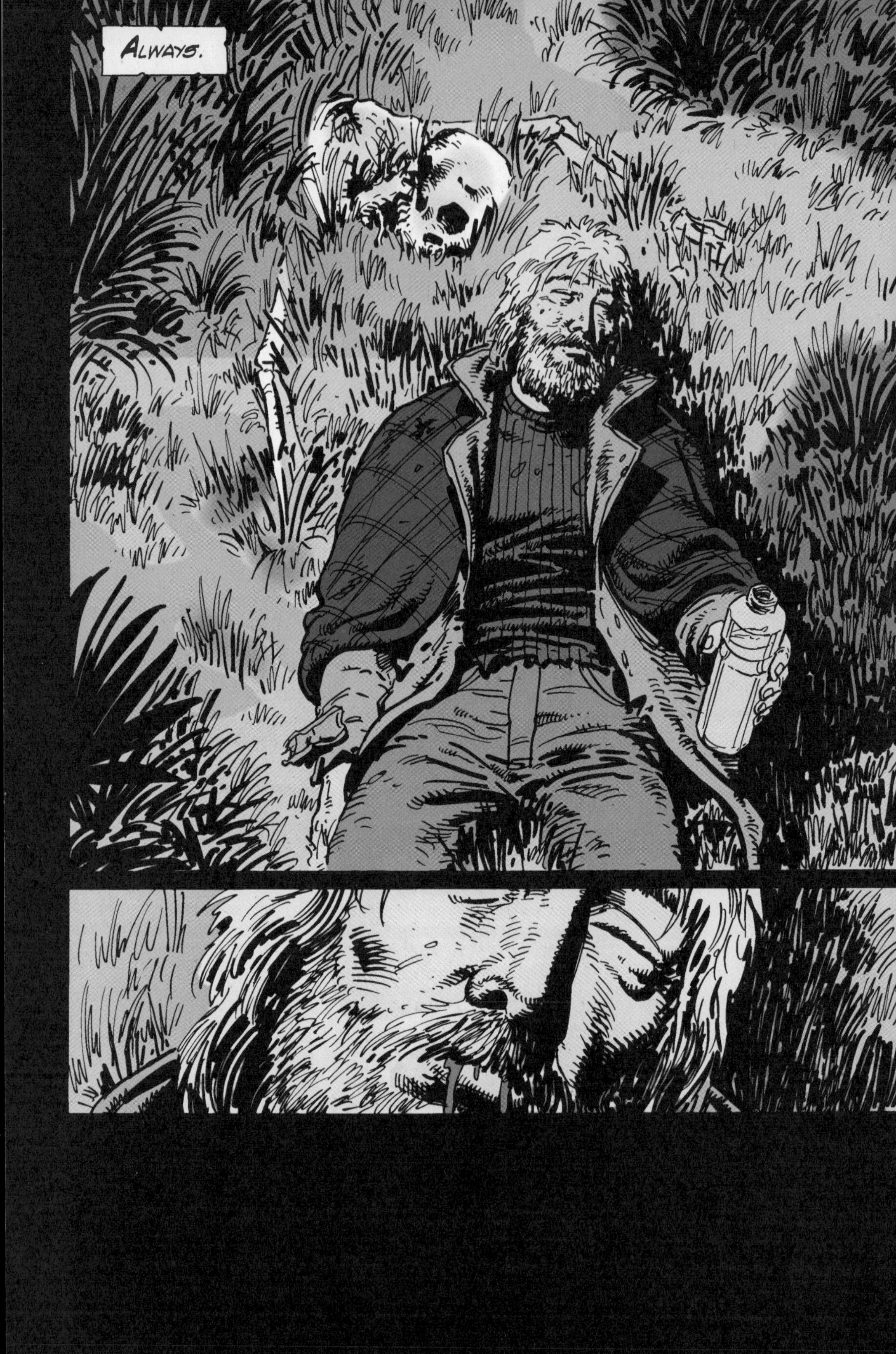
ALWAYS.

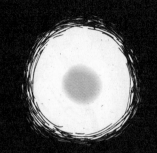

THE LIGHT

GREEN
WHITE
DREAM

WHERE
AM I NOW

WHAT'S GOING ON

WHAT'S GOING ON

MY GOD!

PULL UP!

COME ON, YOU BITCH!
UP! UP!

253

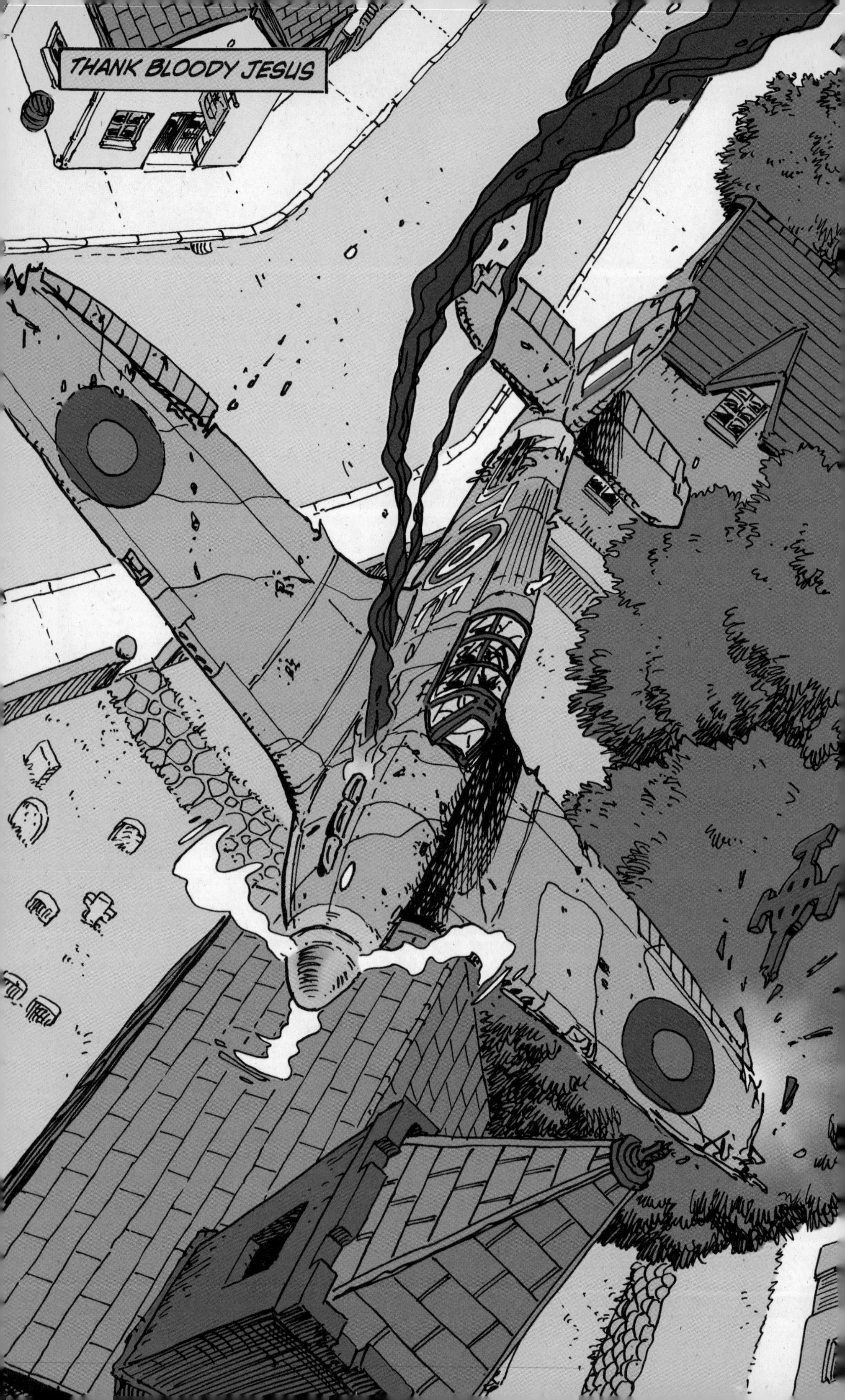
THANK BLOODY JESUS

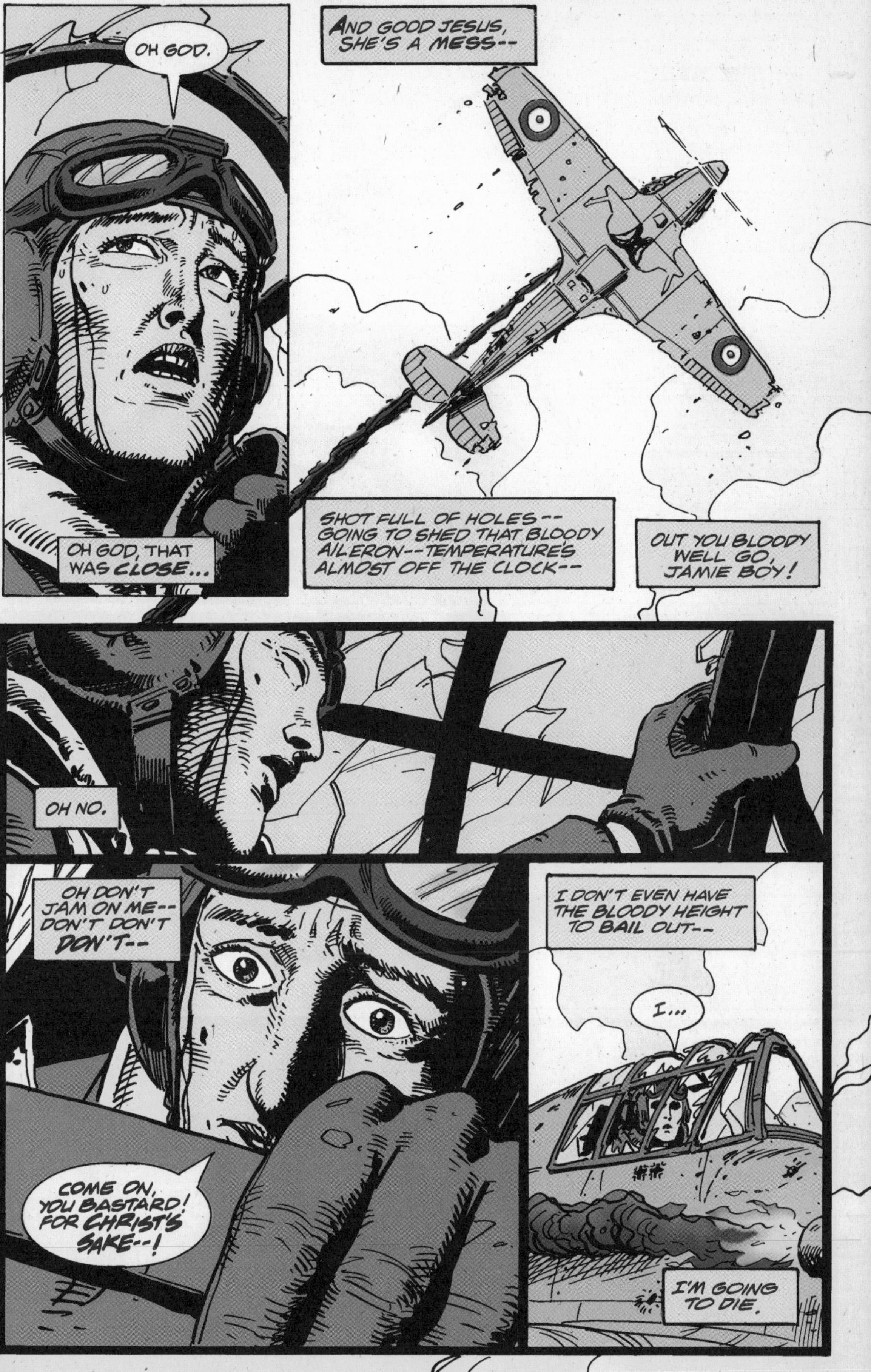
OH GOD.
OH GOD, THAT WAS CLOSE...
AND GOOD JESUS, SHE'S A MESS--
SHOT FULL OF HOLES-- GOING TO SHED THAT BLOODY AILERON--TEMPERATURE'S ALMOST OFF THE CLOCK--
OUT YOU BLOODY WELL GO, JAMIE BOY!
OH NO.
OH DON'T JAM ON ME-- DON'T DON'T DON'T--
COME ON, YOU BASTARD! FOR CHRIST'S SAKE--!
I DON'T EVEN HAVE THE BLOODY HEIGHT TO BAIL OUT--
I...
I'M GOING TO DIE.

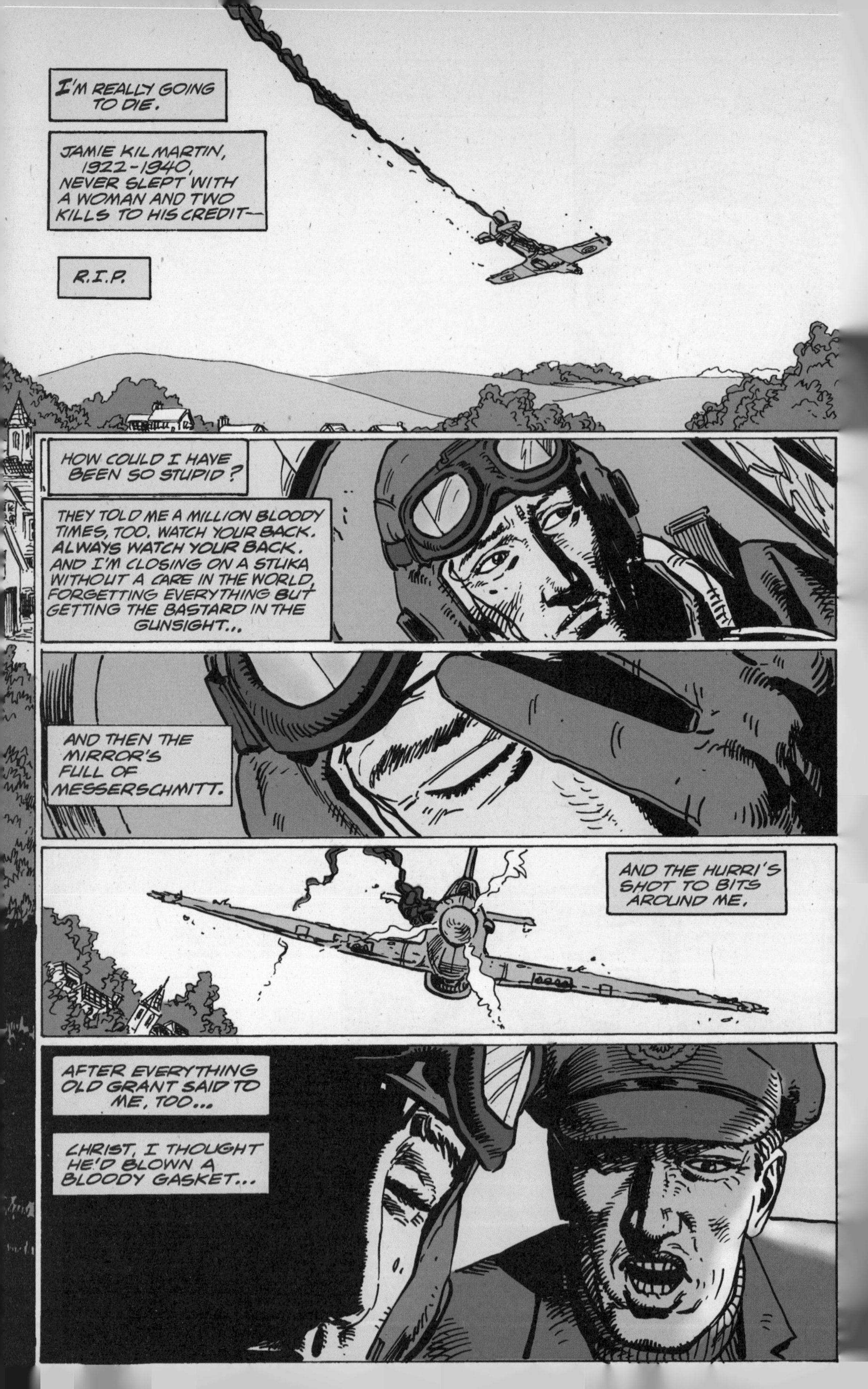
I'M REALLY GOING TO DIE.
JAMIE KILMARTIN, 1922-1940, NEVER SLEPT WITH A WOMAN AND TWO KILLS TO HIS CREDIT—
R.I.P.
HOW COULD I HAVE BEEN SO STUPID?
THEY TOLD ME A MILLION BLOODY TIMES, TOO. WATCH YOUR BACK. ALWAYS WATCH YOUR BACK. AND I'M CLOSING ON A STUKA WITHOUT A CARE IN THE WORLD, FORGETTING EVERYTHING BUT GETTING THE BASTARD IN THE GUNSIGHT...
AND THEN THE MIRROR'S FULL OF MESSERSCHMITT.
AND THE HURRI'S SHOT TO BITS AROUND ME.
AFTER EVERYTHING OLD GRANT SAID TO ME, TOO...
CHRIST, I THOUGHT HE'D BLOWN A BLOODY GASKET...

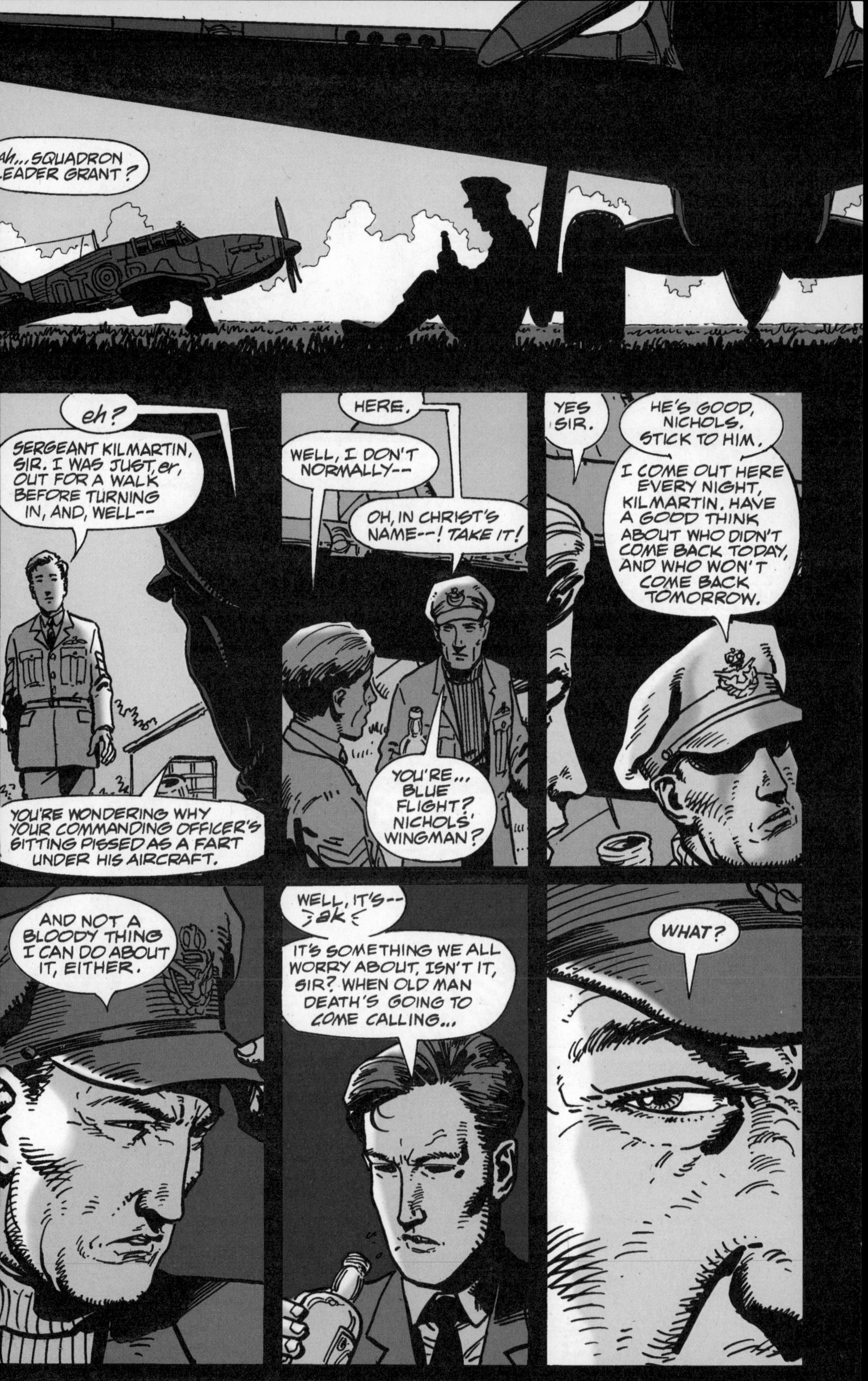

AH... SQUADRON LEADER GRANT?
eh?
SERGEANT KILMARTIN, SIR. I WAS JUST, er, OUT FOR A WALK BEFORE TURNING IN, AND, WELL--
YOU'RE WONDERING WHY YOUR COMMANDING OFFICER'S SITTING PISSED AS A FART UNDER HIS AIRCRAFT.
HERE.
WELL, I DON'T NORMALLY--
OH, IN CHRIST'S NAME--! TAKE IT!
YOU'RE... BLUE FLIGHT? NICHOLS' WINGMAN?
YES SIR.
HE'S GOOD, NICHOLS. STICK TO HIM.
I COME OUT HERE EVERY NIGHT, KILMARTIN. HAVE A GOOD THINK ABOUT WHO DIDN'T COME BACK TODAY, AND WHO WON'T COME BACK TOMORROW.
AND NOT A BLOODY THING I CAN DO ABOUT IT, EITHER.
WELL, IT'S--
ak
IT'S SOMETHING WE ALL WORRY ABOUT, ISN'T IT, SIR? WHEN OLD MAN DEATH'S GOING TO COME CALLING...
WHAT?

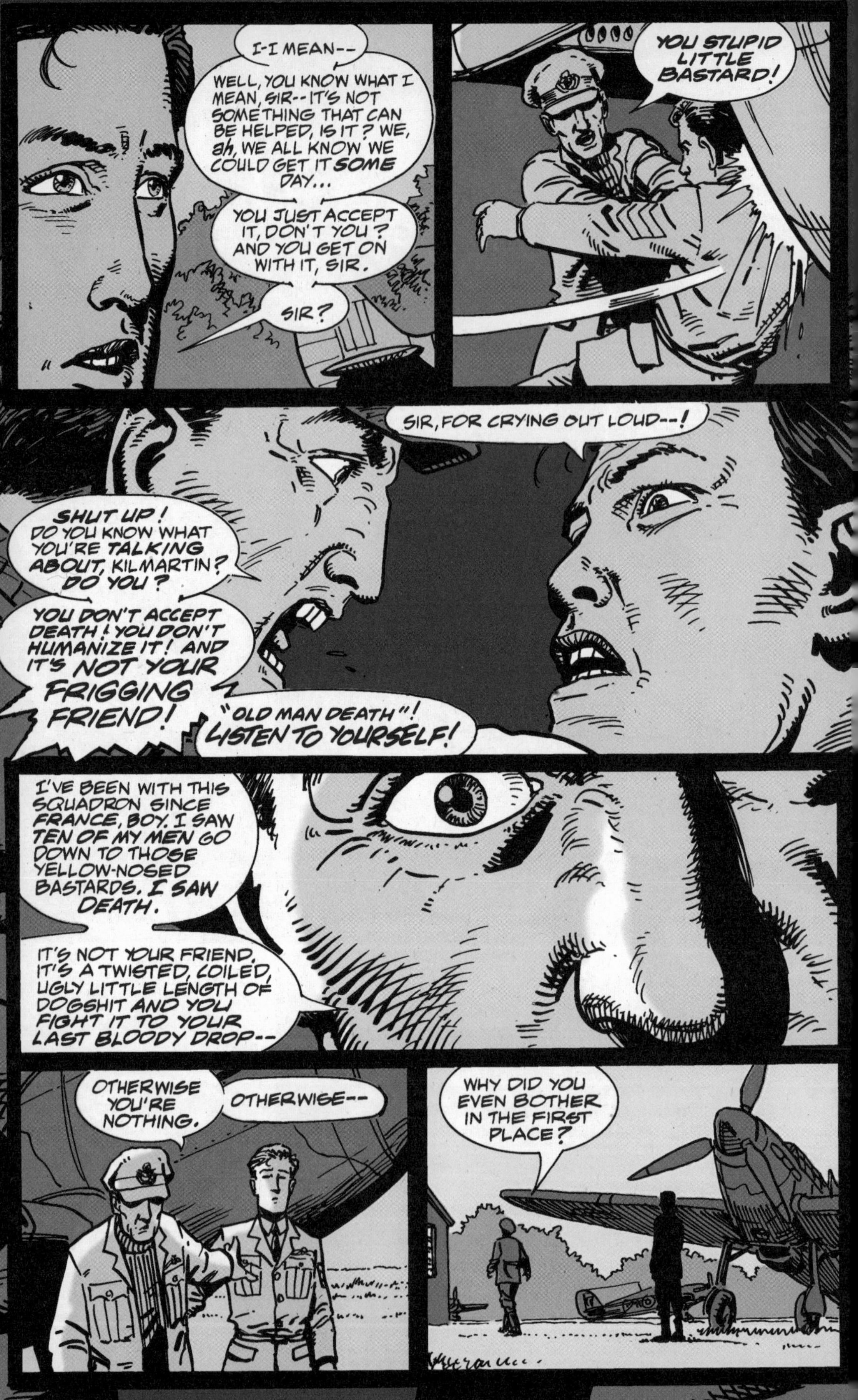
I-I MEAN--
WELL, YOU KNOW WHAT I MEAN, SIR--IT'S NOT SOMETHING THAT CAN BE HELPED, IS IT? WE, ah, WE ALL KNOW WE COULD GET IT SOME DAY...
YOU JUST ACCEPT IT, DON'T YOU? AND YOU GET ON WITH IT, SIR.
SIR?
YOU STUPID LITTLE BASTARD!
SIR, FOR CRYING OUT LOUD--!
SHUT UP! DO YOU KNOW WHAT YOU'RE TALKING ABOUT, KILMARTIN? DO YOU?
YOU DON'T ACCEPT DEATH! YOU DON'T HUMANIZE IT! AND IT'S NOT YOUR FRIGGING FRIEND!
"OLD MAN DEATH"! LISTEN TO YOURSELF!
I'VE BEEN WITH THIS SQUADRON SINCE FRANCE, BOY. I SAW TEN OF MY MEN GO DOWN TO THOSE YELLOW-NOSED BASTARDS. I SAW DEATH.
IT'S NOT YOUR FRIEND. IT'S A TWISTED, COILED, UGLY LITTLE LENGTH OF DOGSHIT AND YOU FIGHT IT TO YOUR LAST BLOODY DROP--
OTHERWISE YOU'RE NOTHING.
OTHERWISE--
WHY DID YOU EVEN BOTHER IN THE FIRST PLACE?

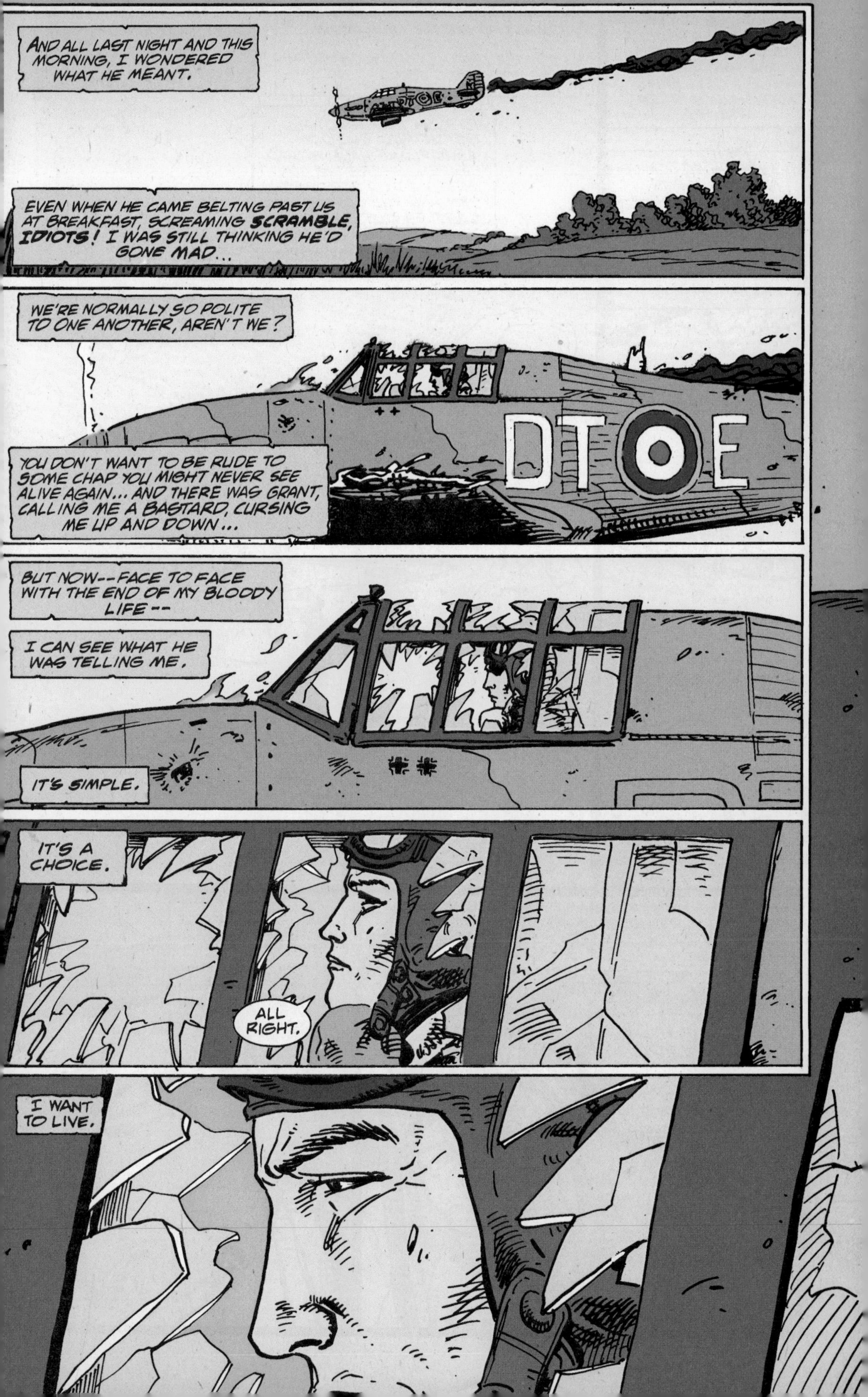
AND ALL LAST NIGHT AND THIS MORNING, I WONDERED WHAT HE MEANT.
EVEN WHEN HE CAME BELTING PAST US AT BREAKFAST, SCREAMING SCRAMBLE, IDIOTS! I WAS STILL THINKING HE'D GONE MAD...
WE'RE NORMALLY SO POLITE TO ONE ANOTHER, AREN'T WE?
YOU DON'T WANT TO BE RUDE TO SOME CHAP YOU MIGHT NEVER SEE ALIVE AGAIN... AND THERE WAS GRANT, CALLING ME A BASTARD, CURSING ME UP AND DOWN...
DTOE
BUT NOW--FACE TO FACE WITH THE END OF MY BLOODY LIFE--
I CAN SEE WHAT HE WAS TELLING ME.
IT'S SIMPLE.
IT'S A CHOICE.
ALL RIGHT.
I WANT TO LIVE.

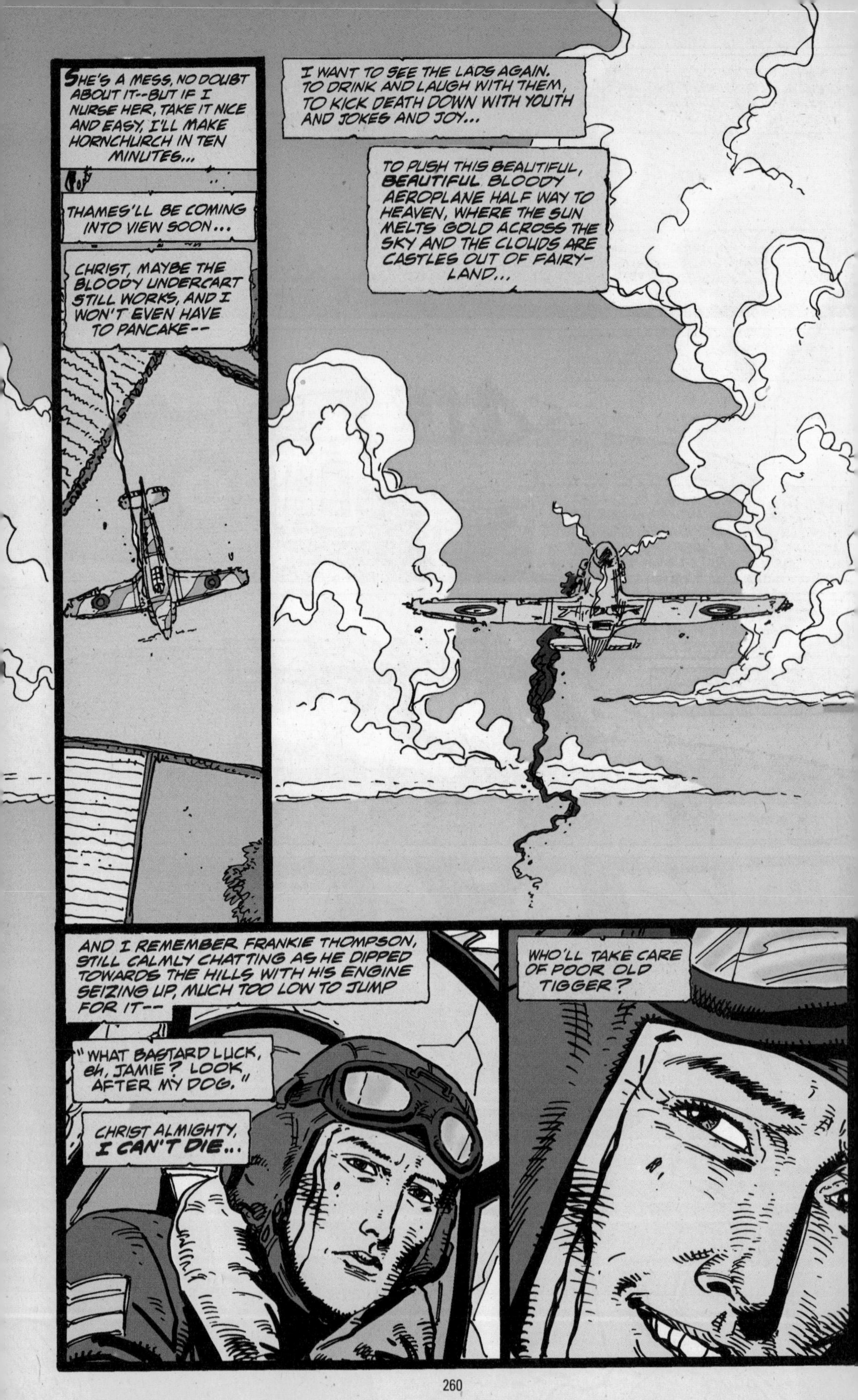
SHE'S A MESS, NO DOUBT ABOUT IT--BUT IF I NURSE HER, TAKE IT NICE AND EASY, I'LL MAKE HORNCHURCH IN TEN MINUTES...
THAMES'LL BE COMING INTO VIEW SOON...
CHRIST, MAYBE THE BLOODY UNDERCART STILL WORKS, AND I WON'T EVEN HAVE TO PANCAKE--
I WANT TO SEE THE LADS AGAIN. TO DRINK AND LAUGH WITH THEM, TO KICK DEATH DOWN WITH YOUTH AND JOKES AND JOY...
TO PUSH THIS BEAUTIFUL, **BEAUTIFUL** BLOODY AEROPLANE HALF WAY TO HEAVEN, WHERE THE SUN MELTS GOLD ACROSS THE SKY AND THE CLOUDS ARE CASTLES OUT OF FAIRY-LAND...
AND I REMEMBER FRANKIE THOMPSON, STILL CALMLY CHATTING AS HE DIPPED TOWARDS THE HILLS WITH HIS ENGINE SEIZING UP, MUCH TOO LOW TO JUMP FOR IT--
"WHAT BASTARD LUCK, eh, JAMIE? LOOK AFTER MY DOG."
CHRIST ALMIGHTY, **I CAN'T DIE...**
WHO'LL TAKE CARE OF POOR OLD TIGGER?

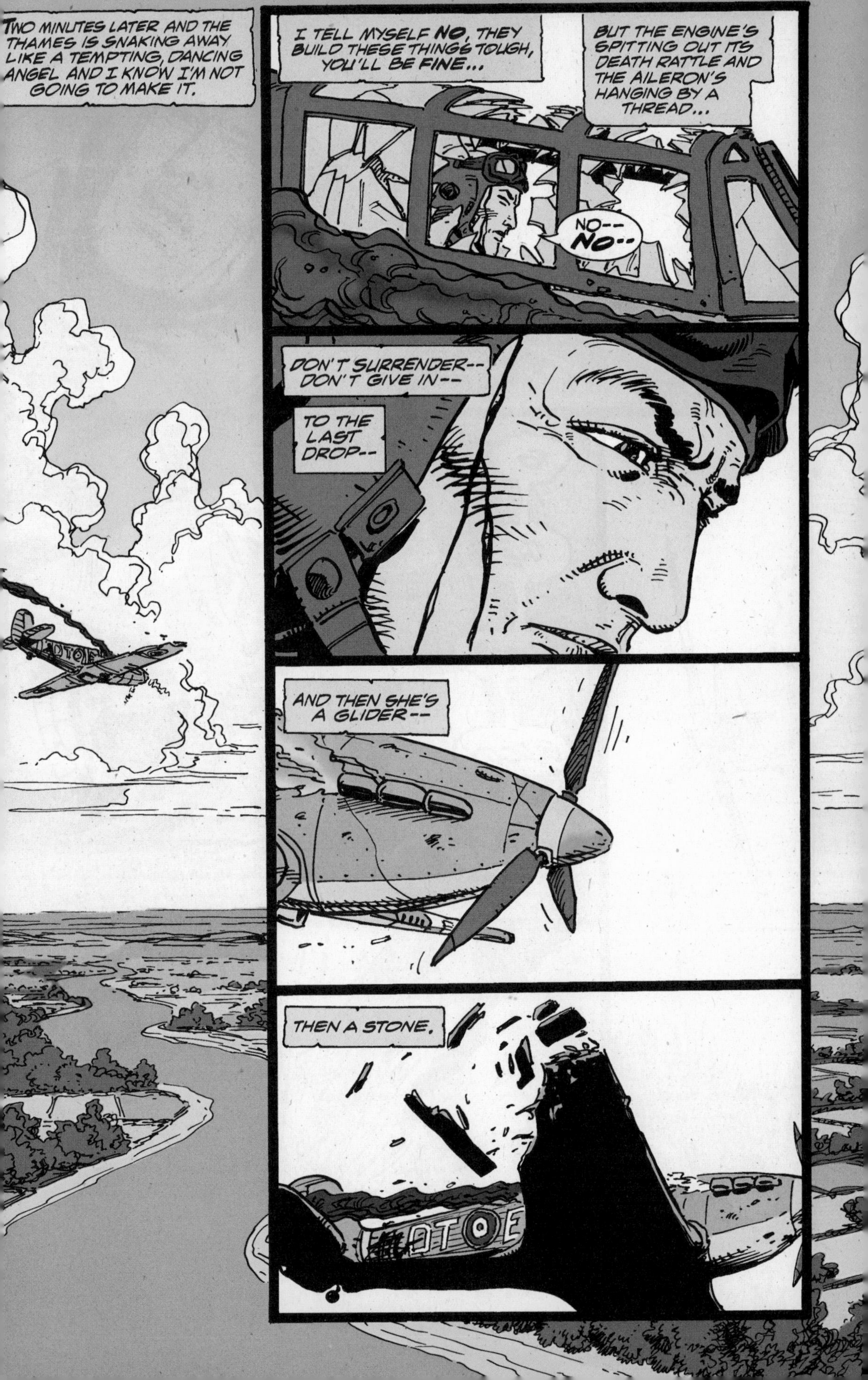
TWO MINUTES LATER AND THE THAMES IS SNAKING AWAY LIKE A TEMPTING, DANCING ANGEL AND I KNOW I'M NOT GOING TO MAKE IT.
I TELL MYSELF NO, THEY BUILD THESE THINGS TOUGH, YOU'LL BE FINE...
BUT THE ENGINE'S SPITTING OUT ITS DEATH RATTLE AND THE AILERON'S HANGING BY A THREAD...
NO-- NO--
DON'T SURRENDER-- DON'T GIVE IN--
TO THE LAST DROP--
AND THEN SHE'S A GLIDER--
THEN A STONE.

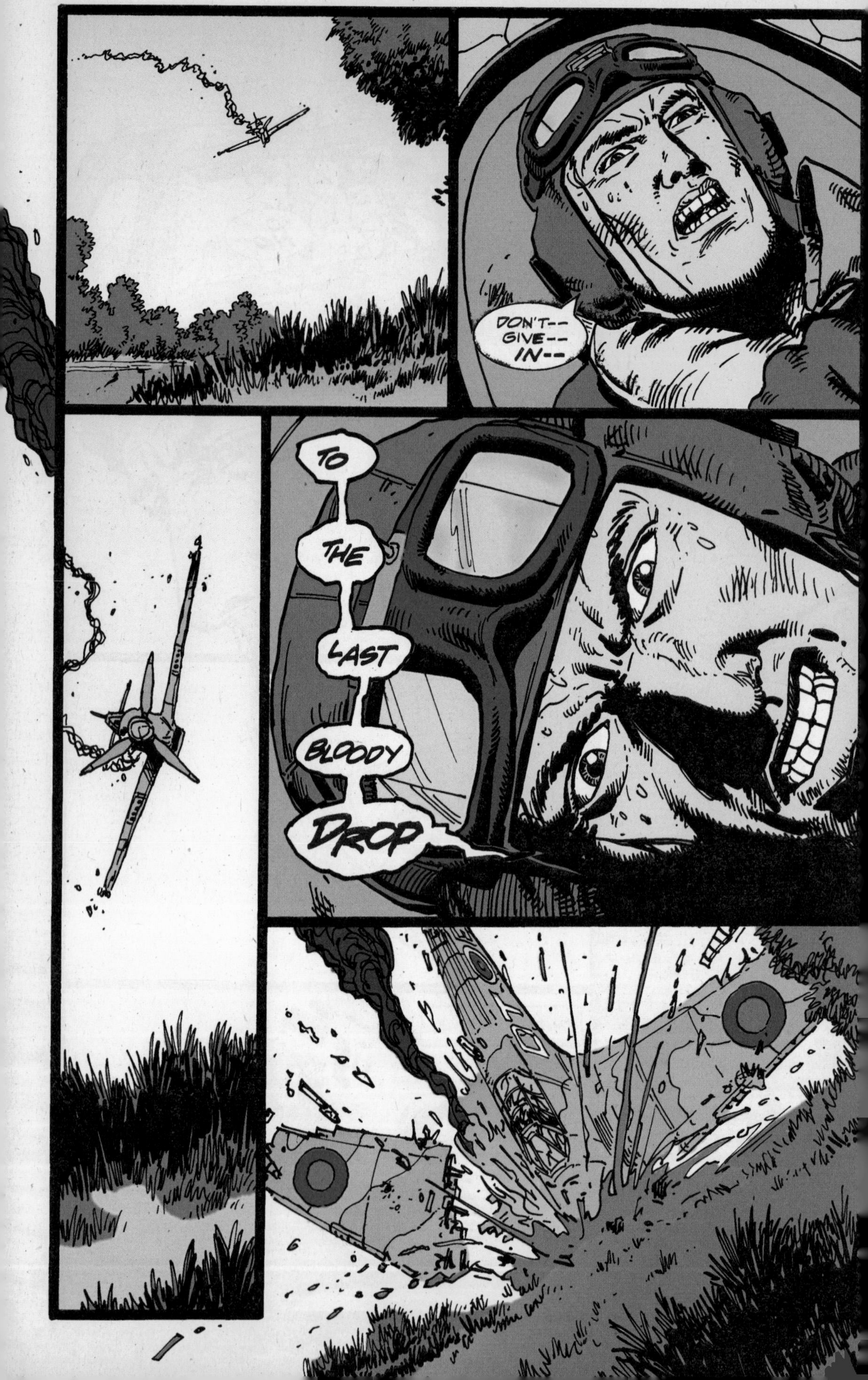
DON'T--
GIVE--
IN--
TO
THE
LAST
BLOODY
DROP

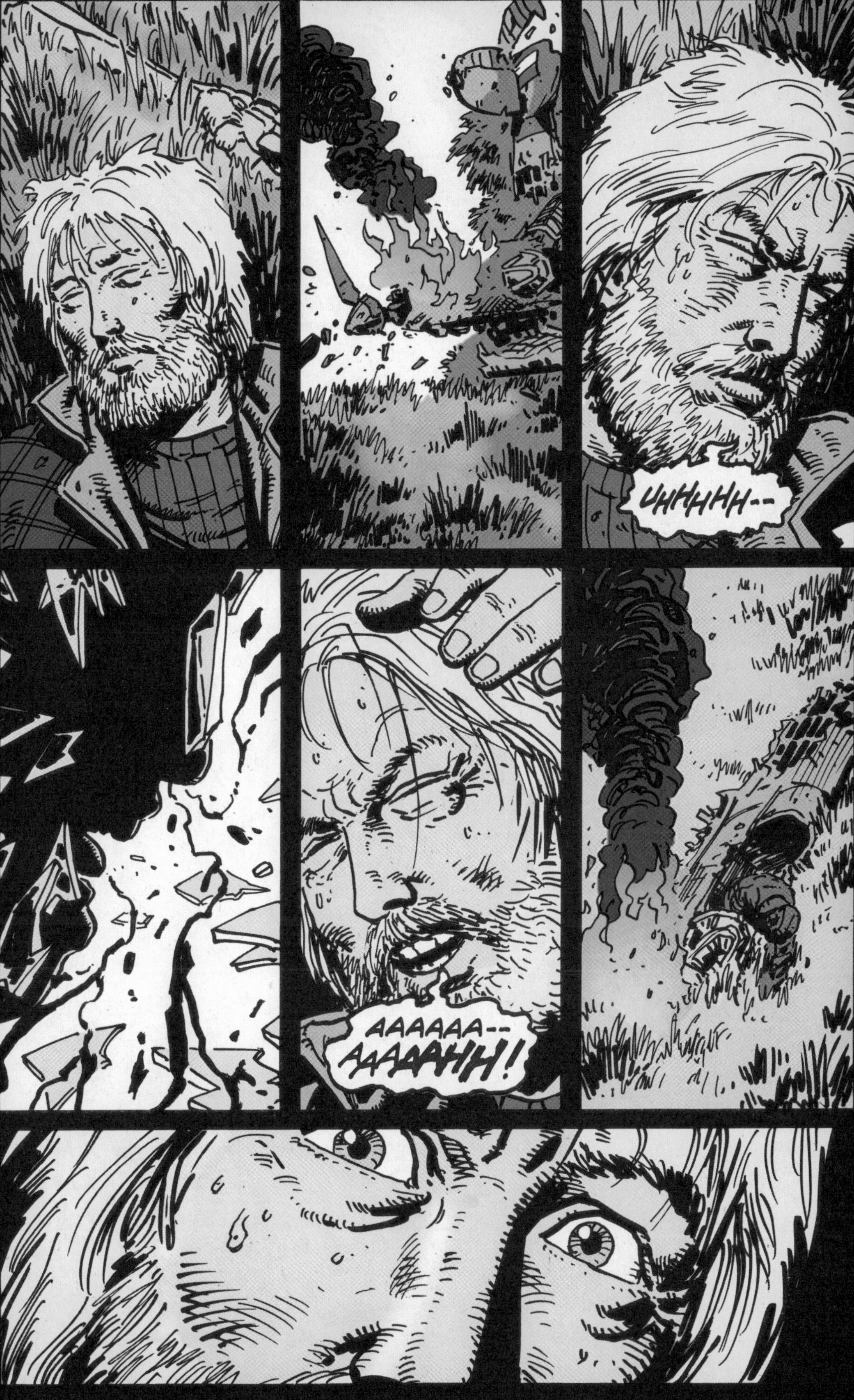
UHHHHH--
AAAAAA--
AAAAAHH!

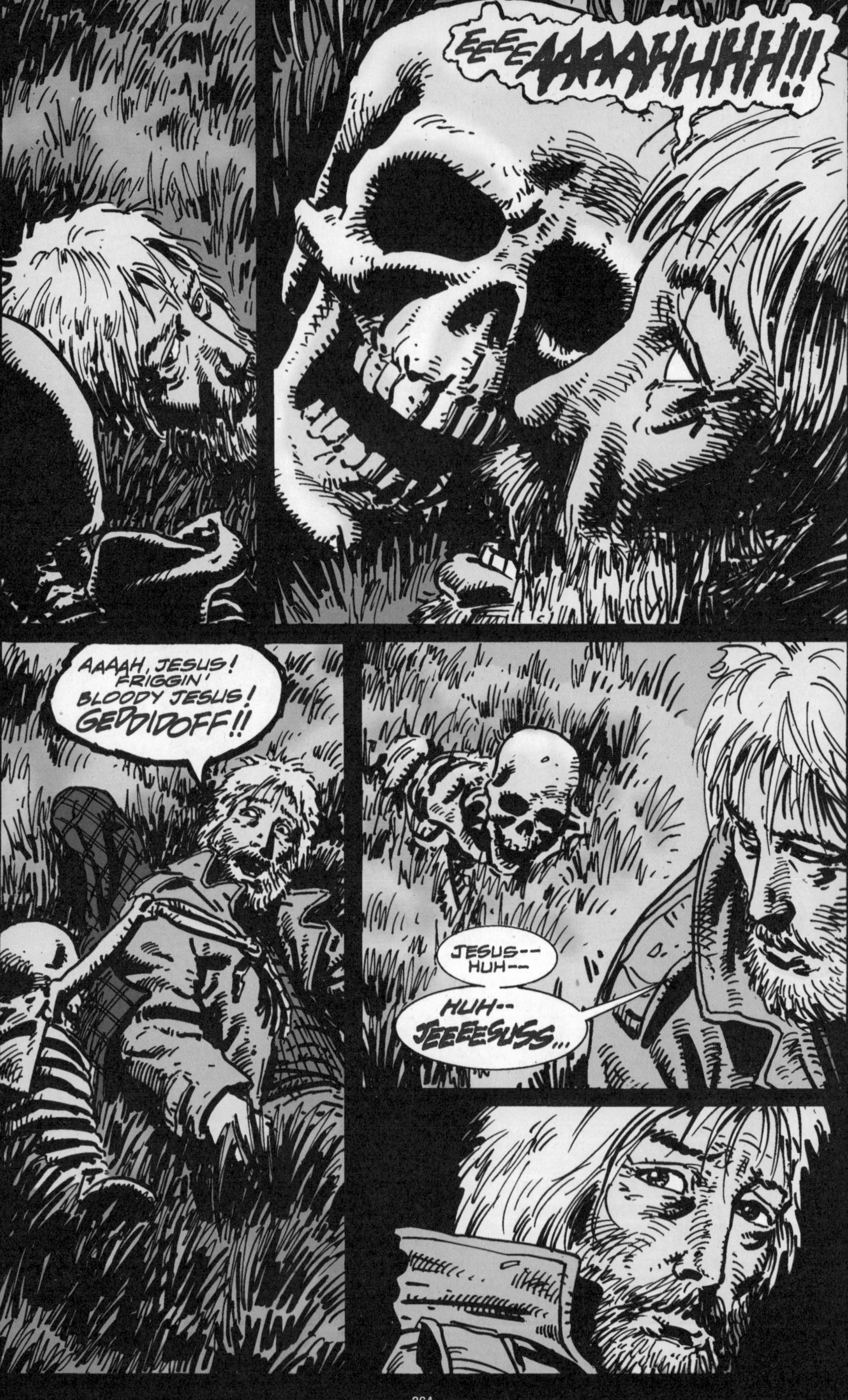
EEEEAAAAHHHH!!
AAAAH, JESUS! FRIGGIN' BLOODY JESUS! GEDDIDOFF!!
JESUS-- HUH--
HUH-- JEEEESUSS...

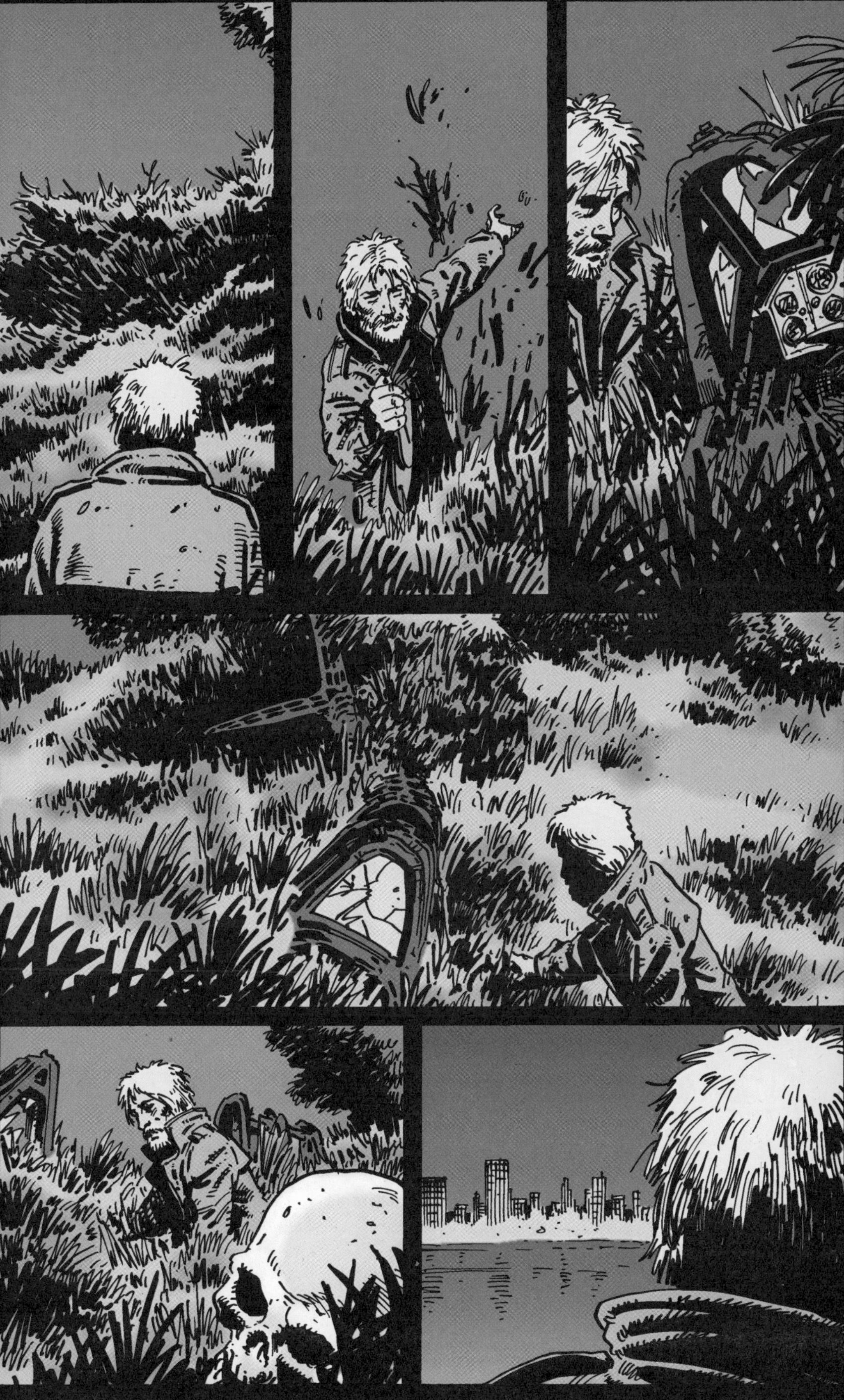

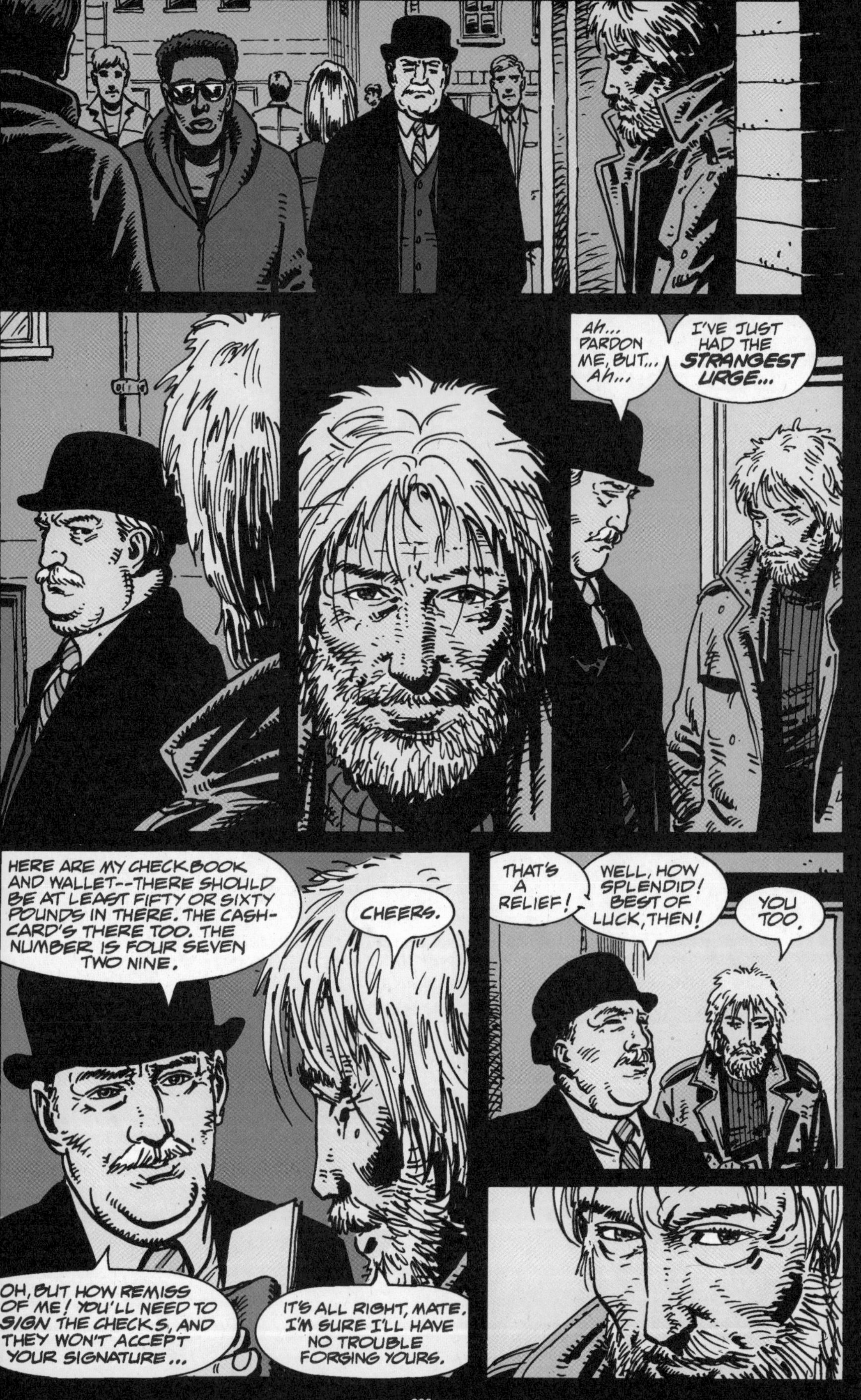
AH... PARDON ME, BUT... AH...
I'VE JUST HAD THE STRANGEST URGE...
HERE ARE MY CHECKBOOK AND WALLET--THERE SHOULD BE AT LEAST FIFTY OR SIXTY POUNDS IN THERE. THE CASH-CARD'S THERE TOO. THE NUMBER IS FOUR SEVEN TWO NINE.
CHEERS.
OH, BUT HOW REMISS OF ME! YOU'LL NEED TO SIGN THE CHECKS, AND THEY WON'T ACCEPT YOUR SIGNATURE...
IT'S ALL RIGHT, MATE. I'M SURE I'LL HAVE NO TROUBLE FORGING YOURS.
THAT'S A RELIEF!
WELL, HOW SPLENDID! BEST OF LUCK, THEN!
YOU TOO.

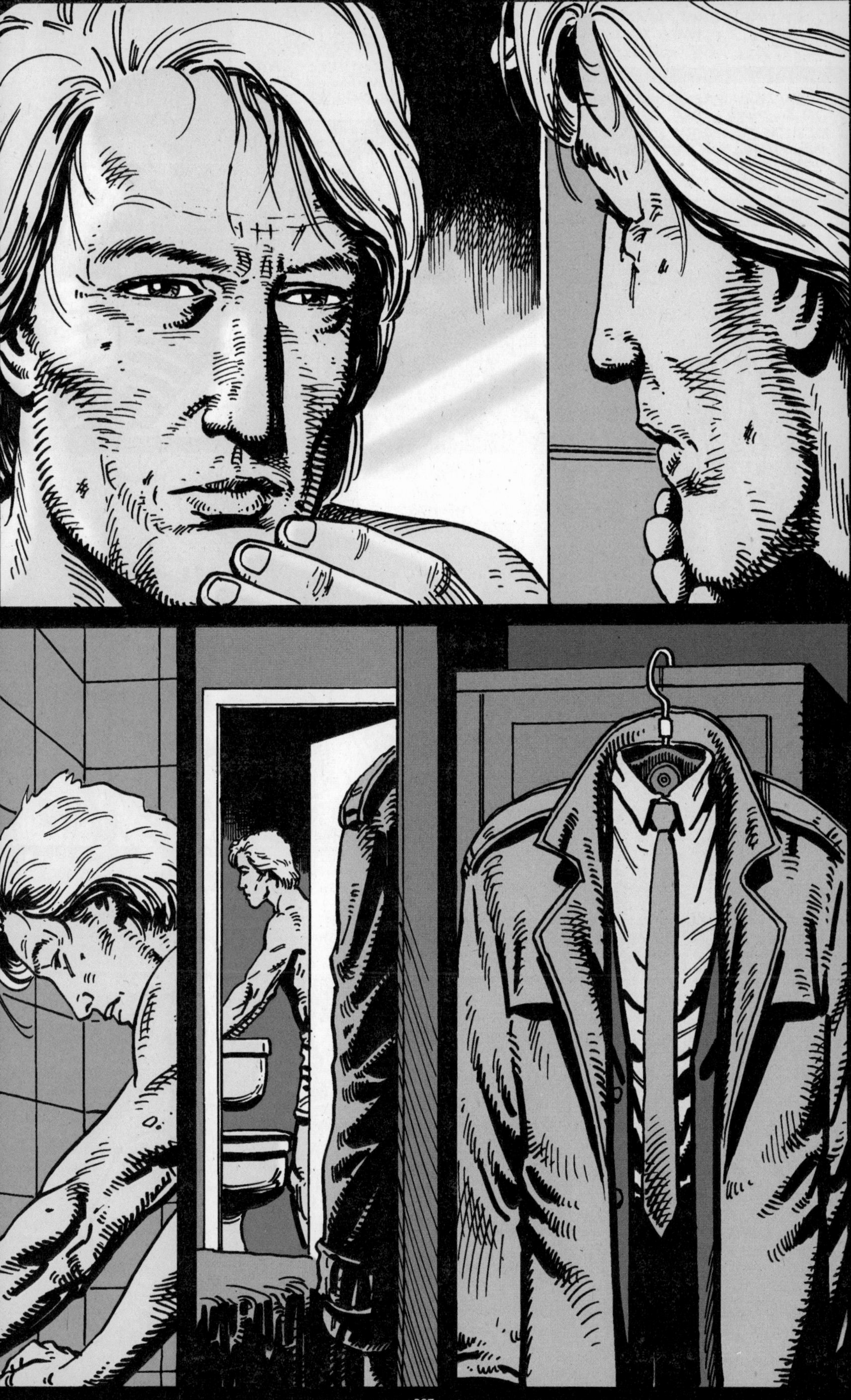

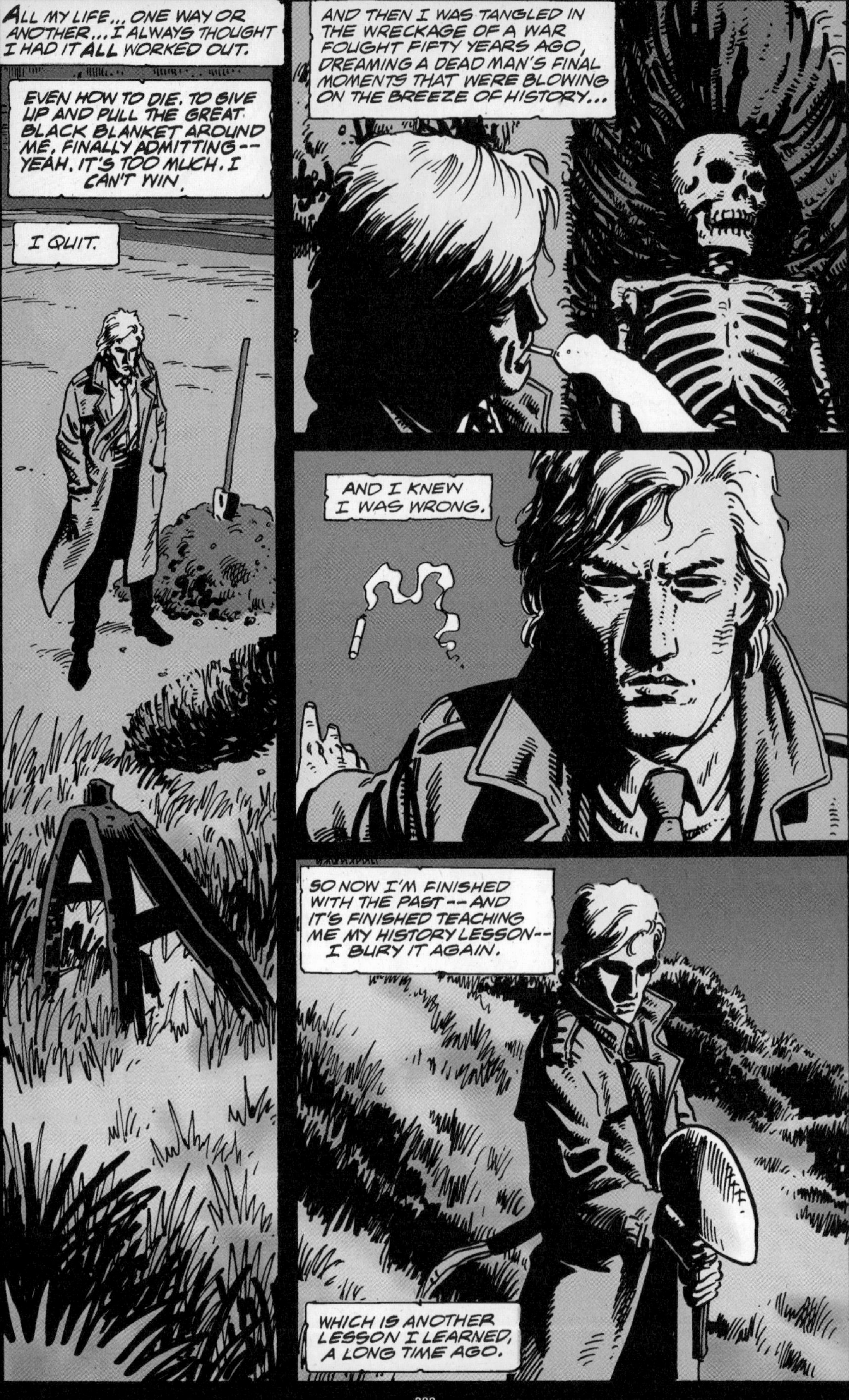
ALL MY LIFE... ONE WAY OR ANOTHER... I ALWAYS THOUGHT I HAD IT ALL WORKED OUT.
EVEN HOW TO DIE. TO GIVE UP AND PULL THE GREAT BLACK BLANKET AROUND ME. FINALLY ADMITTING -- YEAH. IT'S TOO MUCH. I CAN'T WIN.
I QUIT.
AND THEN I WAS TANGLED IN THE WRECKAGE OF A WAR FOUGHT FIFTY YEARS AGO, DREAMING A DEAD MAN'S FINAL MOMENTS THAT WERE BLOWING ON THE BREEZE OF HISTORY...
AND I KNEW I WAS WRONG.
SO NOW I'M FINISHED WITH THE PAST -- AND IT'S FINISHED TEACHING ME MY HISTORY LESSON -- I BURY IT AGAIN.
WHICH IS ANOTHER LESSON I LEARNED, A LONG TIME AGO.

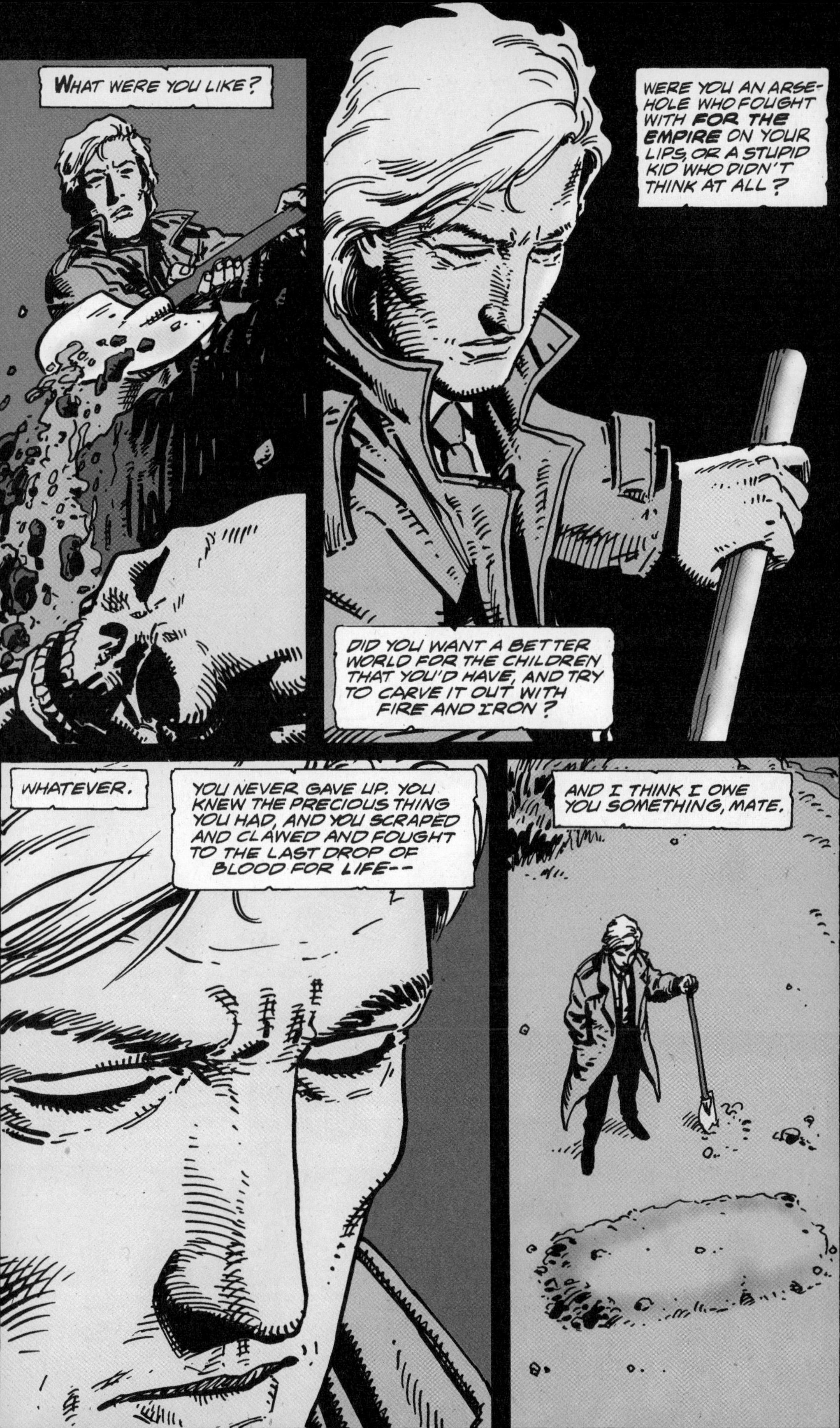
WHAT WERE YOU LIKE?
WERE YOU AN ARSE-HOLE WHO FOUGHT WITH **FOR THE EMPIRE** ON YOUR LIPS, OR A STUPID KID WHO DIDN'T THINK AT ALL?
DID YOU WANT A BETTER WORLD FOR THE CHILDREN THAT YOU'D HAVE, AND TRY TO CARVE IT OUT WITH FIRE AND IRON?
WHATEVER.
YOU NEVER GAVE UP. YOU KNEW THE PRECIOUS THING YOU HAD, AND YOU SCRAPED AND CLAWED AND FOUGHT TO THE LAST DROP OF BLOOD FOR **LIFE**--
AND I THINK I OWE YOU SOMETHING, MATE.

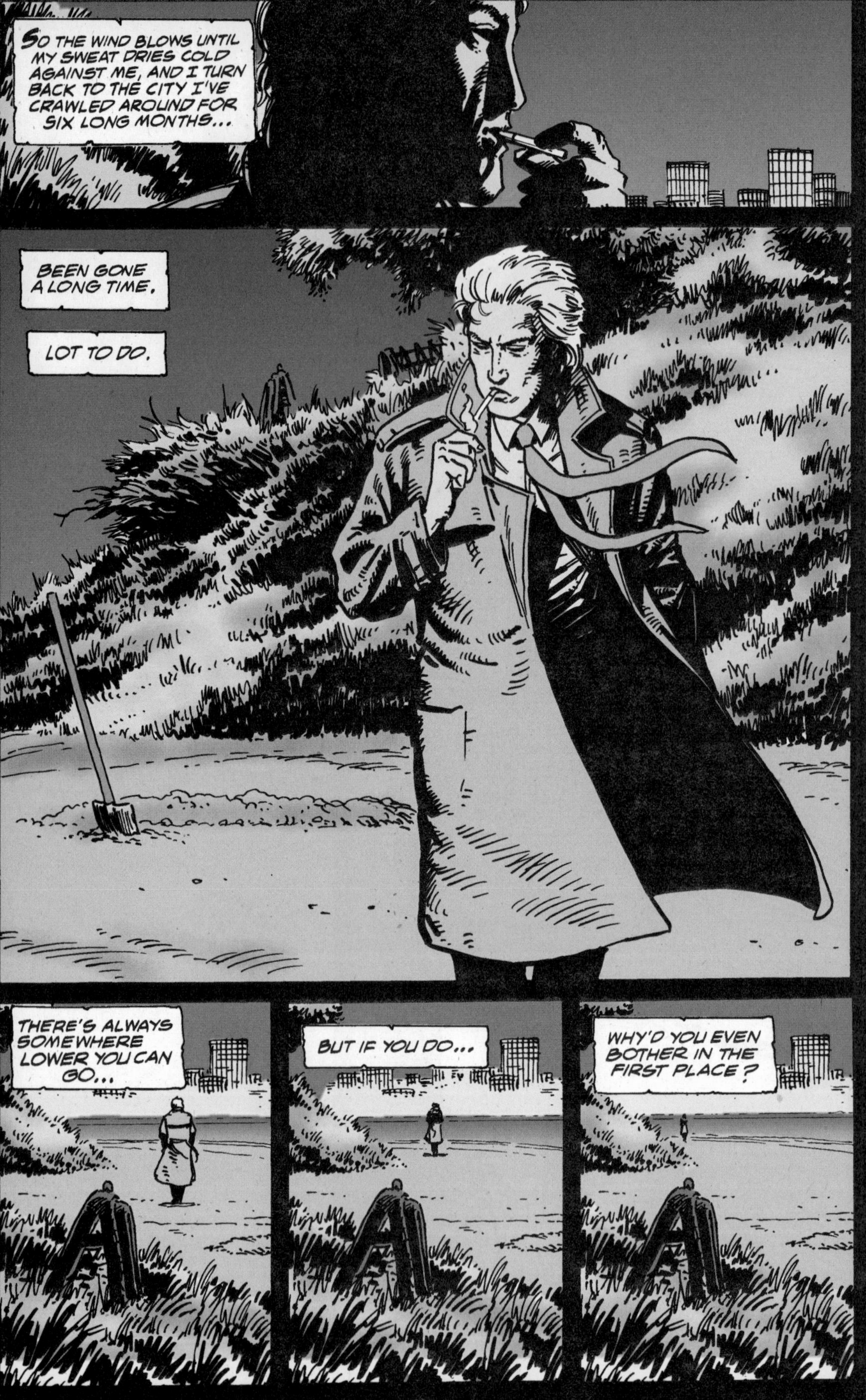
SO THE WIND BLOWS UNTIL MY SWEAT DRIES COLD AGAINST ME, AND I TURN BACK TO THE CITY I'VE CRAWLED AROUND FOR SIX LONG MONTHS...
BEEN GONE A LONG TIME.
LOT TO DO.
THERE'S ALWAYS SOMEWHERE LOWER YOU CAN GO...
BUT IF YOU DO...
WHY'D YOU EVEN BOTHER IN THE FIRST PLACE?

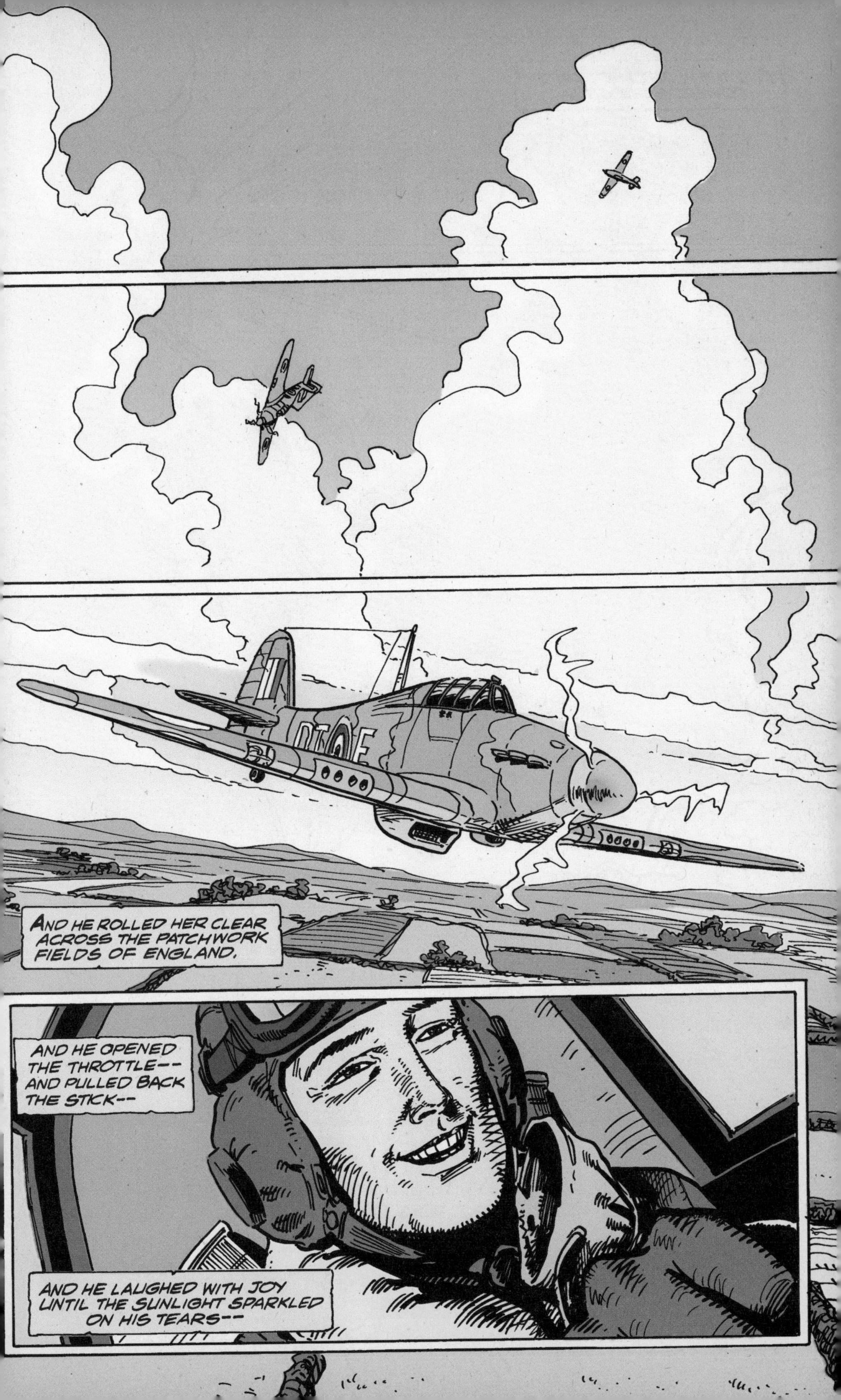

AND HE ROLLED HER CLEAR ACROSS THE PATCHWORK FIELDS OF ENGLAND.
AND HE OPENED THE THROTTLE-- AND PULLED BACK THE STICK--
AND HE LAUGHED WITH JOY UNTIL THE SUNLIGHT SPARKLED ON HIS TEARS--

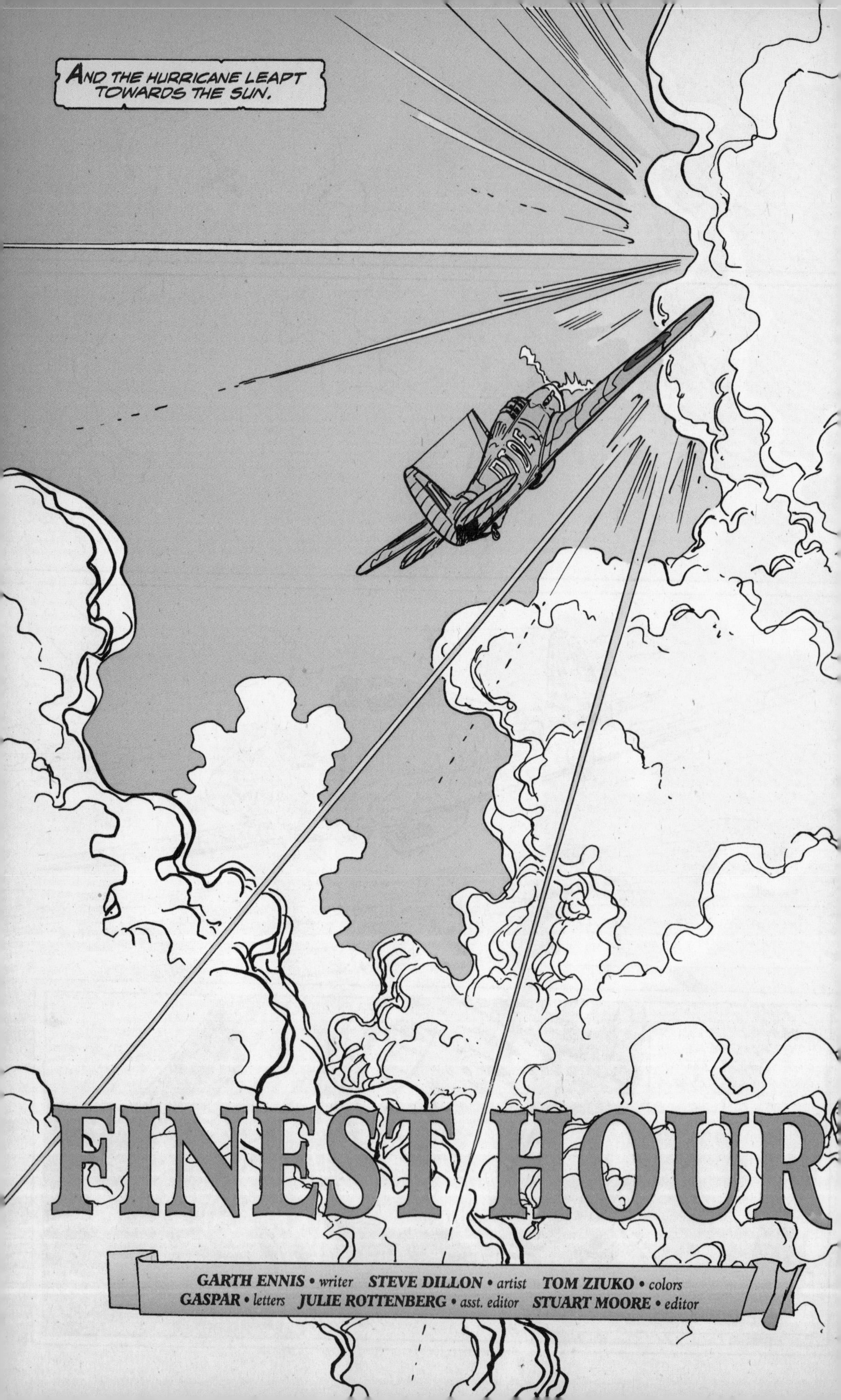

AND THE HURRICANE LEAPT TOWARDS THE SUN.
FINEST HOUR
GARTH ENNIS • writer STEVE DILLON • artist TOM ZIUKO • colors
GASPAR • letters JULIE ROTTENBERG • asst. editor STUART MOORE • editor

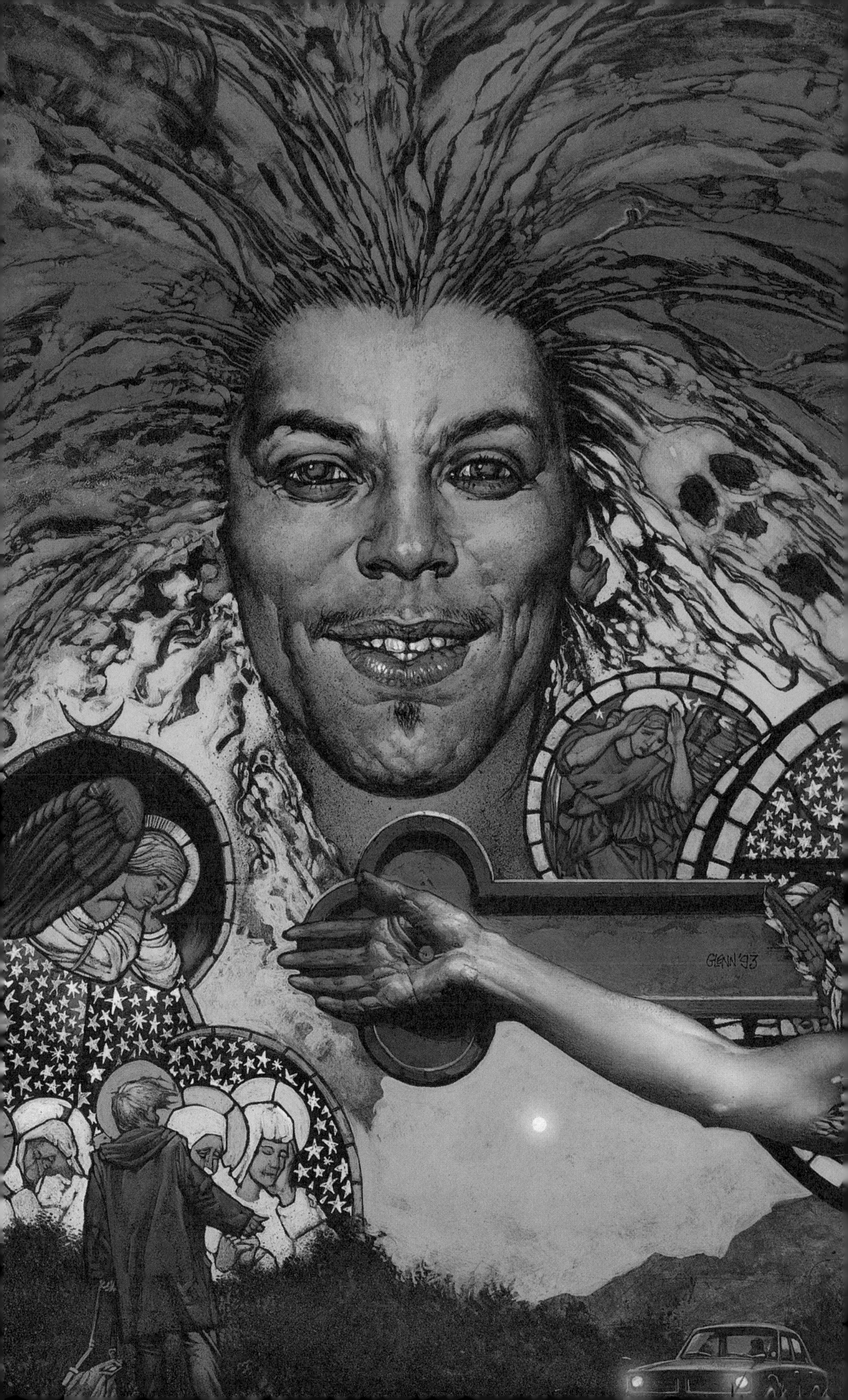
GLENN '93

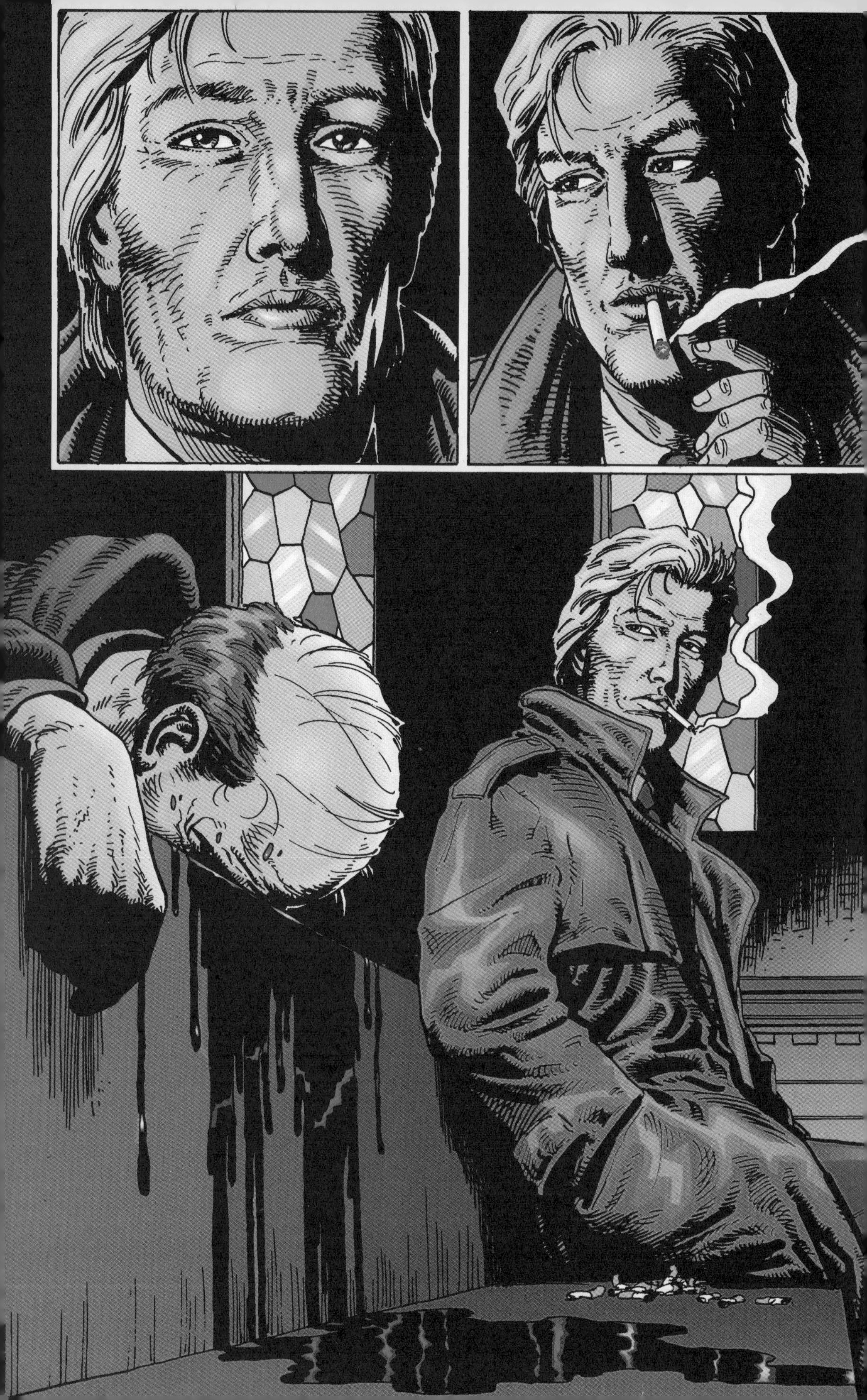

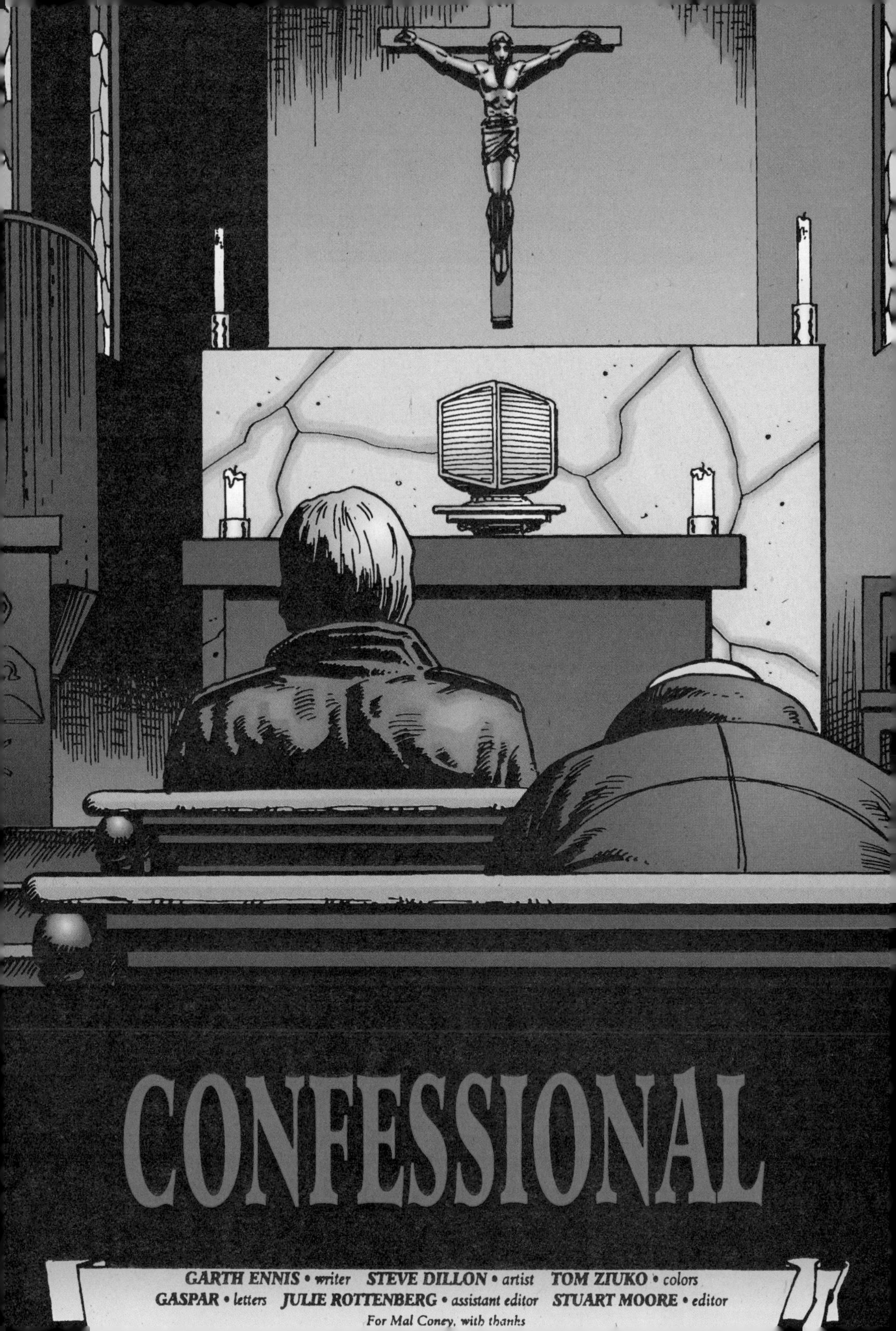
CONFESSIONAL
GARTH ENNIS • writer STEVE DILLON • artist TOM ZIUKO • colors
GASPAR • letters JULIE ROTTENBERG • assistant editor STUART MOORE • editor
For Mal Coney, with thanks

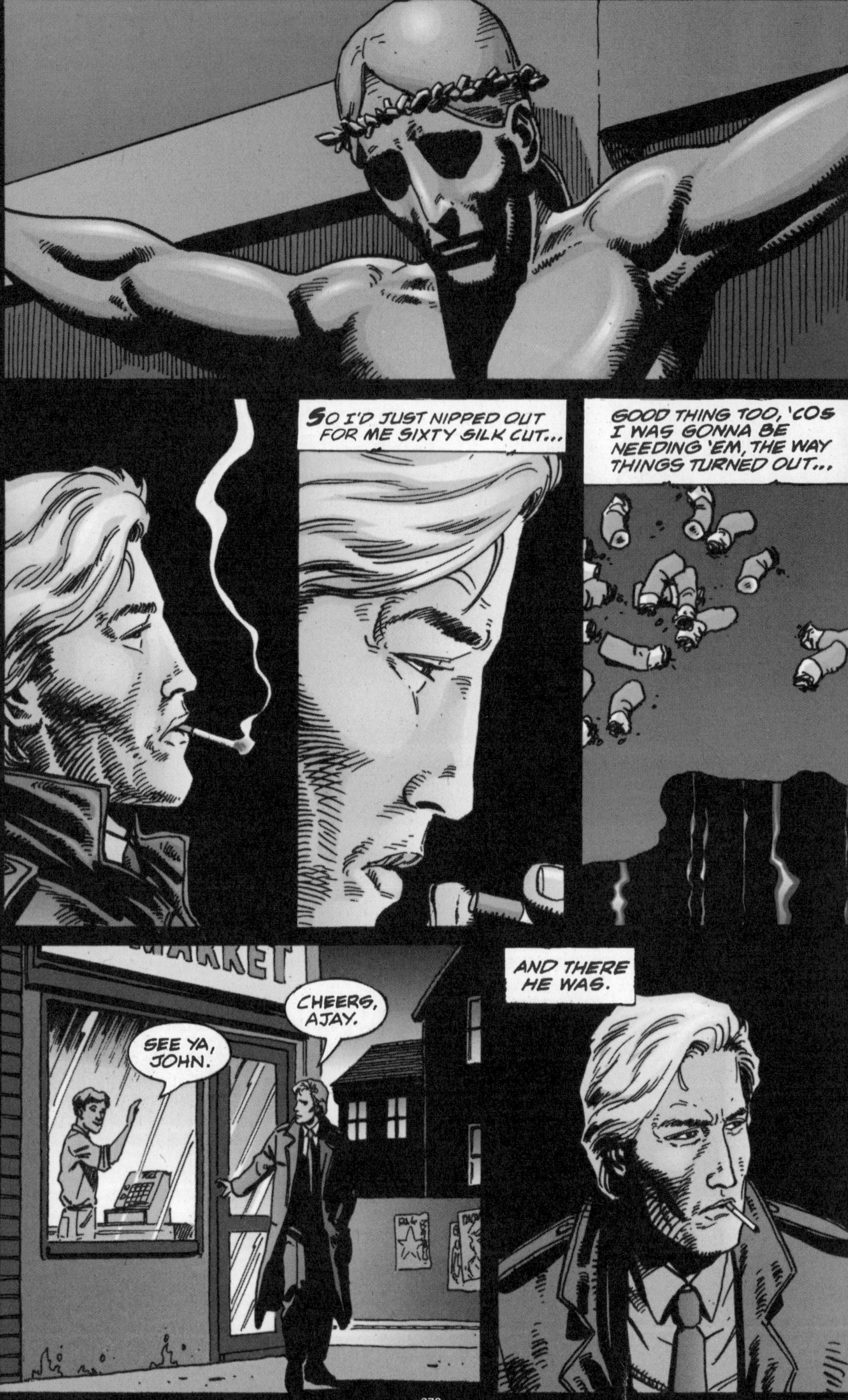
SO I'D JUST NIPPED OUT FOR ME SIXTY SILK CUT...
GOOD THING TOO, 'COS I WAS GONNA BE NEEDING 'EM, THE WAY THINGS TURNED OUT...
SEE YA, JOHN.
CHEERS, AJAY.
AND THERE HE WAS.

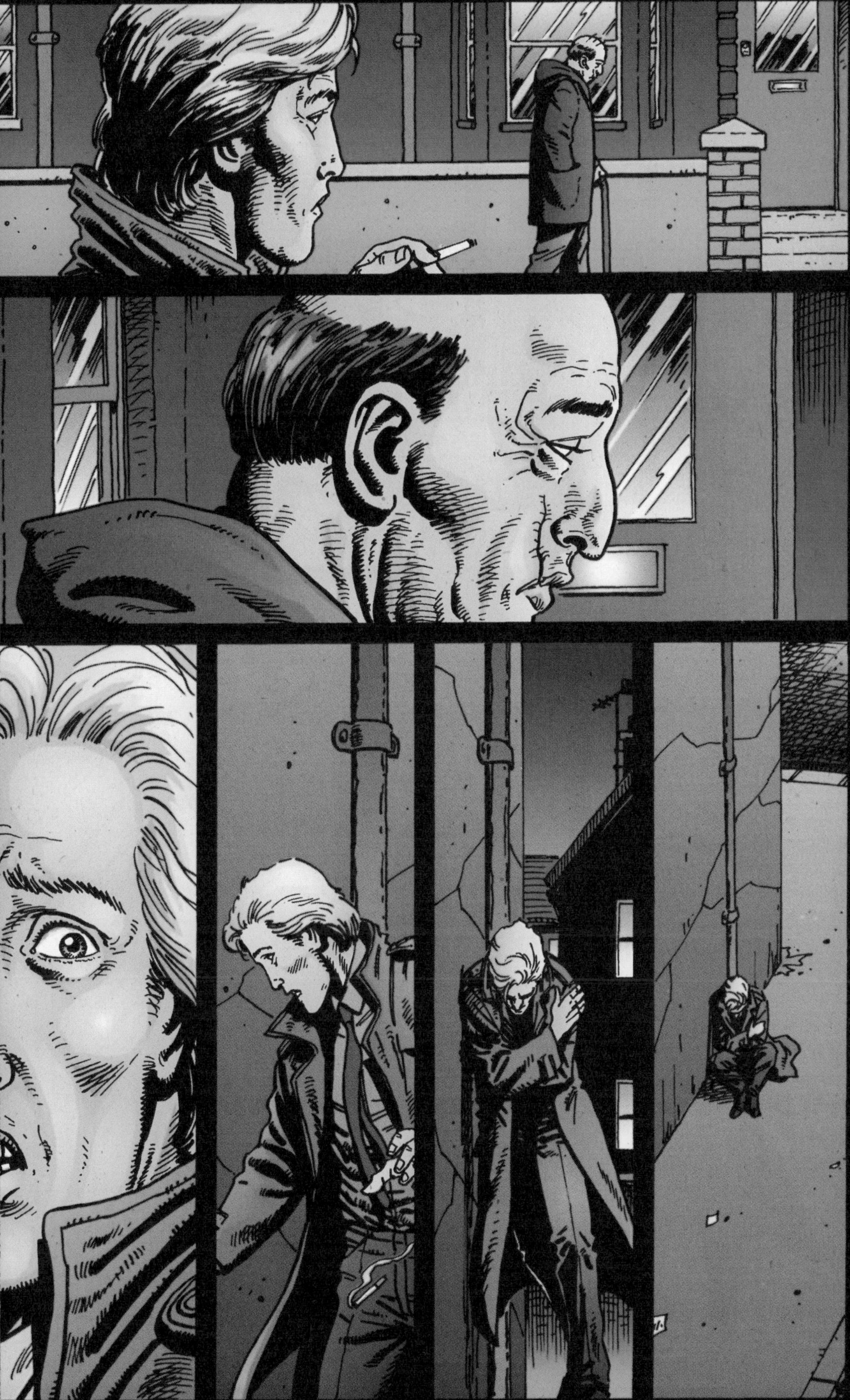

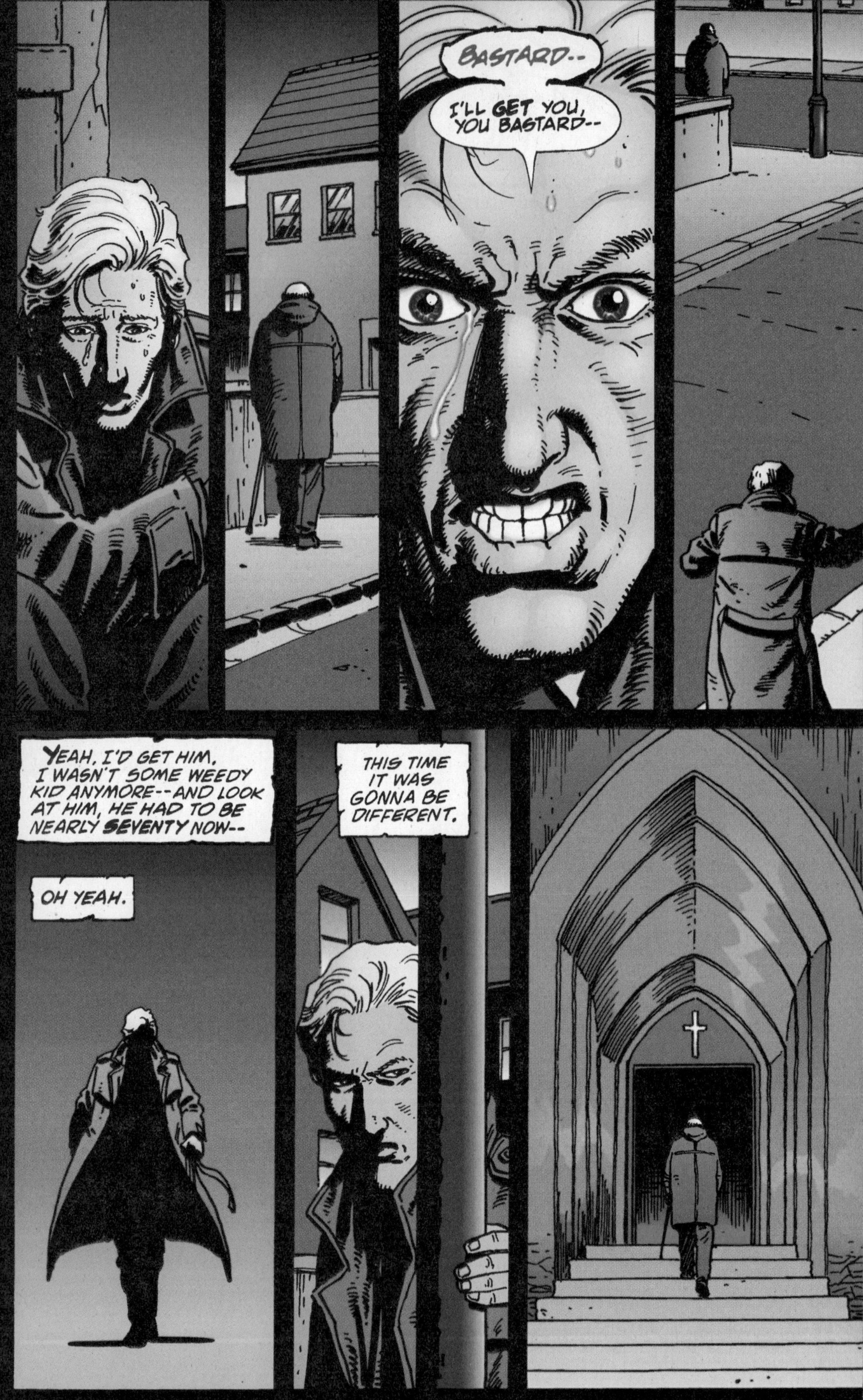
BASTARD--
I'LL GET YOU, YOU BASTARD--
YEAH. I'D GET HIM. I WASN'T SOME WEEDY KID ANYMORE--AND LOOK AT HIM, HE HAD TO BE NEARLY SEVENTY NOW--
OH YEAH.
THIS TIME IT WAS GONNA BE DIFFERENT.

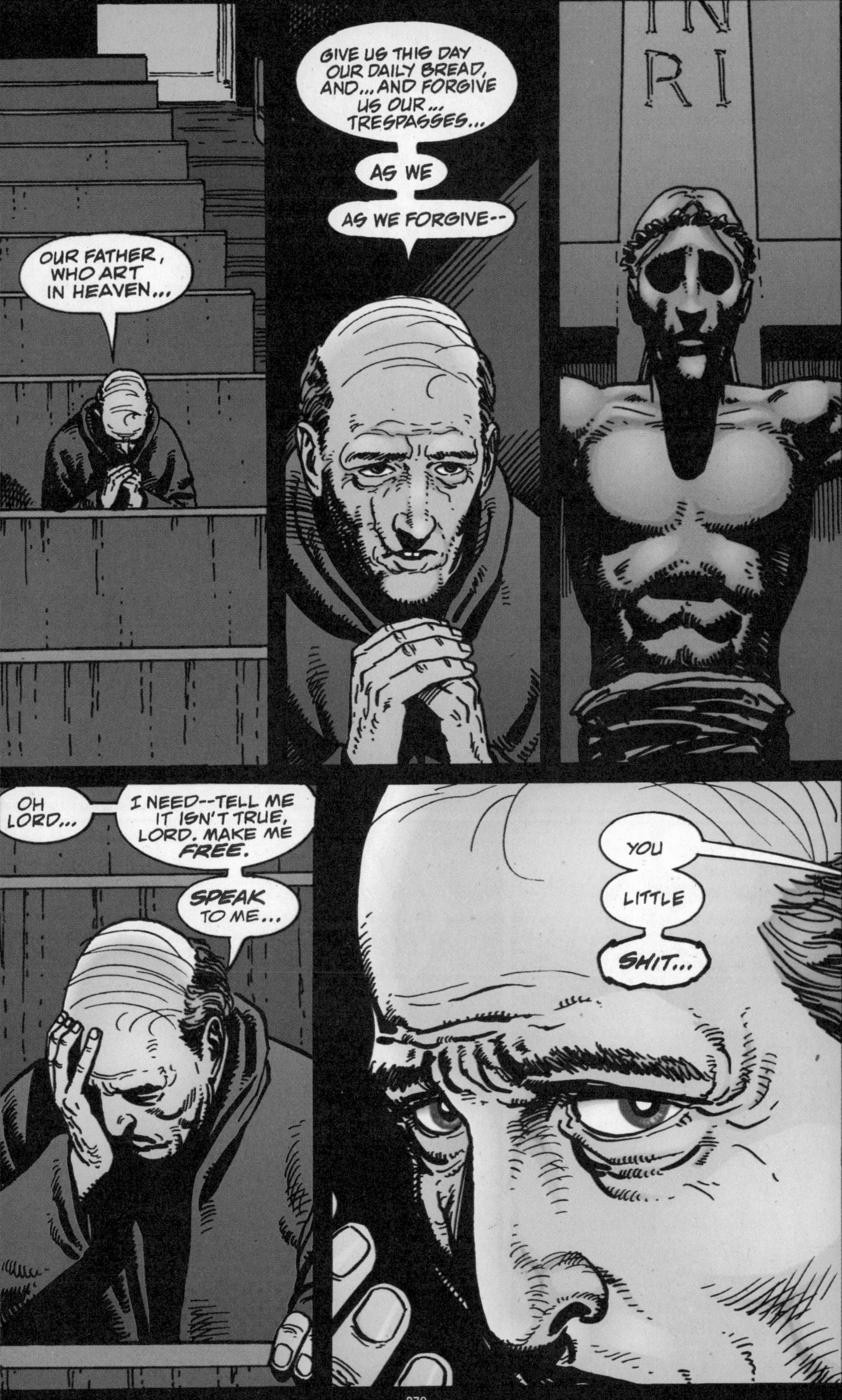
OUR FATHER, WHO ART IN HEAVEN...
GIVE US THIS DAY OUR DAILY BREAD, AND... AND FORGIVE US OUR... TRESPASSES...
AS WE
AS WE FORGIVE--
INRI
OH LORD...
I NEED--TELL ME IT ISN'T TRUE, LORD. MAKE ME FREE.
SPEAK TO ME...
YOU
LITTLE
SHIT...

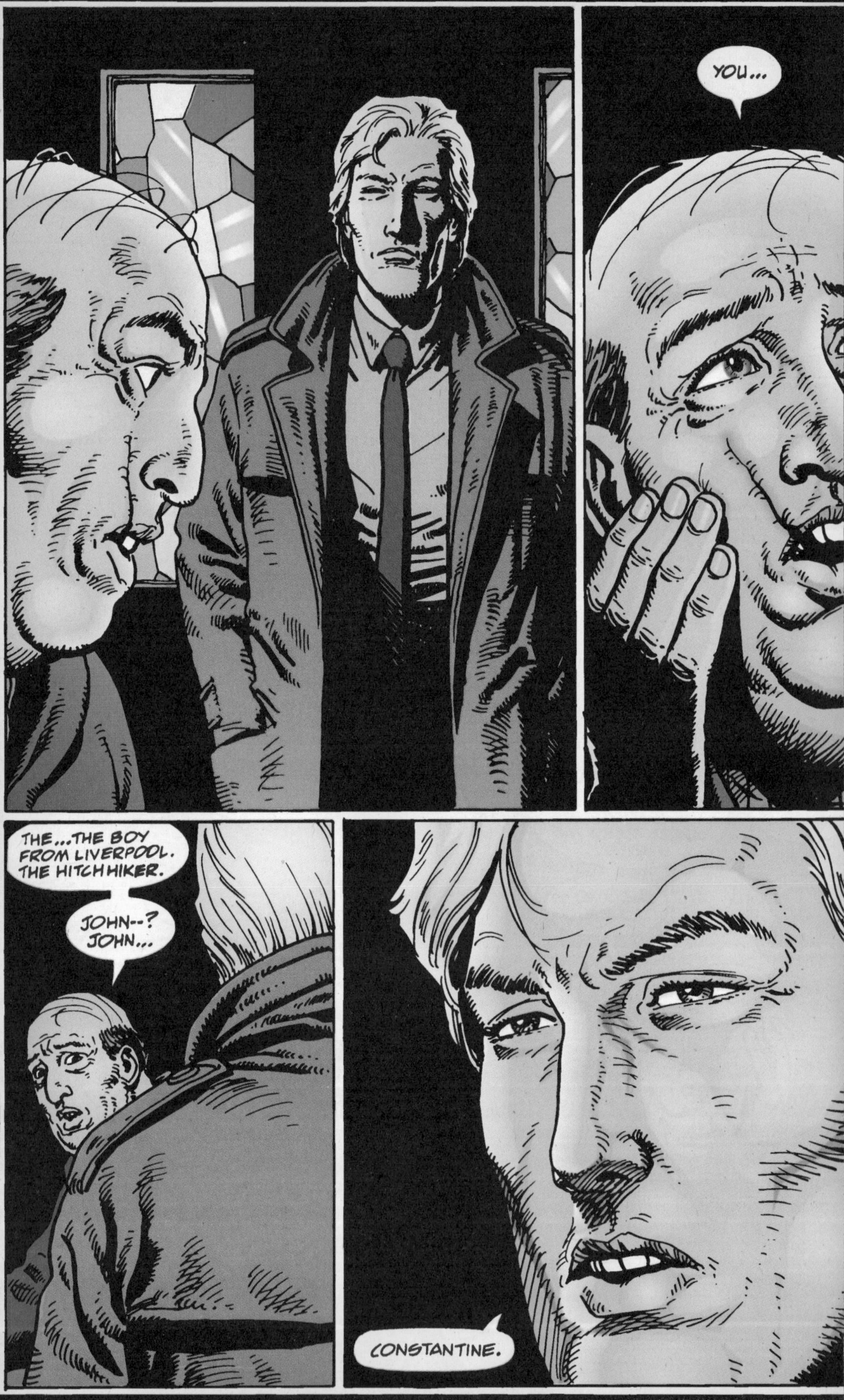
YOU...
THE...THE BOY FROM LIVERPOOL. THE HITCHHIKER.
JOHN--? JOHN...
CONSTANTINE.

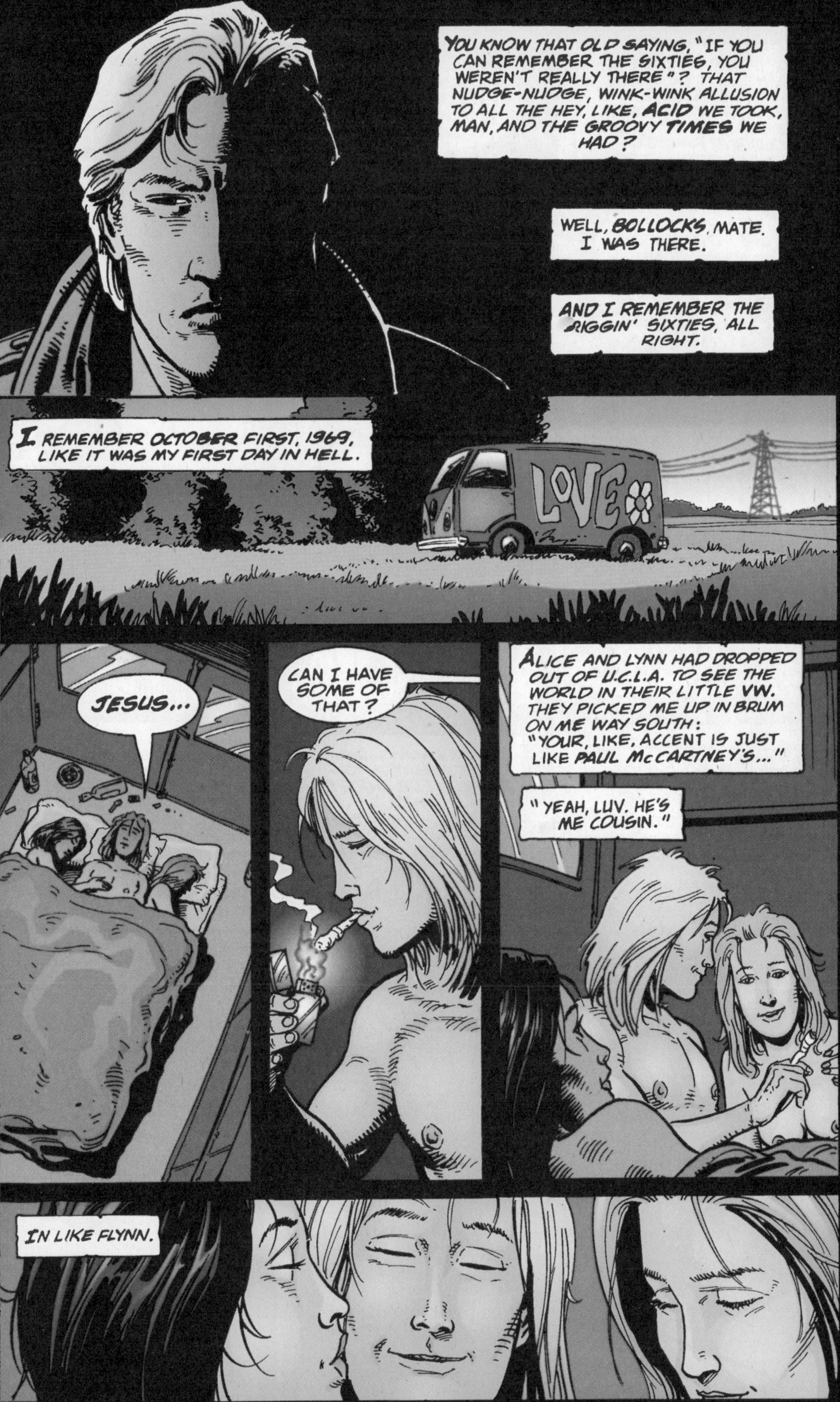
YOU KNOW THAT OLD SAYING, "IF YOU CAN REMEMBER THE SIXTIES, YOU WEREN'T REALLY THERE"? THAT NUDGE-NUDGE, WINK-WINK ALLUSION TO ALL THE HEY, LIKE, ACID WE TOOK, MAN, AND THE GROOVY TIMES WE HAD?
WELL, BOLLOCKS, MATE. I WAS THERE.
AND I REMEMBER THE FRIGGIN' SIXTIES, ALL RIGHT.
I REMEMBER OCTOBER FIRST, 1969, LIKE IT WAS MY FIRST DAY IN HELL.
LOVE
JESUS...
CAN I HAVE SOME OF THAT?
ALICE AND LYNN HAD DROPPED OUT OF U.C.L.A. TO SEE THE WORLD IN THEIR LITTLE VW. THEY PICKED ME UP IN BRUM ON ME WAY SOUTH: "YOUR, LIKE, ACCENT IS JUST LIKE PAUL McCARTNEY'S..."
"YEAH, LUV. HE'S ME COUSIN."
IN LIKE FLYNN.

WE'D STOPPED FOR THE NIGHT OUTSIDE OXFORD, TWO DAYS BEFORE. VODKA, SHITTY ELDER-BERRY WINE, ACAPULCO GOLD AND FAR TOO MANY DEXIES--TOUGH OLD LIFE.

WE GOTTA TURN OFF FOR READING HERE, JOHN. SORRY...

S'OKAY, LUV. LONDON'S ONLY FORTY MILES DOWN THE ROAD. BE PLENTY MORE LIFTS, LIKE.

I FORGOT WE HAD THIS STUFF. YOU GUYS WANT SOME?

YEAH... MMM...'LL KEEP ME GOIN'...

GOOD LUCK MAKING YOUR FORTUNE IN LONDON...

Heh-- HMMMFSH!

PLACE WON'T KNOW WHAT'S HIT IT.

DON'T FORGET TO SEND US PAUL'S AUTOGRAPH.

PROMISE.

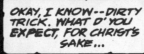

OKAY, I KNOW--DIRTY TRICK. WHAT D'YOU EXPECT, FOR CHRIST'S SAKE...

Heh Heh Heh...

BUT LONDON, YEAH, THAT'S WHERE IT WAS ALL GONNA START HAPPENING. LIVERPOOL, AND DAD, AND ALL THE LITTLE MINDS WERE BEHIND ME.

I WAS HEADING SOUTH TO SET THE WORLD ON FIRE.

NICE DAY FOR IT...

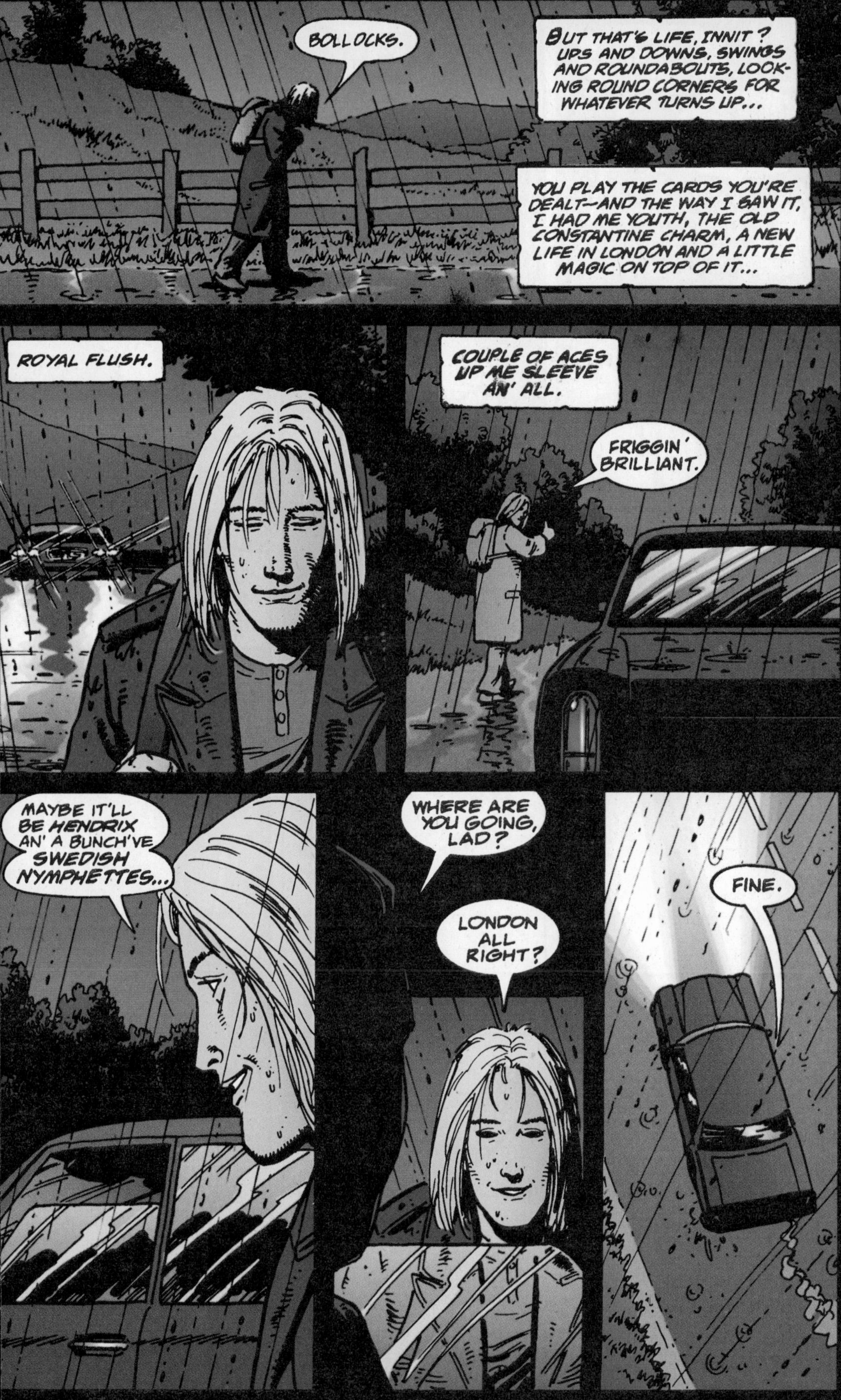
BOLLOCKS.
BUT THAT'S LIFE, INNIT? UPS AND DOWNS, SWINGS AND ROUNDABOUTS, LOOKING ROUND CORNERS FOR WHATEVER TURNS UP...
YOU PLAY THE CARDS YOU'RE DEALT—AND THE WAY I SAW IT, I HAD ME YOUTH, THE OLD CONSTANTINE CHARM, A NEW LIFE IN LONDON AND A LITTLE MAGIC ON TOP OF IT...
ROYAL FLUSH.
COUPLE OF ACES UP ME SLEEVE AN' ALL.
FRIGGIN' BRILLIANT.
MAYBE IT'LL BE HENDRIX AN' A BUNCH'VE SWEDISH NYMPHETTES...
WHERE ARE YOU GOING, LAD?
LONDON ALL RIGHT?
FINE.

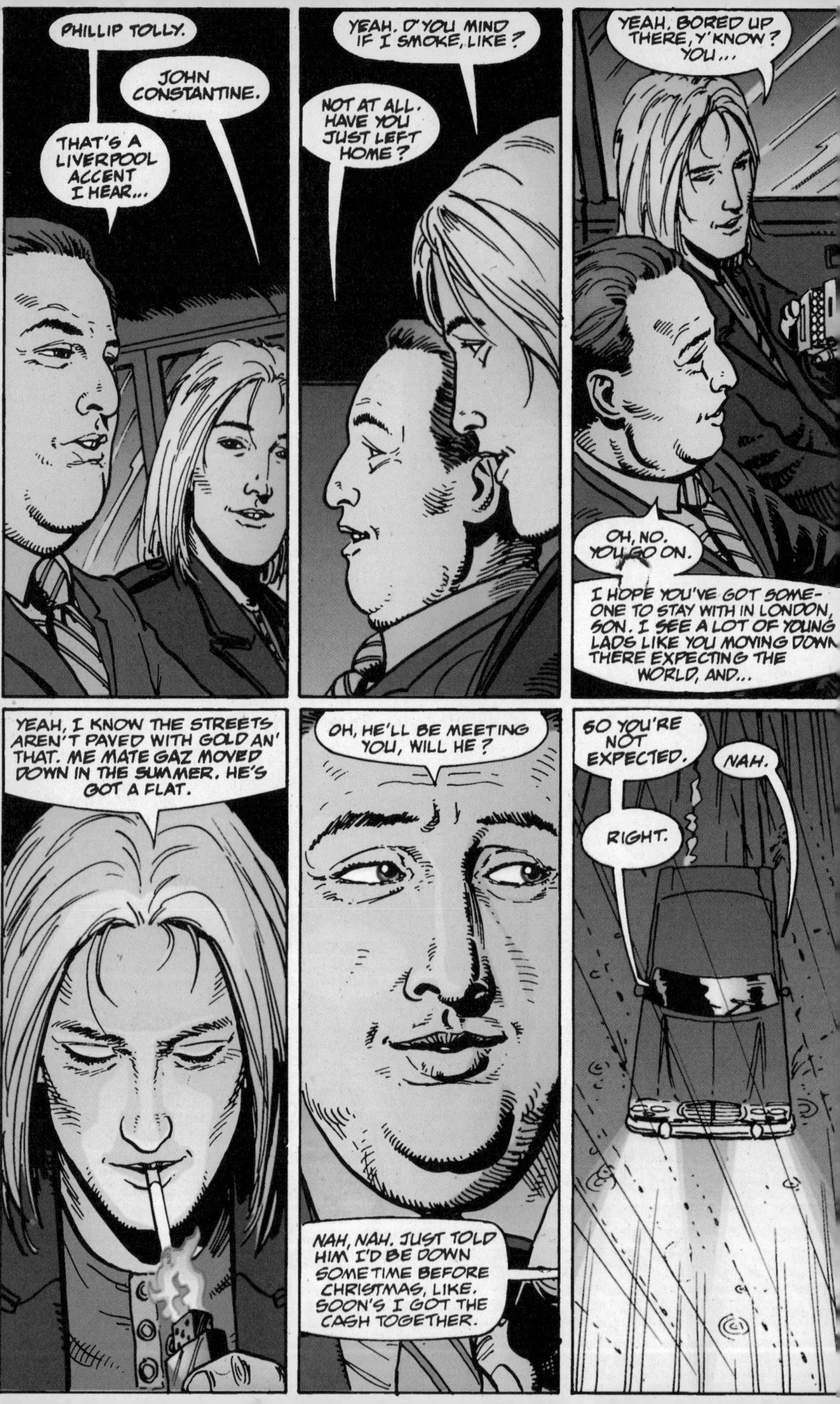
PHILLIP TOLLY.
JOHN CONSTANTINE.
THAT'S A LIVERPOOL ACCENT I HEAR...
YEAH. D'YOU MIND IF I SMOKE, LIKE?
NOT AT ALL. HAVE YOU JUST LEFT HOME?
YEAH. BORED UP THERE, Y'KNOW? YOU...
OH, NO. YOU GO ON.
I HOPE YOU'VE GOT SOMEONE TO STAY WITH IN LONDON, SON. I SEE A LOT OF YOUNG LADS LIKE YOU MOVING DOWN THERE EXPECTING THE WORLD, AND...
YEAH, I KNOW THE STREETS AREN'T PAVED WITH GOLD AN' THAT. ME MATE GAZ MOVED DOWN IN THE SUMMER. HE'S GOT A FLAT.
OH, HE'LL BE MEETING YOU, WILL HE?
NAH, NAH. JUST TOLD HIM I'D BE DOWN SOMETIME BEFORE CHRISTMAS, LIKE. SOON'S I GOT THE CASH TOGETHER.
SO YOU'RE NOT EXPECTED.
NAH.
RIGHT.

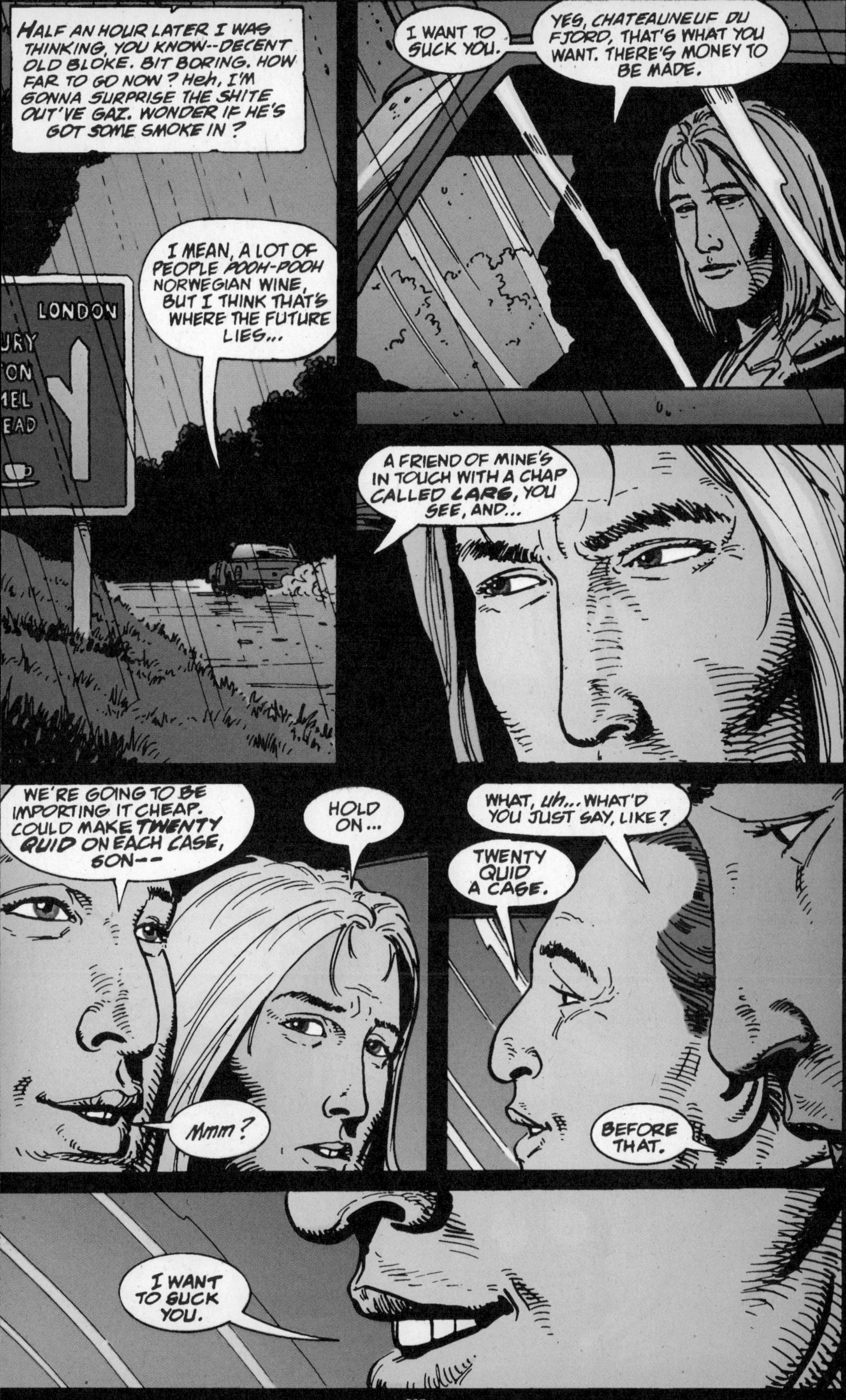
HALF AN HOUR LATER I WAS THINKING, YOU KNOW--DECENT OLD BLOKE. BIT BORING. HOW FAR TO GO NOW? Heh, I'M GONNA SURPRISE THE SHITE OUT'VE GAZ. WONDER IF HE'S GOT SOME SMOKE IN?
LONDON
URY
TON
MEL
EAD
I MEAN, A LOT OF PEOPLE POOH-POOH NORWEGIAN WINE, BUT I THINK THAT'S WHERE THE FUTURE LIES...
I WANT TO SUCK YOU.
YES, CHATEAUNEUF DU FJORD, THAT'S WHAT YOU WANT. THERE'S MONEY TO BE MADE.
A FRIEND OF MINE'S IN TOUCH WITH A CHAP CALLED LARS, YOU SEE, AND...
WE'RE GOING TO BE IMPORTING IT CHEAP. COULD MAKE TWENTY QUID ON EACH CASE, SON--
HOLD ON...
Mmm?
WHAT, uh... WHAT'D YOU JUST SAY, LIKE?
TWENTY QUID A CASE.
BEFORE THAT.
I WANT TO SUCK YOU.

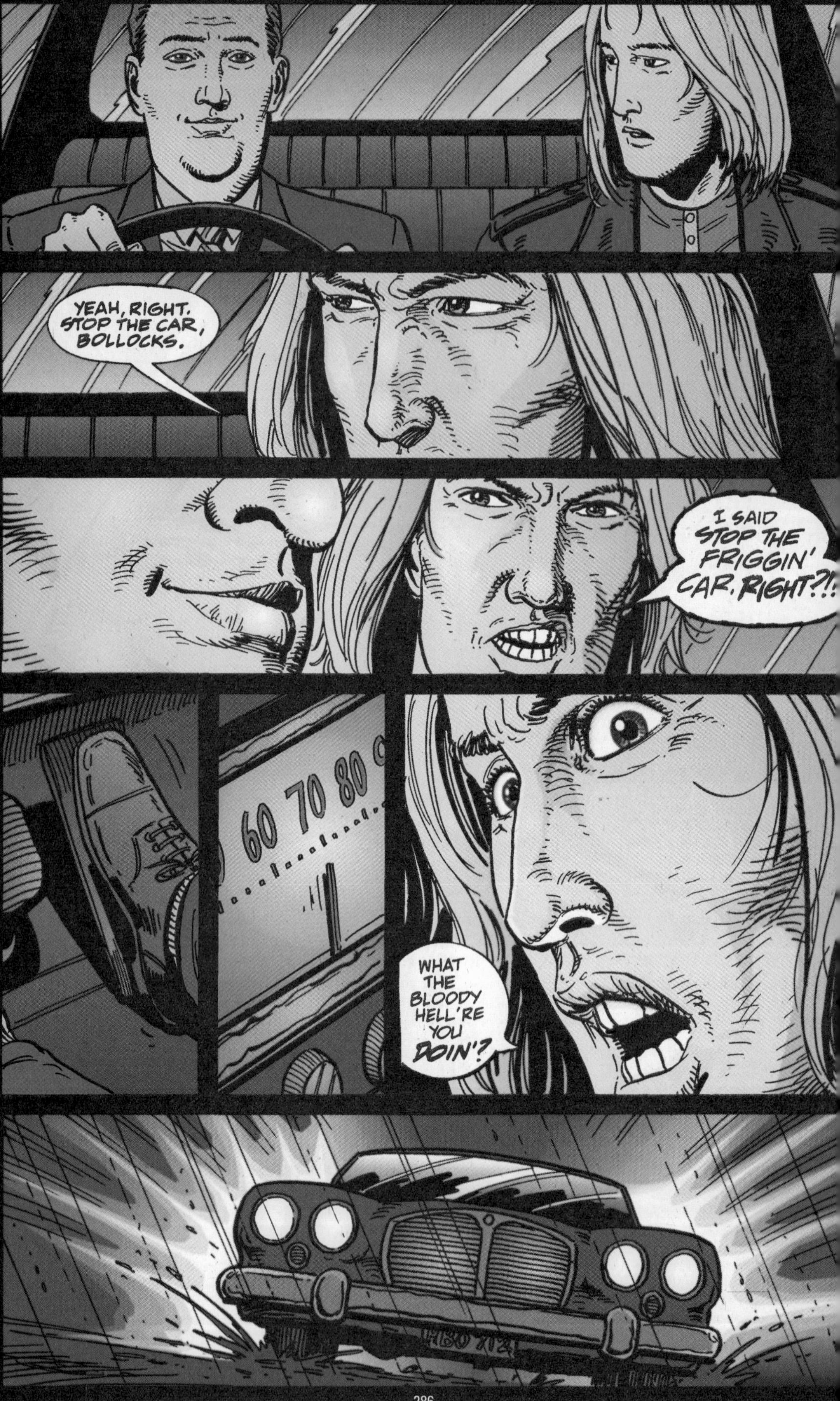
YEAH, RIGHT. STOP THE CAR, BOLLOCKS.
I SAID STOP THE FRIGGIN' CAR, RIGHT?!
60 70 80
WHAT THE BLOODY HELL'RE YOU DOIN'?

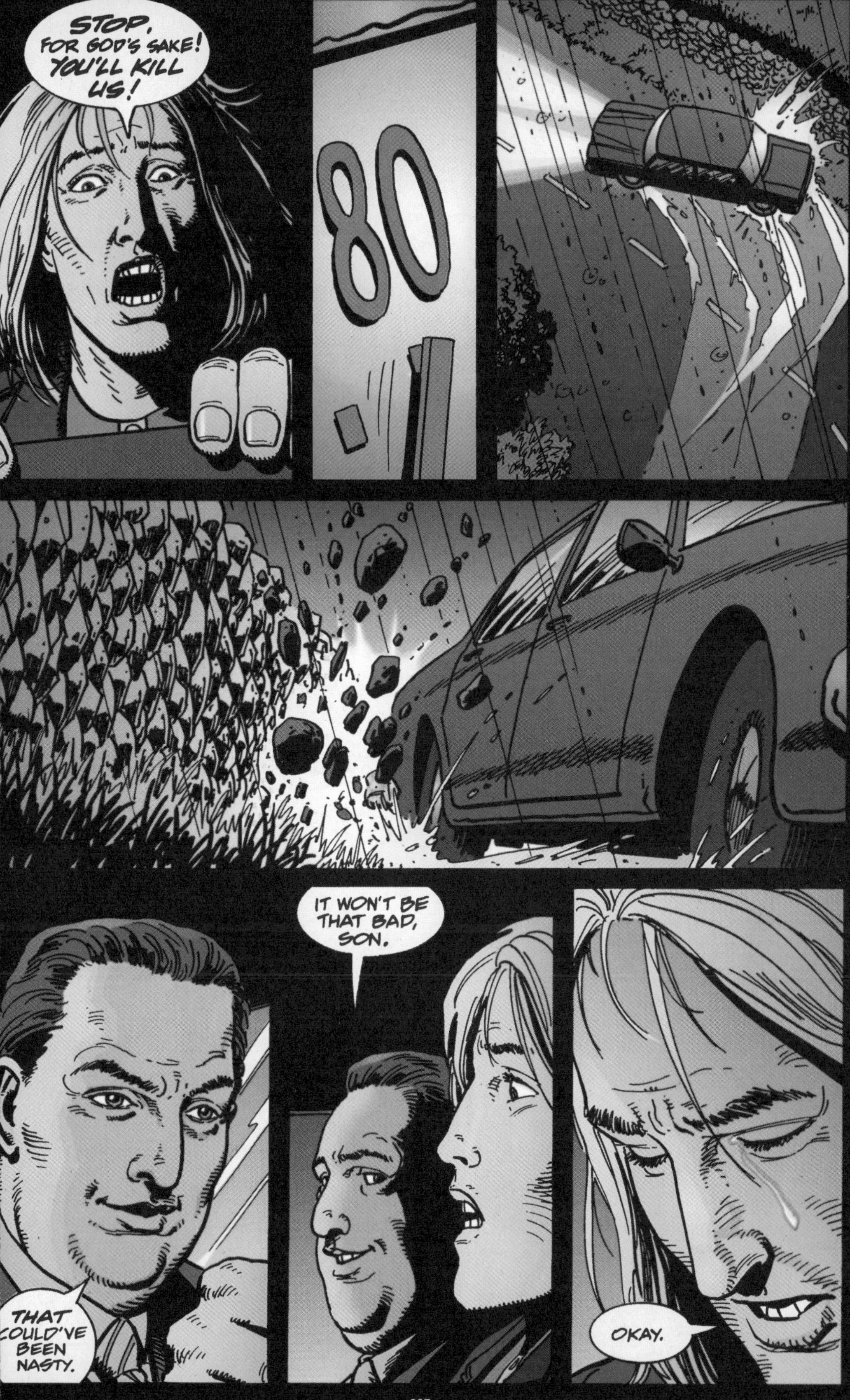
STOP, FOR GOD'S SAKE! YOU'LL KILL US!
80
IT WON'T BE THAT BAD, SON.
THAT COULD'VE BEEN NASTY.
OKAY.

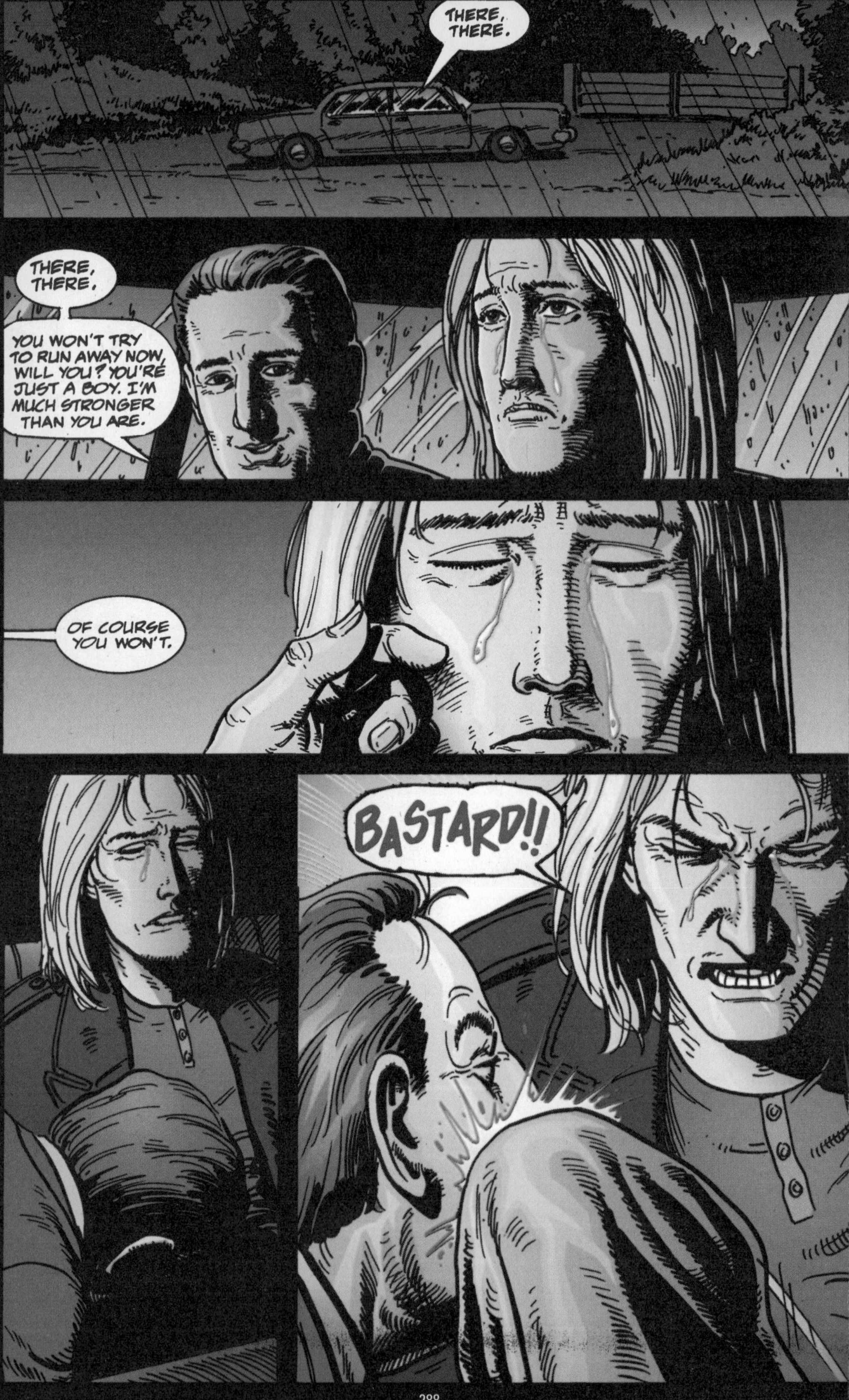

THERE, THERE.
THERE, THERE.
YOU WON'T TRY TO RUN AWAY NOW, WILL YOU? YOU'RE JUST A BOY. I'M MUCH STRONGER THAN YOU ARE.
OF COURSE YOU WON'T.
BASTARD!!

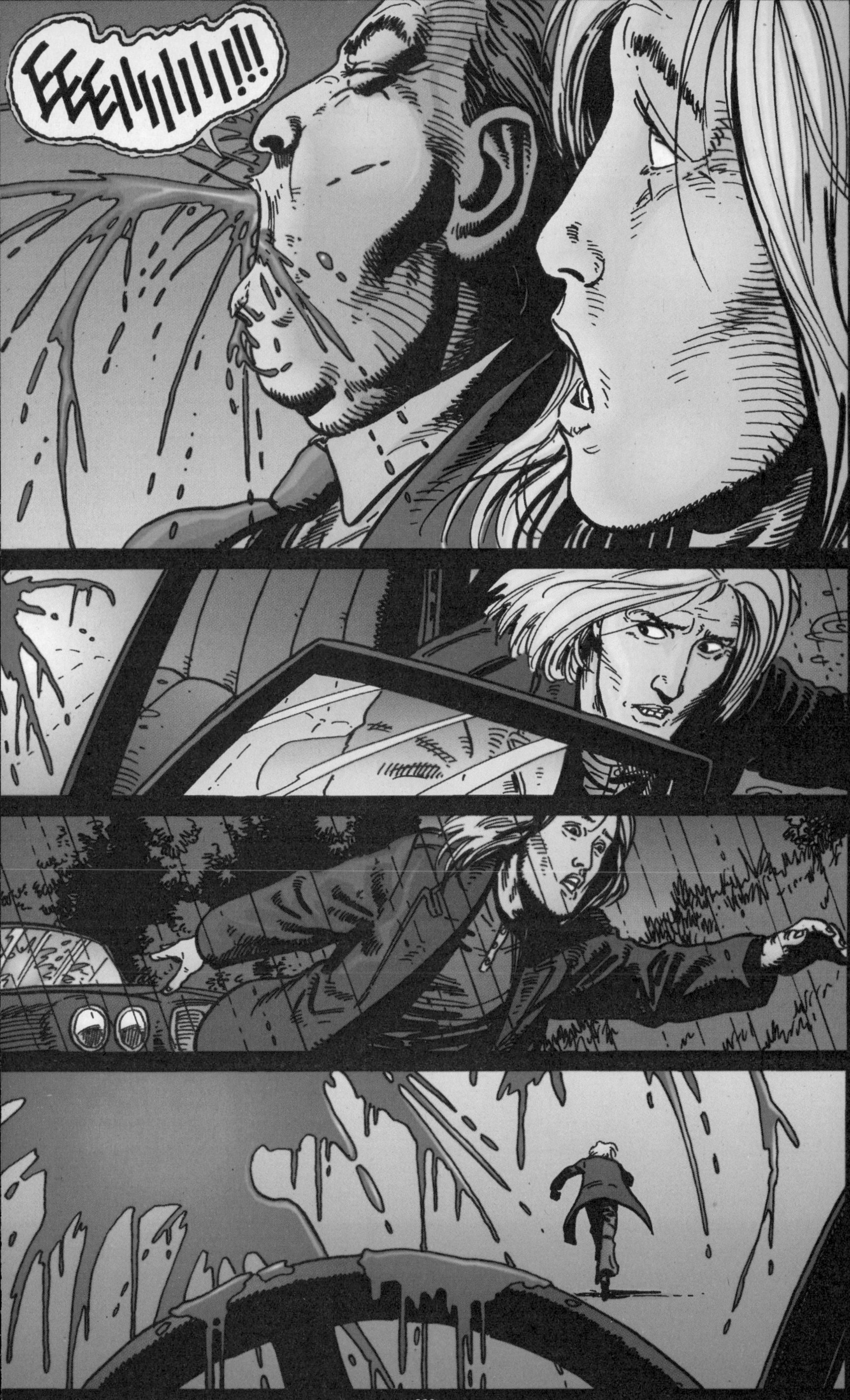
EEEIIIIIII!!!

WHY WAS THERE SO MUCH BLOOD?

THAT'S ALL I COULD THINK OF. NOT "SOME WANKER JUST TRIED TO SUCK ME DICK" OR "I'M STRANDED MILES FROM NOWHERE WITHOUT ME GEAR"--

WHY SO MUCH BLOOD?

YOU DON'T BLEED LIKE THAT WHEN YOU BITE YOUR LIP OR BREAK YOUR NOSE, OR EVEN SEVER YOUR TONGUE--

HUHHHHHHH!!

HUUUUU-HUHHH4HH!

SON?

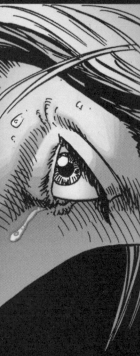

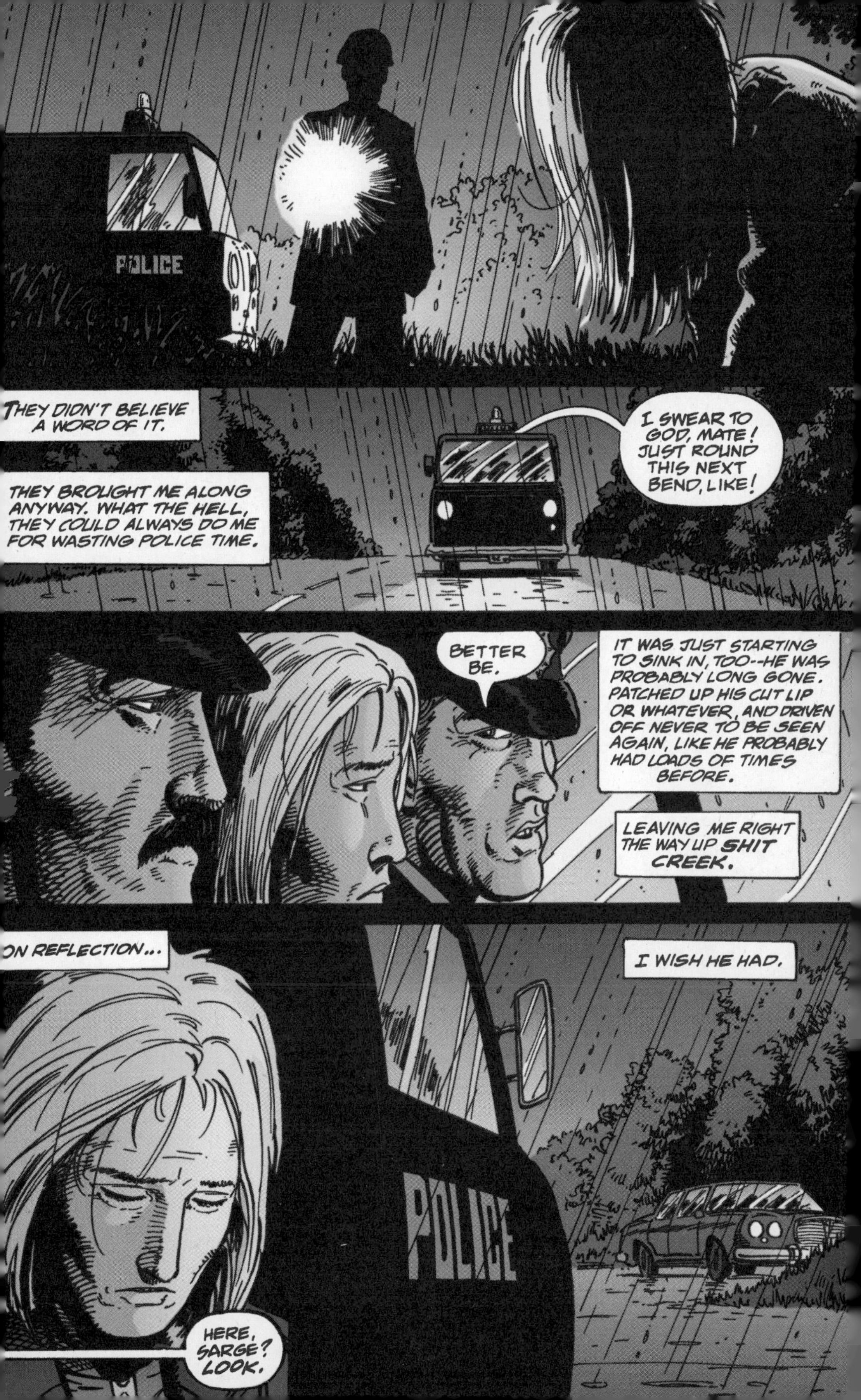
POLICE
THEY DIDN'T BELIEVE A WORD OF IT.
THEY BROUGHT ME ALONG ANYWAY. WHAT THE HELL, THEY COULD ALWAYS DO ME FOR WASTING POLICE TIME.
I SWEAR TO GOD, MATE! JUST ROUND THIS NEXT BEND, LIKE!
BETTER BE.
IT WAS JUST STARTING TO SINK IN, TOO--HE WAS PROBABLY LONG GONE. PATCHED UP HIS CUT LIP OR WHATEVER, AND DRIVEN OFF NEVER TO BE SEEN AGAIN, LIKE HE PROBABLY HAD LOADS OF TIMES BEFORE.
LEAVING ME RIGHT THE WAY UP SHIT CREEK.
ON REFLECTION...
I WISH HE HAD.
POLICE
HERE, SARGE? LOOK.

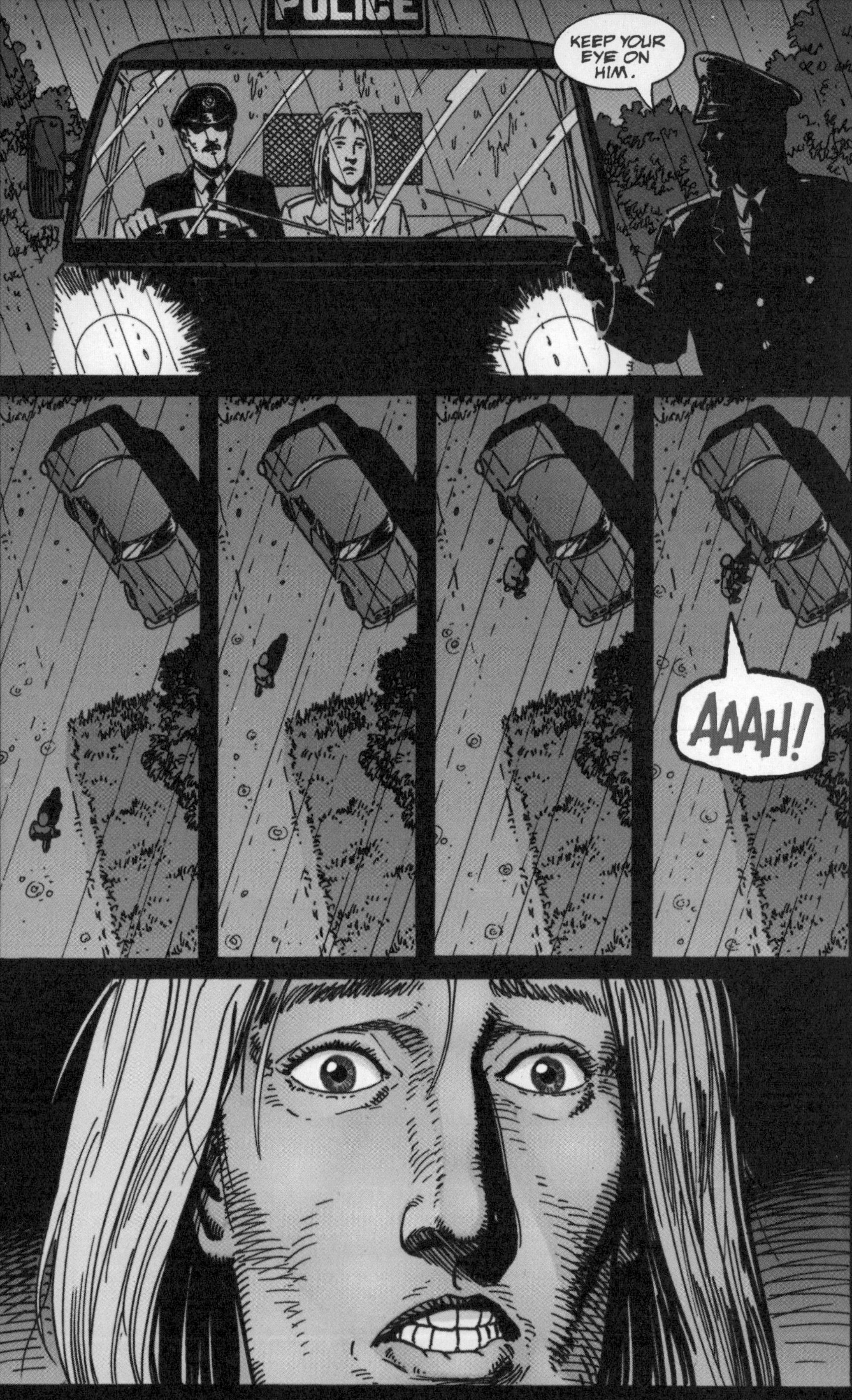
POLICE
KEEP YOUR EYE ON HIM.
AAAH!

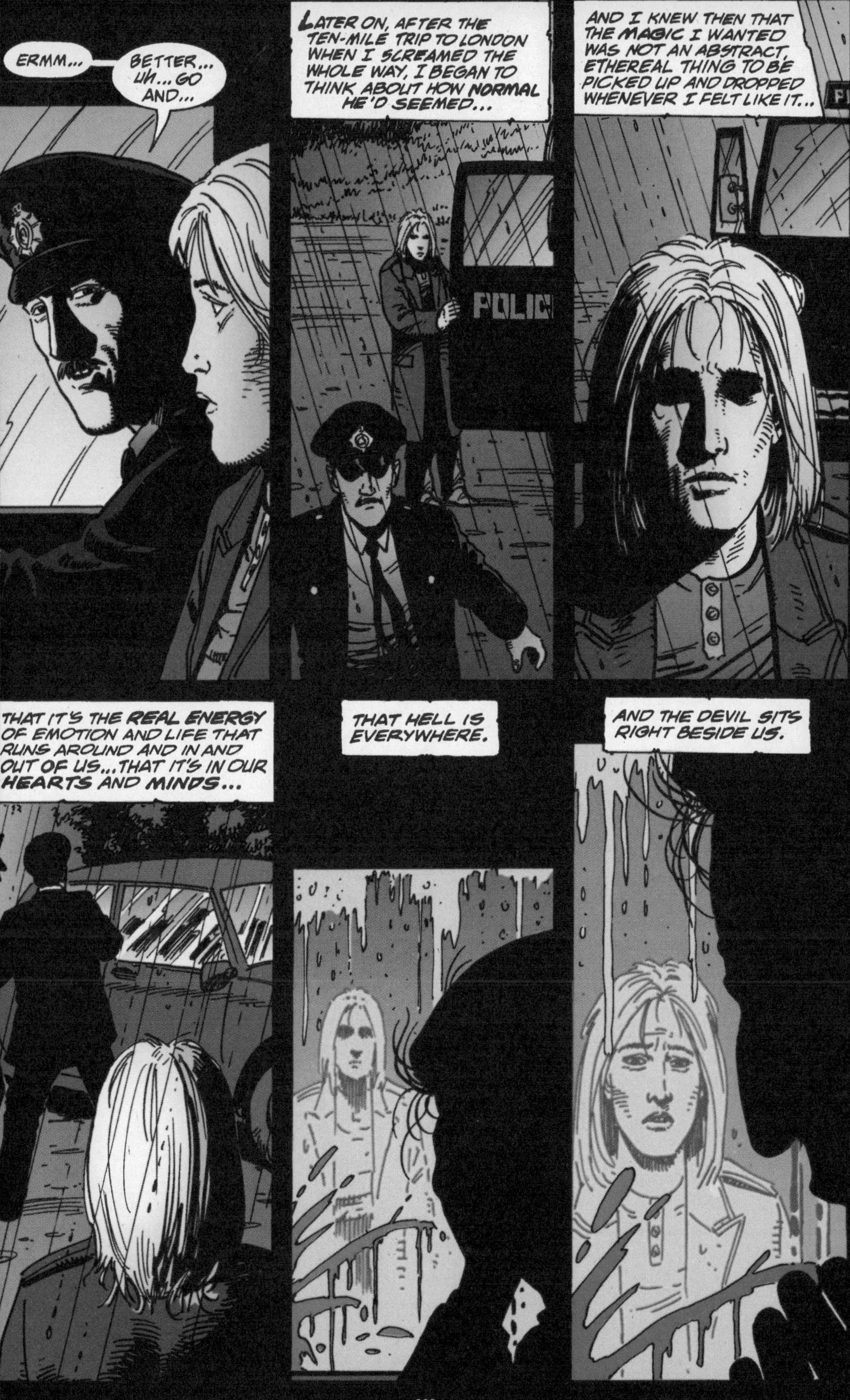
ERMM...
BETTER... UH...GO AND...
LATER ON, AFTER THE TEN-MILE TRIP TO LONDON WHEN I SCREAMED THE WHOLE WAY, I BEGAN TO THINK ABOUT HOW NORMAL HE'D SEEMED...
POLIC
AND I KNEW THEN THAT THE MAGIC I WANTED WAS NOT AN ABSTRACT, ETHEREAL THING TO BE PICKED UP AND DROPPED WHENEVER I FELT LIKE IT...
THAT IT'S THE REAL ENERGY OF EMOTION AND LIFE THAT RUNS AROUND AND IN AND OUT OF US...THAT IT'S IN OUR HEARTS AND MINDS...
THAT HELL IS EVERYWHERE.
AND THE DEVIL SITS RIGHT BESIDE US.

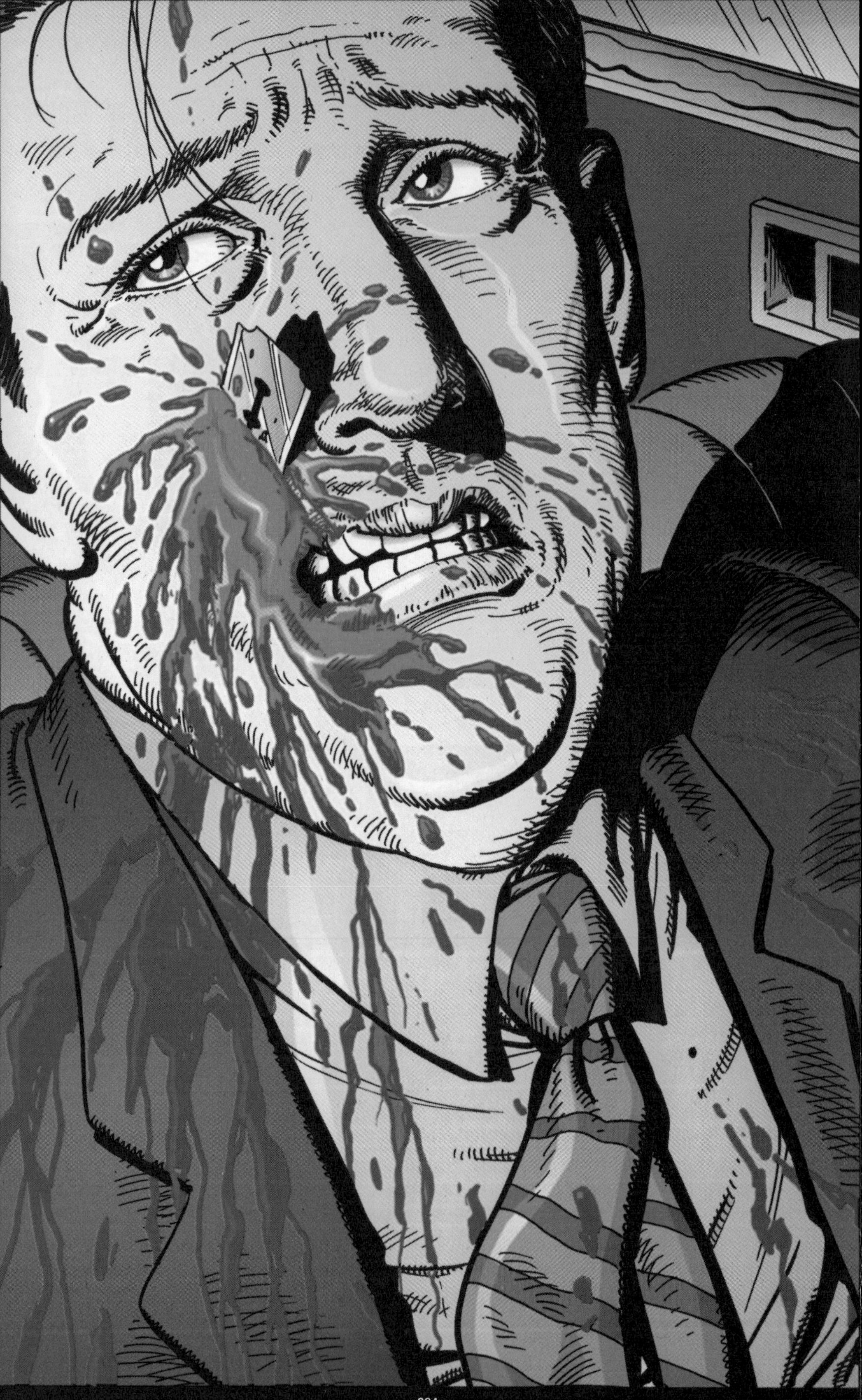

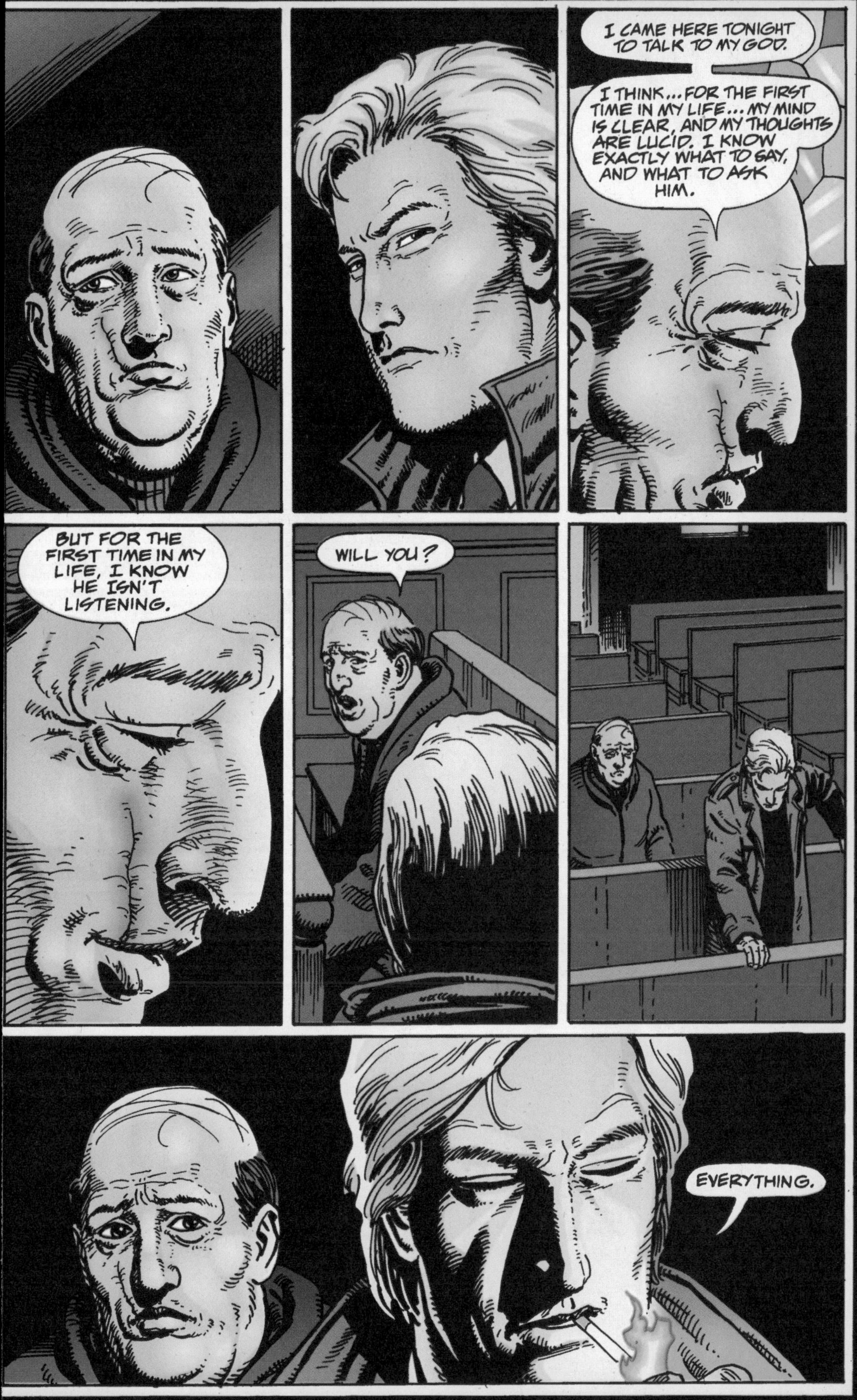
I CAME HERE TONIGHT TO TALK TO MY GOD.
I THINK... FOR THE FIRST TIME IN MY LIFE... MY MIND IS CLEAR, AND MY THOUGHTS ARE LUCID. I KNOW EXACTLY WHAT TO SAY, AND WHAT TO ASK HIM.
BUT FOR THE FIRST TIME IN MY LIFE, I KNOW HE ISN'T LISTENING.
WILL YOU?
EVERYTHING.

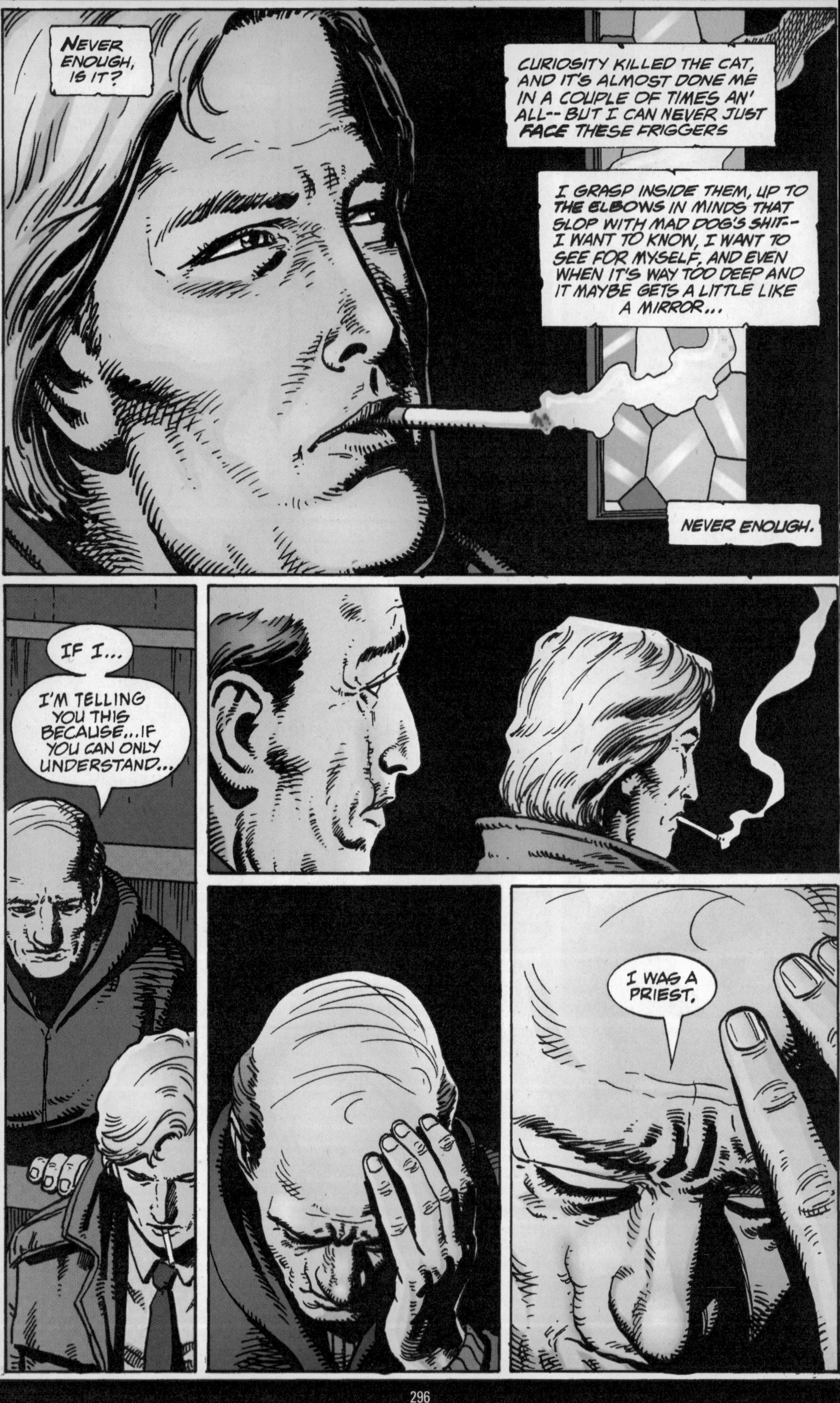
NEVER ENOUGH, IS IT?
CURIOSITY KILLED THE CAT, AND IT'S ALMOST DONE ME IN A COUPLE OF TIMES AN' ALL-- BUT I CAN NEVER JUST FACE THESE FRIGGERS
I GRASP INSIDE THEM, UP TO THE ELBOWS IN MINDS THAT SLOP WITH MAD DOG'S SHIT-- I WANT TO KNOW, I WANT TO SEE FOR MYSELF, AND EVEN WHEN IT'S WAY TOO DEEP AND IT MAYBE GETS A LITTLE LIKE A MIRROR...
NEVER ENOUGH.
IF I...
I'M TELLING YOU THIS BECAUSE...IF YOU CAN ONLY UNDERSTAND...
I WAS A PRIEST.

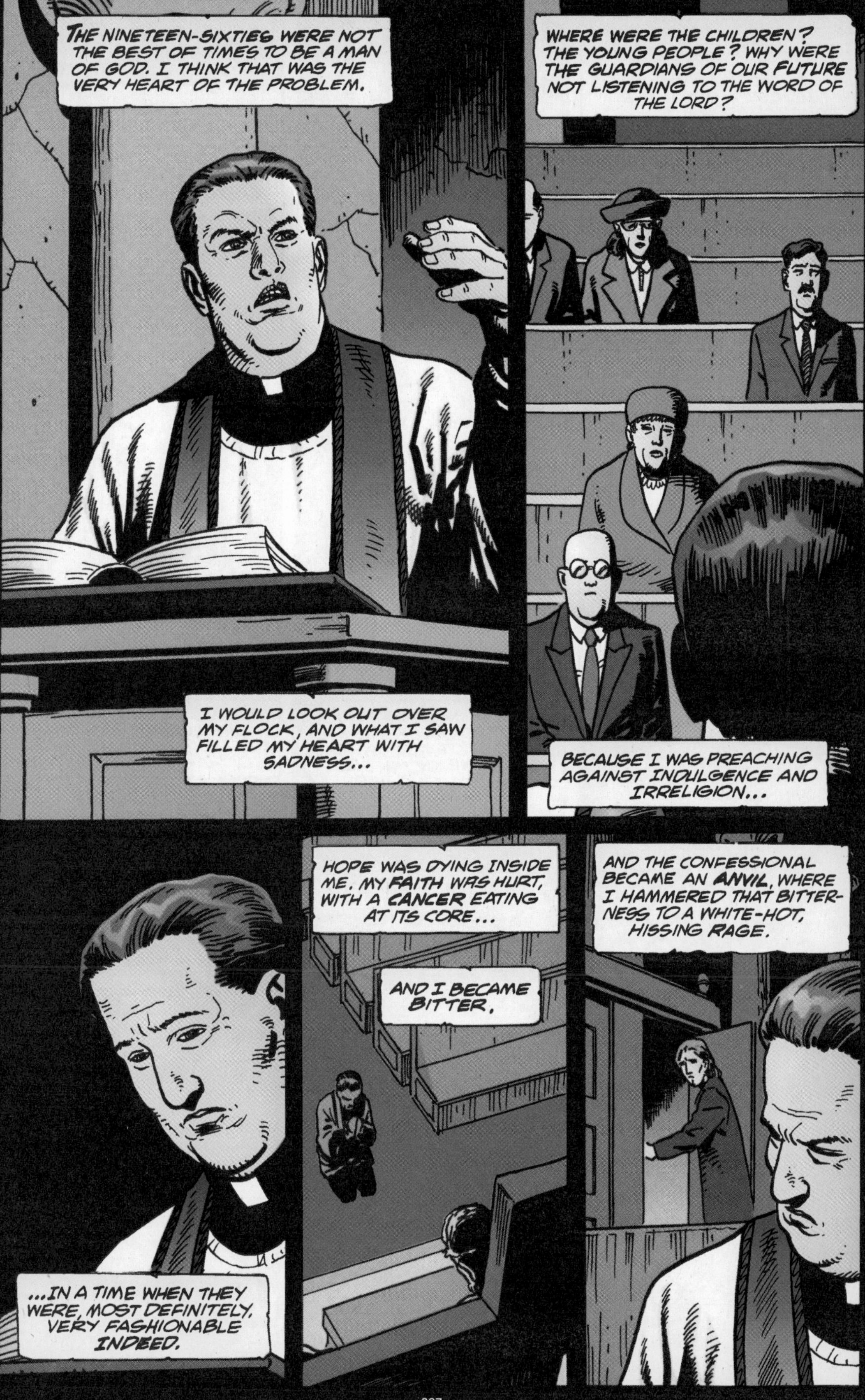
THE NINETEEN-SIXTIES WERE NOT THE BEST OF TIMES TO BE A MAN OF GOD. I THINK THAT WAS THE VERY HEART OF THE PROBLEM.
I WOULD LOOK OUT OVER MY FLOCK, AND WHAT I SAW FILLED MY HEART WITH SADNESS...
WHERE WERE THE CHILDREN? THE YOUNG PEOPLE? WHY WERE THE GUARDIANS OF OUR FUTURE NOT LISTENING TO THE WORD OF THE LORD?
BECAUSE I WAS PREACHING AGAINST INDULGENCE AND IRRELIGION...
...IN A TIME WHEN THEY WERE, MOST DEFINITELY, VERY FASHIONABLE INDEED.
HOPE WAS DYING INSIDE ME. MY FAITH WAS HURT, WITH A CANCER EATING AT ITS CORE...
AND I BECAME BITTER.
AND THE CONFESSIONAL BECAME AN ANVIL, WHERE I HAMMERED THAT BITTERNESS TO A WHITE-HOT, HISSING RAGE.

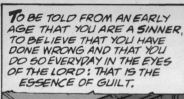

TO BE TOLD FROM AN EARLY AGE THAT YOU ARE A *SINNER*, TO BELIEVE THAT YOU HAVE DONE WRONG AND THAT YOU DO SO EVERYDAY IN THE EYES OF THE LORD: THAT IS THE ESSENCE OF GUILT.

IN THE CATHOLIC CHURCH, WE HAVE HONED IT TO A FINE ART.

FOR A FEW, IMPRESSIONABLE SOULS-- EVEN IN A LIBERAL AGE-- IT IS A DIFFICULT THING TO FORGET.

uh... I'M A BIT... I FEEL, Y'KNOW, CONFUSED AT THE MINUTE--

NO.

uh... SORRY?

YOU MUST BEGIN "FORGIVE ME, FATHER, FOR I HAVE SINNED." THEN YOU MUST TELL ME HOW LONG IT HAS BEEN SINCE YOUR *LAST* CONFESSION.

THEN YOU MAY CONFESS YOUR SINS.

OH.

em... FORGIVE ME, FATHER, FOR I HAVE SINNED. I HAVEN'T CONFESSED IN... IN A FEW YEARS, I SUPPOSE.

I WAS AT THIS PARTY THE OTHER NIGHT, RIGHT? AND ONE OF ME MATES, LIKE, WE'VE KNOWN EACH OTHER SINCE WE WERE NIPPERS...

IT TRANSPIRED THAT, UNDER THE INFLUENCE OF CANNABIS AND L.S.D., THEY HAD MADE WHAT HE CHOSE TO CALL "LOVE".

AND HE WASN'T SURE WHAT TO FEEL ABOUT IT.

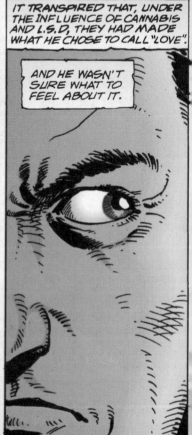

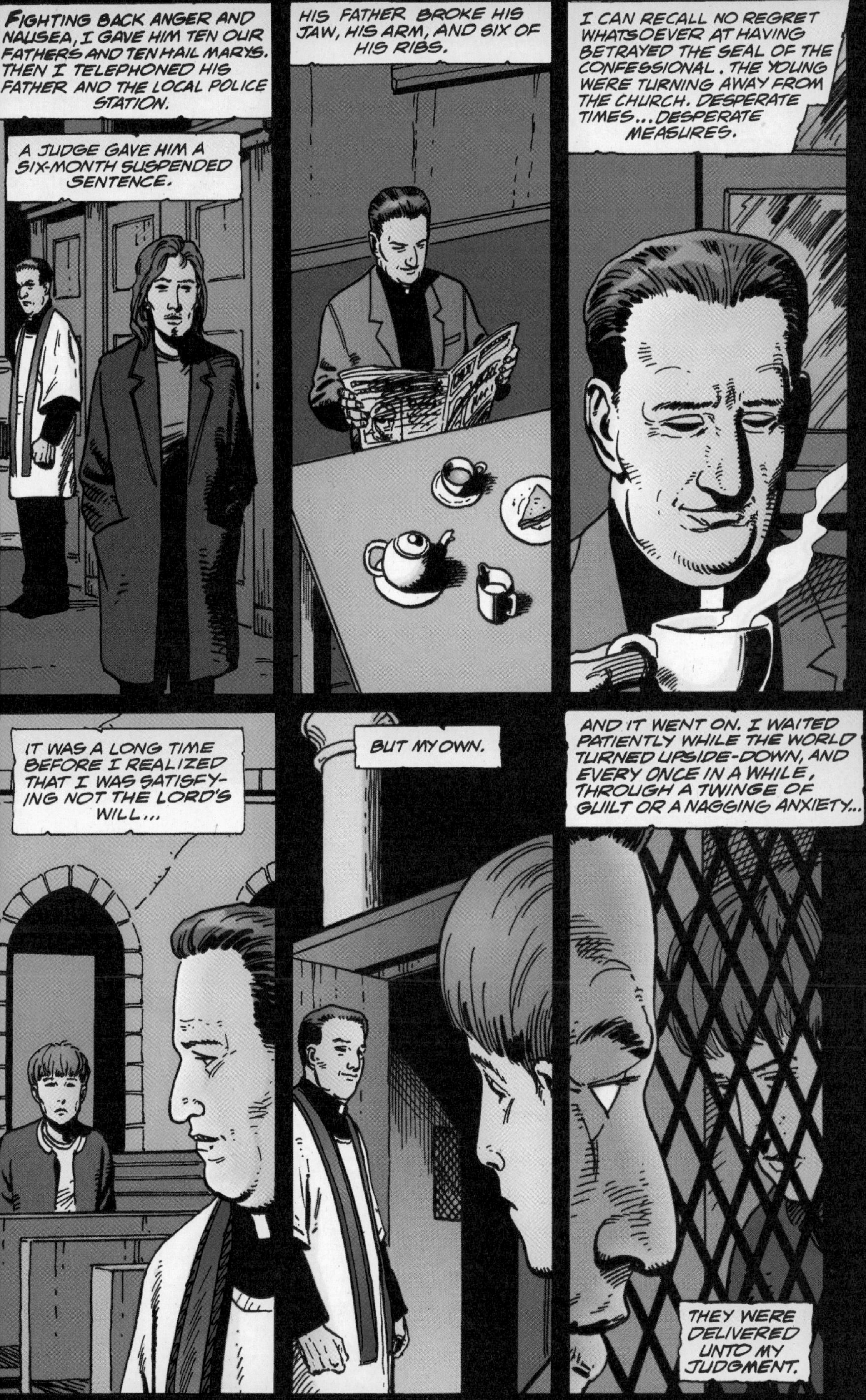
FIGHTING BACK ANGER AND NAUSEA, I GAVE HIM TEN OUR FATHERS AND TEN HAIL MARYS. THEN I TELEPHONED HIS FATHER AND THE LOCAL POLICE STATION.
A JUDGE GAVE HIM A SIX-MONTH SUSPENDED SENTENCE.
HIS FATHER BROKE HIS JAW, HIS ARM, AND SIX OF HIS RIBS.
I CAN RECALL NO REGRET WHATSOEVER AT HAVING BETRAYED THE SEAL OF THE CONFESSIONAL. THE YOUNG WERE TURNING AWAY FROM THE CHURCH. DESPERATE TIMES... DESPERATE MEASURES.
IT WAS A LONG TIME BEFORE I REALIZED THAT I WAS SATISFY-ING NOT THE LORD'S WILL...
BUT MY OWN.
AND IT WENT ON. I WAITED PATIENTLY WHILE THE WORLD TURNED UPSIDE-DOWN, AND EVERY ONCE IN A WHILE, THROUGH A TWINGE OF GUILT OR A NAGGING ANXIETY...
THEY WERE DELIVERED UNTO MY JUDGMENT.

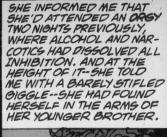

I LISTENED TO THE EVIL OF THE LOVE GENERATION, A LICENTIOUSNESS THAT FILLED ME WITH HATE. MY PUNISHMENTS WERE DELIVERED BY PARENTS AND CONSTABULARY, REQUIRING NOTHING FROM ME BUT A CAREFUL WORD, A SOLICITOUS PHONE CALL...

UNTIL, ONE EVENING, A YOUNG WOMAN CAME TO CONFESS HER SINS TO GOD.

SHE INFORMED ME THAT SHE'D ATTENDED AN ORGY TWO NIGHTS PREVIOUSLY, WHERE ALCOHOL AND NARCOTICS HAD DISSOLVED ALL INHIBITION. AND AT THE HEIGHT OF IT-- SHE TOLD ME WITH A BARELY STIFLED GIGGLE-- SHE HAD FOUND HERSELF IN THE ARMS OF HER YOUNGER BROTHER.

Y'KNOW?

FATHER?

I MEAN, LIKE, HE PROBABLY FEELS WORSE ABOUT IT THAN I DO...

AAAAOW! FATHER--!

HARLOT!

AAAAAH!

Heh.

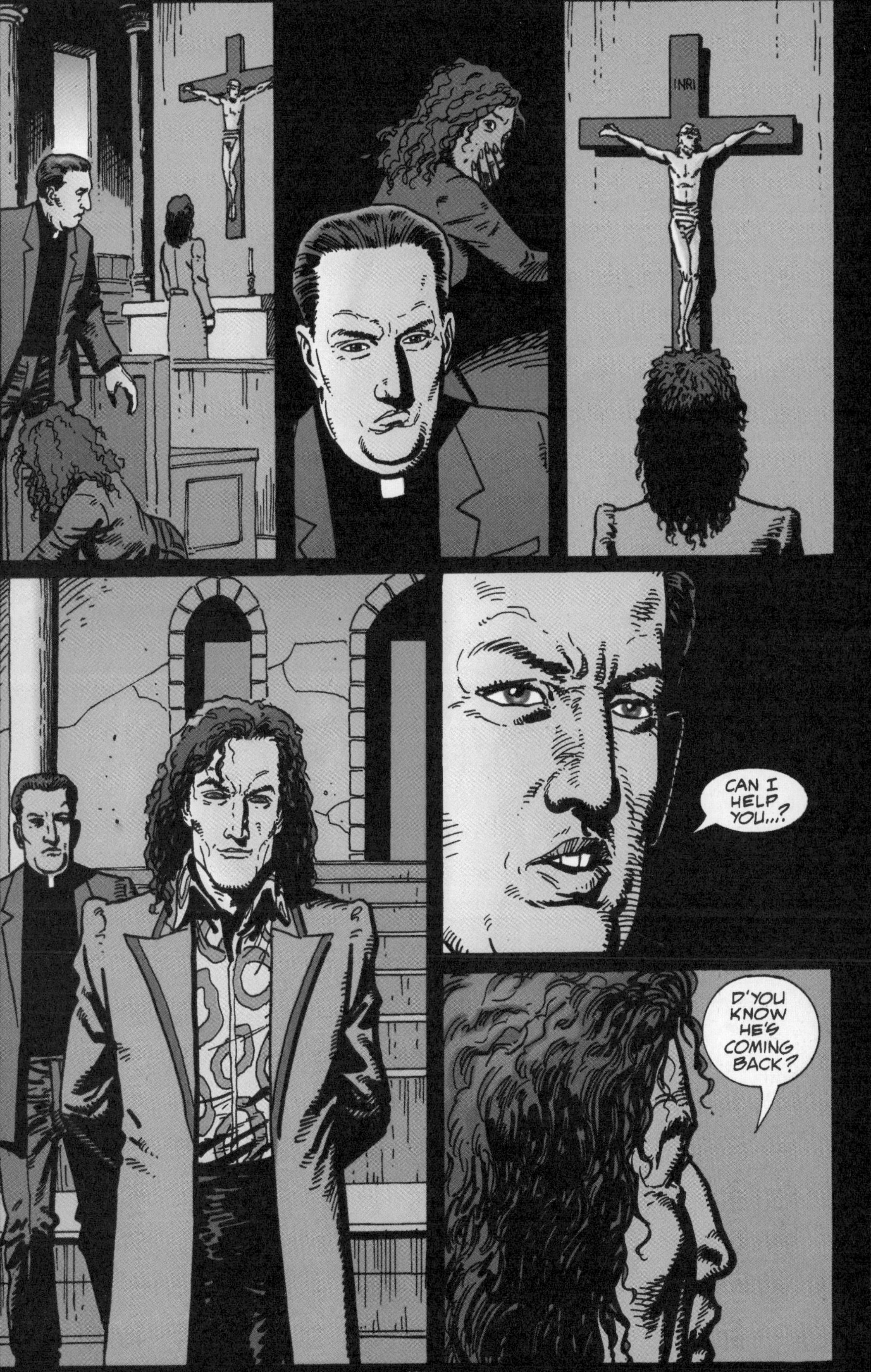
INRI
CAN I HELP YOU...?
D'YOU KNOW HE'S COMING BACK?

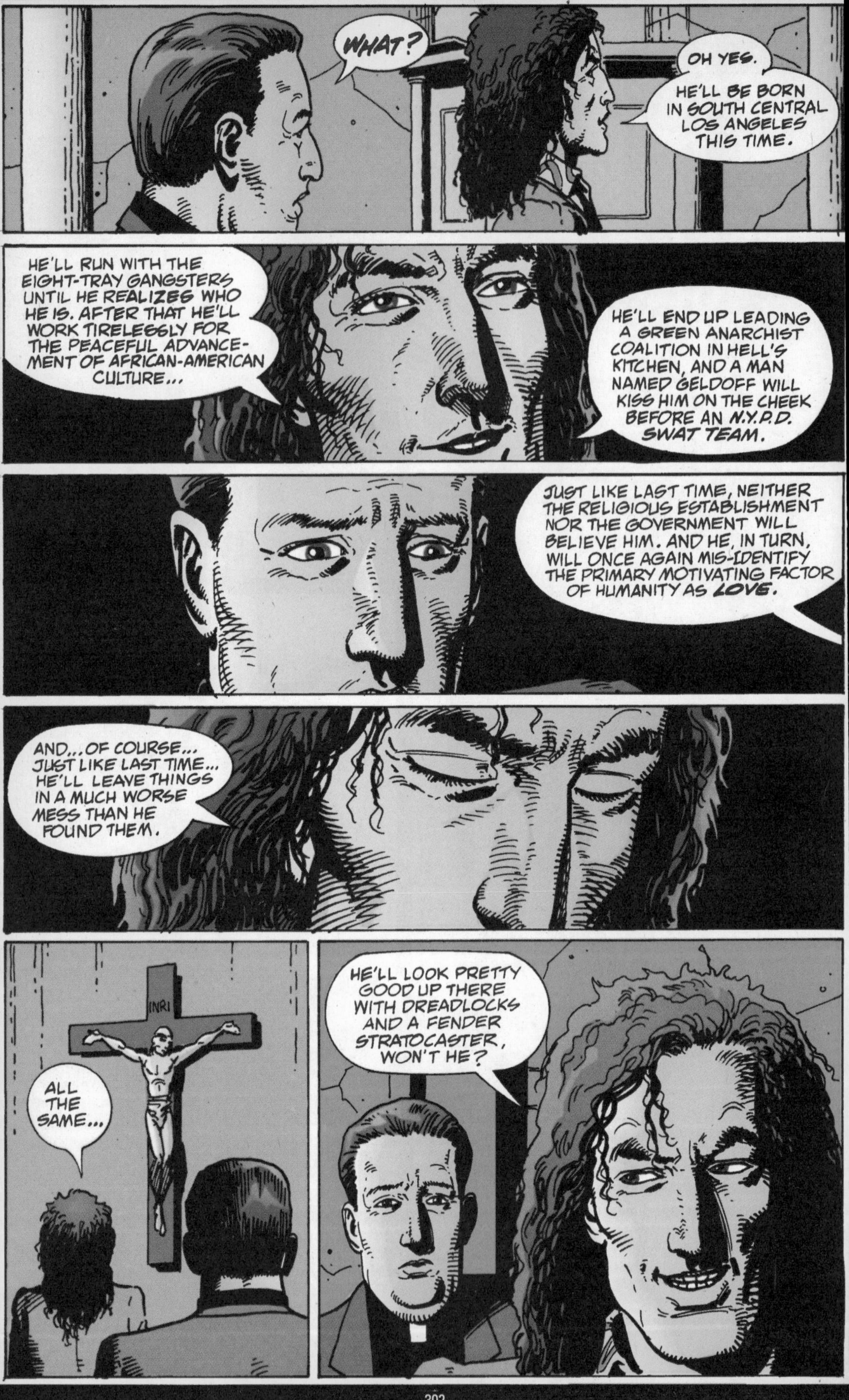
WHAT?
OH YES.
HE'LL BE BORN IN SOUTH CENTRAL LOS ANGELES THIS TIME.
HE'LL RUN WITH THE EIGHT-TRAY GANGSTERS UNTIL HE REALIZES WHO HE IS. AFTER THAT HE'LL WORK TIRELESSLY FOR THE PEACEFUL ADVANCEMENT OF AFRICAN-AMERICAN CULTURE...
HE'LL END UP LEADING A GREEN ANARCHIST COALITION IN HELL'S KITCHEN, AND A MAN NAMED GELDOFF WILL KISS HIM ON THE CHEEK BEFORE AN N.Y.P.D. SWAT TEAM.
JUST LIKE LAST TIME, NEITHER THE RELIGIOUS ESTABLISHMENT NOR THE GOVERNMENT WILL BELIEVE HIM. AND HE, IN TURN, WILL ONCE AGAIN MIS-IDENTIFY THE PRIMARY MOTIVATING FACTOR OF HUMANITY AS LOVE.
AND... OF COURSE... JUST LIKE LAST TIME... HE'LL LEAVE THINGS IN A MUCH WORSE MESS THAN HE FOUND THEM.
INRI
ALL THE SAME...
HE'LL LOOK PRETTY GOOD UP THERE WITH DREADLOCKS AND A FENDER STRATOCASTER, WON'T HE?

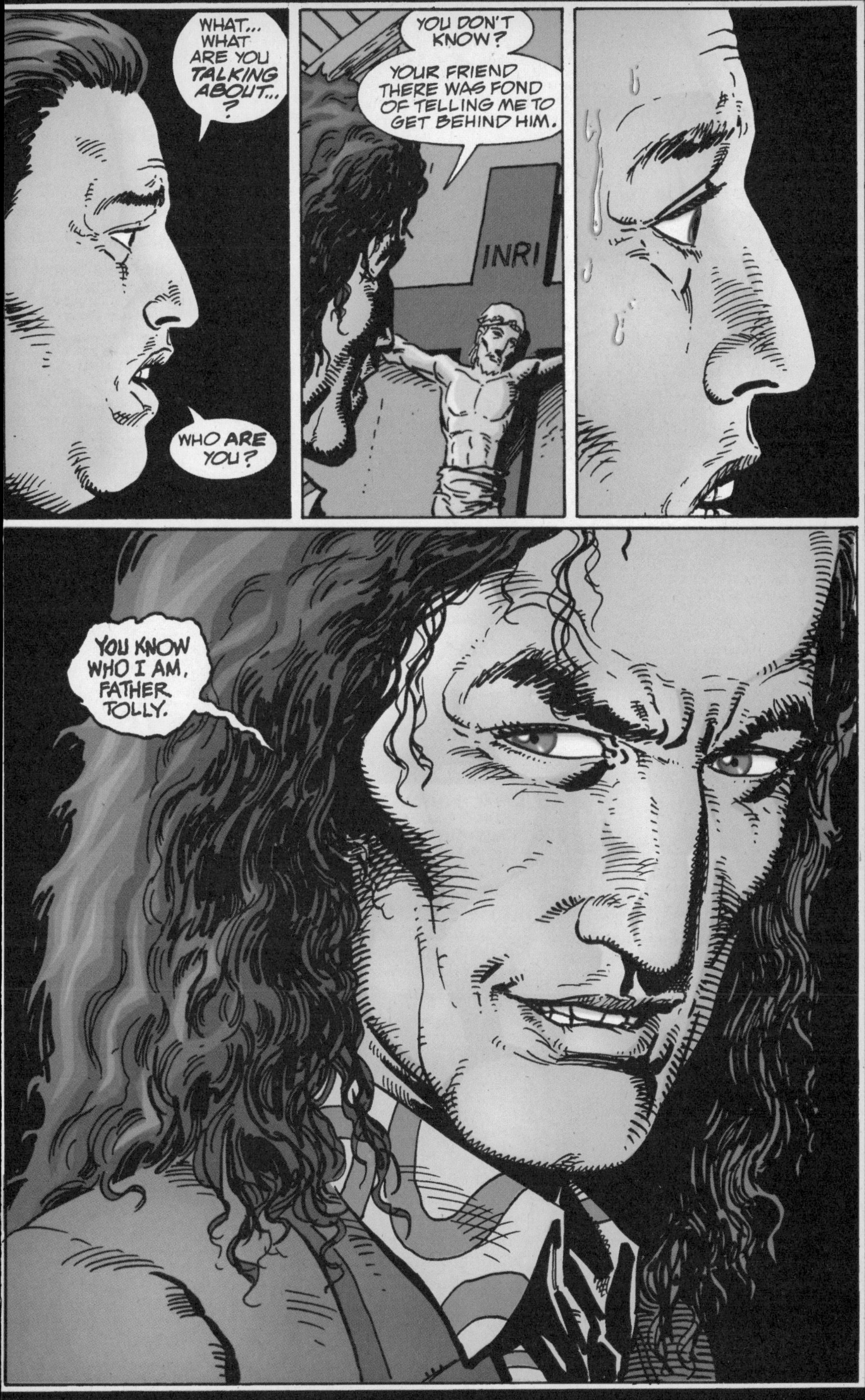

WHAT... WHAT ARE YOU TALKING ABOUT... ?
WHO ARE YOU?
YOU DON'T KNOW?
YOUR FRIEND THERE WAS FOND OF TELLING ME TO GET BEHIND HIM.
INRI
YOU KNOW WHO I AM, FATHER TOLLY.

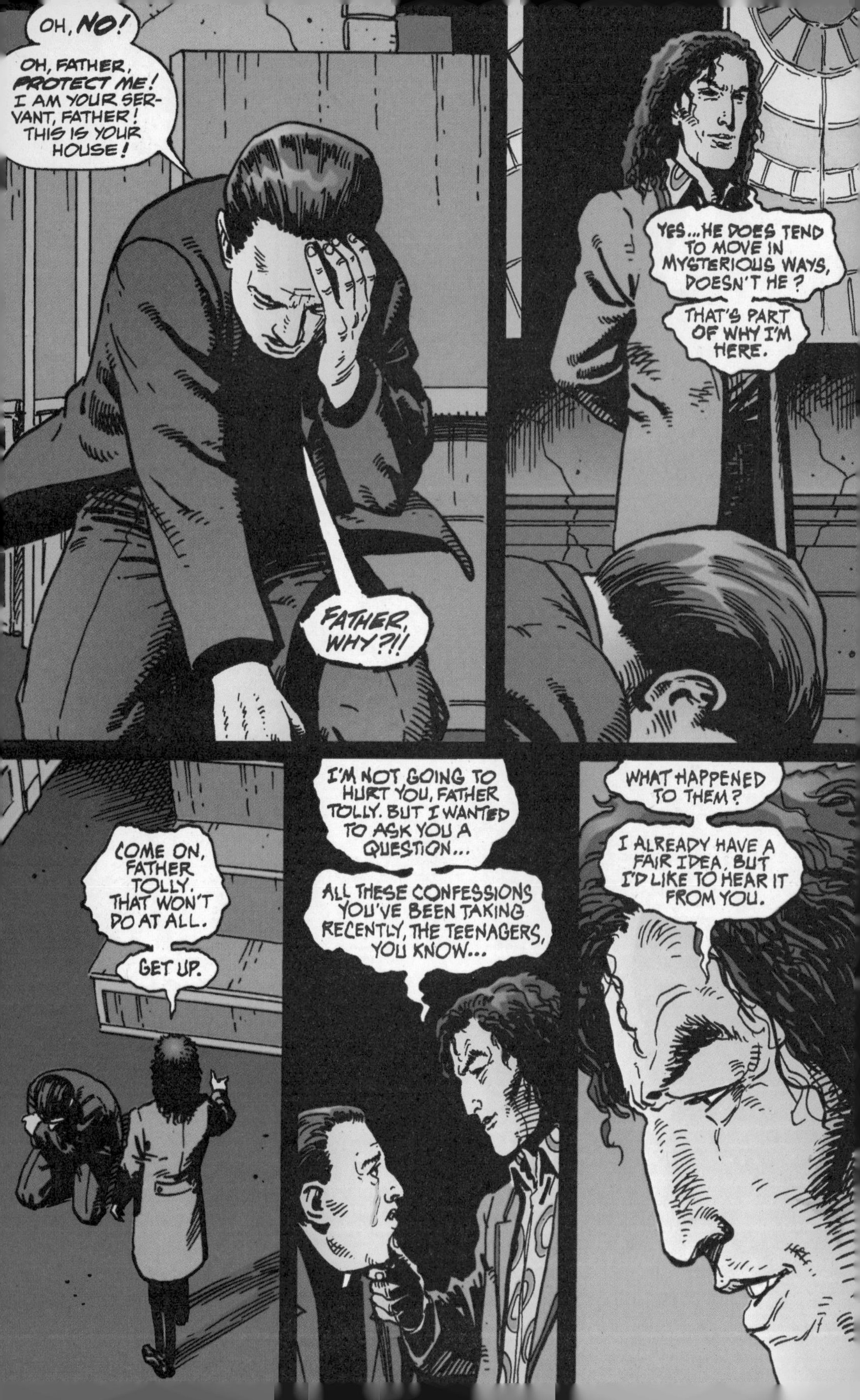
OH, NO!
OH, FATHER, PROTECT ME! I AM YOUR SERVANT, FATHER! THIS IS YOUR HOUSE!
FATHER, WHY?!!
YES... HE DOES TEND TO MOVE IN MYSTERIOUS WAYS, DOESN'T HE?
THAT'S PART OF WHY I'M HERE.
COME ON, FATHER TOLLY. THAT WON'T DO AT ALL.
GET UP.
I'M NOT GOING TO HURT YOU, FATHER TOLLY. BUT I WANTED TO ASK YOU A QUESTION...
ALL THESE CONFESSIONS YOU'VE BEEN TAKING RECENTLY, THE TEENAGERS, YOU KNOW...
WHAT HAPPENED TO THEM?
I ALREADY HAVE A FAIR IDEA, BUT I'D LIKE TO HEAR IT FROM YOU.

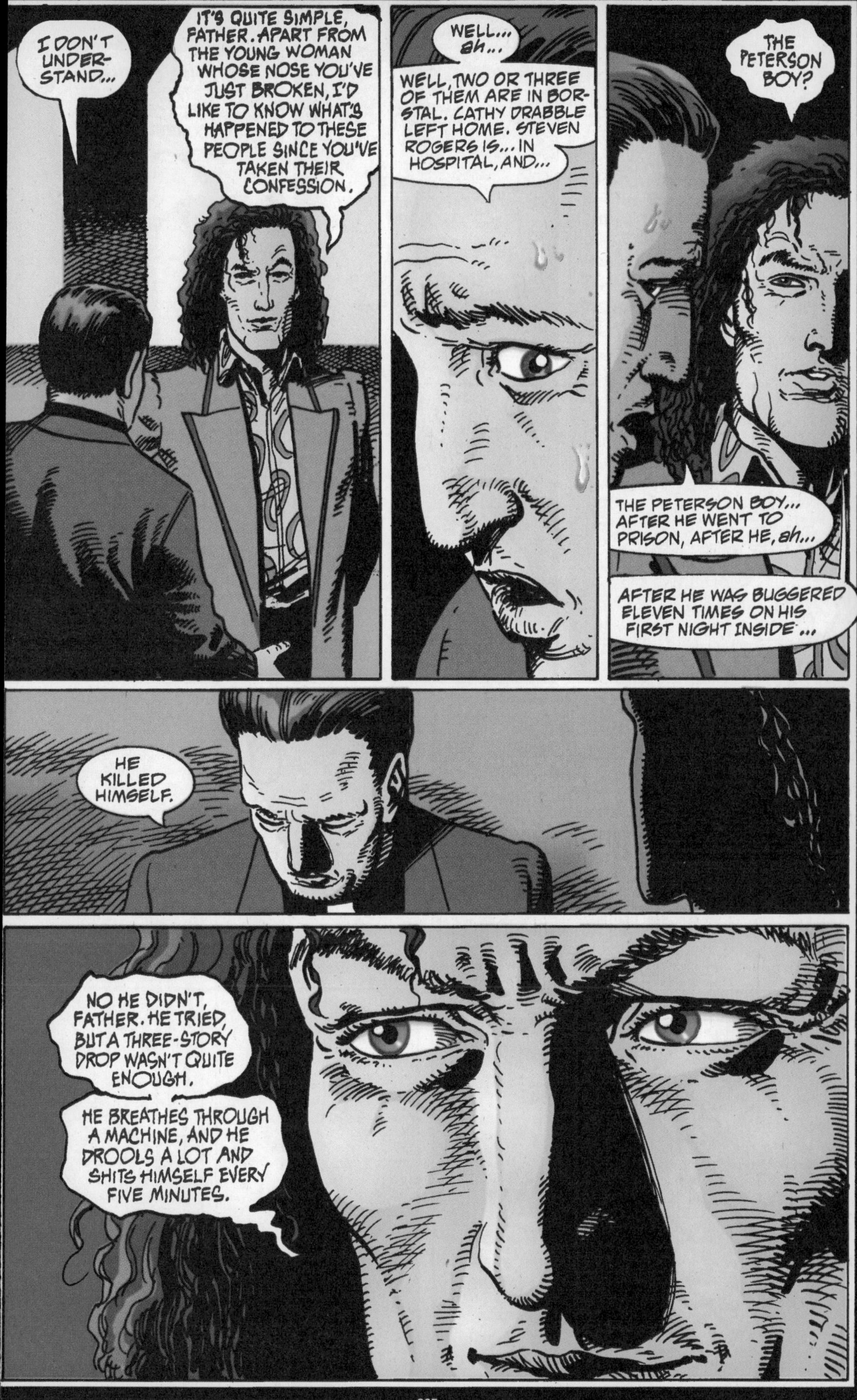
I DON'T UNDER-STAND...
IT'S QUITE SIMPLE, FATHER. APART FROM THE YOUNG WOMAN WHOSE NOSE YOU'VE JUST BROKEN, I'D LIKE TO KNOW WHAT'S HAPPENED TO THESE PEOPLE SINCE YOU'VE TAKEN THEIR CONFESSION.
WELL... ah...
WELL, TWO OR THREE OF THEM ARE IN BOR-STAL. CATHY DRABBLE LEFT HOME. STEVEN ROGERS IS... IN HOSPITAL, AND...
THE PETERSON BOY?
THE PETERSON BOY... AFTER HE WENT TO PRISON, AFTER HE, ah...
AFTER HE WAS BUGGERED ELEVEN TIMES ON HIS FIRST NIGHT INSIDE...
HE KILLED HIMSELF.
NO HE DIDN'T, FATHER. HE TRIED, BUT A THREE-STORY DROP WASN'T QUITE ENOUGH.
HE BREATHES THROUGH A MACHINE, AND HE DROOLS A LOT AND SHITS HIMSELF EVERY FIVE MINUTES.

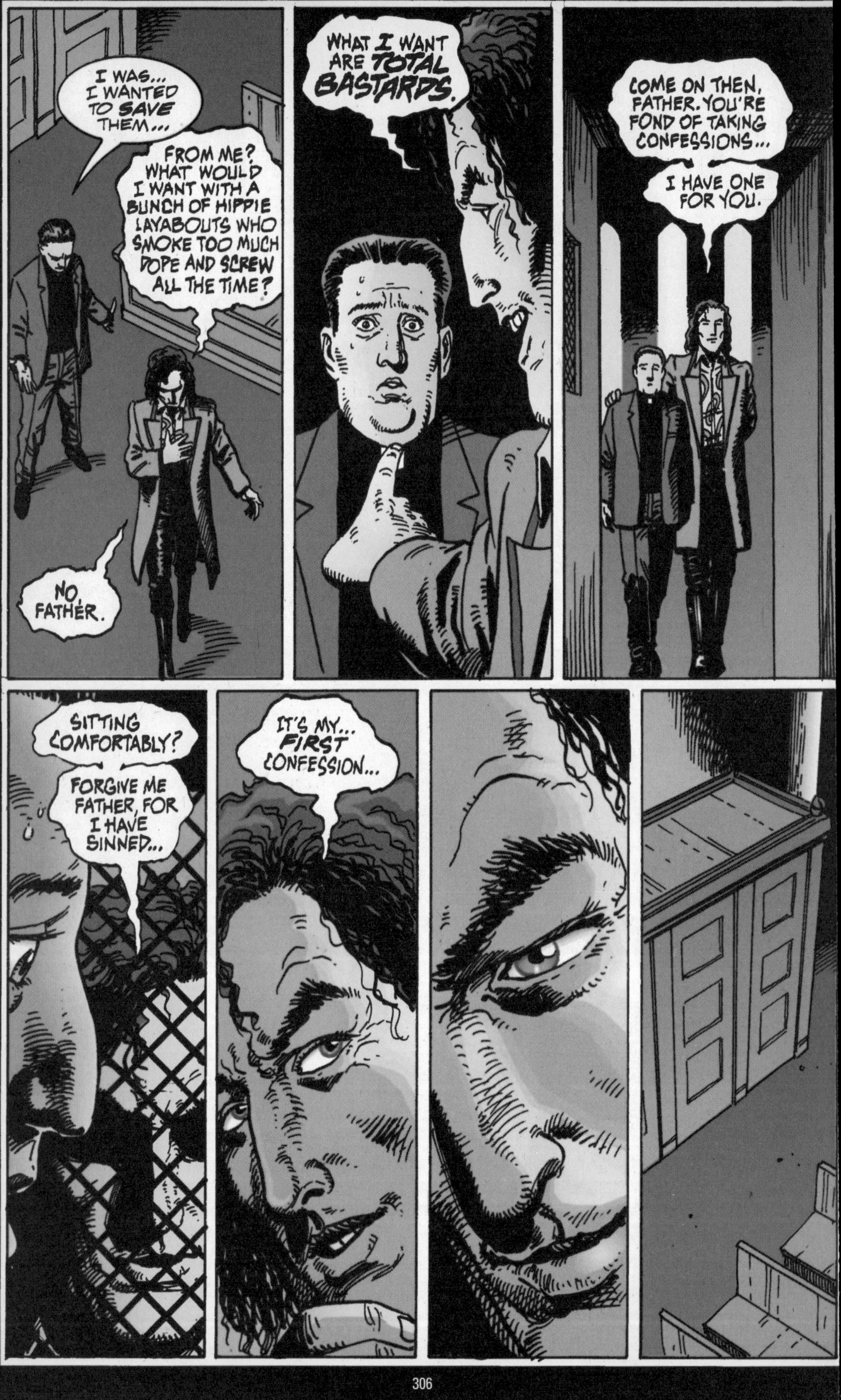
I WAS... I WANTED TO SAVE THEM...
FROM ME? WHAT WOULD I WANT WITH A BUNCH OF HIPPIE LAYABOUTS WHO SMOKE TOO MUCH DOPE AND SCREW ALL THE TIME?
NO, FATHER.
WHAT I WANT ARE TOTAL BASTARDS.
COME ON THEN, FATHER. YOU'RE FOND OF TAKING CONFESSIONS...
I HAVE ONE FOR YOU.
SITTING COMFORTABLY?
FORGIVE ME FATHER, FOR I HAVE SINNED...
IT'S MY... FIRST CONFESSION...

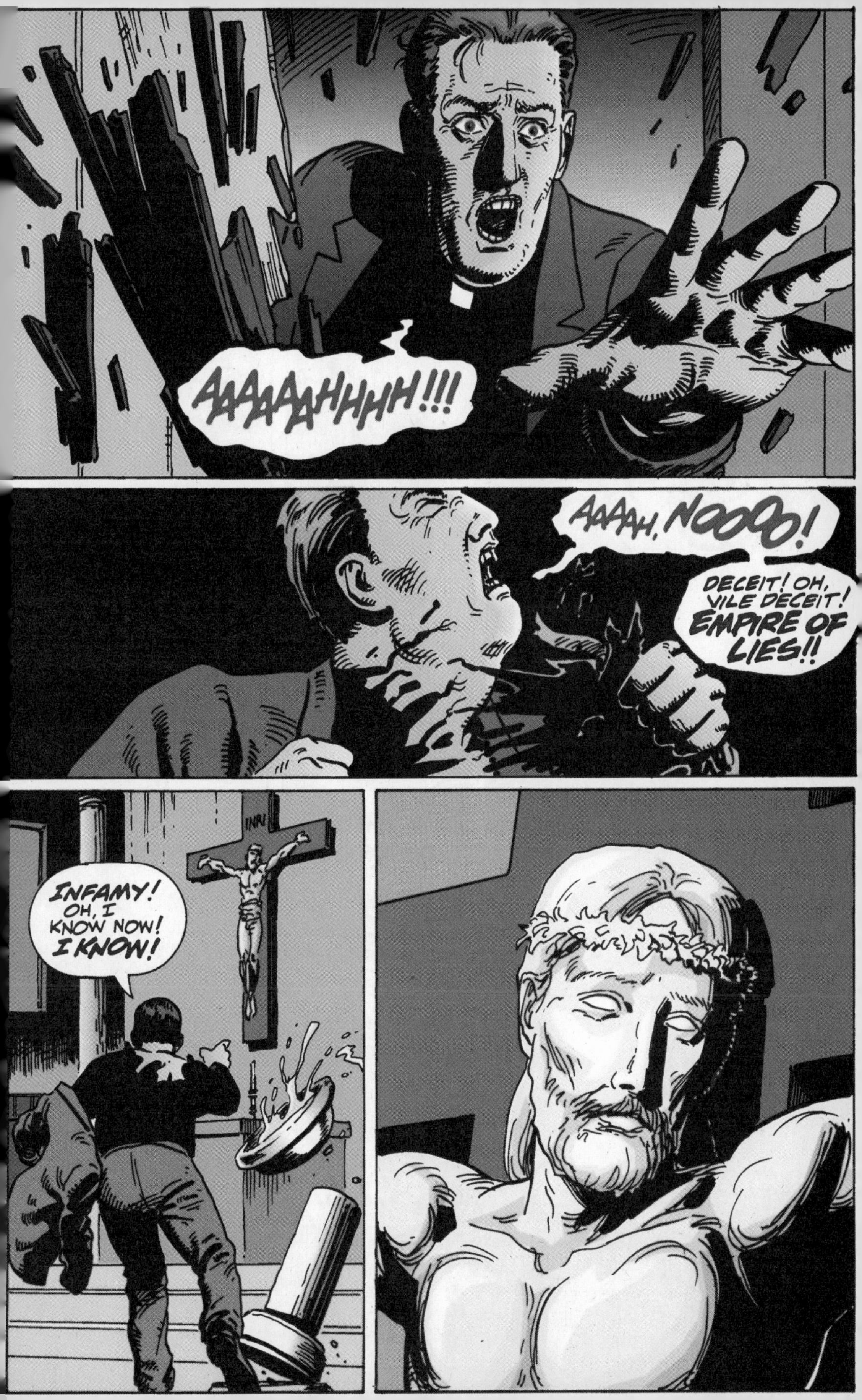
AAAAAAHHHH!!!
AAAAH, NOOOO!
DECEIT! OH, VILE DECEIT! EMPIRE OF LIES!!
INFAMY! OH, I KNOW NOW! I KNOW!
INRI

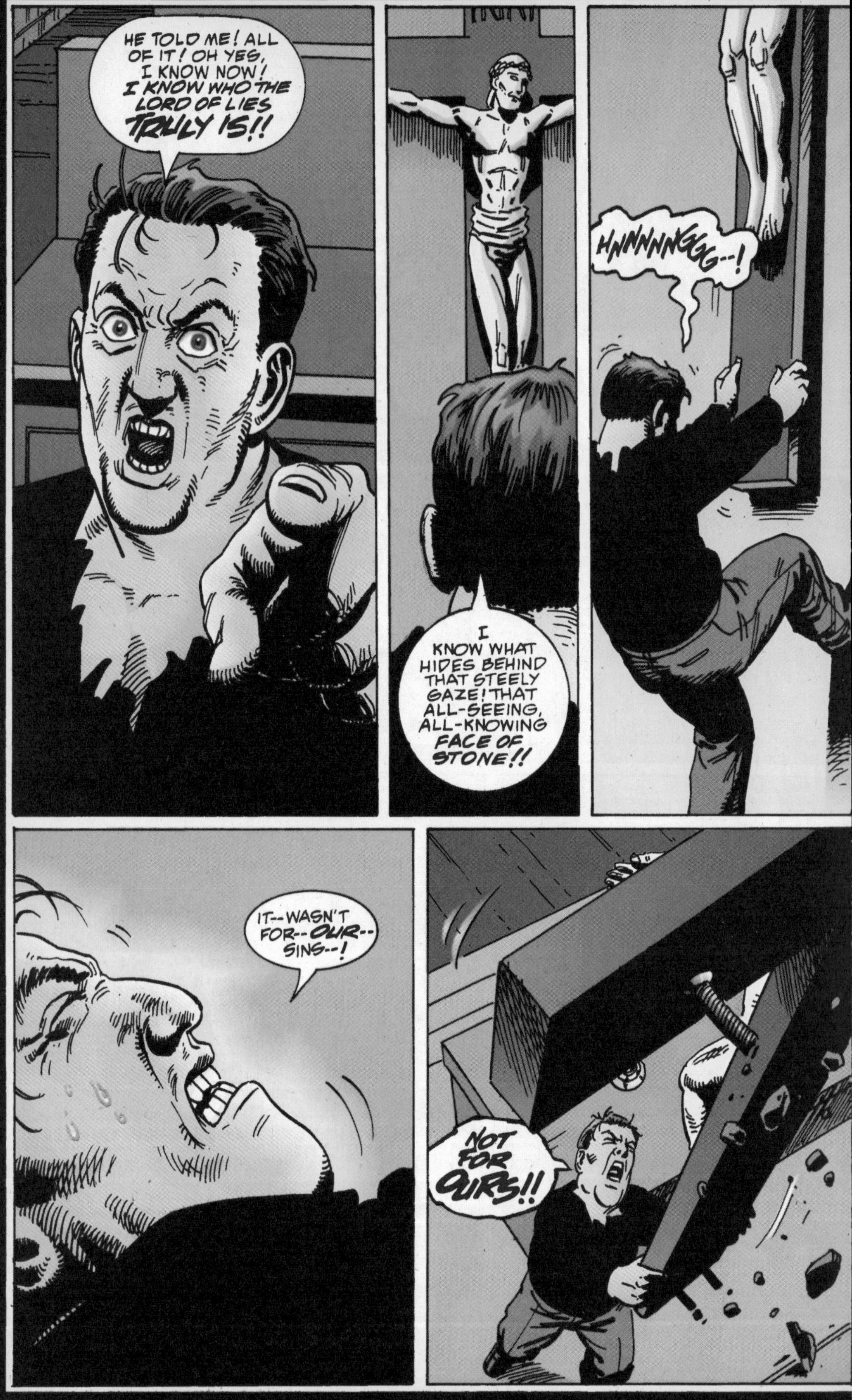
HE TOLD ME! ALL OF IT! OH YES, I KNOW NOW! I KNOW WHO THE LORD OF LIES TRULY IS!!
I KNOW WHAT HIDES BEHIND THAT STEELY GAZE! THAT ALL-SEEING, ALL-KNOWING FACE OF STONE!!
HNNNNNGGG--!
IT--WASN'T FOR--OUR--SINS--!
NOT FOR OURS!!

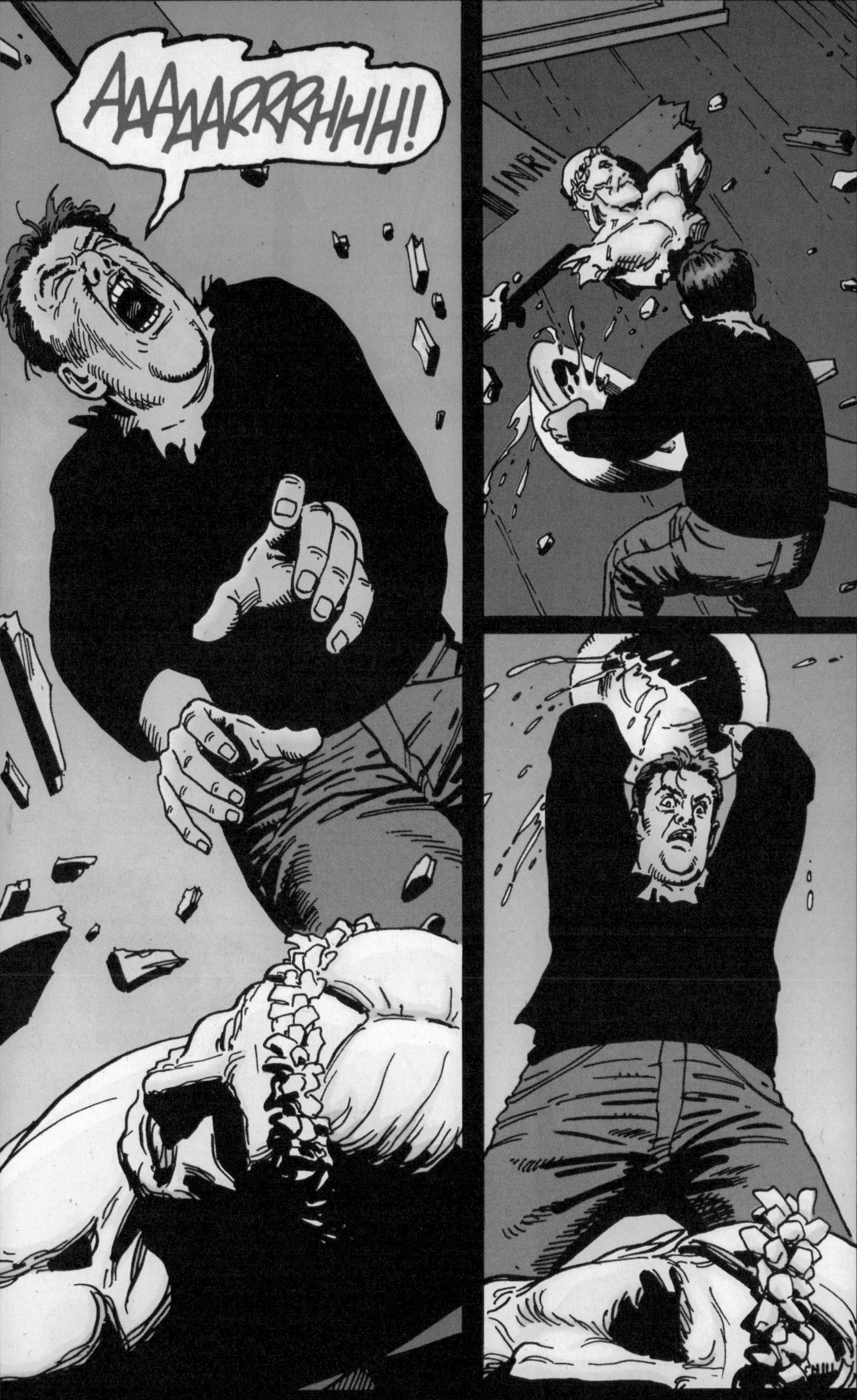
AAAAARRRRHHH!

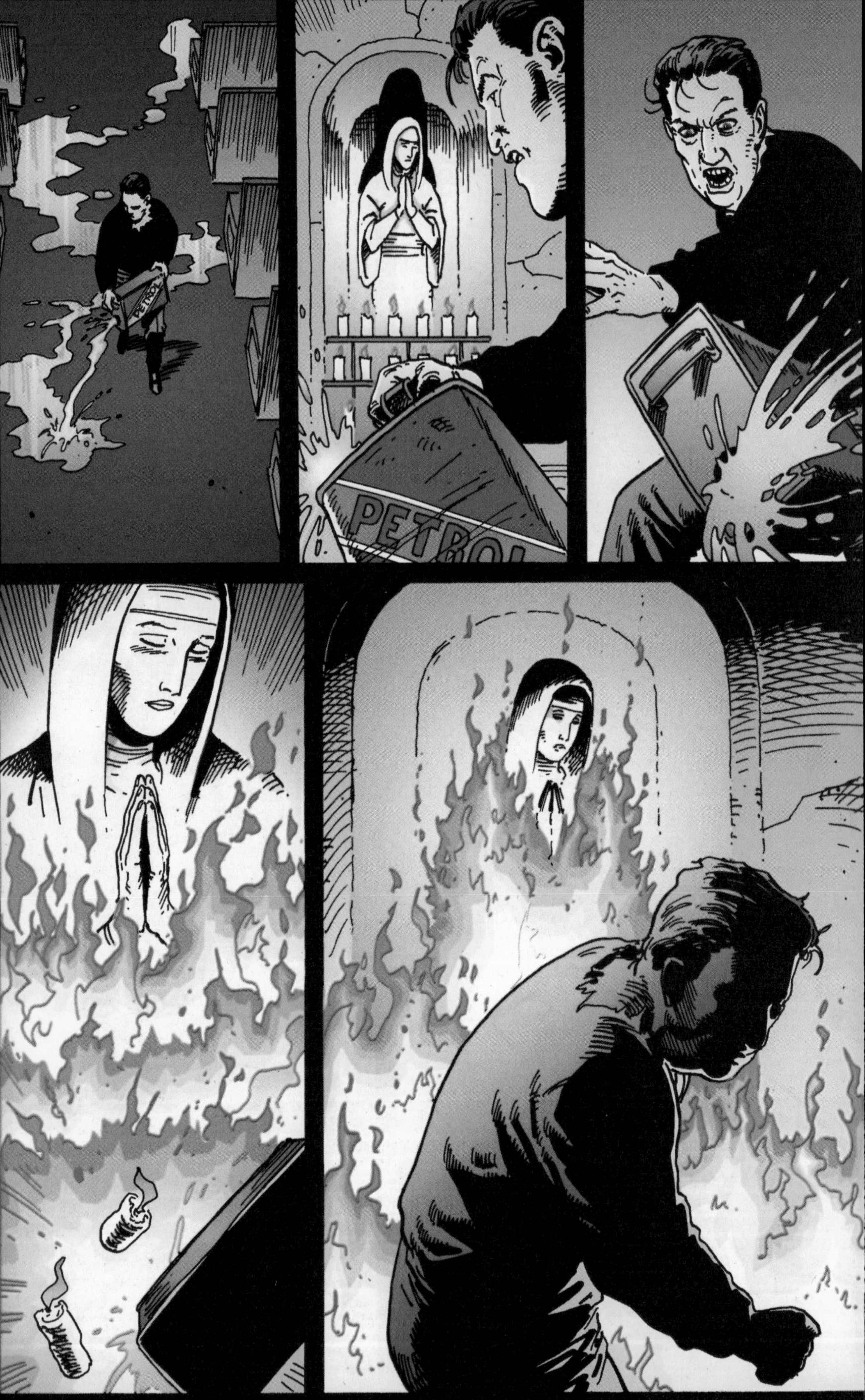
PETROL
PETROL

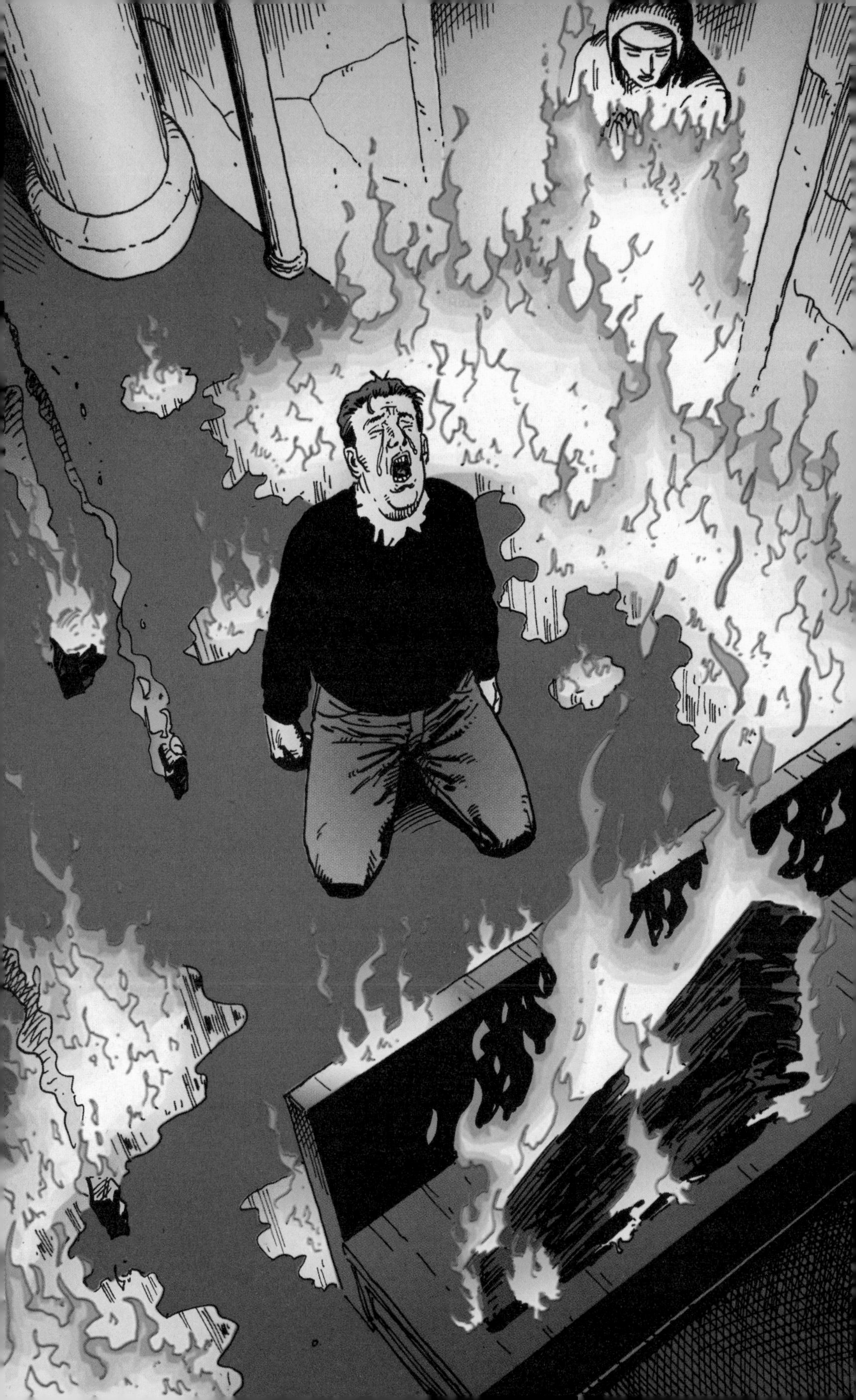

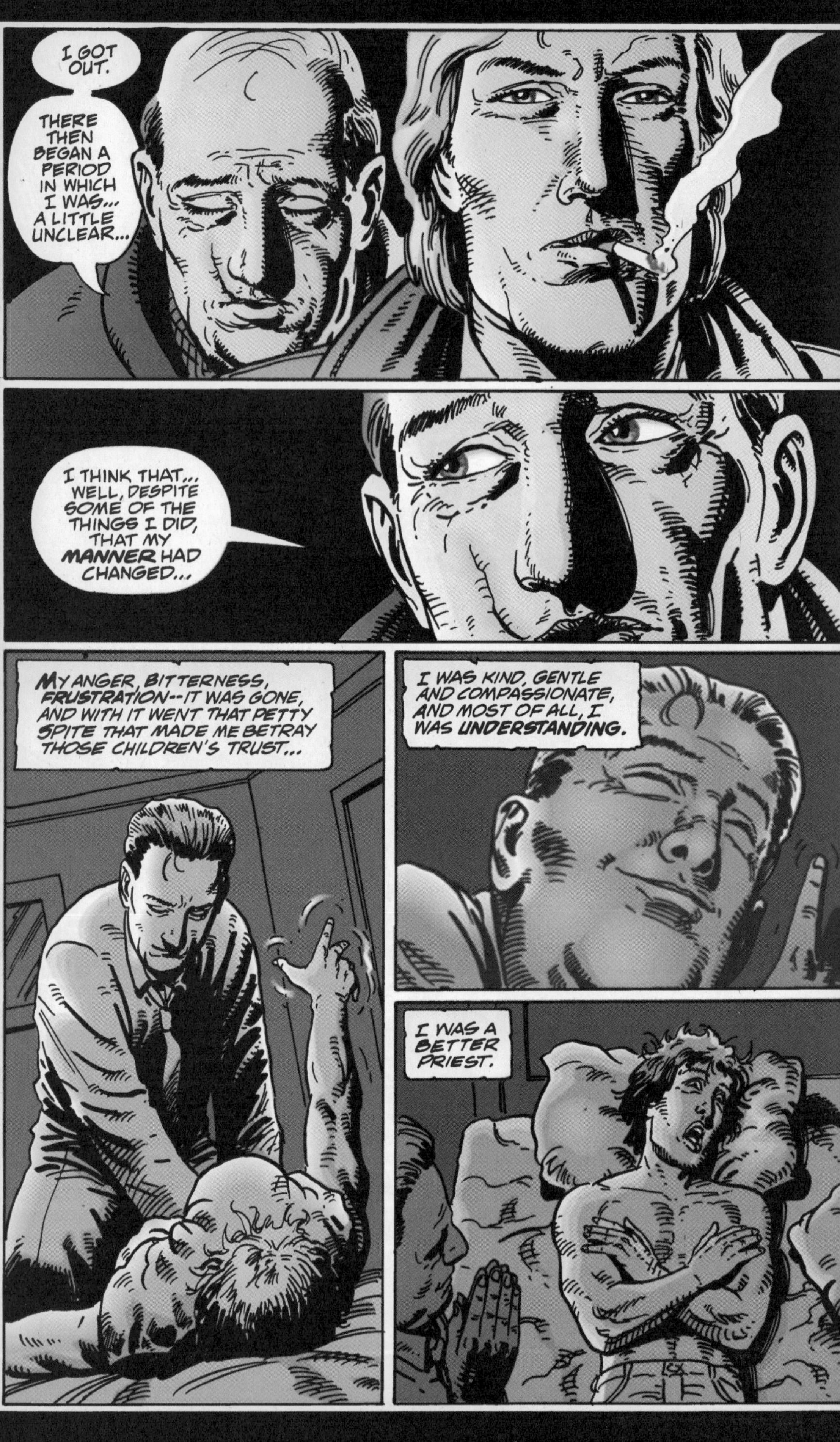
I GOT OUT.
THERE THEN BEGAN A PERIOD IN WHICH I WAS... A LITTLE UNCLEAR...
I THINK THAT... WELL, DESPITE SOME OF THE THINGS I DID, THAT MY MANNER HAD CHANGED...
MY ANGER, BITTERNESS, FRUSTRATION--IT WAS GONE, AND WITH IT WENT THAT PETTY SPITE THAT MADE ME BETRAY THOSE CHILDREN'S TRUST...
I WAS KIND, GENTLE AND COMPASSIONATE, AND MOST OF ALL, I WAS UNDERSTANDING.
I WAS A BETTER PRIEST.

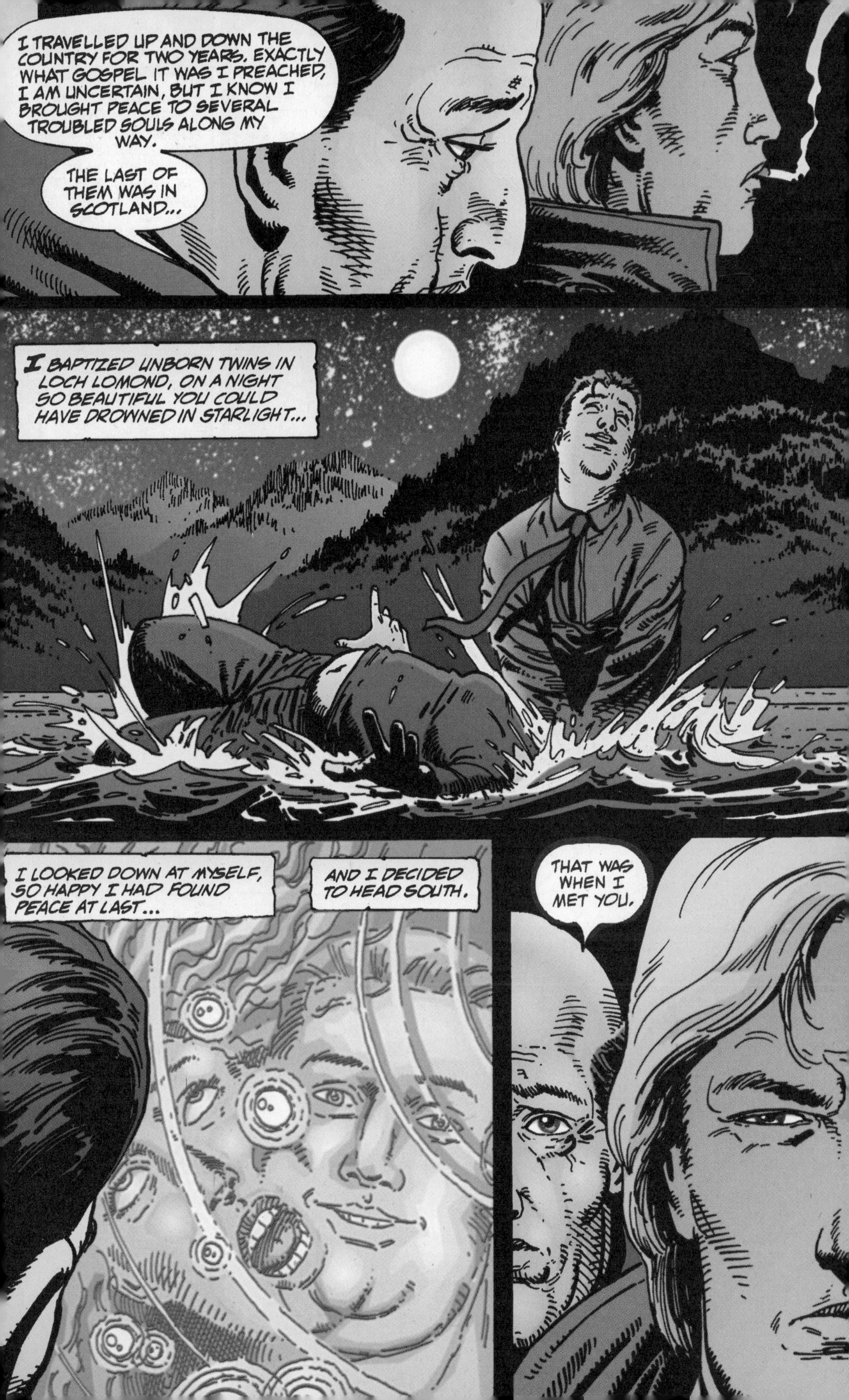
I TRAVELLED UP AND DOWN THE COUNTRY FOR TWO YEARS. EXACTLY WHAT GOSPEL IT WAS I PREACHED, I AM UNCERTAIN, BUT I KNOW I BROUGHT PEACE TO SEVERAL TROUBLED SOULS ALONG MY WAY.
THE LAST OF THEM WAS IN SCOTLAND...
I BAPTIZED UNBORN TWINS IN LOCH LOMOND, ON A NIGHT SO BEAUTIFUL YOU COULD HAVE DROWNED IN STARLIGHT...
I LOOKED DOWN AT MYSELF, SO HAPPY I HAD FOUND PEACE AT LAST...
AND I DECIDED TO HEAD SOUTH.
THAT WAS WHEN I MET YOU.

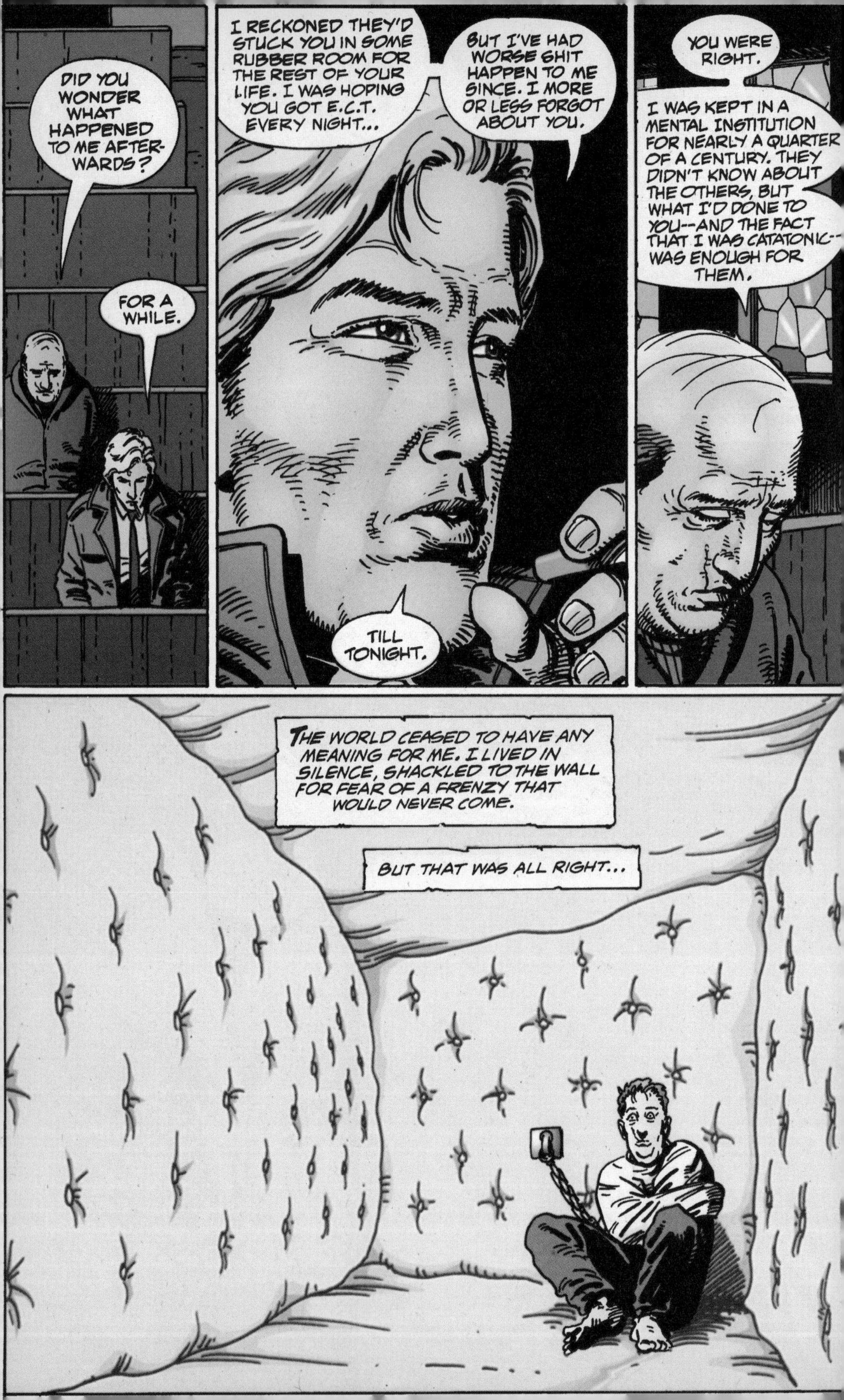
DID YOU WONDER WHAT HAPPENED TO ME AFTER-WARDS?
FOR A WHILE.
I RECKONED THEY'D STUCK YOU IN SOME RUBBER ROOM FOR THE REST OF YOUR LIFE. I WAS HOPING YOU GOT E.C.T. EVERY NIGHT...
BUT I'VE HAD WORSE SHIT HAPPEN TO ME SINCE. I MORE OR LESS FORGOT ABOUT YOU.
TILL TONIGHT.
YOU WERE RIGHT.
I WAS KEPT IN A MENTAL INSTITUTION FOR NEARLY A QUARTER OF A CENTURY. THEY DIDN'T KNOW ABOUT THE OTHERS, BUT WHAT I'D DONE TO YOU--AND THE FACT THAT I WAS CATATONIC--WAS ENOUGH FOR THEM.
THE WORLD CEASED TO HAVE ANY MEANING FOR ME. I LIVED IN SILENCE, SHACKLED TO THE WALL FOR FEAR OF A FRENZY THAT WOULD NEVER COME.
BUT THAT WAS ALL RIGHT...

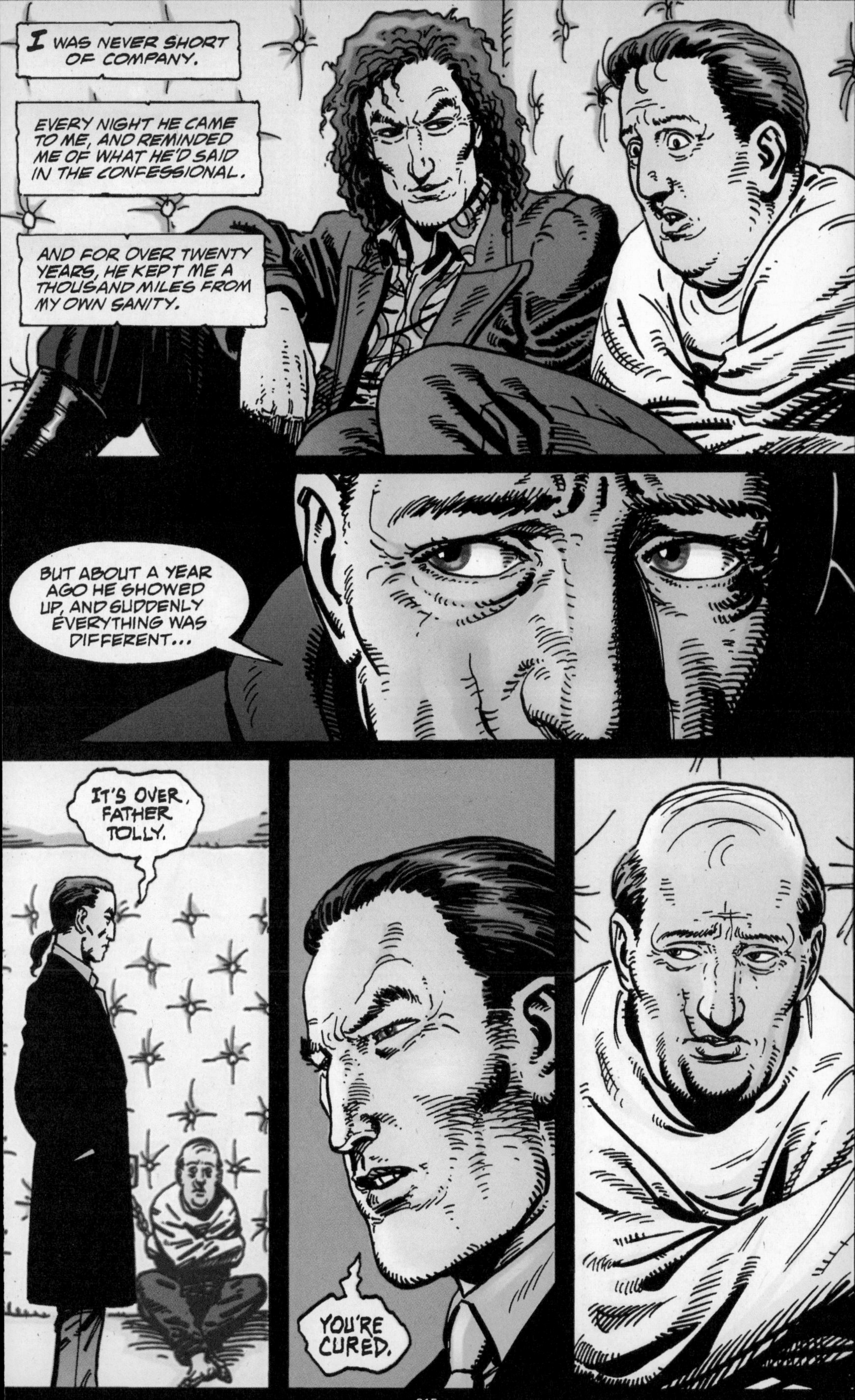
I WAS NEVER SHORT OF COMPANY.
EVERY NIGHT HE CAME TO ME, AND REMINDED ME OF WHAT HE'D SAID IN THE CONFESSIONAL.
AND FOR OVER TWENTY YEARS, HE KEPT ME A THOUSAND MILES FROM MY OWN SANITY.
BUT ABOUT A YEAR AGO HE SHOWED UP, AND SUDDENLY EVERYTHING WAS DIFFERENT...
IT'S OVER, FATHER TOLLY.
YOU'RE CURED.

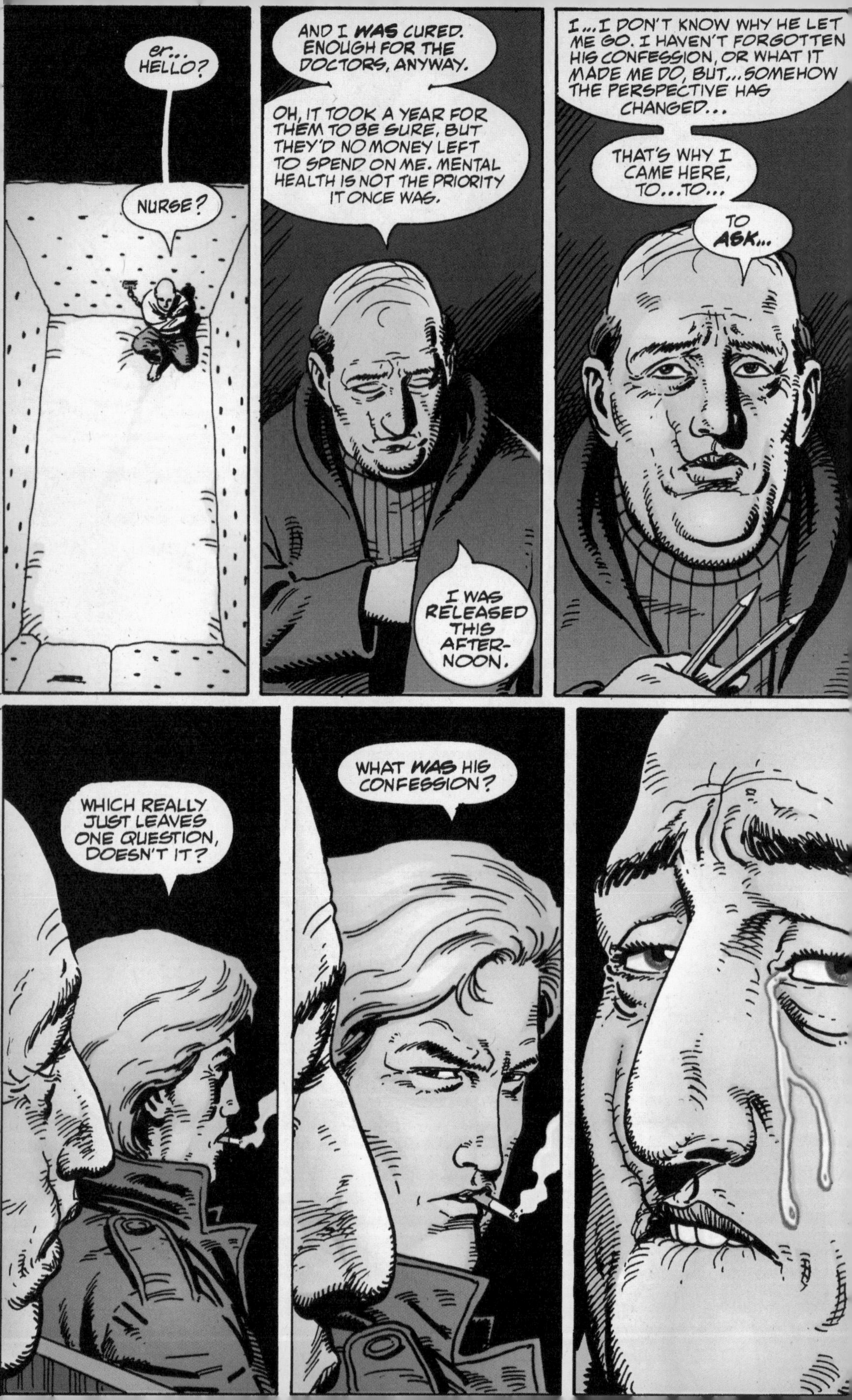
er... HELLO?
NURSE?
AND I WAS CURED. ENOUGH FOR THE DOCTORS, ANYWAY.
OH, IT TOOK A YEAR FOR THEM TO BE SURE, BUT THEY'D NO MONEY LEFT TO SPEND ON ME. MENTAL HEALTH IS NOT THE PRIORITY IT ONCE WAS.
I WAS RELEASED THIS AFTER-NOON.
I...I DON'T KNOW WHY HE LET ME GO. I HAVEN'T FORGOTTEN HIS CONFESSION, OR WHAT IT MADE ME DO, BUT,...SOMEHOW THE PERSPECTIVE HAS CHANGED...
THAT'S WHY I CAME HERE, TO...TO...
TO ASK...
WHICH REALLY JUST LEAVES ONE QUESTION, DOESN'T IT?
WHAT WAS HIS CONFESSION?

AND THEN HE PUTS A PENCIL IN EACH EYE AND HEADBUTTS THE PEW IN FRONT OF HIM.

HE LET YOU GO 'COS HE KNEW YOU'D BE RUNNING INTO ME.

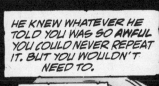

HE KNEW WHATEVER HE TOLD YOU WAS SO AWFUL YOU COULD NEVER REPEAT IT. BUT YOU WOULDN'T NEED TO.

YOU WERE A MESSAGE, TOLLY.

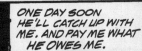

ONE DAY SOON HE'LL CATCH UP WITH ME. AND PAY ME WHAT HE OWES ME.

AND THEN... JUST BEFORE I DIE...

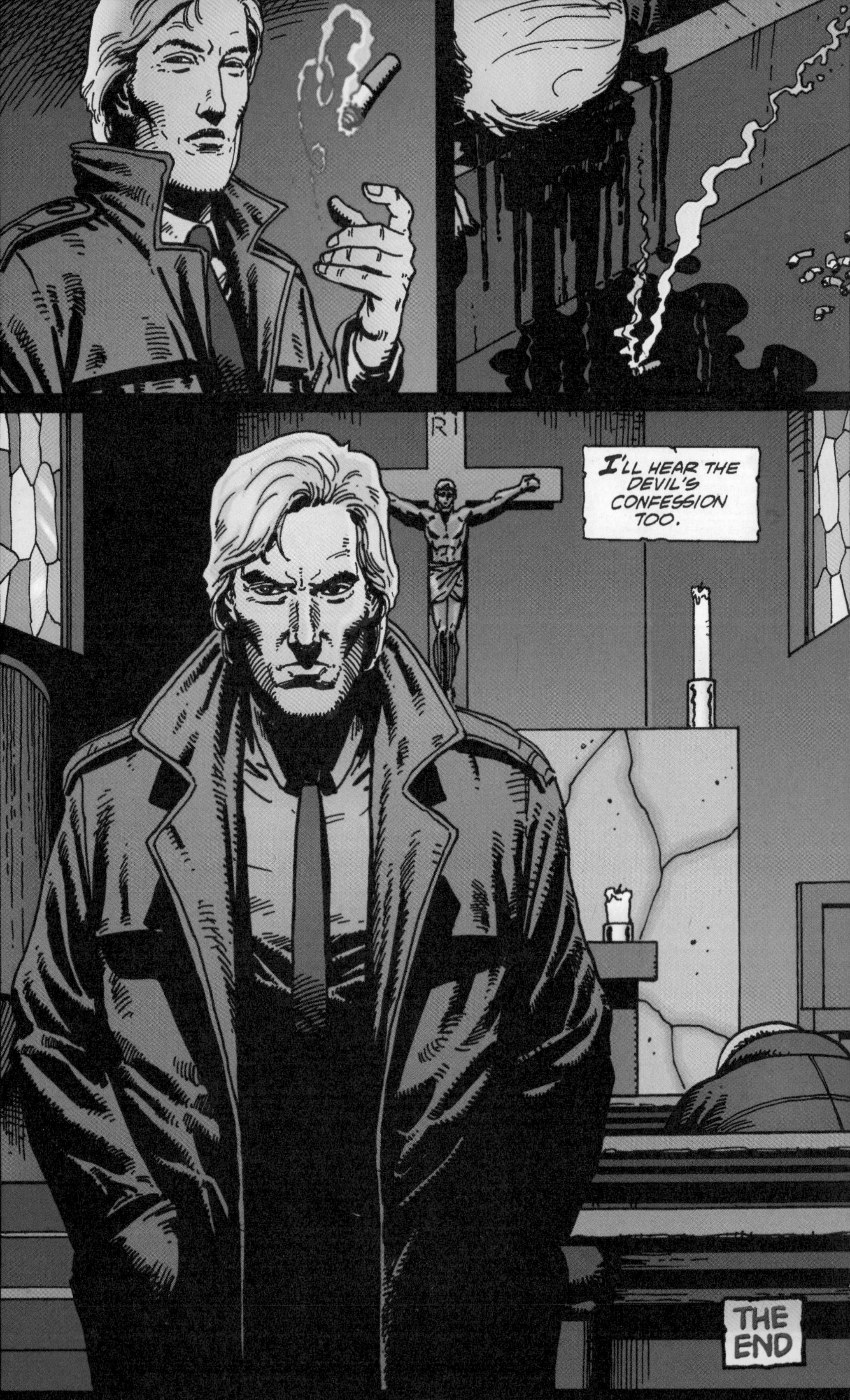
RI
I'LL HEAR THE DEVIL'S CONFESSION TOO.
THE END

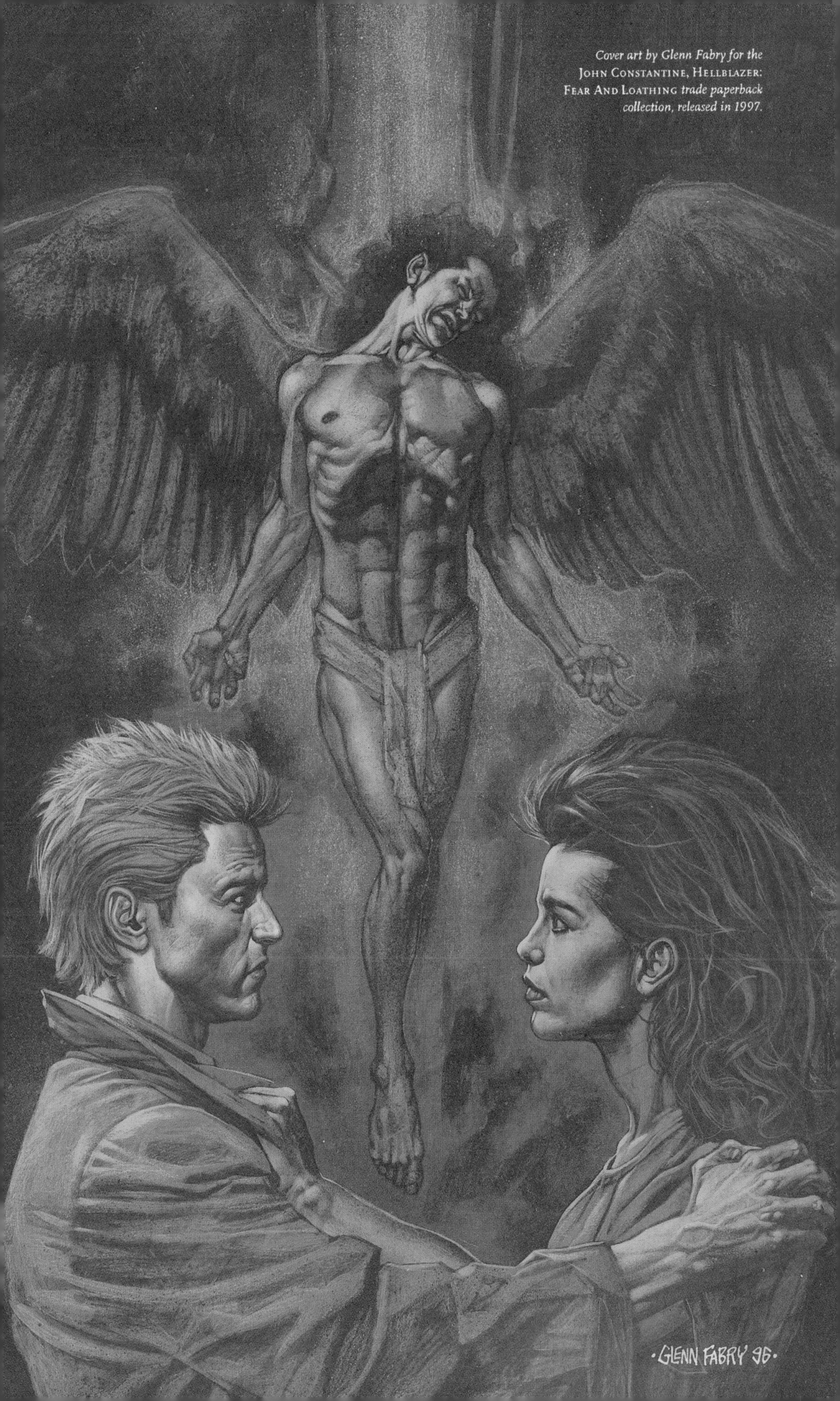
·GLENN FABRY 96·

Cover art by Glenn Fabry for the John Constantine, Hellblazer: Fear And Loathing *trade paperback collection, released in 1997.*

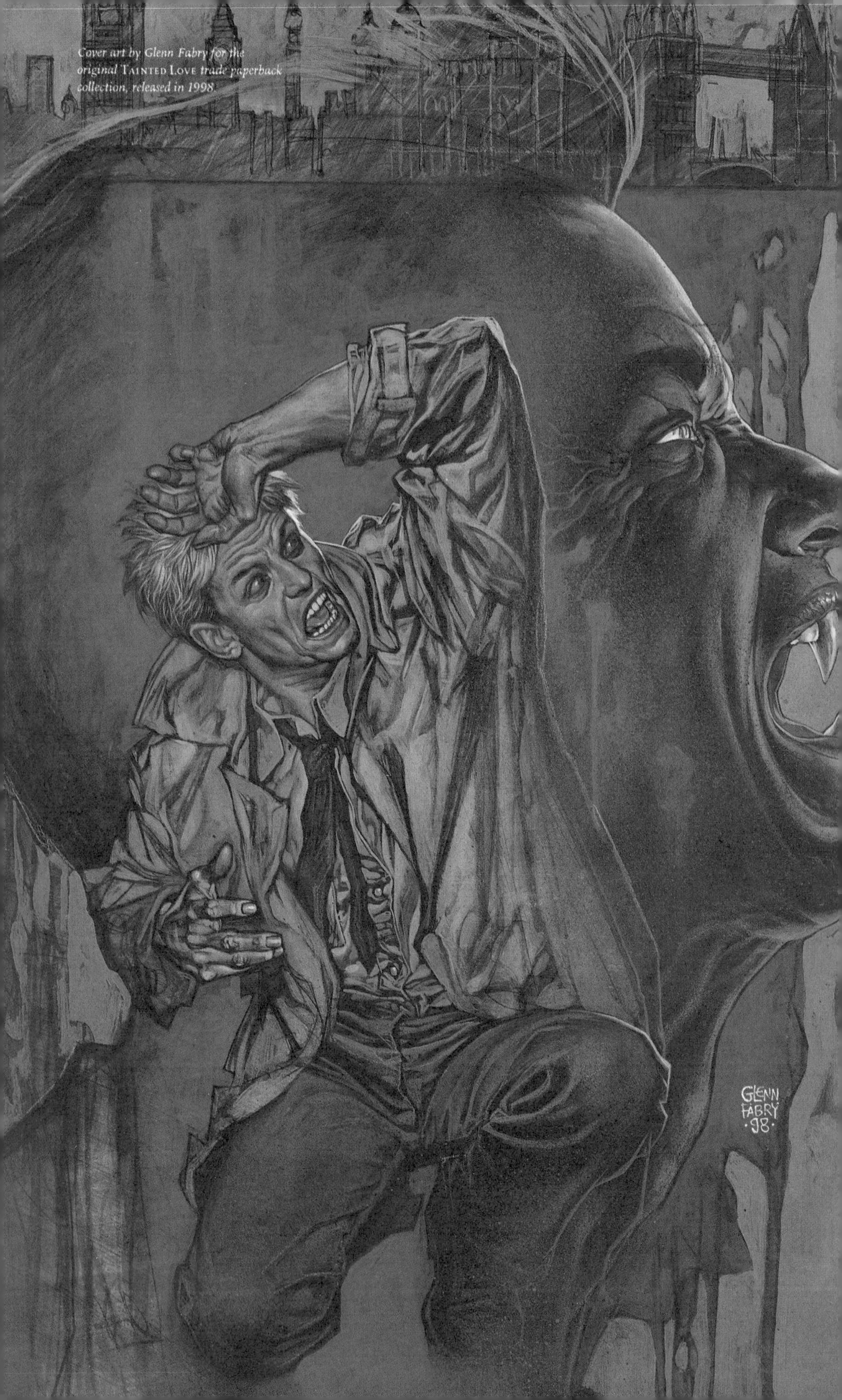
GLENN
FABRY
·98·

Cover art by Glenn Fabry for the original Tainted Love *trade paperback collection, released in 1998.*